Corel® WordPerfect® 9
fast&easy™

Send Us Your Comments

To comment on this book or any other PRIMA TECH title, visit our reader response page on the Web at **www.prima-tech.com/comments**.

How to Order

For information on quantity discounts, contact the publisher: Prima Publishing, P.O. Box 1260BK, Rocklin, CA 95677-1260; (916) 632-4400. On your letterhead, include information concerning the intended use of the books and the number of books you wish to purchase. For individual orders, visit PRIMA TECH's Web site at **www.prima-tech.com**.

Corel® WordPerfect® 9 fast&easy™

Diane Koers

PRIMA TECH

A DIVISION OF PRIMA PUBLISHING

© 1999 by Prima Publishing. All rights reserved. No part of this book may be reproduced or transmitted in any form or by any means, electronic or mechanical, including photocopying, recording, or by any information storage or retrieval system without written permission from Prima Publishing, except for the inclusion of brief quotations in a review.

A Division of Prima Publishing

Prima Publishing and colophon are registered trademarks of Prima Communications, Inc. PRIMA TECH and Fast & Easy are trademarks of Prima Communications, Inc., Rocklin, California 95677.

Publisher: Stacy L. Hiquet
Associate Publisher: Nancy Stevenson
Managing Editor: Dan J. Foster
Senior Acquisitions Editor: Deborah F. Abshier
Senior Editor: Kelli R. Crump
Project Editor: Geneil Breeze
Technical Reviewers: Ray Link and Brian Thomasson
Interior Layout: Marian Hartsough
Cover Design: Prima Design Team
Indexer: Emily Glossbrenner

Corel and WordPerfect are registered trademarks of Corel Corporation.

Important: If you have problems installing or running Corel WordPerfect 9, go to **www.corel.com** on the Web. Prima Publishing cannot provide software support.

Prima Publishing and the author have attempted throughout this book to distinguish proprietary trademarks from descriptive terms by following the capitalization style used by the manufacturer.

Information contained in this book has been obtained by Prima Publishing from sources believed to be reliable. However, because of the possibility of human or mechanical error by our sources, Prima Publishing, or others, the Publisher does not guarantee the accuracy, adequacy, or completeness of any information and is not responsible for any errors or omissions or the results obtained from the use of such information. Readers should be particularly aware of the fact that the Internet is an ever-changing entity. Some facts may have changed since this book went to press.

ISBN: 0-7615-1411-2
Library of Congress Catalog Card Number: 98-67780
Printed in the United States of America

99 00 01 02 03 DD 10 9 8 7 6 5 4 3 2 1

*To Trina,
my wonderful and lovely daughter.*

*Thanks for being you
and for taking such good care
of my son and grandsons.*

Acknowledgments

I am deeply grateful to the many people at Prima Publishing who worked on this book. Thank you for all the time you gave and for your assistance.

Thanks to Debbie Abshier for the opportunity to write this book and her confidence in me, to Ray Link and Brian Thomasson for their assistance in making this book technically correct, and to Geneil Breeze for all her patience and guidance.

Lastly, thanks Vern, for always being who you are.

About the Author

DIANE KOERS owns and operates All Business Service, a software training and consulting business formed in 1988 that services the central Indiana area. Her area of expertise has long been in the word processing, spreadsheet, and graphics areas of computing as well as providing training and support for Peachtree Accounting software. Diane's authoring experience includes numerous *Fast & Easy* guides from Prima Publishing, such as *Windows 98 Fast & Easy*, and other topics, such as Lotus 1-2-3, Lotus SmartSuite, WordPerfect 8, Microsoft Works, Microsoft Office, and Microsoft Word as well as co-authoring Prima's *Essential Windows 98*. She has also developed and written software training manuals for her clients' use.

Active in church and civic activities, Diane enjoys spending her free time traveling and playing with her grandsons and her three Yorkshire Terriers.

Contents at a Glance

Introduction xix

PART I
CREATING THE PERFECT DOCUMENT 1

Chapter 1	Welcome to WordPerfect 3
Chapter 2	Saving, Opening, and Closing WordPerfect 13
Chapter 3	Getting Help 21
Chapter 4	Moving Around in a Document 29
Chapter 5	Editing a Document 39
Chapter 6	Printing Letters and Envelopes 55
Chapter 7	Working with Views 63
Chapter 8	Improving Your Writing 71

PART II
FORMATTING A REPORT 89

Chapter 9	Formatting with Fonts 91
Chapter 10	Changing Paper Sizes and Margins 101
Chapter 11	Modifying Alignment, Indentation, and Spacing ... 109
Chapter 12	Adding Bullets, Numbering, and Borders 117
Chapter 13	Working with Footnotes and Endnotes 127
Chapter 14	Adding Headers, Footers, and Watermarks 137
Chapter 15	Saving Time with Templates 151

CONTENTS AT A GLANCE

PART III
WORKING WITH TABLES 163

Chapter 16	Creating Tabular Tables.	165
Chapter 17	Creating a Perfect Table	175
Chapter 18	Formatting a Table	191
Chapter 19	Using Formulas in a Table	205

PART IV
USING MAIL MERGE 215

Chapter 20	Creating an Address List.	217
Chapter 21	Creating a Form Letter	235
Chapter 22	Merging an Address List and Form Letter	241

PART V
GETTING CREATIVE WITH GRAPHICS 255

Chapter 23	Working with Graphic Lines	257
Chapter 24	Working with Graphic Images.	271
Chapter 25	Working with TextArt	283

PART VI
WORKING ON THE INTERNET. 295

Chapter 26	Using SpeedLinks	297
Chapter 27	Creating a Simple Web Page	311

APPENDIXES 329

Appendix A	Installing WordPerfect.	331
Appendix B	Working with Dragon NaturallySpeaking	349
Appendix C	Discovering WordPerfect Tips and Tricks	381

Glossary.	389
Index	395

Contents

Introduction xix

PART I
CREATING THE PERFECT DOCUMENT 1

Chapter 1 Welcome to WordPerfect 3
    Starting WordPerfect 4
    Typing Text 6
        Typing Short Lines of Text 6
        Entering Date Text 7
        Entering the Body of a Letter 8
    Adding a Special Character 9

Chapter 2 Saving, Opening, and Closing WordPerfect 13
    Saving a WordPerfect Document 14
        Saving a File the First Time 14
        Resaving a Document 16
    Closing a WordPerfect Document 16
    Opening a WordPerfect Document 18
    Exiting the WordPerfect Program 19

Chapter 3 Getting Help 21
    Getting PerfectExpert Help 22
    Using Help Topics 25

CONTENTS

Chapter 4 **Moving Around in a Document** 29
    Moving Around in a Document 30
        Moving Using the Keyboard 30
        Using Autoscroll 32
        Going Forward and Backward 35
        Using the Go To Command 35
    Using the Shadow Cursor 36

Chapter 5 **Editing a Document** 39
    Editing, Selecting, and Deleting Text 40
        Inserting Text 40
        Selecting Text 41
        Deleting Text 42
    Changing Text Case 43
    Using Undo and Redo 44
        Undoing the Previous Step 44
        Redoing the Previous Step 45
    Moving and Copying Text 45
        Moving Text 45
        Copying Text 47
        Using Drag and Drop 48
        Using the Shortcut Menu 49
    Using Find and Replace 50

Chapter 6 **Printing Letters and Envelopes** 55
    Making It Fit 56
    Printing a Document 57
    Creating an Envelope 59
        Starting the Envelope Feature 59
        Adding a Bar Code to an Envelope 60
        Typing a Return Address 61
        Selecting an Envelope Size 62

CONTENTS

Chapter 7 Working with Views 63
    Working in Different Views 64
        Switching from Page View to Draft View 64
        Returning to Page View 65
    Viewing Two Pages at a Time 66
    Zooming Around 67
        Zooming to Full Page View 67
        Zooming In for a Closer Look 70

Chapter 8 Improving Your Writing 71
    Discovering QuickCorrect 72
    Saving Time with QuickWords 73
    Spell-Checking Your Document 76
        Spelling As You Go 76
        Turning Off the Spell-As-You-Go Feature 77
    Working with Spell-Check 78
    Checking Your Grammar 81
    Finding a Synonym with the Thesaurus 83
    Reviewing Document Statistics 85
    Part I Review Questions 87

PART II
FORMATTING A REPORT 89

Chapter 9 Formatting with Fonts 91
    Changing Text Appearance 92
        Changing the Typeface 92
        Changing Font Size 93
        Changing the Style of Text 95
        Making Font Changes from One Location 96
    Using the Highlighter 98
        Selecting a Highlight Color 98
        Applying Highlighter 98
        Removing Highlighting 100

CONTENTS

Chapter 10 Changing Paper Sizes and Margins 101
  Selecting a Paper Size and Orientation 102
  Changing Margins 104
  Adding Page Numbering 105

Chapter 11 Modifying Alignment, Indentation, and Spacing . . . 109
  Justifying Text 110
    Centering a Heading. 110
    Changing Alignment 111
  Indenting a Paragraph. 112
  Centering a Page Vertically 114
  Changing Line Spacing 115

Chapter 12 Adding Bullets, Numbering, and Borders 117
  Adding a Bullet 118
  Creating a Numbered List. 119
  Working with Borders and Fills 120
    Adding a Border to a Paragraph 120
    Adding a Fill Color to a Paragraph. 122
    Putting a Border Around a Page 124

Chapter 13 Working with Footnotes and Endnotes. 127
  Creating Footnotes and Endnotes 128
  Editing Footnotes and Endnotes 131
  Moving Footnotes and Endnotes 132
  Deleting Footnotes and Endnotes 134
  Changing a Footnote to an Endnote 134

Chapter 14 Adding Headers, Footers, and Watermarks 137
  Adding a Header or Footer. 138
  Inserting the Path and Filename 142
  Editing a Header or Footer. 143
  Suppressing a Header or Footer. 143
  Discontinuing a Header or Footer 145
  Adding a Watermark 146

Chapter 15 Saving Time with Templates 151
Creating a Memo.. 152
Creating an Award Certificate............................ 156
Part II Review Questions................................ 162

PART III
WORKING WITH TABLES 163

Chapter 16 Creating Tabular Tables 165
Turning on the Ruler Bar 166
Changing the Default Tabs 166
Adding a Custom Tab Stop................................ 169
Deleting a Tab Stop...................................... 174

Chapter 17 Creating a Perfect Table 175
Inserting a Table in the Document 176
    Inserting a Table Using the Menu.................... 176
    Using Table QuickCreate 178
Entering Information in a Table......................... 180
    Entering Cell Data.................................. 180
    Saving Time with QuickFill 181
Changing Table Size 183
    Adding a Row at the End of a Table.................. 183
    Inserting a Row Elsewhere in a Table 184
    Adding a Column to a Table.......................... 185
    Deleting a Row or Column 187
Importing a Spreadsheet................................. 188

Chapter 18 Formatting a Table............................. 191
Formatting with SpeedFormat 192
Selecting Parts of a Table 194
Changing Column Width................................... 196
Changing Borders 199
Formatting Numbers...................................... 200

Changing Cell Alignment 201
Joining Cells for a Table Heading 202

Chapter 19 Using Formulas in a Table 205
Using QuickSum 206
Adding a Column of Numbers 207
Creating a Simple Formula 209
Copying a Formula 212
Part III Review Questions *214*

PART IV
USING MAIL MERGE 215

Chapter 20 Creating an Address List 217
Creating a Data File. 218
Naming Data Fields. 219
Using Quick Data Entry. 221
Editing a Data File. 224
Changing Fields. 226
    Adding a New Field 226
    Deleting a Field. 229
    Renaming a Field. 232

Chapter 21 Creating a Form Letter 235
Creating a Form Letter 236
Using Automatic Dates 237
Inserting Data Fields. 237

Chapter 22 Merging an Address List and Form Letter. 241
Merging Names and Addresses with a Letter 242
Merging to Specific Conditions. 244
Merging to Selected Records 247
Creating Envelopes for the Merged Records. 249
Part IV Review Questions *253*

PART V
GETTING CREATIVE WITH GRAPHICS 255

Chapter 23 Working with Graphic Lines 257
Adding a Graphic Line 258
Moving a Graphic Line 260
Editing Graphic Lines 262
    Changing the Thickness of a Graphic Line 262
    Changing Line Styles 264
    Editing Line Attributes 265
Deleting Graphic Lines 267
Adding a Shaped Object 268

Chapter 24 Working with Graphic Images 271
Adding a Graphic Image 272
Resizing a Graphic Image 273
Moving a Graphic Image 275
Working with Borders and Fills 276
    Adding a Border 276
    Adding a Shadow to a Graphic Box 277
    Applying Fill Patterns 278
Wrapping Text Around the Graphic Image 279
Tightening Text Contour 281

Chapter 25 Working with TextArt 283
Creating TextArt Text 284
Editing TextArt 285
    Changing TextArt Shapes 285
    Editing TextArt Attributes 287
    Changing 2-D Options 288
    Changing 3-D Options 290
Part V Review Questions 293

PART VI
WORKING ON THE INTERNET 295

Chapter 26 **Using SpeedLinks** 297
    Creating a SpeedLink 298
        Creating an Internet SpeedLink 298
        SpeedLinking to Another Document 300
    Editing a SpeedLink 302
    Adding a SpeedLink to a Document 303
        Typing a SpeedLink 303
        Inserting a SpeedLink 304
    Using a SpeedLink 306
    Deleting a SpeedLink 308

Chapter 27 **Creating a Simple Web Page** 311
    Beginning the PerfectExpert 312
    Changing the Colors 313
    Changing the Wallpaper 314
    Working with Text 315
        Adding and Formatting Text 315
        Creating Bulleted Lists 317
    Adding Graphic Images 318
        Adding Horizontal Lines 318
        Adding Clip Art 320
    Adding Hyperlinks 322
    Publishing to HTML 324
    Viewing the Document in a Web Browser 326
    Part VI Review Questions *328*

APPENDIXES 329

Appendix A **Installing WordPerfect** 331
    System Requirements 332
    Beginning the Installation Process 332
        Installing the Complete WordPerfect Office 2000 ... 335

Installing Only the WordPerfect Component............339
Uninstalling WordPerfect Office 2000 344

Appendix B Working with Dragon NaturallySpeaking 349
Installing Dragon NaturallySpeaking 350
Training to Your Voice 353
    Creating Speech Files.......................353
    Running the Audio Setup Wizard 355
        Testing Speaker Connections..............357
        Testing the Microphone 358
    Running the New User Wizard 361
        Running General Training................361
        Running the Vocabulary Builder 366
Dictating into WordPerfect........................372
    Opening Speech Files.......................372
    Turning the Microphone On and Off 373
Dictating Text 374
Editing Text 376
    Moving Around a Document 376
    Revising Text............................377
    Correcting Recognition Errors 378
Updating Speech Files...........................380

Appendix C Discovering WordPerfect Tips and Tricks 381
Keeping Two Words Together......................382
Looking at All Your Fonts 382
Adding a Drop Cap 384
"Stretching" a Heading..........................386
Adding Dot Leaders to Text on the Right Margin 387

Glossary..................................389

Index....................................395

Introduction

This new *Fast & Easy* book from Prima Publishing will help you use the many and varied features of one of the most popular products on the market today—Corel WordPerfect.

WordPerfect is a powerful word processing program that will take your documents far beyond what you can produce with a typewriter. Whether you want to create a simple letter to a friend, produce a newsletter for a professional organization, or even write a complicated, multipage report containing graphics and tables with numerical data, you will find the information that you need to quickly and easily get the job done in *WordPerfect 9 Fast & Easy*.

This book uses a step-by-step approach with color illustrations of what you will see on your screen, linked with instructions for the next mouse movements or keyboard operations to complete your task. Computer terms and phrases are clearly explained in nontechnical language, and expert tips and shortcuts help you produce professional-quality documents.

WordPerfect 9 Fast & Easy provides the tools you need to successfully tackle the potentially overwhelming challenge of learning to use WordPerfect. Whether you are a novice user or an experienced professional, you will be able to quickly tap into the program's user-friendly integrated design and feature-rich environment.

Who Should Read This Book?

The easy-to-follow, highly visual nature of this book makes it the perfect learning tool for a beginning computer user. However, it is also ideal for those who are new to this version of WordPerfect, or those who feel comfortable with computers and software, but have never used a word processing program before.

In addition, anyone using a software application always needs an occasional reminder about the steps required to perform a particular task. By using *WordPerfect 9 Fast & Easy*, any level of user can look up steps for a task quickly without having to plow through pages of descriptions.

In short, this book can be used by the beginning-to-intermediate computer user as a learning tool or as a step-by-step task reference.

Added Advice to Make You a Pro

You'll notice that this book uses steps and keeps explanations to a minimum to help you learn faster. Included in the book are a few elements that provide some additional comments to help you master the program, without encumbering your progress through the steps:

- **Tips** often offer shortcuts when performing an action, or hints about a feature that might make your work in WordPerfect quicker and easier.
- **Notes** give you a bit of background or additional information about a feature, or advice about how to use the feature in your day-to-day activities.

In addition, three helpful appendixes show you how to install WordPerfect, how to use the newest technology in speech recognition, and how to get the most out of WordPerfect by giving you tips and tricks to make life with WordPerfect easier, faster, and more fun.

Read and enjoy this *Fast & Easy* book. It certainly is the fastest and easiest way to learn WordPerfect 9.

PART I

Creating the Perfect Document

Chapter 1
Welcome to WordPerfect.................... 3

Chapter 2
Saving, Opening, and Closing WordPerfect 13

Chapter 3
Getting Help 21

Chapter 4
Moving Around in a Document 29

Chapter 5
Editing a Document....................... 39

Chapter 6
Printing Letters and Envelopes............. 55

Chapter 7
Working with Views 63

Chapter 8
Improving Your Writing.................... 71

1
Welcome to WordPerfect

Creating a document in WordPerfect involves a couple of steps. Because you will be at the Windows desktop when you start, that's where we will begin in this book as well. In this chapter, you'll learn how to:

- Start the WordPerfect program
- Enter text
- Enter a date
- Add special characters

Starting WordPerfect

Your screen may vary slightly from this figure if you have customized your Windows desktop. You may also see some differences depending on whether you have installed the entire Corel WordPerfect suite or just the WordPerfect program.

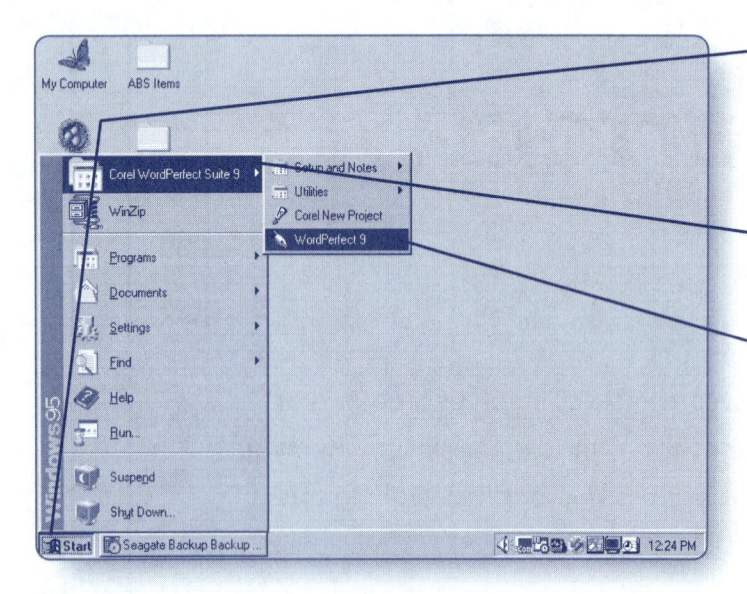

1. Click on the **Start button** in the lower-left corner of your screen. The Start menu will appear.

2. Click on **Corel WordPerfect Suite 9**. A submenu will appear.

3. Click on **WordPerfect 9**. A blank document will open for you to start typing in.

Many items you see when you open a new WordPerfect document are standard to any Windows 95 or 98 program. However, a few items are specific to the WordPerfect program. These include:

- **Toolbar**. A series of commonly used features of the WordPerfect program. These tools remain the same no matter what feature of WordPerfect you are using. You can, however, choose any of WordPerfect's 21 different toolbars to work with—or even create your own!

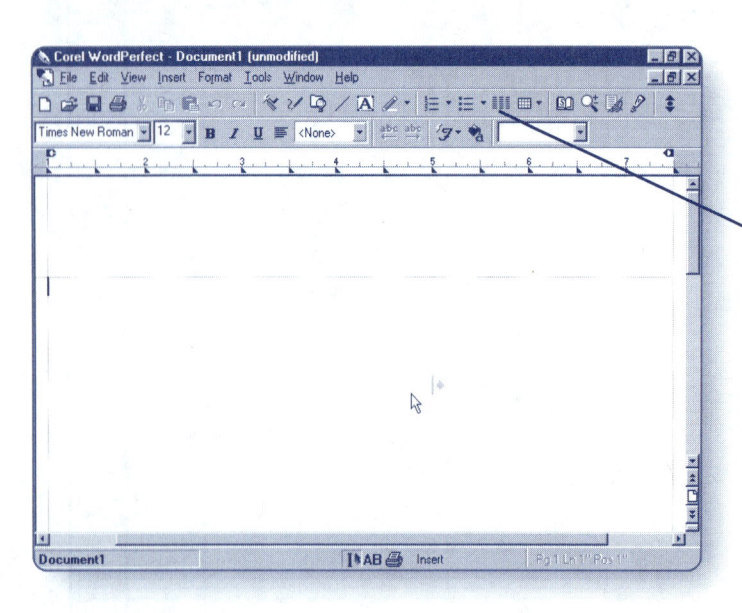

STARTING WORDPERFECT   5

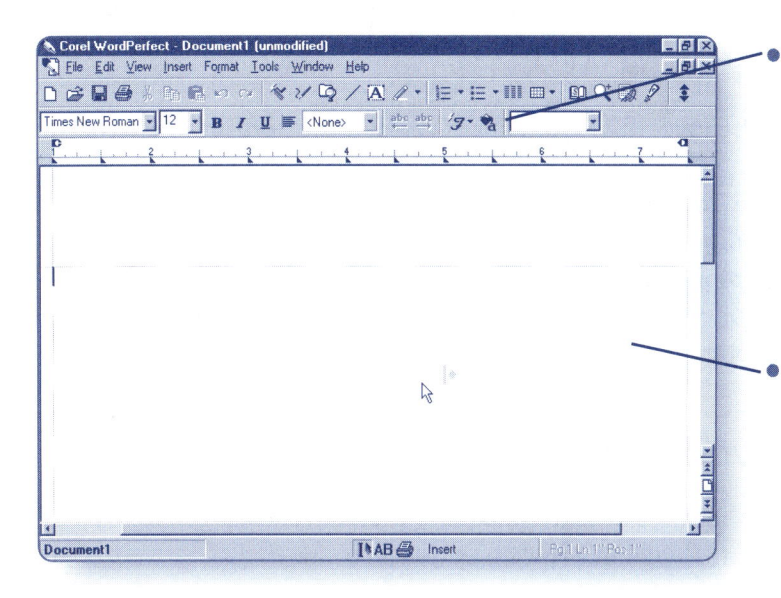

- **Property bar.** A series of tools that change according to the feature you are currently using. For example, if you are working in a table, table tools appear. WordPerfect has 38 different property bars.

- **Document screen.** The white area of the screen where the actual text will appear.

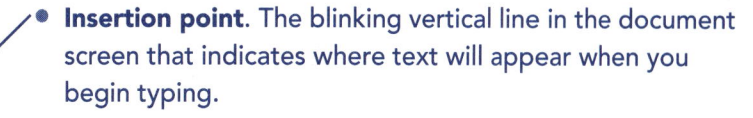

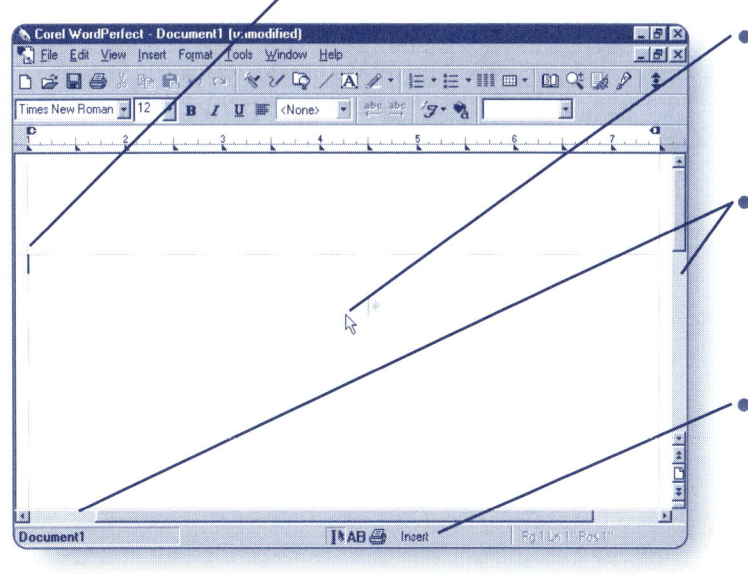

- **Insertion point.** The blinking vertical line in the document screen that indicates where text will appear when you begin typing.

- **Mouse pointer.** The mouse pointer changes as it moves to different locations on the screen.

- **Scroll bars.** Horizontal and vertical bars on the bottom and right side of the screen that allow you to see more of a document.

- **Application bar.** Information about the document currently open in WordPerfect, including filename, printer selection, and insertion point status.

We will examine many of these tools and features in later chapters of this book.

Typing Text

When typing a document in WordPerfect, press the Enter key only when you get to the end of a paragraph. (You can press the Enter key twice if you want an extra blank line between paragraphs.) WordPerfect takes care of the lines within a paragraph. If the word you are typing does not fit entirely on your current line, WordPerfect goes to the next line. This feature is called *word wrap*.

Typing Short Lines of Text

A short line of text—a date or greeting such as "Dear Mr. Smith"—counts as a paragraph all by itself.

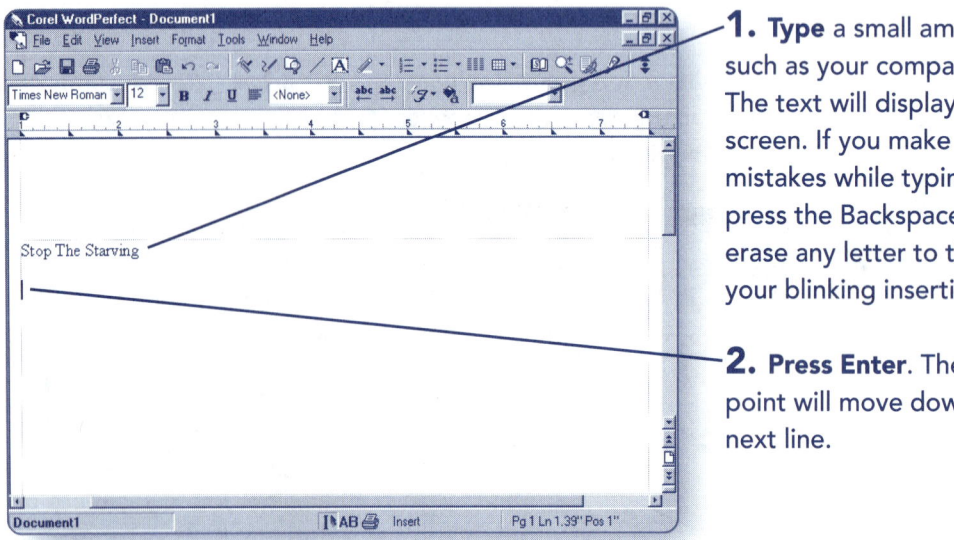

1. Type a small amount of **text** such as your company name. The text will display on the screen. If you make any mistakes while typing, you can press the Backspace key to erase any letter to the left of your blinking insertion point.

2. Press Enter. The insertion point will move down to the next line.

TYPING TEXT 7

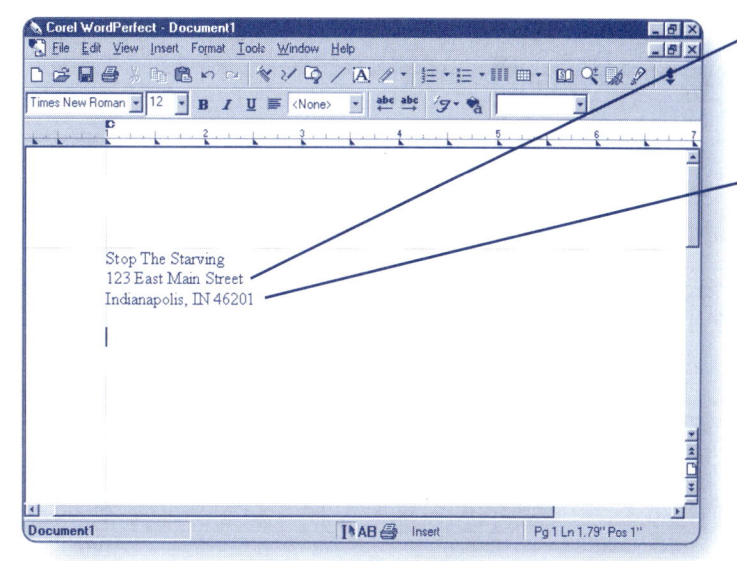

3. Type the next line of **text**. The text will appear in the document.

4. Continue typing any additional short lines of **text**, pressing the Enter key when each line is complete. The text will appear in the document.

Entering Date Text

Instead of fishing around your desk looking for your calendar, let WordPerfect put today's date in your document for you.

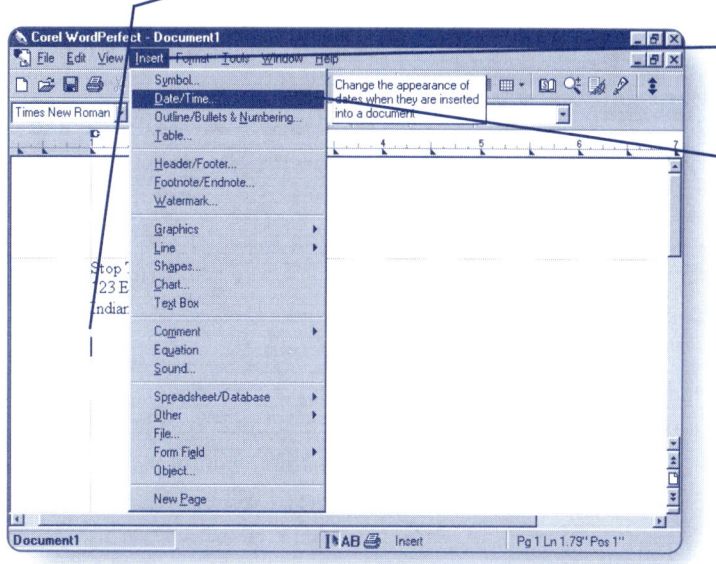

1. Click the **mouse pointer** where you want the date. The blinking insertion point will appear.

2. Click on **Insert**. The Insert menu will appear.

3. Click on **Date/Time**. The Date/Time Dialog box will open.

8 CHAPTER 1: WELCOME TO WORDPERFECT

4. Click on the **Date/Time format** you want to use in your letter. The option will be highlighted.

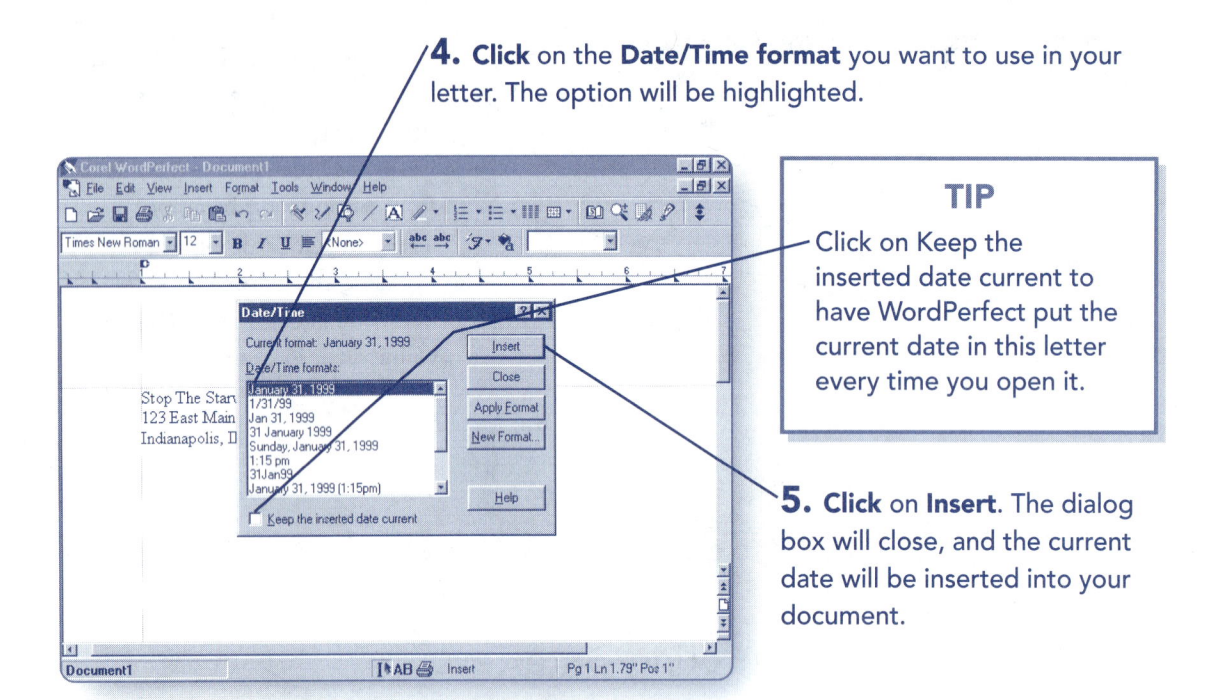

TIP
Click on Keep the inserted date current to have WordPerfect put the current date in this letter every time you open it.

5. Click on **Insert**. The dialog box will close, and the current date will be inserted into your document.

Entering the Body of a Letter

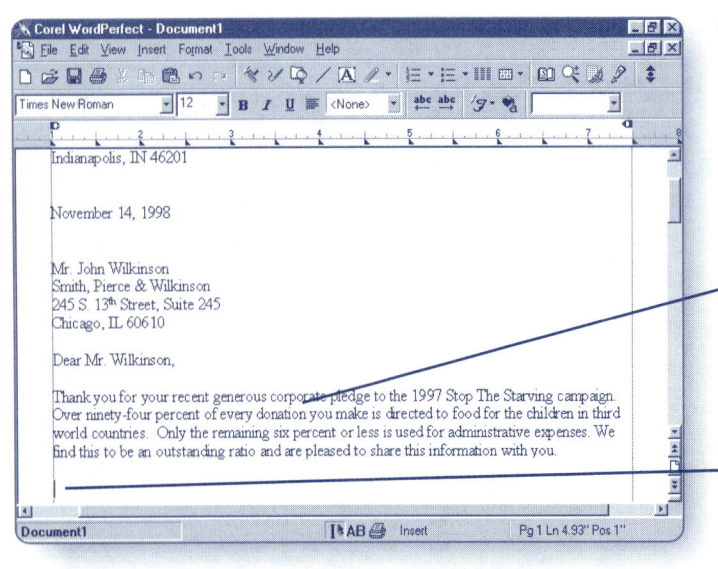

Now word wrap will come into play. Just keep typing when you get to the right side of your screen. Don't worry, WordPerfect will do its job and arrange the paragraph for you.

1. Type a paragraph of text for the first body paragraph. The text will appear in the document.

2. Press the **Enter key twice**. A blank line will be inserted, and the cursor will be moved to the beginning of a new paragraph.

ADDING A SPECIAL CHARACTER 9

3. Type another paragraph of text to serve as the second body paragraph. The text will appear in the document.

4. Press the **Enter key twice**. A blank line will be inserted, and the cursor will be moved to the beginning of a new paragraph.

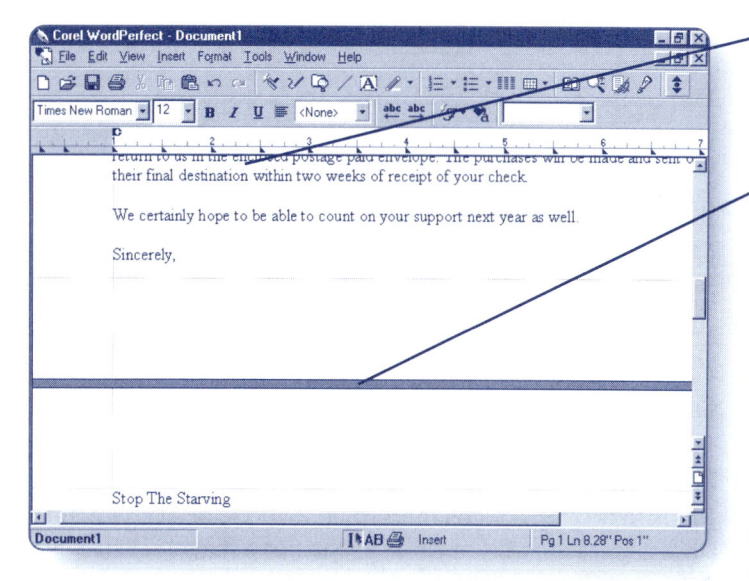

5. Type any **remaining text** for the body of the letter. The text will appear in the document.

Some of the features we will be discussing in the next several chapters only work when you have more than one page of text, so I recommend that you type several paragraphs here, enough to flow to a second page. You can tell you have reached a second page when a gray line appears on your screen. That is called a *page break*.

Adding a Special Character

WordPerfect has many special symbols you can use in your document. You'll find the registered trademark symbol, the copyright symbol, a bunch of multinational alphabet characters, and many more that are just plain fun to use.

10   CHAPTER 1: WELCOME TO WORDPERFECT

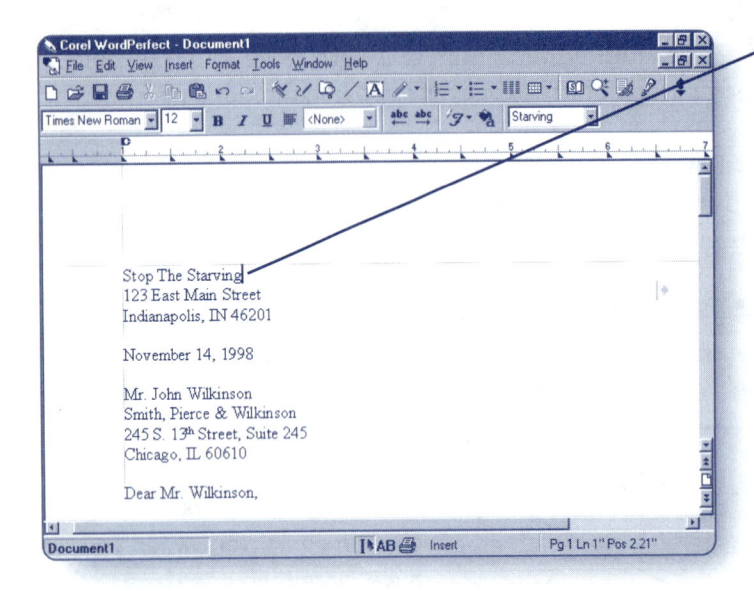

1. Click the **mouse button** at the location you want the special symbol. The insertion point will be moved to that point.

2. Click on **Insert**. The Insert menu will appear.

3. Click on **Symbol**. The WordPerfect Characters dialog box will open. WordPerfect has more than 2,400 special characters available in 15 different categories, including mathematical, multinational, Greek, and Japanese.

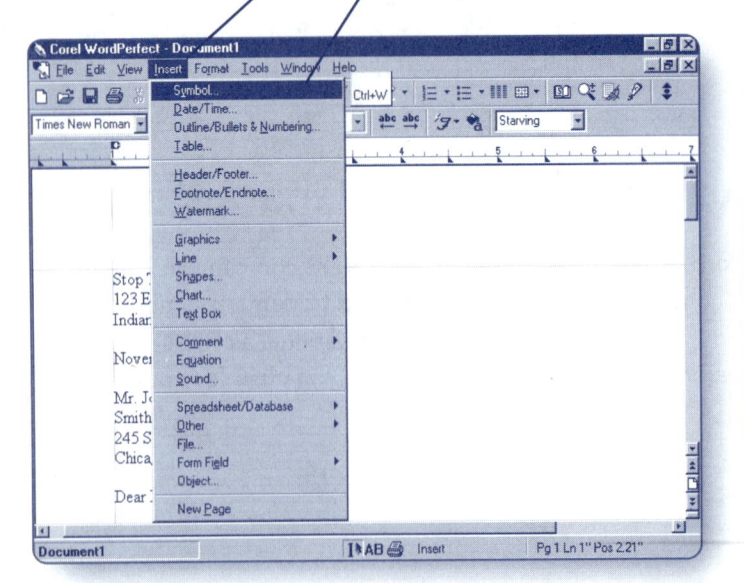

TIP

You can go straight to the WordPerfect special character dialog box by pressing Ctrl+W. Ctrl+W is called a *shortcut key*. Most WordPerfect functions have shortcut keys that let you bypass the menus after you get used to them.

ADDING A SPECIAL CHARACTER   11

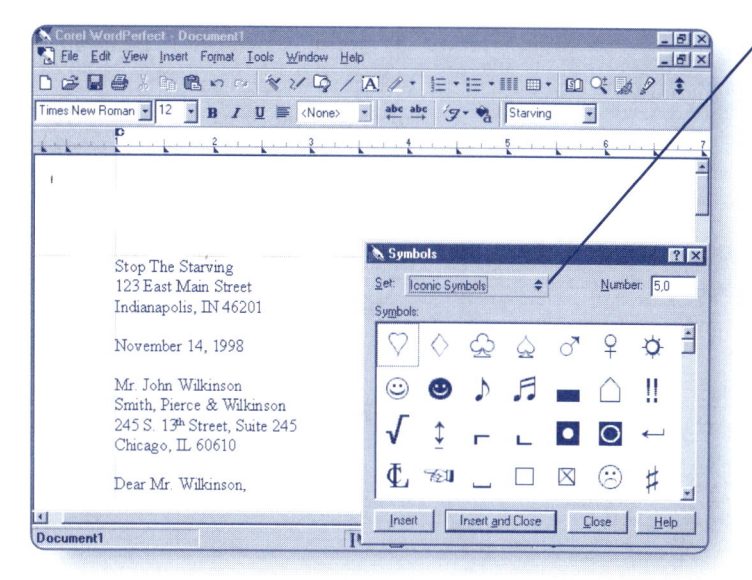

4. Click on the **Set up and down arrow** (◆). A list of categories will appear.

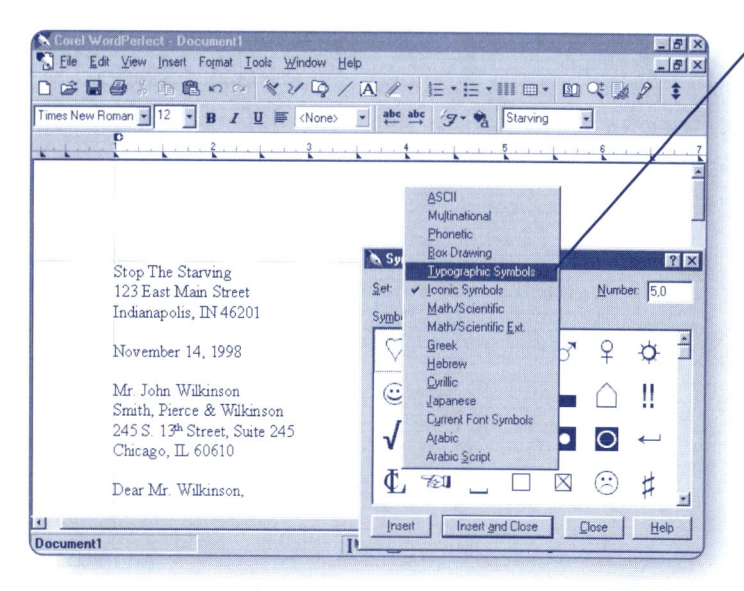

5. Click on **Typographic Symbols** or one of the other categories. A different selection of symbols will appear.

CHAPTER 1: WELCOME TO WORDPERFECT

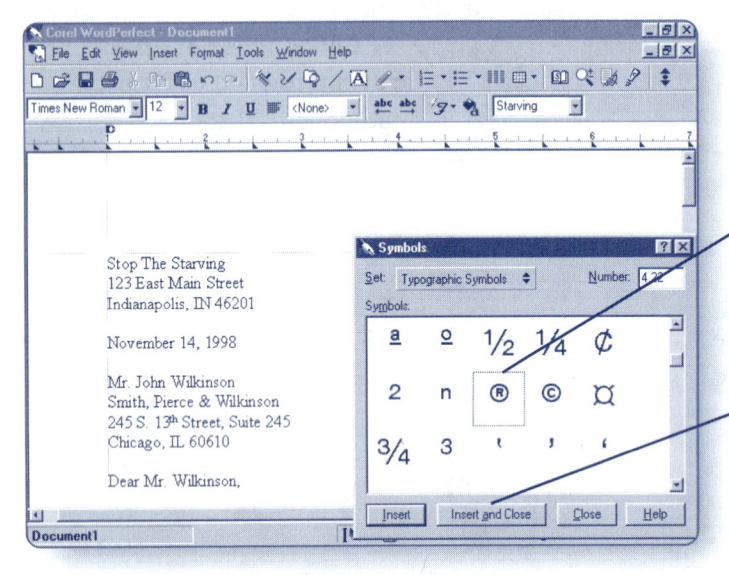

6. Scroll down until you see the desired symbol. The symbols will display in the dialog box.

7. Click on the **symbol** you want placed in your letter. The selected symbol will have a flashing dotted box around it.

8. Click on **Insert and Close**. The WordPerfect character box will close.

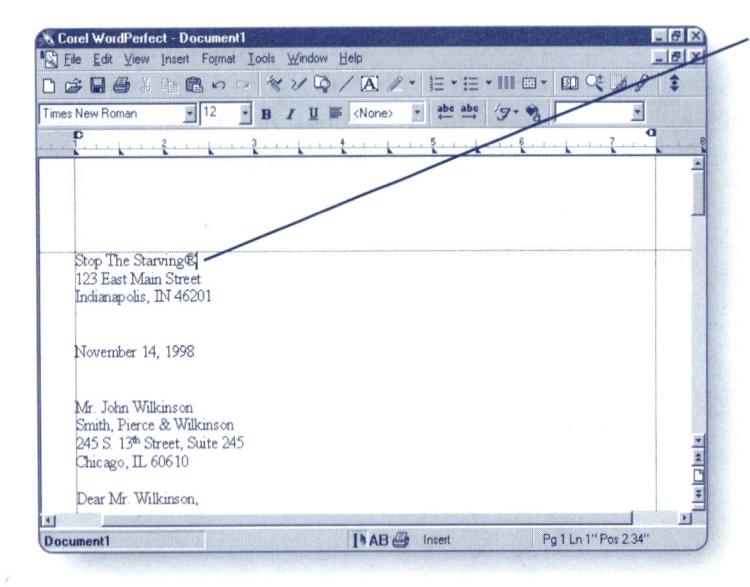

The symbol will be inserted into your document at the insertion point.

2

Saving, Opening, and Closing WordPerfect

When you work on a document in WordPerfect, the changes you make go into a temporary copy in the computer's memory. That memory gets erased when you turn off the computer—or the power fails. To avoid losing your document, you need to save it as a file. In this chapter, you'll learn how to:

- Save a WordPerfect document
- Close a document
- Open a document
- Exit the WordPerfect program

Saving a WordPerfect Document

Anyone who uses a computer has probably lost data at one time or another. If you haven't been saving to disk regularly, it only takes a few seconds to lose hours of work. WordPerfect has built-in features to help protect you against this eventuality. However, you still need to save.

Saving a File the First Time

When you first create a document, it has no name. If you want to be able to get back to that document later, however, it must have a name so that WordPerfect can find it. WordPerfect asks for a filename the first time you save the document; after that, the name you give it appears in the title bar at the top of the screen, as well as at the bottom of the screen in the application bar.

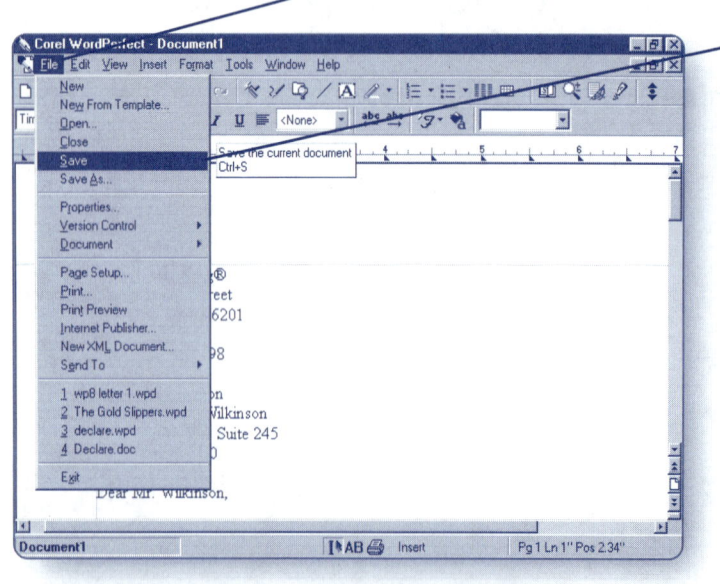

1. Click on **File**. The File menu will appear.

2. Click on **Save**. The Save File dialog box will open.

SAVING A WORDPERFECT DOCUMENT 15

3. Enter a **descriptive name** for the file. The name will appear in the File name: box.

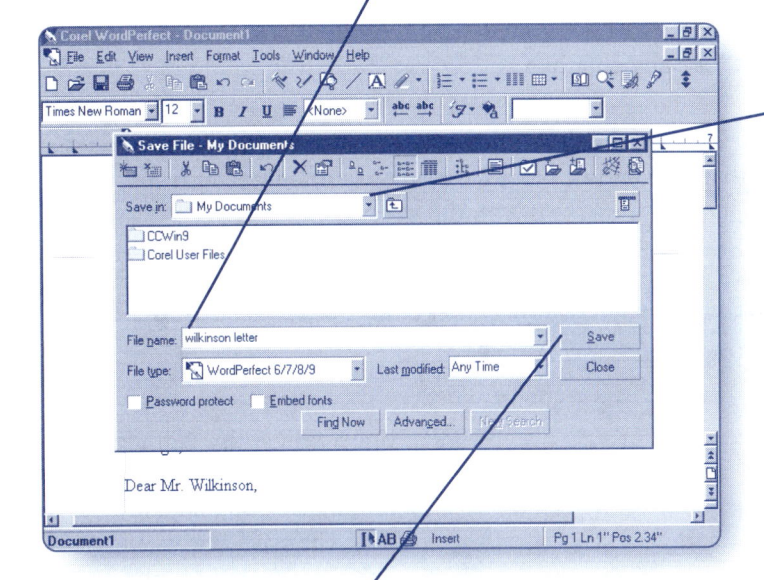

NOTE

The Save in: box lists folder options where you can save the document. The default folder that appears is MyFiles. If you don't want to save it to this folder as in the preceding example, or if you want to save your document to another disk, you can select another one. Click on the down arrow (▼) to browse.

4. Click on **Save**. The file will be saved.

Notice the filename appearing at the top of the window and at the bottom.

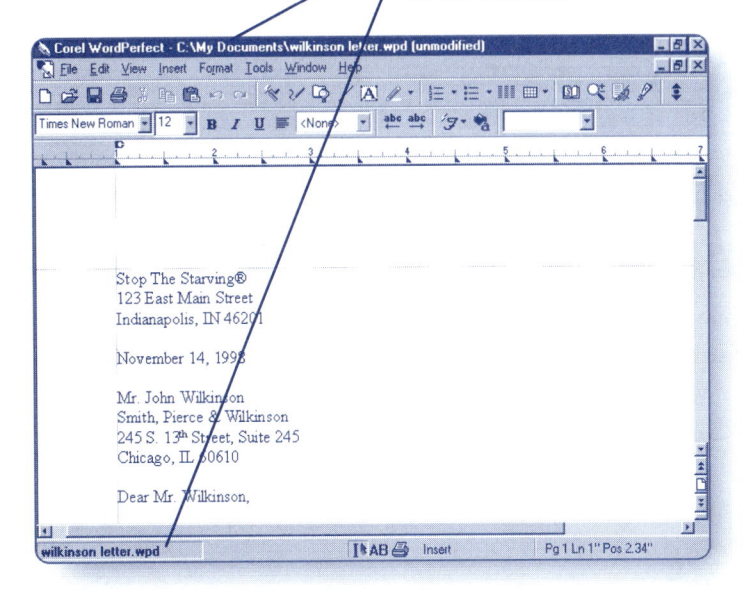

CHAPTER 2: SAVING, OPENING, AND CLOSING WORDPERFECT

Resaving a Document

As you continue to work on your document, you should resave it every ten minutes or so to help ensure that you do not lose any changes.

1. Click on the **Save button**. The document will be resaved with any changes. No dialog box will open because the document is resaved with the same name and in the same folder as previously specified.

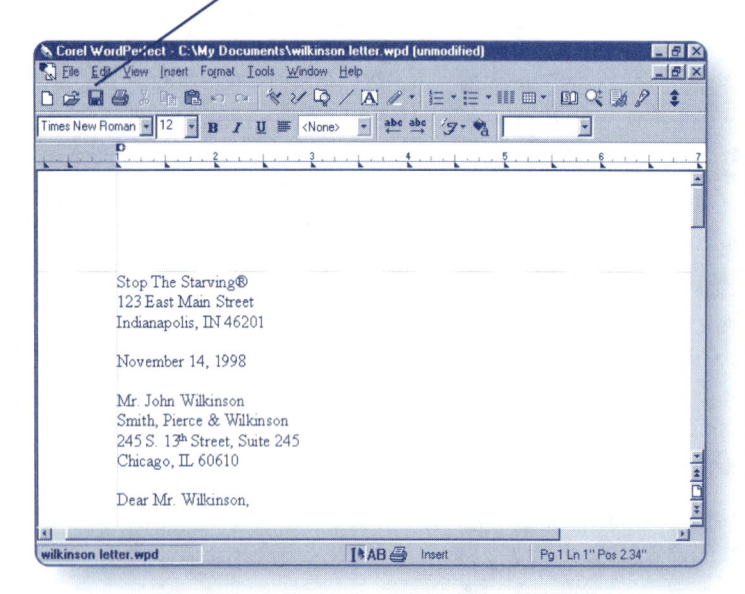

TIP

If you want to save the document with a different name or in a different folder, click on File and then choose Save As. The Save As dialog box prompts you for the new name or folder. The original document remains as well as the new one.

Closing a WordPerfect Document

When you are finished working on a document, you should close it. *Closing* is the equivalent of putting it away for later use. When you close a document, you are putting the document away—not the program. WordPerfect is still active and ready to work for you.

CLOSING A WORDPERFECT DOCUMENT   17

1. Click on **File**. The File menu will appear.

2. Click on **Close**. The document will be put away, and another WordPerfect blank screen will appear ready for you to start on another document.

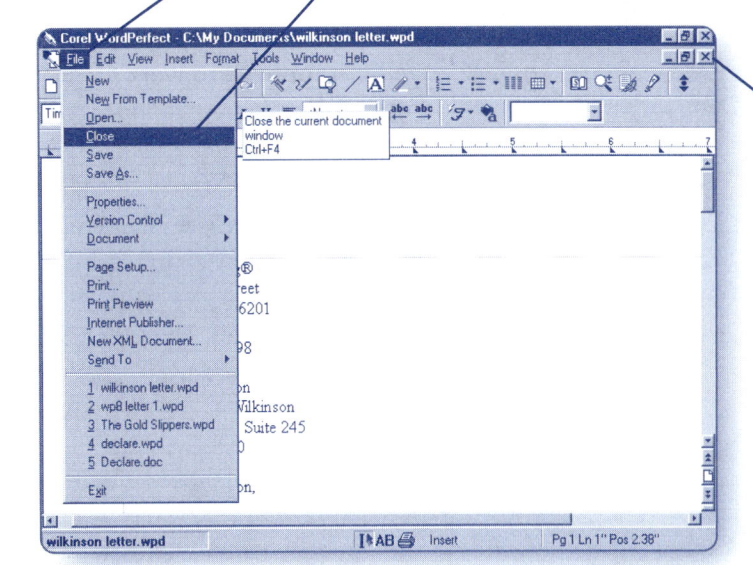

OR

3. Click on the **Close Document button ([X])**. The document will be put away. By choosing this step 3, you skip steps 1 and 2.

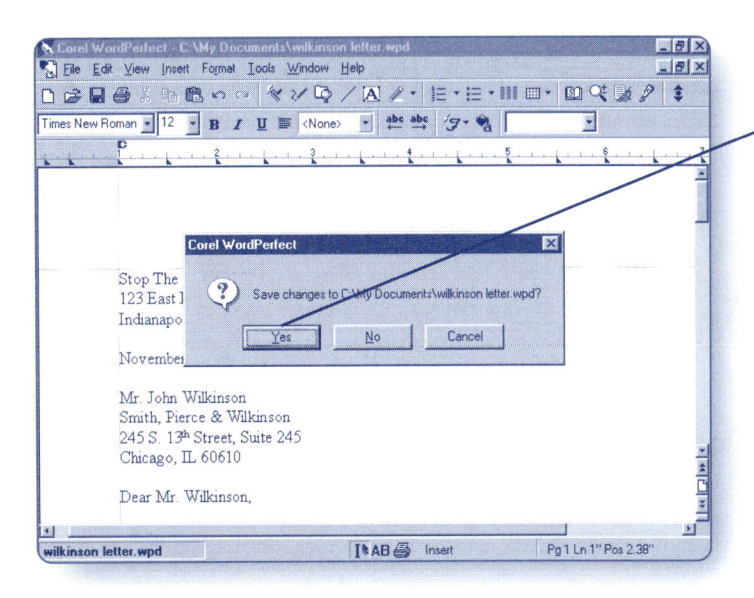

NOTE

If you have not saved any changes to your file, WordPerfect asks whether you want to do so. If you do want to save the file, click on Yes; if you do not want to save it, click on No.

Opening a WordPerfect Document

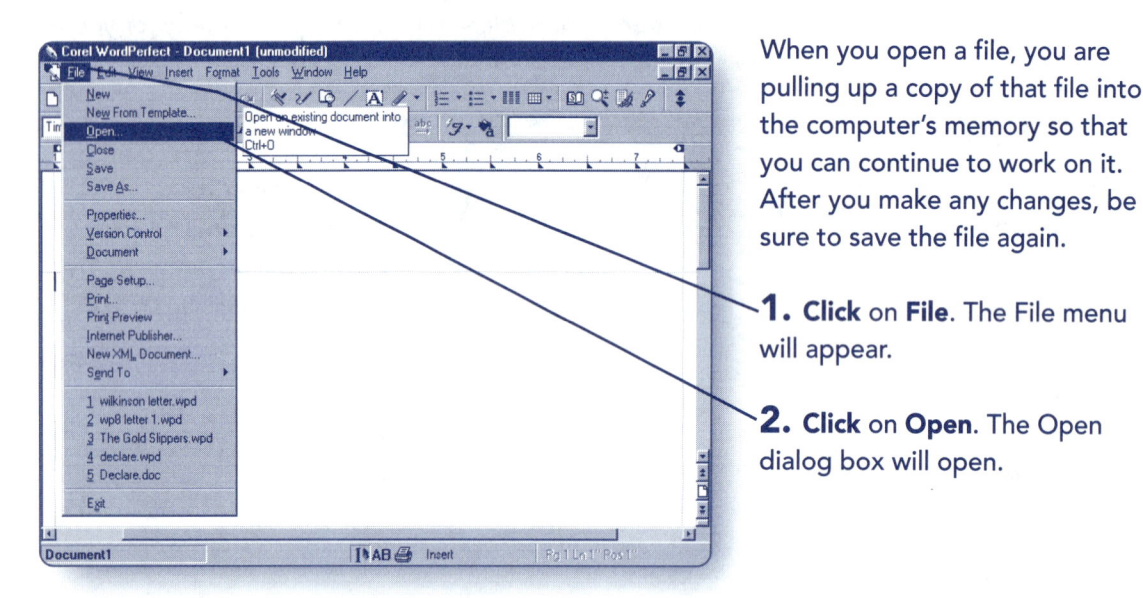

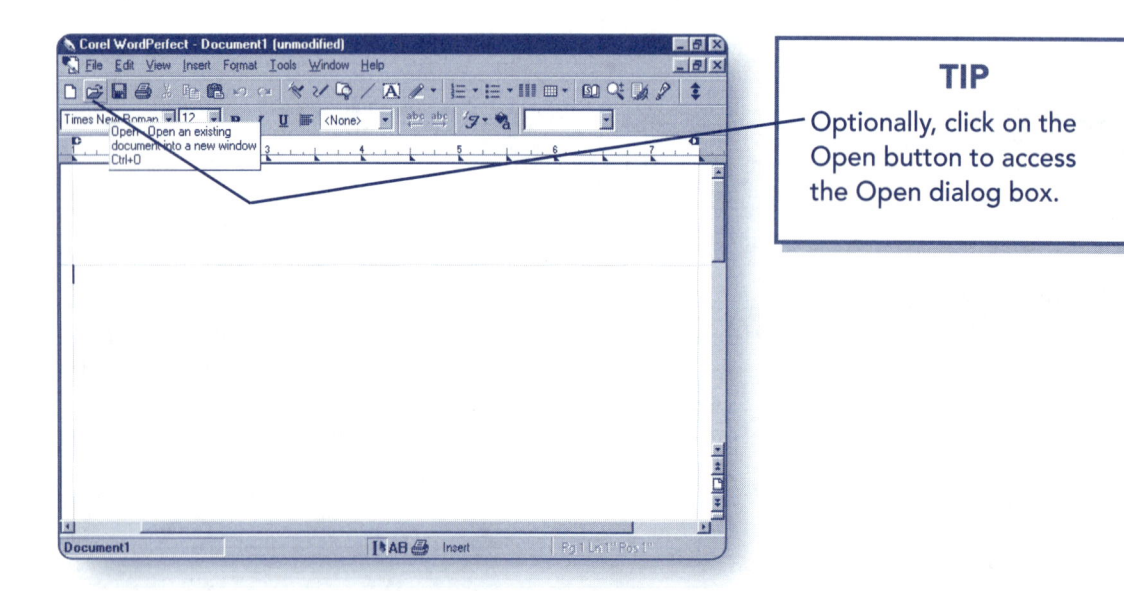

When you open a file, you are pulling up a copy of that file into the computer's memory so that you can continue to work on it. After you make any changes, be sure to save the file again.

1. Click on **File**. The File menu will appear.

2. Click on **Open**. The Open dialog box will open.

TIP
Optionally, click on the Open button to access the Open dialog box.

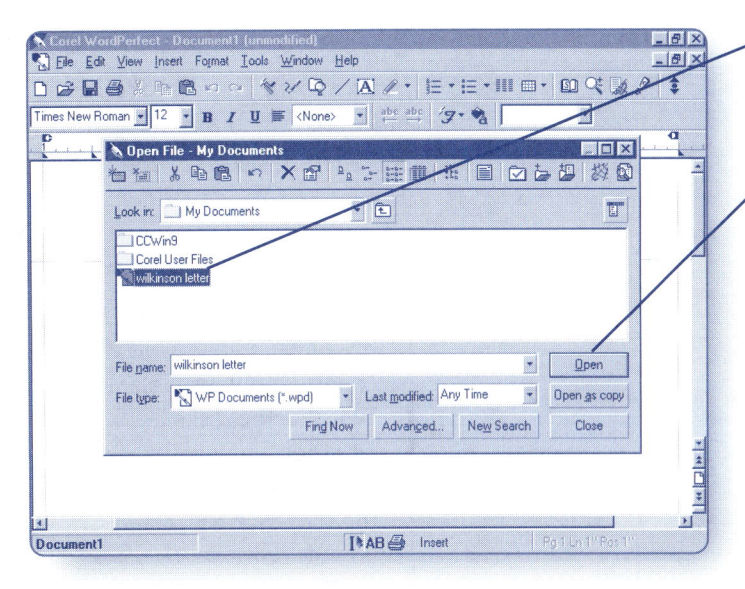

EXITING THE WORDPERFECT DOCUMENT 19

3. Click on the **name** of the file you want to open. The filename will be highlighted.

4. Click on **Open**. The file will be placed on your screen, ready for you to edit.

Exiting the WordPerfect Program

If you are finished working with WordPerfect, exit the WordPerfect program. This procedure protects your data and avoids possible program damage. It also frees up valuable computer memory that can be used for other programs.

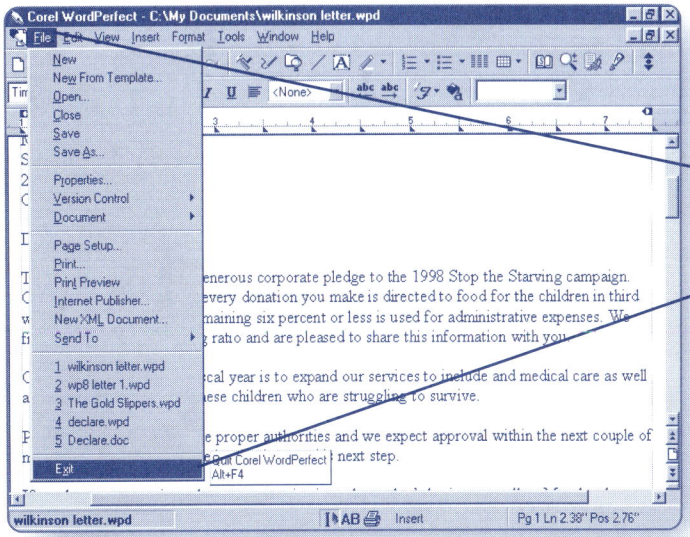

1. Click on **File**. The File menu will appear.

2. Click on **Exit**. The WordPerfect program will be closed down.

OR

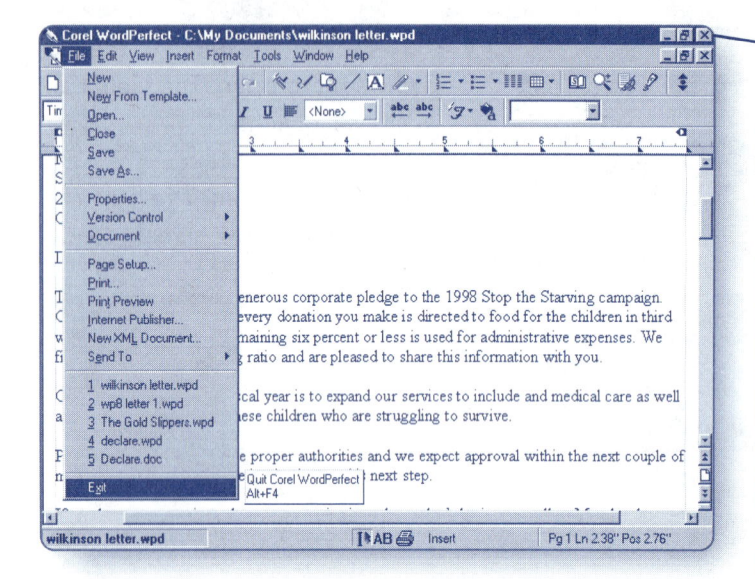

CHAPTER 2: SAVING, OPENING, AND CLOSING WORDPERFECT

3. Click on the **Close Program button ([X])**. The WordPerfect program will be put away. By choosing this step 3, you skip steps 1 and 2.

NOTE

If you have not saved any changes to your file, WordPerfect asks whether you want to do so. If you do want to save the file, click on Yes; if you do not want to save it, click on No. You do not have to close a file before you exit the WordPerfect program. WordPerfect closes the document as you exit the program.

3

Getting Help

Although I sincerely hope you find many answers to your WordPerfect questions in this book, sometimes you need additional information. WordPerfect supplies several types of assistance. In this chapter, you'll learn how to:

- Get PerfectExpert help
- Use Help Topics

CHAPTER 3: GETTING HELP

Getting PerfectExpert Help

Get the expert assistance you need from the PerfectExpert!

1. Click on **Help**. The Help menu will appear.

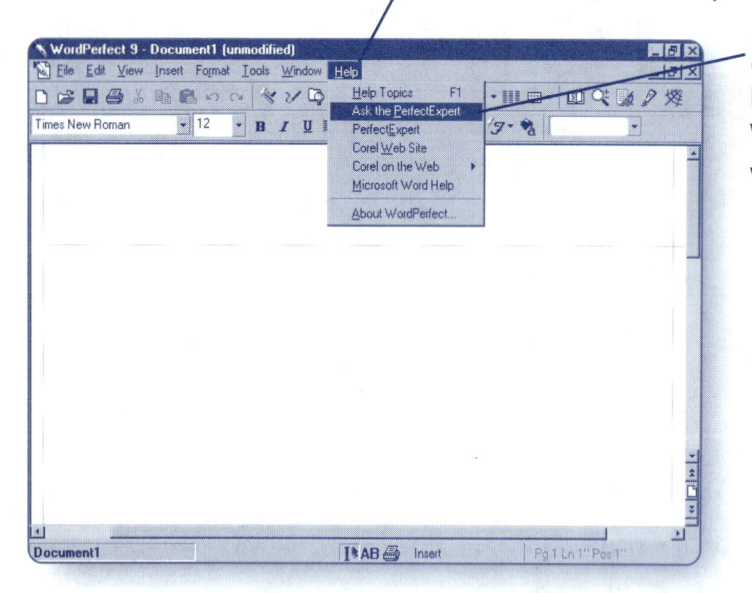

2. Click on **Ask the Perfect Expert**. The Help Topics: WordPerfect 9 Help dialog box will open.

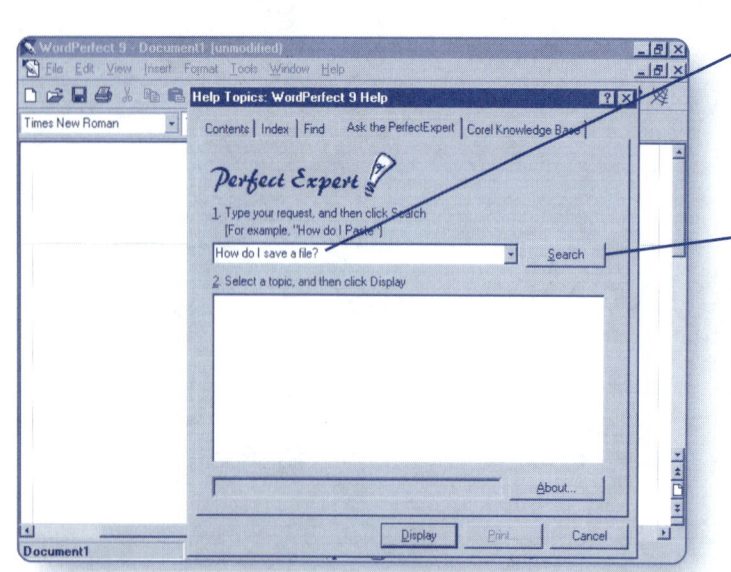

3. Type your question in the Type your request text box. Your request will appear in the text box.

4. Click on **Search**. WordPerfect will search for any topic that might be closely related to your question and display the results in the Search Results box.

GETTING PERFECTEXPERT HELP   23

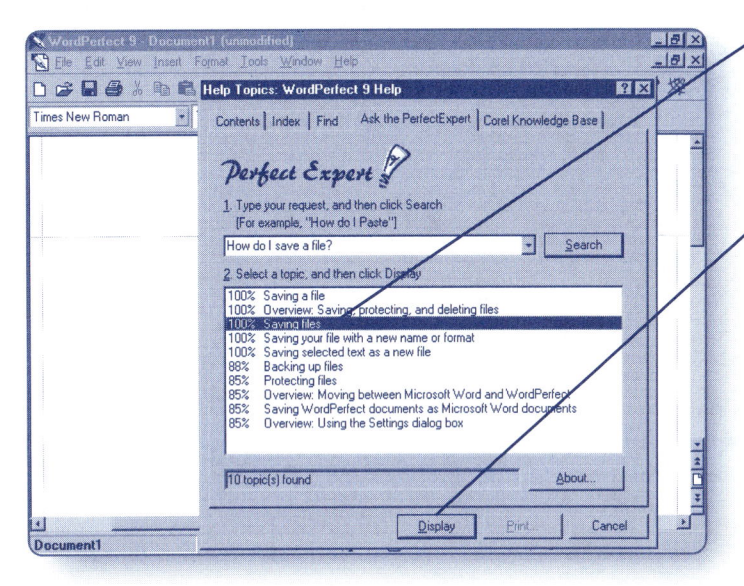

5. Click on the **choice** that most closely resembles the issue you are seeking. The option will be selected.

6. Click on **Display**. A help window will appear with instructions for the feature you asked about.

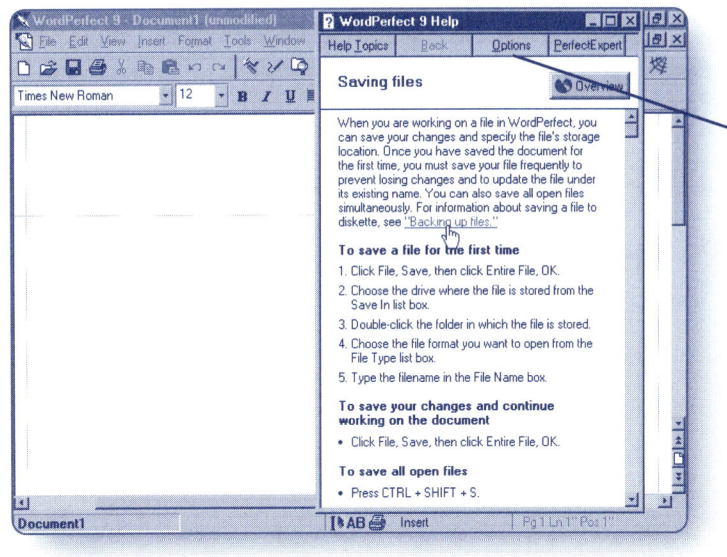

You can print a paper copy of the help instructions.

7. Click on **Options**. The Options menu will appear.

CHAPTER 3: GETTING HELP

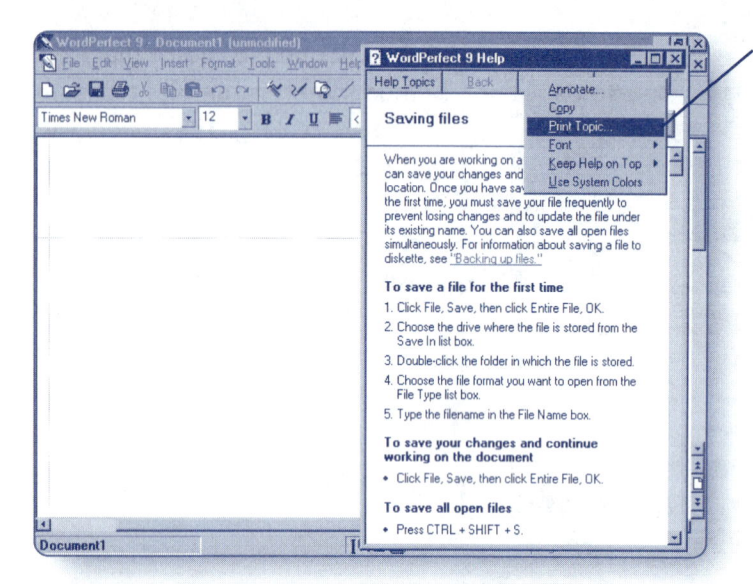

8. Click on **Print Topic**. The Print dialog box will open.

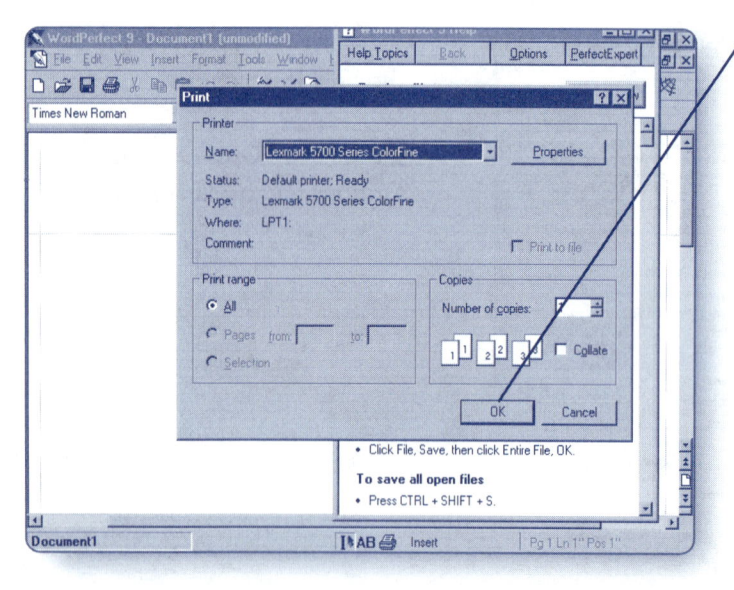

9. Click on **OK**. The topic will be printed.

USING HELP TOPICS 25

TIP
Some help windows have underlined options for you to click on for further or related information.

10. Click on the **Close button** ([X]) of the help topic when you are finished with it. The Help Window will close.

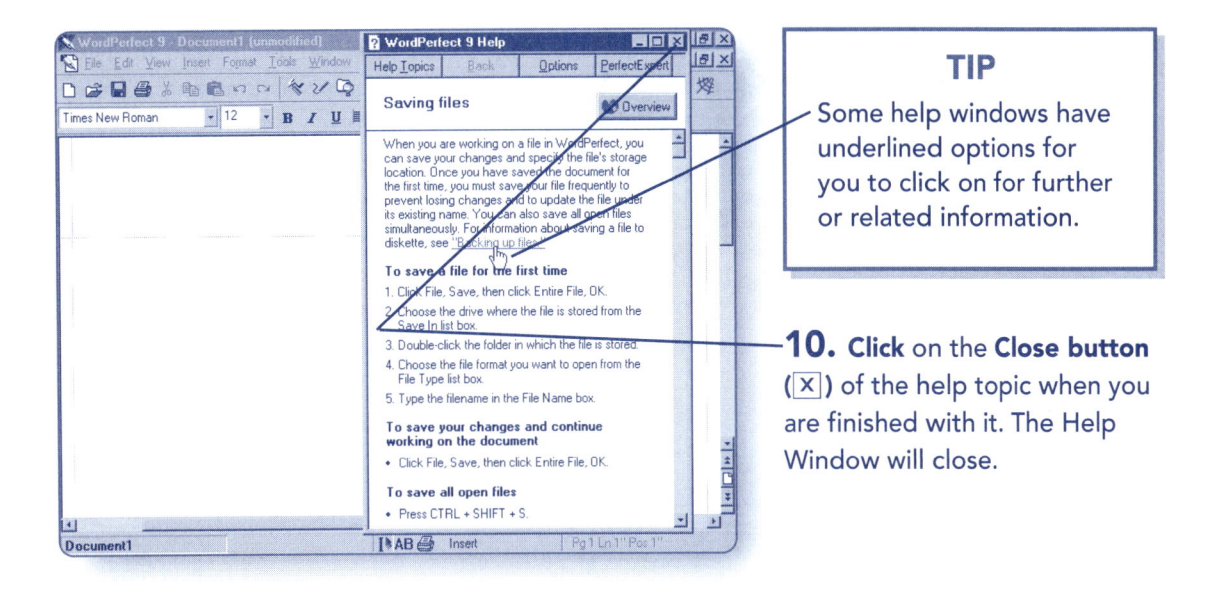

Using Help Topics

Help Topics is an index of all WordPerfect features.

1. Click on **Help**. The Help menu will appear.

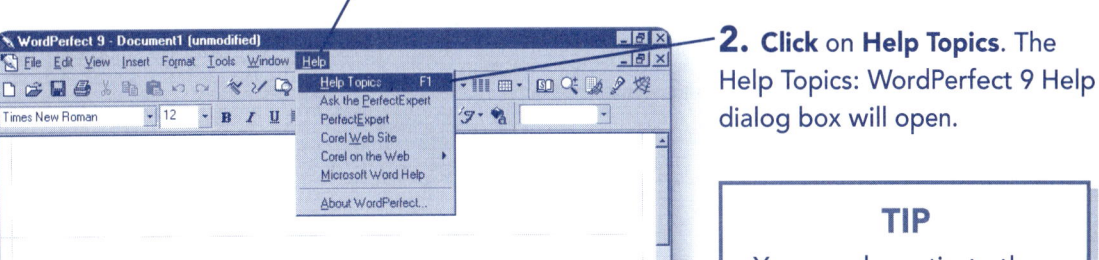

2. Click on **Help Topics**. The Help Topics: WordPerfect 9 Help dialog box will open.

TIP
You can also activate the help feature by pressing the F1 key.

26　CHAPTER 3: GETTING HELP

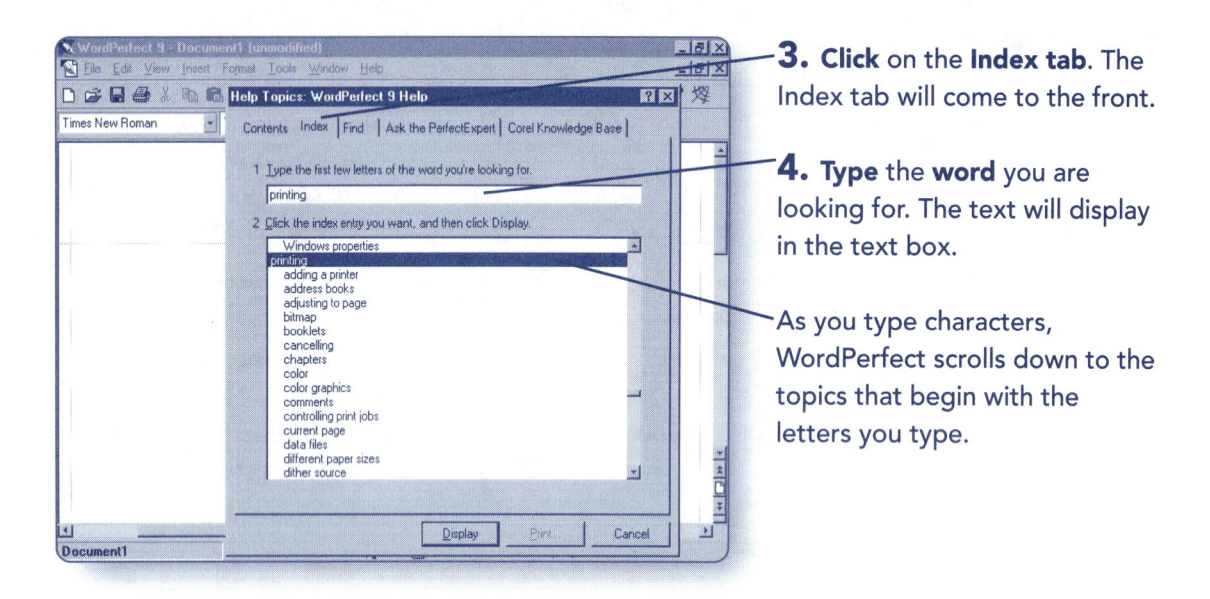

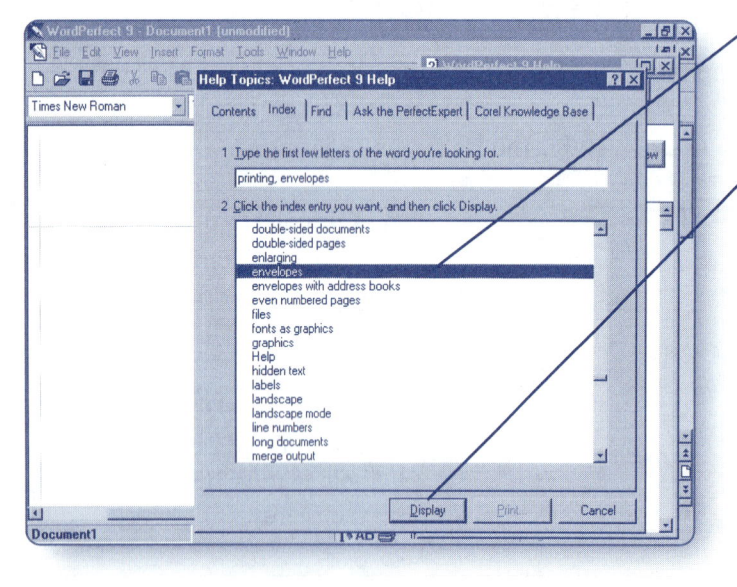

3. Click on the **Index tab**. The Index tab will come to the front.

4. Type the **word** you are looking for. The text will display in the text box.

As you type characters, WordPerfect scrolls down to the topics that begin with the letters you type.

5. Click on the **choice closest** to your topic in the second box. The option will be selected.

6. Click on **Display**. A list of the topics found will appear.

USING HELP TOPICS   27

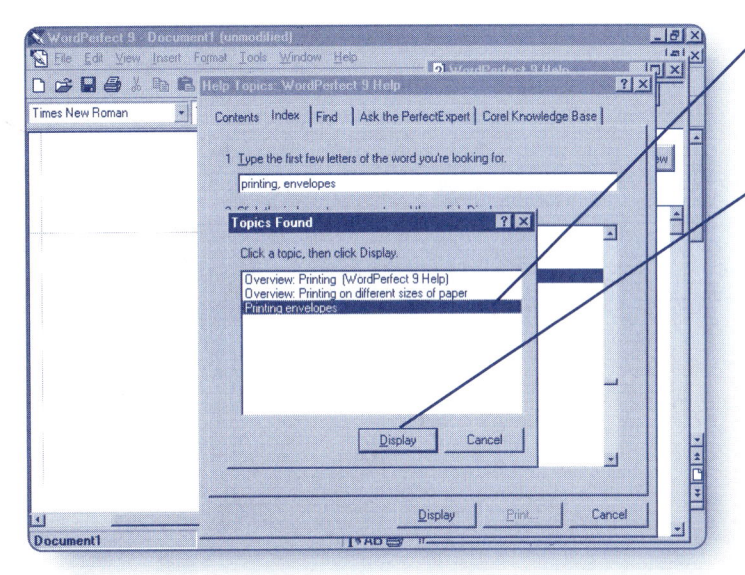

7. **Click** on the **selection** you want to know about. The choice will be selected.

8. **Click** on **Display**. A help window will appear with step-by-step instructions.

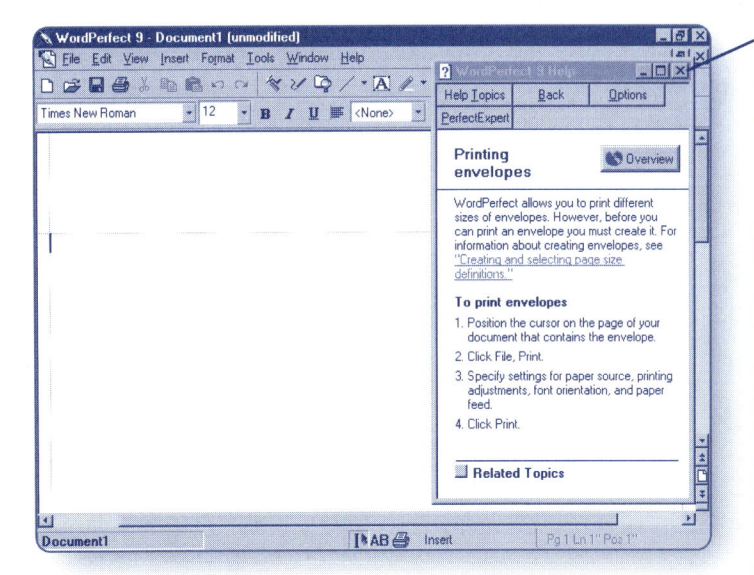

9. **Click** on the **Close button** (⊠) of the help window when you are finished with it. The Help window will close.

TIP

The Corel WordPerfect Web site contains additional help in the form of Technical Support and Tips and Tricks. Click on Corel on the Web from the Help menu for quick access to the Corel WordPerfect Web site.

4

Moving Around in a Document

To edit a document, you'll need to move around freely in it—especially to locate specific text. In this chapter, you'll learn how to:

- Move around in a WordPerfect document
- Use Autoscroll
- Go forward and backward
- Use the Go To command
- Use the shadow cursor

Moving Around in a Document

As you've seen, you can work on any part of the document that shows on your screen simply by clicking the mouse pointer where you want to be. You can also move around in a WordPerfect document by pressing the Up, Down, Right, or Left Arrow keys on the keyboard.

Moving Using the Keyboard

Several shortcut keys speed up the process of moving around in a WordPerfect document. The following table illustrates these shortcut keys.

To Move	Do This
A word at a time	Press Ctrl+Right Arrow or Ctrl+Left Arrow
A paragraph at a time	Press Ctrl+Up Arrow or Ctrl+Down Arrow
A full screen up at a time	Press the PageUp key
A full screen down at a time	Press the PageDown key
To the beginning of a line	Press the Home key
To the end of a line	Press the End key
To the top of the document	Press Ctrl+Home
To the bottom of the document	Press Ctrl+End
To a specified page number	Press Ctrl+G, then enter the page number

Moving Using the Scroll Bar

Two scroll bars are in the document window; a vertical scroll bar and a horizontal scroll bar. Displaying text by using the scroll bars does not, however, move the insertion point. You'll need to click the mouse wherever you want the insertion point to be located.

MOVING AROUND IN A DOCUMENT 31

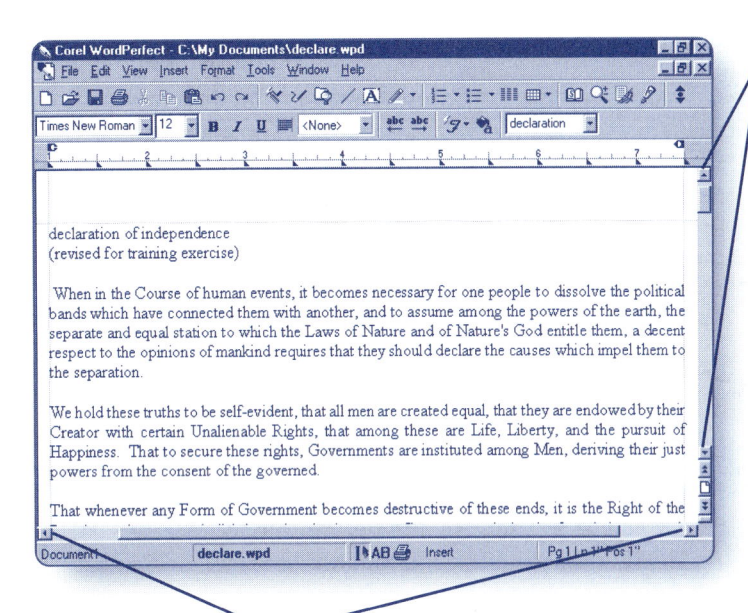

1a. Click on the **arrow** at either end of the vertical scroll bar to move the document up or down in the window.

OR

1b. Click on the **arrow** at either end of the horizontal scroll bar to move the document left or right.

To move the document more quickly, use the scroll box.

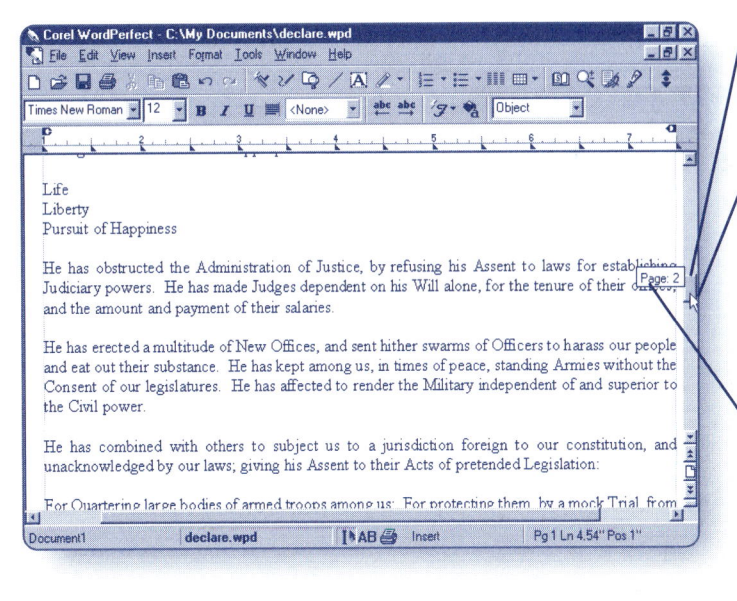

2. Place the mouse **pointer over** the **box** in the vertical or horizontal scroll bar.

3. Press and **hold** the **mouse button** and **drag** the box up or down in the vertical scroll bar, or left or right in the horizontal scroll bar.

Notice that when you move the scroll box in the vertical scroll bar, if you have more than one page, an indicator box appears telling you which page you're on.

4. Release the **mouse button** at your desired location. The screen will move to that location.

32 CHAPTER 4: MOVING AROUND IN A DOCUMENT

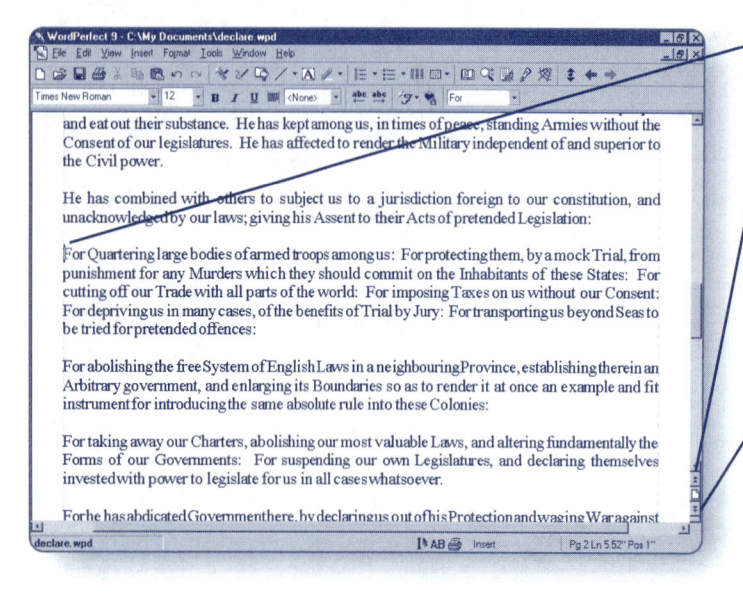

5. Click the **mouse pointer** in the body of the document. The insertion point will be moved.

6a. Click on the **Previous Page button**. Your view will be moved backward in the document one page at a time.

OR

6b. Click on the **Next Page button**. Your view will be moved forward in the document one page at a time.

7. Click the **mouse** in the body of the document. The blinking insertion point will appear.

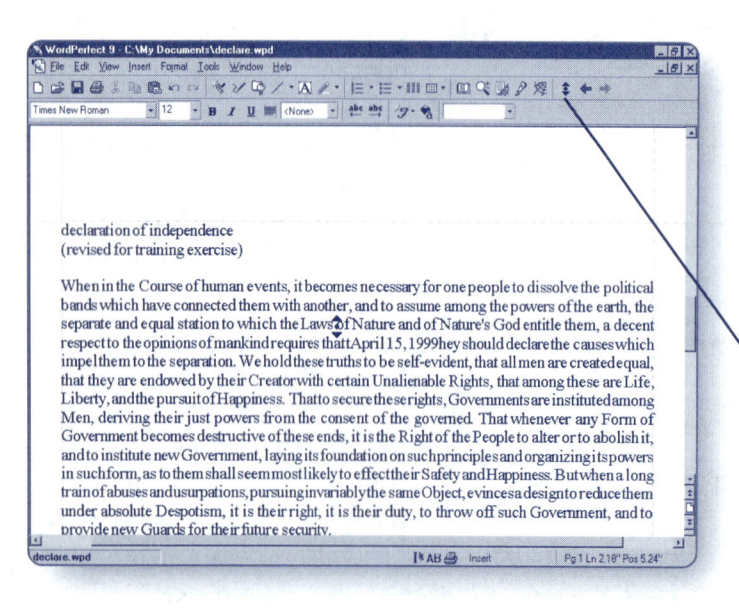

Using Autoscroll

Autoscroll is a new feature of WordPerfect 9. When Autoscroll is activated, the document screen scrolls up or down automatically.

1. Click on the **Autoscroll button**. The mouse will turn into a double-headed black arrow with a dot in the center.

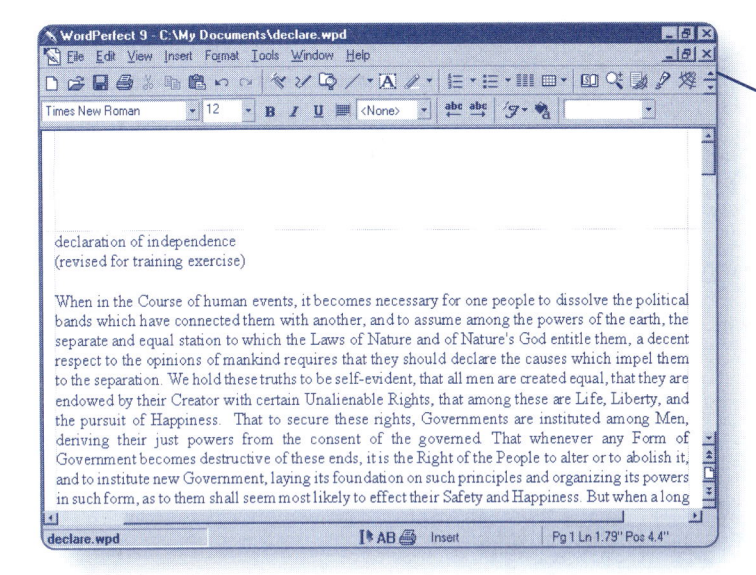

MOVING AROUND IN A DOCUMENT   33

NOTE
Depending on your screen resolution, you may not see the Autoscroll button. Click on the toolbar arrows to see additional buttons.

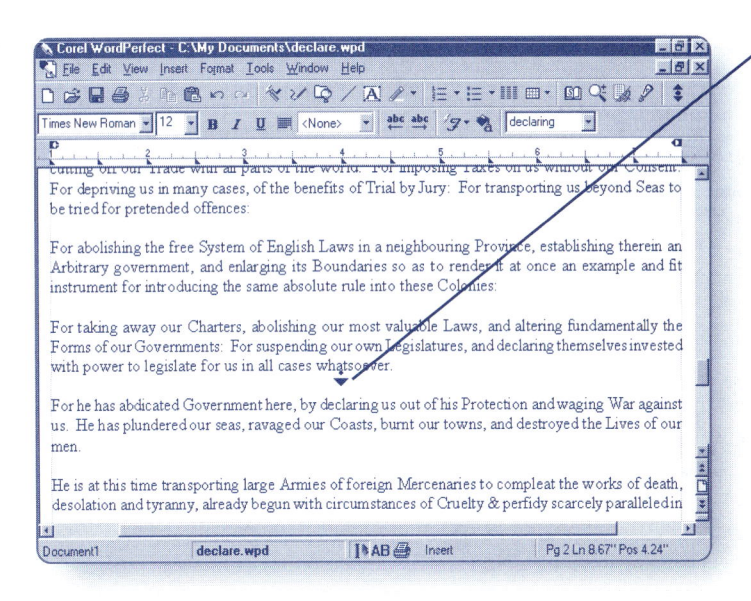

2a. Slowly **move** the **mouse** slightly **downward**. The Autoscroll feature will activate, and your view will scroll toward the bottom of the document.

OR

CHAPTER 4: MOVING AROUND IN A DOCUMENT

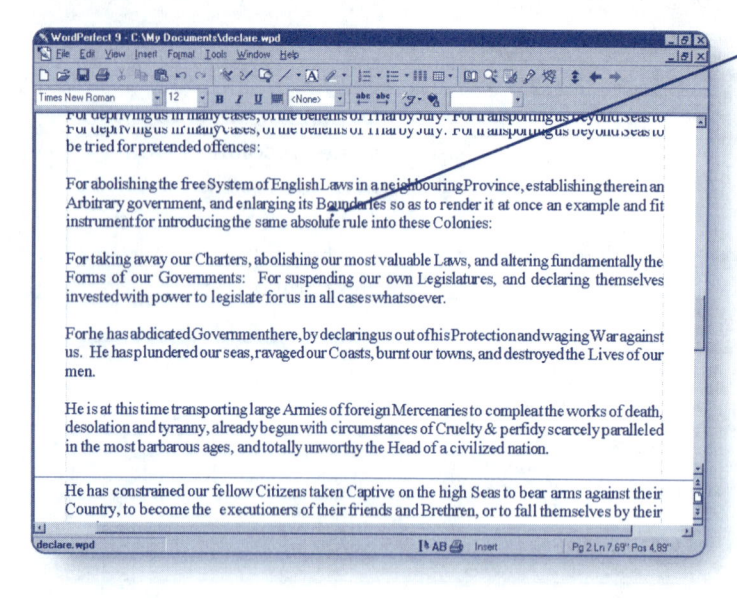

2b. Slowly **move** the **mouse** slightly **upward**. The Autoscroll feature will activate, and your view will scroll toward the top of the document.

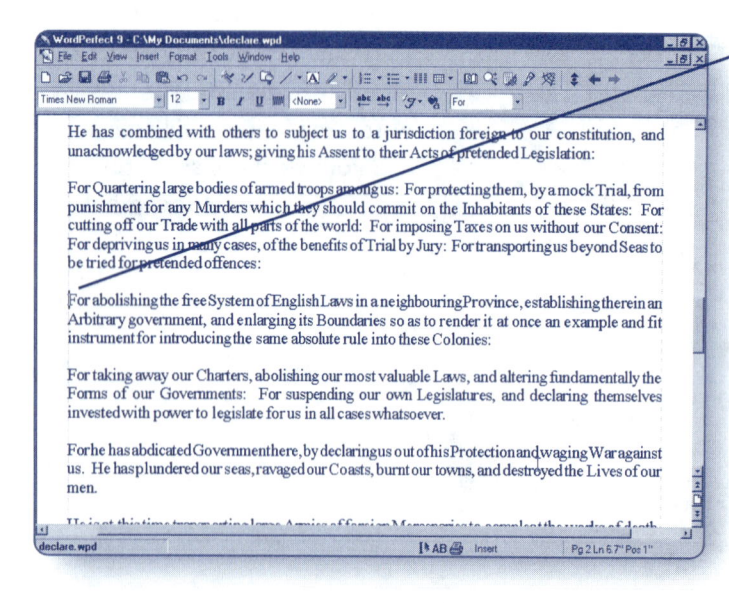

3. Click the **mouse button**. The Autoscroll feature will stop, and a blinking insertion point will appear.

MOVING AROUND IN A DOCUMENT 35

Going Forward and Backward

As you find yourself clicking from one place to the next in your document, the Back and Forward buttons can quickly move the insertion point.

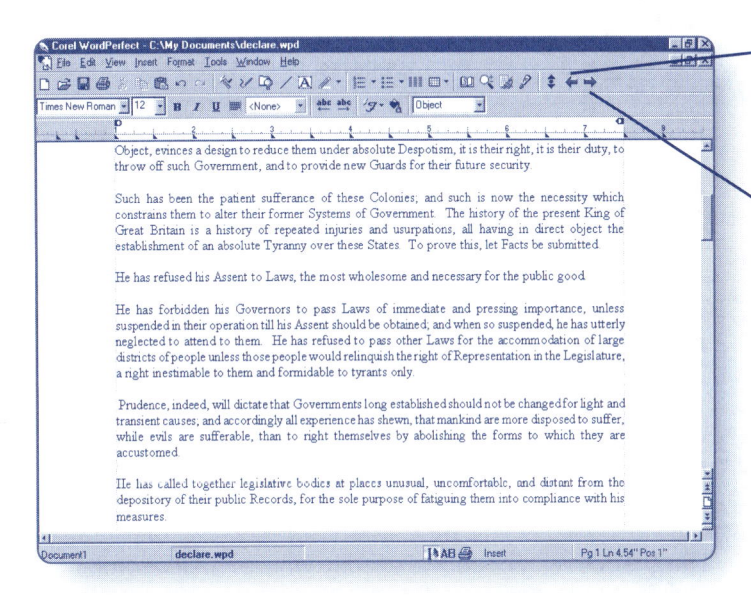

1. Click on the **Back button**. The insertion point will jump to its previous location.

2. Click on the **Forward button**. The insertion point move will redo.

Using the Go To Command

If you have a lengthy document, use the Go To command to jump to a specific location in the document.

1. Click on **Edit**. The Edit menu will appear.

2. Click on **Go To**. The Go To dialog box will open.

TIP
Pressing Ctrl+G also displays the Go To dialog box.

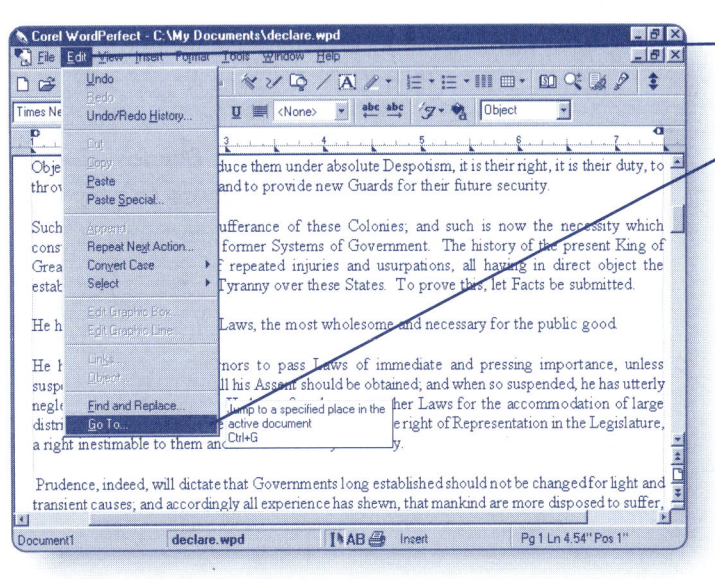

CHAPTER 4: MOVING AROUND IN A DOCUMENT

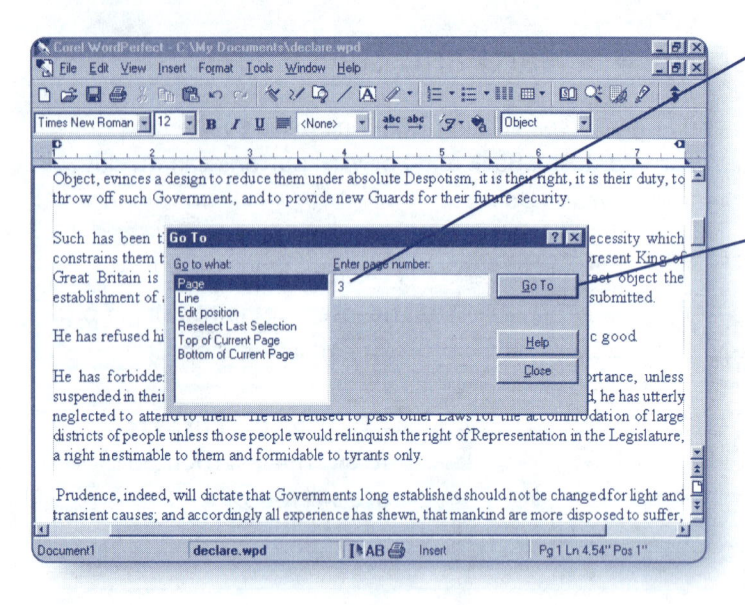

3. Type the **page number** you want to display. The number will appear in the Enter page number: box.

4. Click on **Go To**. The specified page will be displayed. The insertion point will be located at the beginning of the specified page.

Using the Shadow Cursor

The shadow cursor keeps your mouse pointer from getting lost. The shadow cursor shows exactly where the insertion point will go when you click the mouse. You can click anywhere to start typing text, or drag to insert clip art, a text box, or a table.

1. Click on the **Shadow Cursor button**. The mouse pointer will turn from an I-beam into an arrow.

USING THE SHADOW CURSOR   37

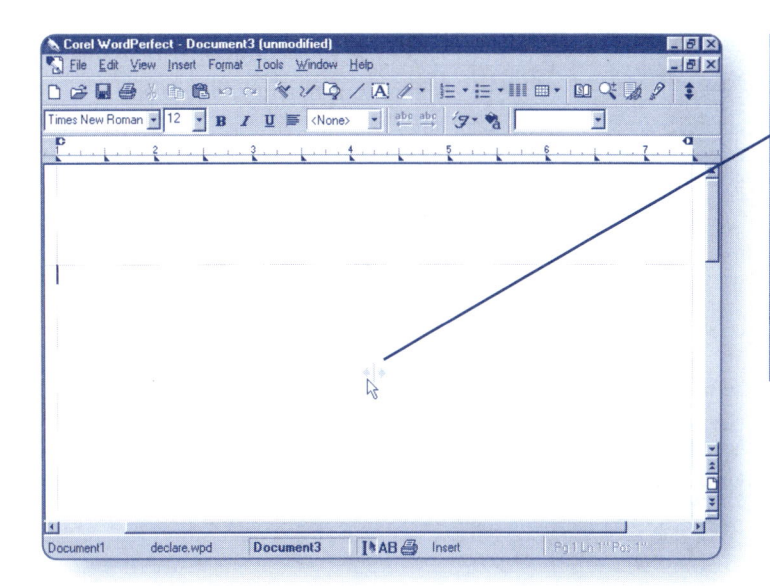

TIP

If the shadow cursor has an arrowhead on both the left and right side of the light line, WordPerfect is indicating that this is the horizontal center of the page.

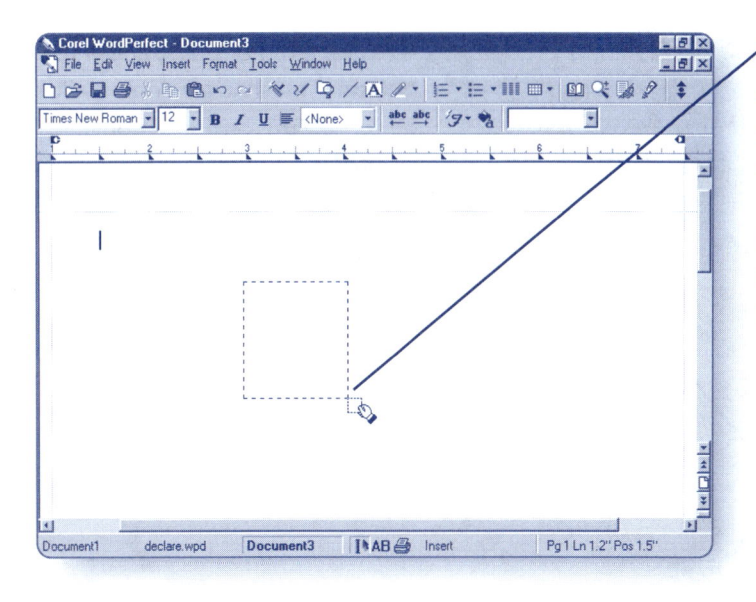

2. Click on the **mouse button** and **drag** a **small rectangle** on your screen. A shortcut menu will appear.

From here, you can add clip art, text boxes, tables, and custom boxes.

38 CHAPTER 4: MOVING AROUND IN A DOCUMENT

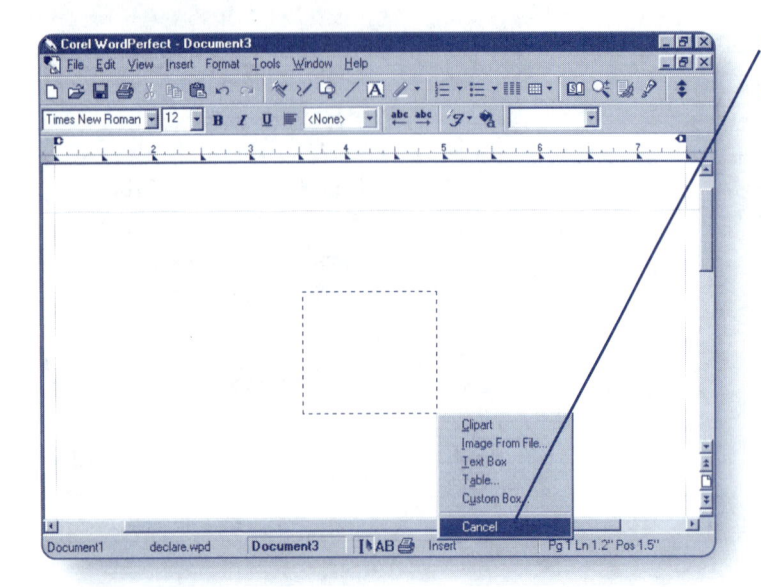

3. Click on **Cancel**. The shortcut menu will close.

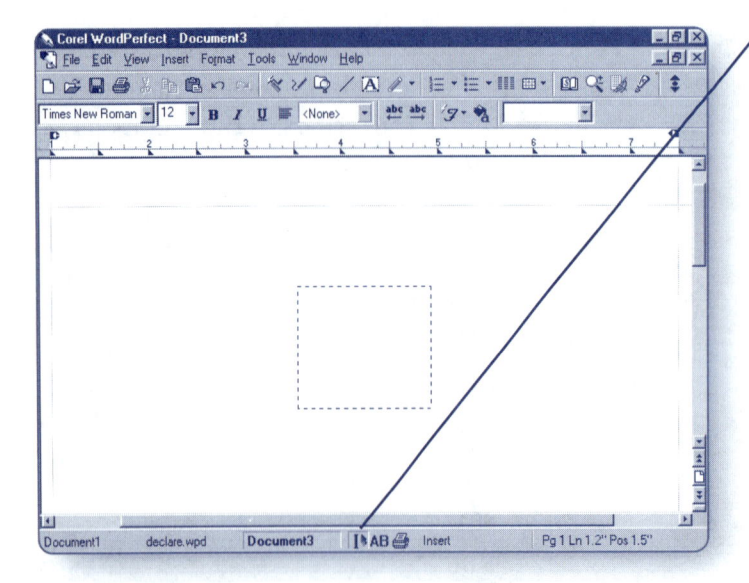

4. Click on the **Shadow Cursor button**. The shadow cursor will be turned off, and the mouse pointer will look like an I.

5

Editing a Document

Unless you're a perfect typist, you probably have a few mistakes in your document. Or perhaps you've changed your mind about some of the text in the document. In a word processing program, these types of changes are easy to make. In this chapter, you'll learn how to:

- Insert, select, delete, and move text
- Reverse mistakes with Undo
- Use the find and replace feature

Editing, Selecting, and Deleting Text

Editing text with WordPerfect is a breeze. Need extra words? Just type them in. Need to delete words? Just highlight them and press the Delete key.

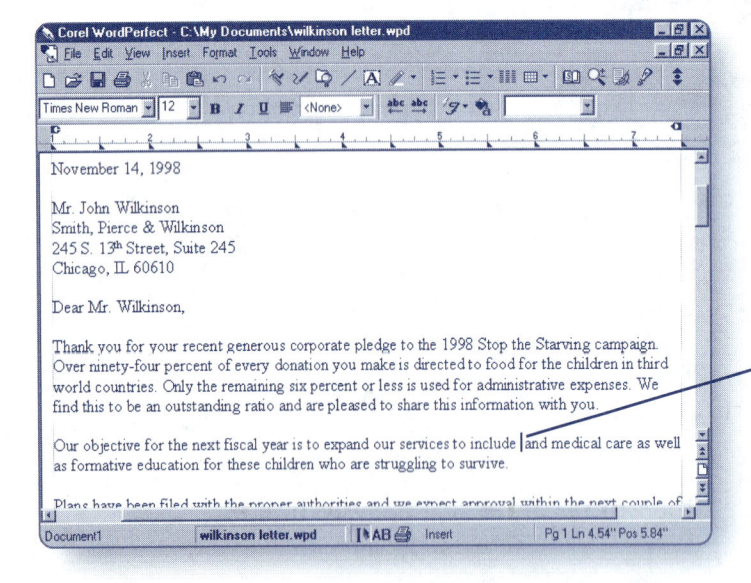

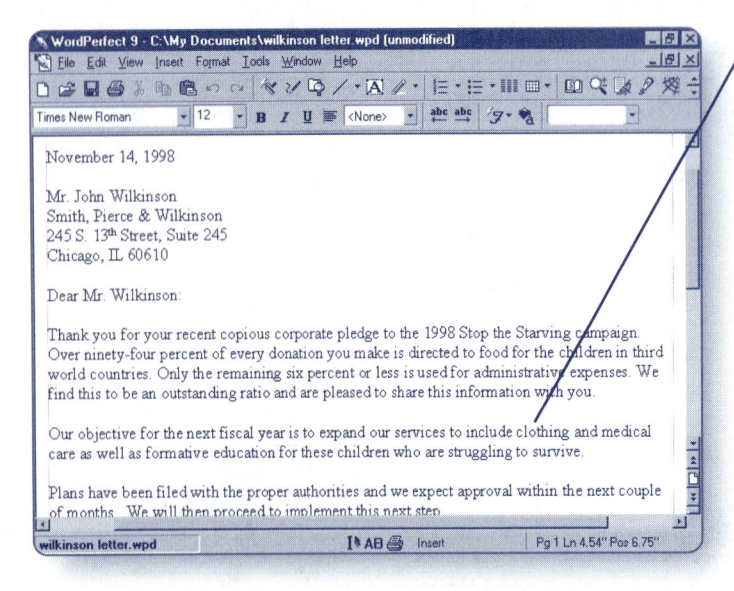

Inserting Text

WordPerfect begins in *insert* mode. This means that when you want to add new text to a document, simply place the insertion point where you want the new text to be and start typing.

1. Click the **mouse pointer** directly in front of the word in the body of the document where you want new text to appear. The blinking insertion point will appear.

2. Type any new **word or phrase**, adding a space before or after as necessary. The new text will be inserted into the document.

WordPerfect will push the existing text to the right and keep moving it over or down to make room for the new text.

EDITING, SELECTING, AND DELETING TEXT 41

Selecting Text

To move, copy, delete, or change the formatting of text, you need to select the text to be edited. When text is selected, it appears as light type on a dark background on your screen, just the reverse of unselected text. You can only select a sequential block of text at a time, not bits of text in different places.

The following list shows different selection techniques:

- To select one word, double-click on the word.

- To select a sentence, click three times (triple-click) anywhere in the paragraph.

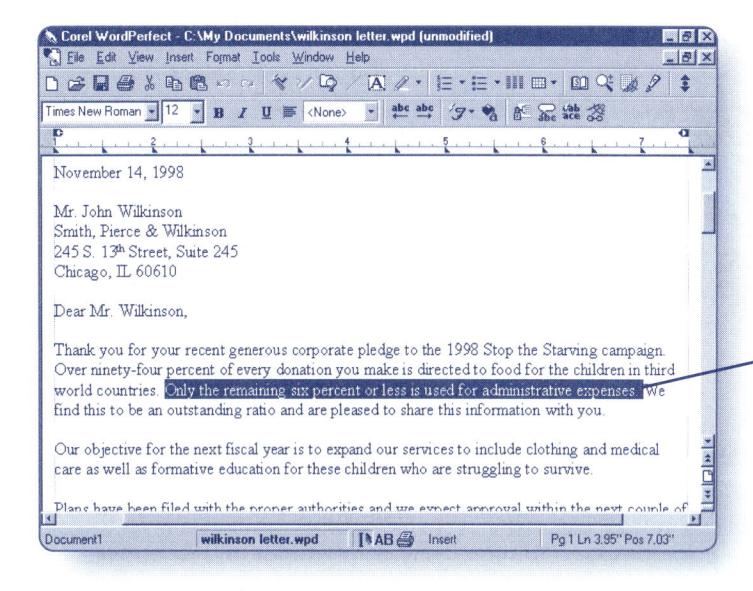

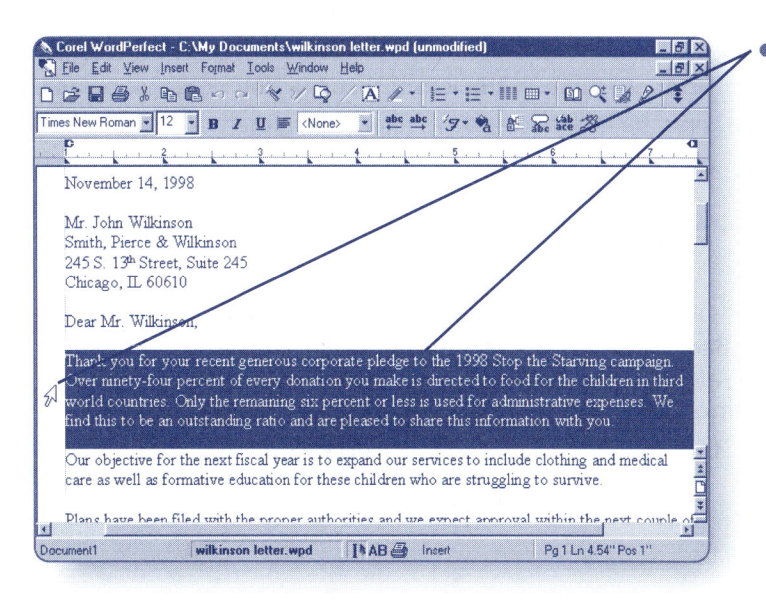

- To select an entire paragraph, double-click in the left margin with the mouse arrow pointing to the text.

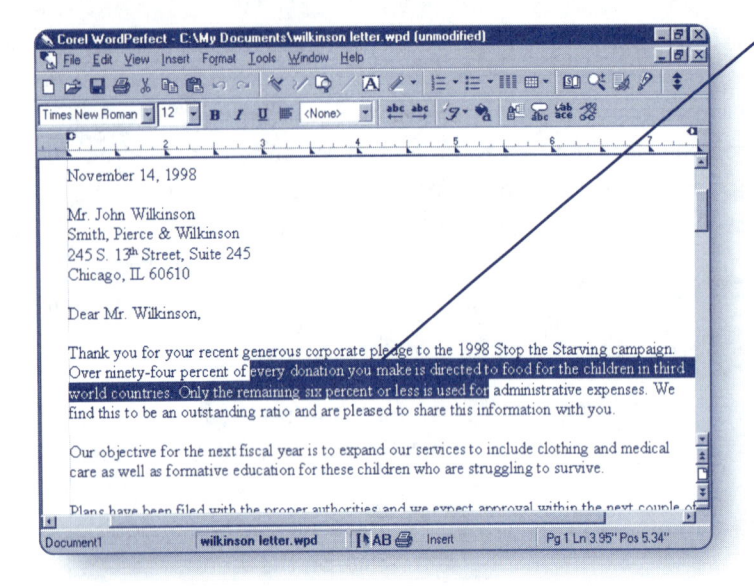

- To select a block of text, click at the beginning of the text, hold down the mouse button, and drag across the balance of the text to be selected.

- To select the entire document, press Ctrl+A or choose Edit, Select All.

TIP
To deselect text, click anywhere in the document where the text is not highlighted.

Deleting Text

You can delete unwanted text one character, one word, or one paragraph at a time; or any combination of the above.

Two common keys used to delete text are the Backspace key and the Delete key. Pressing the Backspace key deletes one character at a time to the left of the insertion point, whereas pressing the Delete key deletes one character at a time to the right of the insertion point.

TIP
An easy way to remember which direction the Backspace key will delete is to look at the arrow printed on the Backspace key (most keyboards). The arrow points to the left, indicating that this is the direction the characters will be deleted.

CHANGING TEXT CASE 43

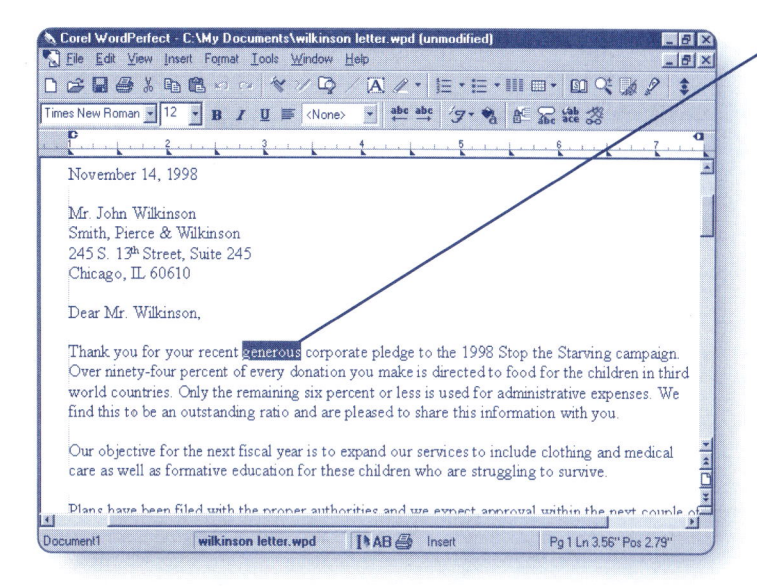

1. Select the **text** to be deleted. The text will be highlighted.

2. Press the **Delete key**. The text will be deleted.

As soon as the deleted text disappears, any text below or to the right of the deleted words will move up to remove any blank space.

Changing Text Case

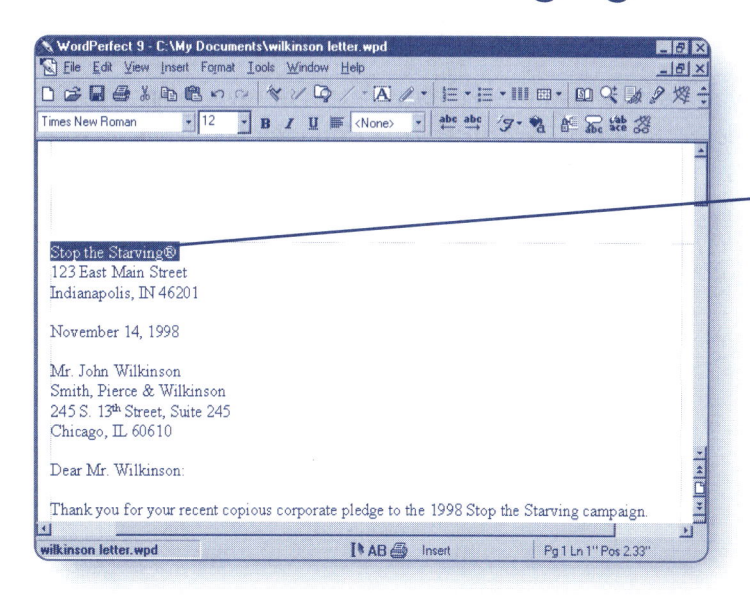

WordPerfect provides an easy way to change the capitalization case of text without retyping.

1. Select the **text** to be changed. The text will be highlighted.

CHAPTER 5: EDITING A DOCUMENT

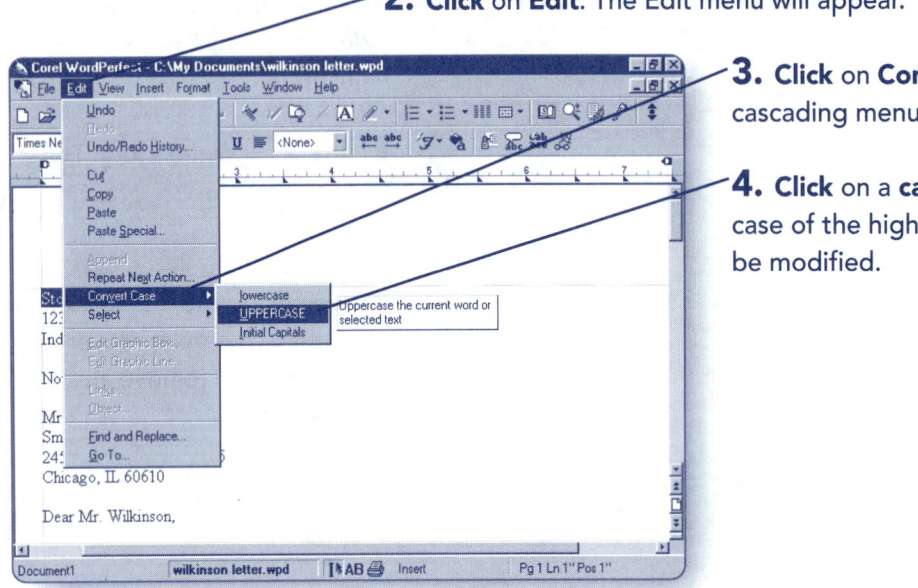

2. Click on **Edit**. The Edit menu will appear.

3. Click on **Convert Case**. A cascading menu will appear.

4. Click on a **case option**. The case of the highlighted text will be modified.

Using Undo and Redo

If you want to restore text you deleted, or reverse an action recently taken, use WordPerfect's Undo feature.

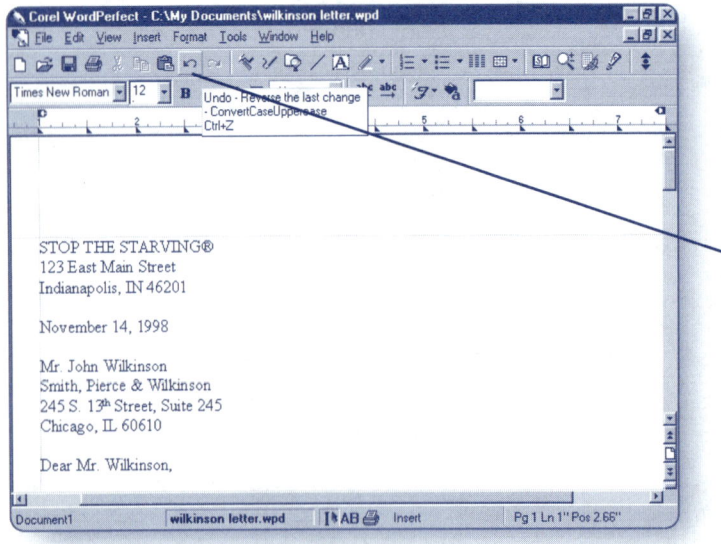

Undoing the Previous Step

You're one click away from reversing your previous action.

1. Click on the **Undo button**. The last action taken will be reversed.

MOVING AND COPYING TEXT | 45

> **NOTE**
> To undo multiple steps at one time, click on the Edit menu and choose Undo/Redo History. Select the steps you want to reverse and click on Undo. Unfortunately, this only works for the most recent steps—you cannot undo the fifth step back without also undoing the last four things you did.

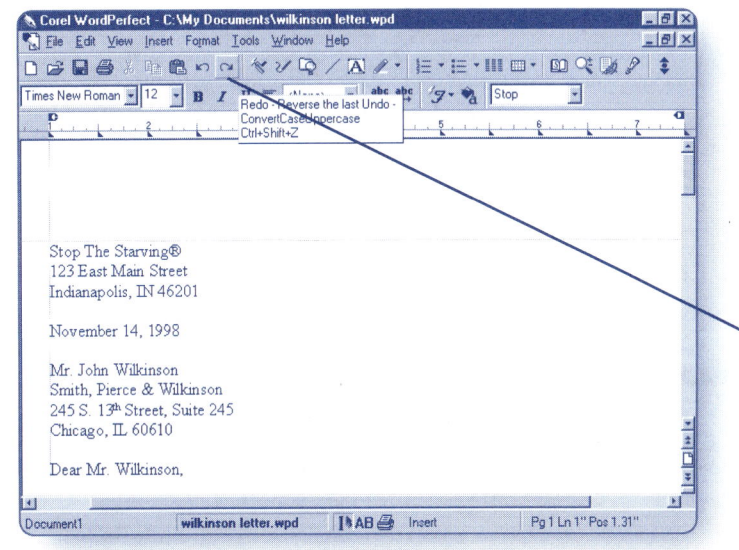

Redoing the Previous Step

If you chose to undo an action and then decided you liked it better the way you had it, use the Redo feature.

1. Click on the **Redo button**. The Undo action will be reversed.

Moving and Copying Text

Windows includes a feature called the *Clipboard*, which holds information temporarily. WordPerfect uses the Clipboard feature effectively to move or copy text from one place to another.

Moving Text

The feature used to move text from one place to another is called *cut and paste*. With cut and paste, the original text is deleted and placed in the new location.

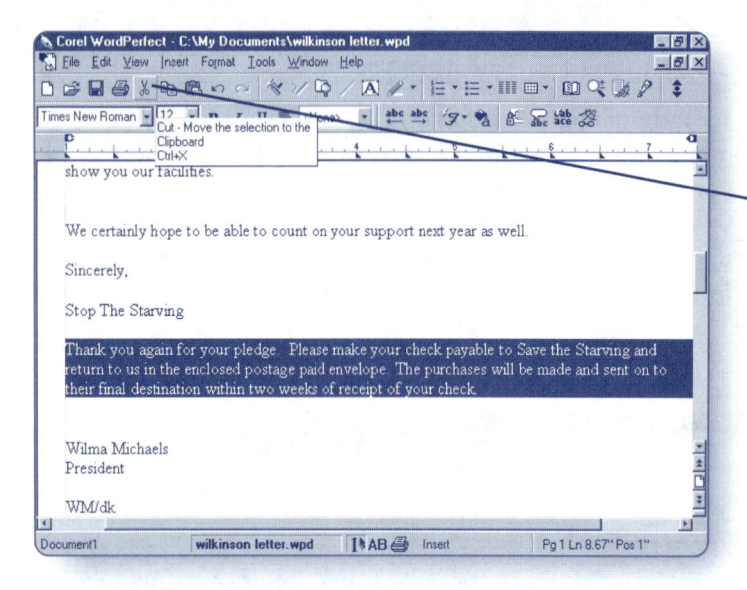

46 CHAPTER 5: EDITING A DOCUMENT

1. Select the **text** to be moved. The text will be highlighted.

2. Click on the **Cut button**. The text will be removed from the document and is stored on the Windows Clipboard.

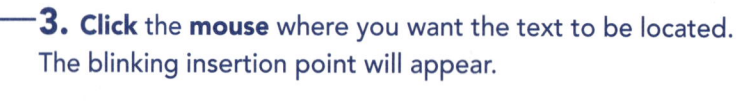

3. Click the **mouse** where you want the text to be located. The blinking insertion point will appear.

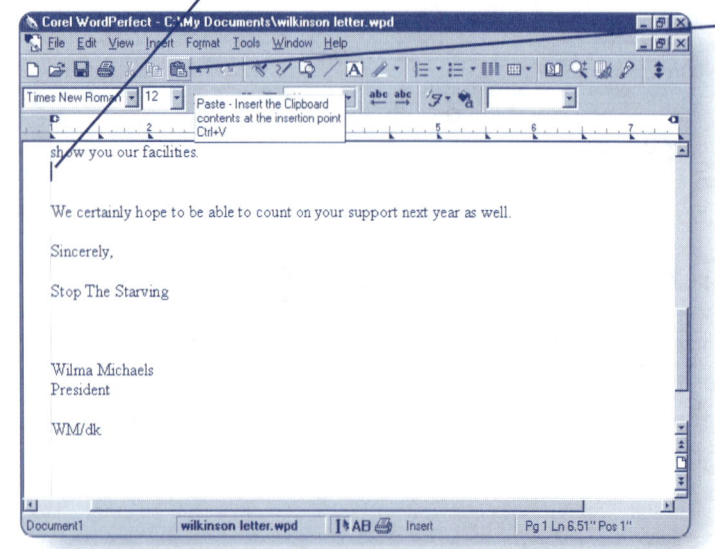

4. Click on the **Paste button**. The text will be placed at the new location.

NOTE

Text or an object placed on the Windows Clipboard remains on the Clipboard even after it's been pasted into a new location. It remains on the Clipboard until other text or objects are placed on the Clipboard, or until the computer is restarted.

Copying Text

Copying text leaves the original text in its original location while a copy of it is placed on the Windows Clipboard.

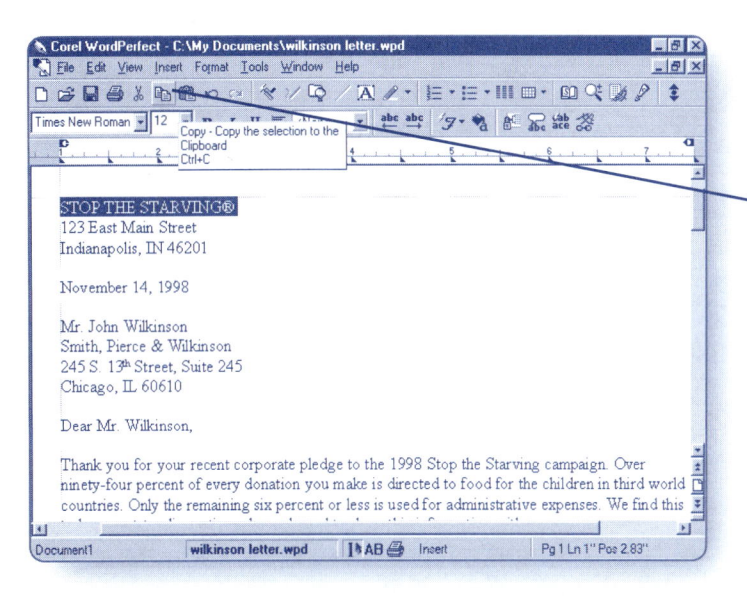

1. Select the **text** to be copied. The text will be highlighted.

2. Click on the **Copy button**. The text will be stored on the Windows Clipboard.

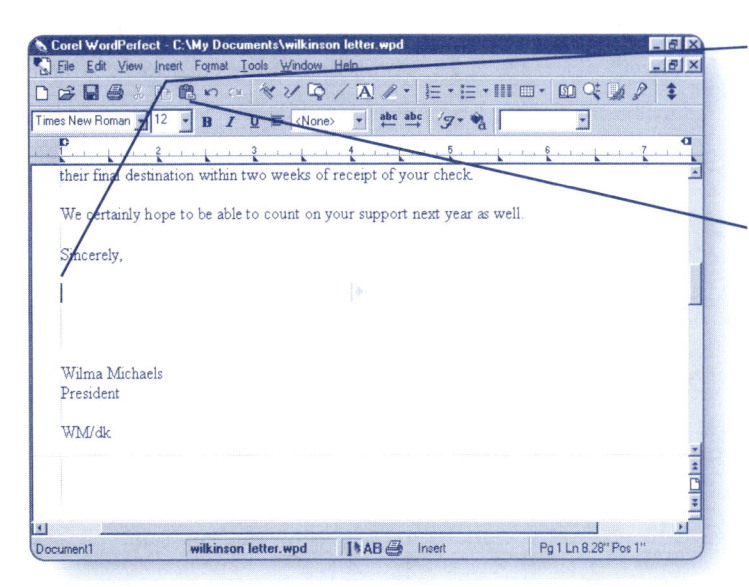

3. Click the **mouse** where you want the text to be located. The blinking insertion point will appear.

4. Click on the **Paste button**. The text will be placed at the new location.

48 CHAPTER 5: EDITING A DOCUMENT

Using Drag and Drop

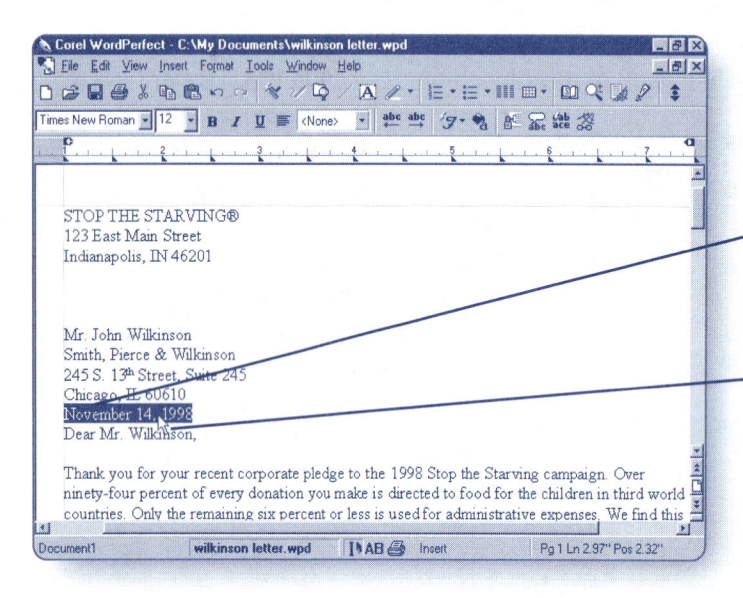

The drag-and-drop method of moving text works best to move a small amount of text a short distance.

1. Select the **text** to be moved. The text will be highlighted.

2. Position the **mouse pointer** on top of the highlighted text. The white mouse arrow will point to the left.

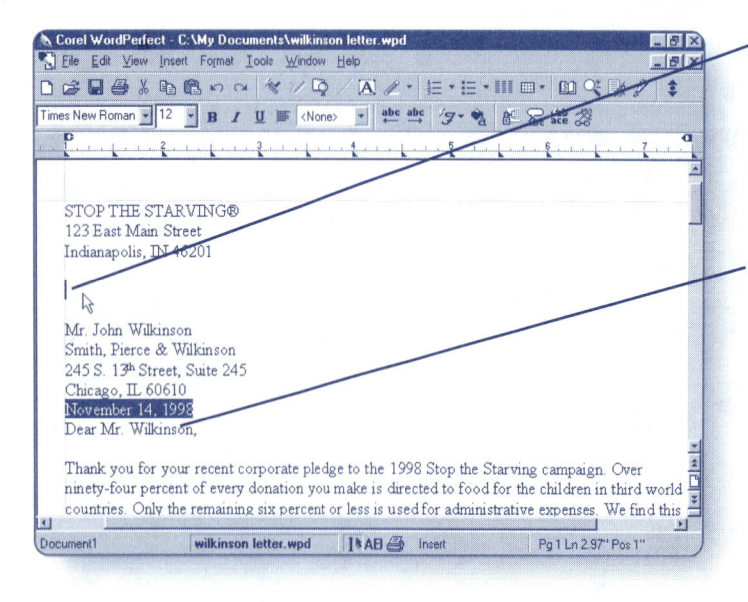

3. Hold down the **mouse button** and **drag** the mouse to the desired location. A gray line will indicate the position of the text.

4. Release the **mouse button**. The text will be moved.

TIP

To copy text with drag and drop, hold down the Ctrl key before dragging the selected text. Release the mouse button before releasing the Ctrl key.

MOVING AND COPYING TEXT 49

Using the Shortcut Menu

A quick way to use cut, copy, and paste is to access it from WordPerfect's shortcut menu. A shortcut menu appears when the right mouse button is clicked.

1. Select the **text** to be cut or copied. The text will be highlighted.

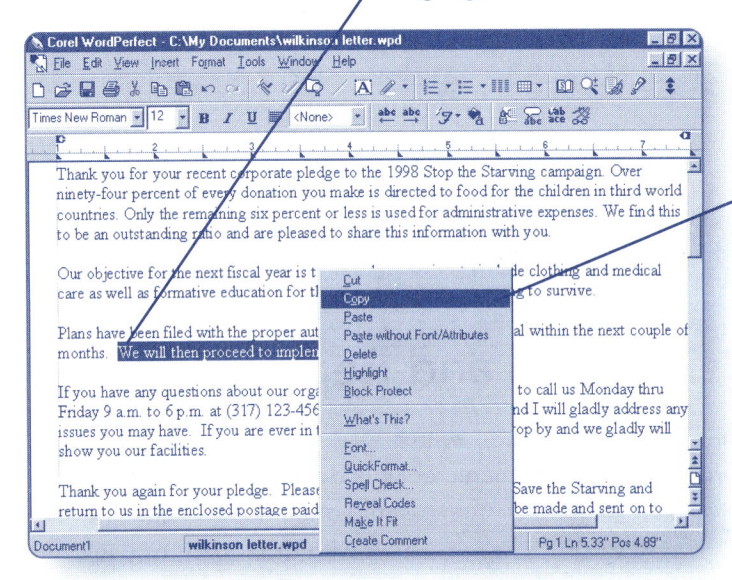

2. Press the **right mouse button**. A shortcut menu will appear.

3. Click on **Cut** or **Copy**. The text will be cut or copied.

NOTE

Choices can be made from a shortcut menu by using either the left or right mouse button.

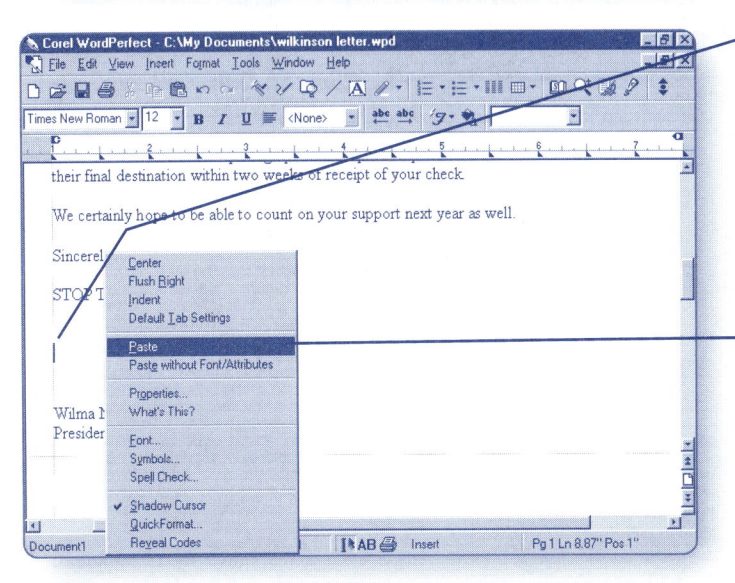

4. Click the **mouse** at the new location. The blinking insertion point will appear.

5. Press the **right mouse button** (*right-click*). A shortcut menu will appear.

6. Click on **Paste**. The text will be pasted into the new location.

CHAPTER 5: EDITING A DOCUMENT

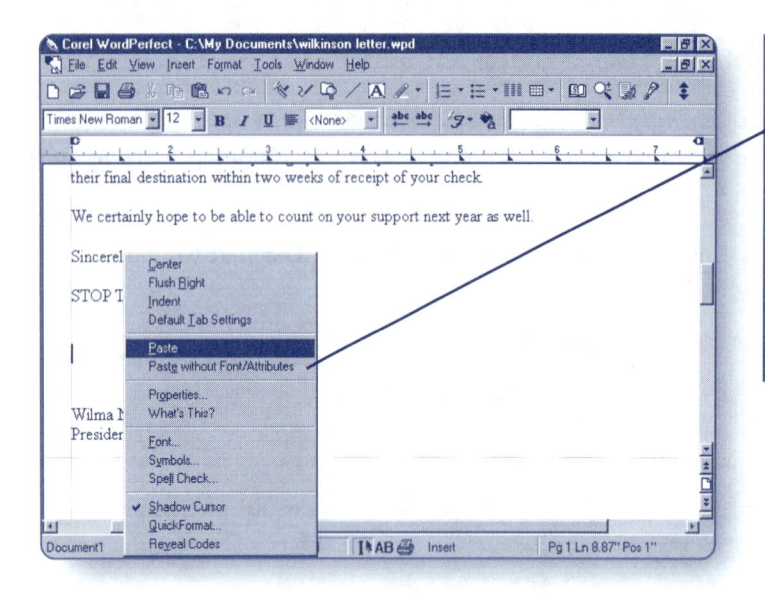

TIP

Optionally, click on Paste without Font/Attributes to paste the text without any formatting. Formatting is discussed in Chapter 9, "Formatting with Fonts."

Using Find and Replace

Use Find and Replace to search for any text, such as phrases, words, or individual characters in a document. You can replace some or all occurrences of the text with other text, or you can delete the text.

1. Click on **Edit**. The Edit menu will appear.

2. Click on **Find and Replace**. The Find and Replace dialog box will open.

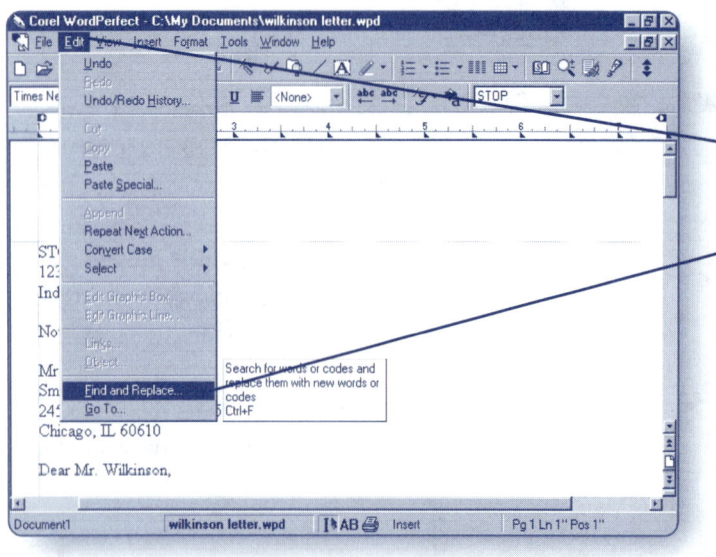

USING FIND AND REPLACE   51

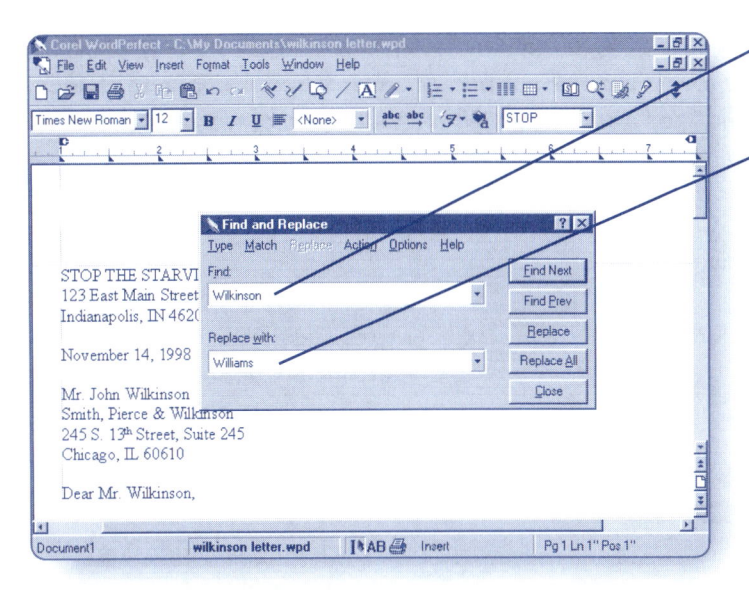

3. Type the **text** you want to find in the Find: text box.

4. Type the **text** you want to replace the found text with in the Replace with: box.

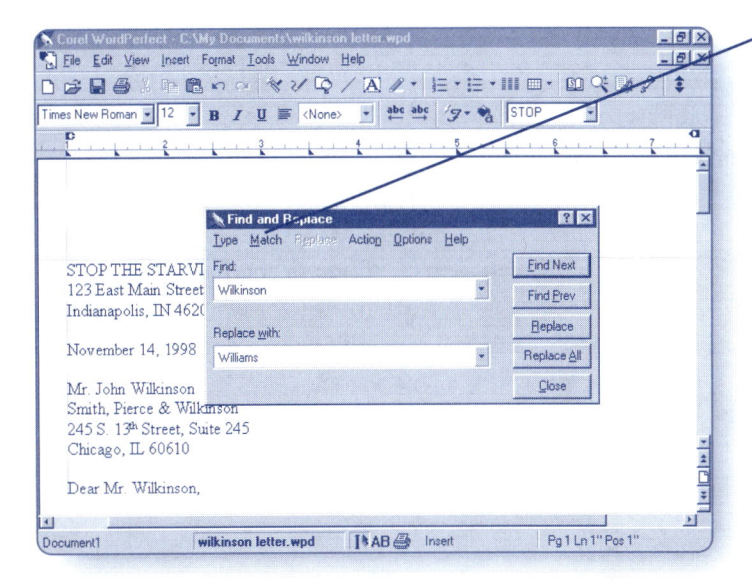

5. Click on **Match** in the Find and Replace dialog box. The Match menu will appear. This menu offers choices for the text you are searching for.

CHAPTER 5: EDITING A DOCUMENT

In a Whole Word match, the replacement occurs only when the text is a word, not part of a word. For example, to change "and" to "also," select Whole Word so that words such as "band" or "Anderson" are not changed.

6. Click on **Whole Word**, if desired. The option will be activated.

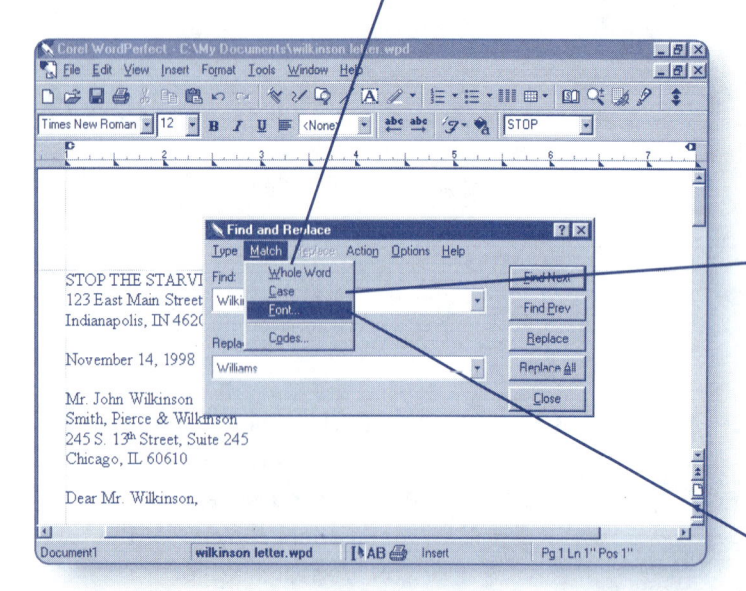

Match Case finds only text that matches the upper- and lowercase letters you type. If you type "Adam" and select Case, you will not find "adam."

7. Click on **Case**, if desired. The option will be activated.

Match Font finds text with specific typeface, style, size, and attributes (such as bold or shadow).

8. Click on **Font**. The Match Font dialog box will open.

9. Choose the **font or attributes** for which you are searching. The options will be selected.

10. Click on **OK**. The Match Font dialog box will close.

USING FIND AND REPLACE 53

A notation of your selection appears below the Find: box.

TIP
If you want to replace text with different fonts, click on the Replace menu and then choose Fonts. You can then select replacement fonts and attributes.

11. Click on **Find Next**. WordPerfect will find and highlight the first occurrence of the found text.

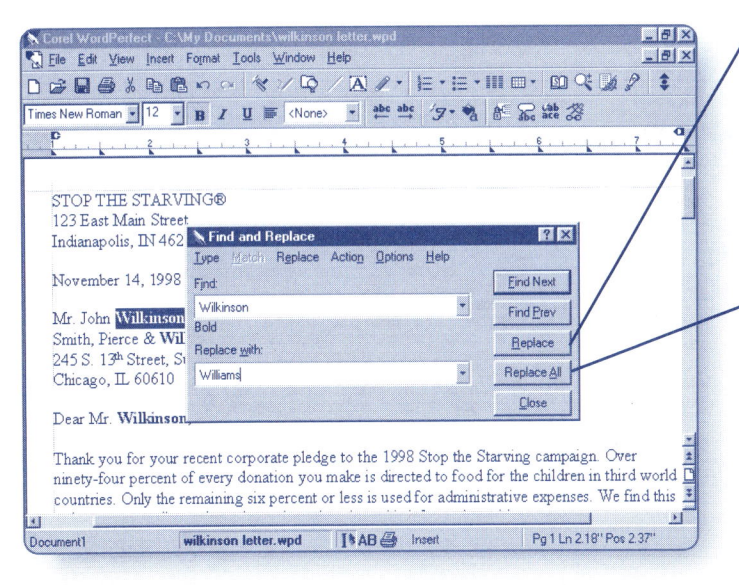

12. Click on **Replace**. WordPerfect will replace the text and jump to the next occurrence.

TIP
Clicking on Replace All automatically replaces all occurrences of the found text with the Replace with: text.

13. Repeat step 12 until the document has been searched. When no more occurrences of the "find" text are located, a message box will appear advising you that the "find" text is not found.

CHAPTER 5: EDITING A DOCUMENT

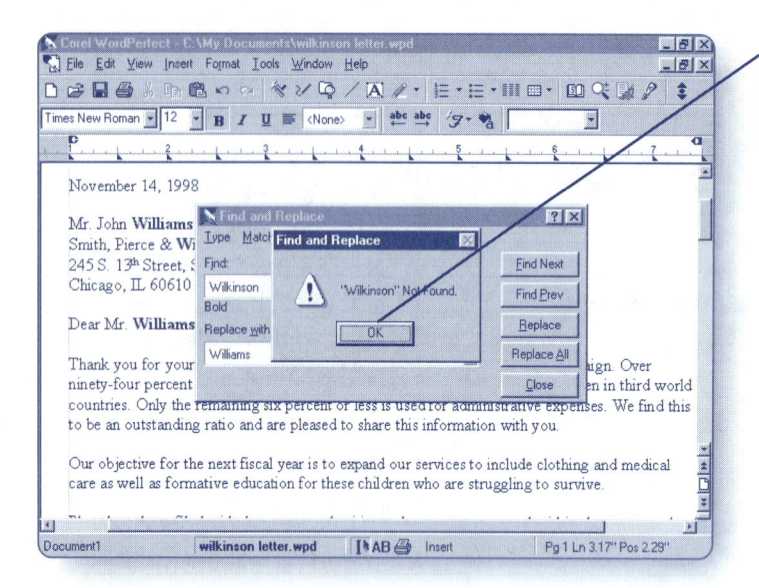

14. Click on **OK**. The message box will close.

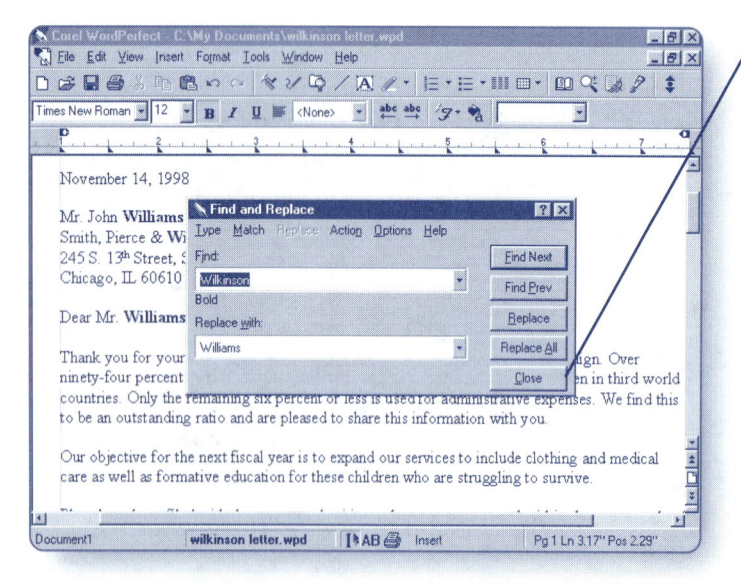

15. Click on **Close**. The Find and Replace dialog box will close.

6
Printing Letters and Envelopes

Now that the letter is complete, it is time to print it. WordPerfect can even create an envelope for your document. In this chapter, you'll learn how to:

- Make a document come out the right size
- Print a document
- Create an envelope
- Select an envelope size

CHAPTER 6: PRINTING LETTERS AND ENVELOPES

Making It Fit

Use the Make It Fit feature to make a document fit a certain number of pages. For example, you can take a letter that is more than one page and shrink it to fit just on one page, or you could expand it to fill two pages.

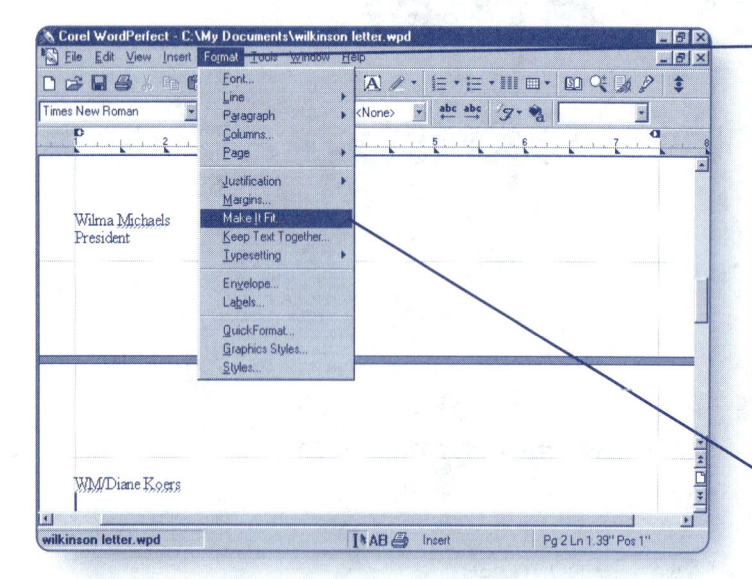

1. Click on **Format**. The Format menu will appear.

TIP
Optionally, before choosing the Format menu, highlight a block of text to be expanded or compressed.

2. Click on **Make It Fit**. The Make It Fit dialog box will open.

The dialog box shows the current number of pages your document takes up. In the Desired number of pages: box, you can enter the number of pages you want the document to be. You can also choose which items to adjust to make it fit.

3. Enter the **Desired number of pages**. The number will be displayed.

WordPerfect can adjust margins, font sizes, and line spacing to make your document the desired size.

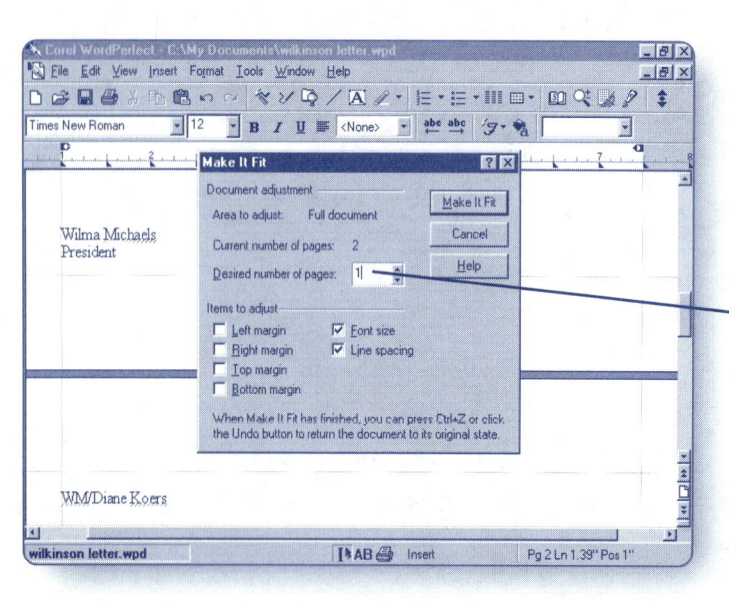

PRINTING A DOCUMENT   57

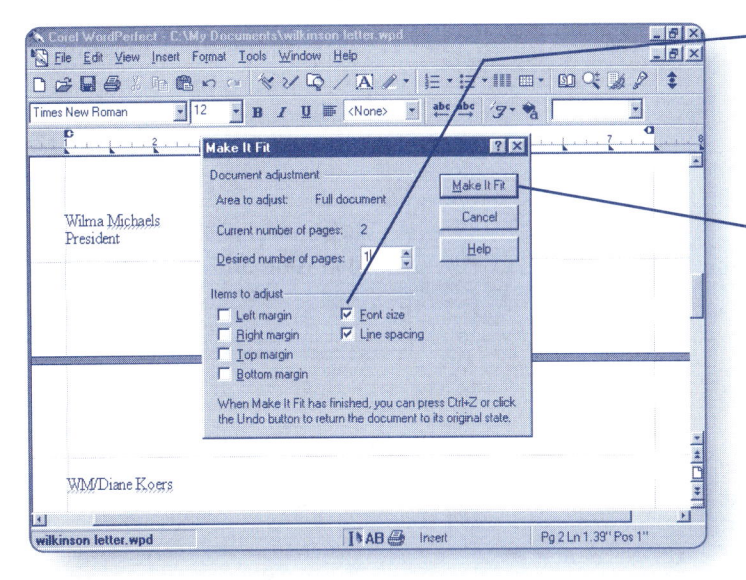

4. Click on **your choices** under Items to adjust. The selected options will display a check mark (✔).

5. Click on **Make It Fit**. The document or selection will be compressed or expanded as you requested.

TIP
Don't try to compress a large document—say, a five-page document into a two-page document. WordPerfect will do it, but you won't be able to read it. The text will be too small.

NOTE
Expansion only works a page at a time. That is, you can compress a five-page document to three pages, but you cannot expand from three pages to five. You must expand from three to four and then do it again to go from four to five.

Printing a Document

If you want a paper copy of your document to send to the recipient or a copy for your records, you can also use the Print feature of WordPerfect.

58   CHAPTER 6: PRINTING LETTERS AND ENVELOPES

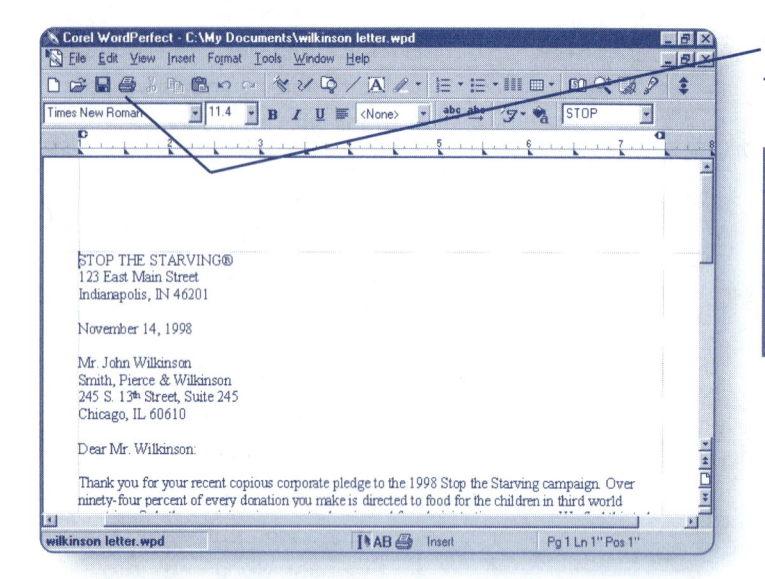

1. Click on the **Print button**. The Print dialog box will open.

> **TIP**
> Optionally, click on the File menu and choose Print.

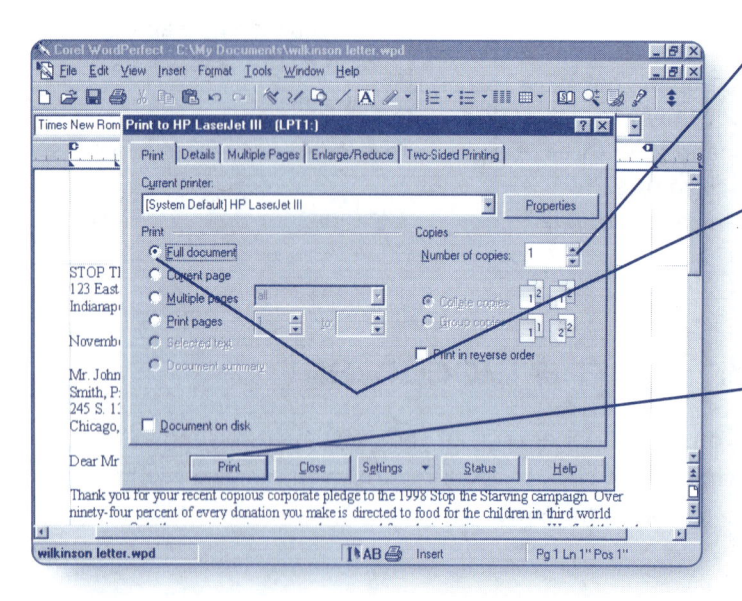

2. Click on the **up** or **down arrow** (◆) to choose the number of copies to print.

3. Select what you want to print: the entire document, the current page, a range of pages, or multiple pages.

4. Click on **Print**. The document will be sent to your printer.

Creating an Envelope

Creating an envelope is easy in WordPerfect. WordPerfect does most of the work for you!

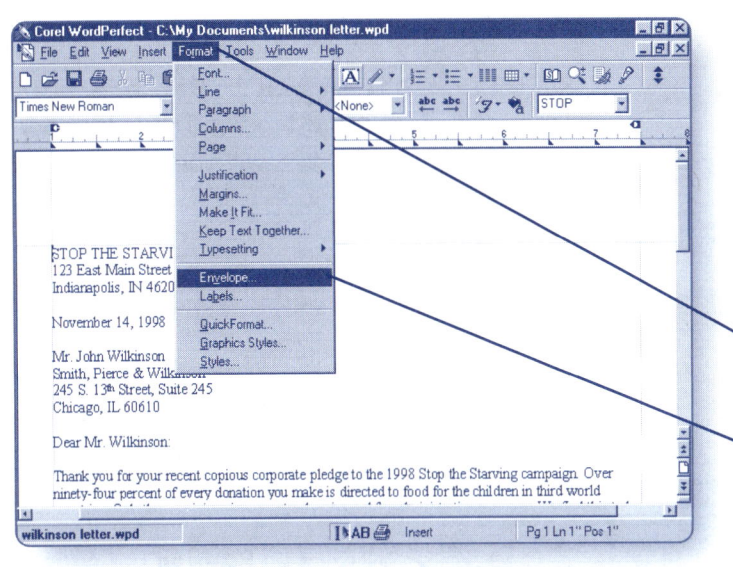

Starting the Envelope Feature

If you are typing a letter, WordPerfect often recognizes who the envelope should be addressed to.

1. Click on **Format**. The Format menu will appear.

2. Click on **Envelope**. The Envelope will be created.

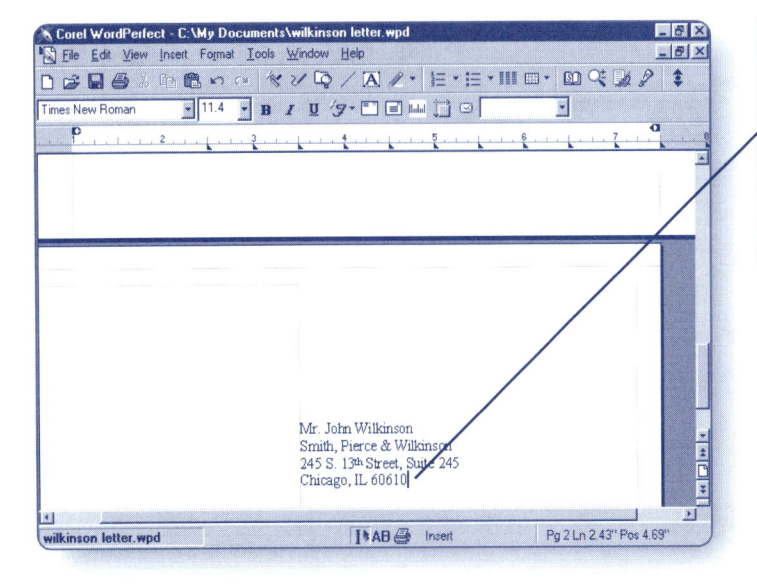

TIP
Edit the recipient address by typing corrections as you would in any other WordPerfect document.

CHAPTER 6: PRINTING LETTERS AND ENVELOPES

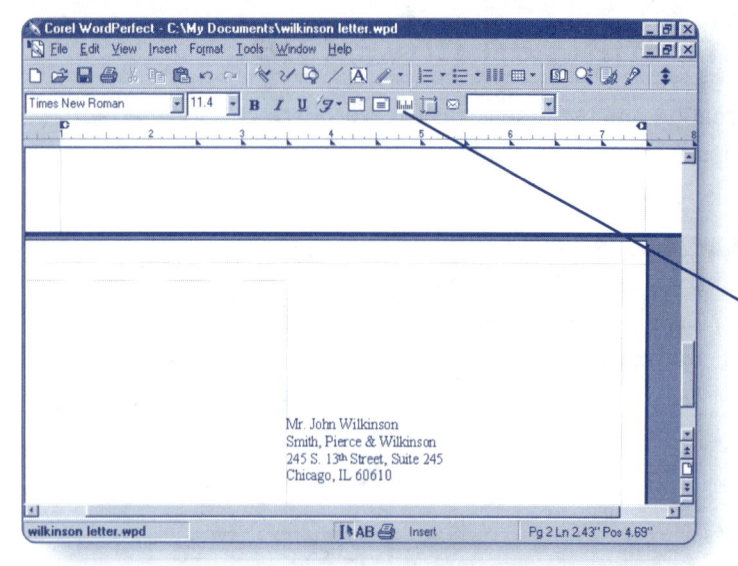

Adding a Bar Code to an Envelope

WordPerfect includes a button to add a professional bar code to the recipient address.

1. Click on the **Bar Code button**. The POSTNET Bar Code dialog box will open.

2. If necessary, **type** any **additions or corrections** to the Zip code. The Zip code will display in the Bar code digits: box.

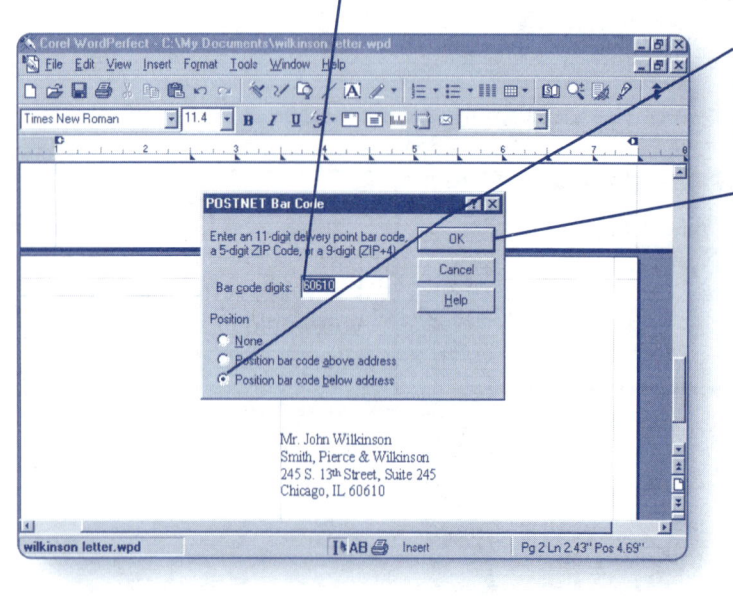

3. Click on **Position bar code below address**. The option will be selected.

4. Click on **OK**. The dialog box will close.

CREATING AN ENVELOPE

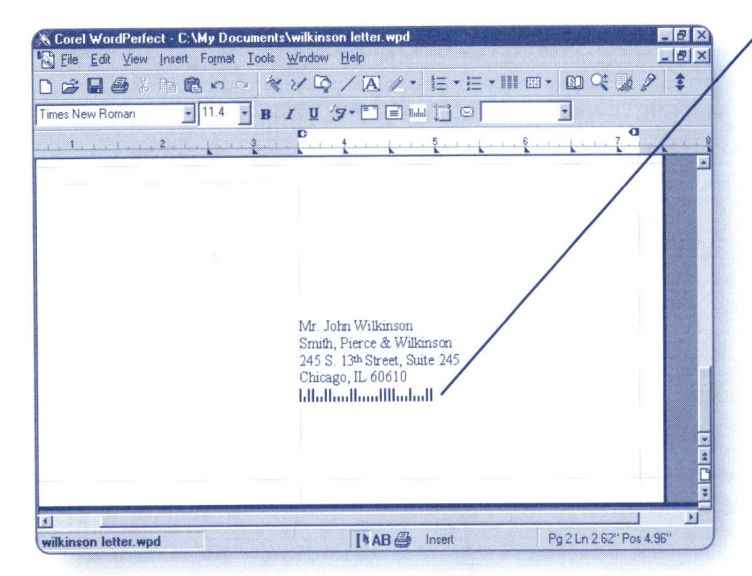

A bar code will be added below the recipient address.

Typing a Return Address

If you're sending the letter in a plain envelope, you may want to include your return address. A space at the top of the envelope is reserved for the return address.

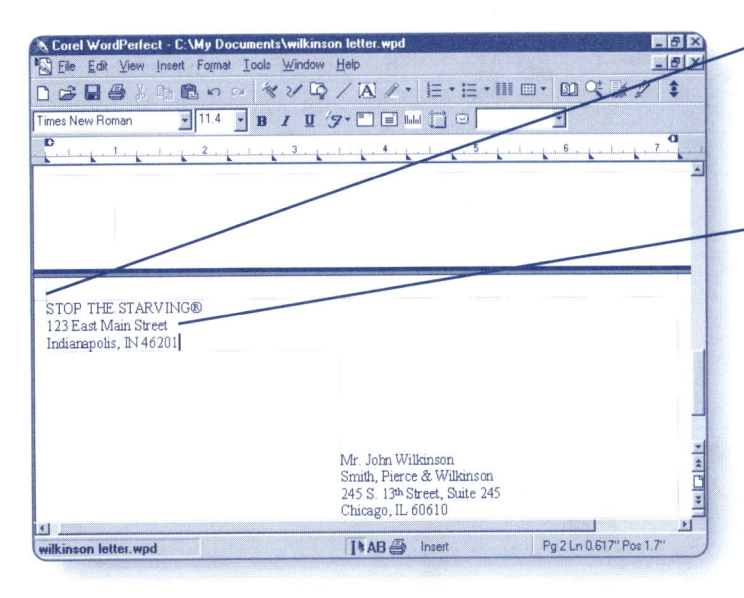

1. Click the **insertion point** at the top left of the envelope. A blinking insertion point will appear.

2. Type the return address **information**. The address will appear on the envelope.

Selecting an Envelope Size

By default, WordPerfect assumes that you want a standard #10 business envelope. If that's not the case, you have a variety of sizes to choose from.

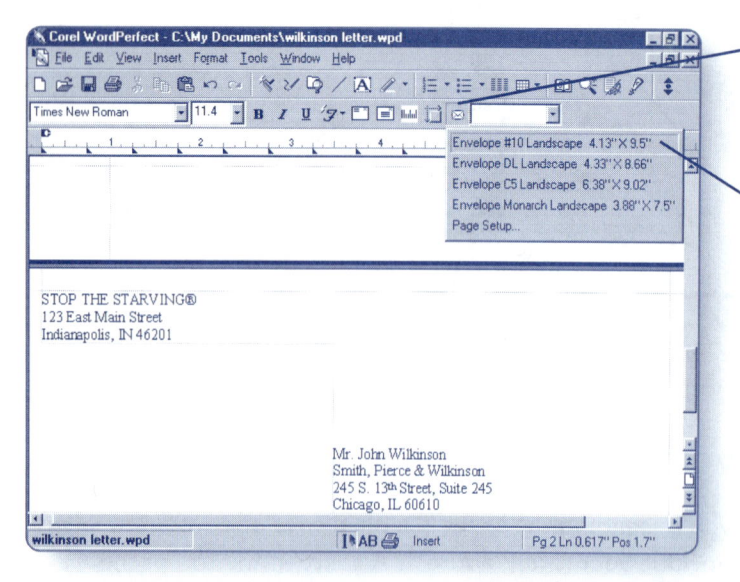

1. Click on the **Envelope Size button**. A list of available envelope sizes will display.

2. Click on a **size**. The current envelope will be reformatted to fit the new size.

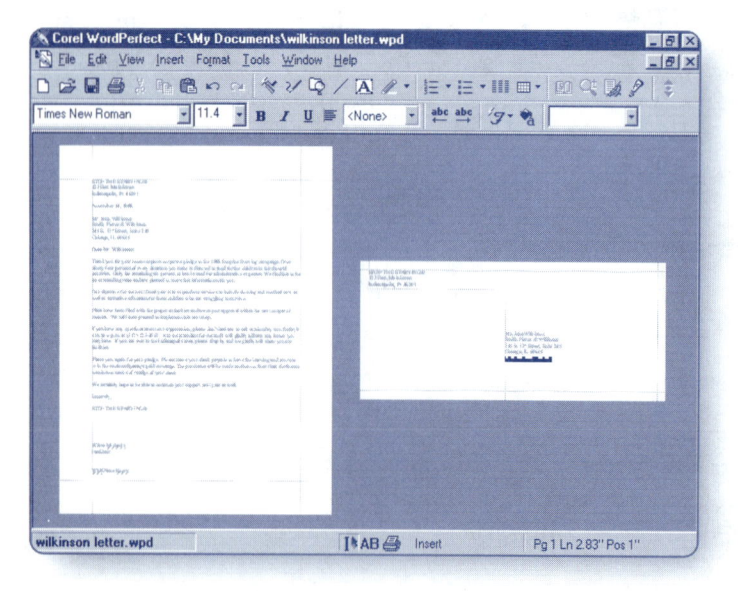

The envelope is now ready to print with your letter. As you can see from this two-page view, the letter will print first and then the envelope.

7
Working with Views

WordPerfect gives you several different perspectives on your document. When you first install the program, it shows your documents in Page view, which lets you see your document as it will look on the printout, with all its headers, footers, footnotes, page numbering, and margins. You can change the view to Draft view, either for one document or for everything you do. You can also see a whole page—or check the layout by looking at two pages at a time, though the text will probably be too small to work with comfortably. In this chapter, you'll learn how to:

- Switch from Page view to Draft view
- Make Draft view the default view
- View two pages at a time
- Zoom to Full Page view
- Zoom in for a closer look

Working in Different Views

If you have used earlier DOS versions of WordPerfect, Draft view is similar to what you may have used—just the text, without the running headers and so on that show up on the printed pages.

Switching from Page View to Draft View

Draft view is similar to Page view except that you cannot see your headers, footers, footnotes, page numbering, or margins. Some people prefer Draft view because it gives them more room on the screen to see their text.

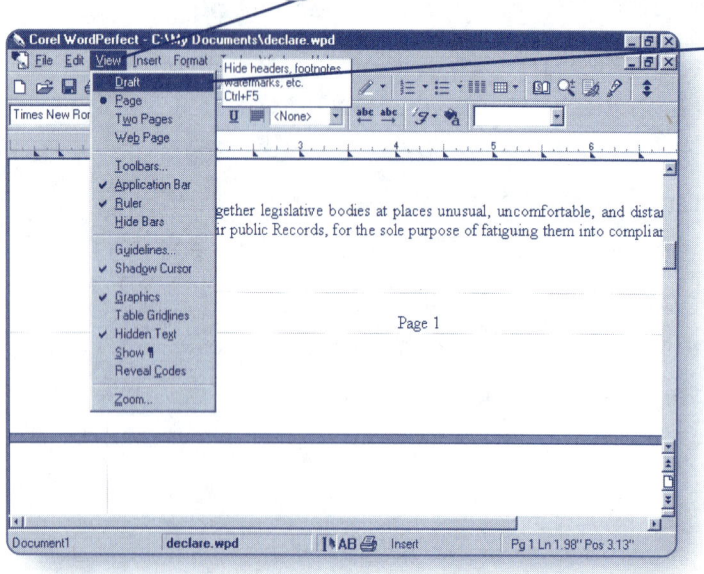

1. Click on **View**. The View menu will appear.

2. Click on **Draft**. The view will change to Draft view.

WORKING IN DIFFERENT VIEWS | **65**

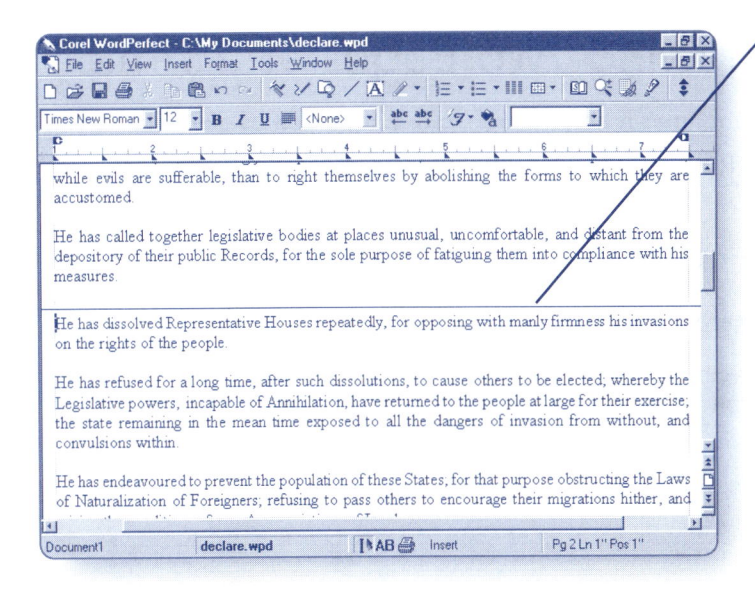

As you scroll down in your document to look at the differences between the two views, do you notice the difference in the page break? Draft view page breaks look like a simple black line across the screen.

Returning to Page View

View settings are saved with each individual document. For example, you may prefer to see your term paper in Page view, but a business letter you're creating is best in Draft view. Whatever view you are using when you save the document is the view it will sustain the next time you open the document.

The next time the WordPerfect program is executed, it will display in the view you last exited WordPerfect.

1. Click on **View**. The View menu will appear.

2. Click on **Page**. The view will return to Page view.

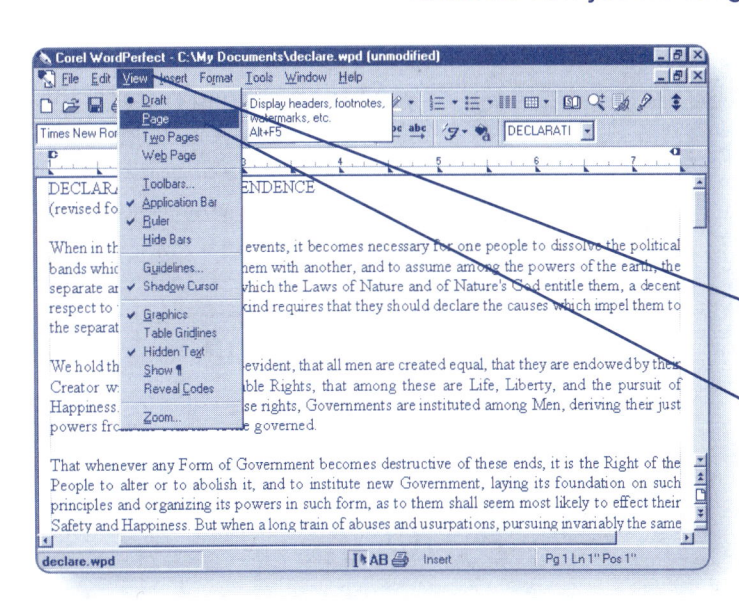

Viewing Two Pages at a Time

Sometimes it helps to see your pages side by side. This can help you in checking that your document has an overall balanced and consistent look to it.

1. Click on **View**. The View menu will appear.

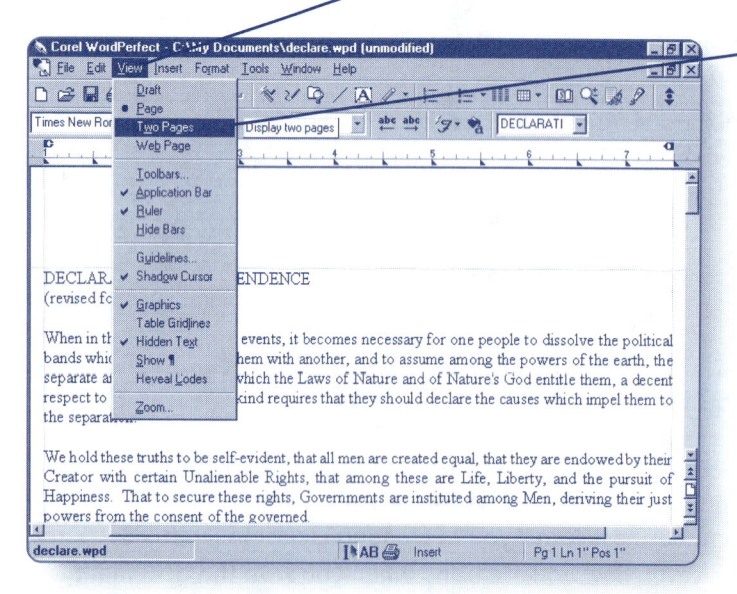

2. Click on **Two Pages**. The view will change to Two Page view. You will see the current page your cursor is on and the page facing it.

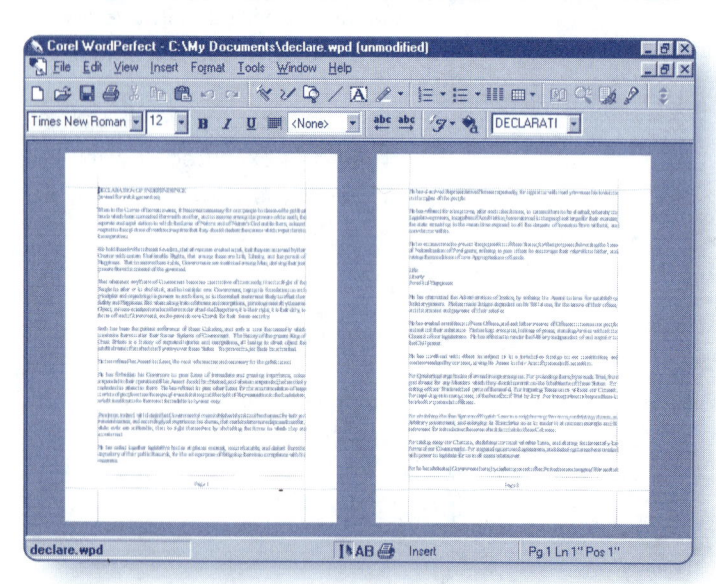

Two Page view is editable, so you have a blinking cursor in the document, and you could continue to type or edit in this view. (That is, if you could actually read the text.)

TIP

Press the PageUp or PageDown keys on your keyboard to view other pages of your document.

ZOOMING AROUND 67

3. Click on **View**. The View menu will appear.

4a. Click on **Page**. The screen will be restored to Page view.

OR

4b. Click on **Draft**. The screen will be restored to Draft view.

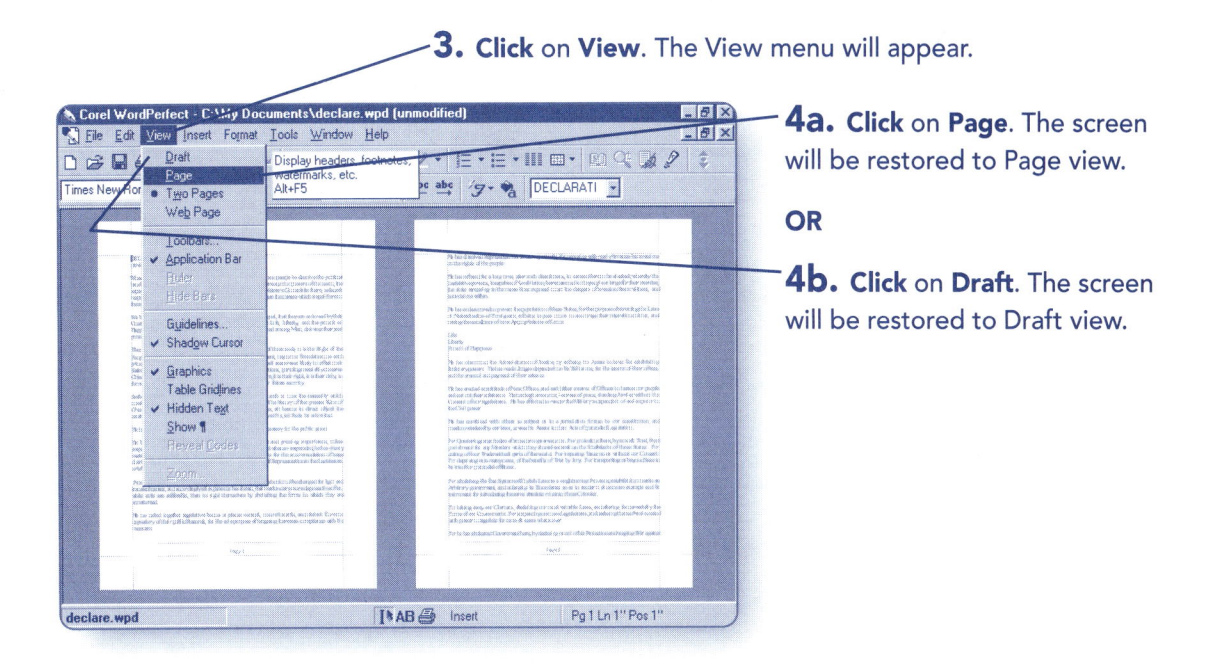

Zooming Around

WordPerfect has the capability to zoom in or out in your document to increase or decrease the size of the characters on the screen. Zooming does not change the way the document is printed.

Zooming to Full Page View

I find it extremely helpful to view my document as a full page. This view is larger than the Two Page view, but smaller than Page or Draft view. A button on the toolbar switches you to various zoom percentages. If you have used an earlier version of WordPerfect, this is similar to the Print Preview feature you used to have.

68 CHAPTER 7: WORKING WITH VIEWS

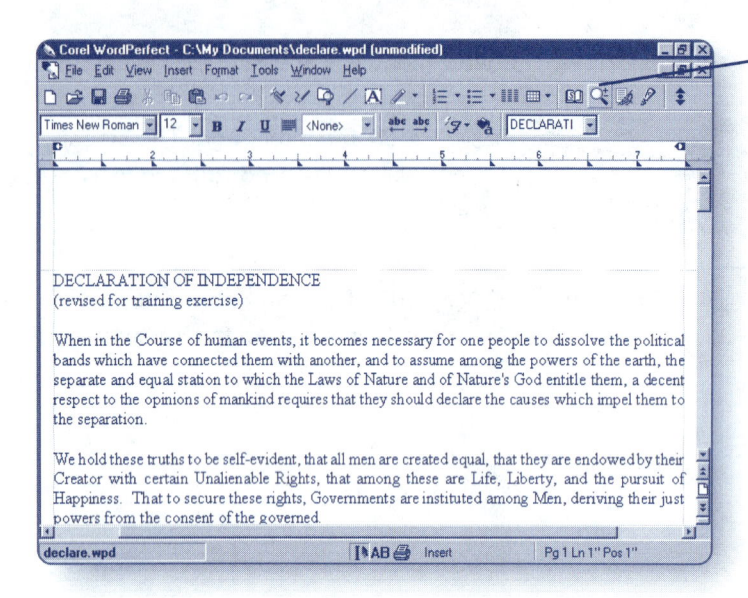

1. Click on the **Zoom button**. The zoom choice menu will appear.

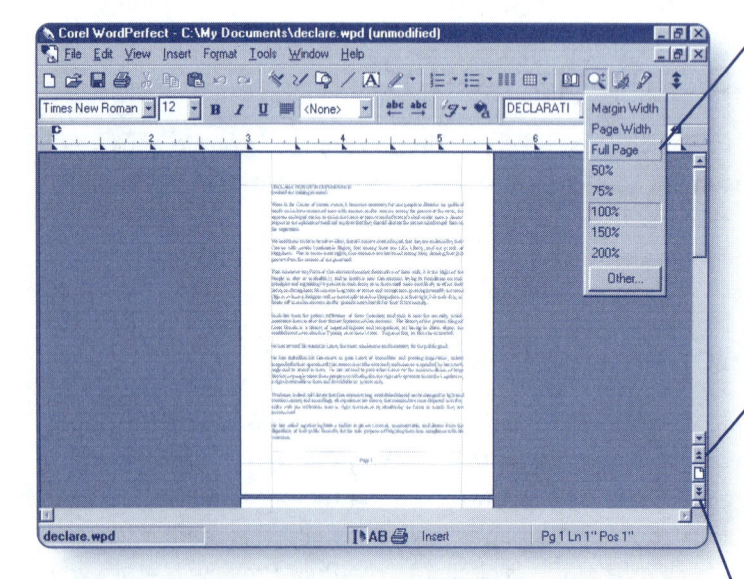

2. Click on **Full Page**. Your document will be displayed one page at a time, at a size that fits each page on the screen all at once. This view is also editable, so you have a blinking cursor in the document, and you could continue to type or edit in this view.

3a. Click on the **Previous Page button** to view the previous page of your document.

OR

3b. Click on the **Next Page button** to view the next page of your document.

ZOOMING AROUND 69

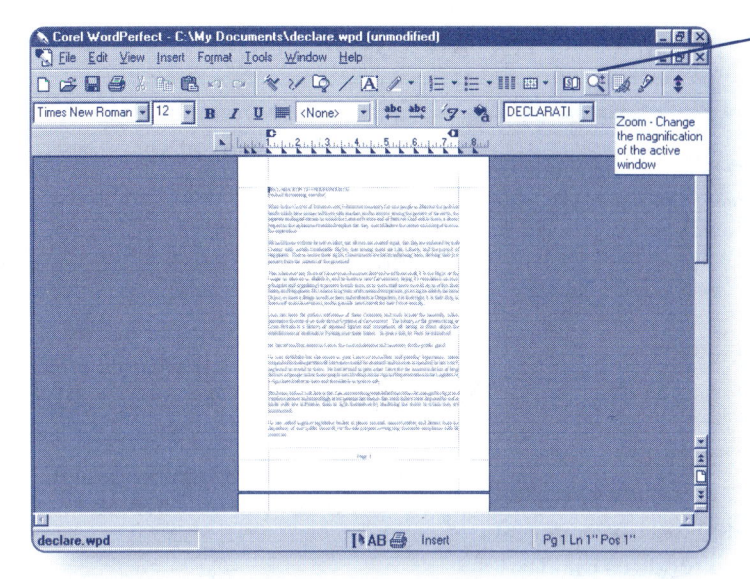

4. Click on the **Zoom button**. The zoom choice menu will appear.

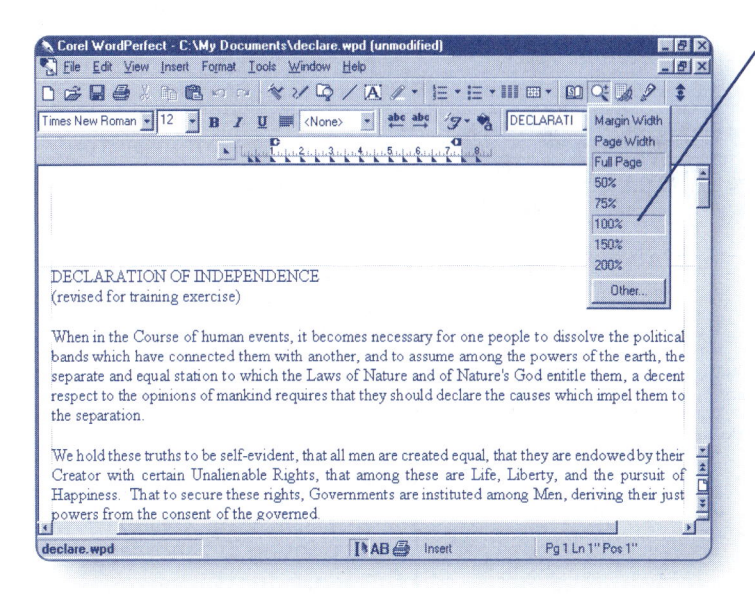

5. Click on **100%**. The view will return to normal.

70 CHAPTER 7: WORKING WITH VIEWS

Zooming In for a Closer Look

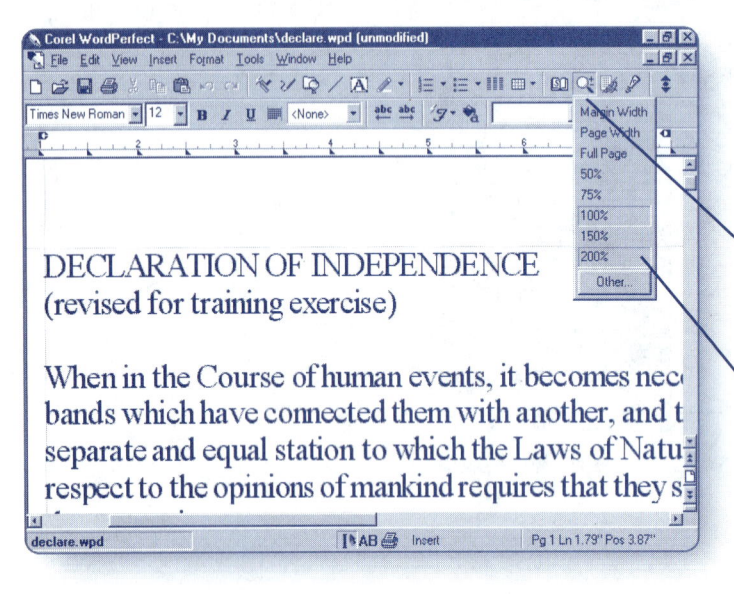

Occasionally, you may need to take a closer look at something in your document, particularly if you are working in a very small font.

1. Click on the **Zoom button**. The zoom choice menu will appear.

2. Click on **200%**. The text on your screen will be doubled in size.

Your text looks larger on the screen, but it will still print in the same size you specified.

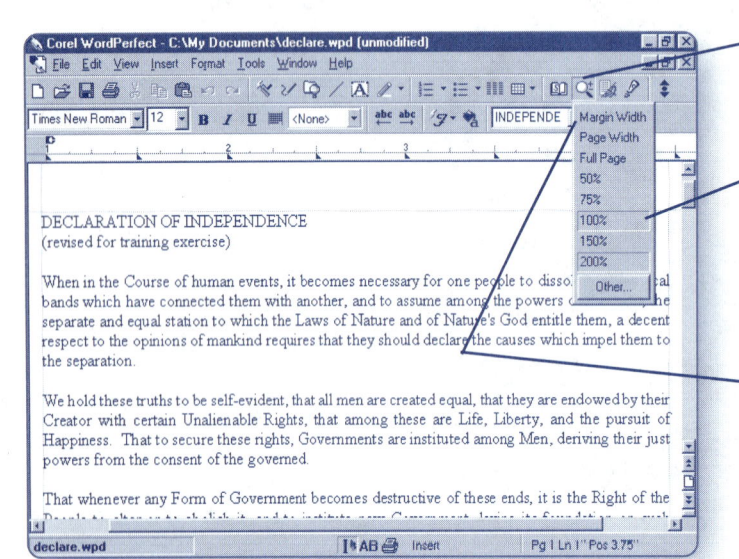

3. Click on the **Zoom button**. The zoom choice menu will appear.

4. Click on **100%**. Your screen will be restored to normal.

TIP

Margin Width is a good zoom choice to use if you are printing in Landscape. Chapter 10, "Changing Paper Sizes and Margins," discusses changing paper size and orientation.

8

Improving Your Writing

Nobody's perfect. As hard as you try to type accurately, you will make mistakes. WordPerfect has several features that can assist you in correcting errors. In this chapter, you'll learn how to:

- Use QuickCorrect
- Save time with QuickWords
- Fix spelling errors
- Check your grammar
- Use the Thesaurus

CHAPTER 8: IMPROVING YOUR WRITING

Discovering QuickCorrect

WordPerfect's QuickCorrect feature can anticipate and fix many common spelling and capitalization errors—for example, exchanging "teh" for "the," "changeing" for "changing," or "monday" for "Monday." Hundreds of words and phrases are included in the predefined list of errors; however, if you commonly make a particular typing mistake, you can have WordPerfect automatically fix it for you.

1. Click on **Tools**. The Tools menu will appear.

2. Click on **QuickCorrect**. The QuickCorrect dialog box will open.

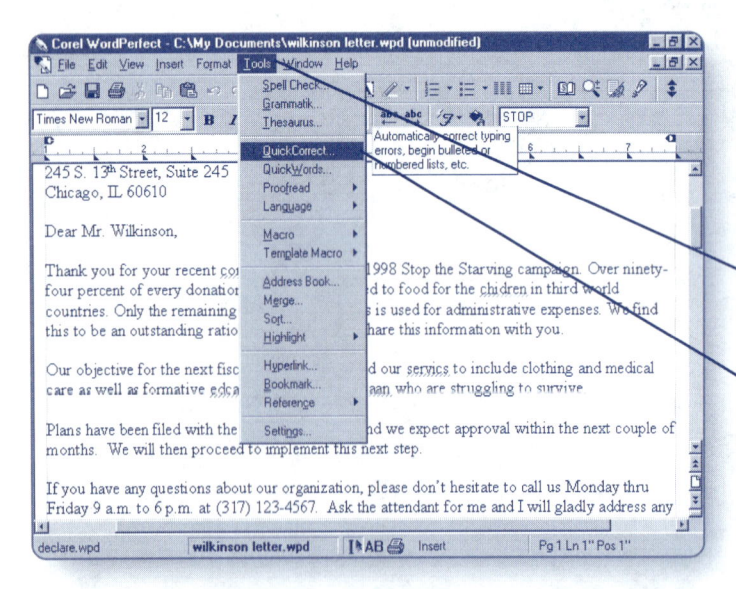

3. If necessary, **click** on the **QuickCorrect tab**. The QuickCorrect tab will come to the front.

4. Type a common **misspelling** in the Replace: box. The text will appear in the Replace: box.

5. Type a **correcting entry** in the With: box. The text will appear in the With: box.

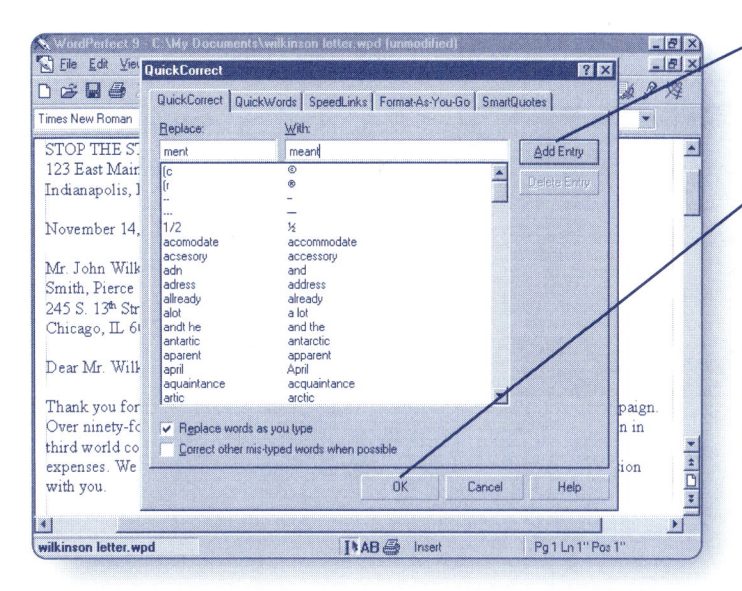

SAVING TIME WITH QUICKWORDS   73

6. Click on **Add Entry**. The entry will be added to the existing QuickCorrect list.

7. Click on **OK**. The QuickCorrect dialog box will close.

The next time you type the incorrect entry followed by a space or punctuation mark, WordPerfect will automatically change it to the correct entry.

Saving Time with QuickWords

Think of QuickWords as abbreviations. Perhaps your company name or address is complicated to type. If you abbreviate it, WordPerfect can do most of the work for you—even add special formatting if you make it part of the abbreviated phrase.

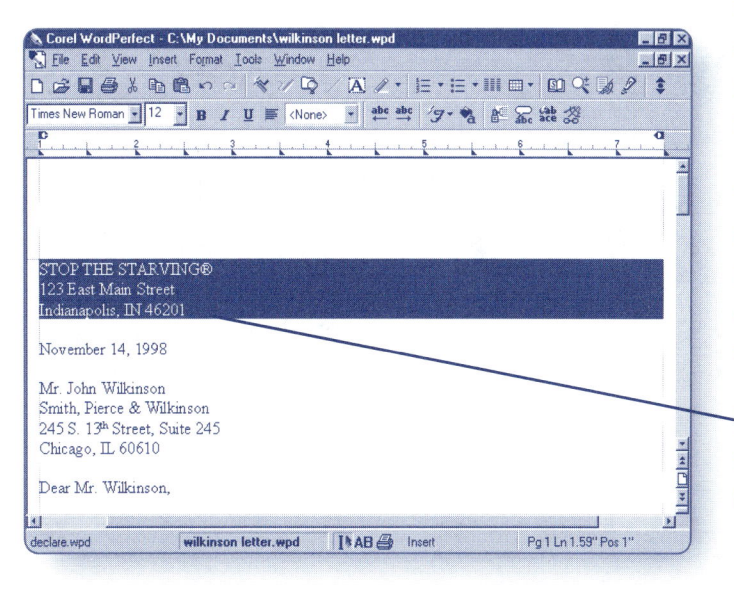

1. Type some **text**. Press the Enter key where necessary and include any formatting you want added to the text. The text will appear on the screen.

2. Select the **text** you just typed. The text will be highlighted.

74 CHAPTER 8: IMPROVING YOUR WRITING

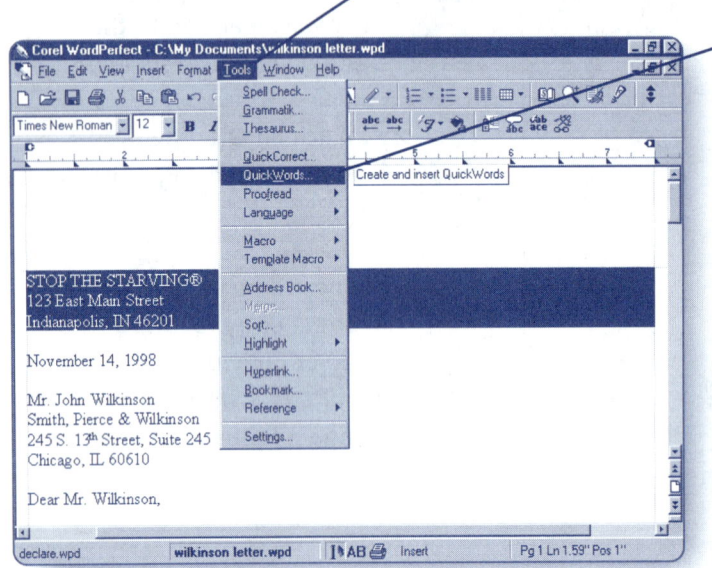

3. Click on **Tools**. The Tools menu will appear.

4. Click on **QuickWords**. The QuickCorrect dialog box will open with the QuickWords tab in the foreground.

5. Type an abbreviation for the selected text in the Abbreviated form area of the dialog box.

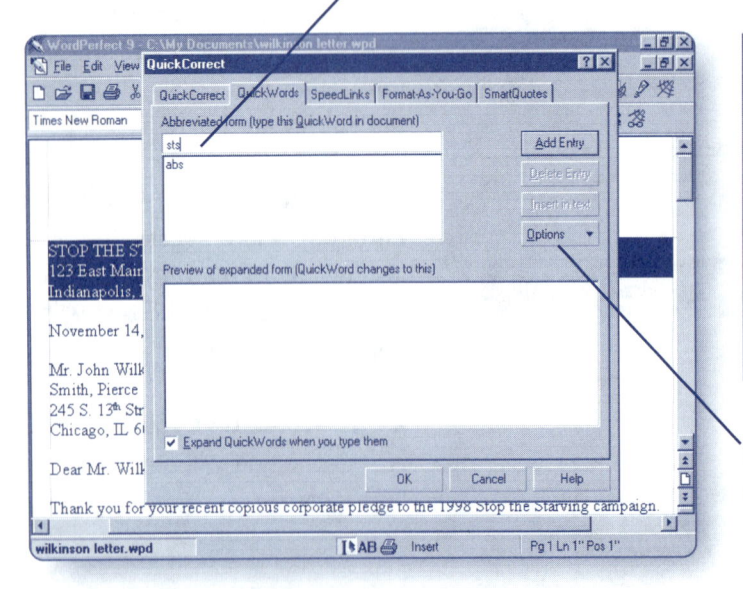

NOTE

Don't use a common word (the, and, my, and so on) for an abbreviation. If so, you won't be able to type those words in a document without the expanded text appearing.

6. Click on **Options.** The options menu will appear.

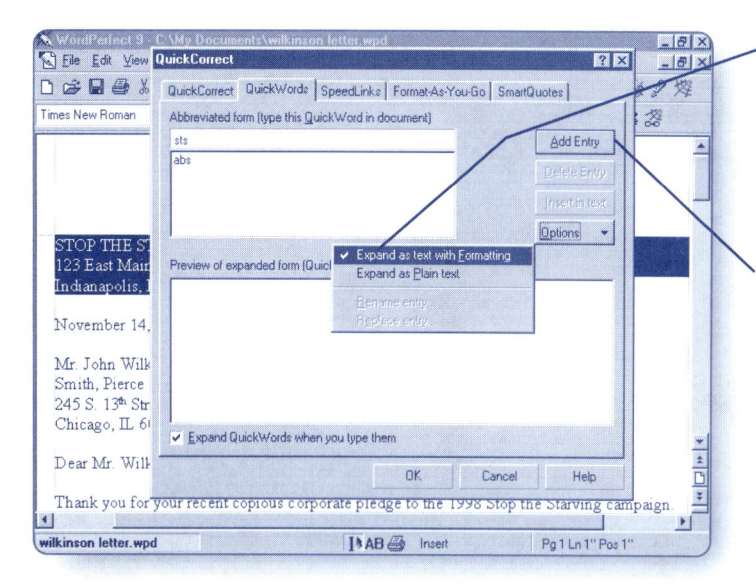

SAVING TIME WITH QUICKWORDS 75

7. Click on **Expand as Text with Formatting** or **Expand as Plain Text**. The selected option will have a check mark (✔) beside it.

8. Click on **Add Entry**. The dialog box will close.

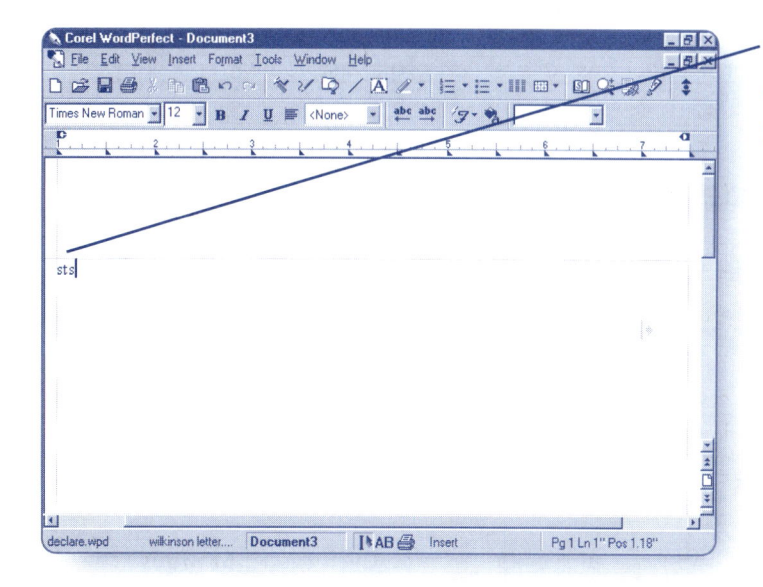

9. Type the **abbreviation**. The abbreviated text will appear in your document.

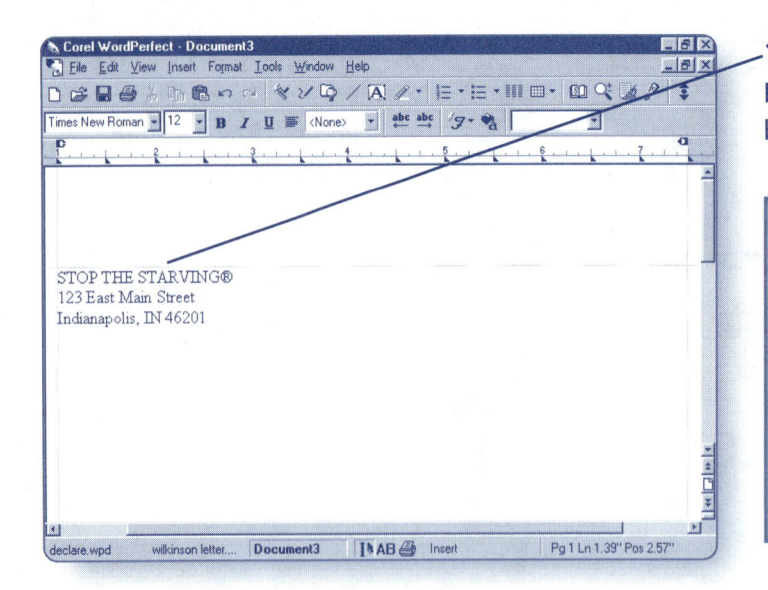

10. Press the **spacebar or Enter key**. The abbreviation will be expanded.

> **NOTE**
>
> The secret to using QuickWords is the spacebar or Enter key. When WordPerfect determines the entire word as the abbreviation you typed, only then will it expand.

Spell-Checking Your Document

WordPerfect has several ways to assist you with spelling issues.

Spelling As You Go

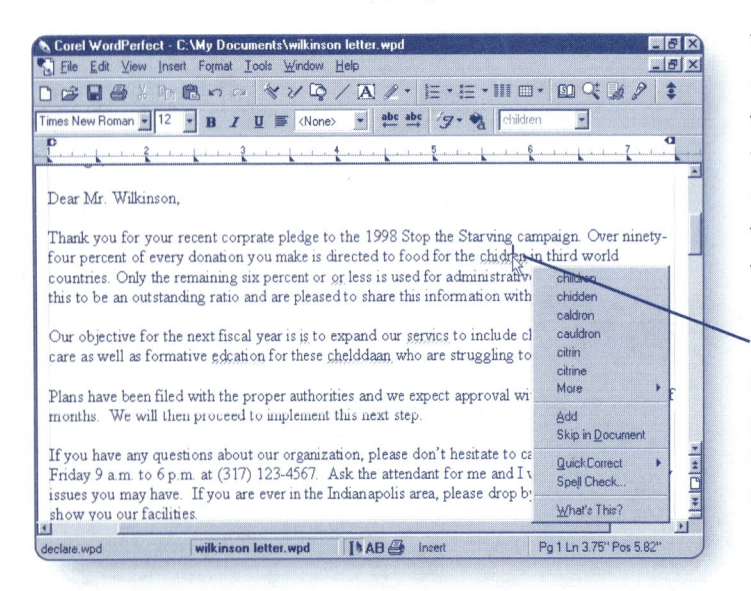

WordPerfect automatically checks your spelling as you type. You may notice some words have a red wavy line under them. You can correct these errors as you go along typing your text.

1. Click the **right mouse button** (*right-click*) while the pointer is positioned over the misspelled word. A shortcut menu will appear.

SPELL-CHECKING YOUR DOCUMENT 77

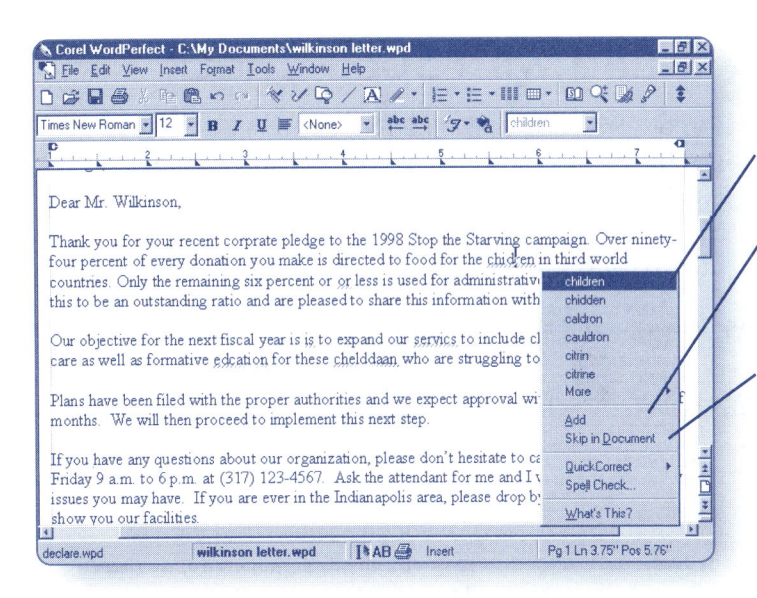

2. Click on one of the **menu choices**:

- Click on one of the suggested replacement words.

- Click on Add to add the word to the WordPerfect dictionary for future reference.

- Click on Skip in Document to tell WordPerfect to ignore this word.

Turning Off the Spell-As-You-Go Feature

You may find the Spell-As-You-Go feature annoying. For example, if you're typing a technical document, almost every word in the document might display the wavy red line. Turn off the Spell-As-You-Go feature.

1. Click on **Tools**. The Tools menu will appear.

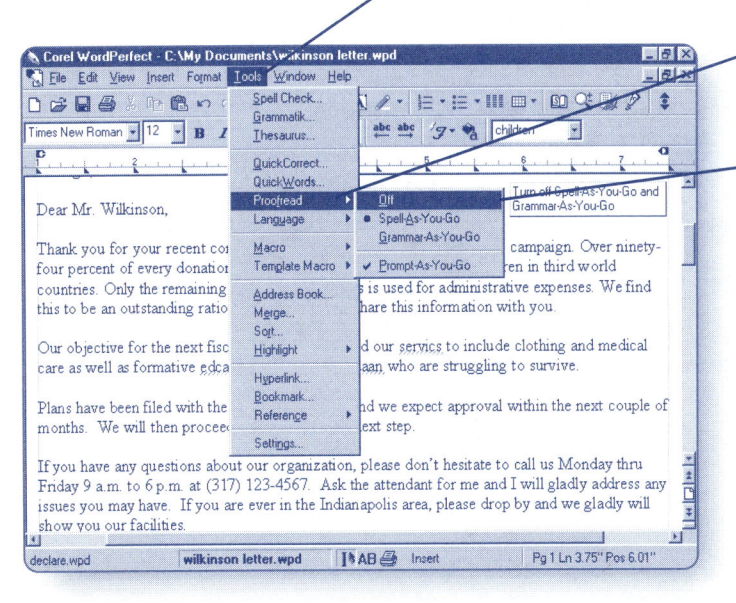

2. Click on **Proofread**. A cascading menu will appear.

3. Click on **Off.** The feature will be turned off.

NOTE
Click on Tools, Proofread, Spell-As-You-Go to reactivate the feature.

CHAPTER 8: IMPROVING YOUR WRITING

Working with Spell-Check

Instead of correcting spelling errors one at a time as you are working on the document, you can check them all at once with the Spell-Check feature.

1. Click on **Tools**. The Tools menu will appear.

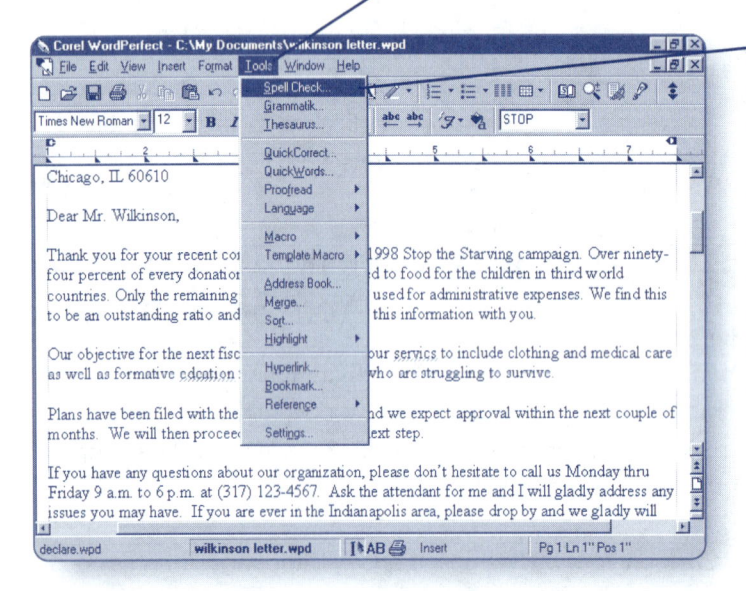

2. Click on **Spell Check**. The language tools dialog box will open.

WordPerfect automatically begins spell-checking your document and stops at the first misspelling, duplicate word, or irregular capitalization in your document.

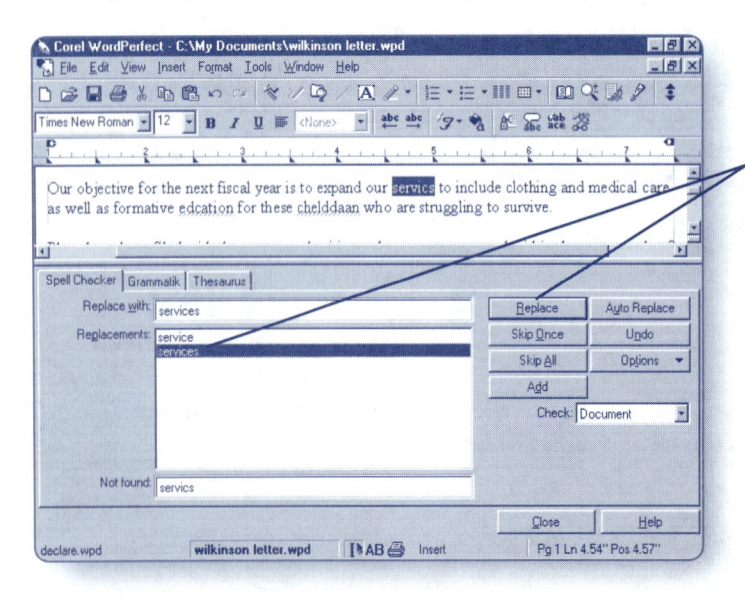

3. Choose one of the following **options**:

- **Replace.** Use this to replace the incorrect word with one you have selected from the Replacements: column.

WORKING WITH SPELL-CHECK 79

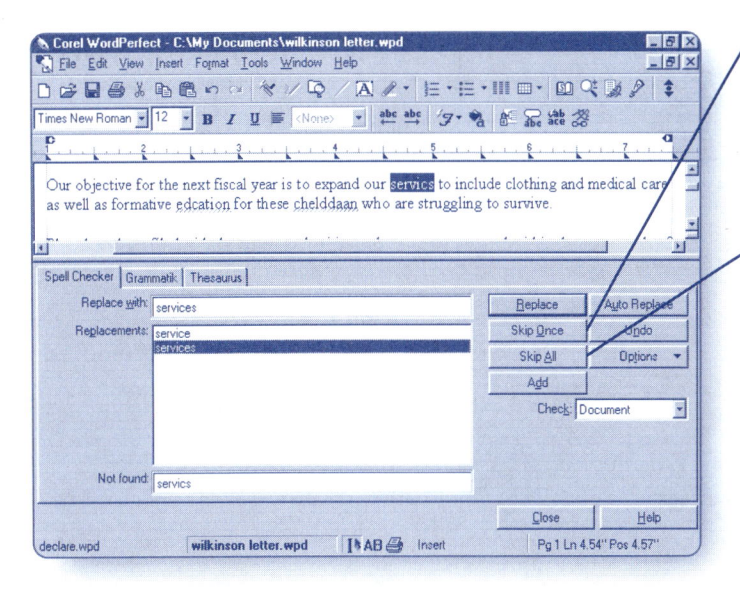

- **Skip Once.** Use this to ignore this occurrence of the word, but stop again the next time it appears. Pertains to the current document only.

- **Skip All.** Use this to ignore all occurrences of the misspelled word during the current spell-check session only.

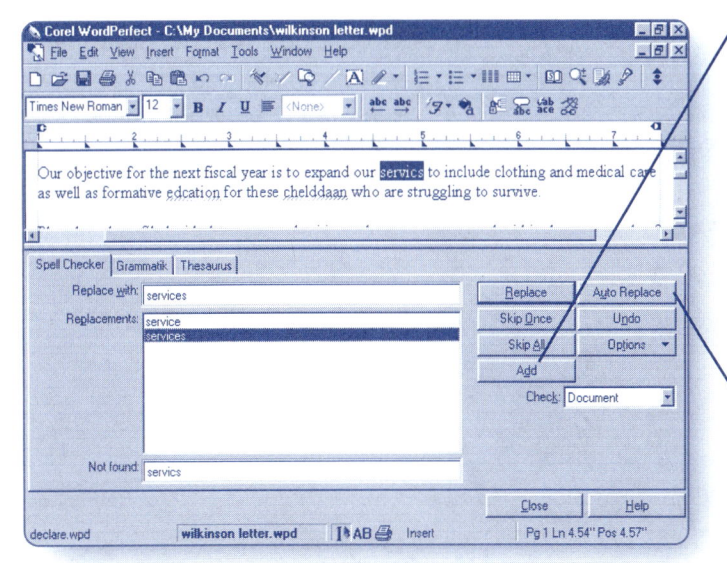

- **Add.** Use this to add the word to the supplemental dictionary. The Spell-Checker will accept this word as correctly spelled in the future—so be sure that you will want it in other documents before you add it to the dictionary.

- **Auto Replace.** Use this to define an automatic replacement for a word. Each time you type the misspelled word, WordPerfect will automatically replace it with the correct spelling.

If none of these options is appropriate, you will need to edit the word yourself.

CHAPTER 8: IMPROVING YOUR WRITING

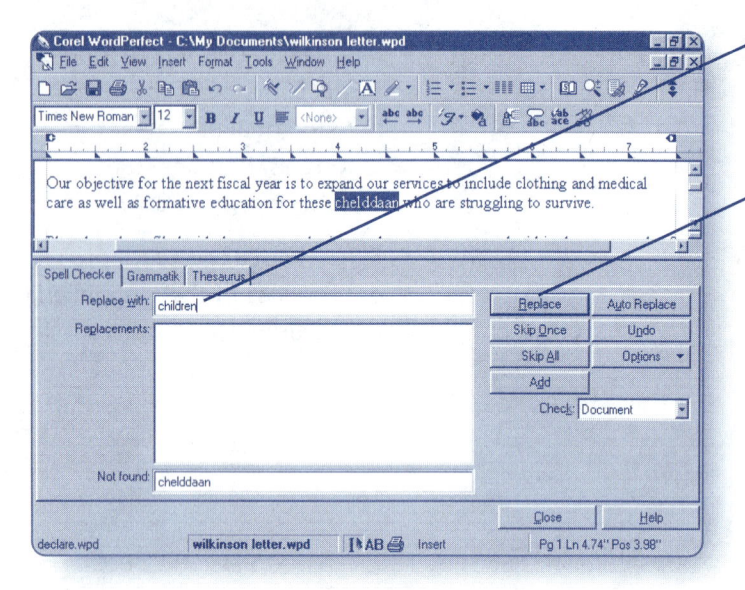

4. Type the **correct spelling** in the Replace with: area of the dialog box.

5. Click on **Replace**. The misspelling will be changed.

When the spell-check is complete, you will be prompted to close the Spell Checker dialog box.

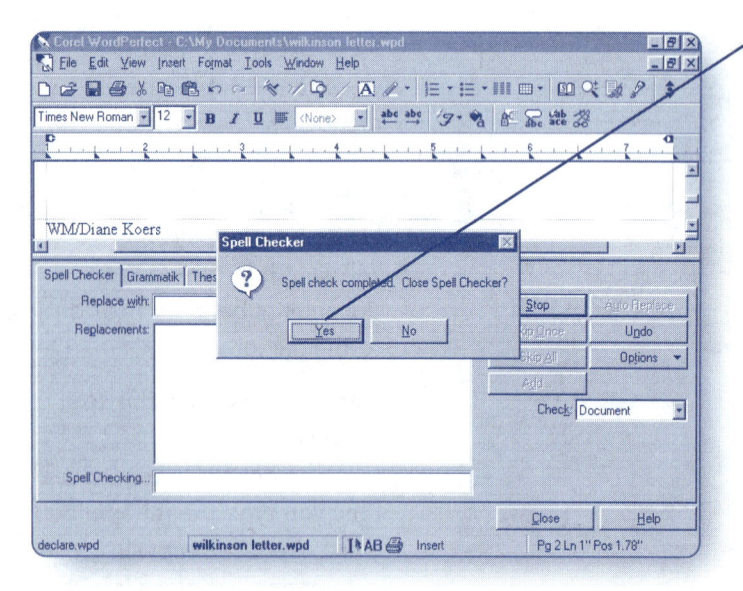

6. Click on **Yes**. The dialog box will close, and you will be returned to your document.

Checking Your Grammar

WordPerfect can correct many kinds of grammatical errors with the Grammatik feature.

1. Click on **Tools**. The Tools menu will appear.

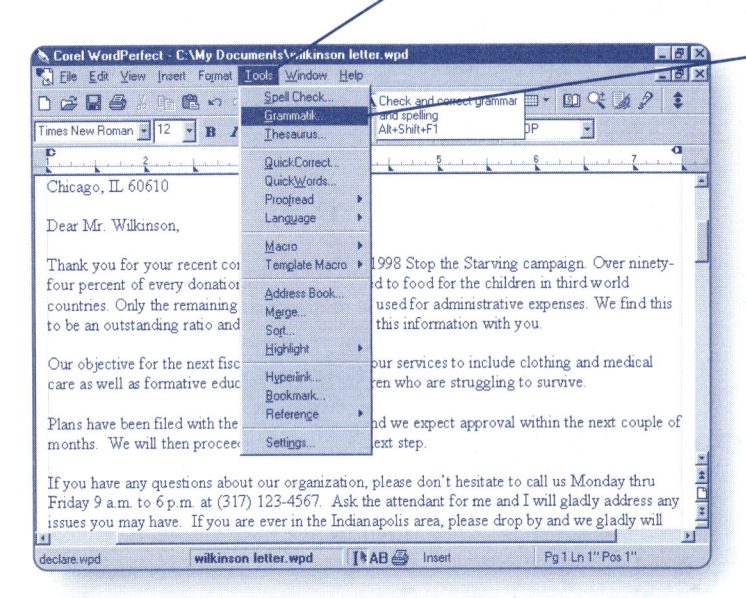

2. Click on **Grammatik**. The language tools dialog box will open.

NOTE

The Grammatik feature will also spell-check your document. Make spelling corrections as instructed in the previous section.

Grammatik stops at the first grammatical error and advises you of the problem at the bottom of the dialog box. It may or may not offer you replacement suggestions. If it does offer one or more suggestions:

3. Click on the **correct suggestion** from the Replacements: list, if available. The replacement suggestion will be highlighted.

4. Click on **Replace**. The text will be changed.

CHAPTER 8: IMPROVING YOUR WRITING

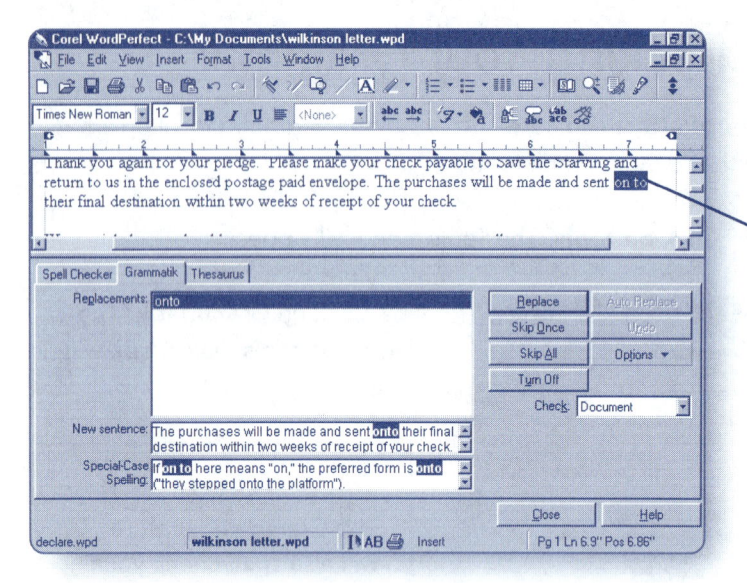

If Grammatik does not offer a replacement suggestion, you may need to edit the sentence manually.

5. Click in the **body of the document** next to the correction you want to make.

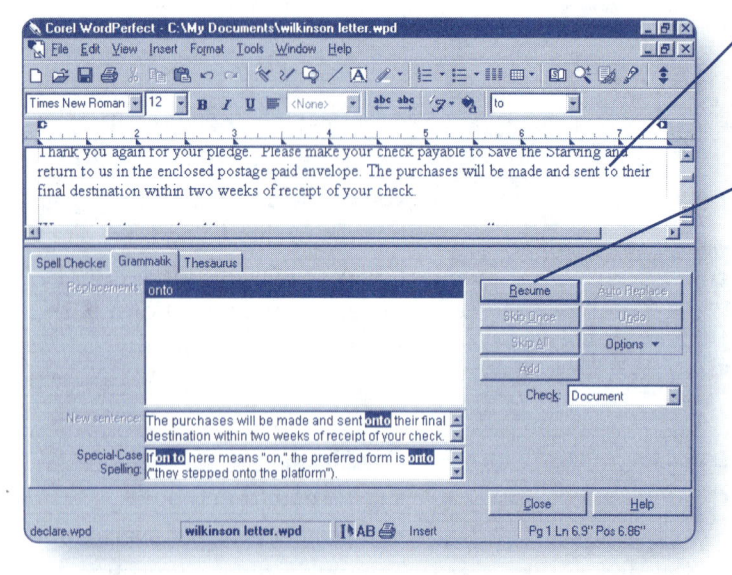

6. Type the **correction.** The typed text will appear in the document.

7. Click on **Resume** to continue the grammar check.

As with the spell-check, you are advised when the grammar check is complete.

FINDING A SYNONYM WITH THE THESAURUS

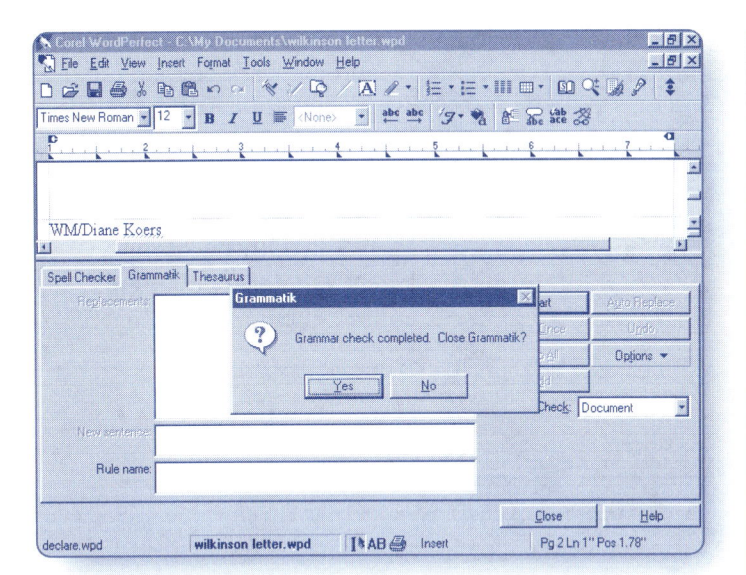

8. Click on **Yes**. The Grammatik dialog box will close.

TIP

Do *not*, repeat do *NOT*, rely on the spell-checker and Grammatik to catch all your errors. They are far from perfect and can miss many items. They can also flag errors when your text is really okay and can suggest wrong things to do to fix both real problems and false error reports. You alone are the one who knows what your document is intended to say. Proofread it yourself!

Finding a Synonym with the Thesaurus

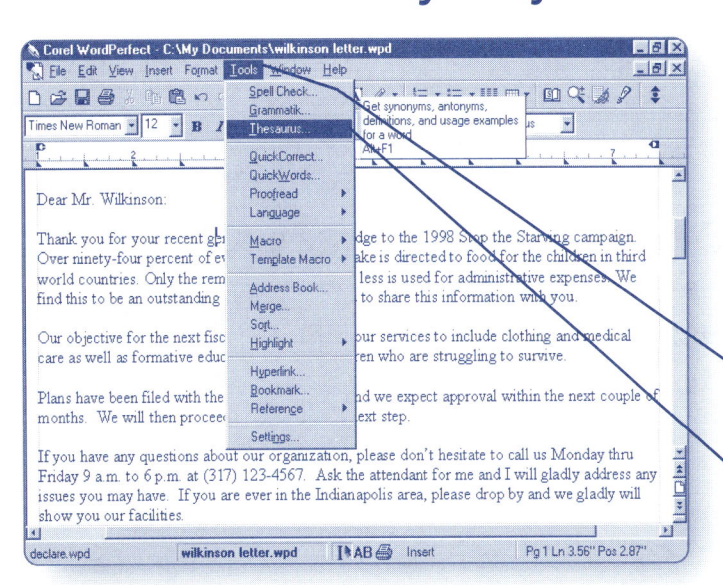

The WordPerfect Thesaurus not only gives synonyms of a word, but antonyms, definitions, and usage examples as well.

1. Position the **insertion point** in the word for which you want to find a synonym.

2. Click on **Tools**. The Tools menu will appear.

3. Click on **Thesaurus**. The language tools dialog box will open, and definitions of the selected word will display.

CHAPTER 8: IMPROVING YOUR WRITING

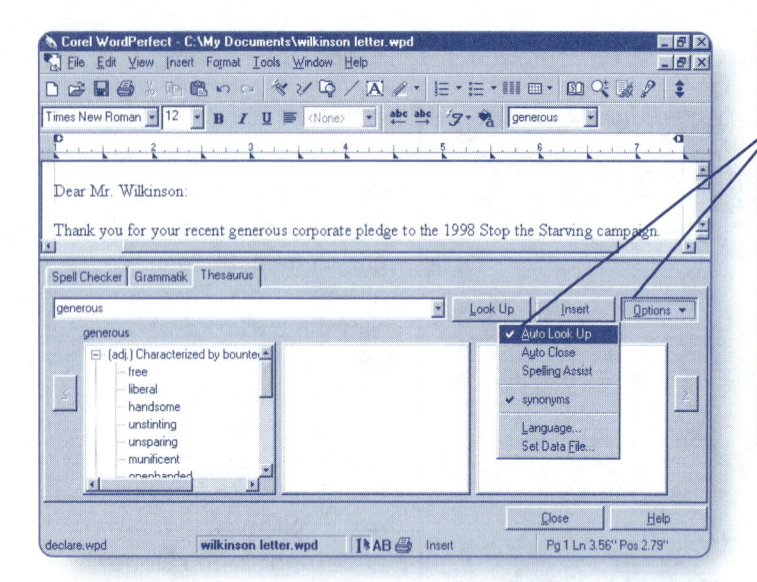

NOTE

If the definitions do not automatically appear, you'll need to activate the Auto Look Up feature. Click on Options and choose Auto Look Up. You should only have to activate this feature the first time.

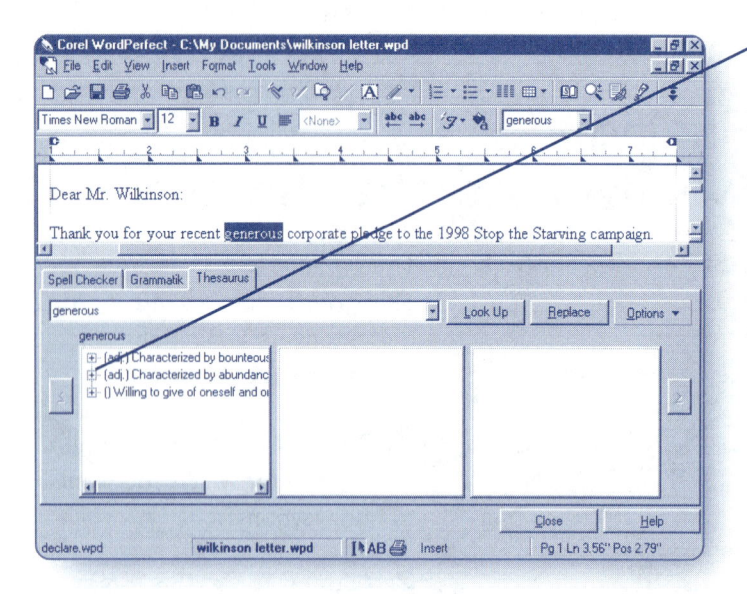

4. If necessary, **click** on the **plus sign** next to the correct definition of your word. A list of synonyms will appear below the definition.

REVIEWING DOCUMENT STATISTICS   85

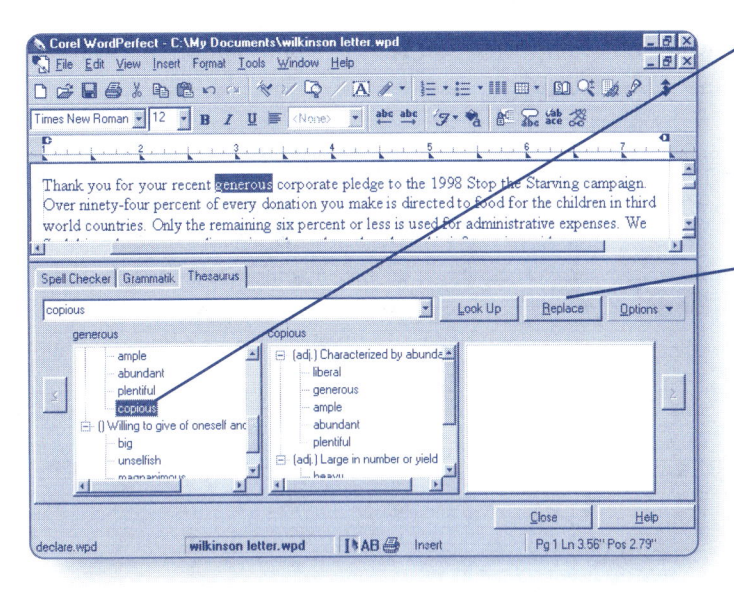

5. Click on the desired **replacement word**. The word will be highlighted, and synonyms of it will display in the second box.

6. Click on **Replace**. The dialog box will close, and the original word will be replaced with your selection.

Reviewing Document Statistics

There may be occasions when you need to know how many words you've typed. Possibly, you're finishing a term paper that needs to be at least 1,000 words, or perhaps you're creating advertising copy for which you'll be paid by the word.

1. Click on **File**. The File menu will appear.

2. Click on **Properties**. The Properties dialog box will open.

3. Click on the **Information tab**. The Information tab will come to the front.

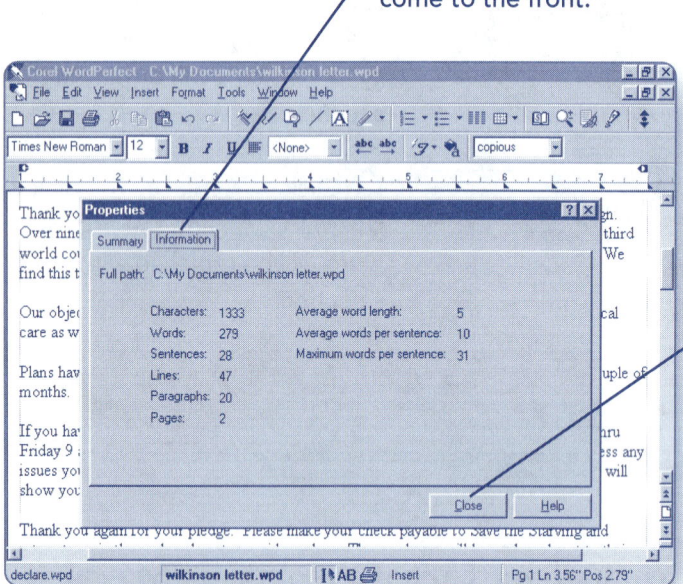

The information box tells you exactly how many pages, words, paragraphs, lines, characters, and sentences you have in your document. It even includes averages!

4. Click on **Close**. The Properties dialog box will close.

Part I Review Questions

1. Which item on the screen changes according to the feature you are currently using? *See "Starting WordPerfect" in Chapter 1*

2. What feature does WordPerfect have that inserts the current date for you? *See "Entering Date Text" in Chapter 1*

3. On what two places onscreen does the name of your saved document appear? *See "Saving a File the First Time" in Chapter 2*

4. What is Autoscroll? *See "Using Autoscroll" in Chapter 4*

5. What does the shadow cursor do? *See "Using the Shadow Cursor" in Chapter 4*

6. What feature allows you to reverse the last action you took? *See "Undoing the Previous Step" in Chapter 5*

7. What Windows feature does WordPerfect use to move or copy text from one place to another? *See "Moving and Copying Text" in Chapter 5*

8. What feature adjusts a document to fit a certain number of pages? *See "Making It Fit" in Chapter 6*

9. How can you view two pages of your document at the same time? *See "Viewing Two Pages at a Time" in Chapter 7*

10. What feature can anticipate and fix many common spelling and capitalization errors? *See "Discovering QuickCorrect" in Chapter 8*

PART II

Formatting a Report

Chapter 9
    Formatting with Fonts.................. **91**

Chapter 10
    Changing Paper Sizes and Margins....... **101**

Chapter 11
    Modifying Alignment, Indentation,
    and Spacing........................ **109**

Chapter 12
    Adding Bullets, Numbering, and Borders... **117**

Chapter 13
    Working with Footnotes and Endnotes ... **127**

Chapter 14
    Adding Headers, Footers,
    and Watermarks **137**

Chapter 15
    Saving Time with Templates **151**

9

Formatting with Fonts

In the past, when people first typed letters on typewriters, there was usually only one font choice available. Later, you could change fonts—if you stopped to put in a new type ball or daisy wheel. Computers make it easy to use unusual typefaces. Not only can you pick and choose the font you want, but you can also modify the size and style as well. In this chapter, you'll learn how to:

- Change typeface
- Change font size
- Change the style of text
- Use the Highlighter

Changing Text Appearance

Changing the appearance of your text could involve changing the typeface, size, style, or any combination of these features.

Changing the Typeface

The default font for WordPerfect is Times New Roman, but WordPerfect comes with many additional fonts. Other software installed on your machine may give you still more fonts as well.

1. Click the **mouse pointer** at the location where you want the font change to begin. The blinking insertion point will appear.

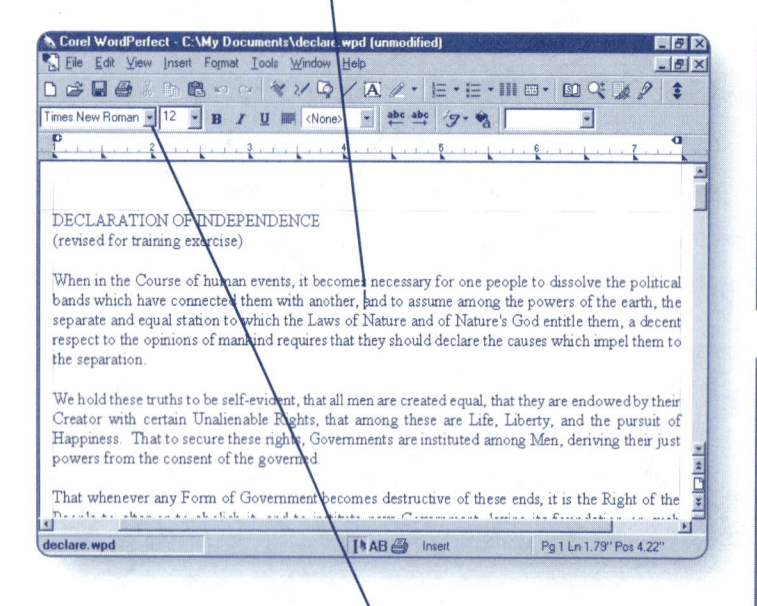

NOTE
Be very careful where the insertion point is located. WordPerfect changes the font from the point of the insertion point.

TIP
If you select a block of text before choosing a new typeface, the change affects only the selected block.

2. Click on the **Font Face down arrow (▼)**. A drop-down list of your font choices will appear. As you move your mouse across the font names, you will see a sample of that typeface.

CHANGING TEXT APPEARANCE 93

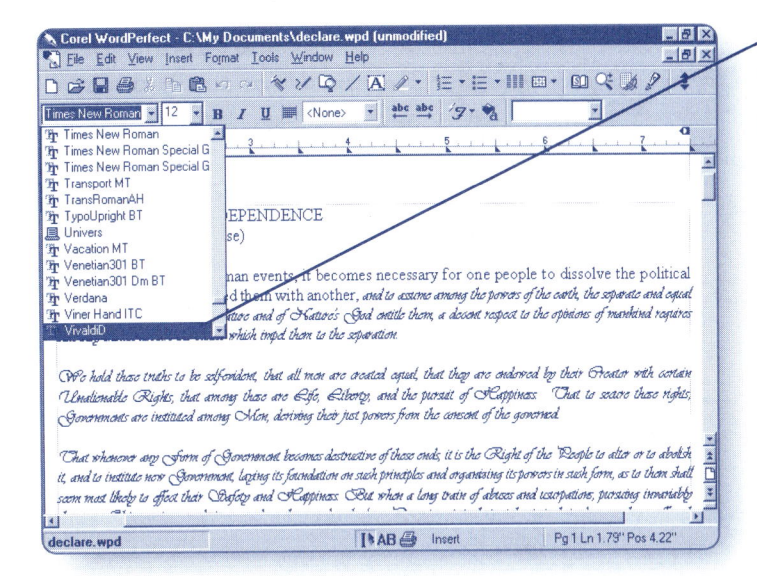

3. Click on the **desired font**. The text after the insertion point will change.

Changing Font Size

The default is a 12-point font—roughly ⅙ of an inch tall. The larger the point size of the font, the larger the text will print. Text that is 72 points is just about 1 inch tall.

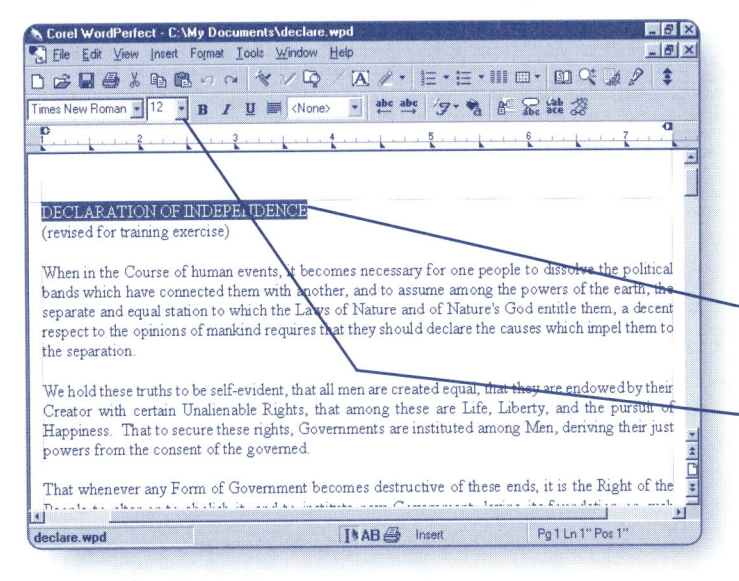

1a. Click the **mouse pointer** at the location where you want the font change to begin. The blinking insertion point will appear.

OR

1b. Select some **text**. The text will be highlighted.

2. Click on the **Font Size drop-down arrow (▼)**. A list of available sizes will appear. These sizes may vary depending on what typeface you are using and what printer you have installed.

CHAPTER 9: FORMATTING WITH FONTS

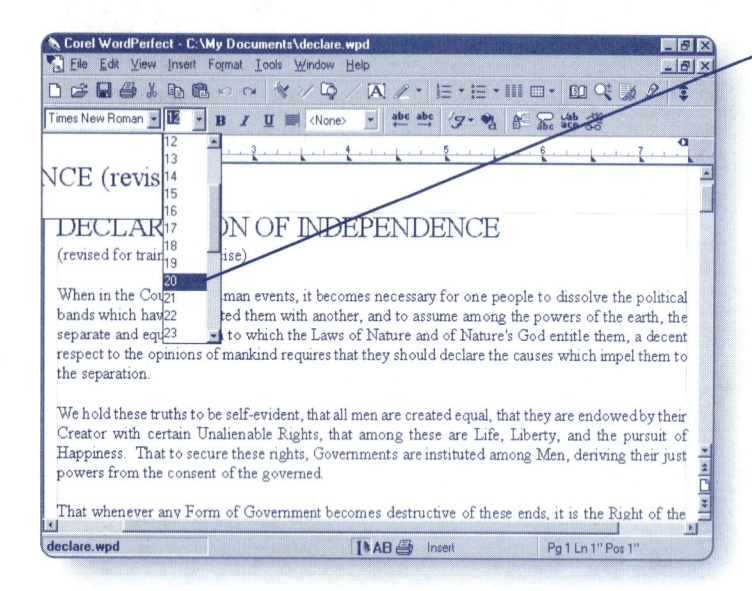

3. Click on the **desired size**. The text will be changed to the new size.

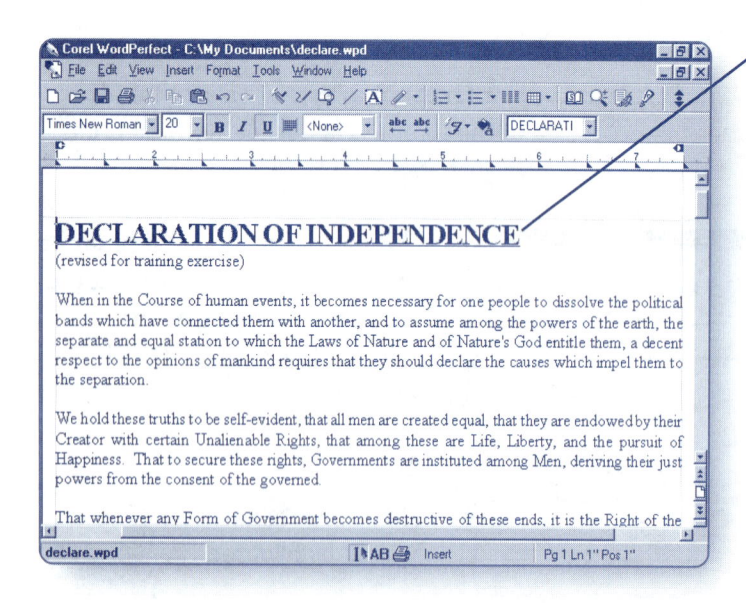

Notice how just the heading changed to the new size. The heading was selected or highlighted before the size selection was made, so that's the only text WordPerfect touched.

CHANGING TEXT APPEARANCE   95

Changing the Style of Text

The style of text includes features such as **bold,** underline, or *italics*. You must highlight the text to be modified before changing the style of it.

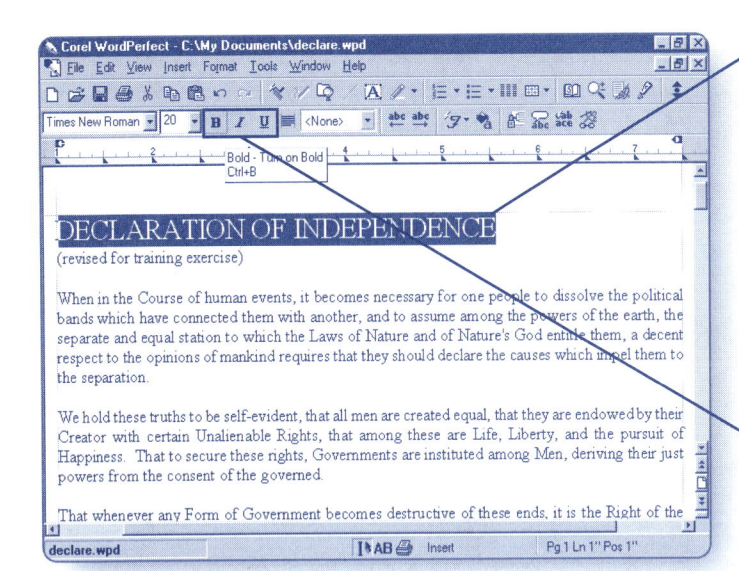

1. Select the **text** you want to change. The text will be highlighted.

Buttons on the property bar make it easy to add style to your text. The button with the "B" is for **bold**, the "I" is for *italics*, and the "U" is for underline.

2. Click on the **Bold, Italics,** or **Underline button**. The text will be changed according to your selection.

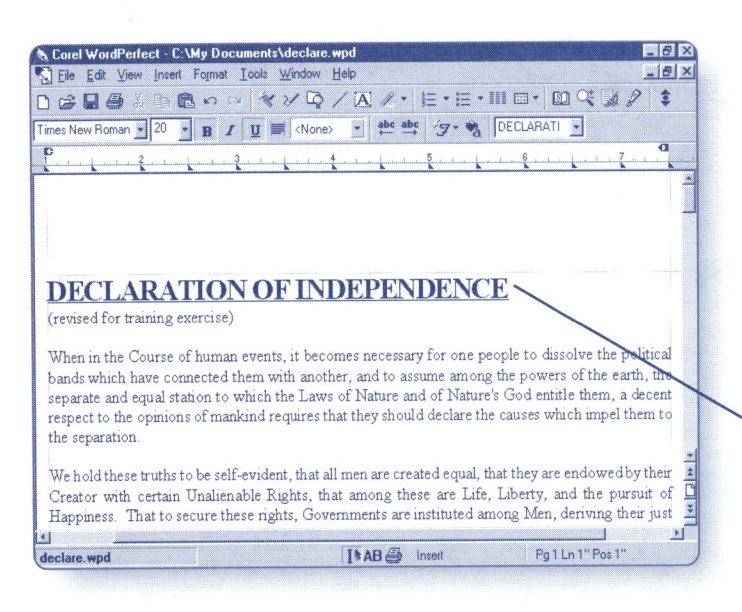

TIP

Shortcut keys also exist for bold, italics, and underlining. Press Ctrl+B for bold, Ctrl+I to italicize, and Ctrl+U to underline your text.

The title in this figure has both bold and underlining applied to it.

CHAPTER 9: FORMATTING WITH FONTS

> **NOTE**
> These buttons are like toggle switches. Notice how the buttons look "pressed" if the feature is turned on. If you click one of them on and decide not to use it, click it again, and the style will be turned off.

> **TIP**
> If you just want to bold, underline, or italicize a single word, you do not need to select it first. Just place the insertion point somewhere in the middle of the word and click the desired style button.

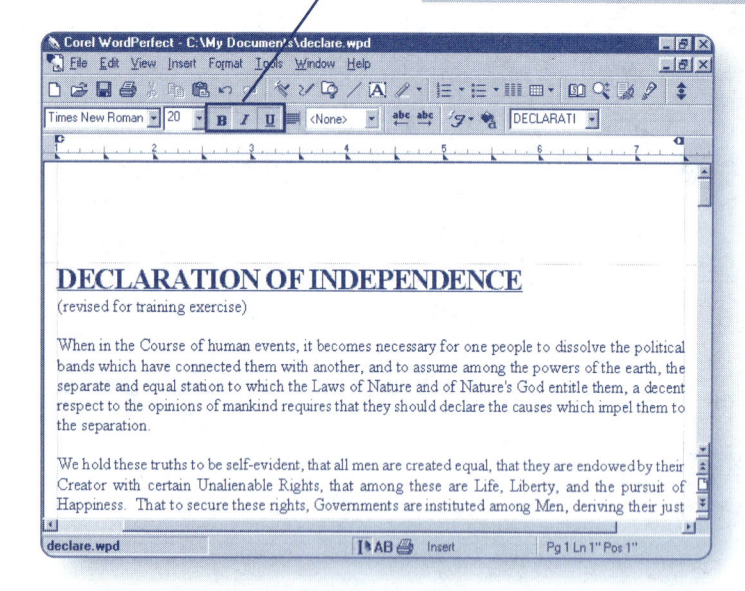

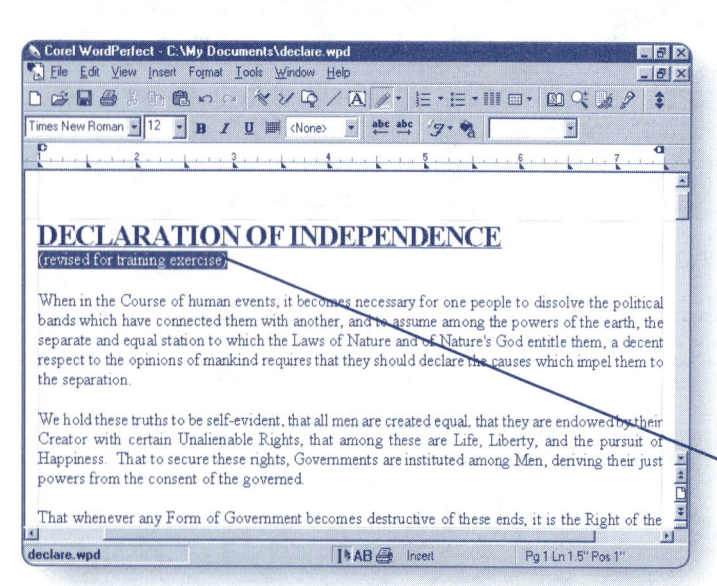

Making Font Changes from One Location

If you want to make all these types of changes at one time, you can use the Font dialog box to make your selections. This method also gives you the advantage of a Preview window to let you see an example of your selection before you actually change the text.

1. Select the **text** to be modified. The text will be highlighted.

CHANGING TEXT APPEARANCE 97

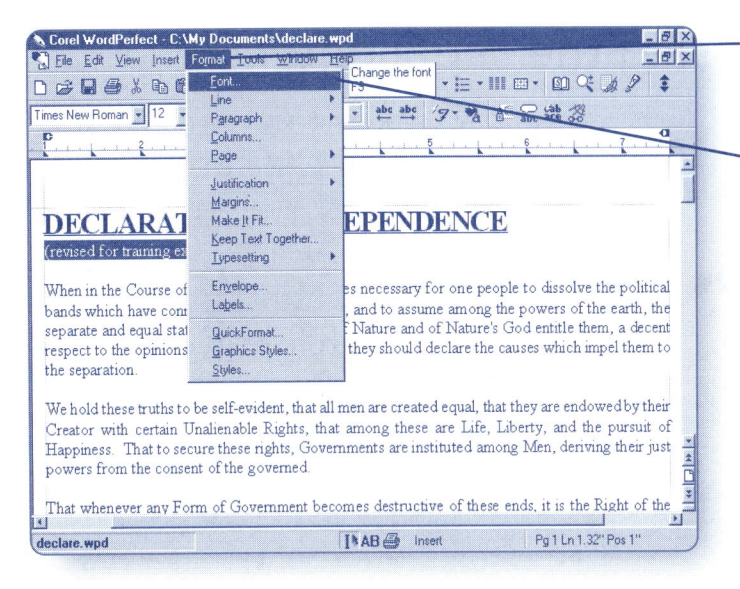

2. Click on **Format**. The Format menu will appear.

3. Click on **Font**. The Font dialog box will open.

4. Choose any of the following **items**:

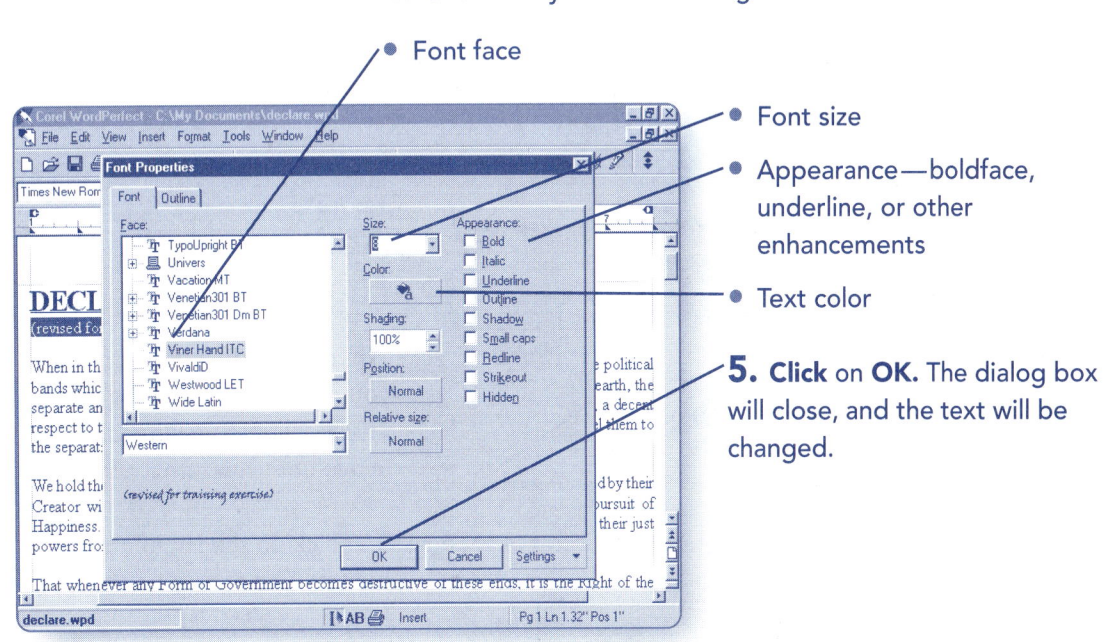

- Font face
- Font size
- Appearance—boldface, underline, or other enhancements
- Text color

5. Click on **OK**. The dialog box will close, and the text will be changed.

Using the Highlighter

Highlighting puts a bar of transparent color over text. If you have a color printer, the highlight colors will print. Black-and-white printers print the colors in gray.

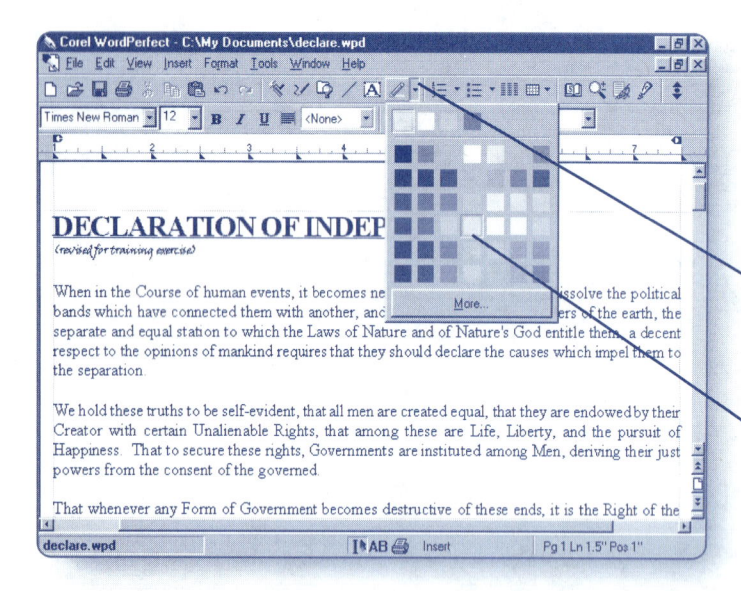

Selecting a Highlight Color

You can choose from a variety of highlight colors.

1. Click on the **Highlight down arrow (▼)**. A palette of colors will appear.

2. Click on a **color**. The highlight button will assume the new color.

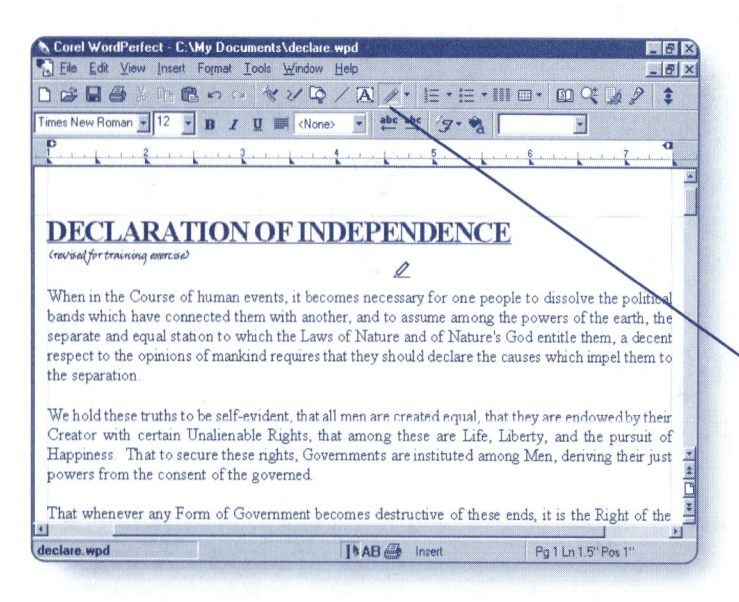

Applying Highlighter

When applying highlighting, you'll use the mouse like a pen. The highlighter will remain active until you turn it off.

1. Click on the **Highlight button**. The mouse pointer will appear as a small pen.

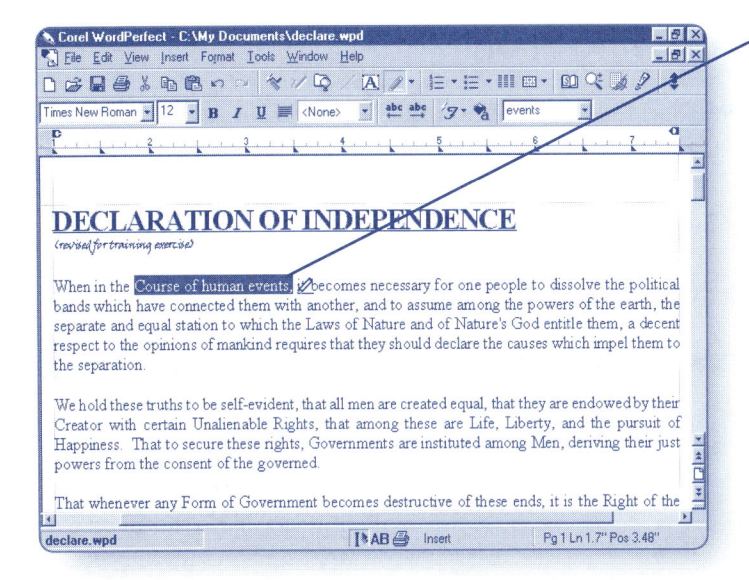

USING THE HIGHLIGHTER   99

2. Drag the **mouse pointer** across the text to be highlighted. The text will have a highlighted wash put over it.

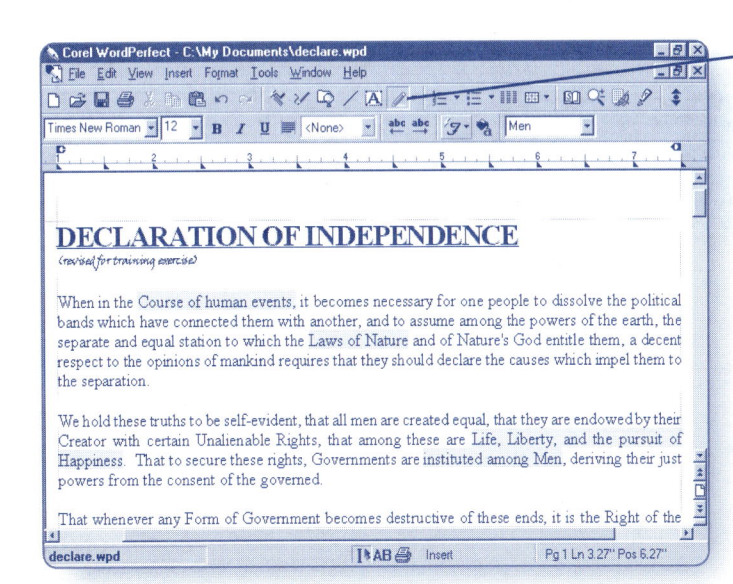

3. Click on the **Highlight button again** to turn off the highlighter pen.

TIP
A quick way to highlight a block of text is to select it first and then click once on the highlight button.

Removing Highlighting

Removing the highlighting from text is just as easy as adding it.

1. Select the **text** to have highlighting removed.

2. Click on **Tools**. The Tools menu will appear.

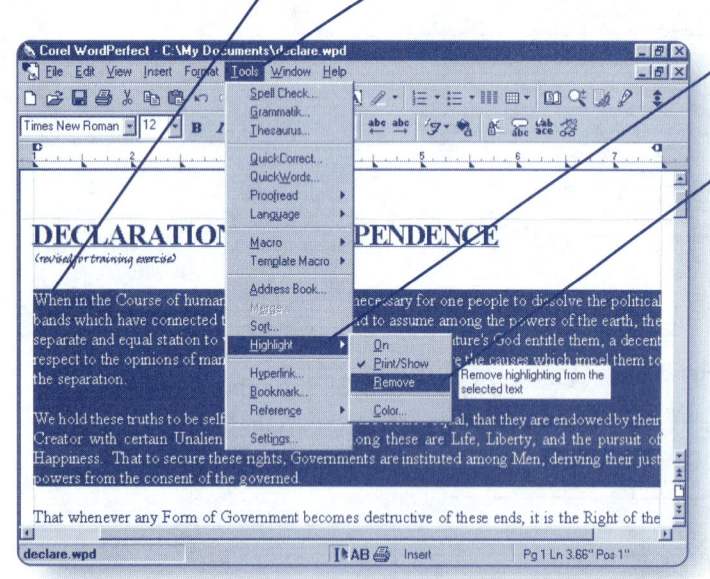

3. Click on **Highlight**. A cascading menu will appear.

4. Click on **Remove**. The highlighting will be removed from the text.

10

Changing Paper Sizes and Margins

WordPerfect has default settings for many things, including the size of the paper and the margin settings it assumes you are using. Both of these are easy to change. In this chapter, you'll learn how to:

- Select a paper size and orientation
- Change margins
- Add page numbering

102 CHAPTER 10: CHANGING PAPER SIZES AND MARGINS

Selecting a Paper Size and Orientation

WordPerfect assumes that you are using $8\frac{1}{2} \times 11$-inch paper in a portrait orientation. Although this is standard for many items, you can select a different size or orientation at any point in your document.

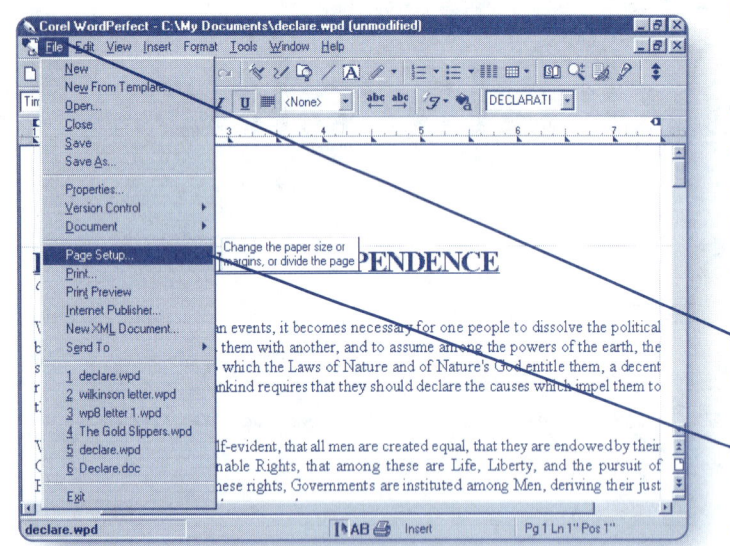

1. Click the **mouse pointer** at the beginning of the page where you want the new paper size setting to take effect. The blinking insertion point will appear.

2. Click on **File**. The File menu will appear.

3. Click on **Page Setup**. The Page Setup dialog box will open.

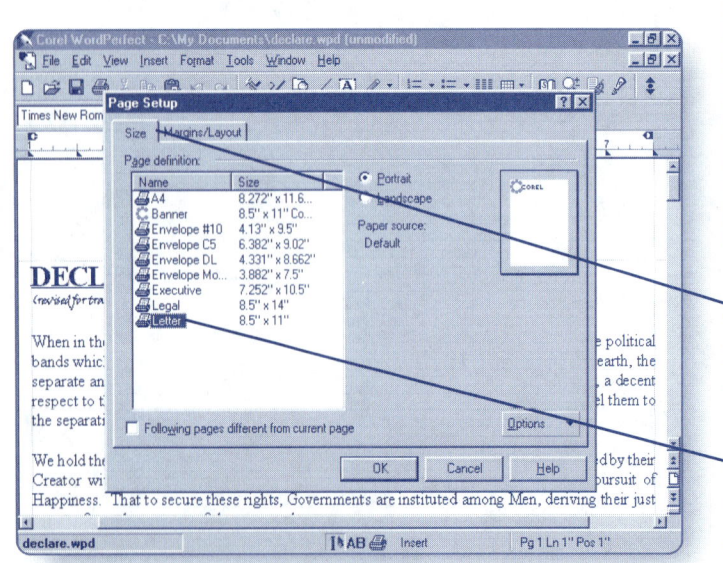

TIP
You can also get to this same dialog box by clicking on Format, Page, and Page Setup.

4. If necessary, **click** on the **Size tab**. The Size tab will come to the front.

5. Click on a **paper size** in the Page definition: box. The selection will be highlighted.

SELECTING A PAPER SIZE AND ORIENTATION 103

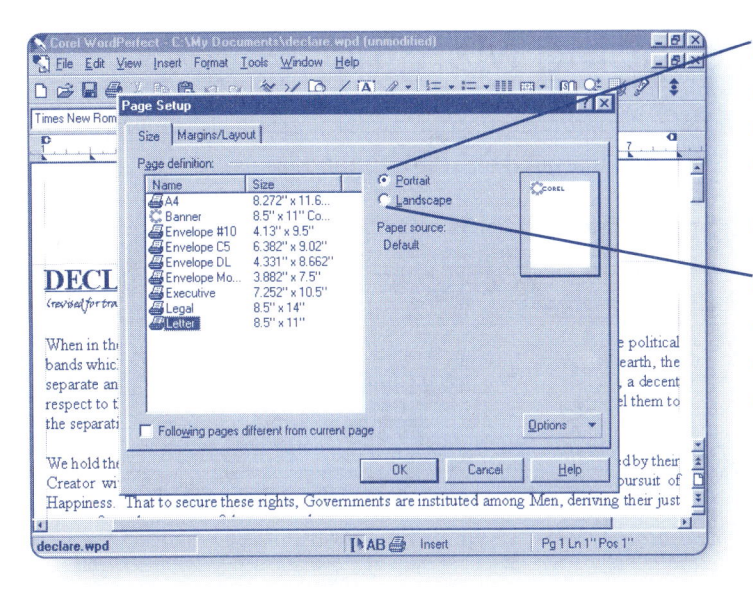

6a. Click on **Portrait** in the orientation area if you want the document to print in the usual vertical layout.

OR

6b. Click on **Landscape** in the orientation area if you want the document to print horizontally across the page.

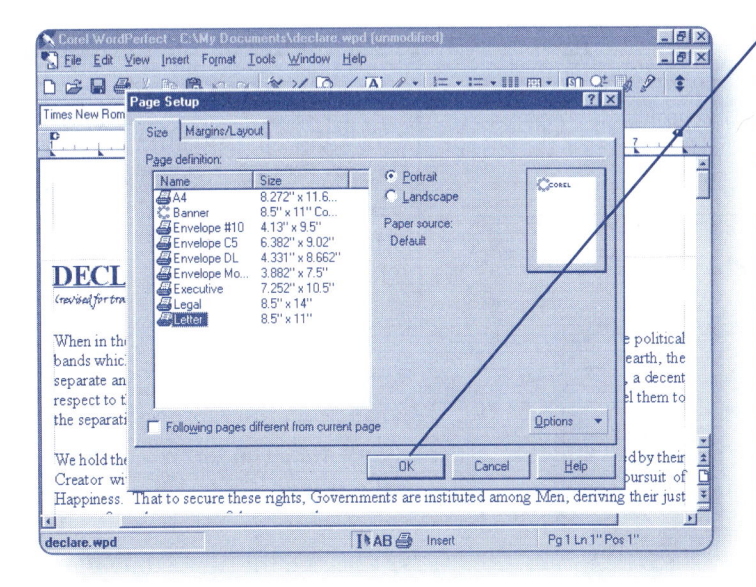

7. Click on **OK**. Your document will be tagged with the print size and orientation you selected.

TIP

You can mix and match paper sizes and orientations in a WordPerfect document. Position your cursor at the beginning of the page you want to change, make the change as in the preceding steps 2 through 7, and then position the insertion point where you want another change to take effect and repeat these steps again.

104 CHAPTER 10: CHANGING PAPER SIZES AND MARGINS

Changing Margins

The default margin settings in a WordPerfect document are 1 inch on each margin: left, right, top, and bottom.

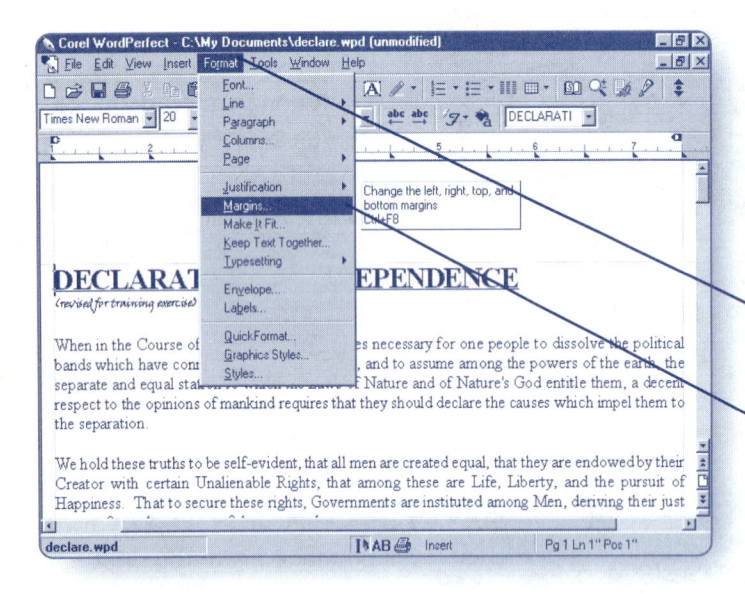

1. Click the **mouse pointer** at the beginning of the page where you want the new paper size setting to take effect. The blinking insertion point will appear.

2. Click on **Format**. The Format menu will appear.

3. Click on **Margins**. The Page Setup dialog box will open.

NOTE

This dialog box is the same Page Setup dialog box used in the previous section, but with the Margins tab in front.

4. Click on the **Margins/Layout tab**. The tab will come to the front.

5. Click on the **up** or **down arrow (♦)** next to the margins you want to change until the box next to it shows your desired choice.

ADDING PAGE NUMBERING   105

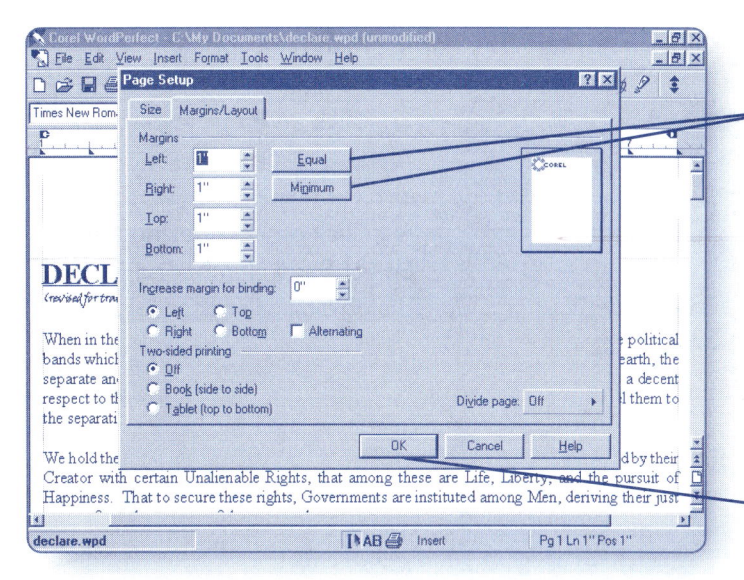

TIP

Click on the Equal button after changing one margin to have all four margins change to the same setting, or click on the Minimum button to set the margins to the smallest amount allowed by your printer.

6. Click on **OK**. The Margins dialog box will close, and the new settings will take effect.

Adding Page Numbering

Page numbering can be added to the top or bottom of the page in your document. You can also add page numbering in a header or footer. Headers and footers are discussed in Chapter 14, "Adding Headers, Footers, and Watermarks."

1. Click the **mouse pointer** at the beginning of the page where you want the page numbering to take effect. The blinking insertion point will appear.

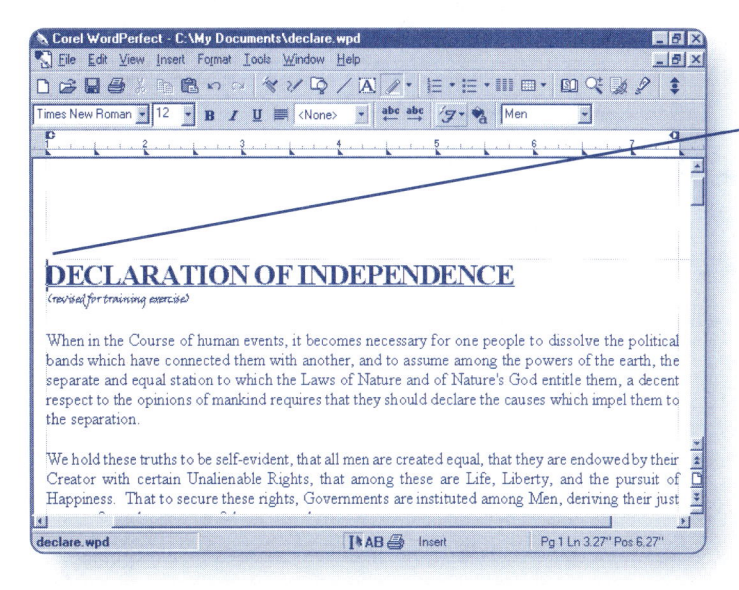

106 CHAPTER 10: CHANGING PAPER SIZES AND MARGINS

2. Click on **Format**. The Format menu will appear.

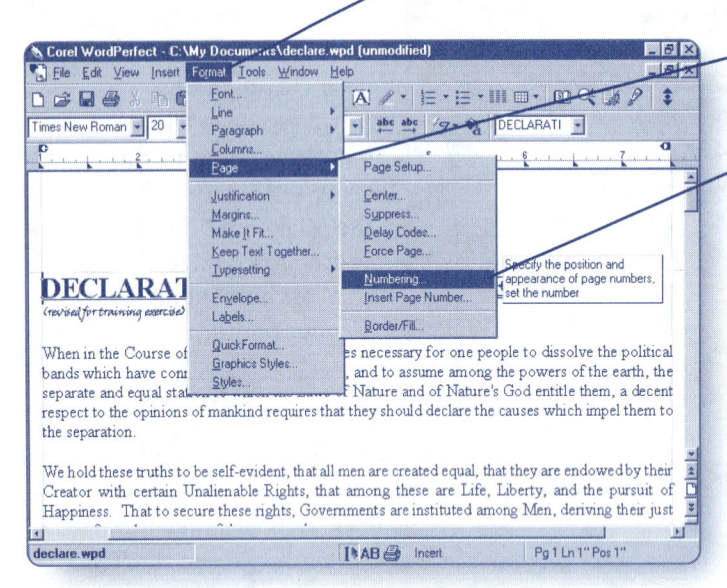

3. Click on **Page**. A cascading menu will appear.

4. Click on **Numbering**. The Select Page Numbering Format dialog box will open.

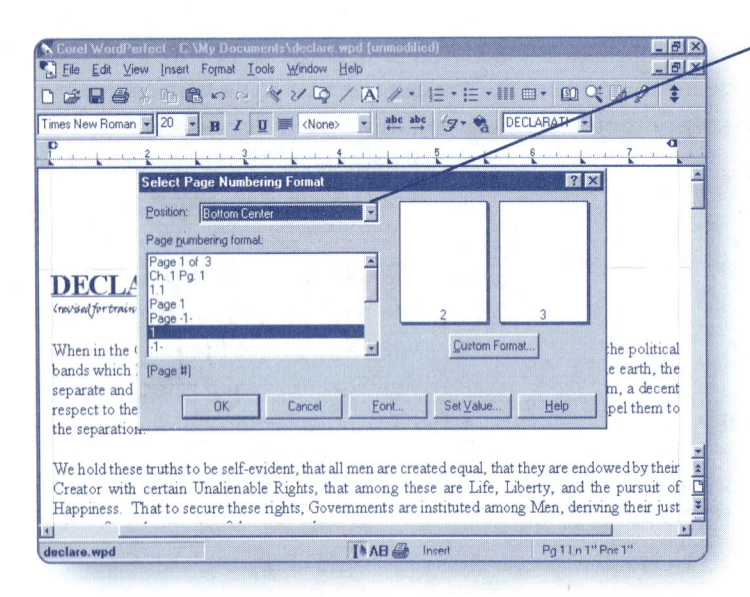

5. Click on the **down arrow** (▼) next to the Position: list box. A list of available choices will appear.

ADDING PAGE NUMBERING 107

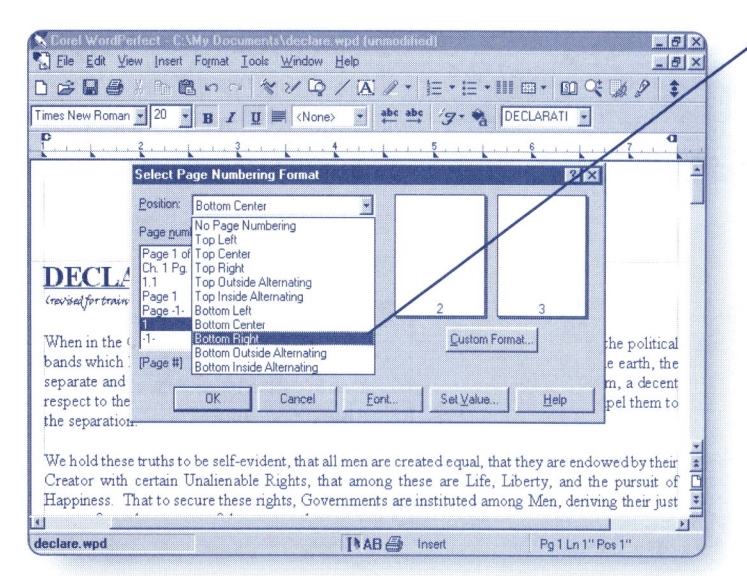

6. Click on the **location** where you want the page number to appear.

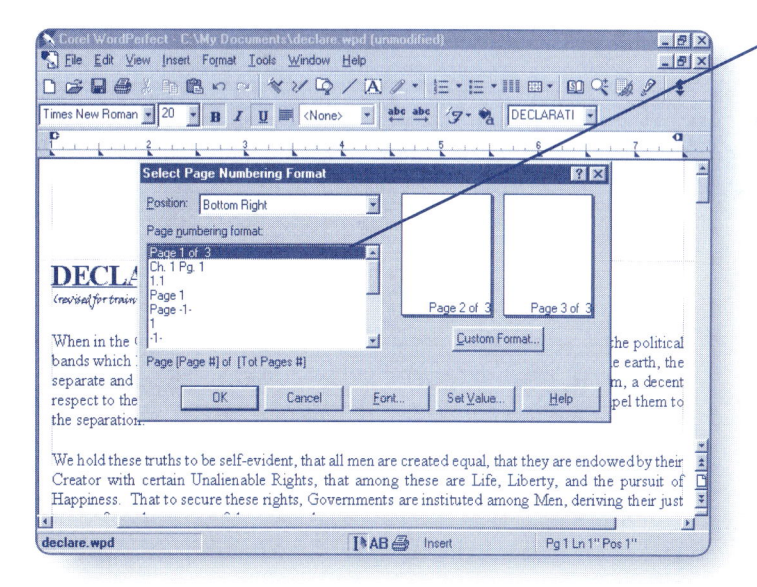

7. Click on a **numbering format** in the Page numbering format: list box.

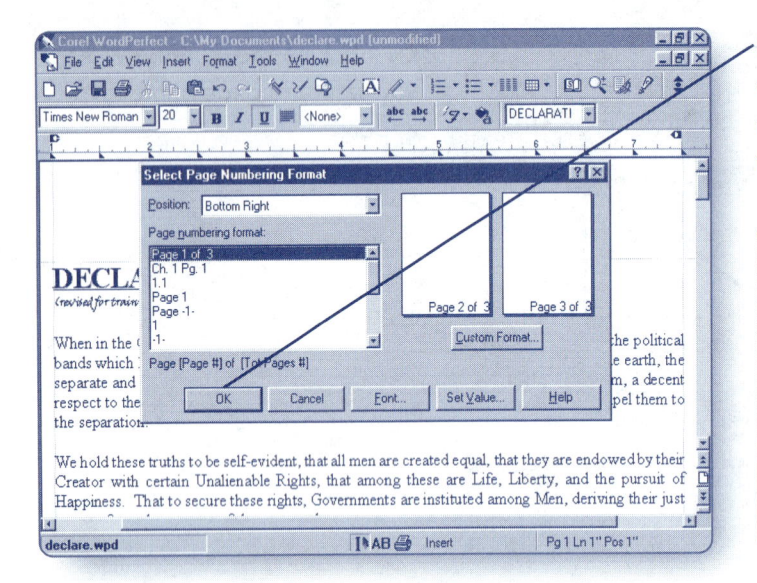

8. Click on **OK**. The dialog box will close, and page numbering will begin on the current page at the location you specify.

> **NOTE**
>
> Page numbering does not appear on the screen if you are using Draft view. Views are discussed in Chapter 7, "Working with Views."

11

Modifying Alignment, Indentation, and Spacing

Alignment of text can be changed both horizontally and vertically to add a pleasing appearance to your document. Indentation and spacing modifications can make a document easier to read. In this chapter, you'll learn how to:

- Center a heading
- Change justification
- Change the indentation of a paragraph
- Center a page vertically
- Change line spacing

Justifying Text

Document text can be modified so that it is even on the left side (*left justified*), even on the right side (*right justified*), or even on both sides (*full justified*). You can even make text S T R E T C H across the page (*all justified*).

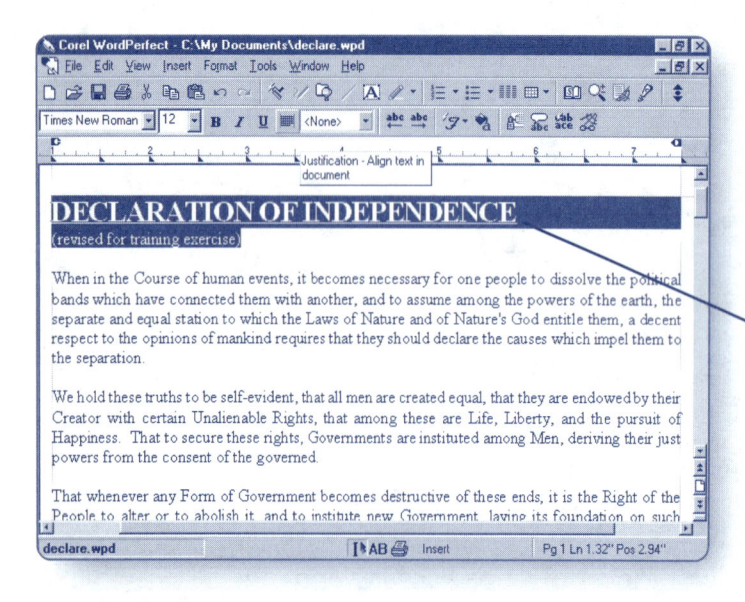

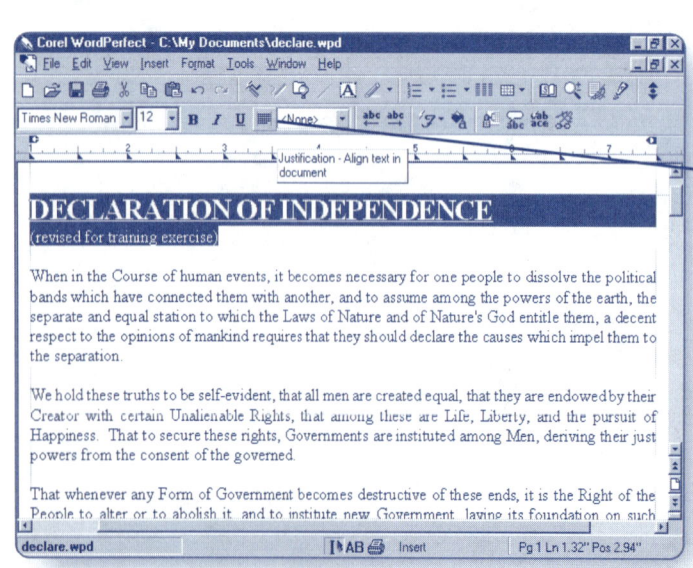

Centering a Heading

Centering a heading of a report lets the readers know they are beginning a new section.

1. Select the **text** to be centered. The text will be highlighted.

> **TIP**
> If you do not select the text first, everything from the insertion point forward will be centered.

2. Click on the **Justification button**. A list of choices will appear.

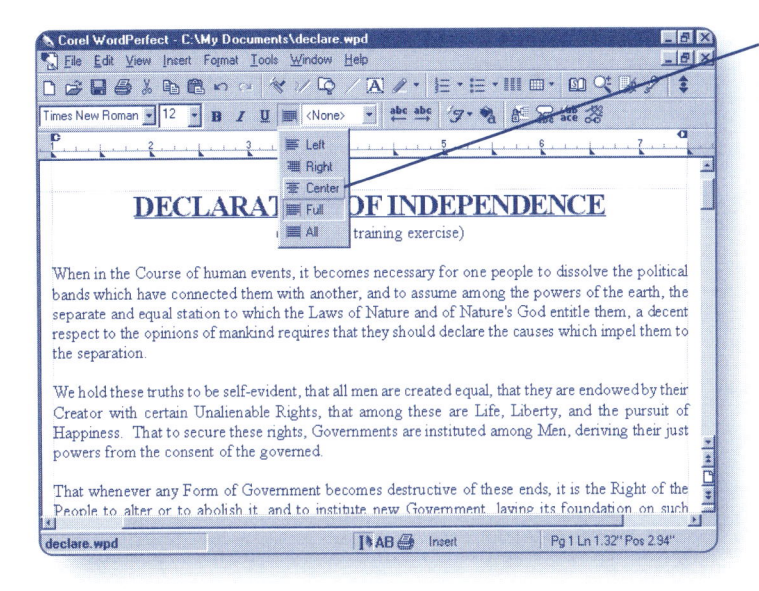

JUSTIFYING TEXT   111

3. Click on **Center**. The text you selected will be centered.

Changing Alignment

Alignment arranges the text to line up at one or both margins, or centers it across the page.

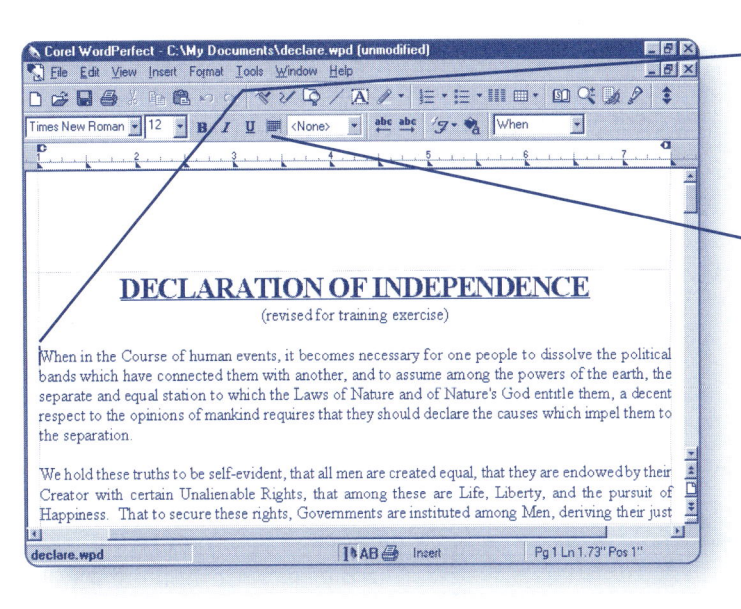

1. Click the **mouse pointer** where you want the justification change to begin. The blinking insertion point will appear.

2. Click on the **Justification button**. A list of choices will appear.

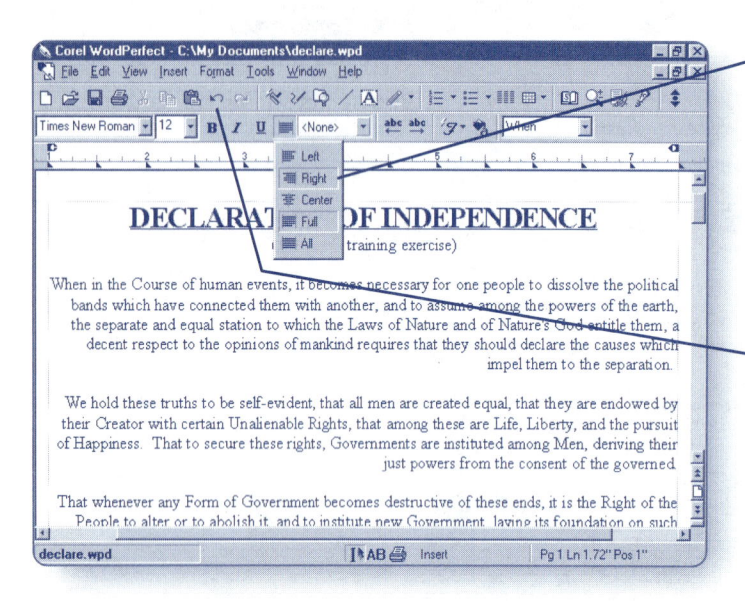

112 CHAPTER 11: MODIFYING ALIGNMENT, INDENTATION, AND SPACING

3. Click on the **desired choice**: Left, Right, Center, Full, or All. The document will be changed from the insertion point downward.

TIP

Don't forget! If you make a change you don't want, you can undo it by clicking on the Undo button on the toolbar.

Indenting a Paragraph

Indents are different from tabs. A tab moves just one line of text. An indent moves all the lines in a paragraph. Use *Indent* to move a complete paragraph one tab stop or a specified distance to the right. Use *Hanging Indent* to move all but the first line of a paragraph one tab stop or a specified distance to the right. A hanging indent is often used to format bibliography entries. Use *Double Indent* to move an entire paragraph in one tab stop from both the left and right margins. A double indent is often used to format a quotation.

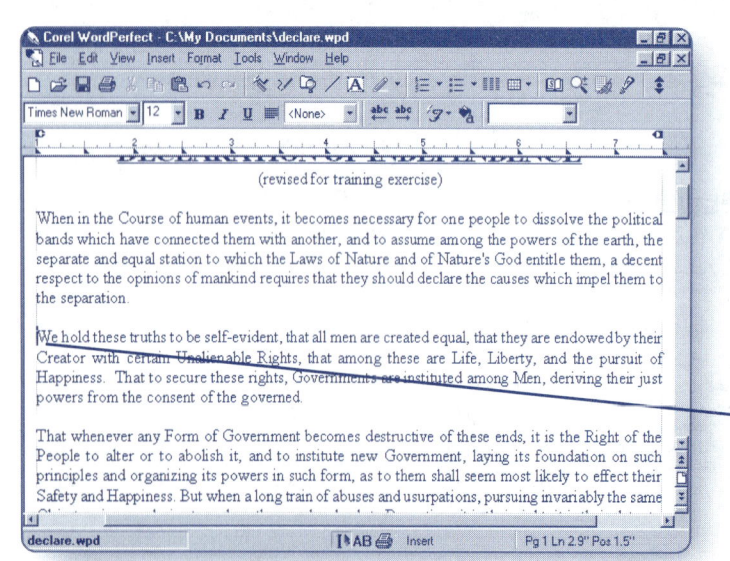

1. Click at the **beginning** of the **paragraph** you want to indent. The blinking insertion point will appear.

INDENTING A PARAGRAPH   113

TIP
If you want to apply indenting to several paragraphs, highlight those paragraphs first.

2. Click on **Format**. The Format menu will appear.

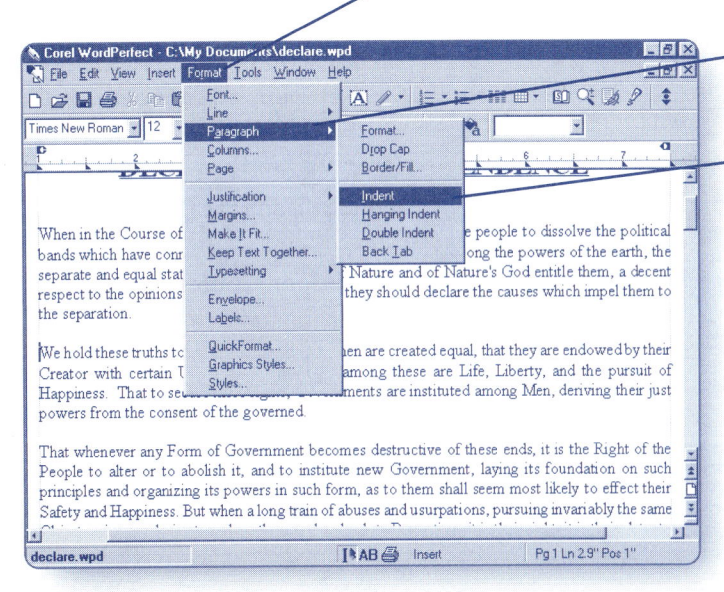

3. Click on **Paragraph**. A cascading menu will appear.

4. Click on **Indent**, **Hanging Indent**, or **Double Indent**. The menus will close.

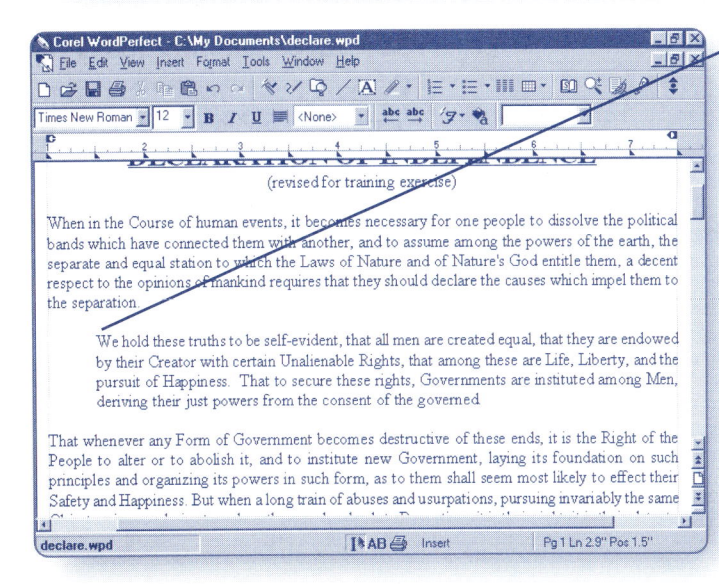

The paragraph will be indented per your selection.

CHAPTER 11: MODIFYING ALIGNMENT, INDENTATION, AND SPACING

Centering a Page Vertically

Aesthetically, title pages look better when centered vertically. You may even want to vertically center the first page of a letter.

1. Position the **insertion point** on the page to be centered vertically. The blinking insertion point will appear.

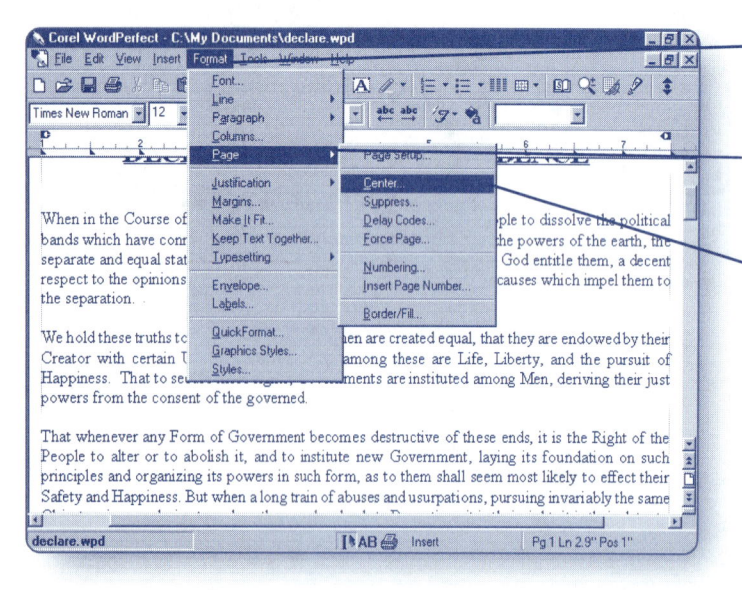

2. Click on **Format**. The Format menu will appear.

3. Click on **Page**. A cascading menu will appear.

4. Click on **Center**. The Center Page(s) dialog box will open.

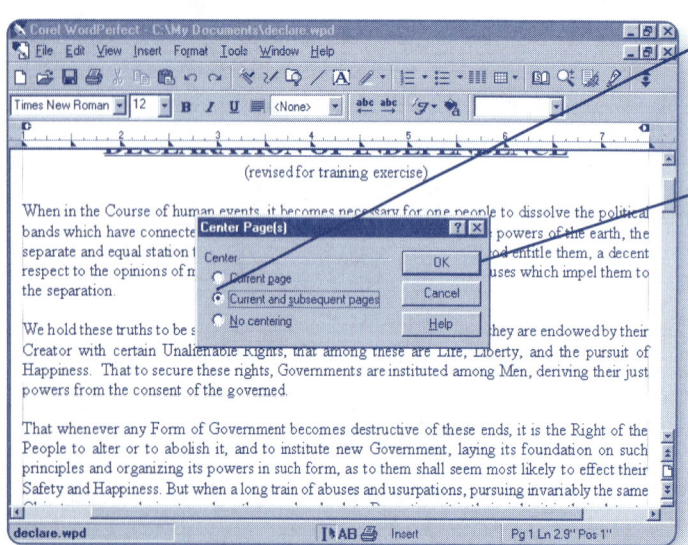

5. Click on **Current Page** or **Current and subsequent pages**, depending on your needs.

6. Click on **OK**. The dialog box will close, and the page will be centered vertically from top to bottom margin.

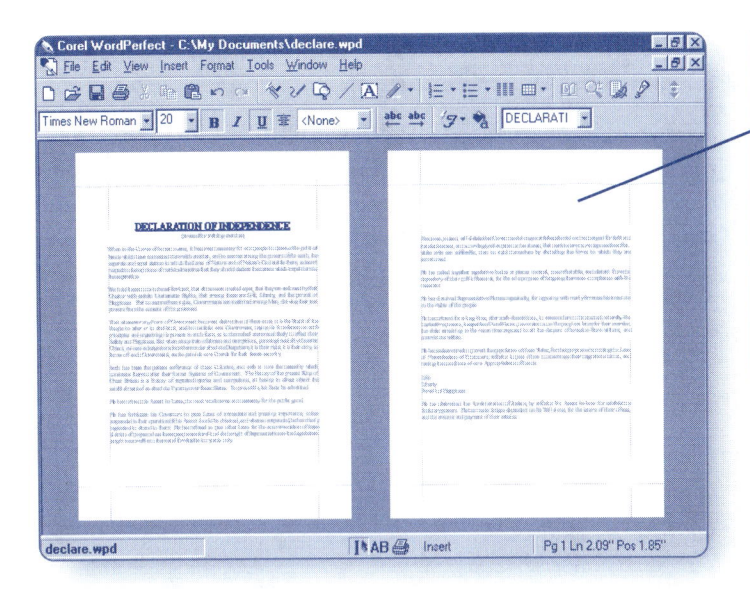

CHANGING LINE SPACING 115

TIP

The best way to see a page that has been centered vertically is to use Two Page view or Full Page view. Views are covered in Chapter 7, "Working with Views."

Changing Line Spacing

TIP

If you only want a section of the document to have the new line spacing, highlight that section first.

Line spacing changes the distance between lines of text from the position of your cursor downward in your document. The default choice in WordPerfect is single spacing.

1. Click the **mouse pointer** where you want the line spacing change to begin. The blinking insertion point will appear.

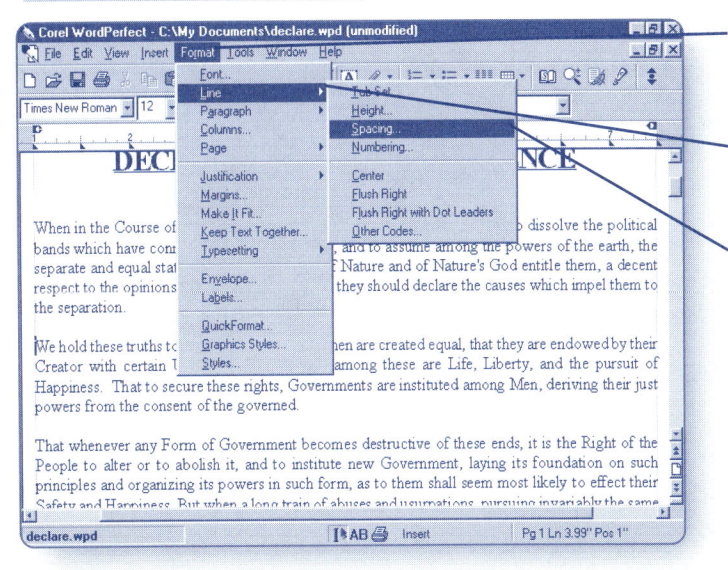

2. Click on **Format**. The Format menu will appear.

3. Click on **Line**. A cascading menu will appear.

4. Click on **Spacing**. The Line Spacing dialog box will open.

116 CHAPTER 11: MODIFYING ALIGNMENT, INDENTATION, AND SPACING

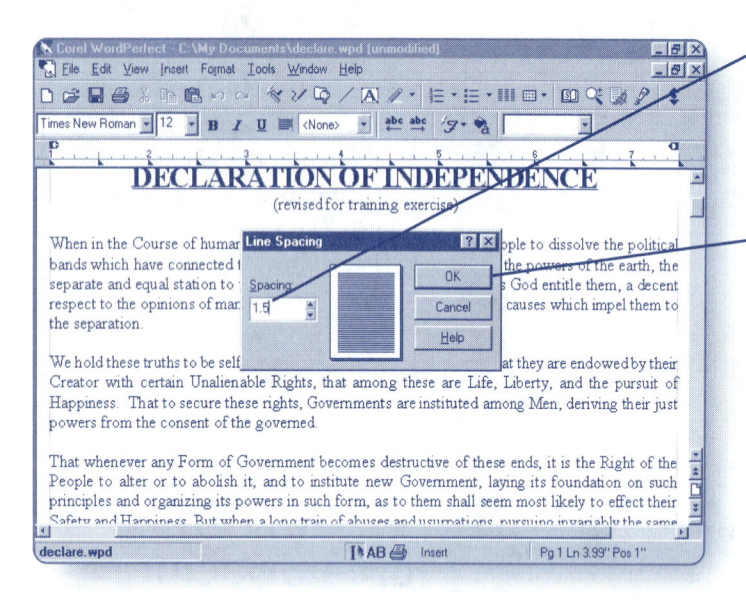

5. Type the **desired spacing** in the Spacing: box. Type 2 for double spacing, 1.5 for one and one-half line spacing, and so on.

6. Click on **OK**. The dialog box will close.

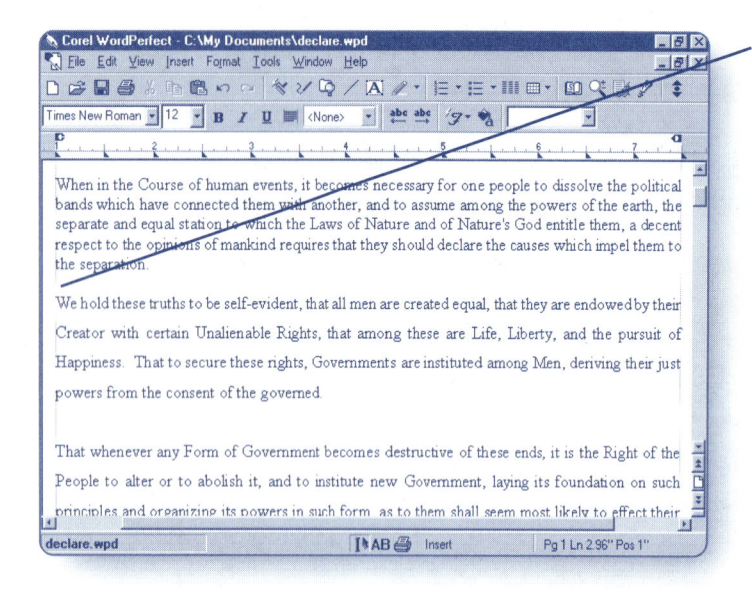

The document from the insertion point downward will have the new line spacing.

12
Adding Bullets, Numbering, and Borders

Bullets and borders call attention to points in a document. Numbered lists allow the reader to follow steps in a sequential order. In this chapter, you'll learn how to:

- Add a bullet
- Create a numbered list
- Add a border to a paragraph
- Add a fill color to a paragraph
- Put a border around a page

CHAPTER 12: ADDING BULLETS, NUMBERING, AND BORDERS

Adding a Bullet

Bullets call attention to a list of items. Adding bullets is only a mouse click away when you use the WordPerfect toolbar. Bullets come in several styles, so you can use different kinds of lists or suit the bullets to your subject.

1. Select the **text** to be bulleted. The text will be highlighted.

2. Click on the **Bullet down arrow (▼)**. A list of bullet styles will display.

NOTE

Your selection of bullets may vary from the ones displayed in this figure.

3. Click on a **bullet style**. The style will be applied to the selected paragraphs.

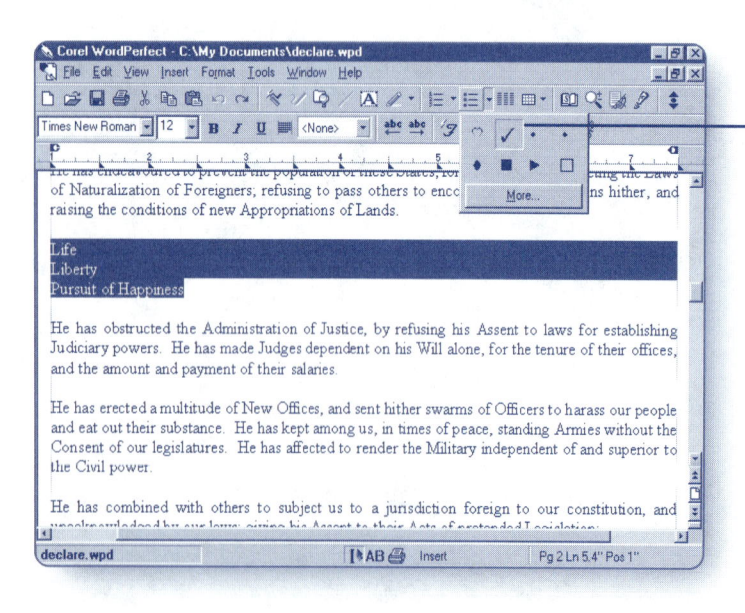

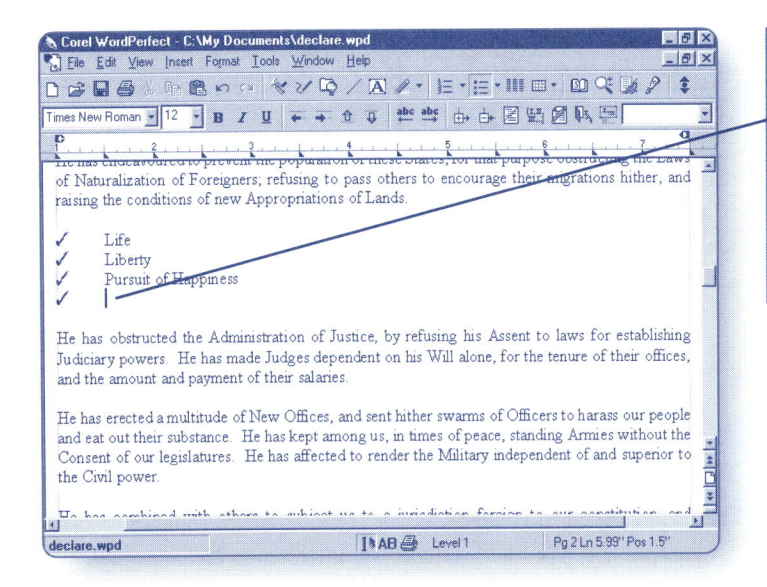

CREATING A NUMBERED LIST   119

TIP
If you click the mouse at the end of a bulleted item and then press Enter, the next item you type will have a bullet as well.

Creating a Numbered List

Numbered lists are frequently used to list steps of a project. The sequencing makes reading easier. There are nine different styles of numbering, including Roman numerals.

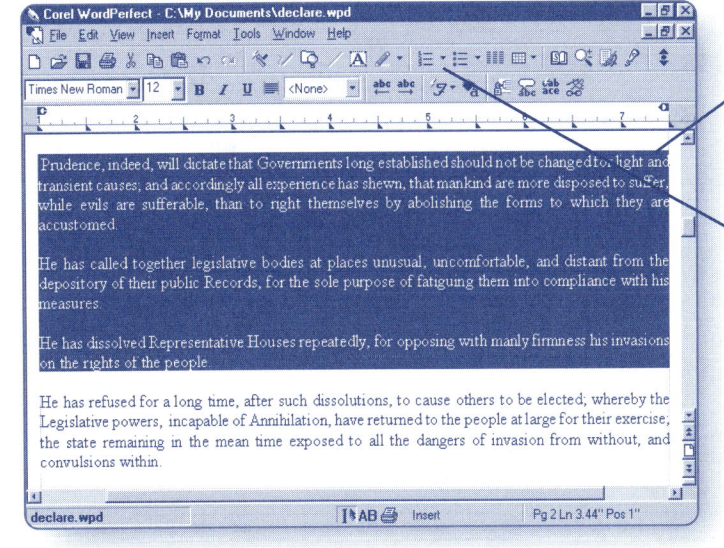

1. Select the **text** to be numbered. The text will be highlighted.

2. Click on the **Numbering button down arrow (▼)**. A list of numbering styles will appear.

NOTE
Your selection of numbering choices may vary from the ones displayed in this figure.

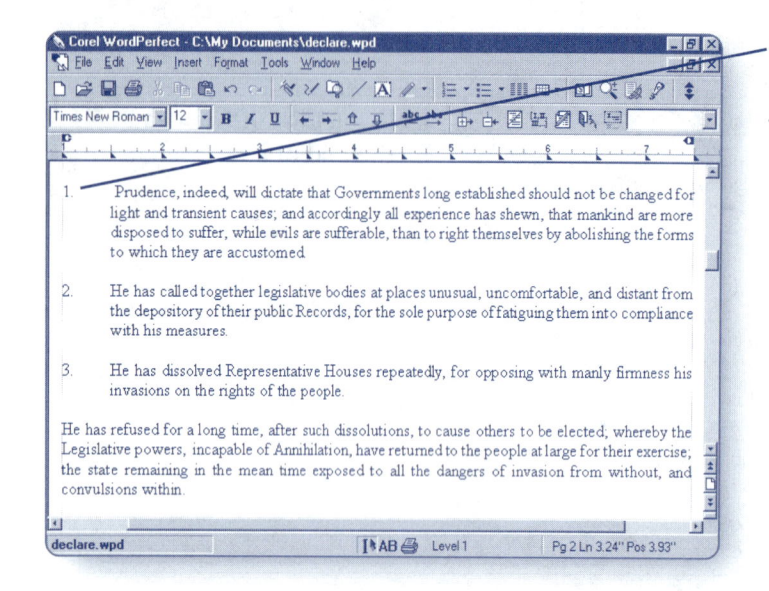

CHAPTER 12: ADDING BULLETS, NUMBERING, AND BORDERS

The selected text will be indented and have numbers in front.

Working with Borders and Fills

WordPerfect can put borders around paragraphs or pages. For additional special effects, add background fill to the paragraphs or pages.

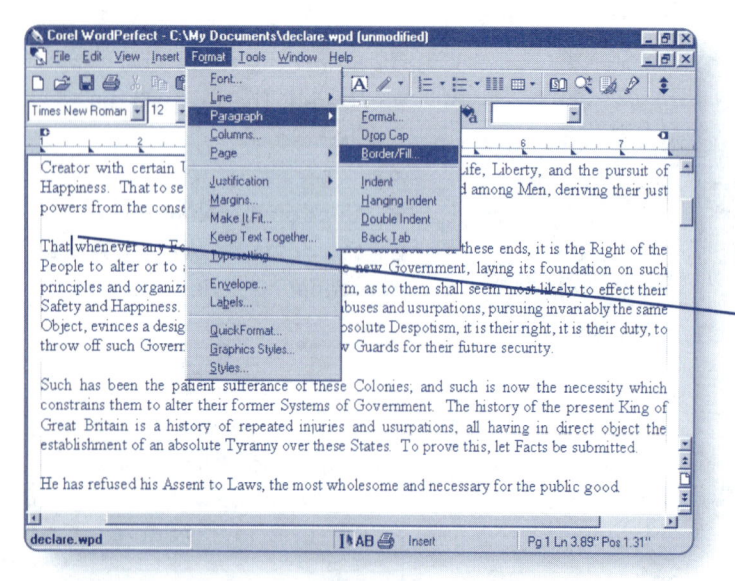

Adding a Border to a Paragraph

Another way to call attention to specific text is to put a border around it.

1. Click the **mouse pointer** in the paragraph to have a border. The blinking insertion point will appear.

WORKING WITH BORDERS AND FILLS   121

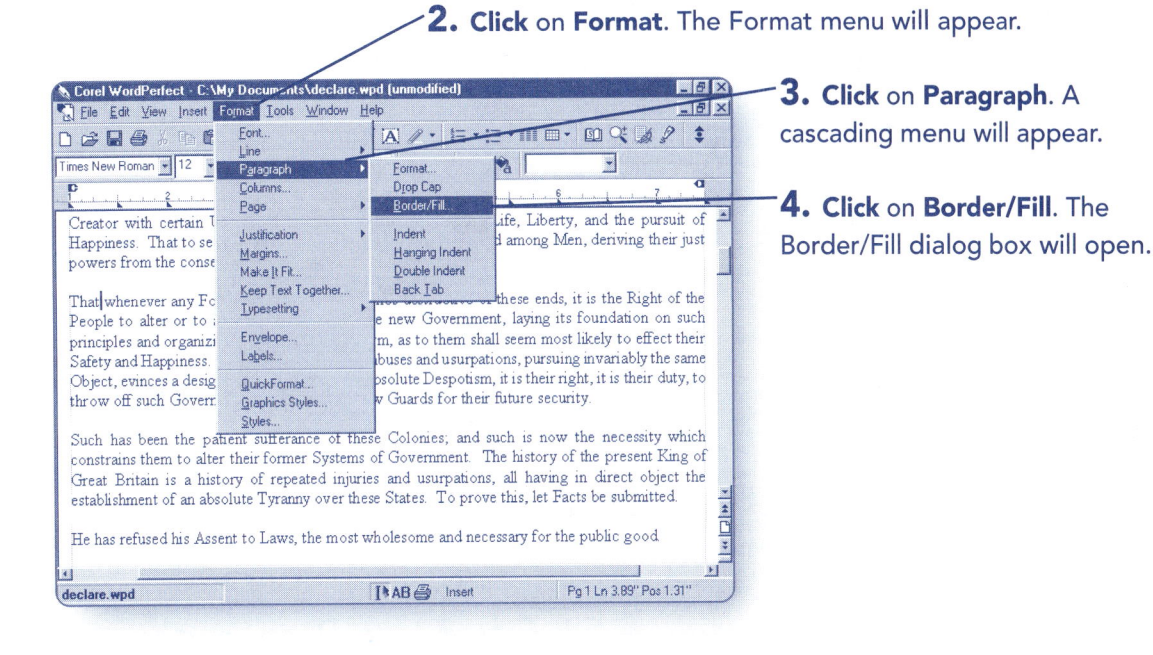

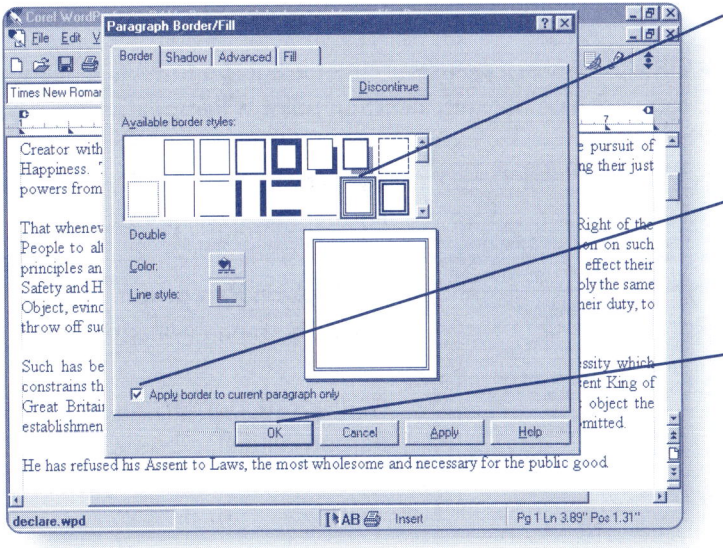

2. Click on **Format**. The Format menu will appear.

3. Click on **Paragraph**. A cascading menu will appear.

4. Click on **Border/Fill**. The Border/Fill dialog box will open.

5. Click on a **style** from the Available border styles: box. A dark line will appear around your selection.

6. If necessary, **click** on **Apply to Current Paragraph Only**. A ✔ will appear in the check box.

7. Click on **OK**. The dialog box will close.

122 CHAPTER 12: ADDING BULLETS, NUMBERING, AND BORDERS

The paragraph will have a border around it.

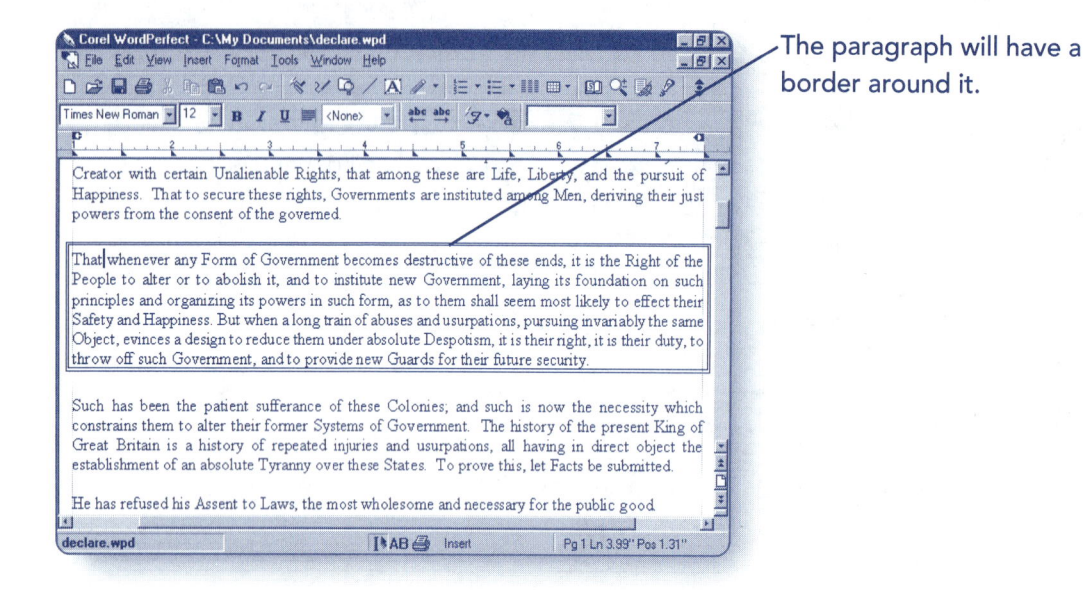

Adding a Fill Color to a Paragraph

Adding fill color to a paragraph puts the text on a different background from the rest of the page.

1. Click the **mouse pointer** in the paragraph to have a filled background. The blinking insertion point will appear.

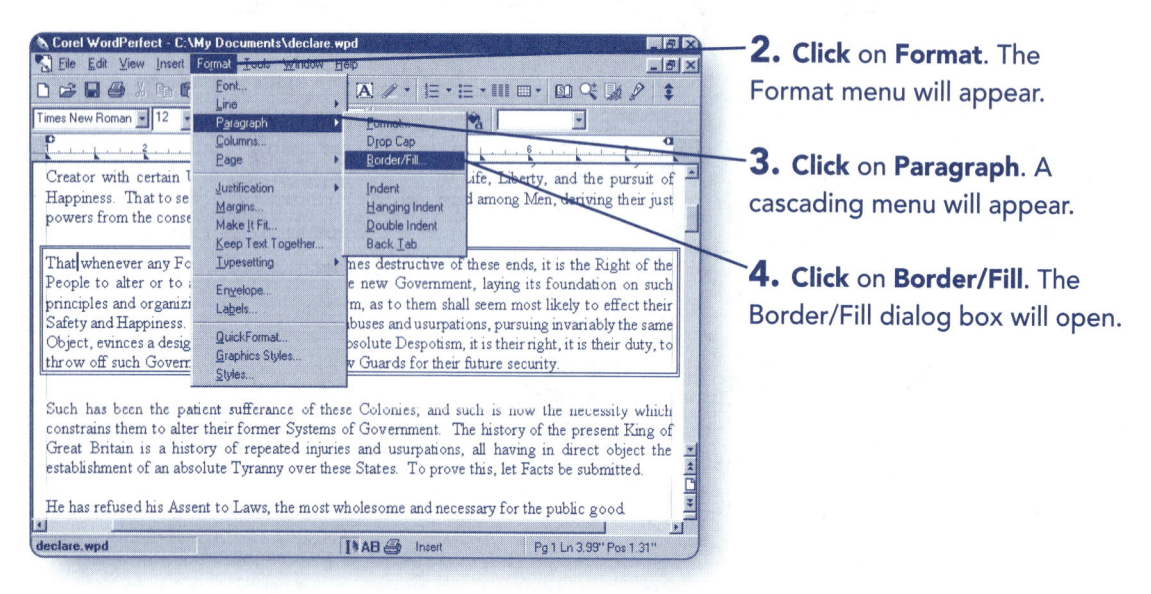

2. Click on **Format**. The Format menu will appear.

3. Click on **Paragraph**. A cascading menu will appear.

4. Click on **Border/Fill**. The Border/Fill dialog box will open.

WORKING WITH BORDERS AND FILLS   123

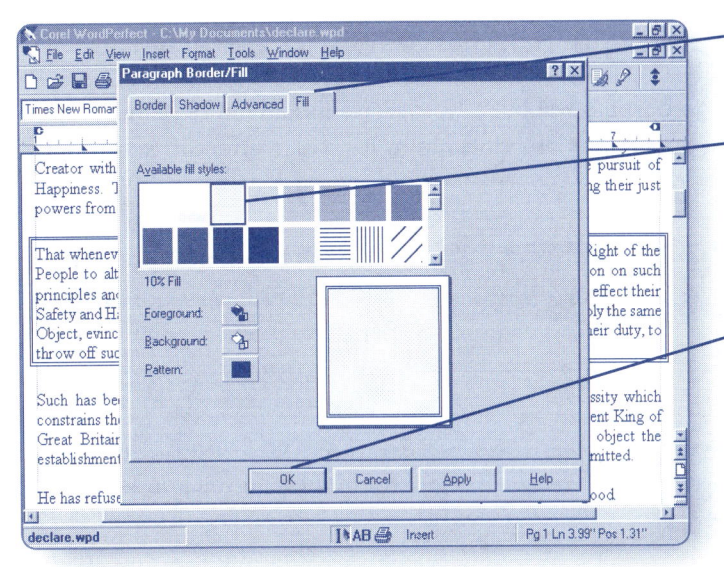

5. Click on the **Fill tab**. The tab will come to the front.

6. Click on a **style** from the Available fill styles: box. A dark line will appear around your selection.

7. Click on **OK**. The dialog box will close, and the paragraph will have a filled background.

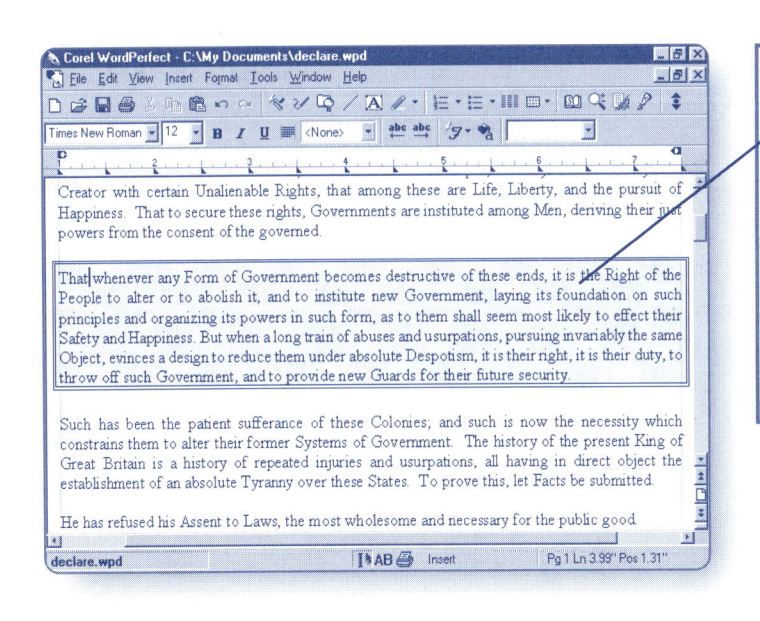

TIP

Keep the fill color light and solid if your text is to be black; otherwise, you won't be able to read the text. If you do want a dark background, for example 100% black, change the text color to white.

Putting a Border Around a Page

Page borders will put a border around an entire page or multiple pages of a document. It's a nice effect to add to the title page of a report.

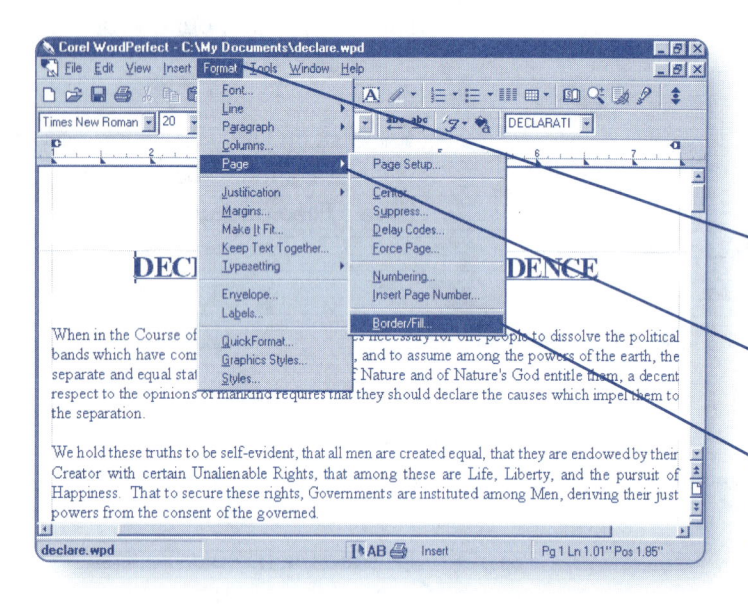

1. Click the **mouse pointer** in the page to have a border. The blinking insertion point will appear.

2. Click on **Format**. The Format menu will appear.

3. Click on **Page**. A cascading menu will appear.

4. Click on **Border/Fill**. The Page Border/Fill dialog box will open.

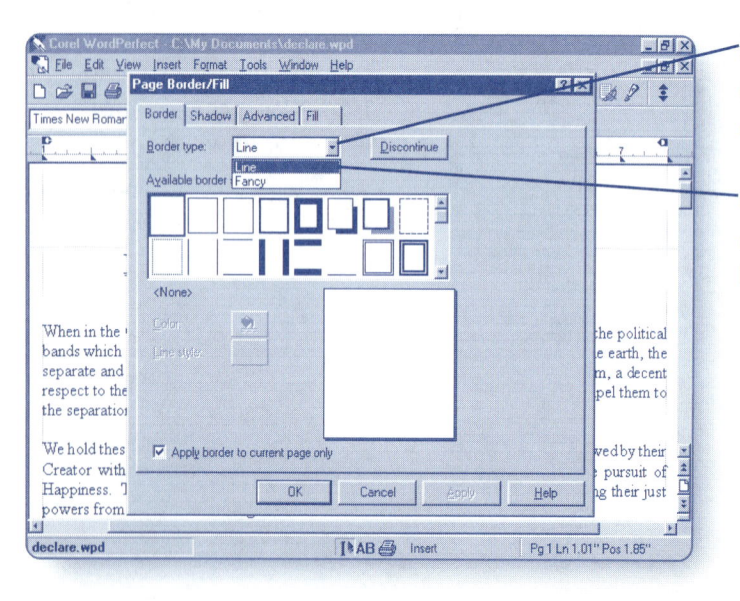

5. Click on the **Border type: down arrow (▼)**. A list of choices will appear.

6. Click on a **border type**. The option will be displayed in the Border type: box.

WORKING WITH BORDERS AND FILLS 125

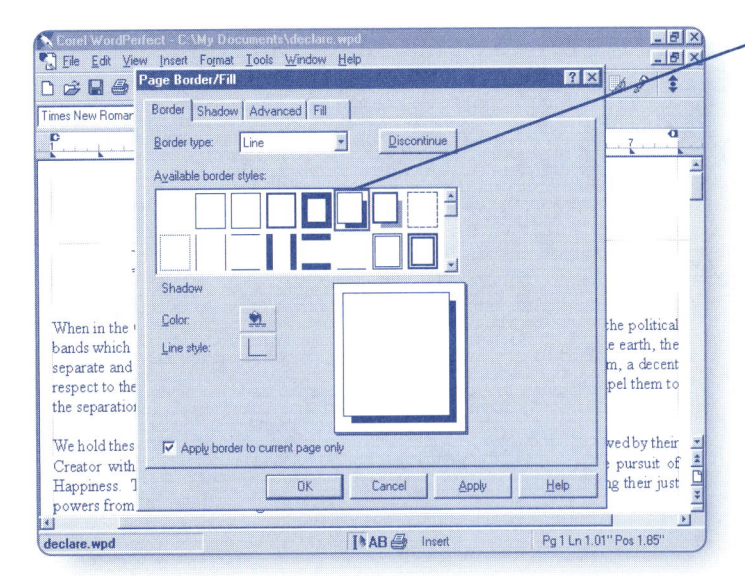

7. Click on a **style** from the Available border styles: box. A dark line will appear around your selection.

TIP

Scroll down the Available border styles: box to see additional selections.

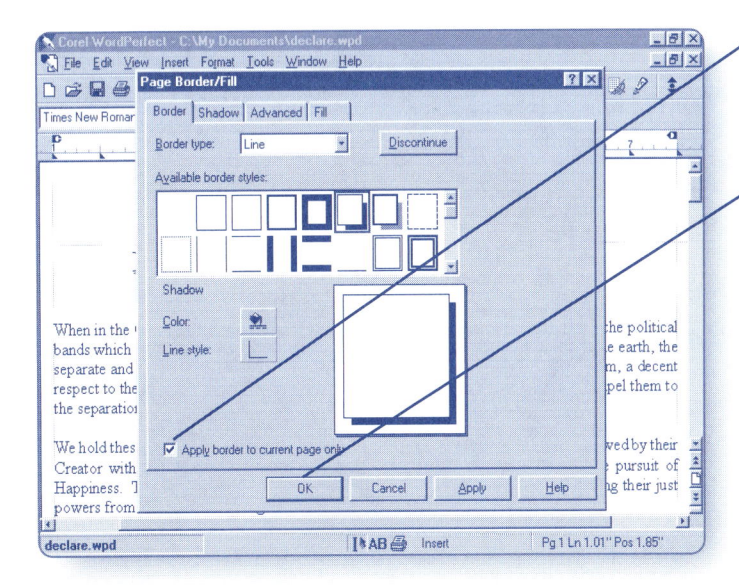

8. If desired, **click** on **Apply border to current page only**. A ✔ will appear in the check box.

9. Click on **OK**. The dialog box will close, and the page will have a border around it.

13

Working with Footnotes and Endnotes

Footnotes and endnotes are all about giving credit where credit is due. Footnotes appear at the bottom of the page the reference is on, and endnotes traditionally occur at the end of the report. In this chapter, you'll learn how to:

- Create and edit a footnote or endnote
- Move and delete a footnote or endnote
- Change a footnote to an endnote

CHAPTER 13: WORKING WITH FOOTNOTES AND ENDNOTES

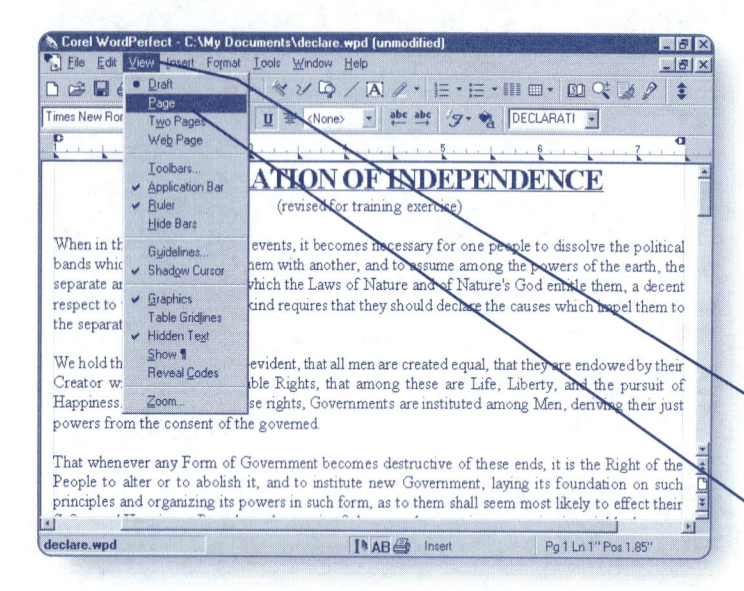

Creating Footnotes and Endnotes

It will be easier to work on footnotes or endnotes if you are in Page view.

1. Click on **View**. The View menu will appear.

2. Click on **Page**. If you are not already in Page view, the screen will switch to Page view.

3. Position the **insertion point** at the location where the footnote reference number should appear.

4. Click on **Insert**. The Insert menu will appear.

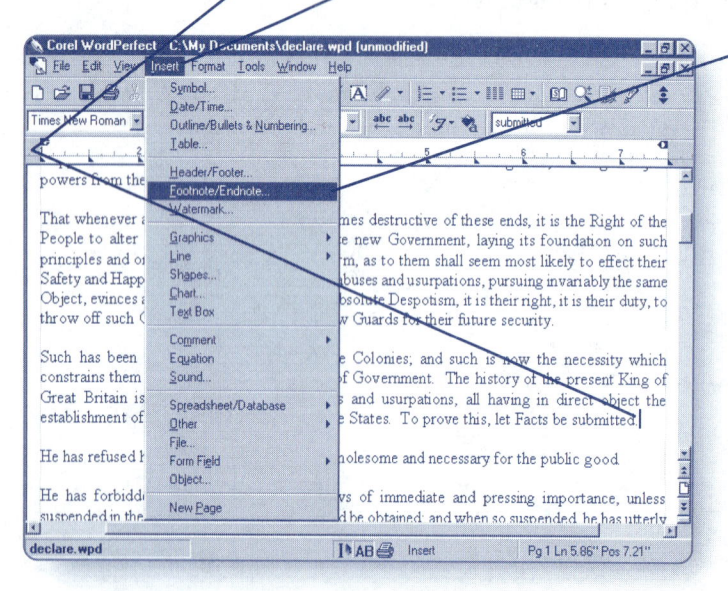

5. Click on **Footnote/Endnote**. The Footnote/Endnote dialog box will open.

CREATING FOOTNOTES AND ENDNOTES 129

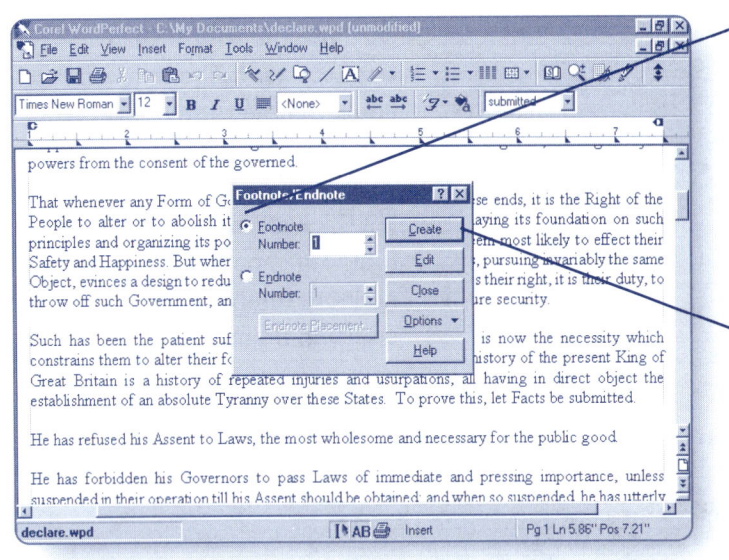

6. Click on the **option button** next to Footnote Number: or Endnote Number: depending on which item you want to create. WordPerfect will automatically number the footnotes and endnotes for you.

7. Click on **Create**. The insertion point will jump to the bottom of the screen if you are creating a footnote or to the end of the document if you are creating an endnote.

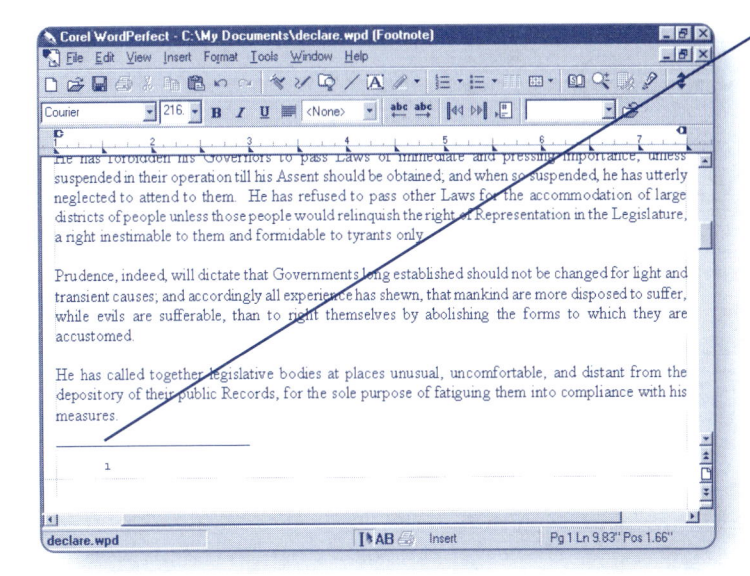

If this is a footnote, you will see a separating line for the footnote text, and the reference number will appear. For either footnotes or endnotes, the reference is automatically numbered and superscripted for you.

CHAPTER 13: WORKING WITH FOOTNOTES AND ENDNOTES

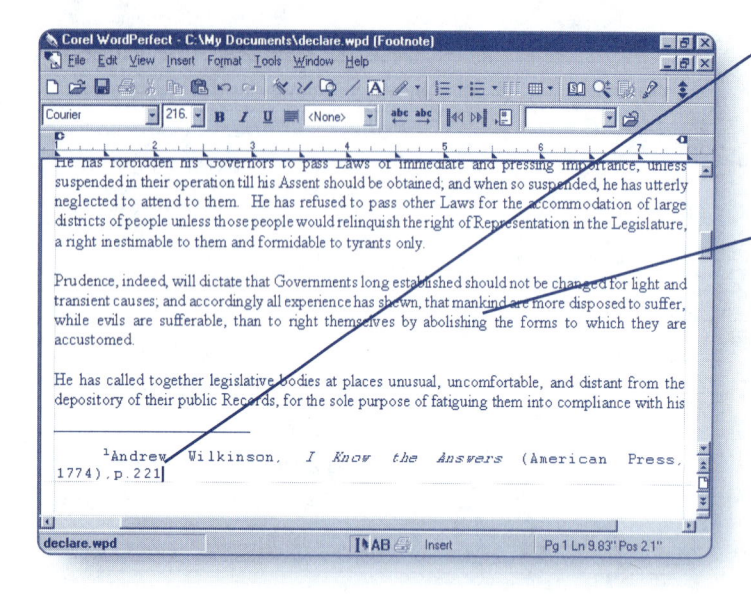

8. Type the **footnote** or **endnote text**. The text will appear in the footnote or endnote area.

9. Click anywhere above the footnote separator line or the endnote reference number. The insertion point will return to your document.

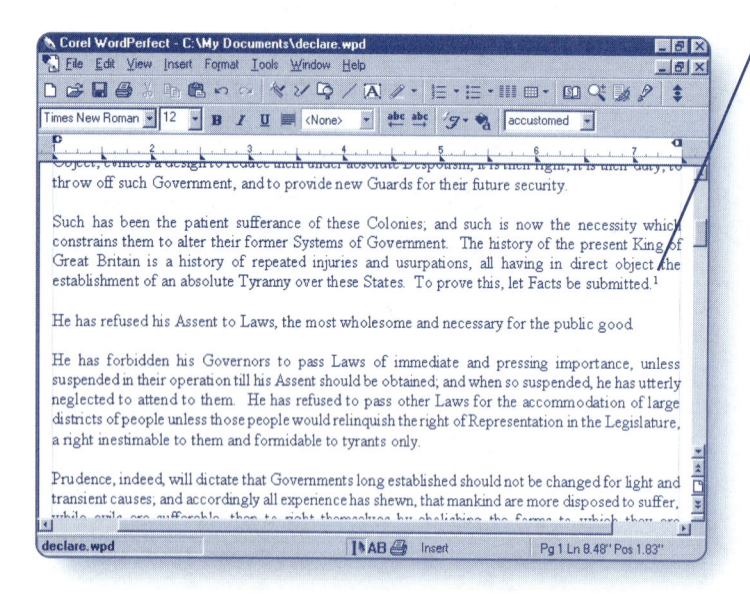

The reference number also appears in the body of your document.

Editing Footnotes and Endnotes

Editing a footnote or endnote is like editing any other text in a WordPerfect document.

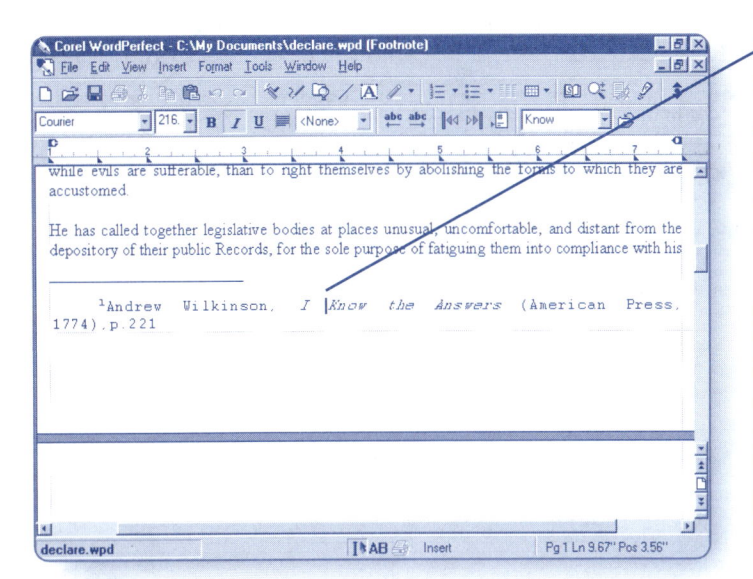

1. Click the **mouse pointer** in the footnote text at the bottom of the page or in the endnote text at the bottom of the document. The blinking insertion point will appear.

NOTE

If you are not in Page view, you will not be able to see the footnote text at the bottom of the page.

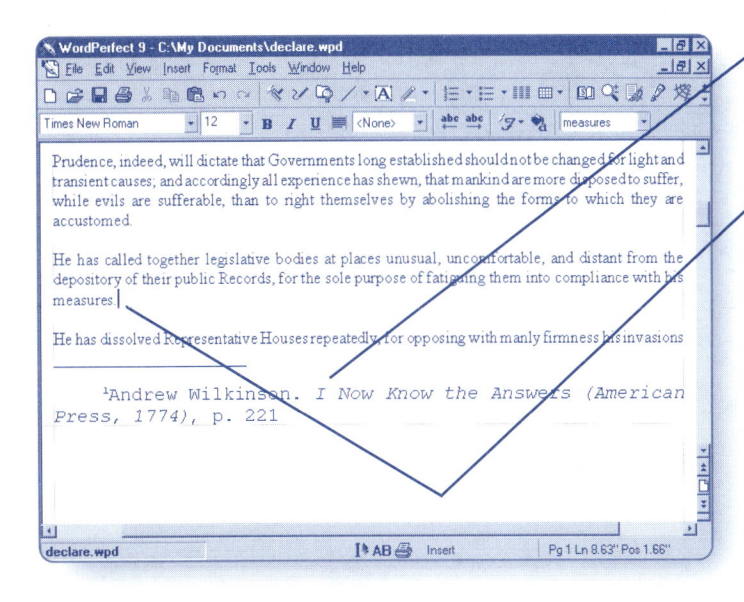

2. Type any necessary **corrections** or **changes**. The text will be modified.

3. Click anywhere in the body of your document. The insertion point will return to your document.

Moving Footnotes and Endnotes

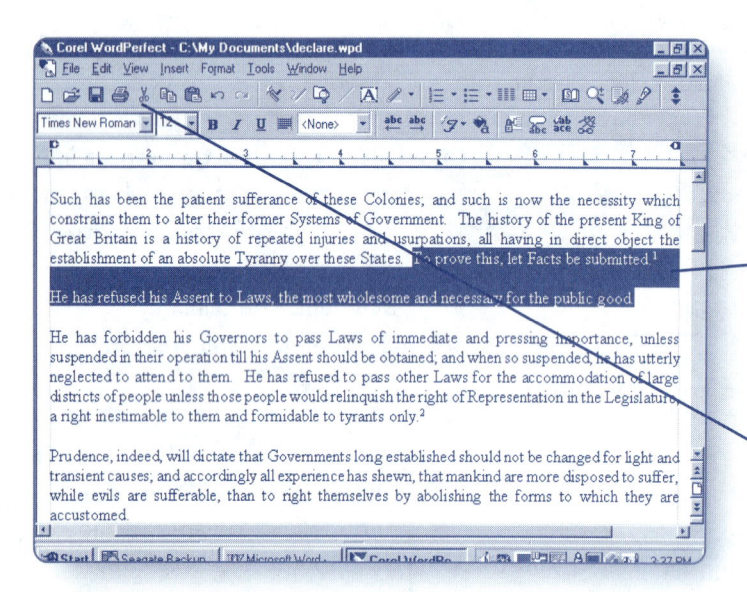

If you move text that contains a footnote or endnote, WordPerfect changes the reference number automatically if necessary.

1. Select the **text to be moved,** including the reference number. The text will be highlighted.

2. Click on the **Cut button.** The text including the footnote reference information will be placed on the Clipboard.

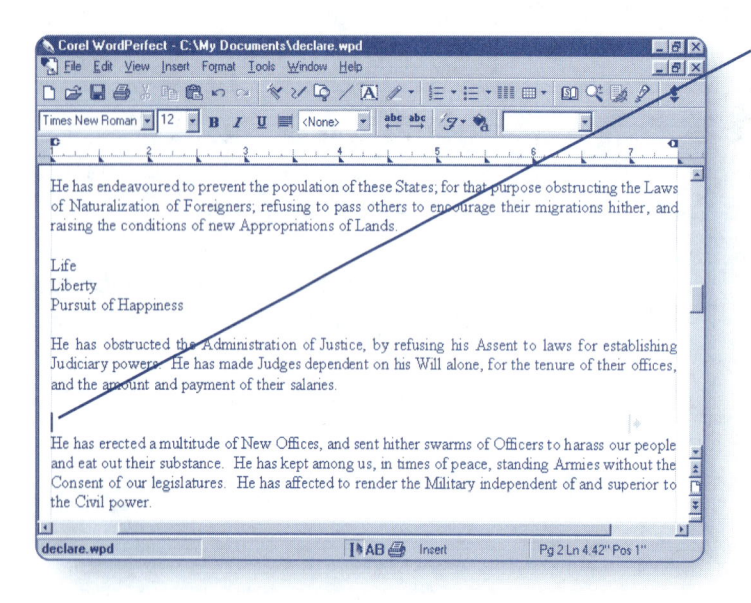

3. Position the **insertion point** where the text is to be placed. The blinking insertion point will appear.

MOVING FOOTNOTES AND ENDNOTES   133

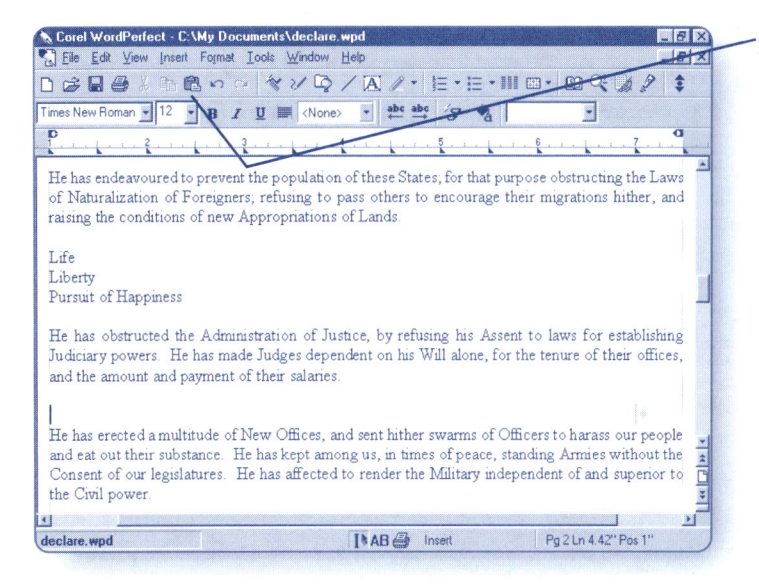

4. Click on the **Paste button**. The text and footnote or endnote reference will be placed in the new location.

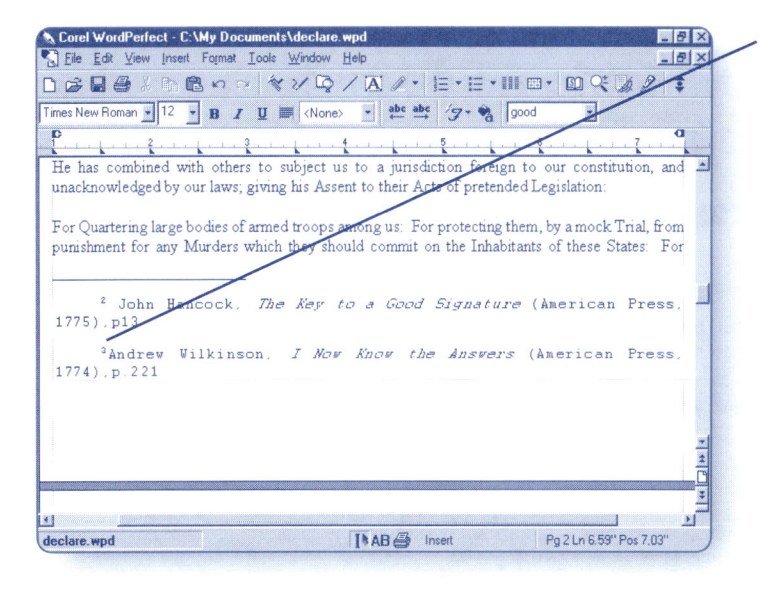

If necessary, WordPerfect renumbers the footnote.

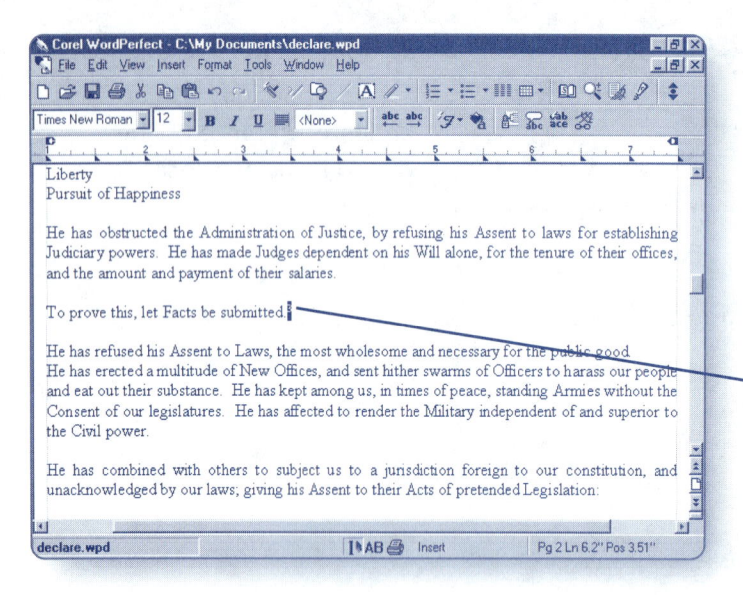

Deleting Footnotes and Endnotes

Deleting a footnote or endnote is as easy as deleting regular text from a document.

1. Select the **footnote** or **endnote reference number** in the body of your document. The text will be highlighted.

2. Press the **Delete key**. The reference and the footnote or endnote text will be deleted.

Changing a Footnote to an Endnote

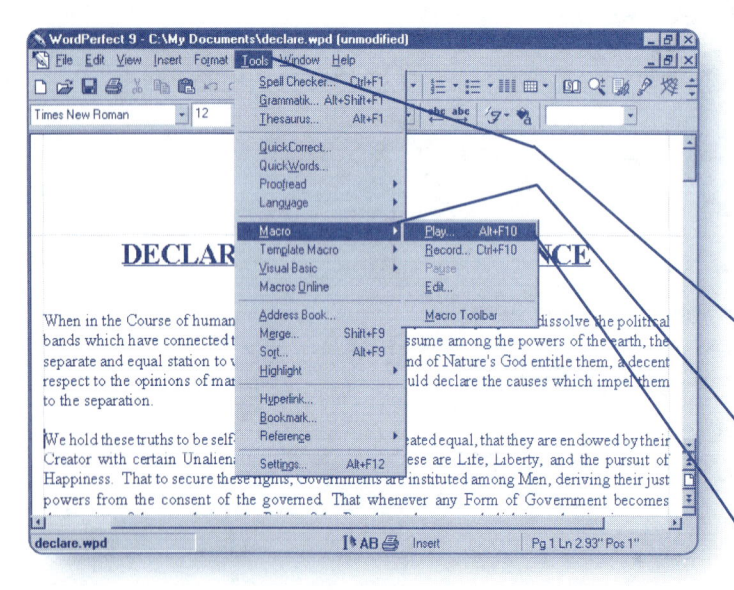

If you need to change your footnotes to endnotes (or vice versa), you do not have to delete the footnotes and retype them as endnotes. WordPerfect includes a macro to convert them for you.

1. Click on **Tools**. The Tools menu will appear.

2. Click on **Macro**. A cascading menu will appear.

3. Click on **Play**. The Play Macro dialog box will open.

CHANGING A FOOTNOTES TO AN ENDNOTE   135

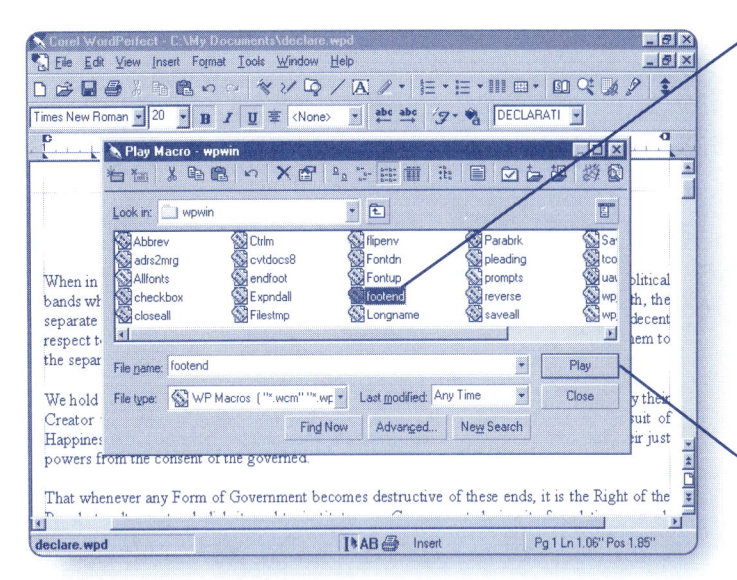

4. Click on **footend**. This is the macro to convert footnotes to endnotes.

TIP
Choose the macro named endfoot to convert endnotes to footnotes.

5. Click on **Play**. The macro will execute, and all footnotes will be changed to endnotes.

NOTE
If you only want certain footnotes or endnotes to be converted, highlight the text containing the reference number before you execute the macro. WordPerfect then converts the footnotes or endnotes in the selected text, leaving the others alone.

14

Adding Headers, Footers, and Watermarks

One time-saving feature of WordPerfect is its capability to add a header or footer. You only need to create the header or footer information one time, and WordPerfect inserts it at the top or bottom of each page of your document. Watermarks allow you to insert text or graphics underneath the body of your document creating an almost subliminal effect. In this chapter, you'll learn how to:

- Add a header or footer
- Insert the path and filename
- Edit a header or footer
- Suppress a header or footer
- Discontinue a header or footer
- Add a watermark

CHAPTER 14: ADDING HEADERS, FOOTERS, AND WATERMARKS

Adding a Header or Footer

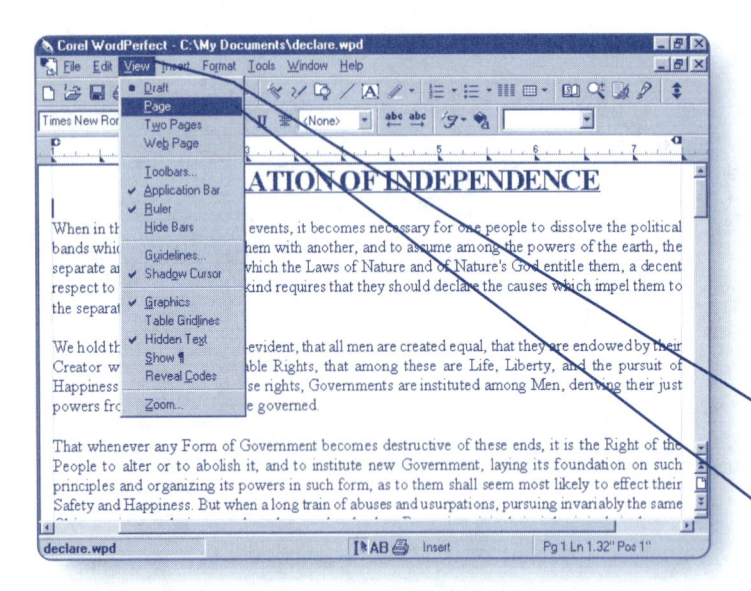

If you have text or graphics you want to appear at the top or bottom of each page, you can add a header or footer. Headers appear at the top of every page, whereas footers appear at the bottom of every page. Headers and footers are best created in Page view.

1. Click on **View**. The View menu will appear.

2. Click on **Page**. The document will be displayed in Page view.

3. Click the **mouse pointer** on the page where you want the header or footer to begin. For example, position it at the top of the document. The blinking insertion point will appear.

4. Click on **Insert**. The Insert menu will appear.

5. Click on **Header/Footer**. The Headers/Footers dialog box will open. Notice that the title bar at the top reflects that you are in the header or footer.

ADDING A HEADER OR FOOTER   139

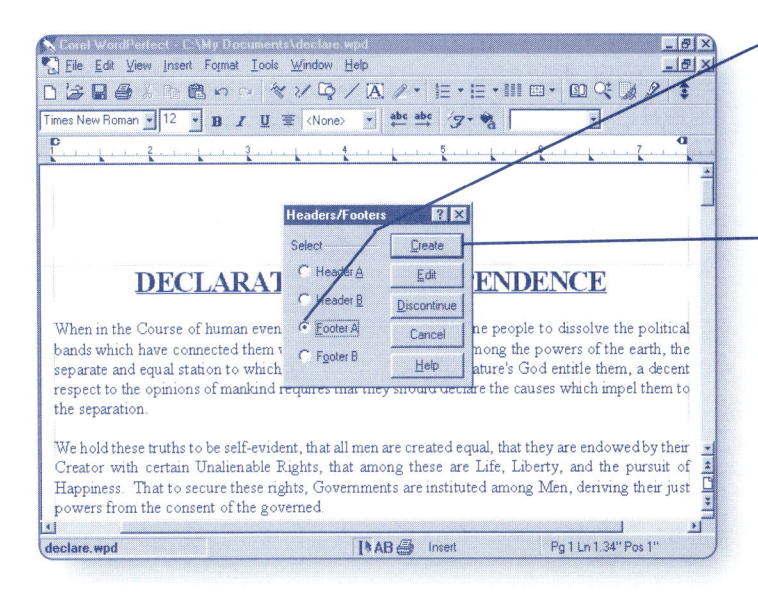

6. Click on **Header A** or **Footer A**, whichever you want to insert. The option will be selected.

7. Click on **Create**. The insertion point will jump to the top or bottom margin of the page.

Notice the title bar of the window reflects you are in the header (or footer) area.

8. Type the **text** desired for the header or footer. The text will display in the header or footer area.

Do not type a page number here. Let WordPerfect fill in the correct page number for you. When you are ready for the page number, perform the following steps.

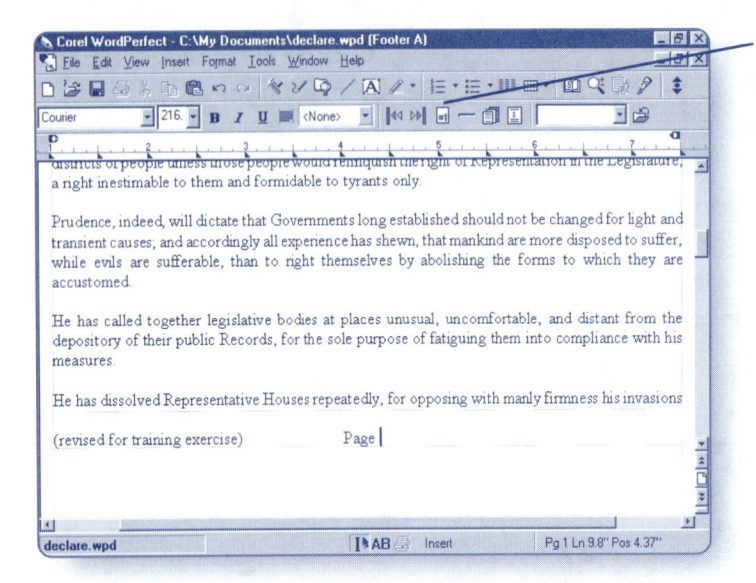

9. Click on the **Page Numbering button**. A list of choices will appear.

10. Click on **Page Number**. The current page number will be entered. This is really a code to WordPerfect and will update as the pages actually change.

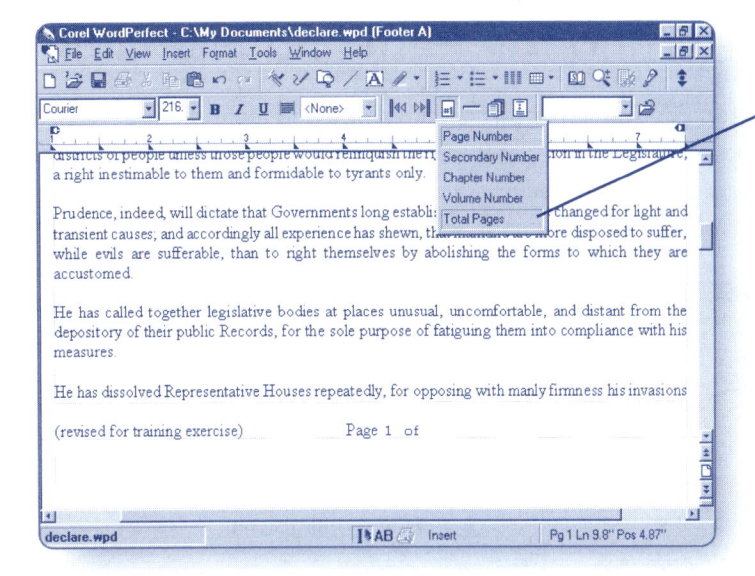

ADDING A HEADER OR FOOTER

TIP
If you want to enter the total number of pages such as Page *x* of *y*, where *x* is the current page number, and *y* is the total number of pages: type the word *Page* and a space; click on the Page Number button and choose Page Number; type a space followed by the word *of* and another space; then click on the Page Number button and choose Total Pages.

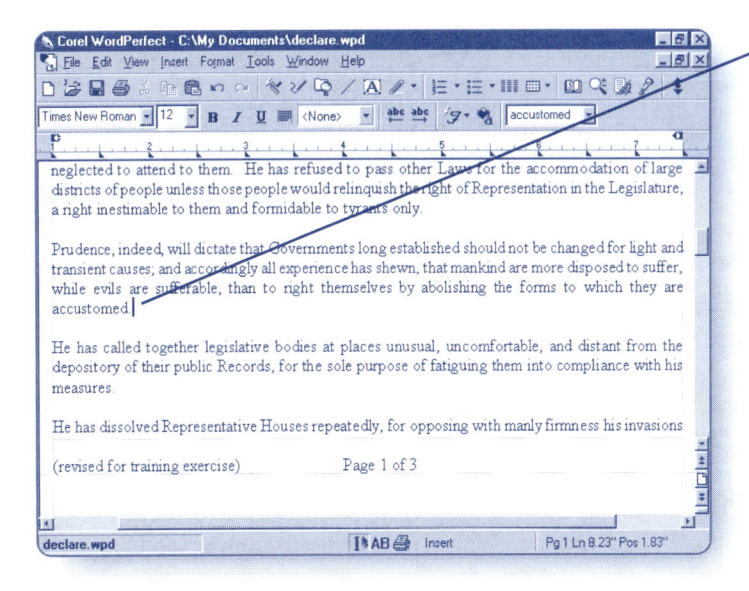

11. Click anywhere in your document outside the header/footer area to exit the header or footer.

Inserting the Path and Filename

Often you want to insert the filename and location of a document. You can put it in the header or footer, or in the body text of the document. To use this feature, you must have first saved the document and given it a name.

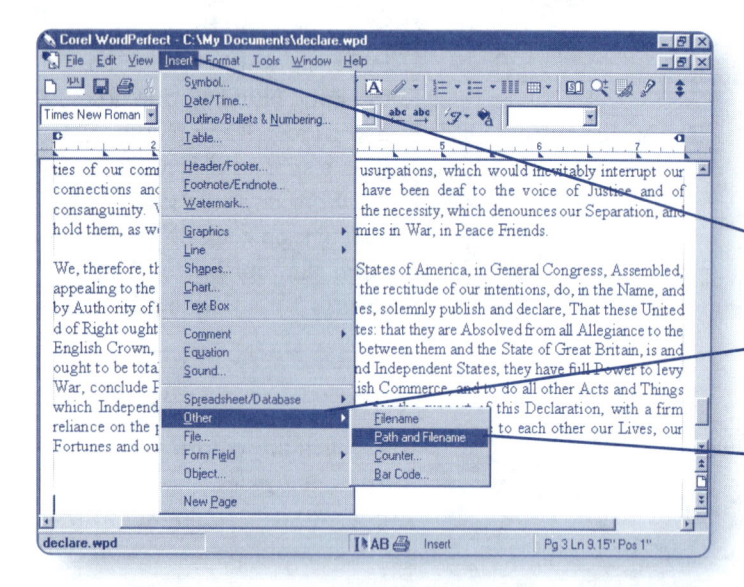

1. Click the **mouse pointer** where you want the location and filename to be. The blinking insertion point will appear.

2. Click on **Insert**. The Insert menu will appear.

3. Click on **Other**. A cascading menu will appear.

4. Click on **Path and Filename**. The document path and filename will be placed at the insertion point.

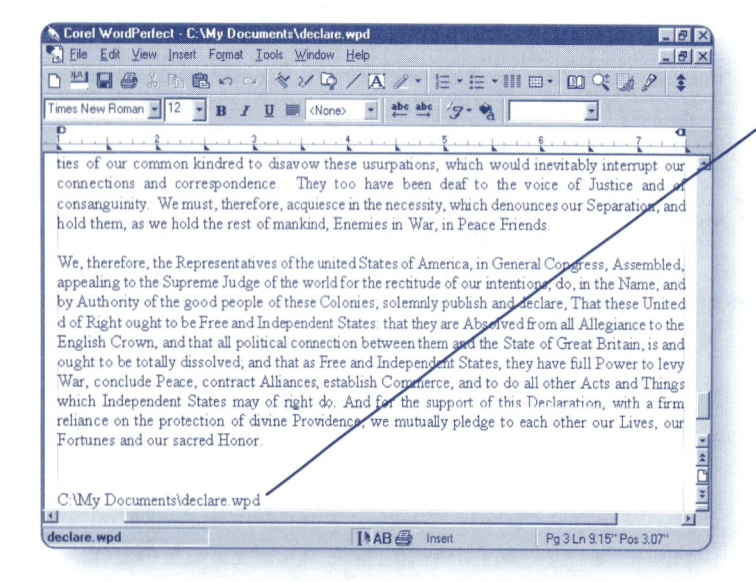

NOTE

The path and filename are *dynamic*, which means that if you move the document to another folder or give it a different name, that change will be reflected in the document as well.

Editing a Header or Footer

Editing a header or footer is easy as long as you are in Page view.

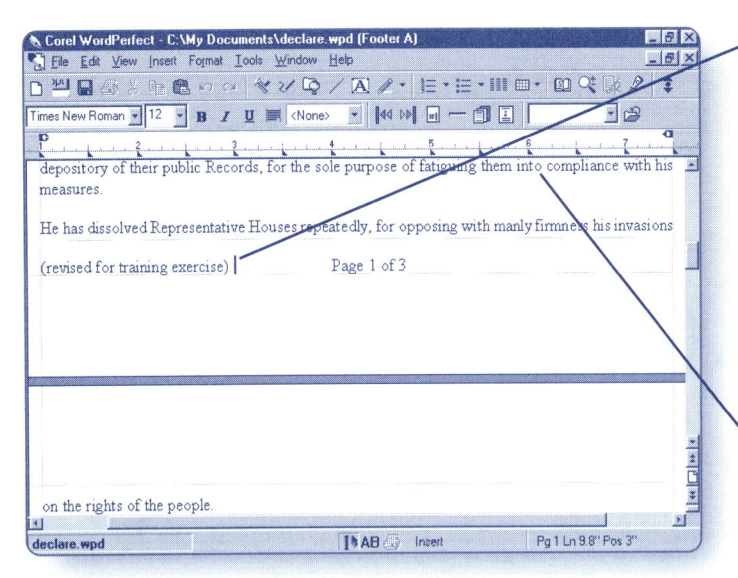

1. Click in the **header** or **footer area** on the screen. Notice the title bar at the top reflects that you are in the header or footer.

2. Make any desired changes or corrections to the header or footer text. The text will be modified.

3. Click anywhere in the body of the document. The insertion point will return to the body of the document.

Suppressing a Header or Footer

Occasionally there is a page that you do not want the header, footer, page numbering, or watermark to print on. It could be the first page of a letter or report, or it could be any page in the middle of the report. WordPerfect allows you to suppress the printing for a specific page.

144 CHAPTER 14: ADDING HEADERS, FOOTERS, AND WATERMARKS

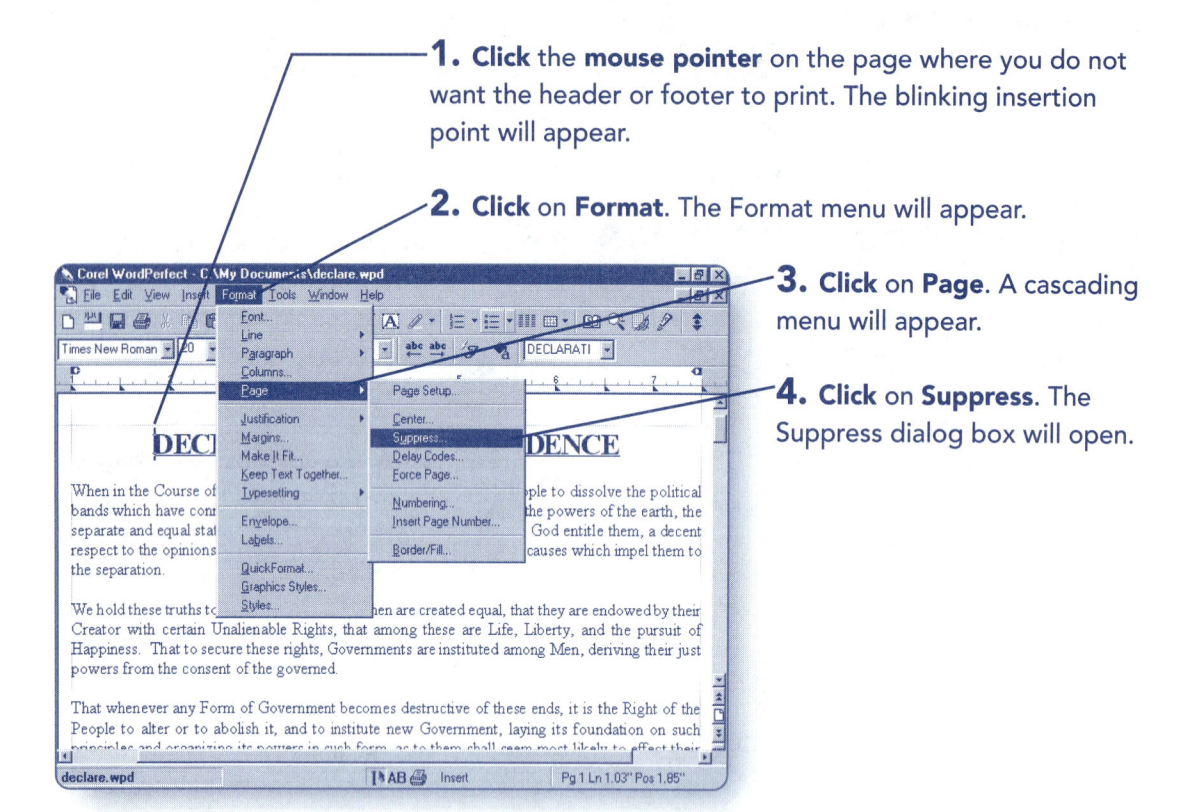

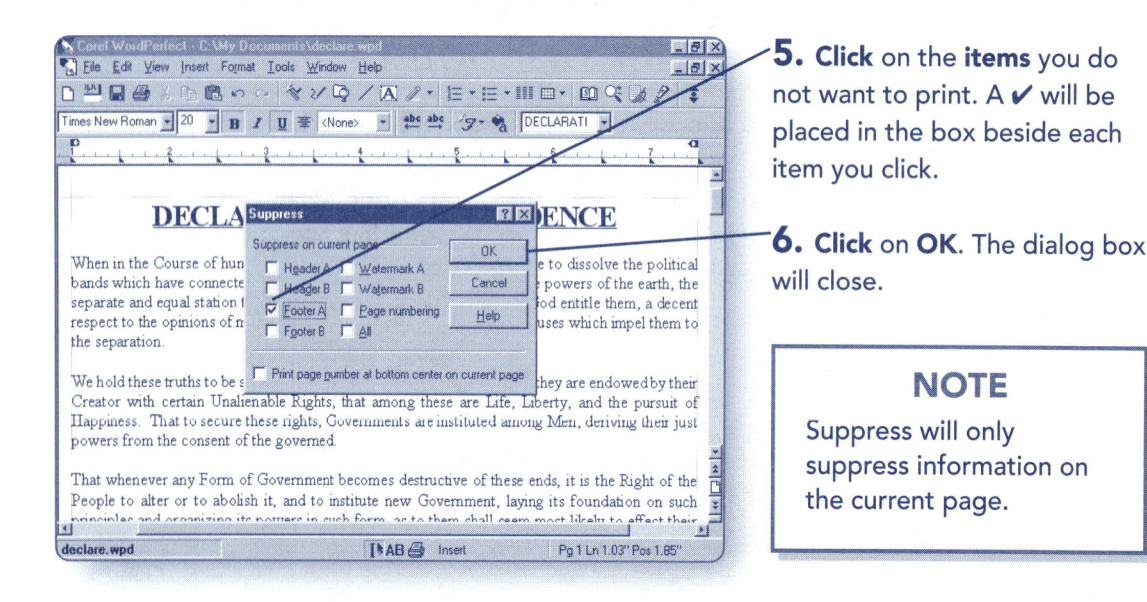

1. Click the **mouse pointer** on the page where you do not want the header or footer to print. The blinking insertion point will appear.

2. Click on **Format**. The Format menu will appear.

3. Click on **Page**. A cascading menu will appear.

4. Click on **Suppress**. The Suppress dialog box will open.

5. Click on the **items** you do not want to print. A ✔ will be placed in the box beside each item you click.

6. Click on **OK**. The dialog box will close.

NOTE
Suppress will only suppress information on the current page.

Discontinuing a Header or Footer

If you want to stop the printing of a header or footer, you can discontinue it.

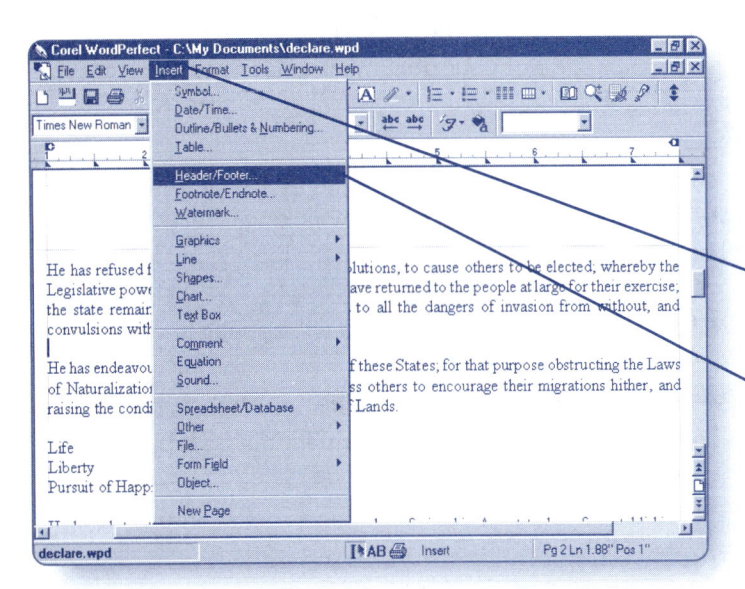

1. Click the **mouse pointer** on the page where you want the header or footer to discontinue printing. The blinking insertion point will appear.

2. Click on **Insert**. The Insert menu will appear.

3. Click on **Header/Footer**. The Headers/Footers dialog box will open.

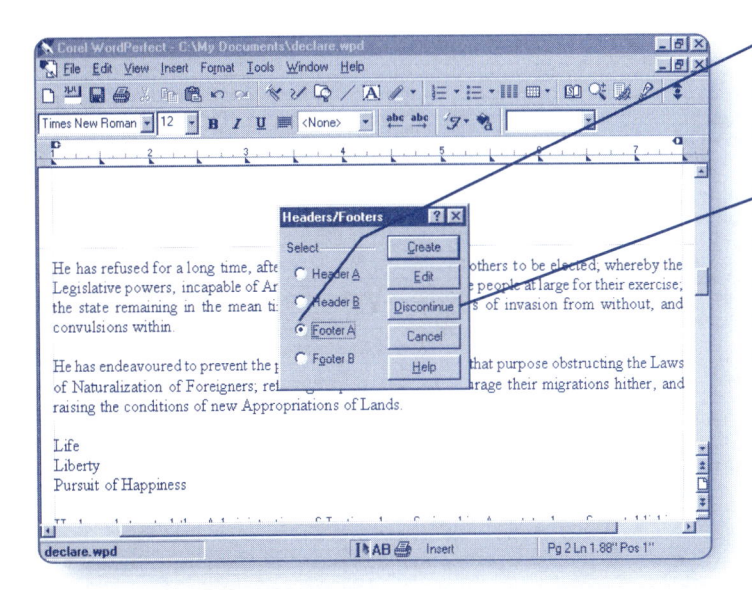

4. Click on the **Header/Footer item** to be discontinued. The option will be selected.

5. Click on **Discontinue**. The dialog box will close, and the header or footer will be discontinued from that point downward in your document.

Adding a Watermark

You can print a watermark (background image) behind the text on a page. You can use clip art images, an existing file, or text for the watermark. You can also adjust the shading (or lightness) of the watermark. A watermark is like a header or footer in that it will begin on a specified page and continue through each page of your document unless you suppress or discontinue it.

1. Click the **mouse pointer** on the page where you want the watermark to begin appearing. The blinking insertion point will appear.

2. Click on **Insert**. The Insert menu will appear.

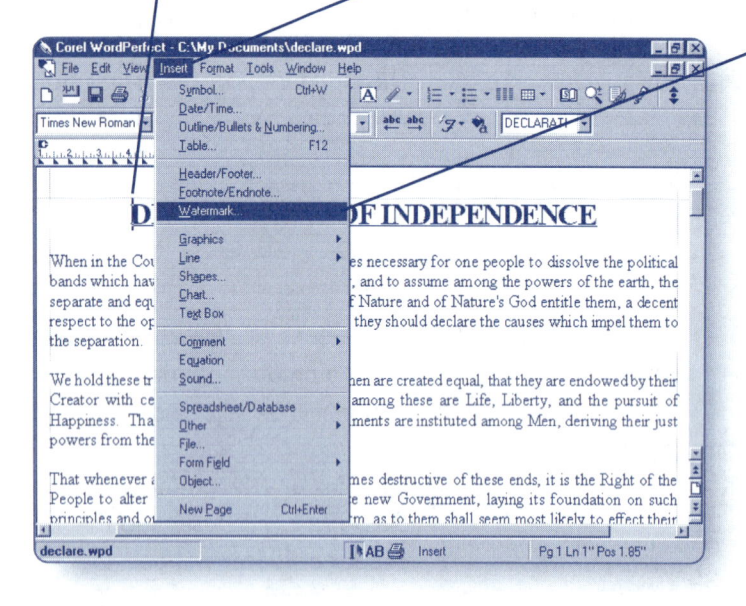

3. Click on **Watermark**. The Watermark dialog box will open.

ADDING A WATERMARK 147

4. Choose Watermark A. The option will be selected.

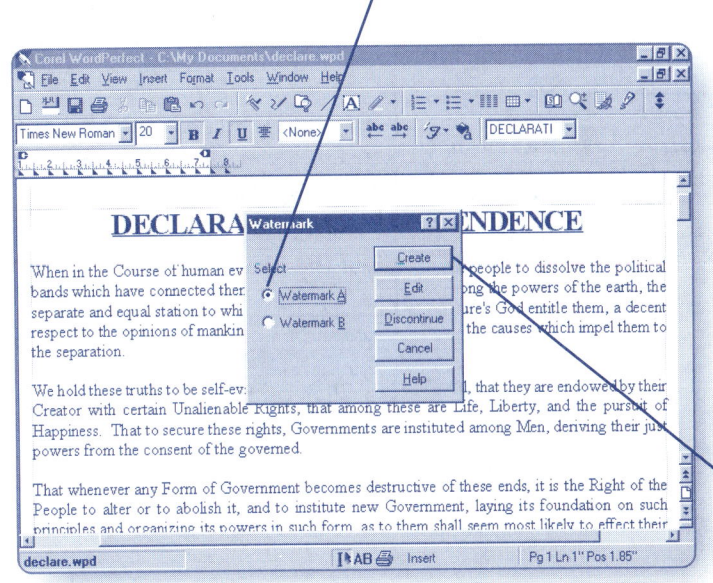

NOTE
By default, the watermark will appear on every page; however, you can have two different watermarks—one on the odd-numbered pages, and the other on the even-numbered pages.

5. Click on **Create**. A blank page will be displayed in Full Page view.

Don't panic! You did not lose your text. Look at the top of your window. The title bar at the top shows that you are in the watermark area.

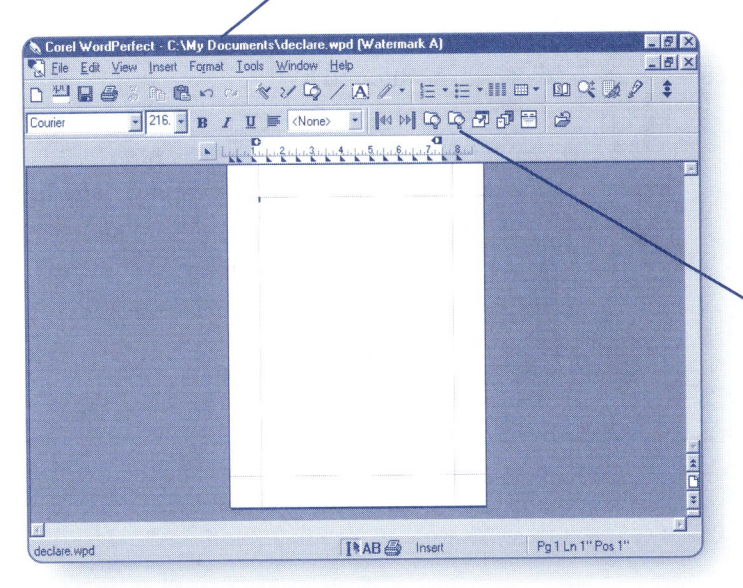

You are seeing the background of your document displayed in Full Page view. You are now ready to add a graphic image to the background of your document.

6. Click on the **Image button**. The Insert Image-ClipArt dialog box will open.

148 CHAPTER 14: ADDING HEADERS, FOOTERS, AND WATERMARKS

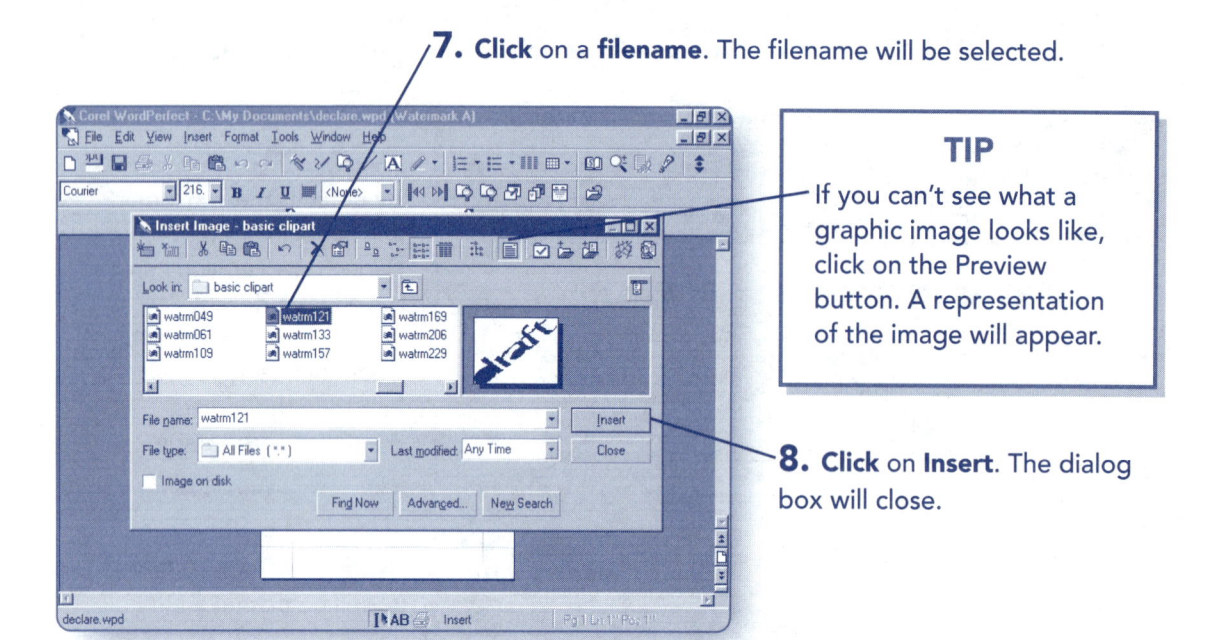

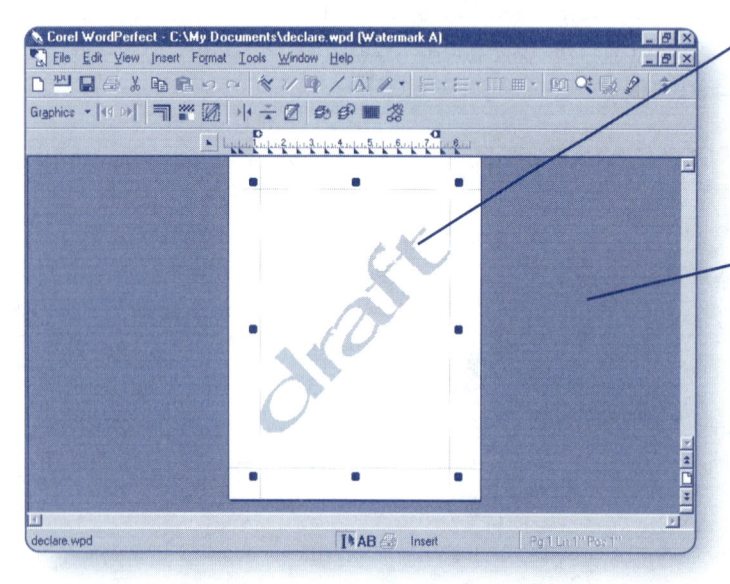

7. Click on a **filename**. The filename will be selected.

TIP

If you can't see what a graphic image looks like, click on the Preview button. A representation of the image will appear.

8. Click on **Insert**. The dialog box will close.

The graphic image appears on the background page in a light gray shading with eight small black dots called *handles* around it.

9. Click in the **gray area** outside the background page to deselect the graphic image. The small black handles around the graphic image will disappear.

ADDING A WATERMARK   149

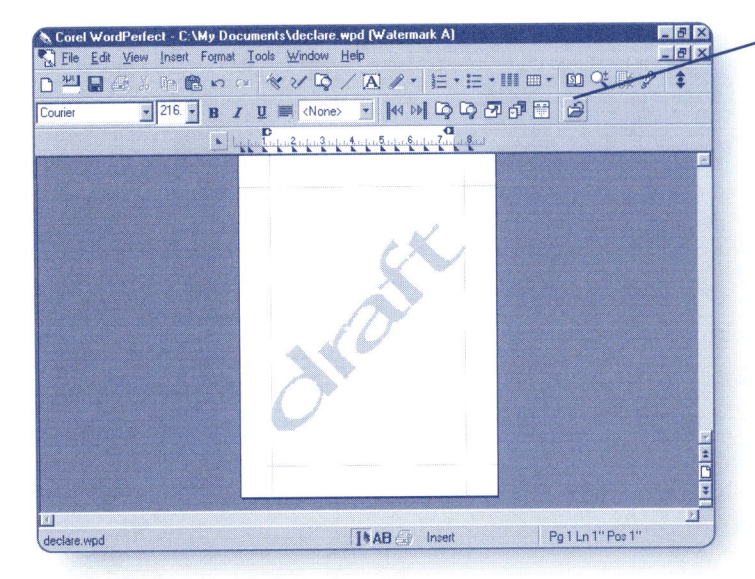

10. **Click** on the **Close button**. The insertion point will return to the body of the document.

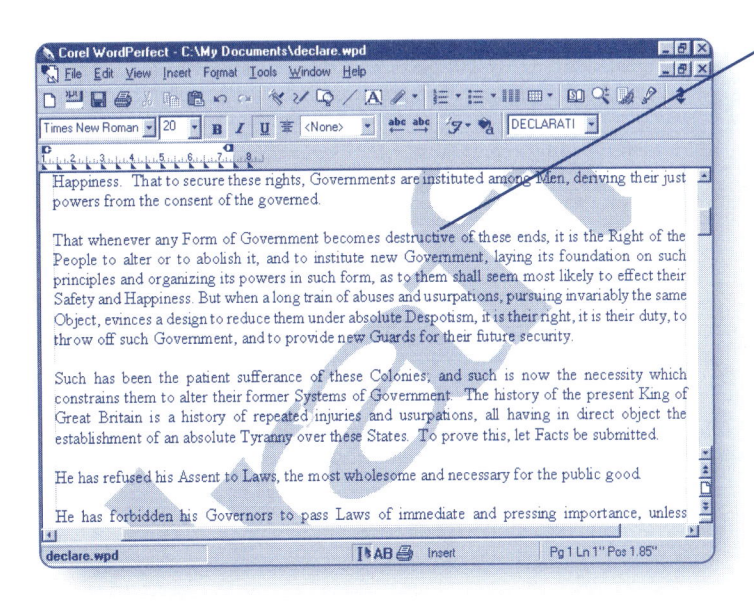

The image appears underneath the text of your document.

NOTE
Watermarks, headers, and footers do not show on your screen if you are in Draft view.

15

Saving Time with Templates

WordPerfect has some great time-saving templates—sample documents with all sorts of special formatting. WordPerfect does most of the work for you; a feature called PerfectExpert guides you in using templates. In this chapter, you'll learn how to:

- Create a memo
- Create an award certificate

CHAPTER 15: SAVING TIME WITH TEMPLATES

Creating a Memo

The memo template contains several predesigned looks for your memos. Try them all out to find your favorite!

1. Click on **File**. The File menu will appear.

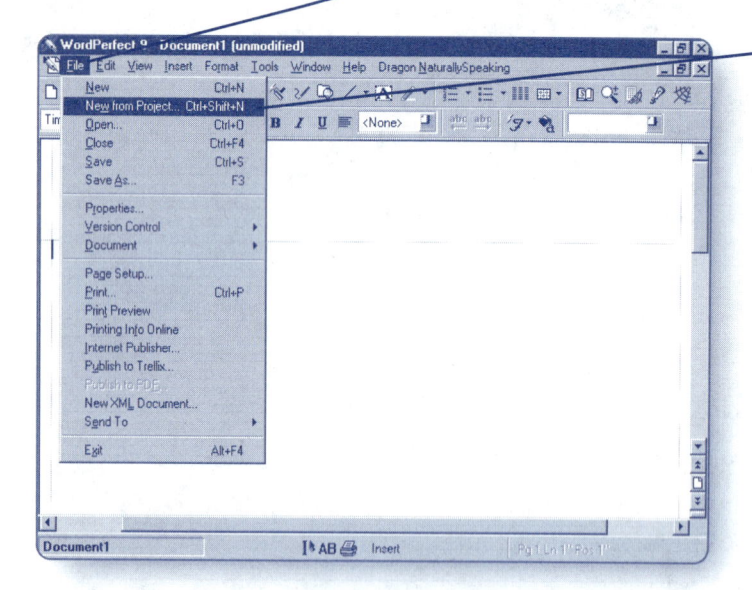

2. Click on **New from Project**. The PerfectExpert dialog box will open.

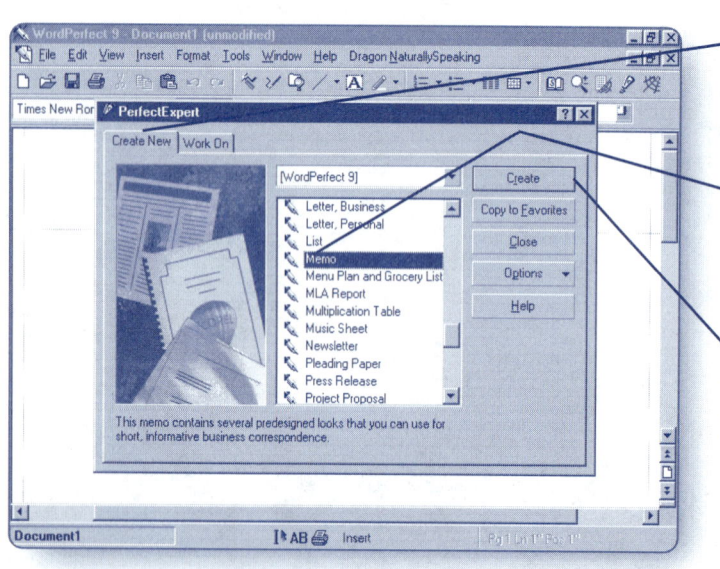

3. If necessary, **click** on the **Create New tab**. The Create New tab will come to the front.

4. Click on **Memo**. This is the template you need for this project.

5. Click on **Create**. A memo will appear onscreen ready for you to enter your information.

CREATING A MEMO 153

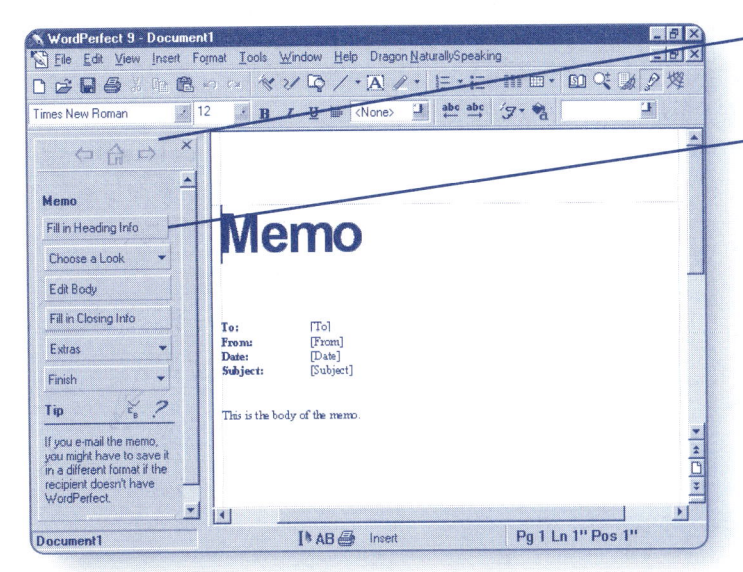

The PerfectExpert appears on the left side.

6. Click on **Fill in Heading Info**. The memo heading dialog box will open.

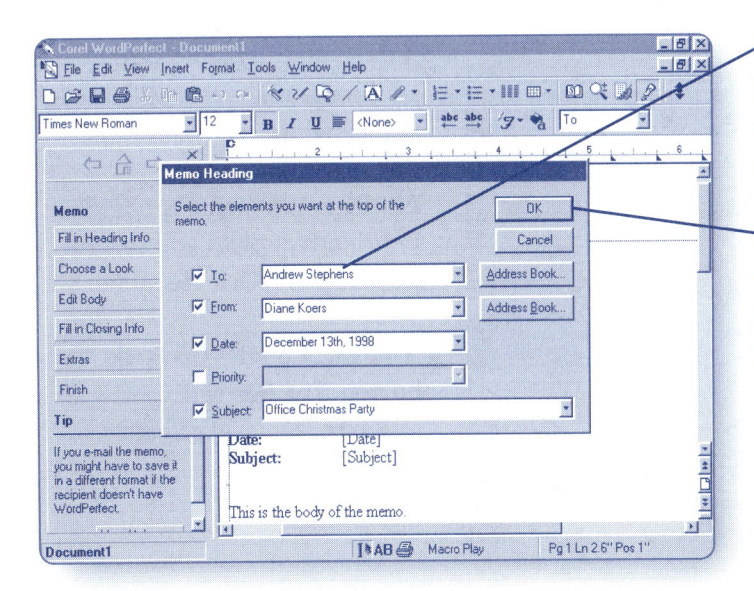

7. Type the **heading information** in the To:, From:, and Subject: boxes. The text will display on each line of the box.

8. Click on **OK**. The dialog box will close, and the heading information will be entered into your memo.

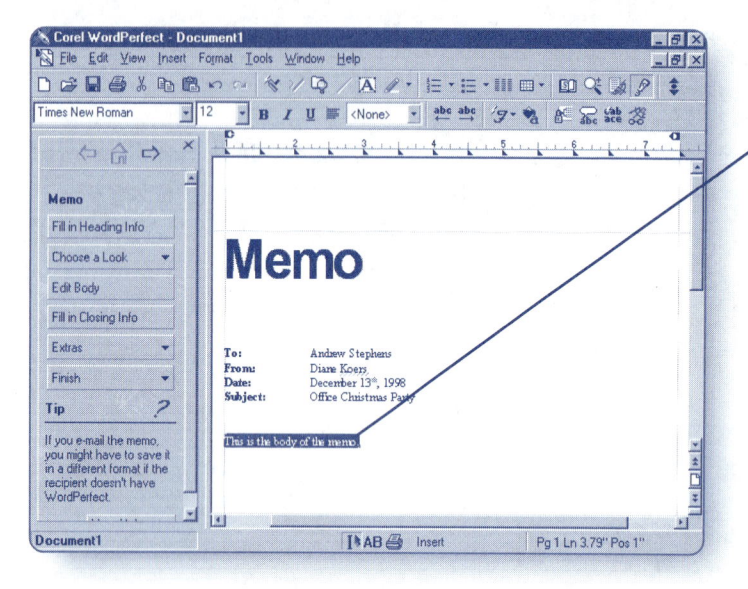

The insertion point will jump down to the body of the memo.

9. Highlight and **delete** the **text** "This is the body of the memo." The text will be deleted.

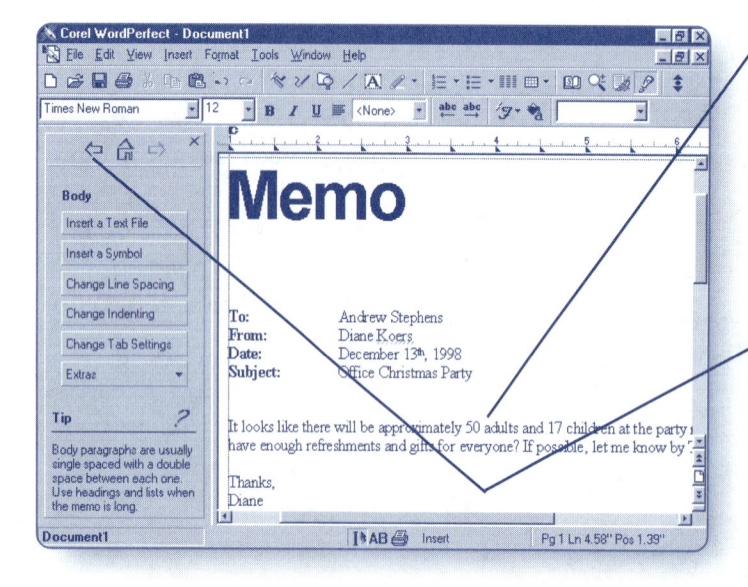

10. Type the **memo body** information. The text will display in the memo.

Although the memo is typed, WordPerfect gives you several ways to embellish the memo.

11. Click on the **Go Back button**. The PerfectExpert will return to the main selection.

CREATING A MEMO 155

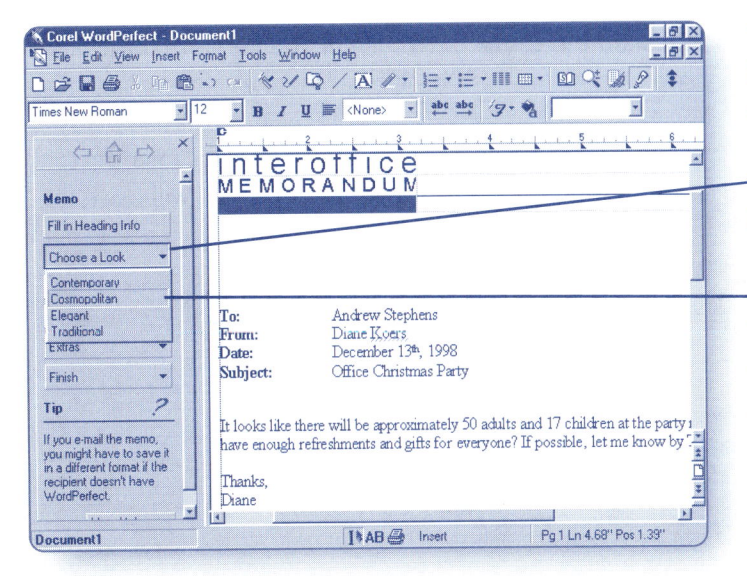

You can choose different looks for your memo. The default style is Traditional.

12. **Click** on **Choose a Look**. A list of memo styles will appear.

13. **Click** on a **memo style**: Traditional, Contemporary, Cosmopolitan, or Elegant. The appearance of the memo will change according to the selection you made.

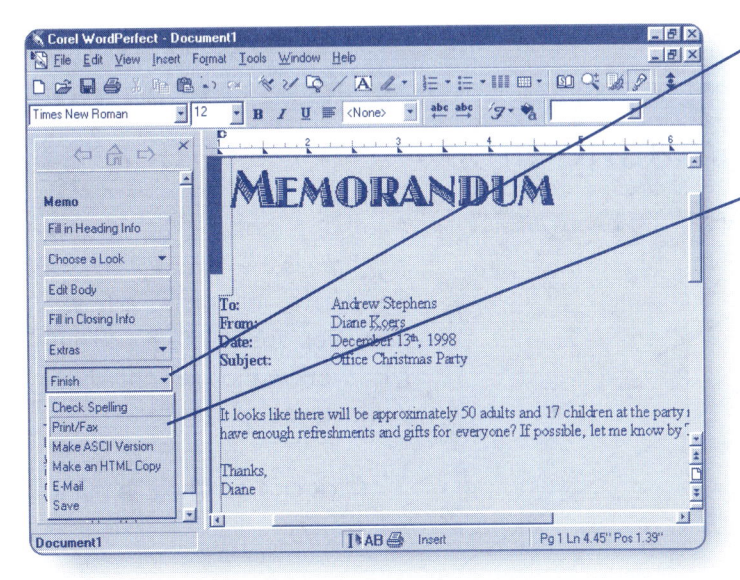

14. **Click** on **Finish** on the PerfectExpert window. A list of choices will appear.

15. **Click** on any **step** you want WordPerfect to take next: Check the spelling in the memo, Print or Fax the memo, E-mail the memo, or Save the memo.

156 CHAPTER 15: SAVING TIME WITH TEMPLATES

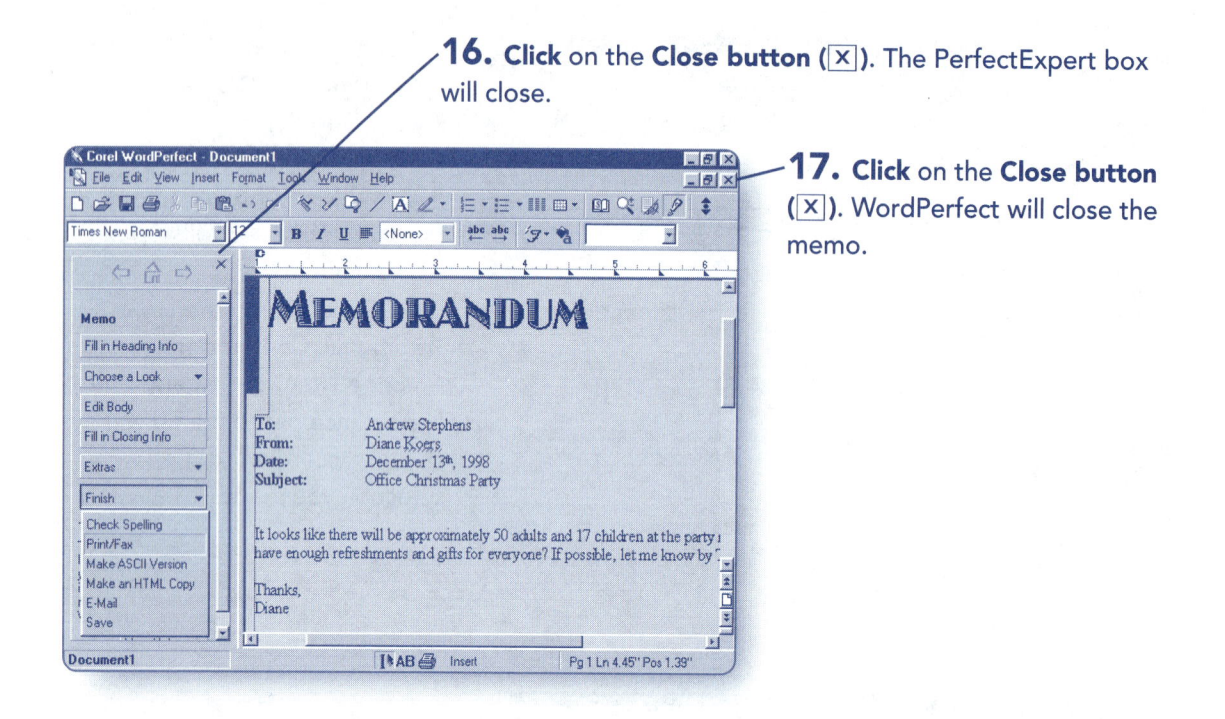

16. **Click** on the **Close button** ([X]). The PerfectExpert box will close.

17. **Click** on the **Close button** ([X]). WordPerfect will close the memo.

Creating an Award Certificate

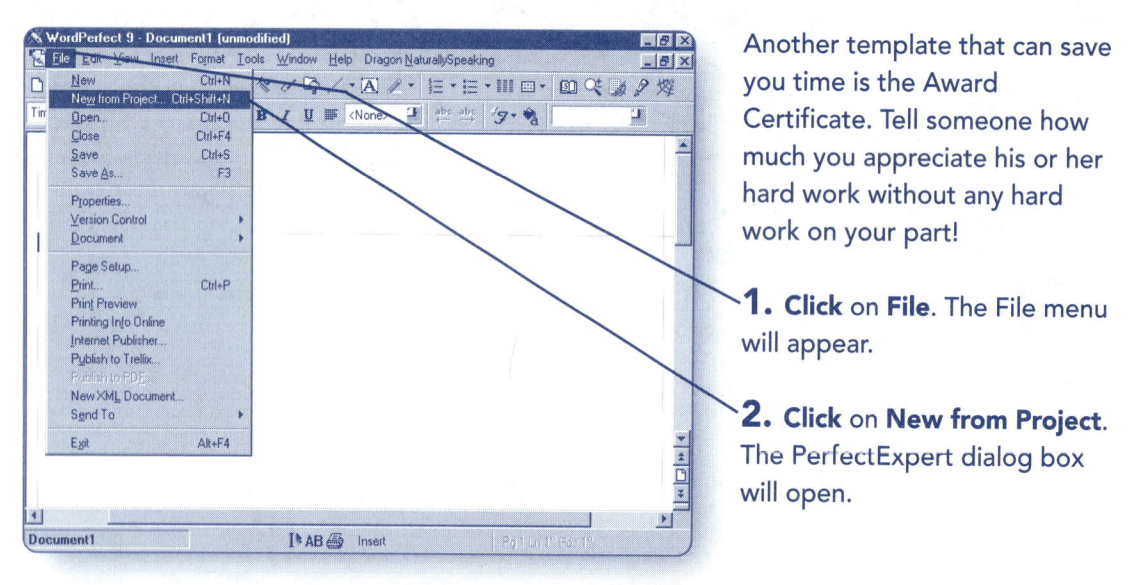

Another template that can save you time is the Award Certificate. Tell someone how much you appreciate his or her hard work without any hard work on your part!

1. **Click** on **File**. The File menu will appear.

2. **Click** on **New from Project**. The PerfectExpert dialog box will open.

CREATING AN AWARD CERTIFICATE 157

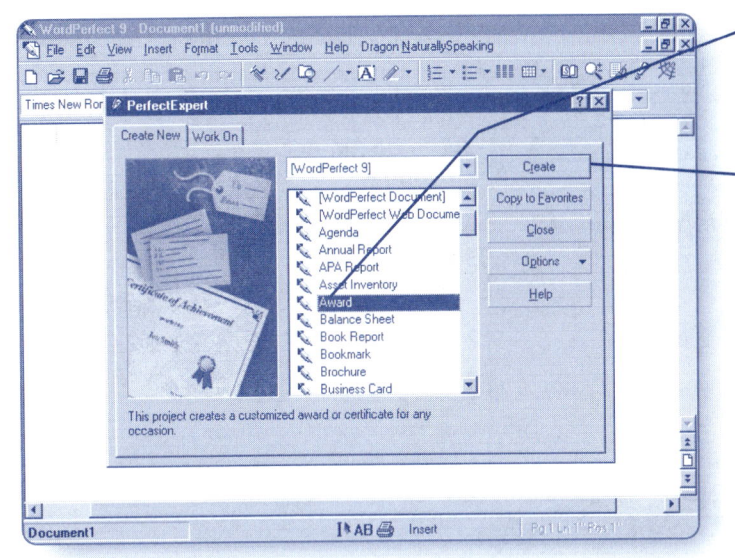

3. Click on **Award**. This is the template to help you create a certificate.

4. Click on **Create**. A Certificate of Achievement will appear in Full Page view as well as the PerfectExpert to help you make any changes.

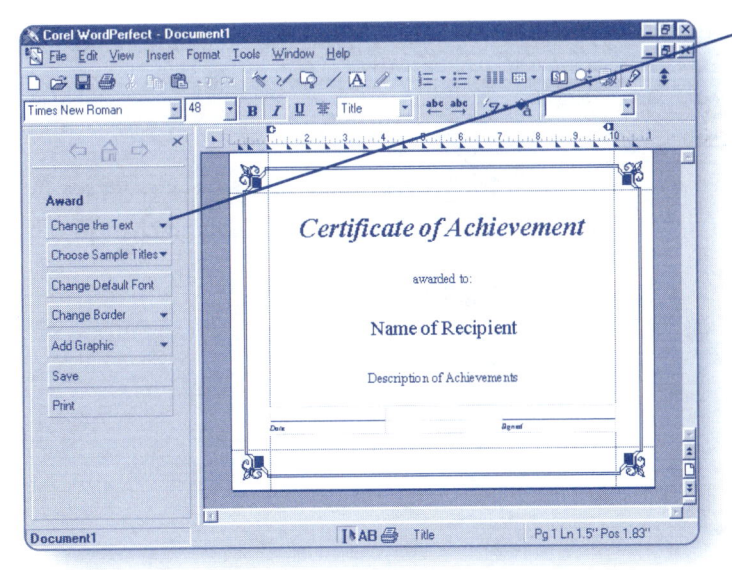

5. Click on **Change the Text**. A selection of items to change will appear.

158 CHAPTER 15: SAVING TIME WITH TEMPLATES

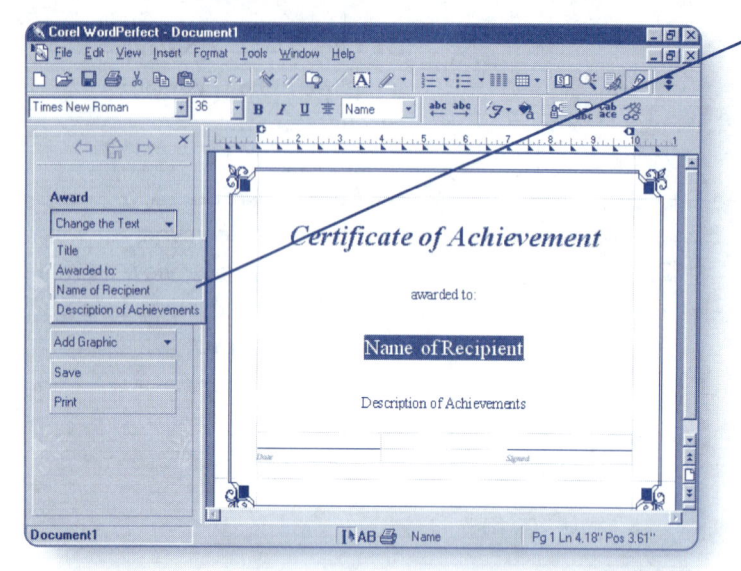

6. Click on **Name of Recipient**. The words *Name of Recipient* will be highlighted in the document.

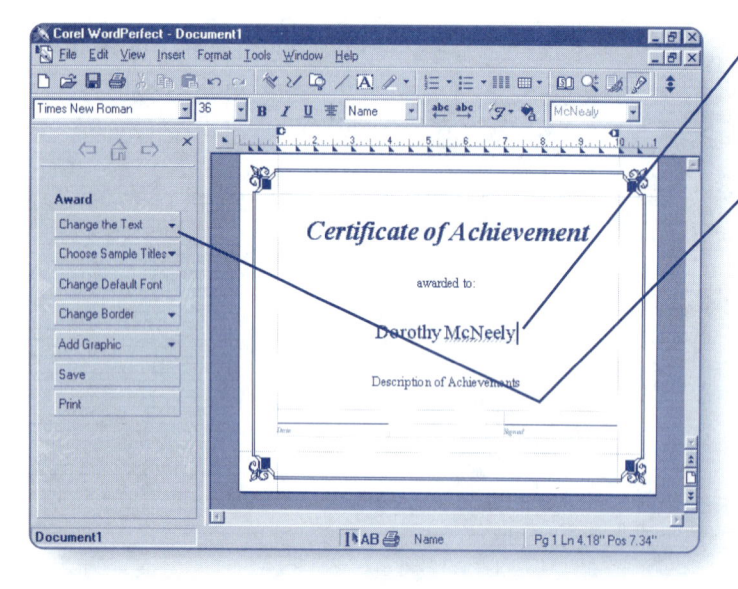

7. Type the recipient **name**. The name will display on the certificate.

8. Click on **Change the Text**. A selection of items to change will appear.

CREATING AN AWARD CERTIFICATE   159

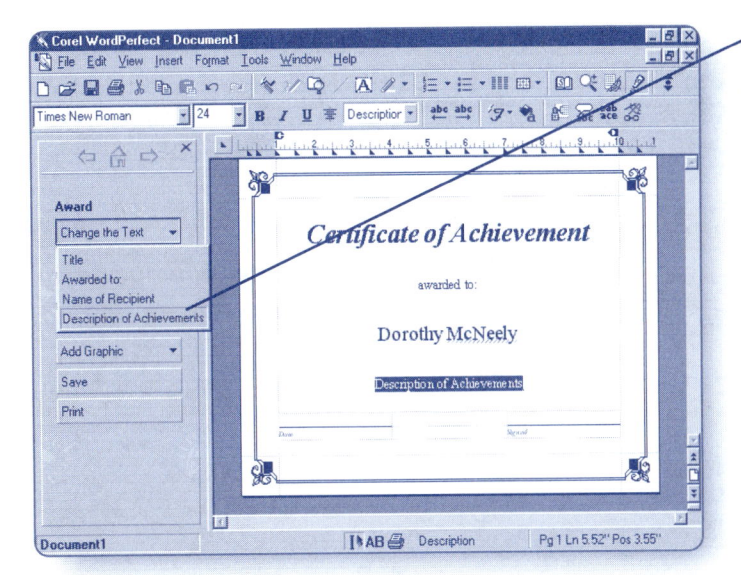

9. Click on **Description of Achievements**. The words will be highlighted in the document.

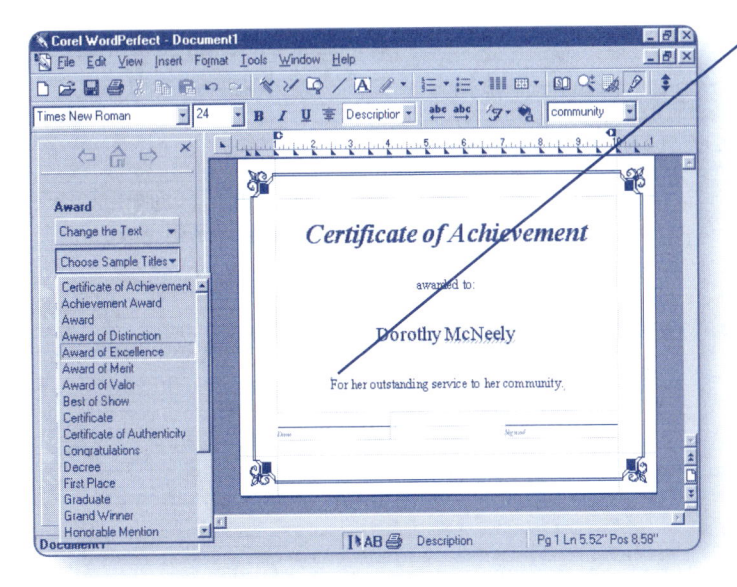

10. Type a **description** of the award. The typed text will replace the highlighted text.

CHAPTER 15: SAVING TIME WITH TEMPLATES

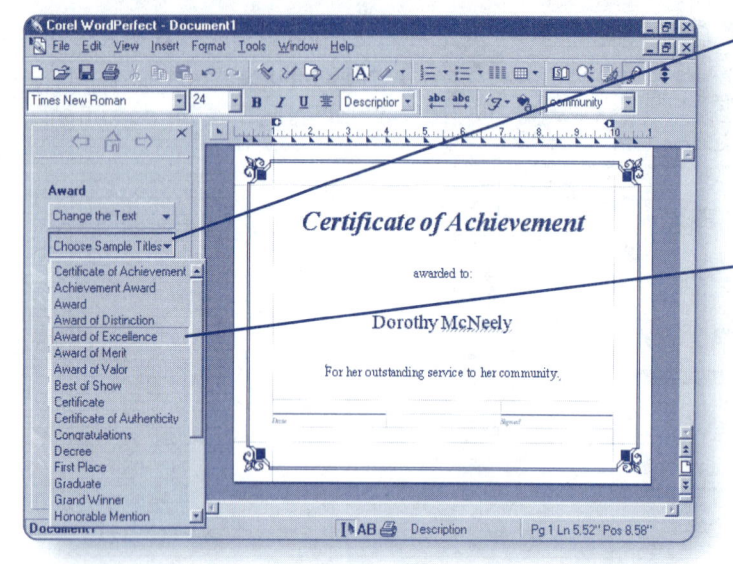

11. Click on **Choose Sample Titles** to change the certificate type. Be sure to scroll down the list to look at all 23 possible titles.

12. Click on an appropriate **title** for your certificate. The title of the certificate will automatically change for you.

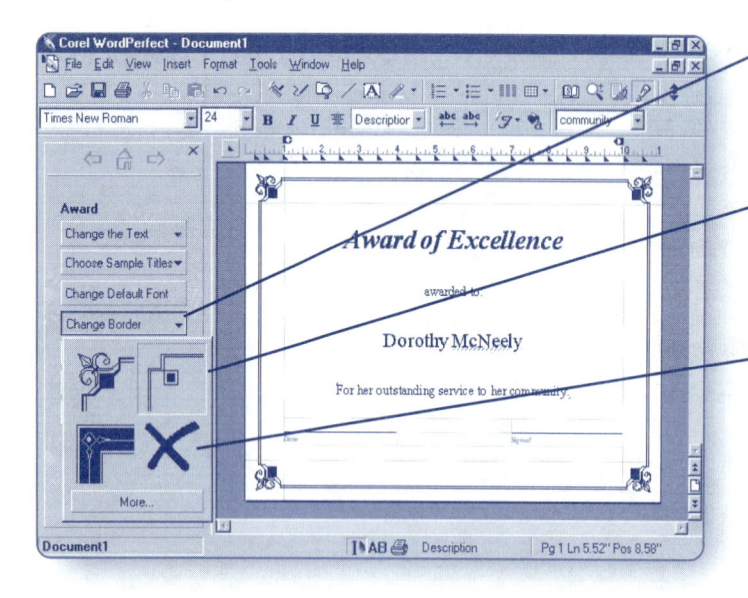

13. Click on **Change Border**. A list of available border styles will appear.

14. Click on the desired style of **border**. The border around the certificate will change.

The selection with the big X means "no border" on the certificate.

You can further enhance the certificate by adding a graphic.

CREATING AN AWARD CERTIFICATE 161

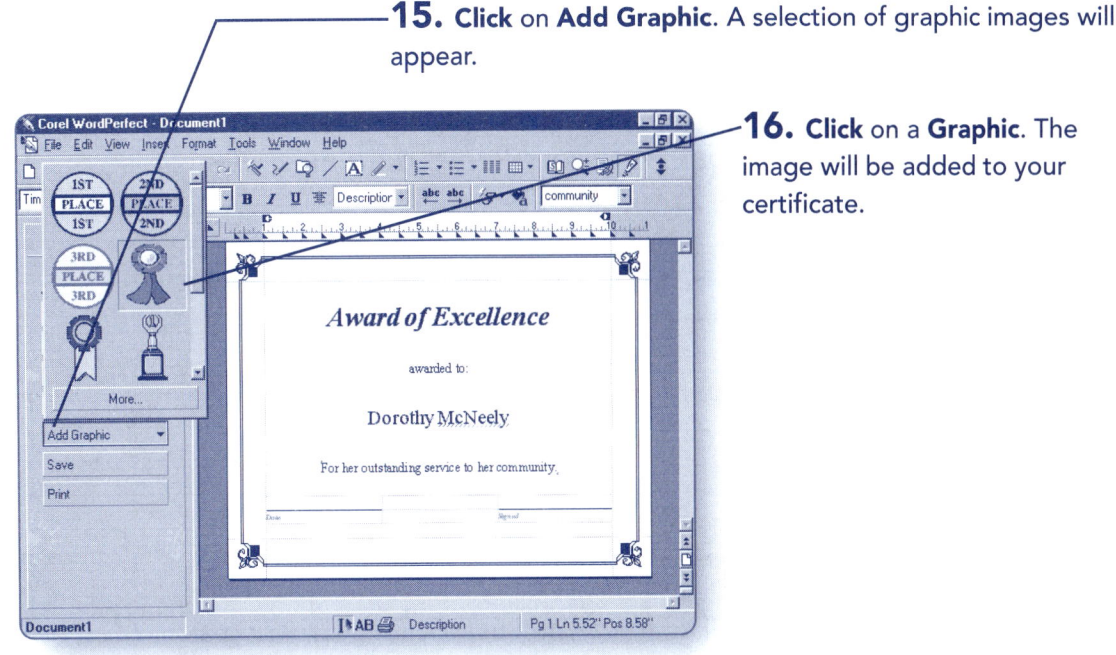

15. Click on **Add Graphic**. A selection of graphic images will appear.

16. Click on a **Graphic**. The image will be added to your certificate.

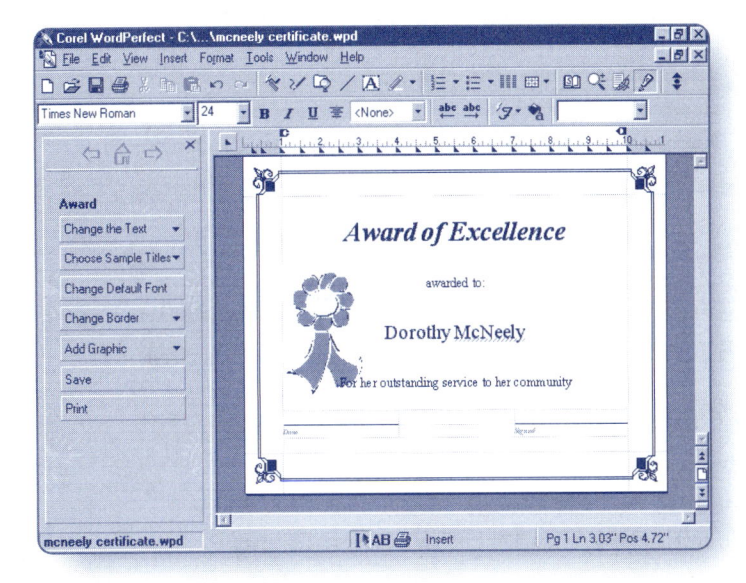

Your certificate is now complete and can be printed and/or saved.

Part II Review Questions

1. What is the default font for a WordPerfect document? *See "Changing the Typeface" in Chapter 9*

2. Approximately how tall is a 72-point font? *See "Changing Font Size" in Chapter 9*

3. Which view does page numbering not appear in? *See "Adding Page Numbering" in Chapter 10*

4. Why should you select text first before choosing to center a heading? *See "Centering a Heading" in Chapter 11*

5. When are numbered lists frequently used? *See "Creating a Numbered List" in Chapter 12*

6. What happens when you add a fill color to a paragraph? *See "Adding a Fill Color to a Paragraph" in Chapter 12*

7. Which feature shows a separating line at the bottom of a page—a footnote or an endnote? *See "Creating Footnotes and Endnotes" in Chapter 13*

8. What is the name of the macro that converts a footnote to and endnote? *See "Changing a Footnote to an Endnote" in Chapter 13*

9. How many pages does the suppress feature affect? *See "Suppressing a Header or Footer" in Chapter 14*

10. What feature does WordPerfect use to guide you in using templates? *See the introduction in Chapter 15*

PART III

Working with Tables

Chapter 16
　　　Creating Tabular Tables. **165**

Chapter 17
　　　Creating a Perfect Table **175**

Chapter 18
　　　Formatting a Table **191**

Chapter 19
　　　Using Formulas in a Table **205**

16

Creating Tabular Tables

WordPerfect has built-in default tab settings although you can also create your own settings. There are four styles of tab settings, and each of those can have dot leaders in front of it, if desired. In this chapter, you'll learn how to:

- Turn on the ruler bar
- Work with the default tabs
- Add a custom tab stop
- Delete a tab stop

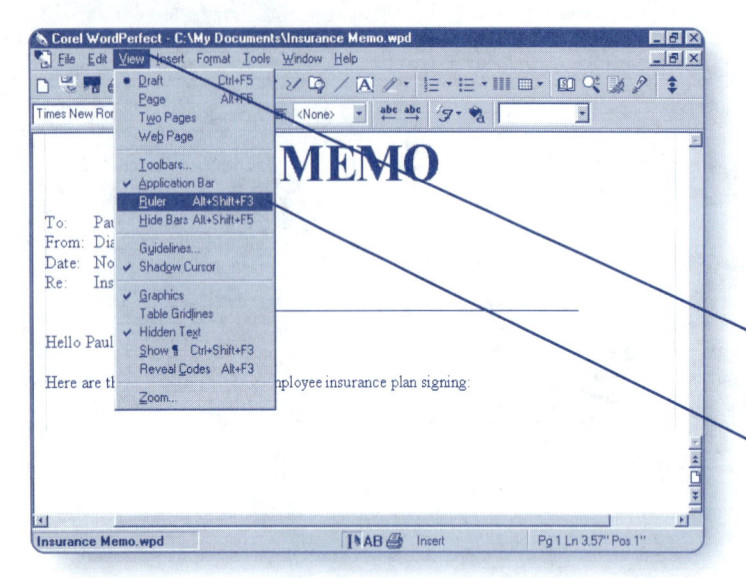

Turning on the Ruler Bar

If you are going to modify tabs, it is extremely helpful to turn on the ruler bar.

1. Click on **View**. The View menu will appear.

2. Click on **Ruler**. The ruler bar will appear with the current tab settings.

Changing the Default Tabs

By default, WordPerfect assigns left-aligned tabs at half-inch intervals. If you want to change that, for example, to quarter-inch intervals, use the Tab Set dialog box.

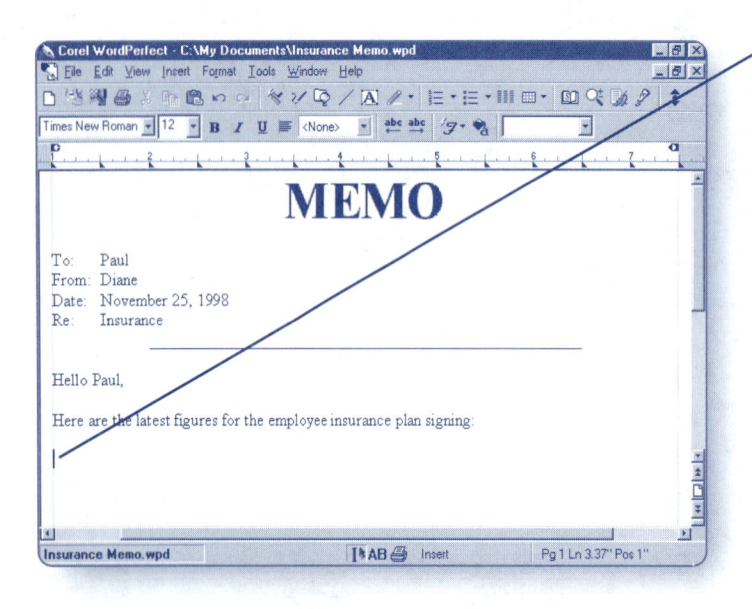

1. Click the **mouse pointer** where you want the new tab settings to go into effect. The blinking insertion point will appear.

CHANGING THE DEFAULT TABS 167

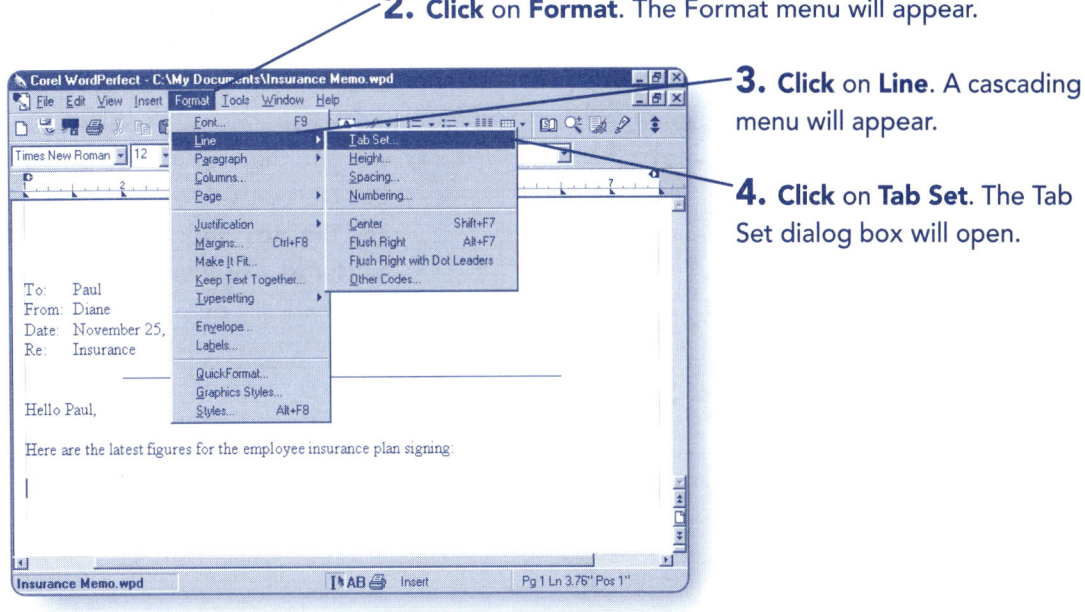

2. Click on **Format**. The Format menu will appear.

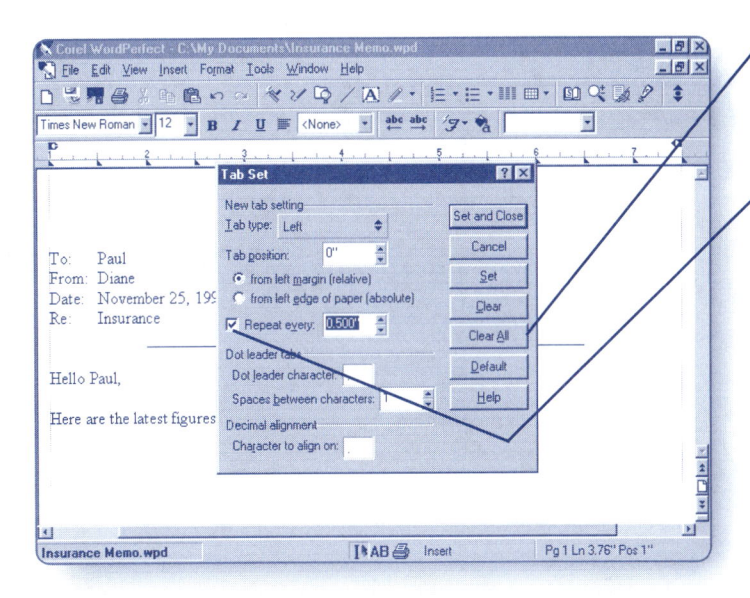

3. Click on **Line**. A cascading menu will appear.

4. Click on **Tab Set**. The Tab Set dialog box will open.

5. Click on **Clear All**. The existing default tabs will disappear.

6. Click on **Repeat every:**. A ✔ will appear in the box, and the measurement box to the right will now be available.

CHAPTER 16: CREATING TABULAR TABLES

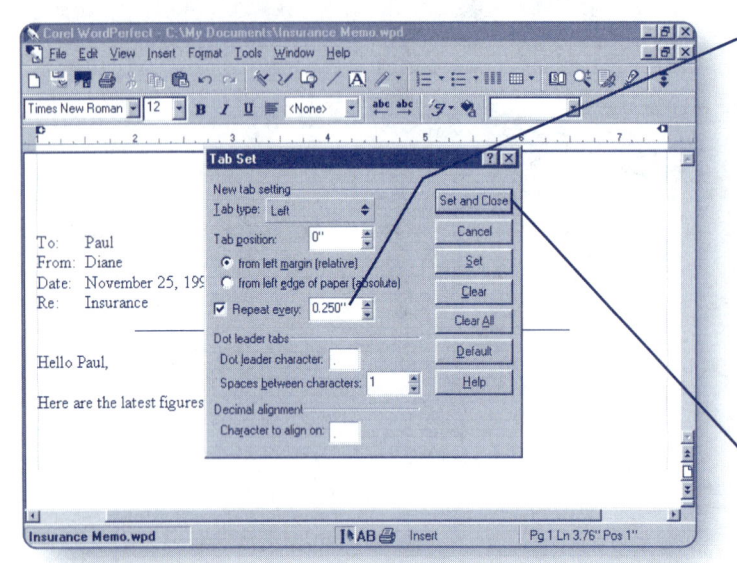

7. Type the **desired increment** in the measurement box. Use a decimal format. You could type in 0.25 or .25 or .25". Whether you add the zero in front of the decimal point or whether you add the inch mark (") doesn't matter to WordPerfect. It will automatically put them in for you.

8. Click on **Set and Close**. The new setting will go into effect.

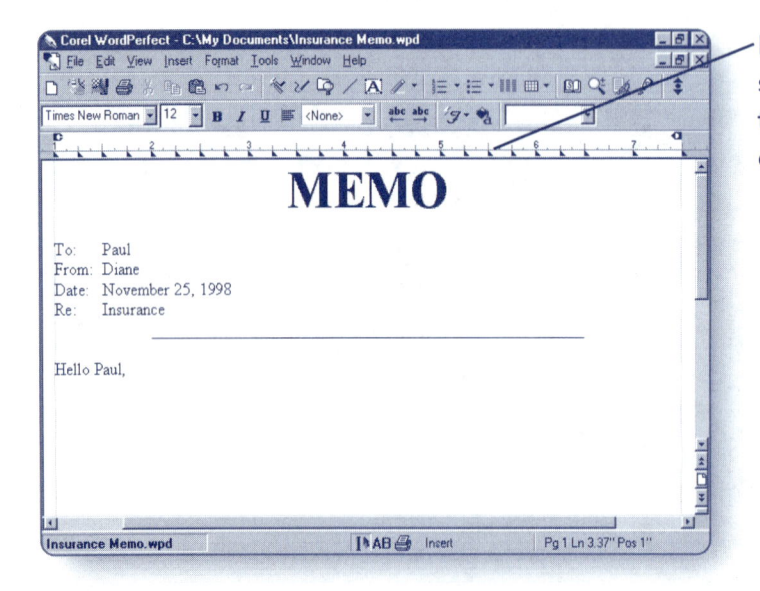

Look at the ruler bar. The small triangles that represent tab settings are at every quarter-inch.

Adding a Custom Tab Stop

Four different types of tabs are available: left aligned, right aligned, center aligned, and decimal aligned. Tabs can have dot leaders added to keep the eye focused on a particular line of the document. You can create a custom tab setting using any combination of these tabs.

The following figure illustrates different types of tabs.

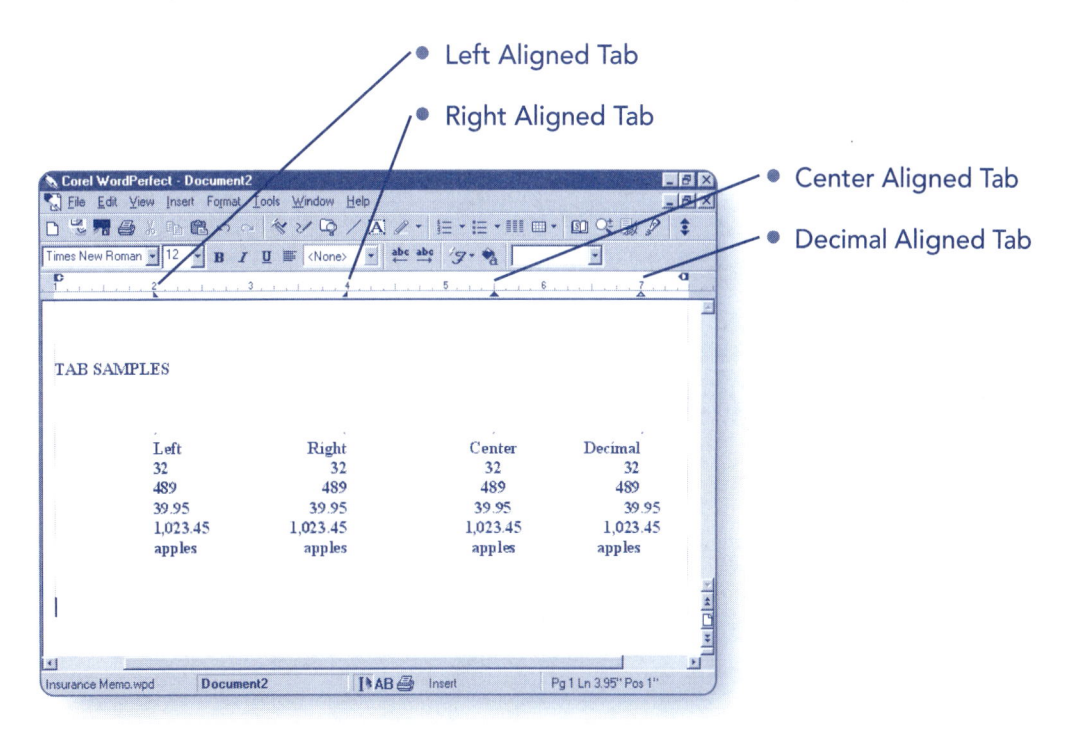

- Left Aligned Tab
- Right Aligned Tab
- Center Aligned Tab
- Decimal Aligned Tab

CHAPTER 16: CREATING TABULAR TABLES

1. Click the **mouse pointer** where you want the new tab settings to take effect. The blinking insertion point will appear.

2. Click on **Format**. The Format menu will appear.

3. Click on **Line**. A cascading menu will appear.

4. Click on **Tab Set**. The Tab Set dialog box will open.

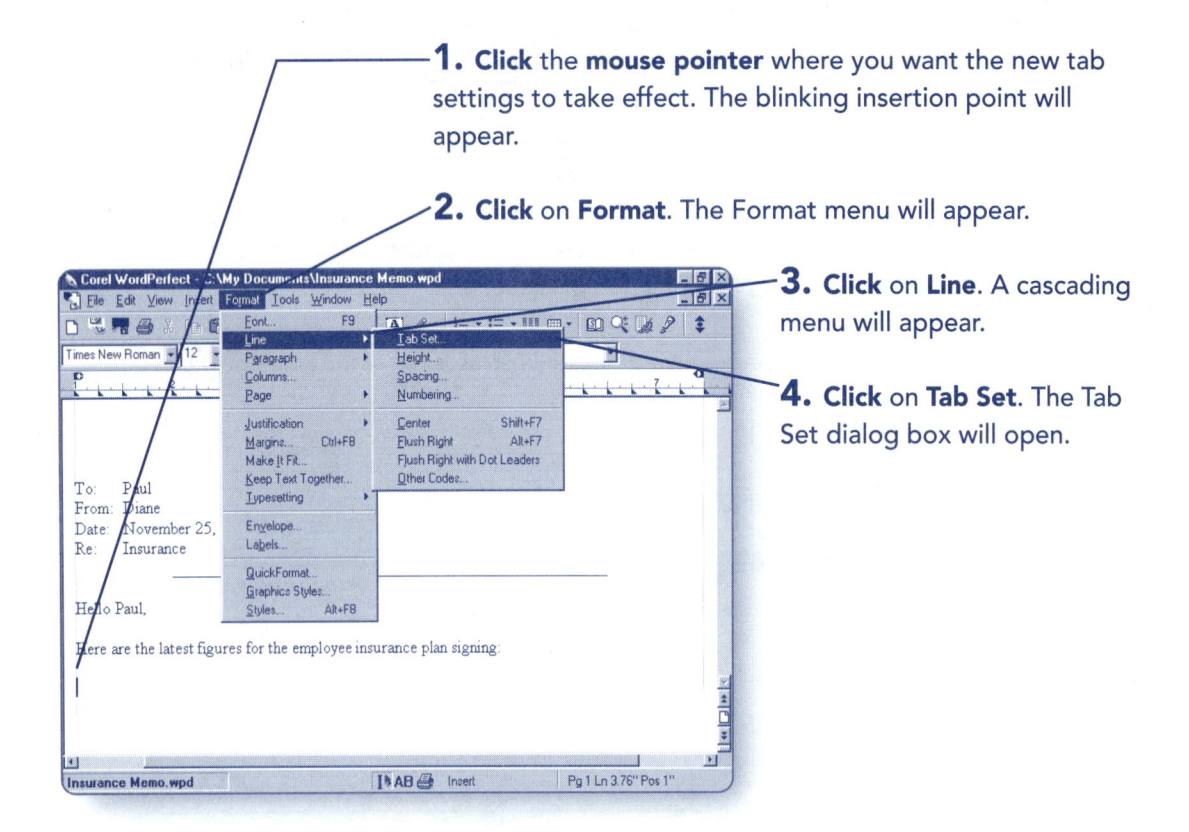

5. Click on **Clear All**. All existing tabs will be deleted.

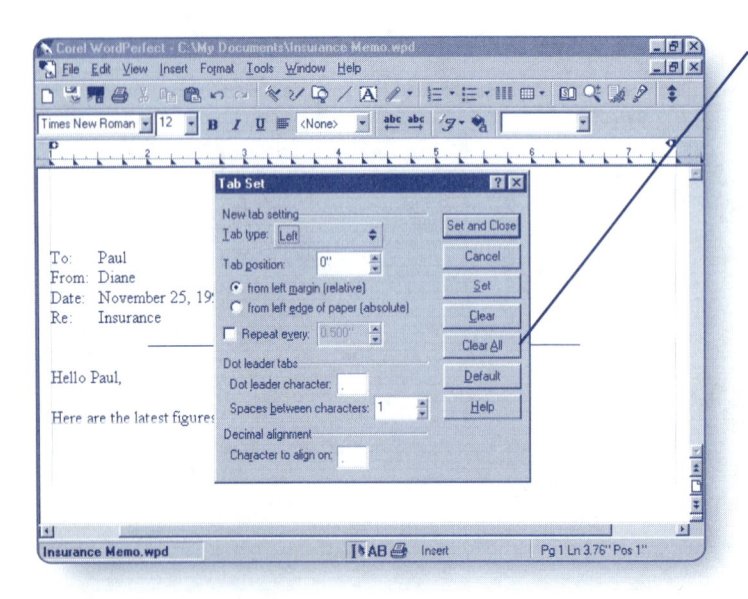

ADDING A CUSTOM TAB STOP   171

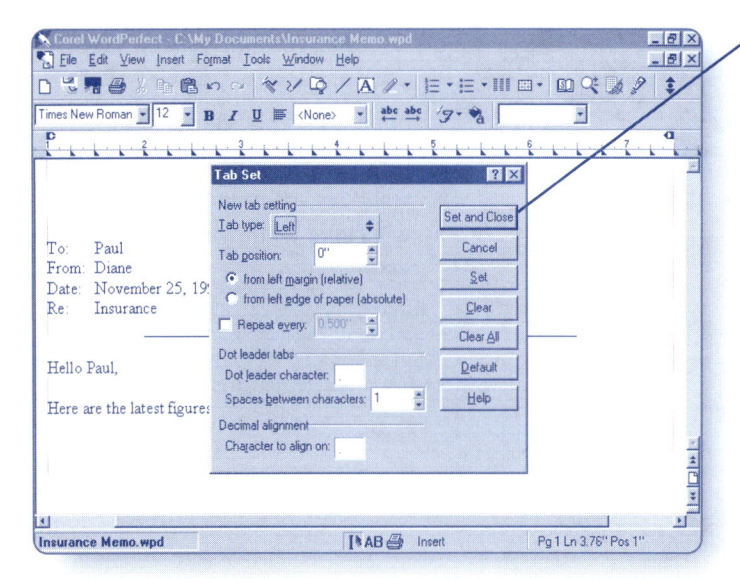

6. Click on **Set and Close.** The Tab Set dialog box will close.

7. Position the **mouse pointer** on the tab area of the ruler line. Be sure that you are in the tab area, which is directly below the bottom of the ruler line. The mouse pointer will turn into a white arrow.

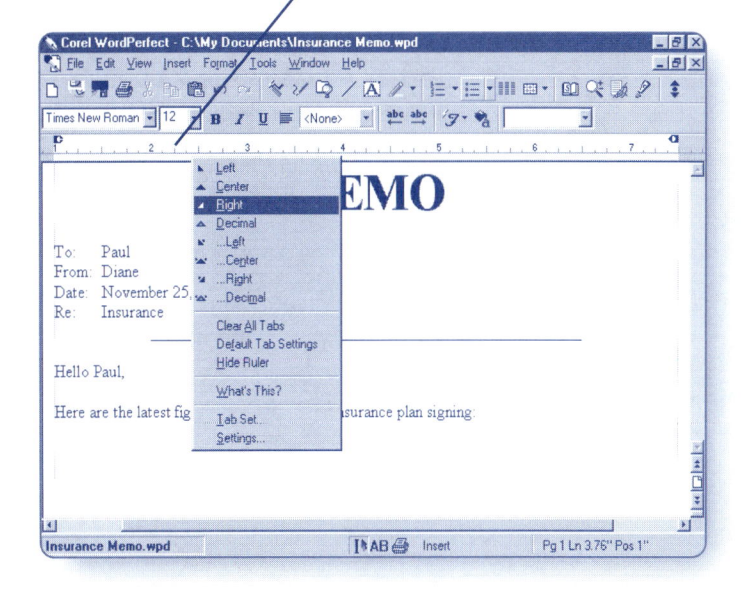

8. Click the **right mouse button**. The tab shortcut menu will appear.

NOTE

Make sure that the menu you see is like the one in this figure. If not, try again. You may not have been exactly in the tab area of the ruler line.

CHAPTER 16: CREATING TABULAR TABLES

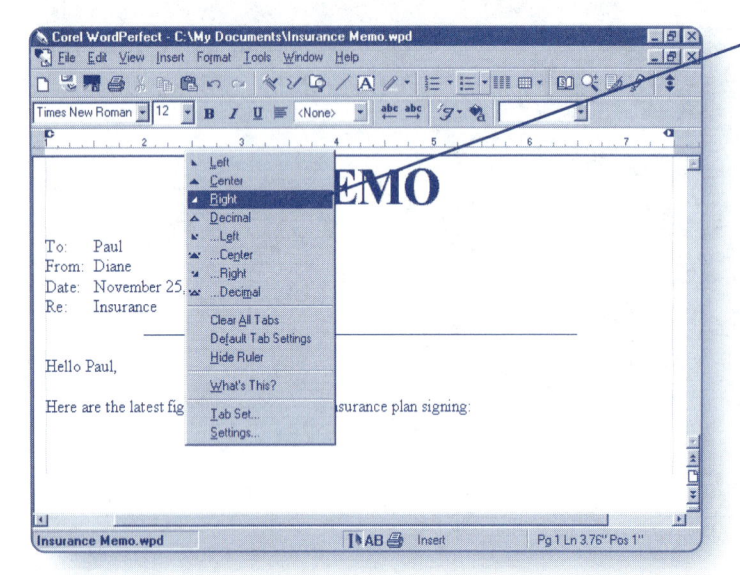

9. Click on the **style of tab** you want to use. The first four will have no dot leader in front of them, but the next four choices will have a dot leader. The menu will close when you have made a selection.

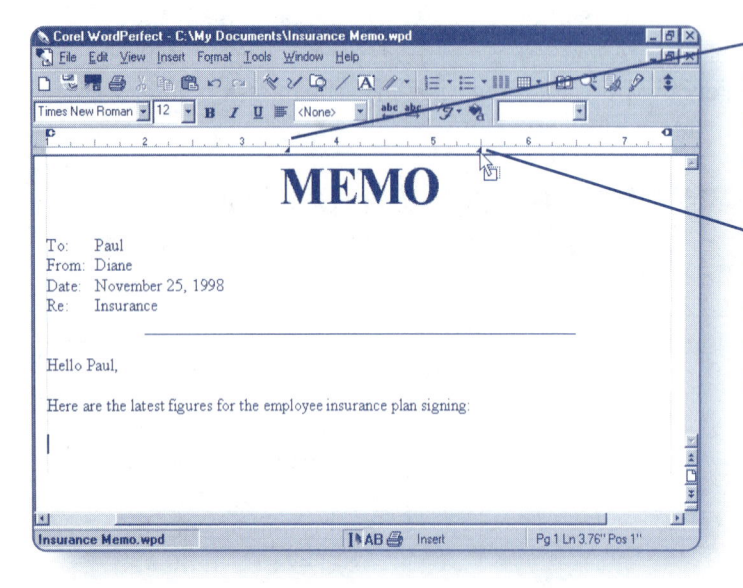

10. Click on the **tab area** of the ruler bar wherever you want the new tab setting to appear. A small triangle will appear.

11. Repeat steps 7 through **10** for each additional tab stop you want to place. The tab stops will appear on the ruler bar.

ADDING A CUSTOM TAB STOP

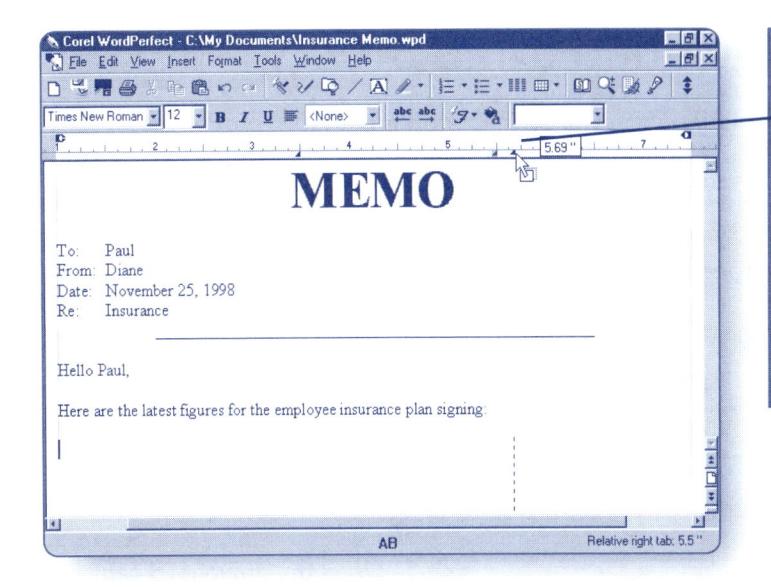

TIP

To move a tab stop, position the mouse pointer on top of the tab stop. The mouse pointer turns into an arrow with a rectangular box at the bottom of it. Drag the tab stop to the new position.

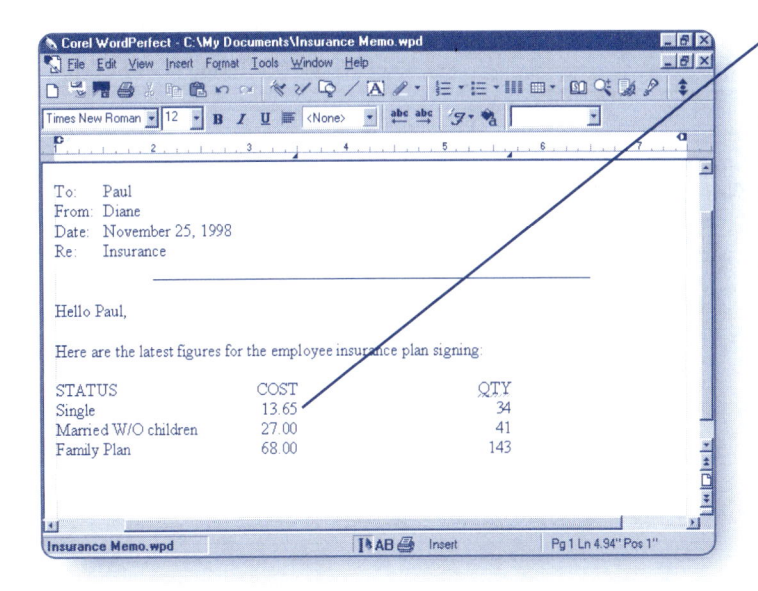

You are now ready to begin typing your text into your document, pressing the Tab key whenever you want to jump to the next tab stop. Look how neatly the figures line up in this table!

Deleting a Tab Stop

Deleting an unwanted tab stop is easy in WordPerfect!

1. Click the **mouse pointer** where you want the new tab settings to take effect. The blinking insertion point will appear.

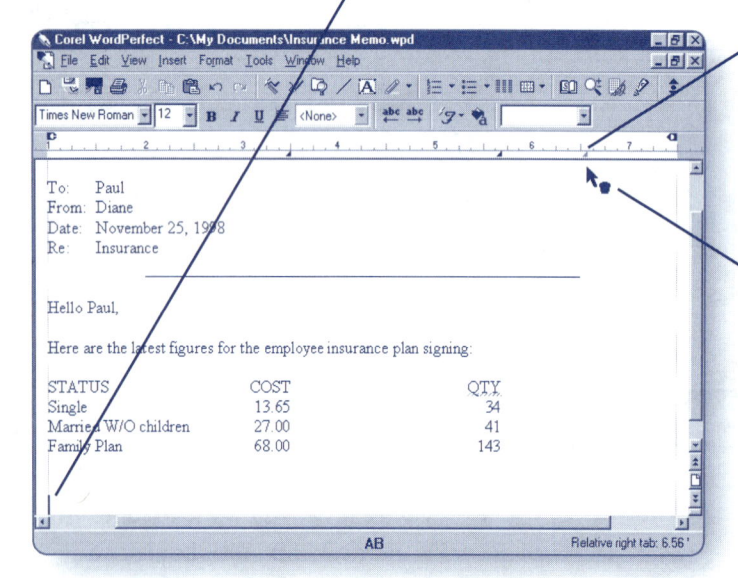

2. Position the **mouse** over the **unwanted tab stop.** The mouse pointer turns into an arrow with a rectangular box at the bottom of it.

3. Drag the **unwanted tab stop** off the ruler bar into the white part of the WordPerfect document. The mouse pointer will turn into a small trash can.

4. Release the **mouse button**. The tab stop will be deleted.

17

Creating a Perfect Table

WordPerfect tables are like small spreadsheets built right into your documents. Tables have formulas and functions just like your spreadsheet program. If you have already created a file with your spreadsheet program, you can even insert it into your WordPerfect document. In this chapter, you'll learn how to:

- Insert a table in the document
- Enter information in a table
- Save time with QuickFill
- Add and delete rows and columns
- Insert an existing spreadsheet into a document

Inserting a Table in the Document

WordPerfect has two ways you can insert a table; one uses the menu, whereas the other method uses the mouse.

Inserting a Table Using the Menu

When creating a table, you'll specify the number of rows and columns needed. If you don't create the table exactly the right size, you'll learn how to enlarge or reduce the table later in this chapter. The maximum table size is 64 columns by 32,767 rows. That ought to be big enough!

1. Click the **mouse pointer** at the location where you want the table. The blinking insertion point will appear.

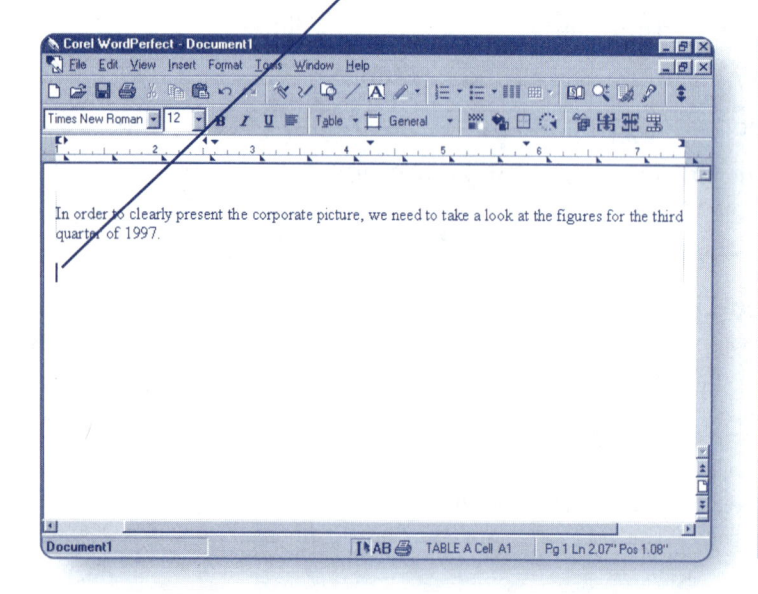

> **TIP**
> If you plan on placing the table at the beginning of your document, press the Enter key once before you create the table. This gives you a small space at the top in the event you decide to add something ahead of the table. If you decide not to keep that space, you can always delete it later.

INSERTING A TABLE IN THE DOCUMENT   177

2. Click on **Insert**. The Insert menu will appear.

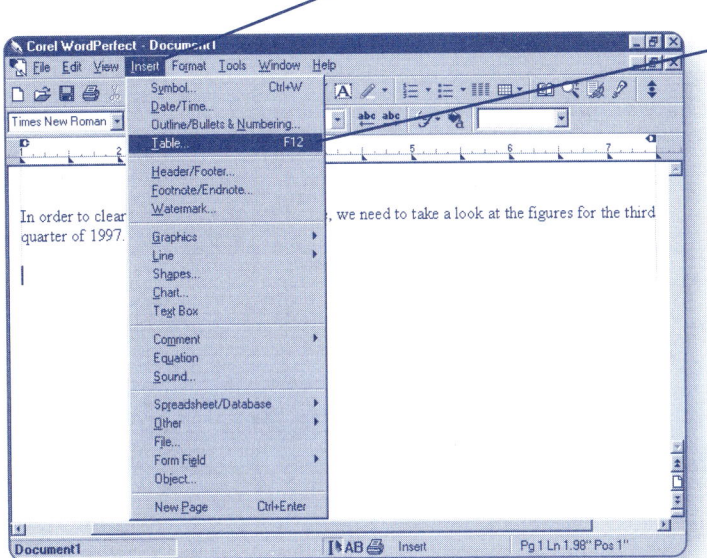

3. Click on **Table**. The Create Table dialog box will open.

4. Click on the **up/down arrows** (◆) to specify the number of table columns. The specified number will display.

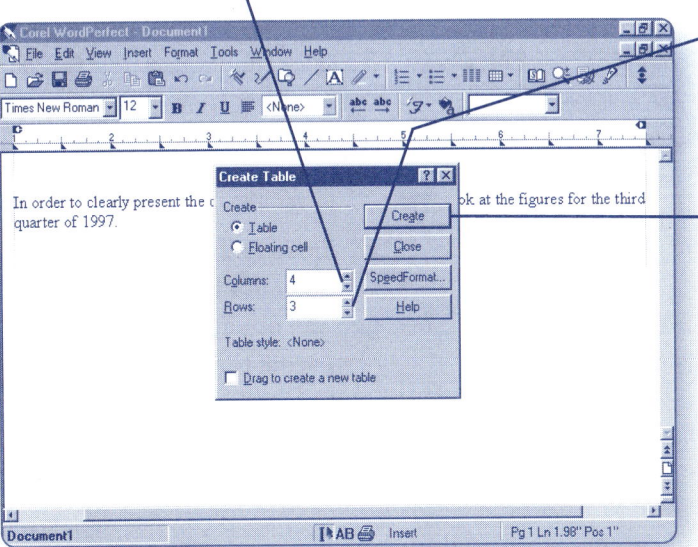

5. Click on the **up/down arrows** (◆) to specify the number of table rows. The specified number will display.

6. Click on **Create**. The table will be created.

178 CHAPTER 17: CREATING A PERFECT TABLE

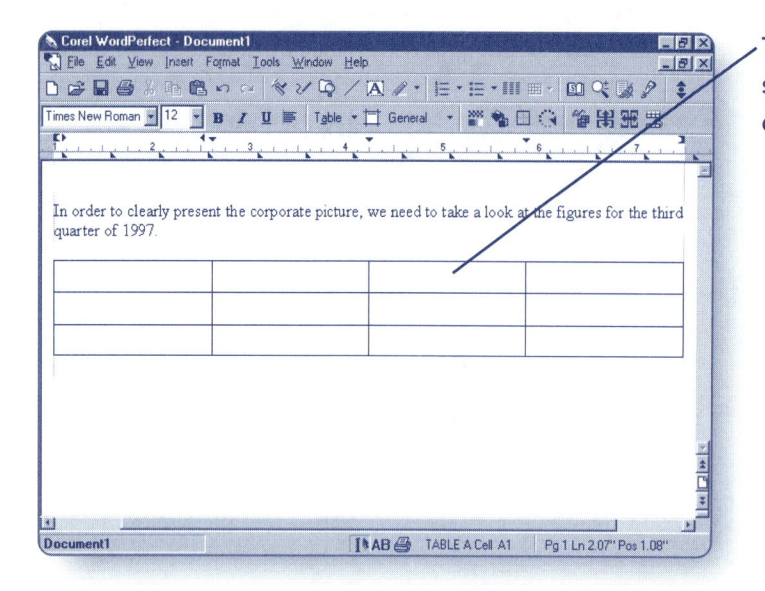

The table will display with the specified number of rows and columns.

Using Table QuickCreate

The maximum table size that can be added with this method is 32 columns by 45 rows. If you need more than that, you must use the menu method.

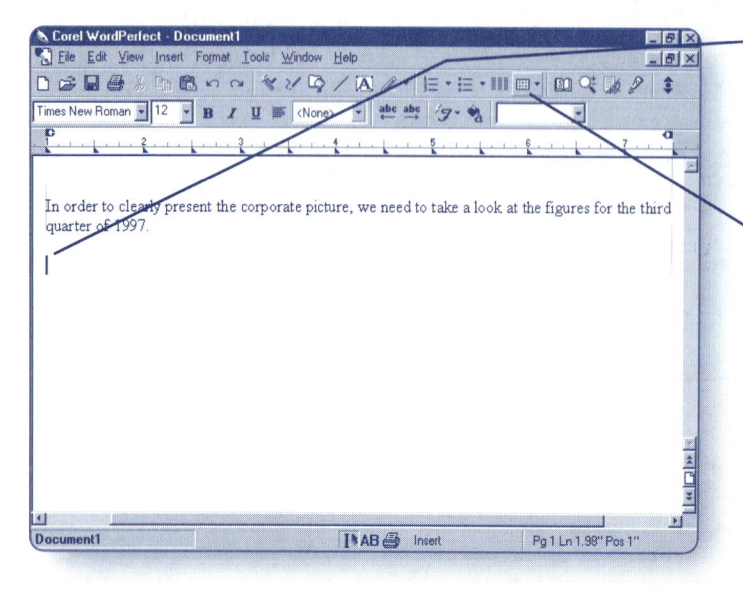

1. Click the **mouse pointer** at the location where you want the table. The blinking insertion point will appear.

2. Press and hold the **Table QuickCreate button**. A small grid will open. This grid represents the columns and rows of a table.

INSERTING A TABLE IN THE DOCUMENT   179

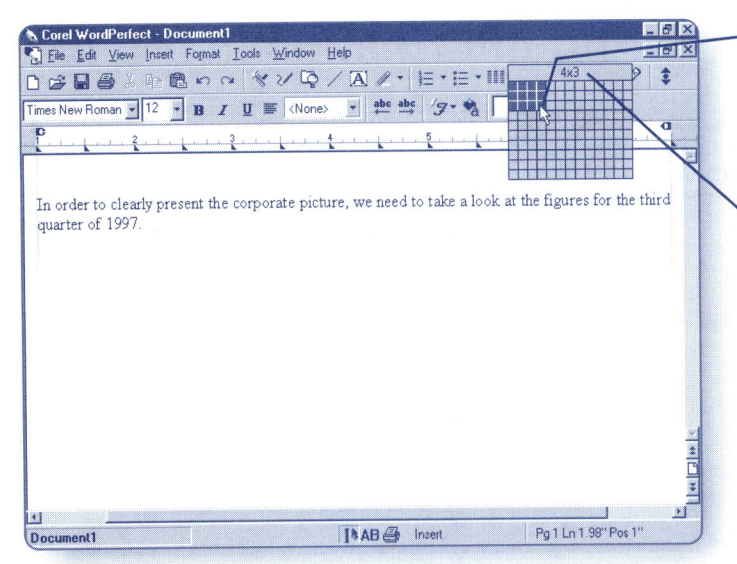

3. Drag the **mouse pointer** over the squares of the grid until you have covered enough to represent the size of your table.

As you are dragging across the grid, notice the numbers at the top. These represent how many columns and rows you have selected. For example, 4 x 3 will give you a table with four columns and three rows.

4. Release the **mouse button**. A table will be inserted into your document.

Notice the property bar has changed. It now contains buttons for working with tables.

Entering Information in a Table

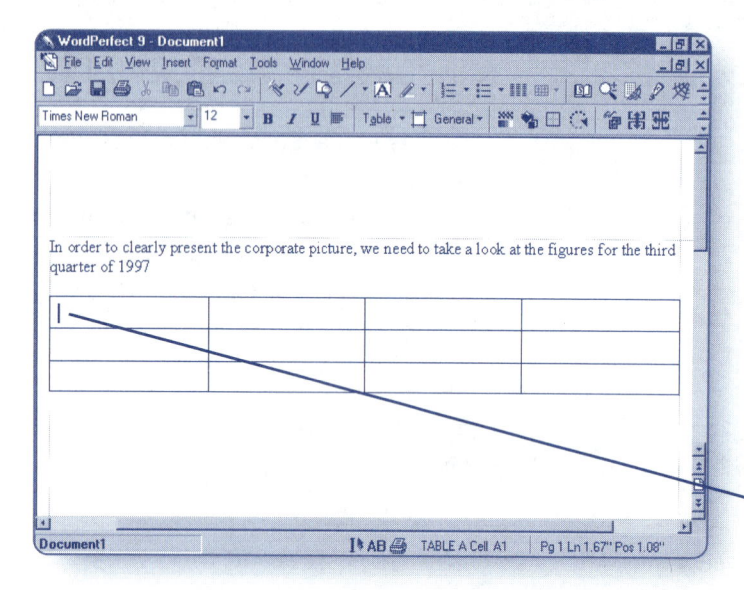

You can type data into the table cells, or you can allow WordPerfect to automatically fill in areas of your table.

Entering Cell Data

Entering information in a table is similar to entering information in any other part of your WordPerfect document.

1. Click the **mouse pointer** in the cell to receive information. The blinking insertion point will appear.

2. Type some **text**. The text will display in the cell.

When you get to the edge of the cell, the text will wrap to the next line of that cell.

NOTE

If you don't want the text to wrap to the next line of the cell, let it wrap anyway. In Chapter 18, "Formatting a Table," you will discover how to change the width of cells as well as join cells together.

ENTERING INFORMATION IN A TABLE   181

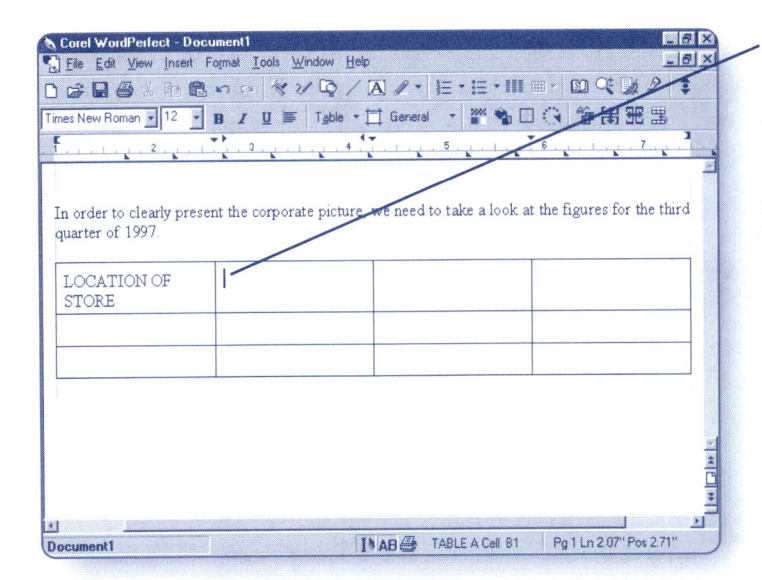

3. Press the **Tab key.** The insertion point will be moved to the next cell.

TIP
Press and hold the Shift key while pressing the Tab key to move to a previous cell.

4. Type some **text** in the next cell. The text will display in the cell.

Saving Time with QuickFill

Use QuickFill to continue a pattern of values across a row or down a column. You can use days of the week, months, quarters, numbers, or Roman numerals.

1. Type the **beginning value** (Monday, January, Qtr 1, 1st Quarter, and so on) in a cell of the table. The typed value will display in the table cell.

NOTE
If you are going to increment regular numbers, you must enter them into two cells. For example, you must enter 1 in the first cell and 2 in the second cell. WordPerfect needs to pick up a pattern from your numbers.

CHAPTER 17: CREATING A PERFECT TABLE

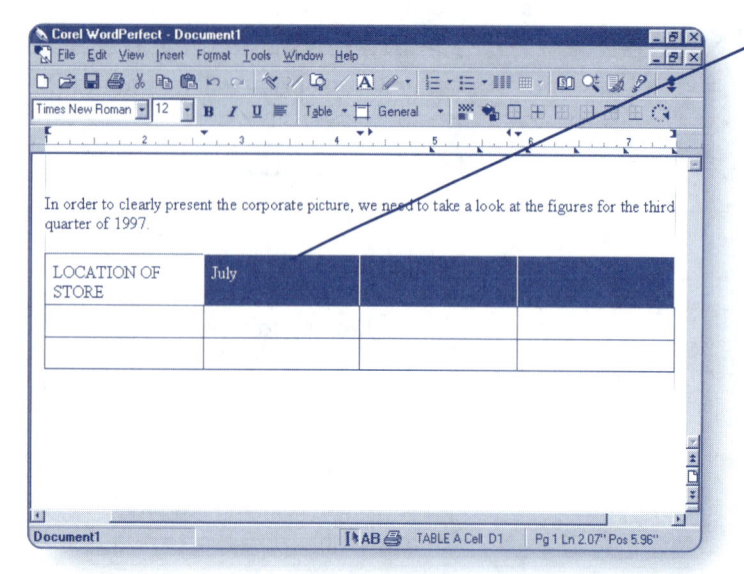

2. Select the **cell or cells** that contain the beginning value and the cells to contain the incrementing values. The cells will be highlighted.

> **TIP**
> To select cells, click at the beginning of the first cell, hold down the Shift key and press the Right Arrow key across (or down) to the ending cell. The cells will be black when they are selected.

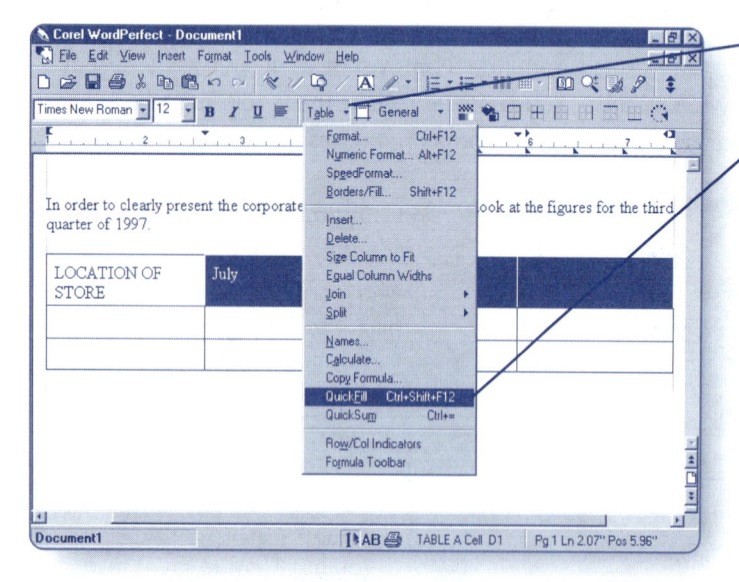

3. Click on the **Table button**. The table menu will appear.

4. Click on **QuickFill**. The cells will be filled in with the incrementing values.

CHANGING TABLE SIZE 183

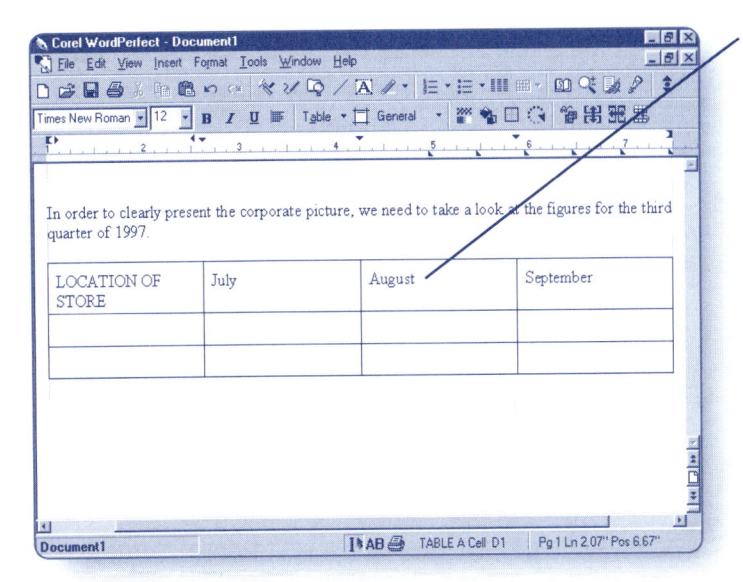

If you typed an abbreviation for the month or day, WordPerfect will use the corresponding abbreviations.

TIP

To deselect cells in a table, click anywhere in the table outside the selected area.

Changing Table Size

The size of your WordPerfect table can be easily modified. The method you'll use depends on where in the table you want the size modification to take place.

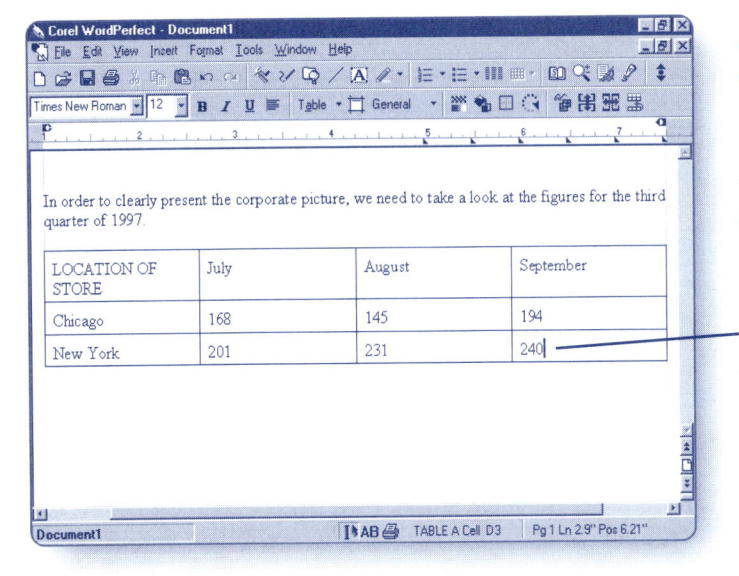

Adding a Row at the End of a Table

If you need additional rows when you reach the end of your table, WordPerfect can quickly add them for you.

1. Click the **mouse pointer** at the end of any text in the last cell of the table. The blinking insertion point will appear.

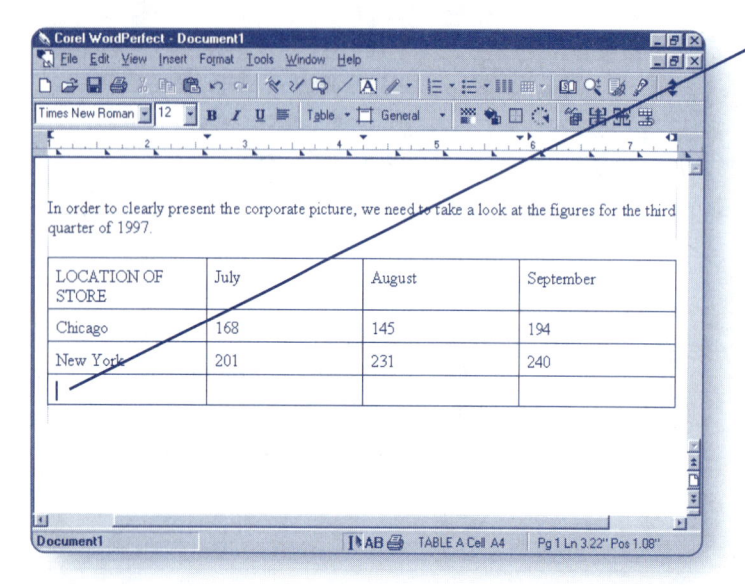

CHAPTER 17: CREATING A PERFECT TABLE

2. Press the **Tab key**. A new row will be added to the end of the table.

3. Repeat steps 1 and **2** for as many additional rows as needed.

Inserting a Row Elsewhere in a Table

Adding a row at the beginning or in the middle of a table is just as simple as adding one at the end of a table.

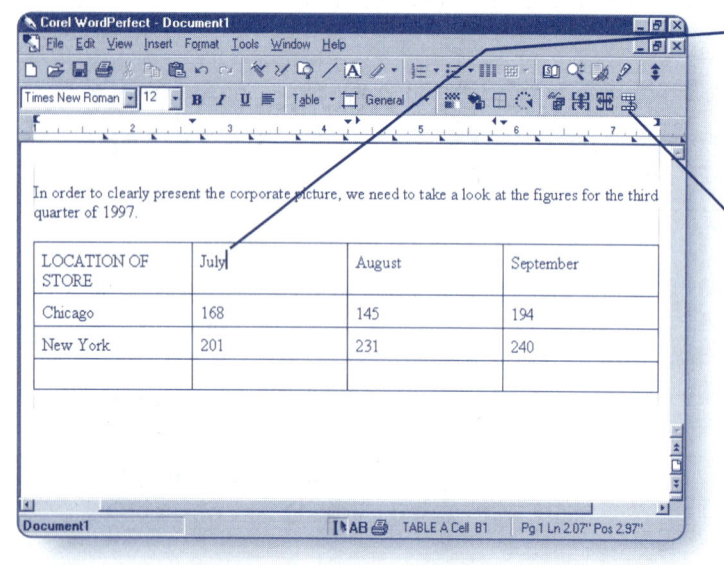

1. Click the **mouse pointer** in any cell where you want the new row to appear. The blinking insertion point will appear.

2. Click on the **Insert Row button**. A new row will be inserted above the current one.

CHANGING TABLE SIZE   185

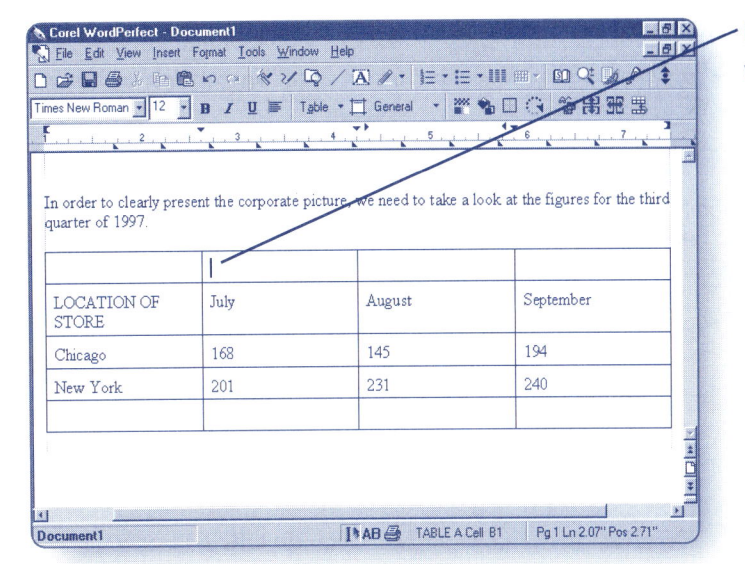

Notice how the existing rows were moved down in the table.

Adding a Column to a Table

A column can be inserted anywhere in the table.

1. Click the **mouse pointer** in the column where the new column is to be placed. The blinking insertion point will appear.

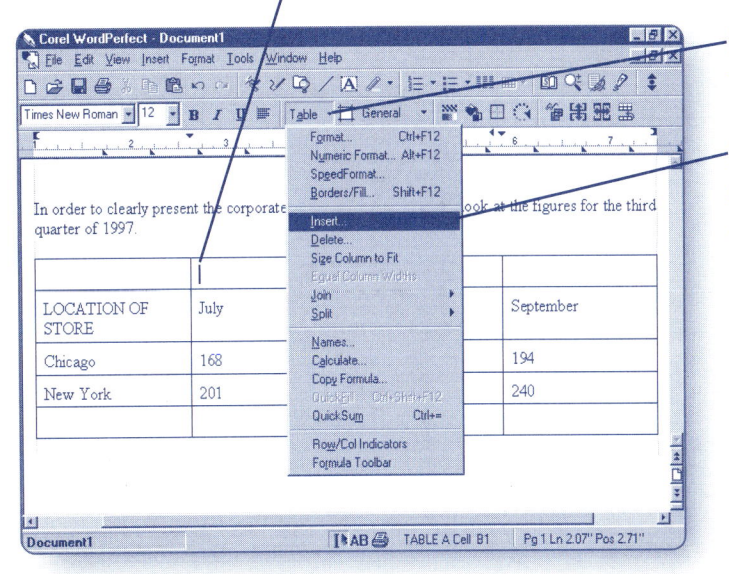

2. Click on the **Table button**. The Table menu will appear.

3. Click on **Insert**. The Insert Columns/Rows dialog box will open.

CHAPTER 17: CREATING A PERFECT TABLE

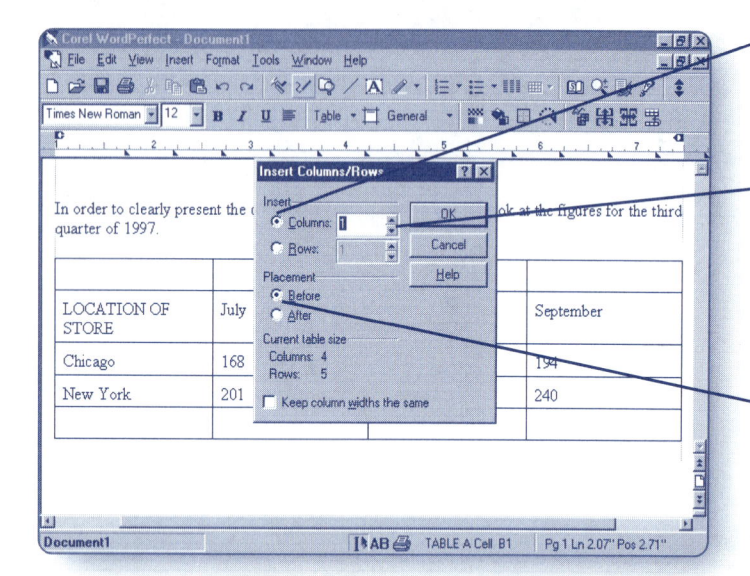

4. Click on **Columns** in the Insert area. The option will be selected.

5. Click the **up/down arrow** (♦) until the box reads the number of columns you want to insert. The number of columns will be displayed.

6. Click on **Before** in the Placement area. The option will be selected.

7. Click on **OK**. The new columns will be inserted into the table.

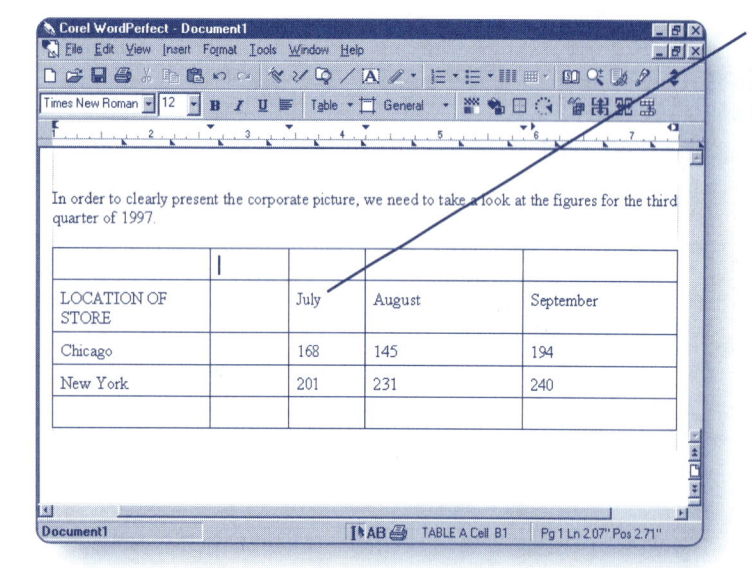

Notice how the column you had your insertion point in has been moved to the right.

Deleting a Row or Column

Unwanted rows or columns can be deleted quickly.

1. Click the **mouse pointer** in the row or column you want to delete. The blinking insertion point will appear.

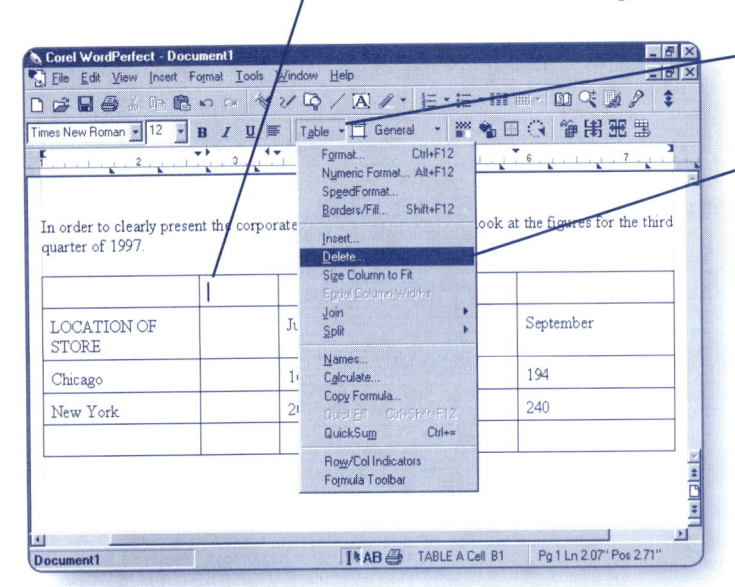

2. Click on the **Table button**. The Table menu will appear.

3. Click on **Delete**. The Delete Structure/Contents dialog box will open.

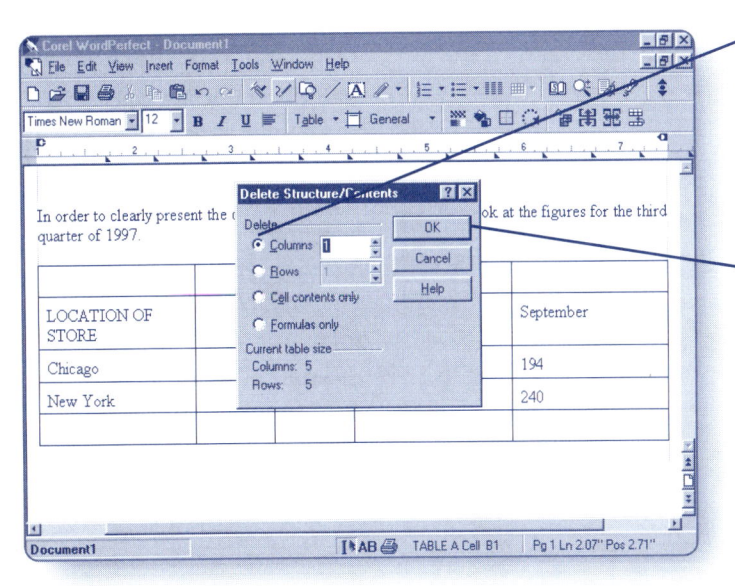

4. Click on **Rows** or **Columns** in the Delete area, depending on whether you want to delete a row or a column. The option will be selected.

5. Click on **OK**. The dialog box will close, the unwanted row or column will be deleted, and existing rows or columns will be pulled up or over.

Importing a Spreadsheet

If you have already created a spreadsheet in another program such as Corel Quattro Pro, Lotus 1-2-3, or Microsoft Excel, you can insert it into a WordPerfect document.

1. Click the **mouse pointer** where you want the spreadsheet to appear. The blinking insertion point will appear.

2. Click on **Insert**. The Insert menu will appear.

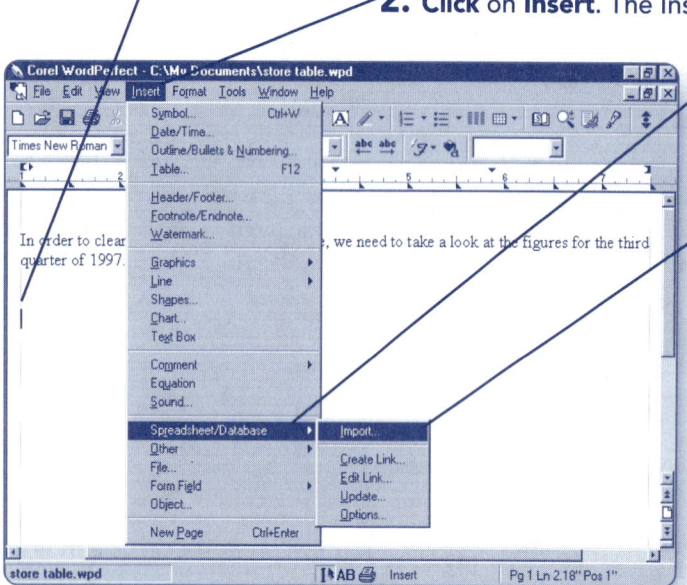

3. Click on **Spreadsheet/Database**. A cascading menu will appear.

4. Click on **Import**. The Import Data dialog box will open.

TIP

If you choose Create Link instead of Import, the spreadsheet will be linked to the WordPerfect document. This means that if you update the original spreadsheet, WordPerfect will update the copy in your document the next time you open it. If you Import only, the WordPerfect document does not get updated if the original spreadsheet changes.

IMPORTING A SPREADSHEET 189

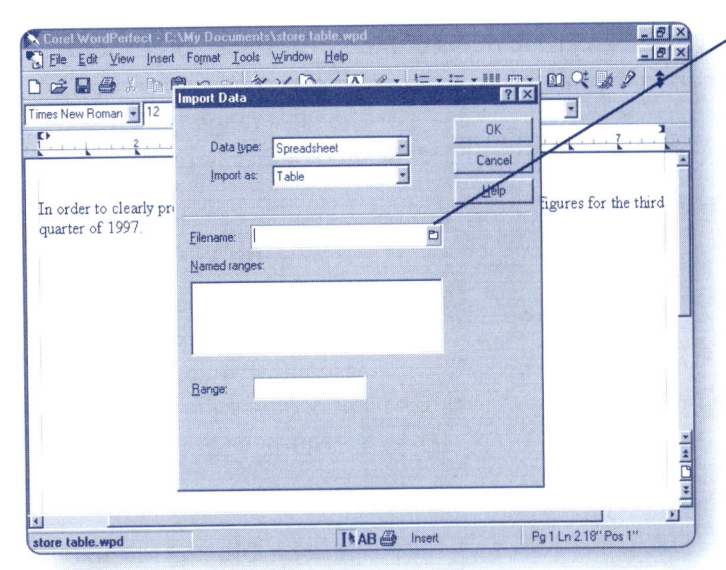

5. Click on the **lookup box** in the Filename: text box. The Select Data Filename dialog box will open.

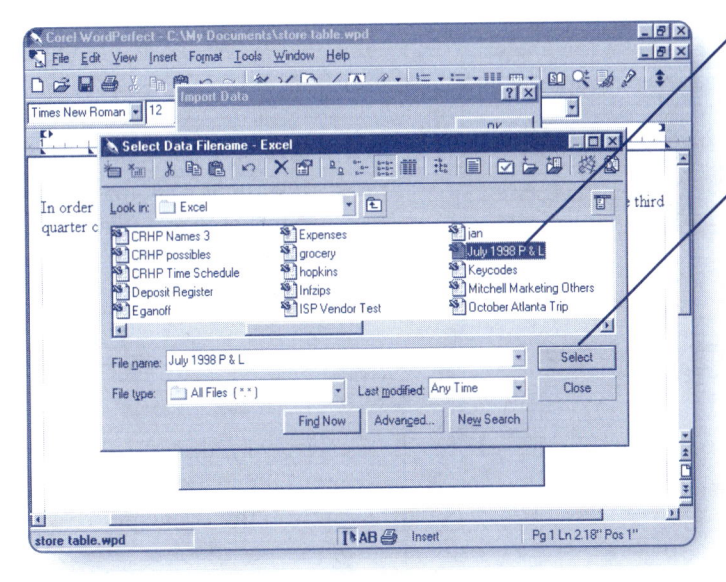

6. Click on the **filename** of your spreadsheet. The filename will be highlighted.

7. Click on **Select**. The dialog box will close, and the filename will be inserted into the Import Data dialog box.

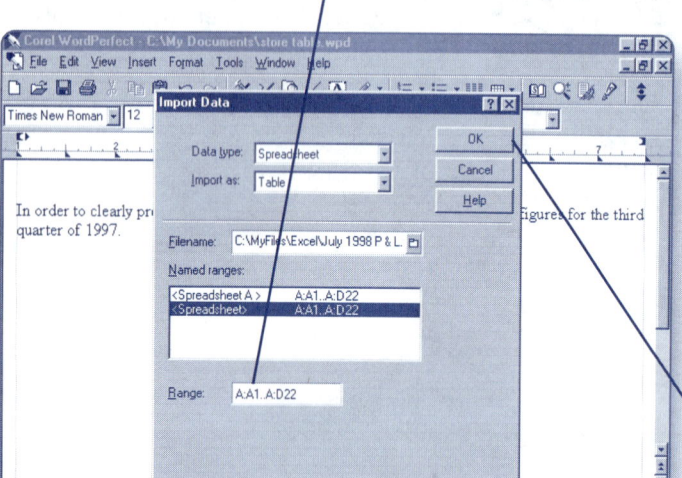

CHAPTER 17: CREATING A PERFECT TABLE

8. Type the **cell locations** of the spreadsheet you want to import in the Range: box. Either type a range such as B5:C16 or choose a range from the Named ranges: area.

NOTE

If you do not specify a range area, WordPerfect assumes that you want to import the entire spreadsheet.

9. Click on **OK.** The dialog box will close.

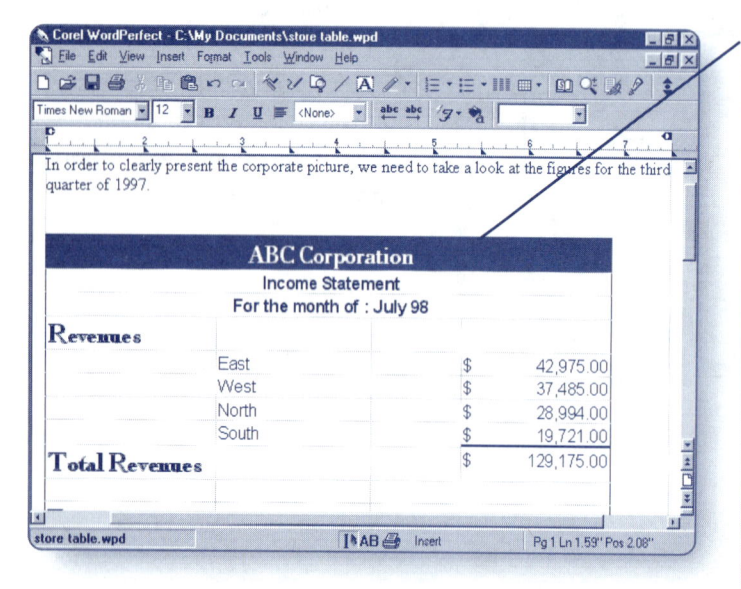

The spreadsheet will be inserted in your document as a WordPerfect table including any formatting applied in the spreadsheet.

NOTE

Occasionally, the formatting changes slightly in the conversion from spreadsheet to WordPerfect table. You will still be able to modify it in WordPerfect if that happens.

18

Formatting a Table

The appearance of a WordPerfect table can be changed. You can quickly change the way a table looks by applying a style to the whole table, or you can also change the look of specific parts of the table, such as a border or certain cells. In this chapter, you'll learn how to:

- Format with SpeedFormat
- Change column width in a table
- Change lines in a table
- Format and align numbers in a table
- Join cells for a table heading

CHAPTER 18: FORMATTING A TABLE

Formatting with SpeedFormat

WordPerfect's SpeedFormat feature gives you 40 different formats to choose from to save you time. Using SpeedFormat is the fastest way to make your table look wonderful!

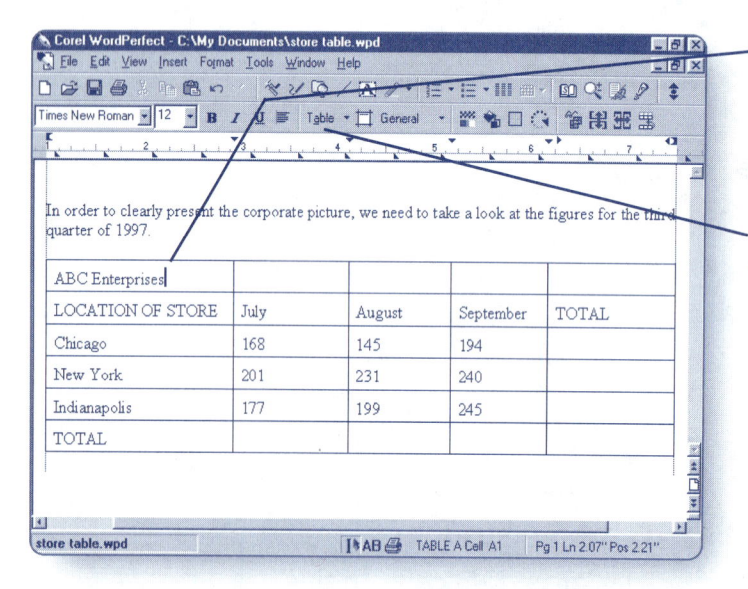

1. Click the **mouse pointer** anywhere in the table. The blinking insertion point will appear.

2. Click on the **Table button**. The Table menu will appear.

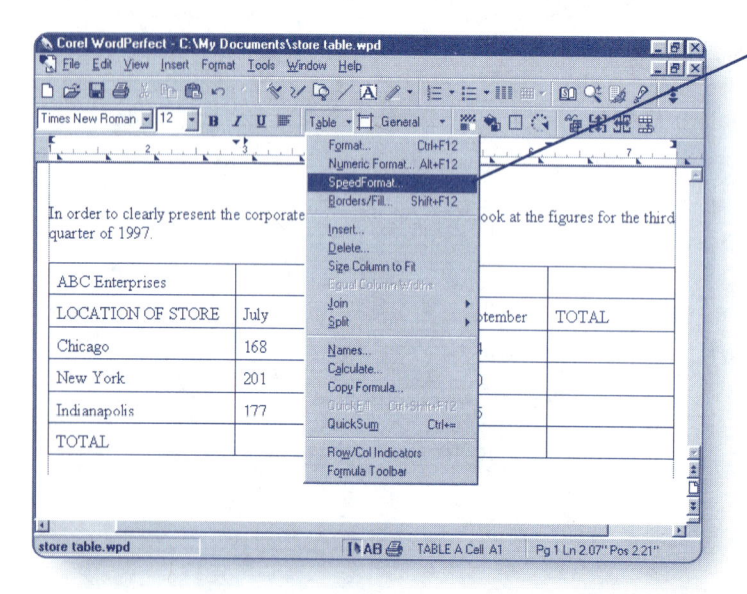

3. Click on **SpeedFormat**. The Table SpeedFormat dialog box will open.

FORMATTING WITH SPEEDFORMAT   193

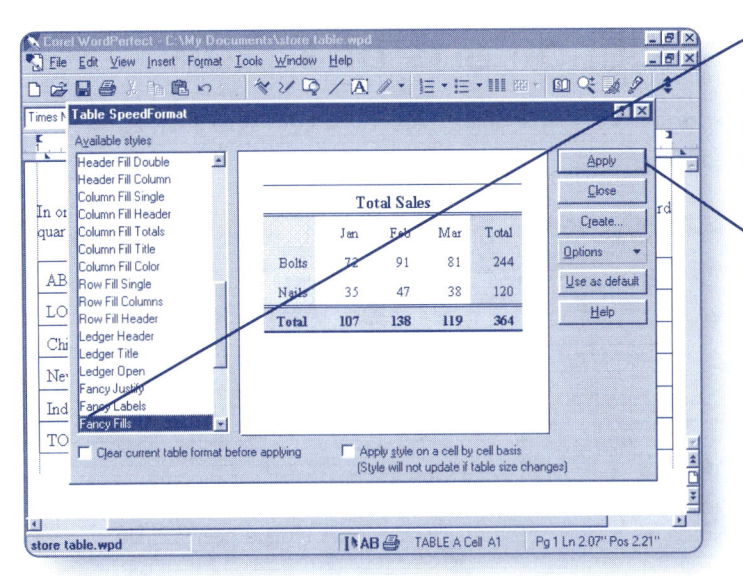

4. Click on one of the **Available styles**. You can see a sample representation in the Preview box.

5. Click on **Apply**. The dialog box will close.

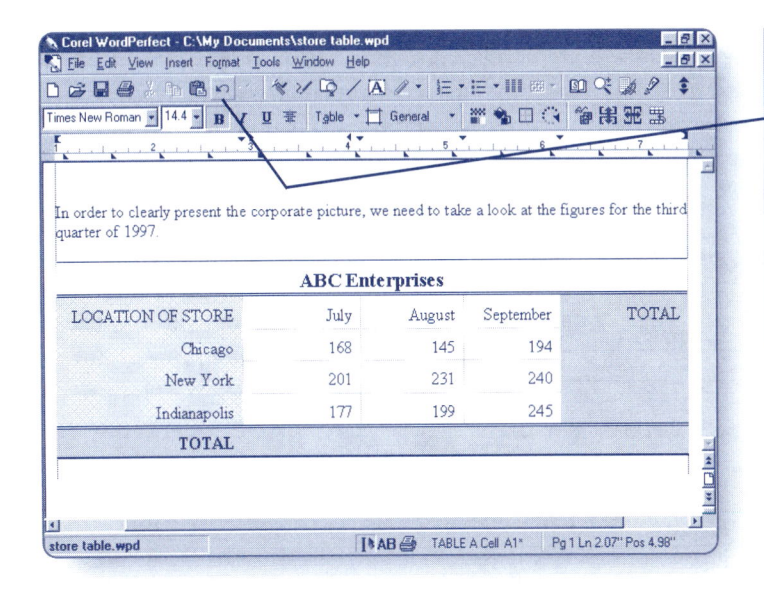

NOTE

So that you will have a plain table to practice on for the rest of this chapter, click on the Undo button to undo the SpeedFormat.

Selecting Parts of a Table

To modify parts of a table, select the cells you want to change.

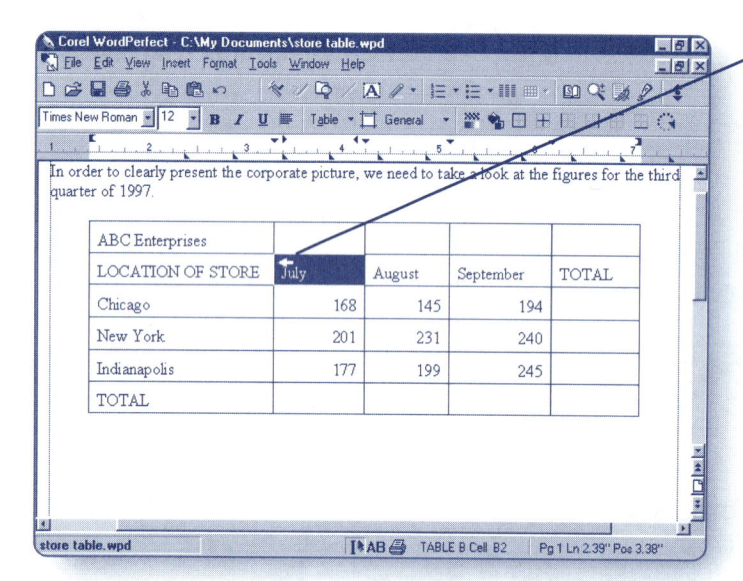

1. Position the **mouse pointer** in a cell near the top or left edge. The mouse pointer will turn into a cell selection arrow—a white arrow pointing up or to the left.

2. Click the **mouse button** once. A single cell will be selected, and the cell will turn dark.

TIP

To deselect a cell, click the mouse pointer in any other cell.

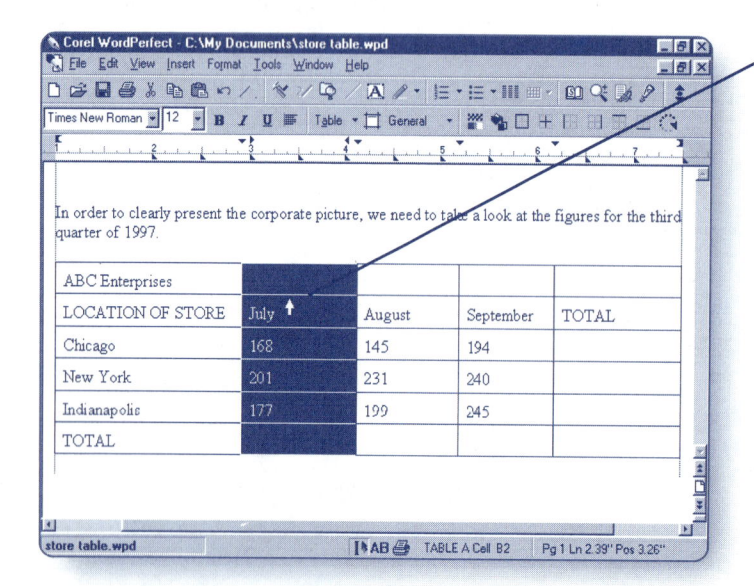

3. With the **cell selection arrow** pointing up, **double-click** the **mouse**. The entire column will be highlighted.

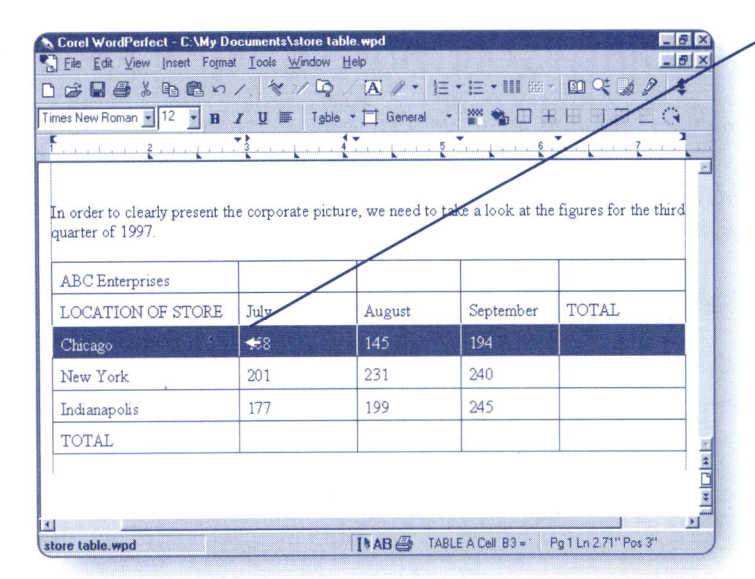

SELECTING PARTS OF A TABLE

4. With the **cell selection arrow** pointing to the left, **double-click** the **mouse**. The entire row will be highlighted.

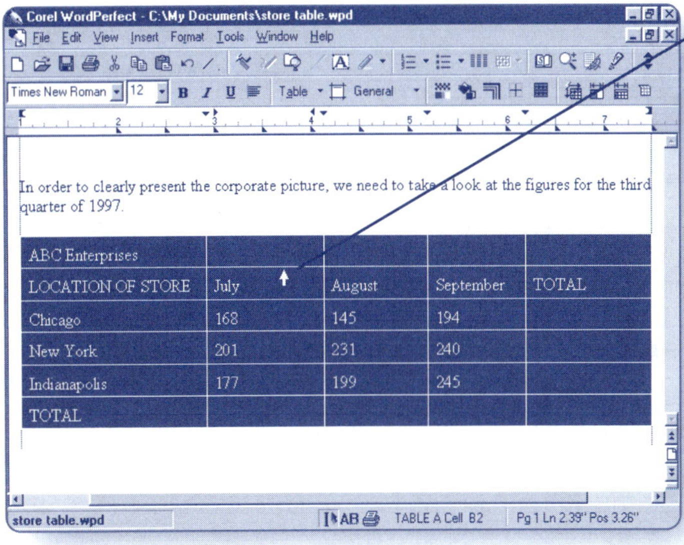

5. With the **cell selection arrow** pointing up or to the left, **triple-click** the **mouse**. The entire table will be highlighted.

NOTE

When a cell or row or column has been selected, you can continue to drag across other cells, rows, or columns to select additional ones.

CHAPTER 18: FORMATTING A TABLE

Changing Column Width

By default, all columns are equally spaced, and the table expands across the entire width of the document. You can change a column to any width you want, but first you must tell WordPerfect not to expand the table to fill the width of the document.

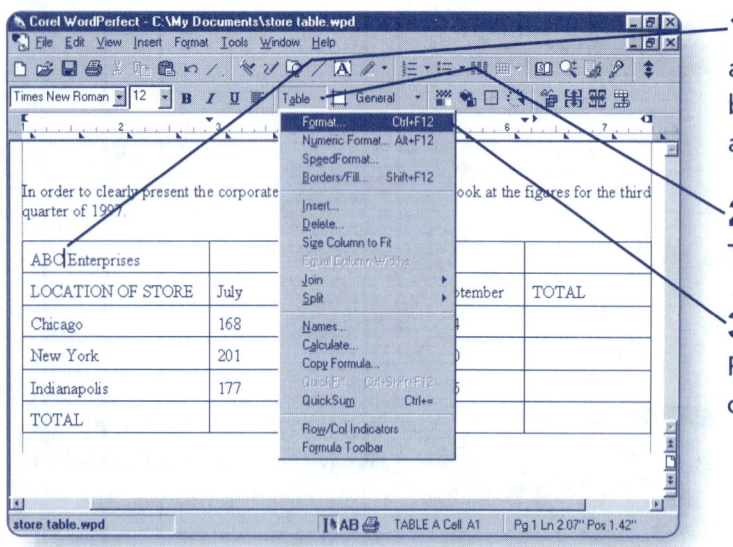

1. Click the **mouse pointer** anywhere in the table. The blinking insertion point will appear.

2. Click on the **Table button**. The Table menu will appear.

3. Click on **Format**. The Properties for Table Format dialog box will open.

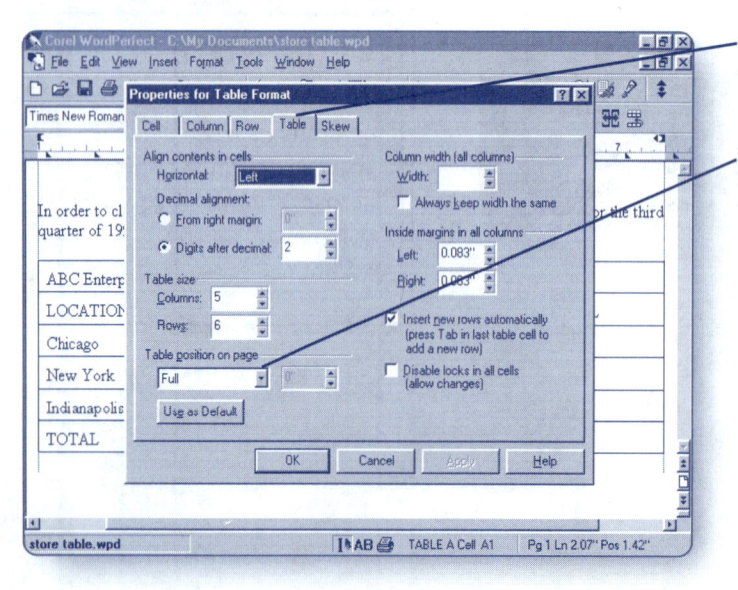

4. Click on the **Table tab**. The tab will come to the front.

5. Click on **Table position on page**. A list of available choices will appear.

CHANGING COLUMN WIDTH 197

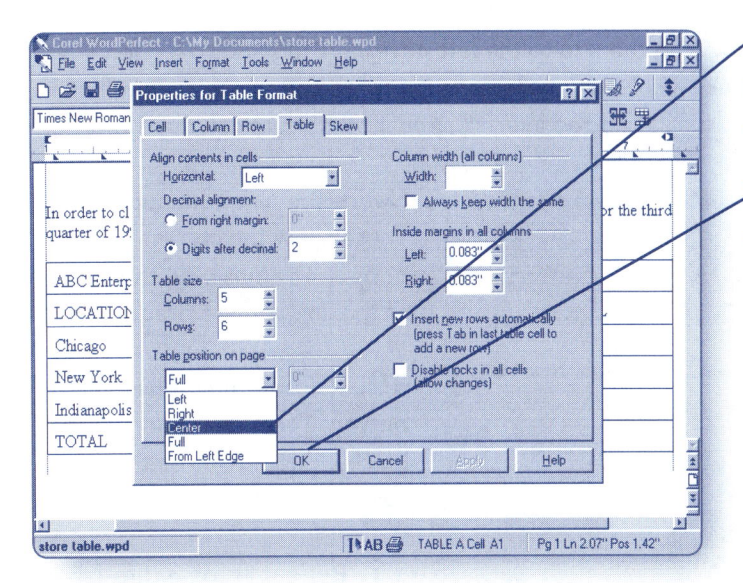

6. Click an alignment **option**: Left, Center, Right, or Full. The option will be selected.

7. Click on **OK**. The dialog box will close.

8. Position the **mouse pointer** on the line to the right of the column you want to change. The mouse pointer will turn into a black cross with two small arrowheads on it.

9. Drag the **line** to the **left or right**. Dragging to the left will make a column smaller, whereas dragging to the right will make it wider. A dotted line will appear to indicate column width.

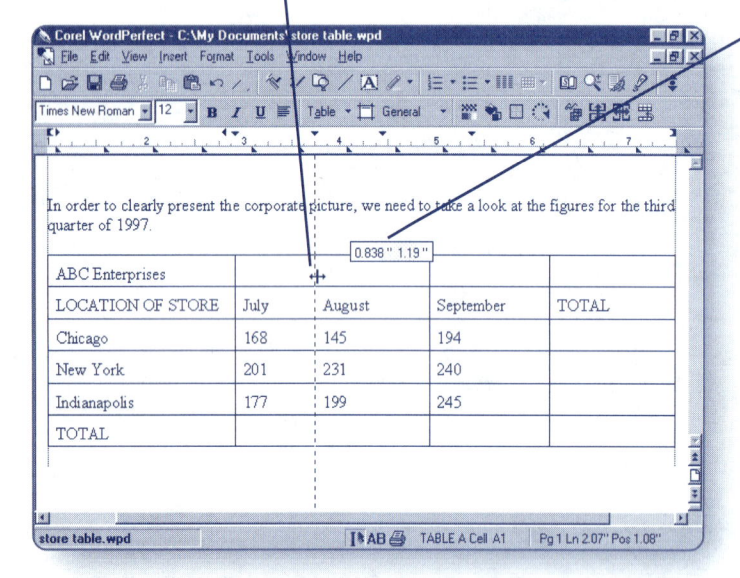

Notice the numbers appearing. These show the column widths of both columns on either side of the line you are dragging.

10. Release the **mouse button**. The entire column will be changed as well as the column next to it.

11. Repeat steps 8 through **10** for all columns you want to change. The column widths will be modified.

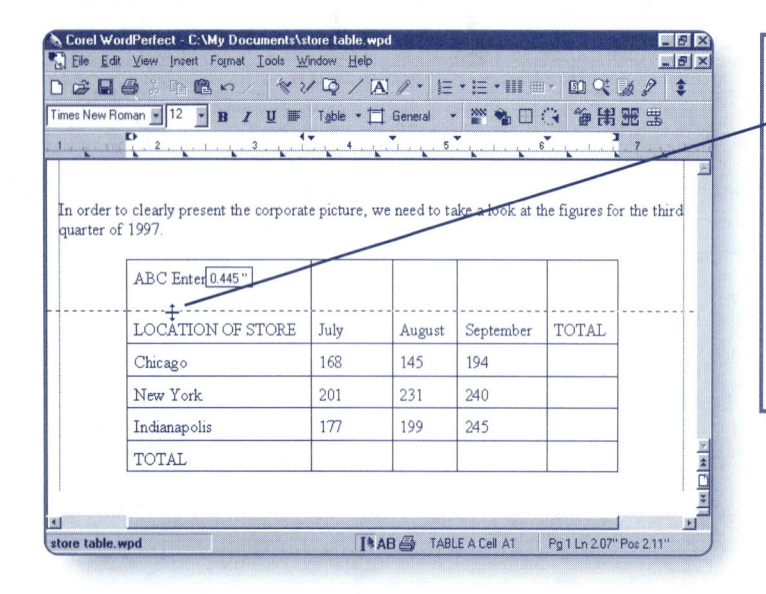

TIP

Row Height can be modified the same way by positioning the mouse pointer on the line below the row to be modified and following steps 8 and 9 except to drag the line up or down.

CHANGING BORDERS 199

Changing Borders

The default choice is to have a single-line border around each cell of a table.

1. Select the **cells** you want to modify. The property bar will change, giving you several choices of lines to modify.

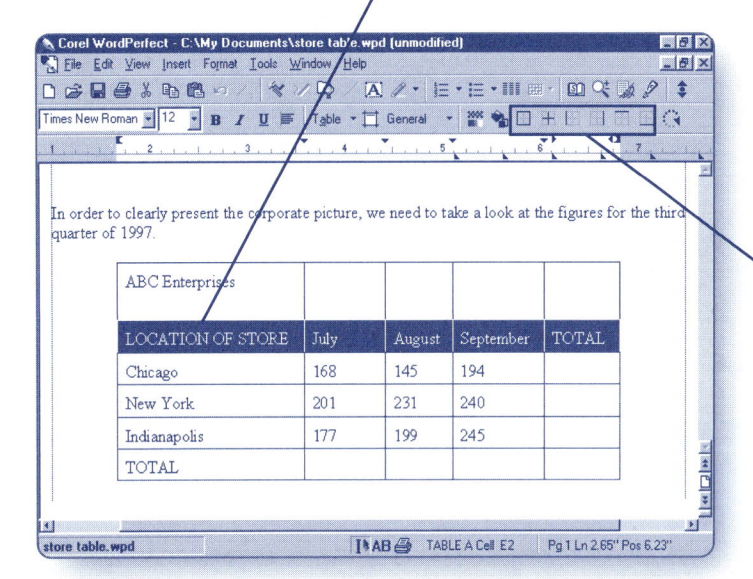

You can modify the outside lines of your selection, or you can modify the inside lines. You can even modify the left, right, top, or bottom lines only.

2. Click on the **line button** for the line you want to modify. For example, click on the Outside Lines button. A menu will appear with different line styles to choose from.

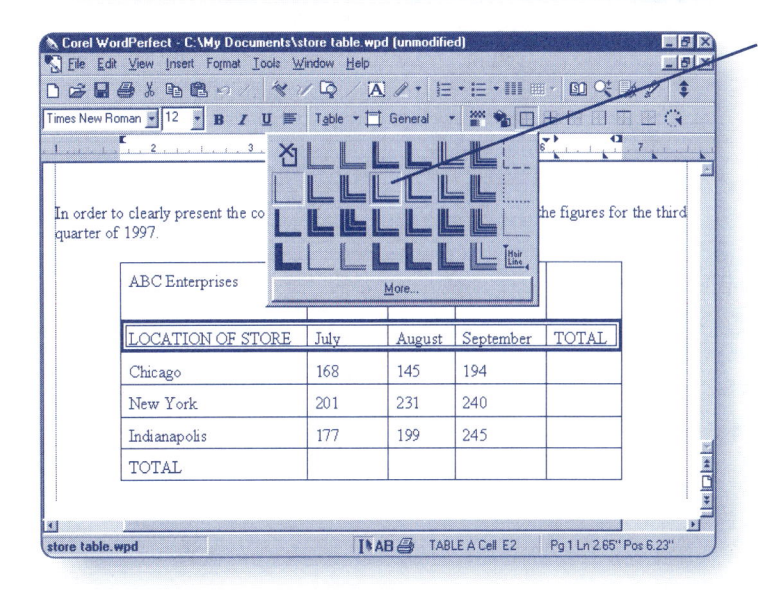

3. Click on the **style of line** best suited for your selection. The new line style will be applied to your selection.

Formatting Numbers

You have the option of changing the format of any numbers you enter in your table.

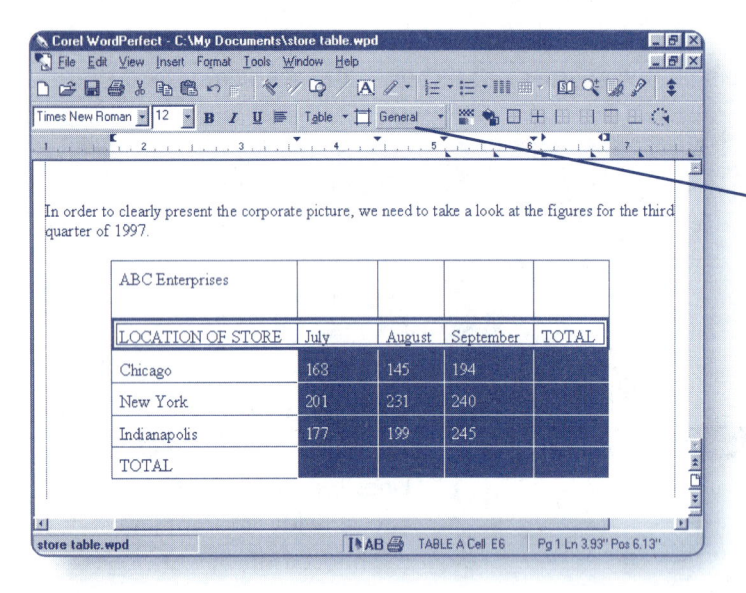

1. Select the **cells** you want to modify. The cells will be highlighted.

2. Click on **General**. A list of available formats will appear.

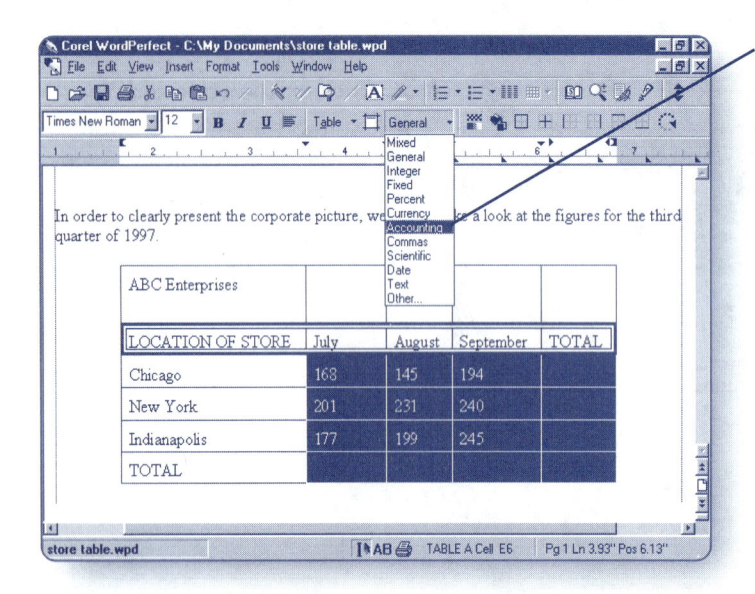

3. Choose a **number style**. The format you select will be applied to the highlighted cells.

Changing Cell Alignment

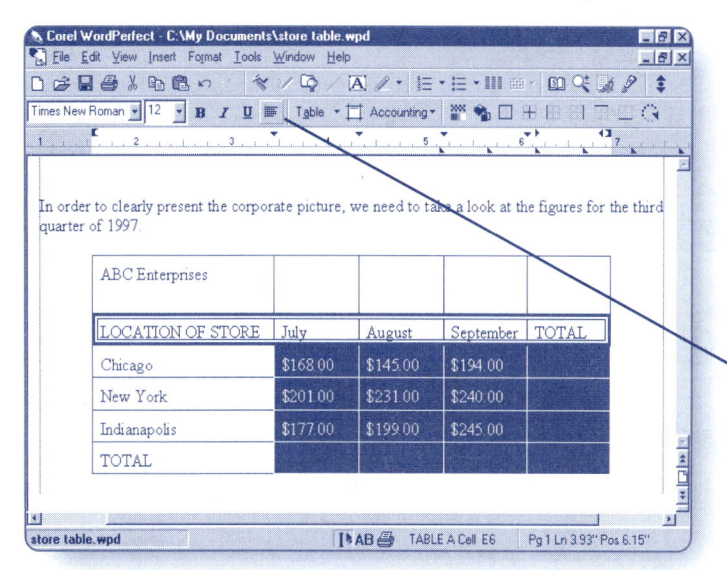

Traditionally, numbers are aligned on the right side of a cell, whereas text-filled cells are left aligned or centered.

1. Select the **cells** to be modified. The cells will be highlighted.

2. Click on the **Justification button**. The Justification menu will appear.

3. Choose an **alignment**: Left, Right, Center, Full, or All. The cell alignment will be changed.

202　CHAPTER 18: FORMATTING A TABLE

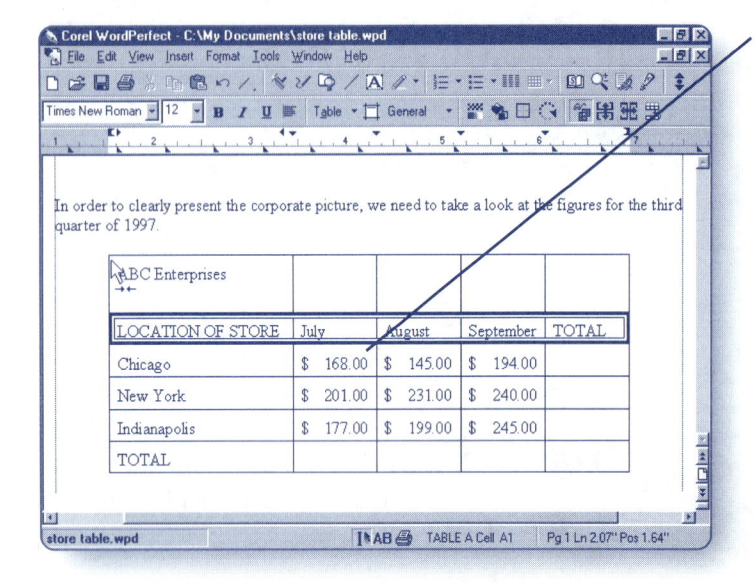

In this figure, the numeric cells were right aligned.

Joining Cells for a Table Heading

Any two or more cells can be joined together to form a larger cell.

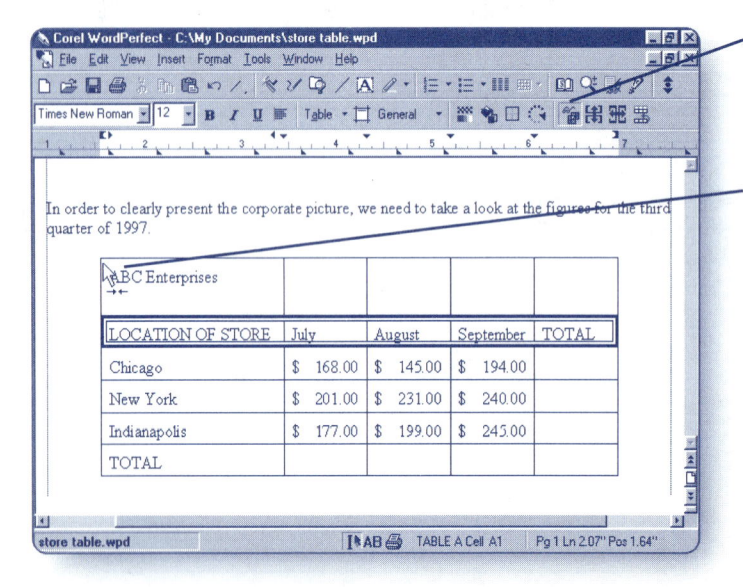

1. Click on the **QuickJoin button**. The feature will be activated.

The mouse pointer will display two small arrows at the bottom of it.

JOINING CELLS FOR A TABLE HEADING 203

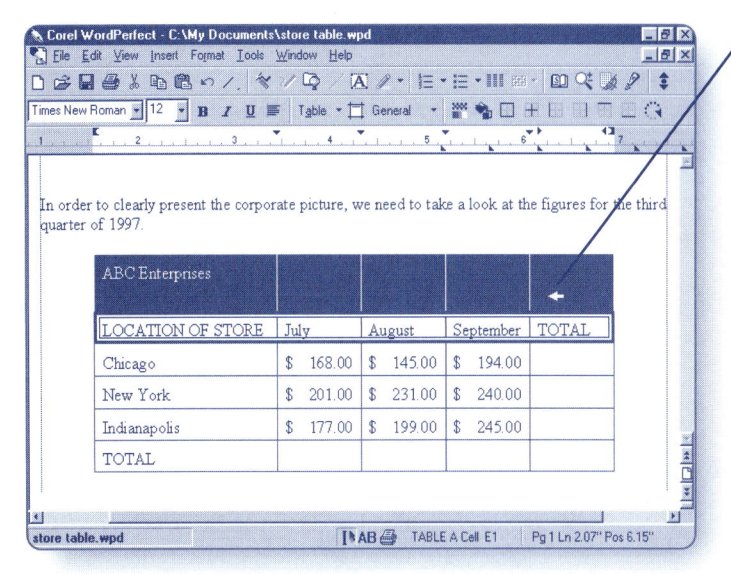

2. Drag the **mouse pointer** across the **cells to be joined**—for example, the top row of the table. The cells will be selected.

3. Release the **mouse button**. The cells will be joined together to form one large cell.

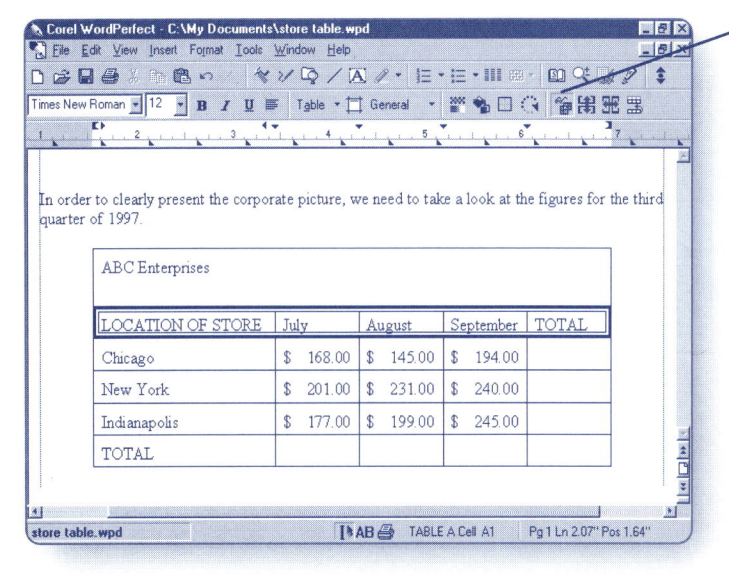

4. Click on the **QuickJoin button** again. The feature will be turned off.

19

Using Formulas in a Table

You can create different kinds of formulas in a WordPerfect table to do your math for you! A formula can do addition, subtraction, multiplication, and division as well as make logical decisions for you. In this chapter, you'll learn how to:

- Use QuickSum
- Add a column of numbers
- Create a simple formula
- Copy a formula

Using QuickSum

QuickSum is the fastest method to add a sequential column or row of numbers.

1. Click the **mouse pointer** in the cell where you want the mathematical answer. The blinking insertion point will appear.

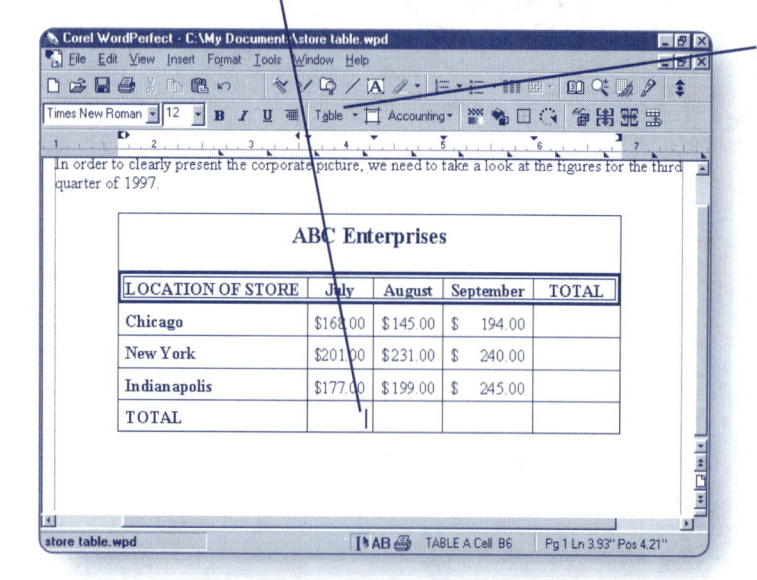

2. Click on the **Table button**. The Table menu will appear.

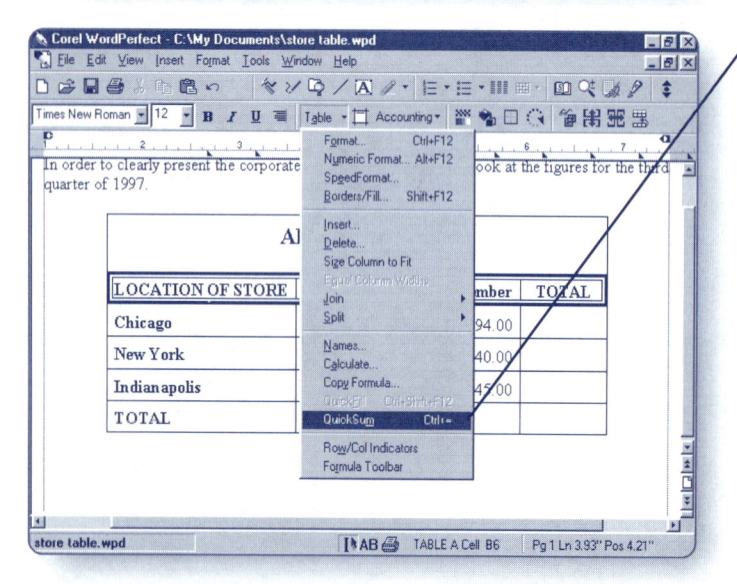

3. Click on **QuickSum**. The answer will appear in the empty cell.

ADDING A COLUMN OF NUMBERS   **207**

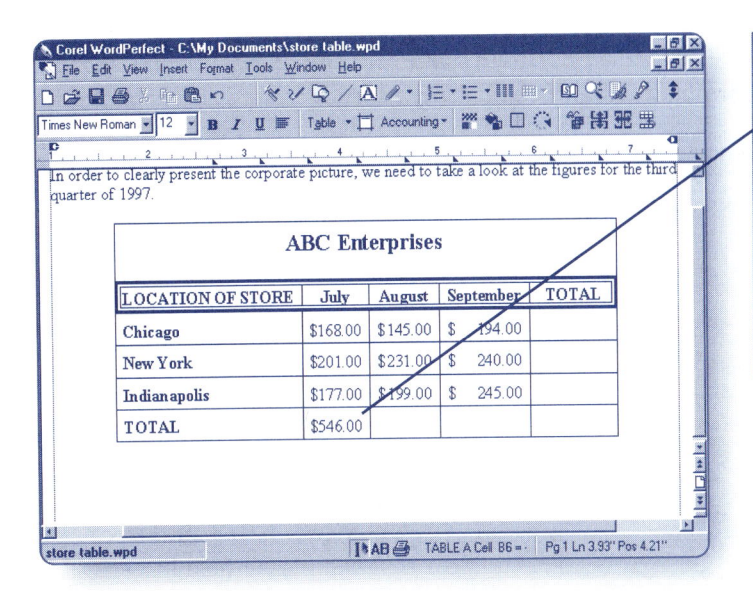

NOTE

QuickSum adds the numbers directly above the current cell. If no numbers are directly above it, QuickSum adds the numbers in the cells to the left of the current cell.

Adding a Column of Numbers

Occasionally, QuickSum cannot determine the cells you want to add. WordPerfect has a built-in function to assist you.

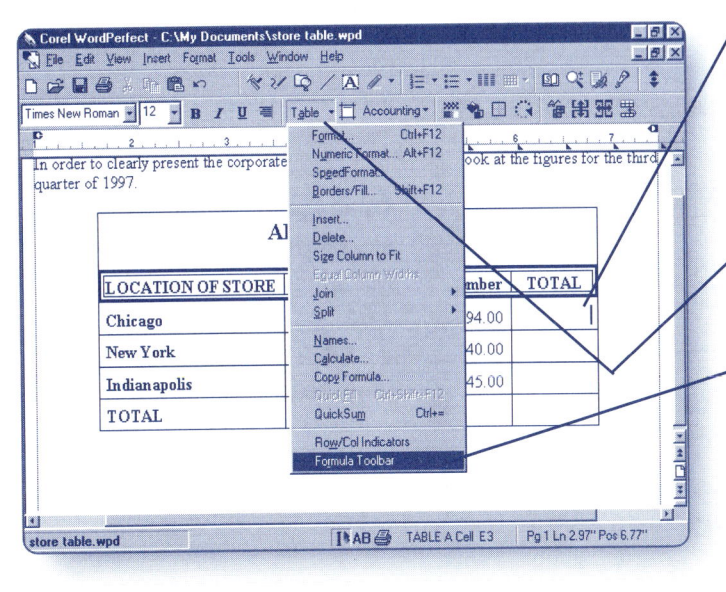

1. Click the **mouse pointer** in the cell where you want the mathematical answer. The blinking insertion point will appear.

2. Click on the **Table button**. The Table menu will appear.

3. Click on **Formula Toolbar**. The WordPerfect Formula toolbar will appear.

CHAPTER 19: USING FORMULAS IN A TABLE

4. Click in the **Formula box**—the long white box in the Formula toolbar. The blinking insertion point will appear.

5. Type the following **formula**: **+SUM(xx:XX)** where xx is the beginning cell address, and XX is the ending cell address.

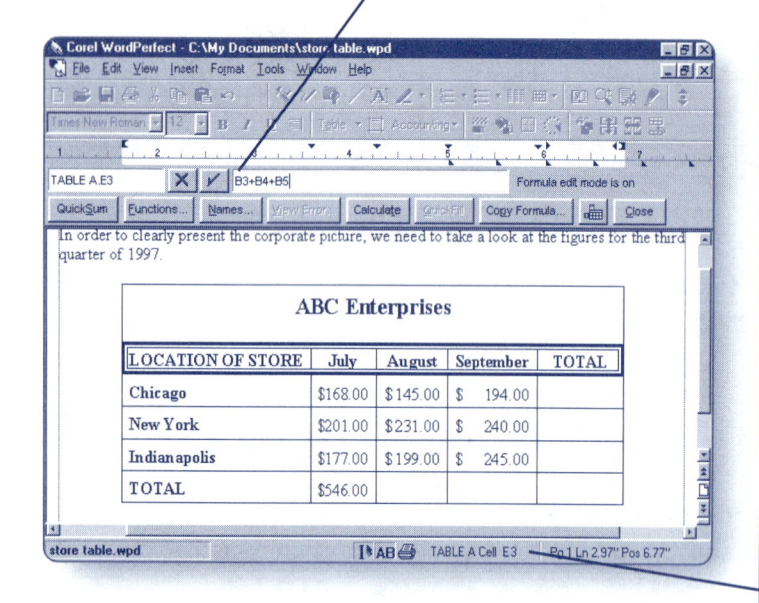

NOTE
WordPerfect tables use addresses just like spreadsheets. The columns are alphabetic: A, B, C, and so on, and the rows are numeric: 1, 2, 3, and so on. A sample formula for adding part of a column might be SUM(B2:B16).

TIP
If you are not sure of a cell's address, look in the status bar.

6. Press the **Enter key** to accept the formula. The answer will appear in the current cell.

7. Click on **Close**. The Formula toolbar will disappear.

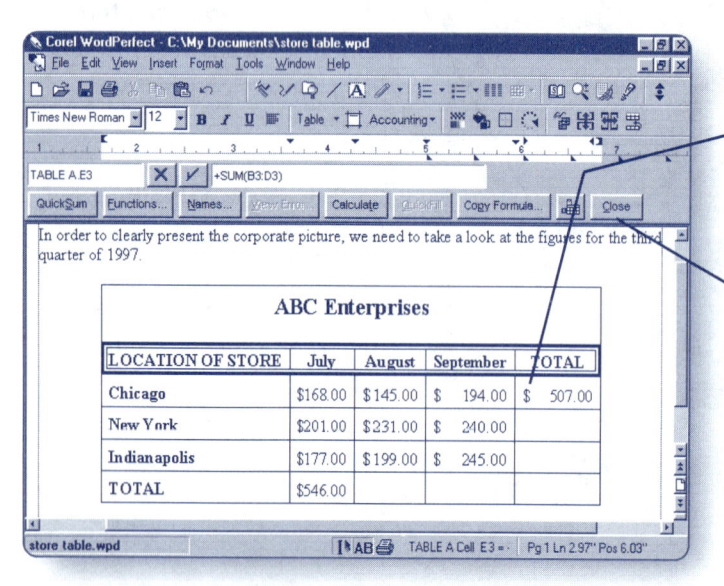

CREATING A SIMPLE FORMULA   209

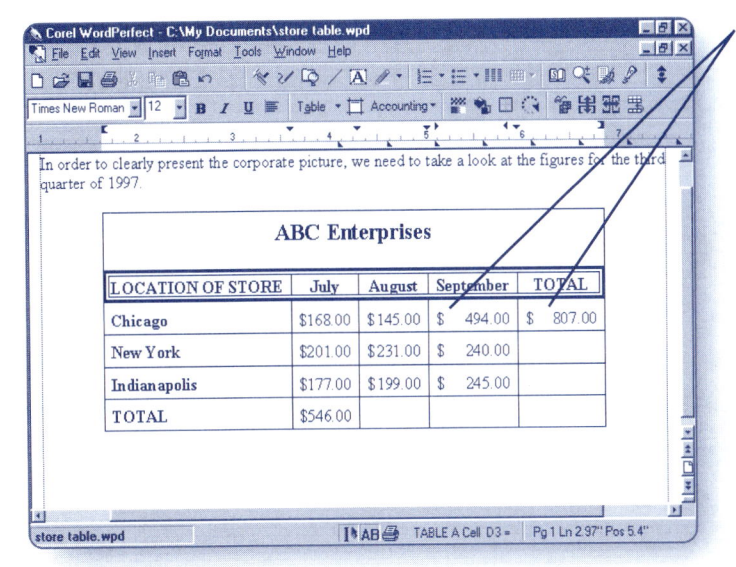

Like a spreadsheet, WordPerfect automatically recalculates a formula if the data changes.

Creating a Simple Formula

Not all formulas involve addition. You can also create formulas to do subtraction, multiplication, or division.

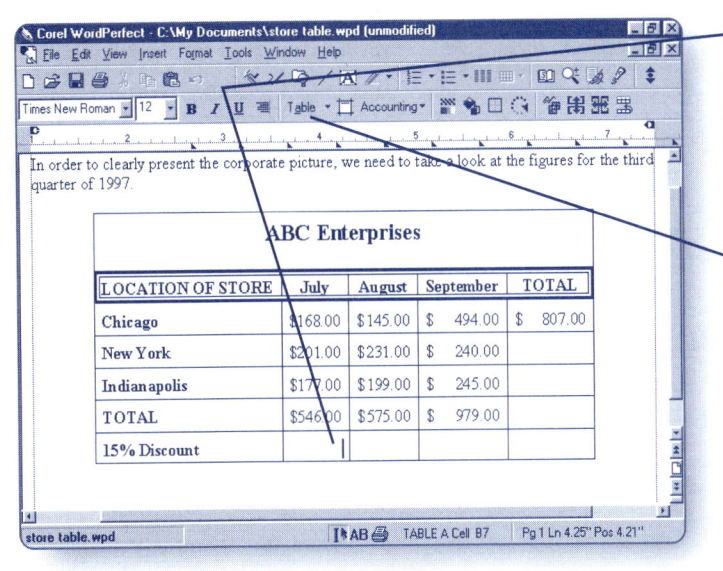

1. Click the **mouse pointer** in the cell where you want the mathematical answer. The blinking insertion point will appear.

2. Click on the **Table button**. The Table menu will appear.

CHAPTER 19: USING FORMULAS IN A TABLE

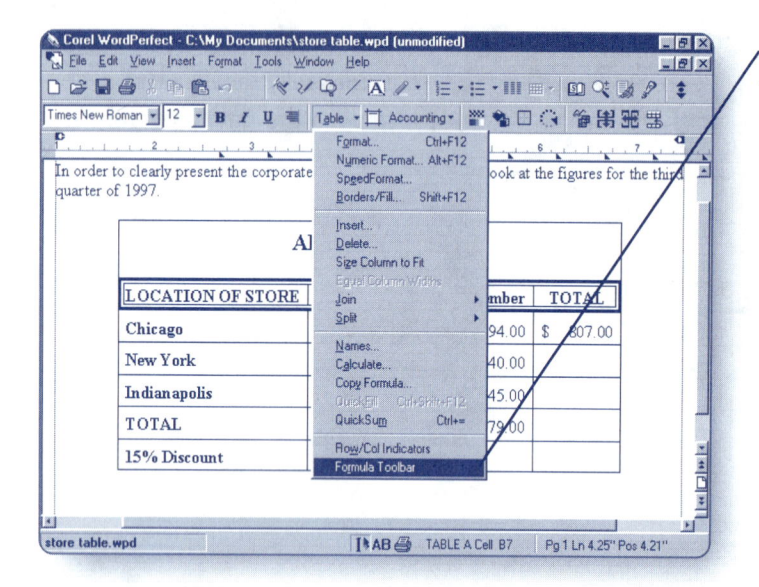

3. Click on **Formula Toolbar.** The Formula Toolbar will appear.

4. Click in the **Formula box.** The blinking insertion point will appear.

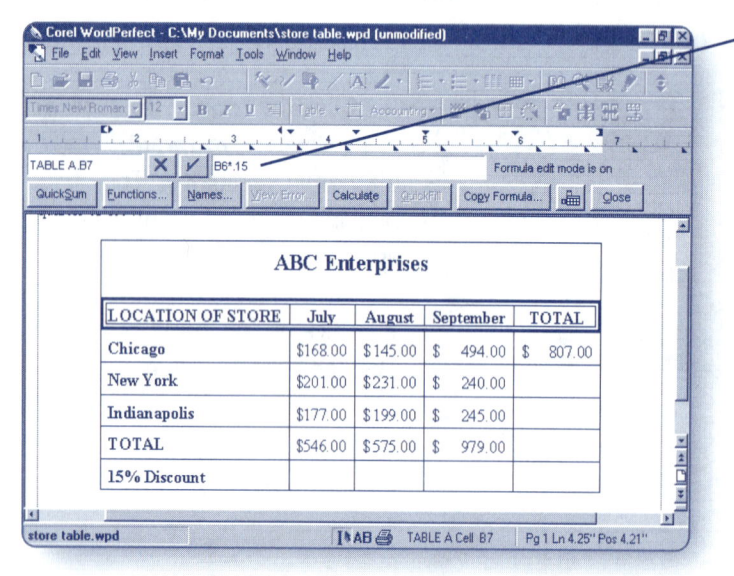

5. Type a formula using the table cells as references. Use the plus sign (+) for addition, the minus sign or hyphen character (-) for subtraction, the asterisk key (*) for multiplication, and the slash key (/) for division.

A sample formula might be A3*B5 or C2/C3 or even A3*B3-C3. Formulas can also include static numbers such as B6*.15.

CREATING A SIMPLE FORMULA

> **NOTE**
>
> For a compound formula such as the last sample listed in step 5, WordPerfect tables follow the rules of priorities from your old high school algebra class. This means that multiplication and division are done before addition and subtraction. Put portions of the formula you want calculated first into parentheses to give them priority in calculation sequence.

6. Press the **Enter key** to accept the formula. The answer will appear in the current cell.

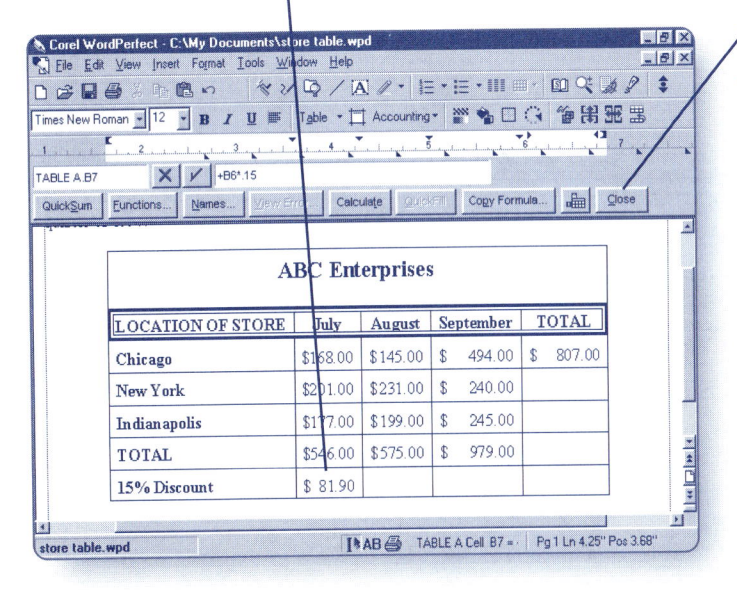

7. Click on **Close**. The Formula toolbar will disappear.

Copying a Formula

It is not necessary to type a formula more than once. Use the Copy Formula feature instead.

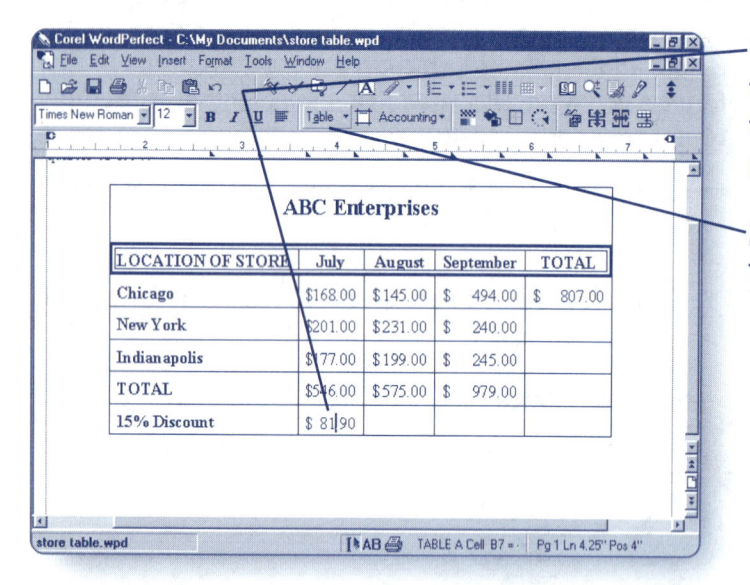

1. **Click** the **mouse pointer** in the cell that already has the formula. The blinking insertion point will appear.

2. **Click** on the **Table button**. The Table menu will appear.

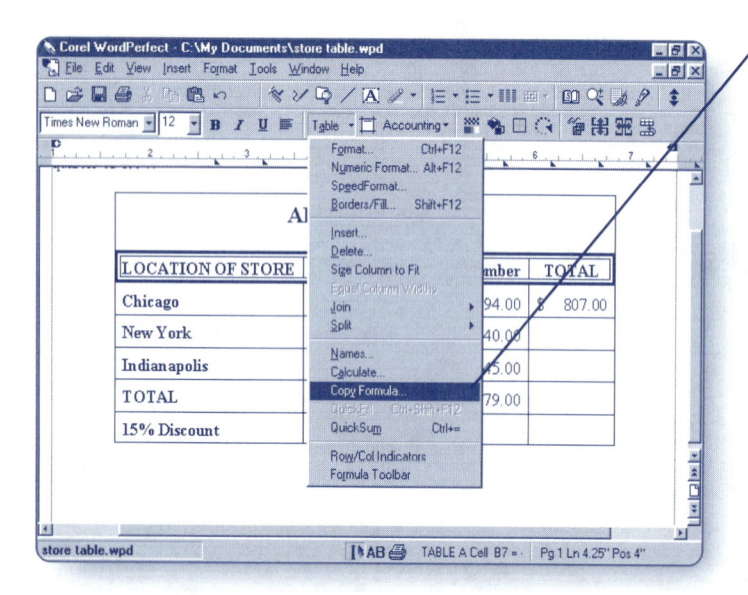

3. **Click** on **Copy Formula**. The Copy Formula dialog box will open.

COPYING A FORMULA 213

4. Click on a **destination**. In our sample figure, we need to copy the formula to the right two times.

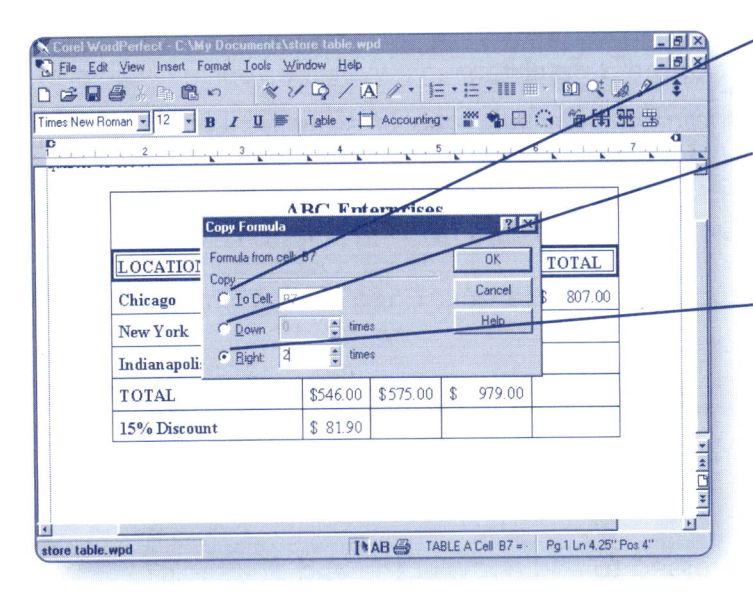

From here, you can copy the formula to a specific cell.

From here, you can copy a formula to the cells below the selected cell.

From here, you can copy a formula to the cells to the right of the selected cell.

5. Click on **OK**. The dialog box will close.

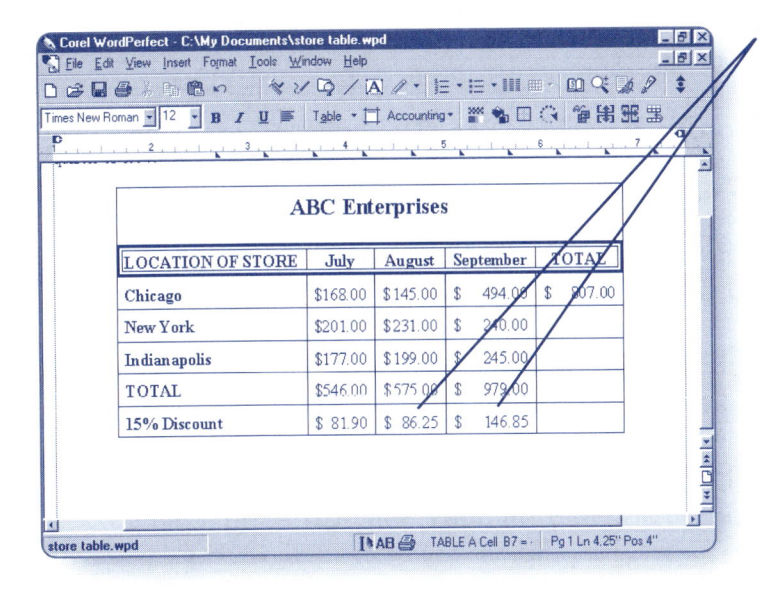

The formula will be duplicated, and the answers inserted in the desired cells.

Part III Review Questions

1. What is the alignment of the default tabs in a WordPerfect document? *See "Changing the Default Tabs" in Chapter 16*

2. What icon does the mouse pointer turn into as you are removing a tab from the ruler? *See "Deleting a Tab Stop" in Chapter 16*

3. What button on the toolbar creates a table? *See "Using Table QuickCreate" in Chapter 17*

4. What feature can be used to continue a pattern of values across a row or down a column? *See "Saving Time with QuickFill" in Chapter 17*

5. What key should be pressed to add a row at the end of a table? *See "Adding a Row at the End of a Table" in Chapter 17*

6. How do you deselect a cell in a table? *See "Selecting Parts of a Table" in Chapter 18*

7. What is the default border in a table? *See "Changing Borders" in Chapter 18*

8. What is the fastest method to add a sequential column of numbers? *See "Using QuickSum" in Chapter 19*

9. What key is used to designate multiplication in a formula? *See "Creating a Simple Formula" in Chapter 19*

10. When creating a compound formula, what math functions are calculated before addition and subtraction? *See "Creating a Simple Formula" in Chapter 19*

PART IV

Using Mail Merge

Chapter 20
    Creating an Address List............**217**

Chapter 21
    Creating a Form Letter.............**235**

Chapter 22
    Merging an Address List
    and Form Letter **241**

20

Creating an Address List

You know the letter you get from the celebrity telling you that you have won TEN MILLION DOLLARS! (Okay, in teeny tiny print it says you "may" have won ten million dollars.) It has your name printed in big letters right there on the certificate!

Those letters are created using a feature called Mail Merge. Mail Merge consists of three parts: a list of names and addresses, called a *data file*; the generic letter, called the *form file*; and the actual merged letter, made up of parts one and two. We will start with part one of this process. In this chapter, you'll learn how to:

- Create a data file
- Name data fields
- Use Quick Data Entry
- Edit a data file
- Change a data field name

CHAPTER 20: CREATING AN ADDRESS LIST

Creating a Data File

The data file is where your addresses and other variable information will be stored. You need to begin the merge process with a blank document on the screen.

1. Click on **Tools**. The Tools menu will appear.

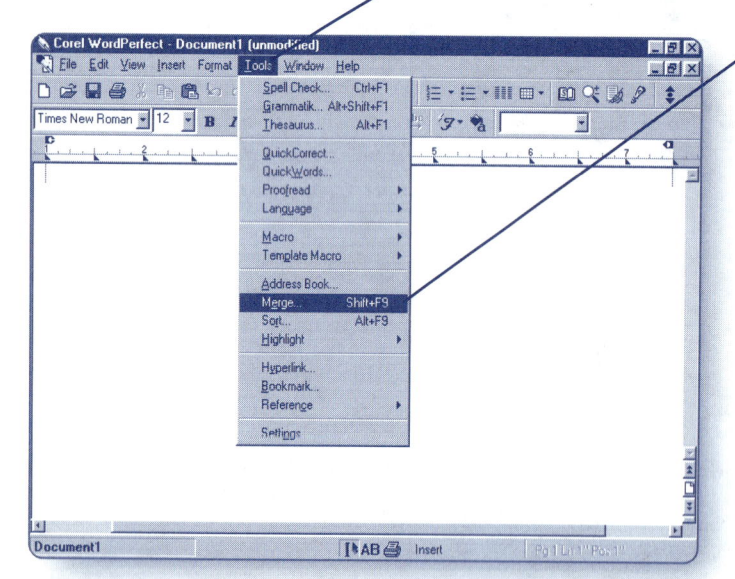

2. Click on **Merge**. The Merge dialog box will open.

From this dialog box, you can create either of the two parts to a mail merge or even complete the process by combining the two together to create the finished letter.

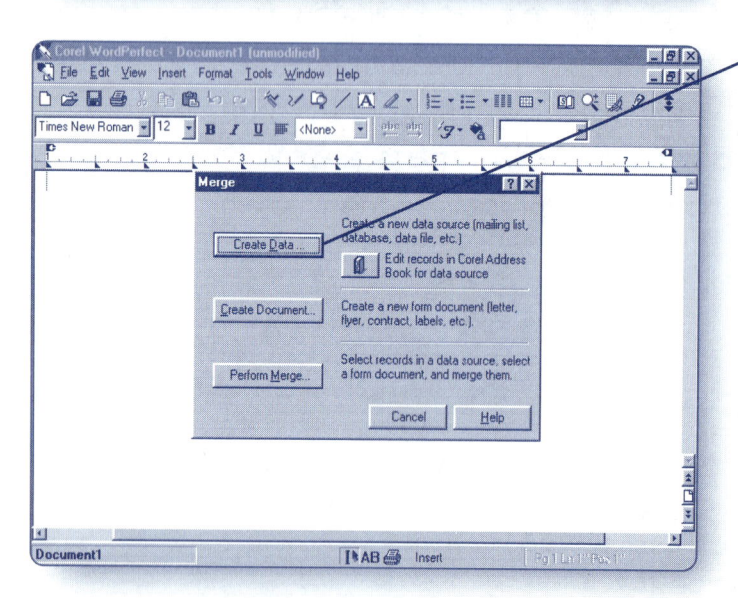

3. Click on **Create Data**. The Create Data File dialog box will open.

Naming Data Fields

Fields and records are two of the common terms used with merge data files. A *field* is an individual piece of information about someone, such as zip code or first name. A *record* is the complete picture of information about someone with all the fields put together.

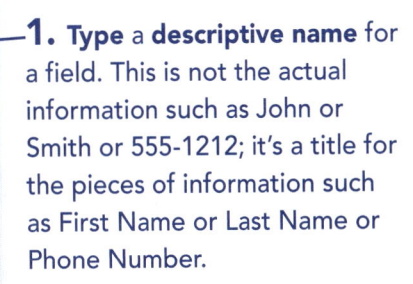

1. Type a **descriptive name** for a field. This is not the actual information such as John or Smith or 555-1212; it's a title for the pieces of information such as First Name or Last Name or Phone Number.

2. Click on **Add**. The field name will be added to the Fields used in merge: box, and you are ready to add another field.

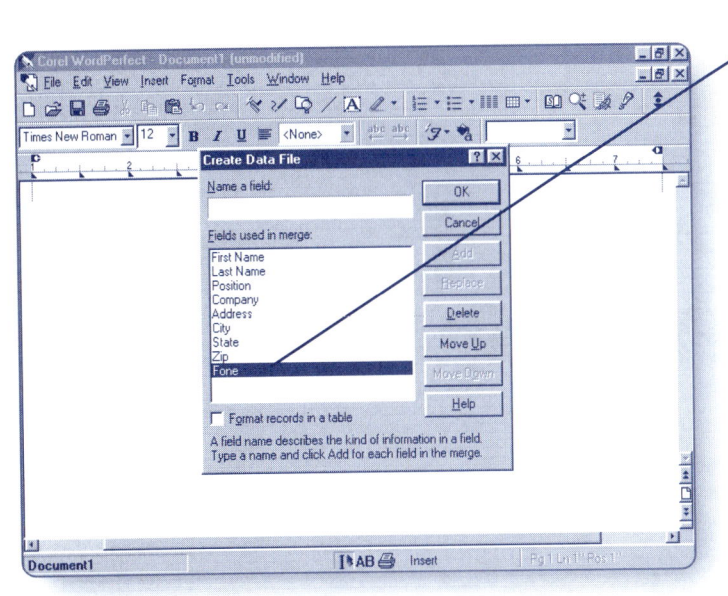

3. Repeat steps 1 and **2** for as many fields you need for your address list.

You can create the data in a table format. In a table format, each column of the table will contain a field. Each row will contain a record.

CHAPTER 20: CREATING AN ADDRESS LIST

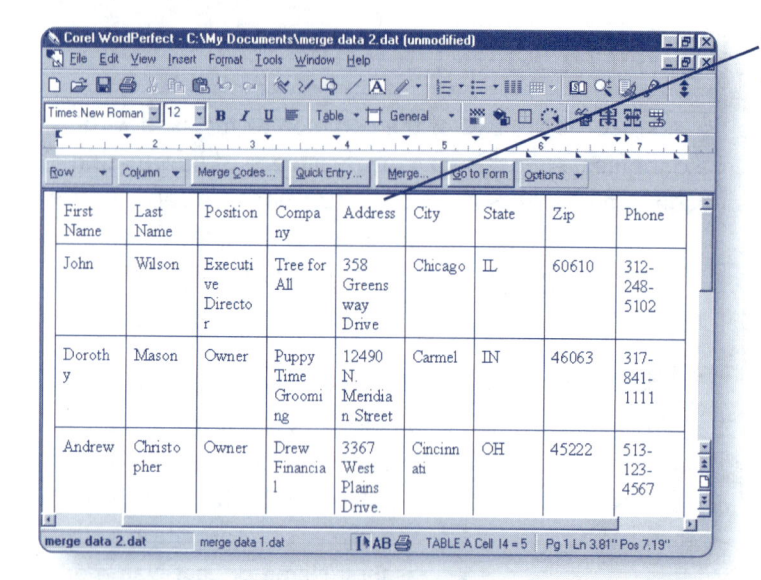

— This figure shows what data in a table format looks like.

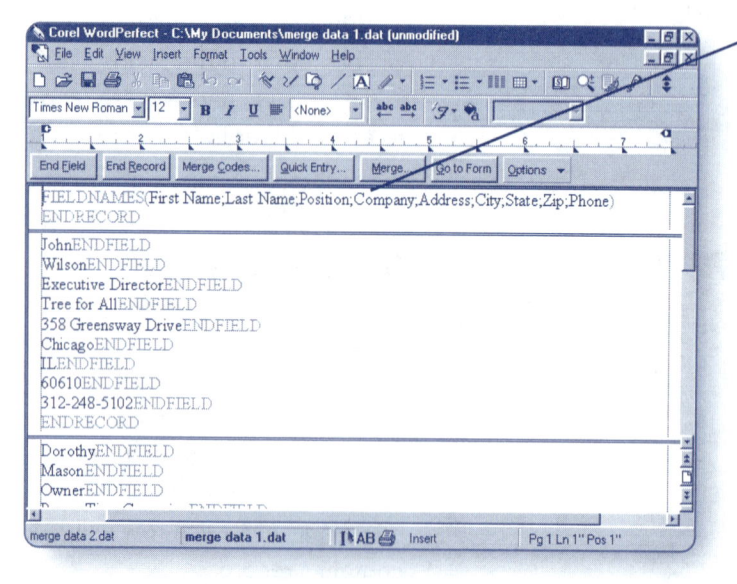

— This figure shows what data in a text (non-table) format looks like. This is similar to earlier versions of WordPerfect.

USING QUICK DATA ENTRY

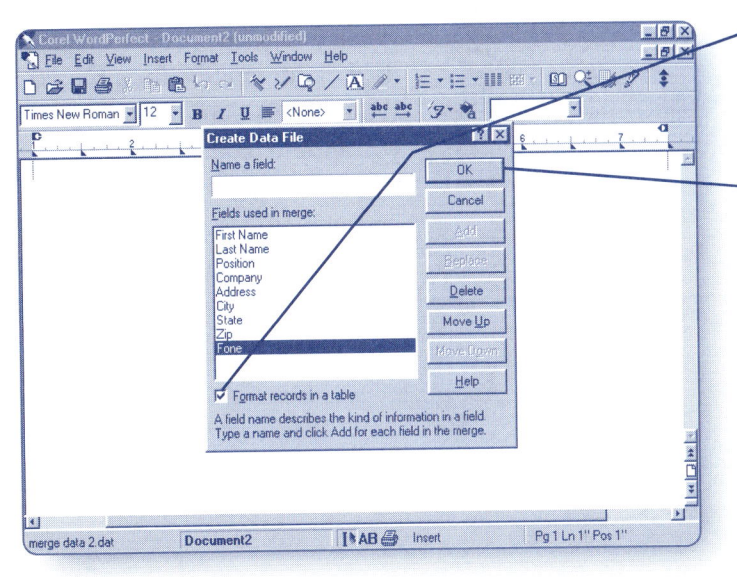

4. Click on **Format records in a table** to turn on this feature. A ✔ will appear in the box.

5. Click on **OK**. The Quick Data Entry dialog box will open.

Using Quick Data Entry

You enter the actual information about someone, such as name or address, in the Quick Data Entry dialog box.

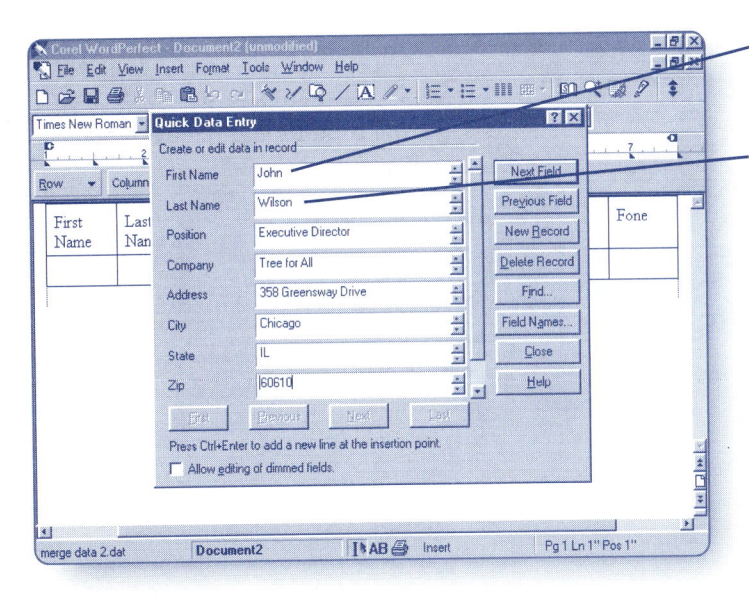

1. Type the **information** for the first field. The text will display.

2. Press the **Enter key**. The insertion point will move to the next field.

3. Continue typing the information for the first record in the appropriate field, pressing the Enter key to move to the next field.

CHAPTER 20: CREATING AN ADDRESS LIST

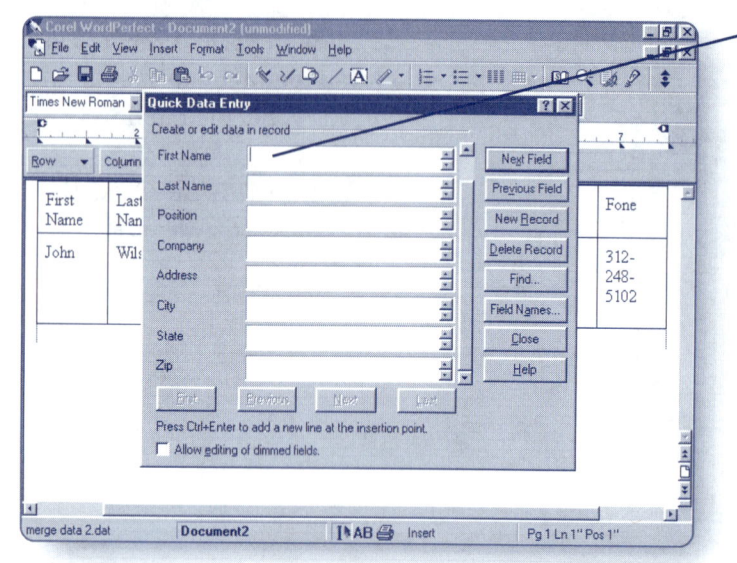

When you have entered the last field of information for a record, WordPerfect automatically gives you another blank record to begin entering the next person's information.

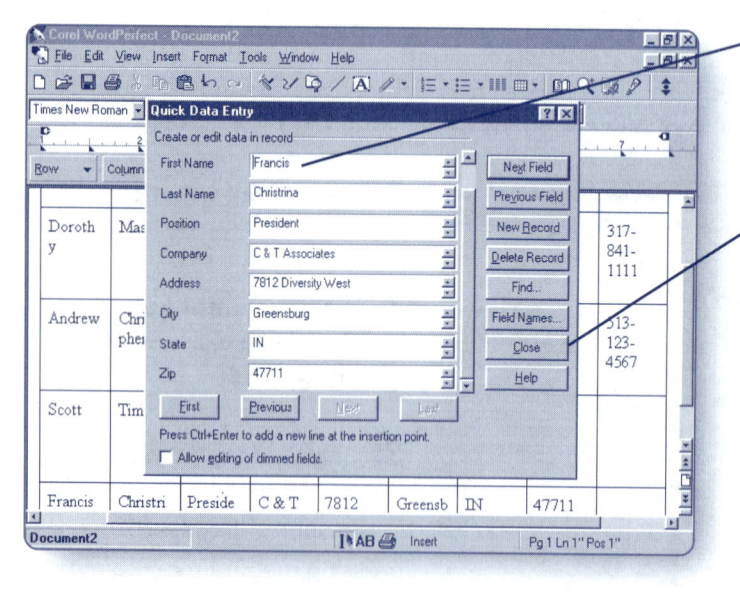

4. Continue entering the **records** for your address file following the preceding steps 1 through 3.

5. Click on **Close**. WordPerfect will prompt you to save your file.

USING QUICK DATA ENTRY   223

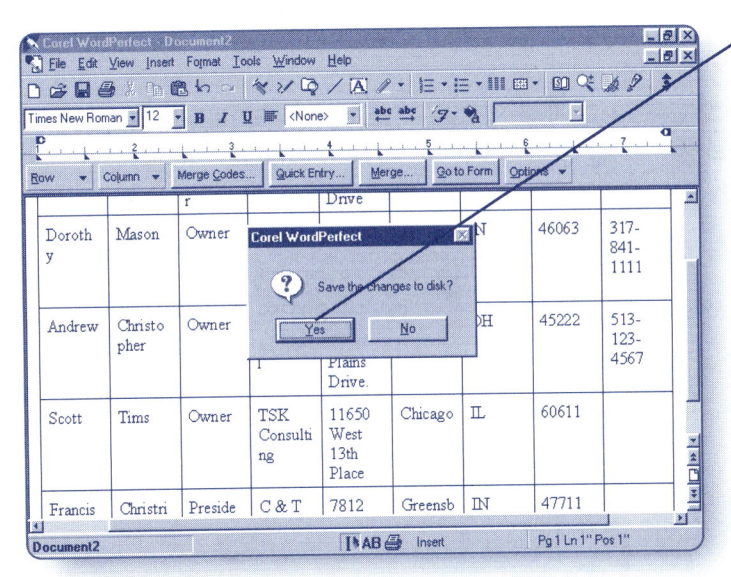

6. Click on **Yes** to save this file. The Save File dialog box will open.

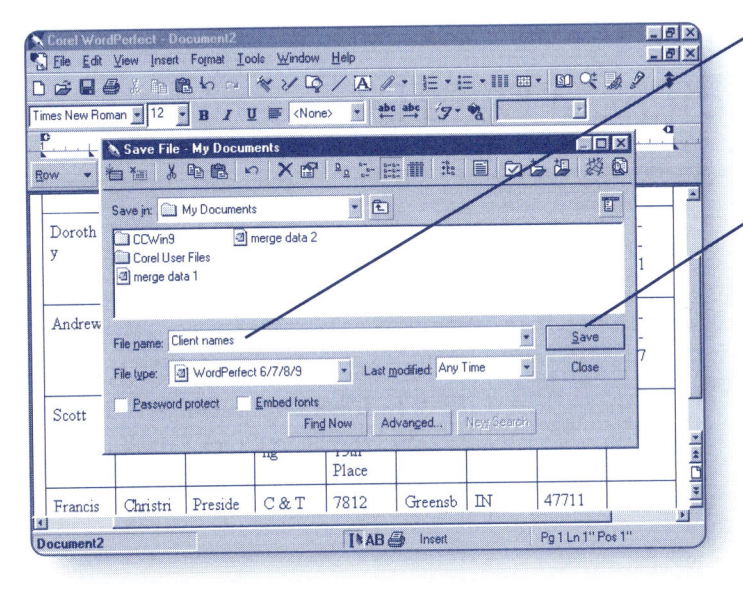

7. Type a **name** for the data file. WordPerfect will add .dat at the end to identify this file as a data file.

8. Click on **Save**. The file will be saved, and the dialog box will close.

CHAPTER 20: CREATING AN ADDRESS LIST

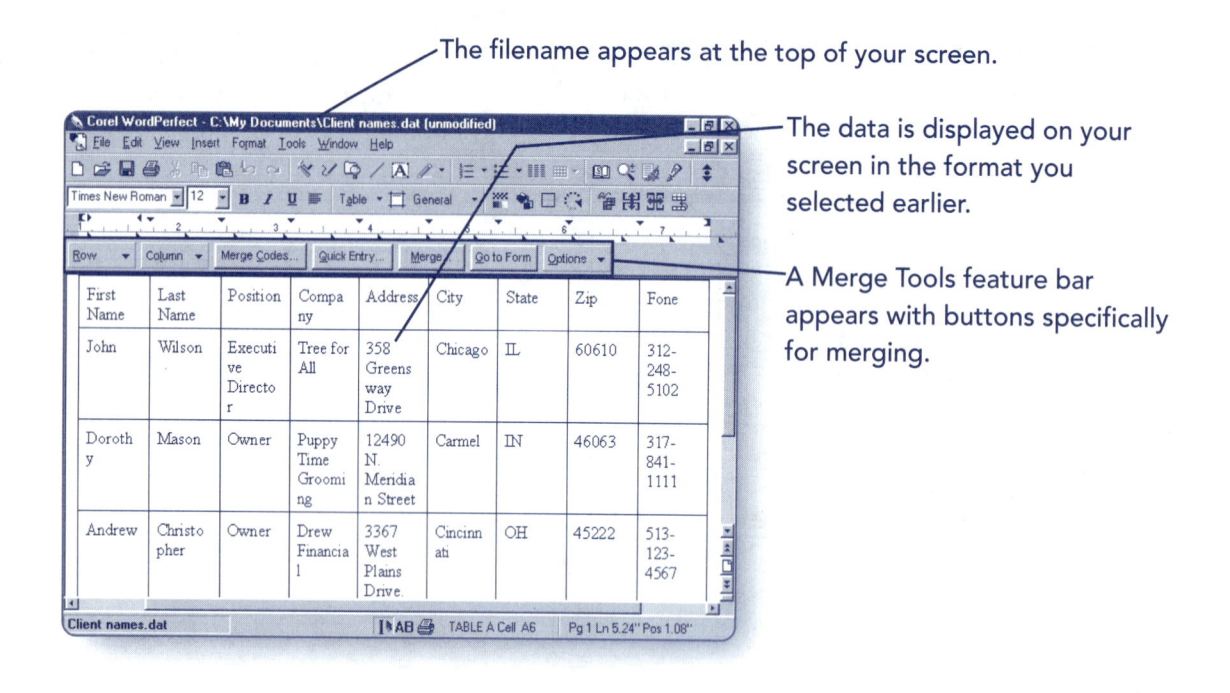

The filename appears at the top of your screen.

The data is displayed on your screen in the format you selected earlier.

A Merge Tools feature bar appears with buttons specifically for merging.

Editing a Data File

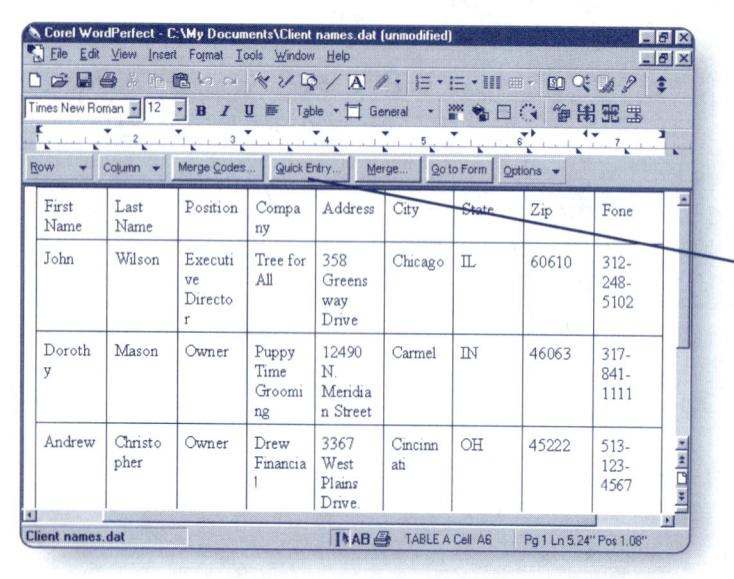

If you need to add or delete a record or change an address in the data file, the fastest way is to use the Quick Data Entry box.

1. Click on the **Quick Entry button**. The Quick Data Entry dialog box will open.

EDITING A DATA FILE

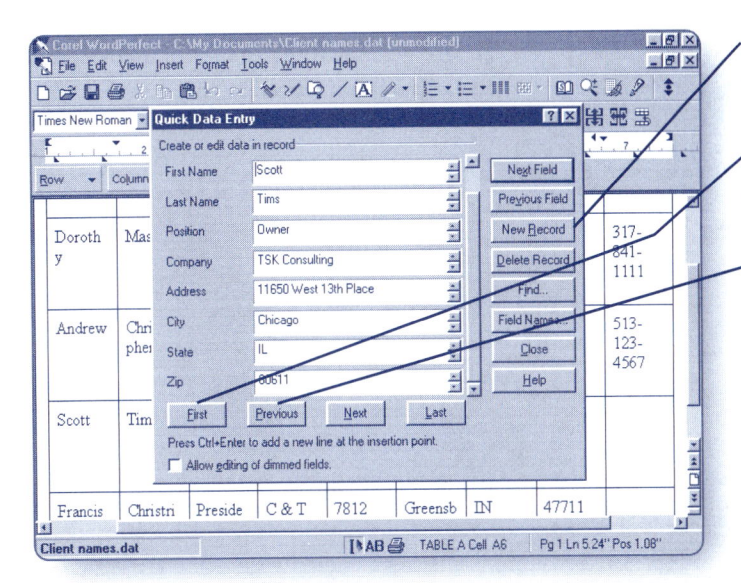

Click on New Record to add a new person to the data file.

Click on First to go to the first record in the data file.

Click on Previous to go to the previous record in the data file.

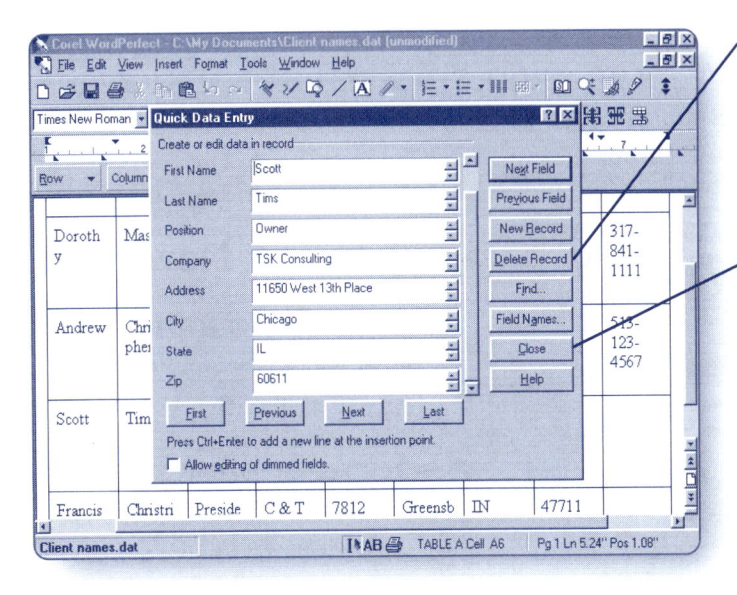

Click on Delete Record to delete the current record.

2. Click in any field and type any necessary changes.

3. Click on Close to close the dialog box. You will be prompted to save the file.

226 CHAPTER 20: CREATING AN ADDRESS LIST

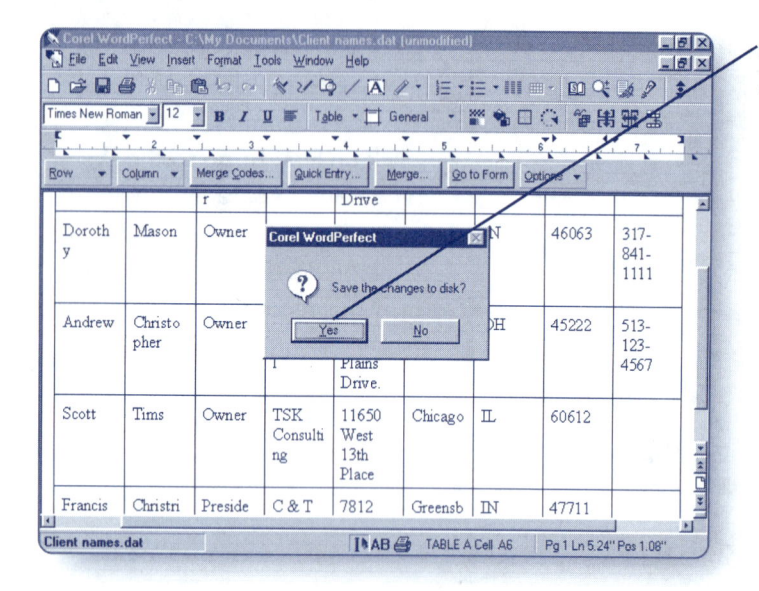

4. Click on **Yes**. The changes will be saved.

Changing Fields

You can change, delete, or even add a new field to the data file. Your changes will affect all existing records as well as new ones.

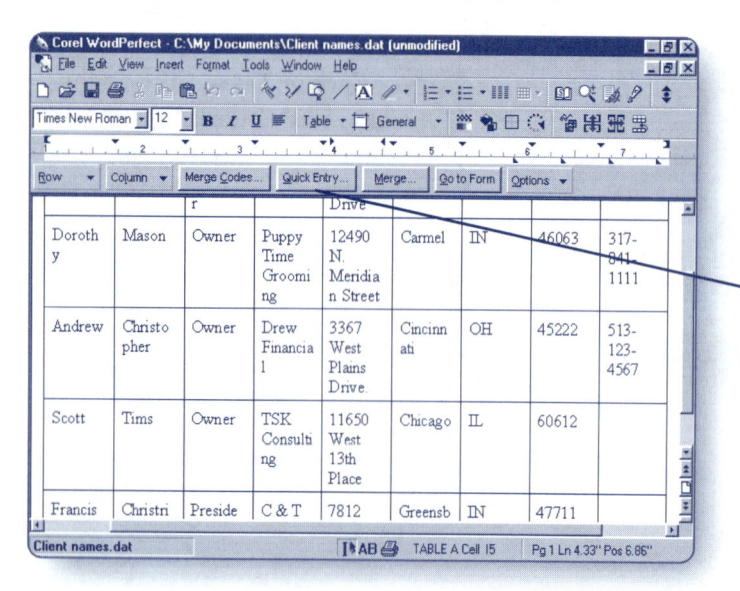

Adding a New Field

Did you think of another field to add? It's simple to add fields to a merge data file.

1. Click on the **Quick Entry button.** The Quick Data Entry dialog box will open.

CHANGING FIELDS 227

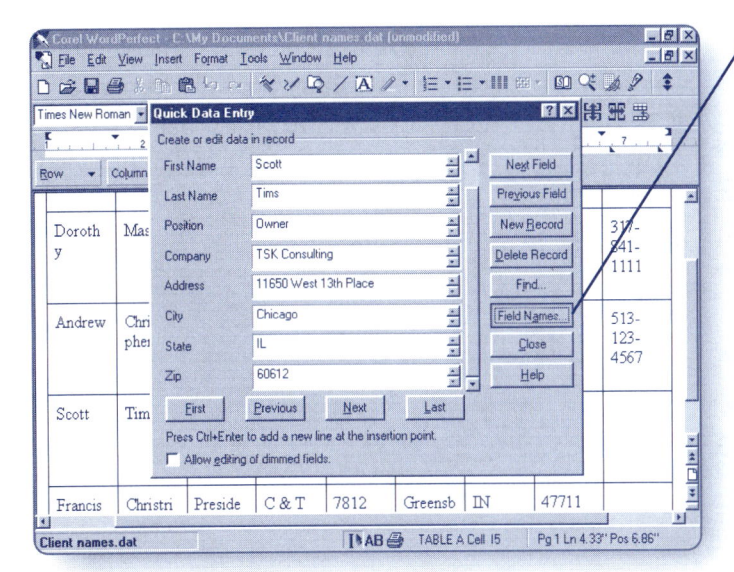

2. Click on **Field Names**. The Edit Field Names dialog box will open.

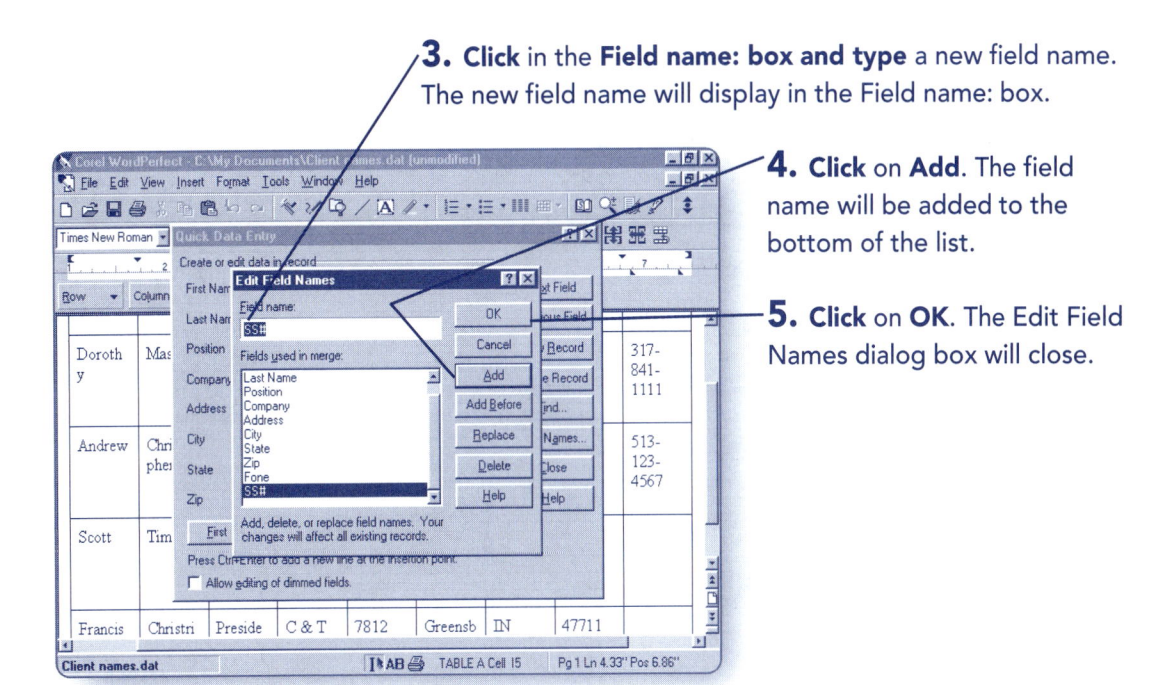

3. Click in the **Field name: box and type** a new field name. The new field name will display in the Field name: box.

4. Click on **Add**. The field name will be added to the bottom of the list.

5. Click on **OK**. The Edit Field Names dialog box will close.

CHAPTER 20: CREATING AN ADDRESS LIST

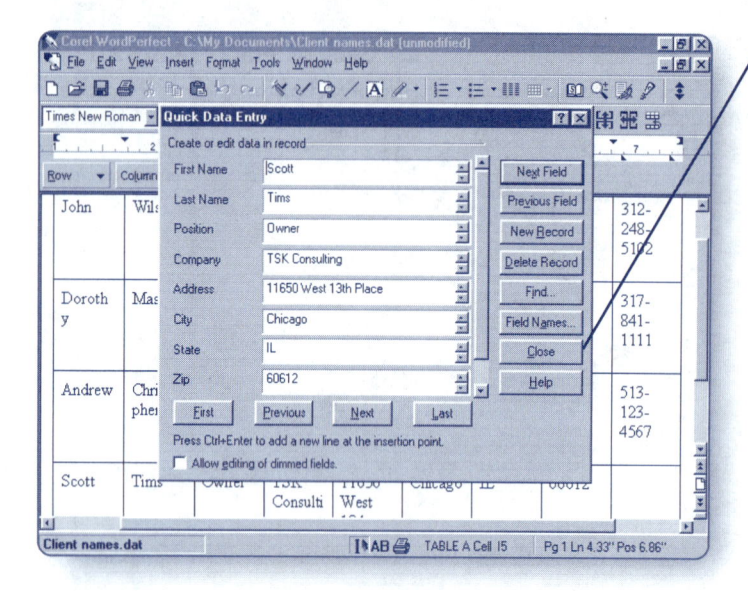

6. Click on **Close**. The Quick Data Entry box will close, and you will be prompted to save your changes.

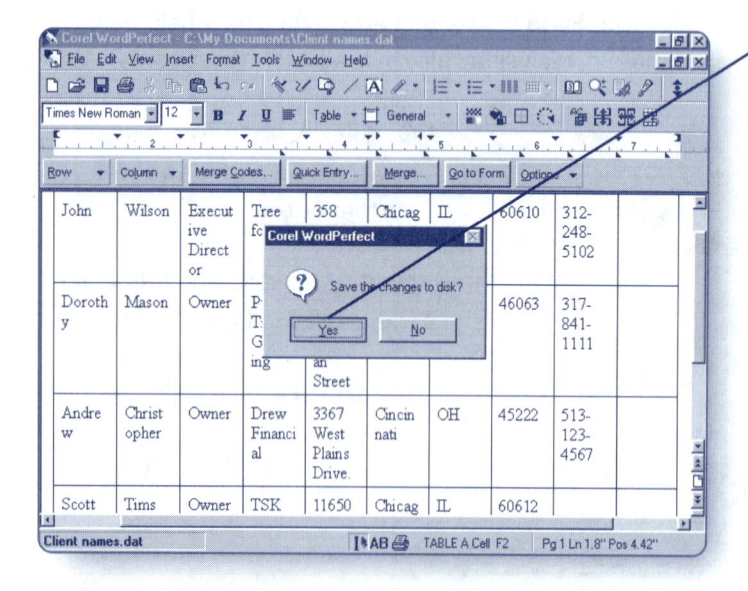

7. Click on **Yes**. The changes will be saved.

CHANGING FIELDS   229

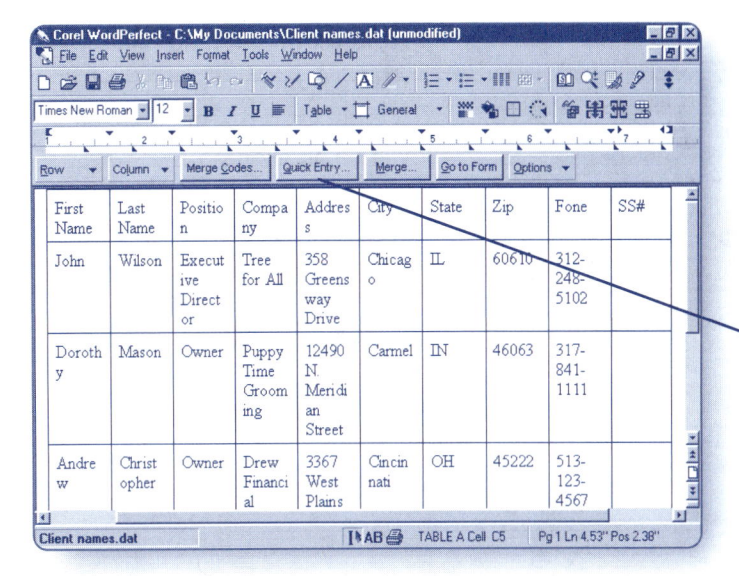

Deleting a Field

If you have a field of data that you no longer need, you can delete it. Deleting a field also deletes all data for that field in every record.

1. Click on the **Quick Entry button** on the feature bar. The Quick Data Entry dialog box will open.

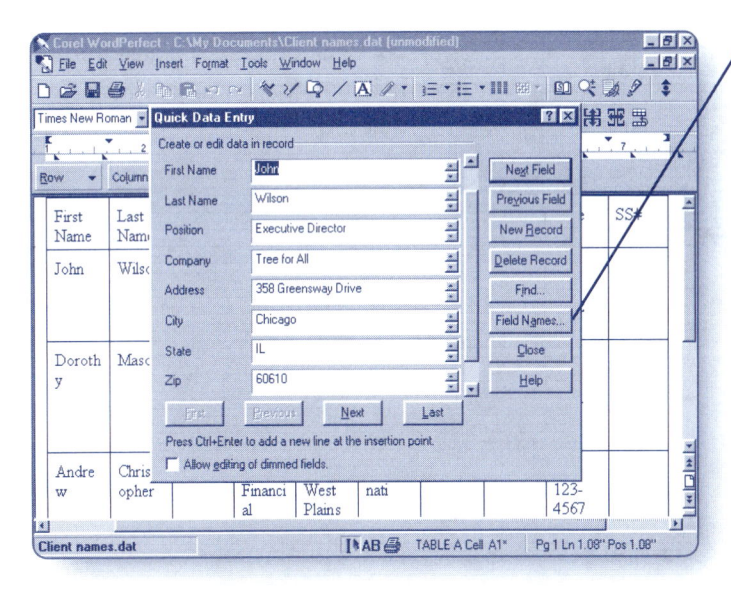

2. Click on **Field Names**. The Edit Field Names dialog box will open.

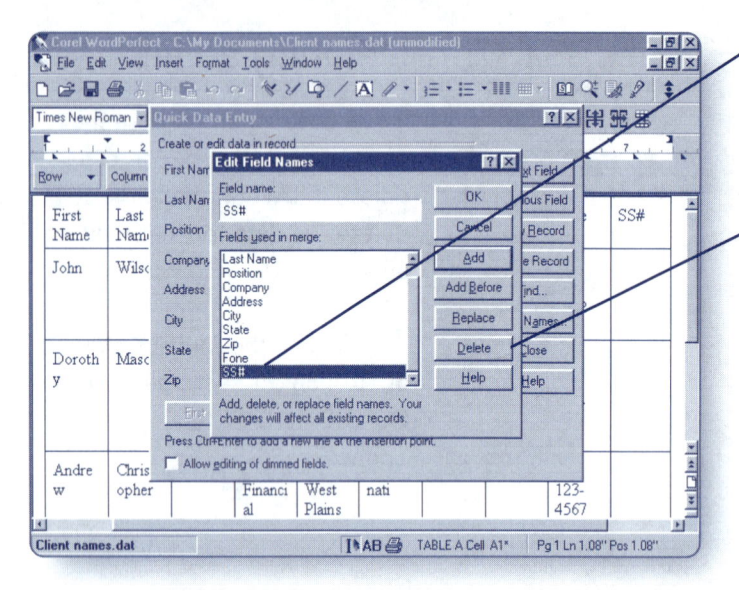

3. Click on the **field name** to delete from the Fields used in merge: list box. The field name will be highlighted.

4. Click on **Delete**. A dialog box will open warning you that the field contents will be deleted from every existing record.

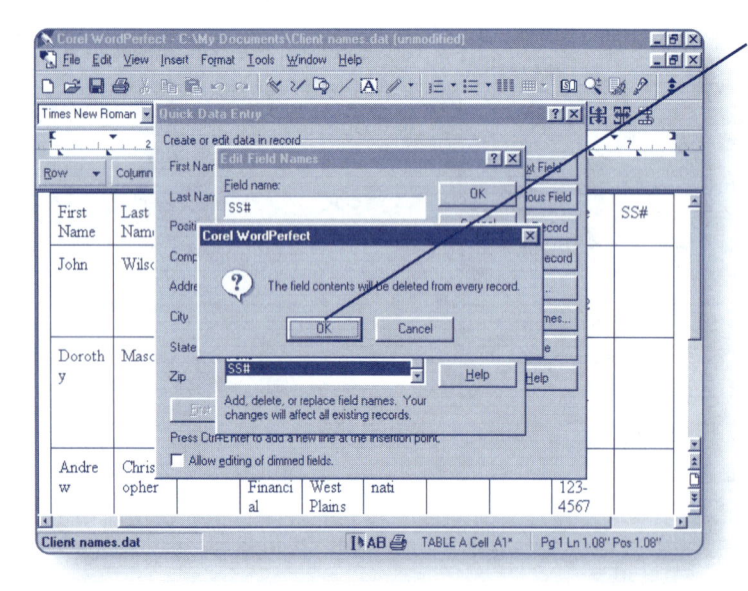

5. Click on **OK**. The selected field and its contents will be deleted.

CHANGING FIELDS   231

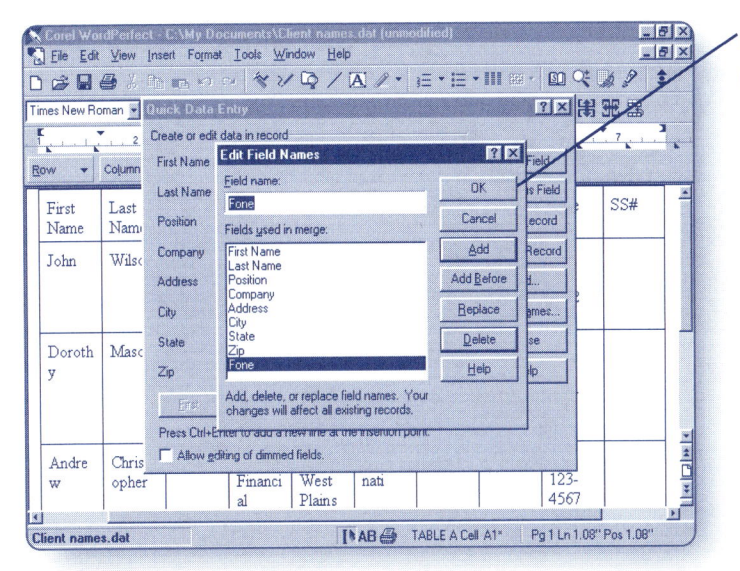

6. Click on **OK**. The Edit Field Names dialog box will close.

7. Click on **Close**. The Quick Data Entry box will close, and you will be prompted to save your changes.

CHAPTER 20: CREATING AN ADDRESS LIST

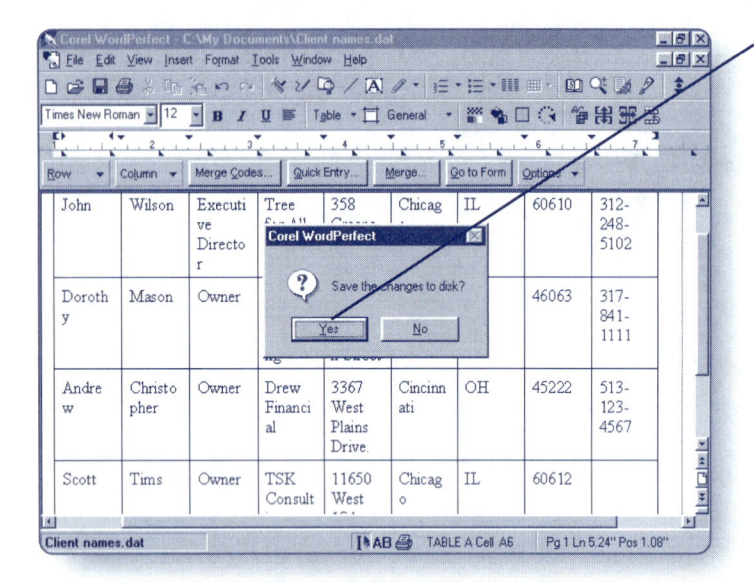

8. Click on **Yes**. The changes will be saved.

Renaming a Field

The fastest and easiest way to rename a field is to change it in the table heading.

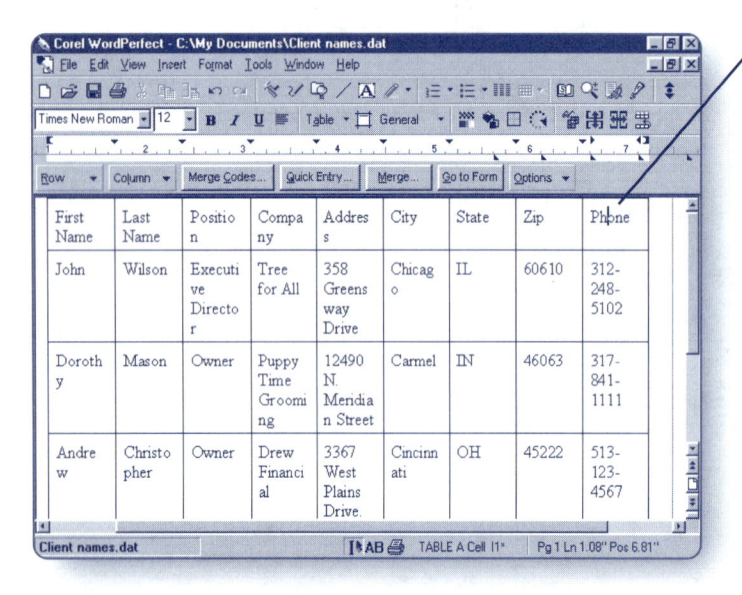

1. Click in the **cell** containing the field name to be changed. The blinking insertion point will appear.

2. Type a modified **field name**. The field name will be changed. In this example, the field name "Fone" is changed to "Phone."

CHANGING FIELDS 233

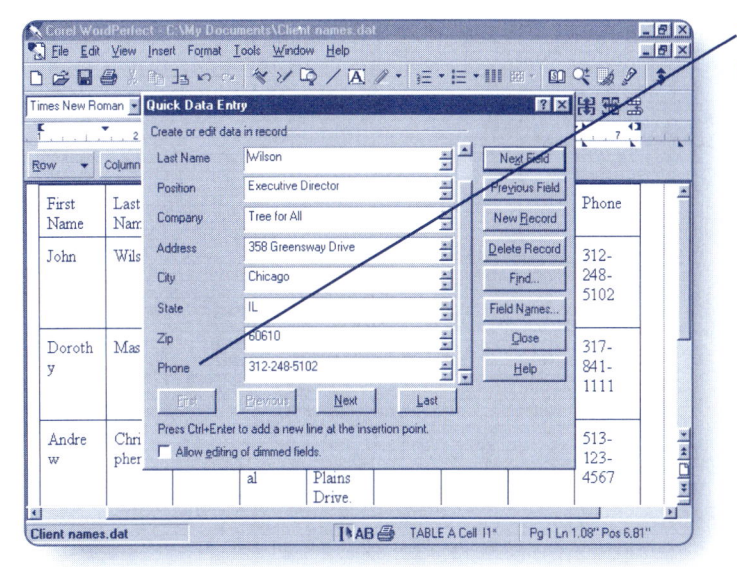

The field name is even changed in the Quick Data Entry box!

21

Creating a Form Letter

The second step in Mail Merge is creating the form letter. The form document contains the information that does not change from letter to letter. It also includes *data fields* to tell WordPerfect where to put the information from the data file. In this chapter, you'll learn how to:

- Create a form letter
- Use automatic dates
- Insert data fields

Creating a Form Letter

First you need to *associate* the data file with a form file. When you merge that form file in the future, the associated source file is used.

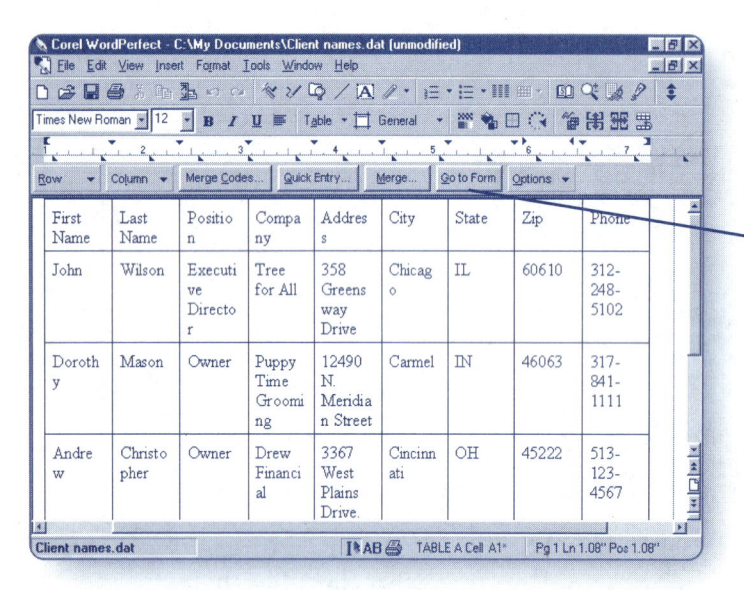

1. If not already opened, **open** the **data file** you have already created. The data file will be displayed on the screen.

2. Click on the **Go To Form button**. A dialog box will open advising you that WordPerfect doesn't know which form file to associate with the open data file.

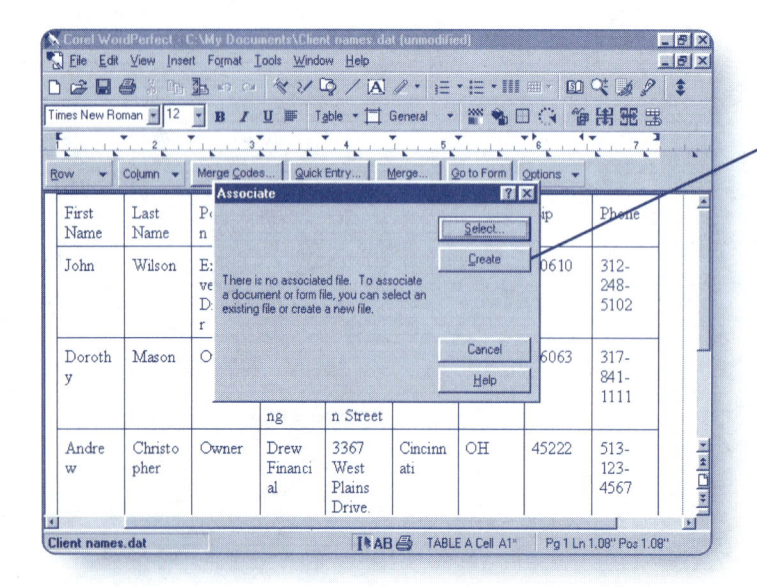

You can either select an existing file or create a new one.

3. Click on **Create** to create a new file. A blank WordPerfect document will open on the screen, with the Merge feature bar displayed.

Using Automatic Dates

One of the first items listed in a letter is usually a date. WordPerfect gives you two types of dates to use. You learned about using a *date text* in Chapter 1, "Welcome to WordPerfect." Another type of date is called the *merge date*. The merge date is *dynamic*, which means that it changes to the current date when you merge the two documents.

1. Click the **mouse pointer** where you want the date to appear in the letter. The blinking insertion point will appear.

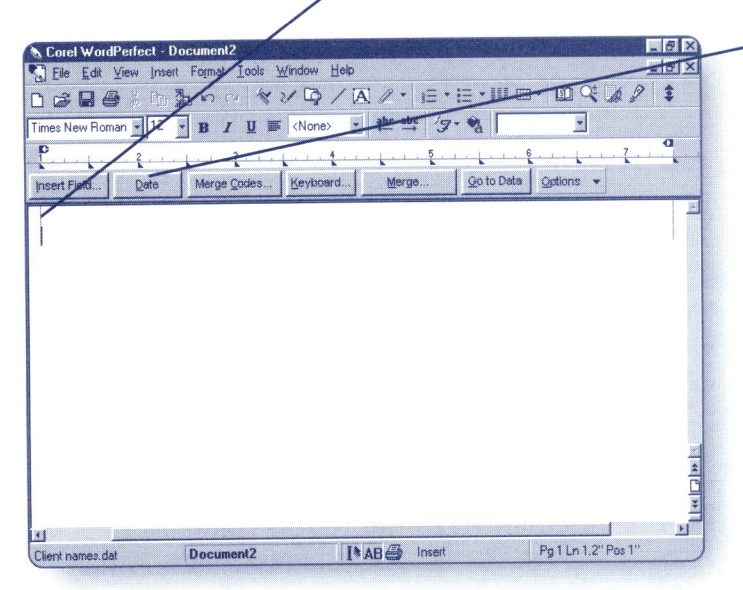

2. Click on **Date**. The word DATE will appear in the document in red letters. In reality, this is a WordPerfect code.

Inserting Data Fields

You are now ready to tell WordPerfect where to insert the data from the data file you created. Because of the association you made earlier in this chapter, WordPerfect knows what field names you used in your data file.

CHAPTER 21: CREATING A FORM LETTER

1. Click the **mouse pointer** where you want the first field of information to appear in the letter. The blinking insertion point will appear.

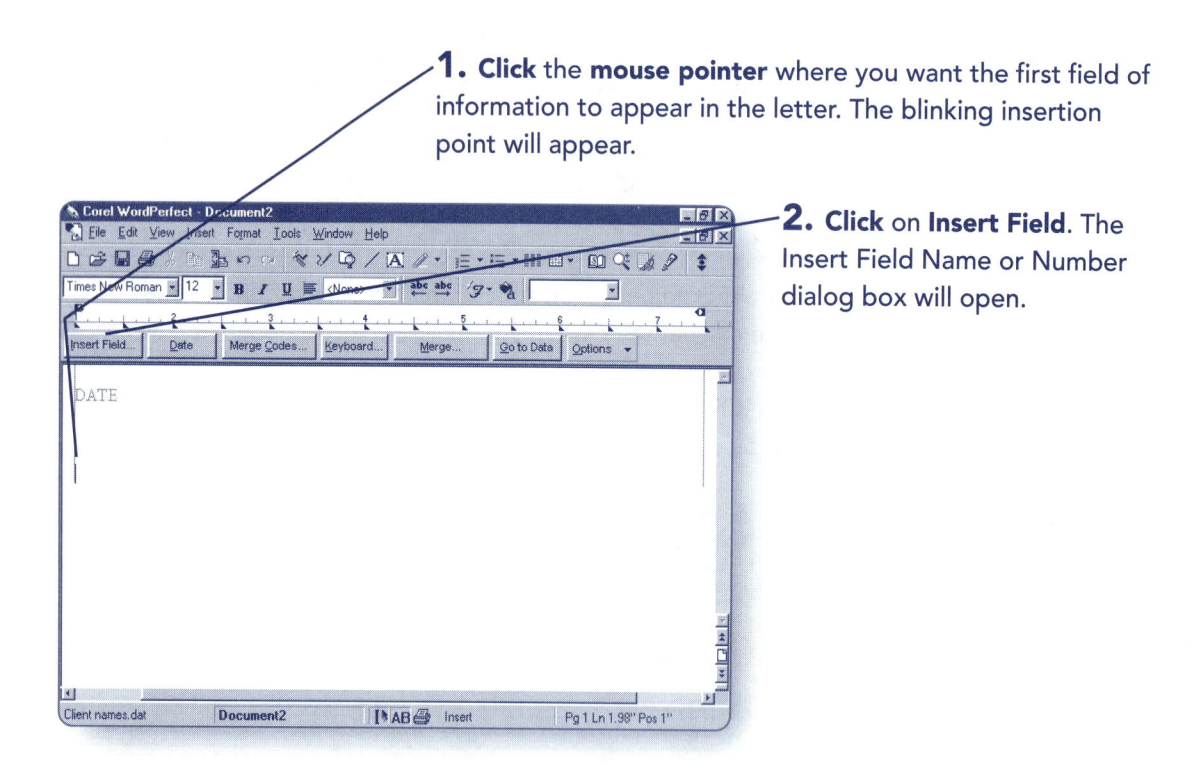

2. Click on **Insert Field**. The Insert Field Name or Number dialog box will open.

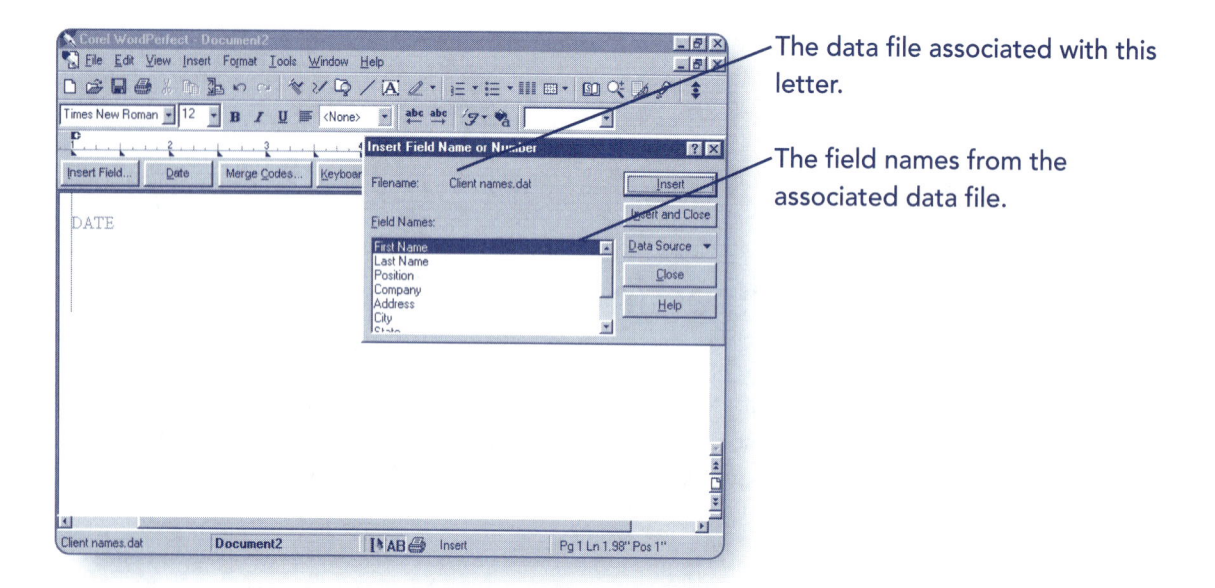

The data file associated with this letter.

The field names from the associated data file.

INSERTING DATA FIELDS

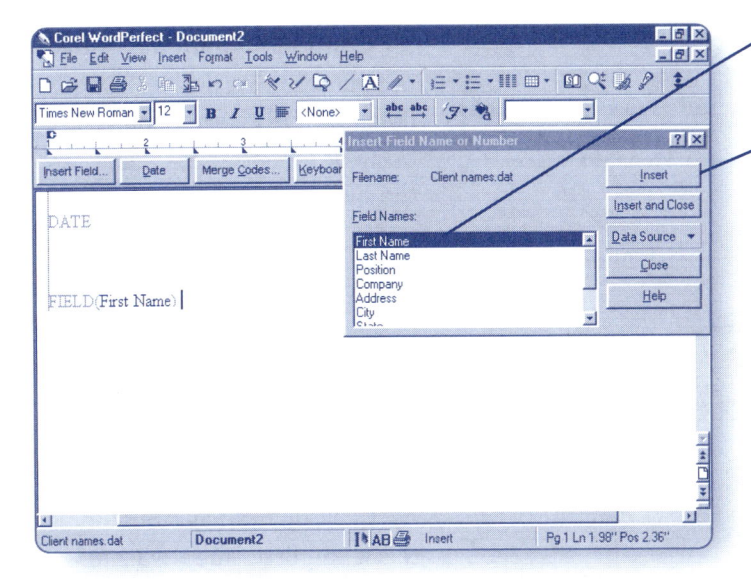

3. Click on the first **data field** you want in your letter.

4. Click on **Insert**. The field name will be inserted into your document, and the dialog box will remain open.

5. Repeat steps 1, **3**, and **4** for each additional field in your letter.

You will need to add punctuation as necessary between the fields but not in the actual fields.

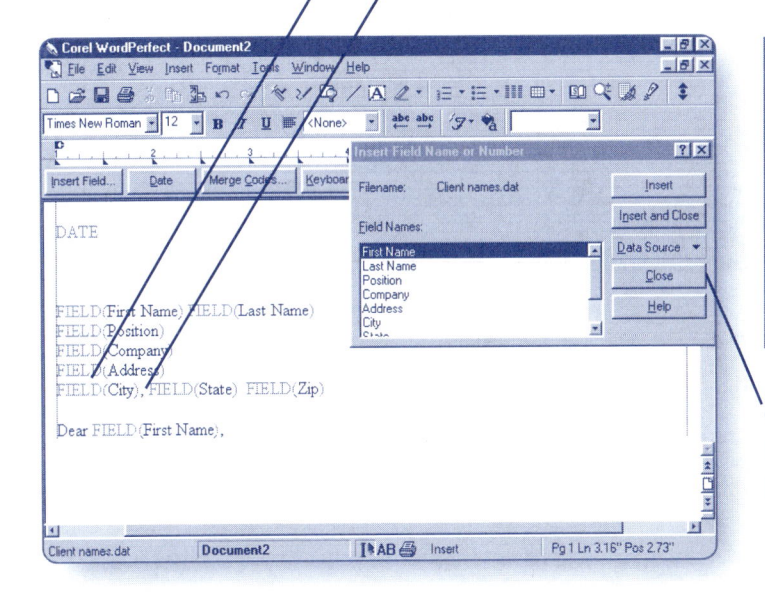

NOTE

You do not have to use every field in the form file, and you can use fields more than once. In this example, I used the First Name field twice.

6. Click on **Close**. The Insert Field Name or Number dialog box will close.

240 CHAPTER 21: CREATING A FORM LETTER

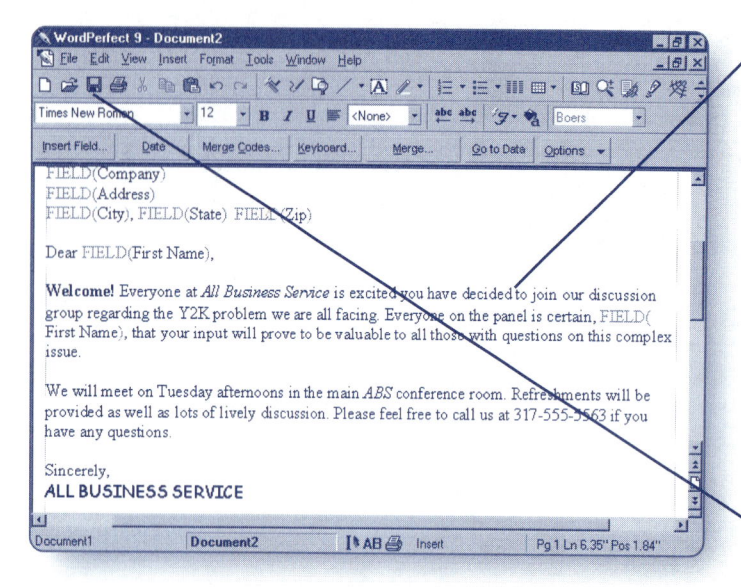

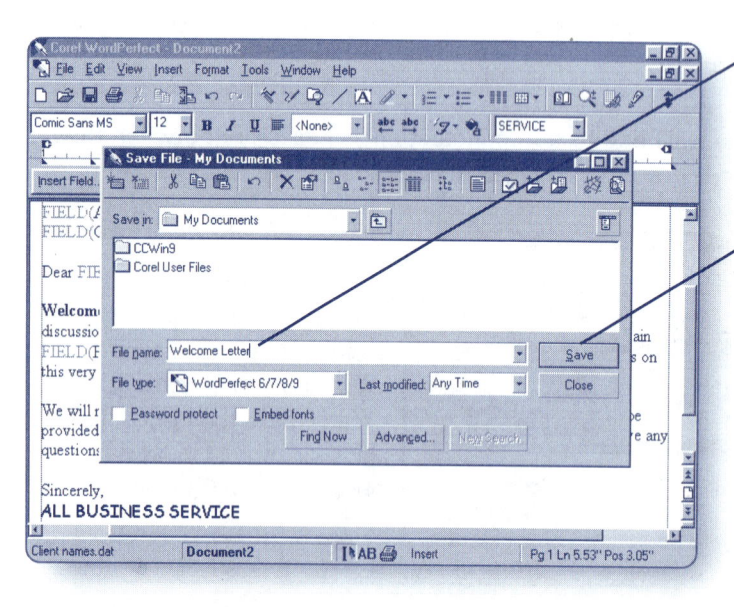

7. Continue typing the **body** of your letter as desired. Data fields can be inserted in the body of the letter as well as at the beginning.

TIP

Any formatting should be done in the form document, not the data document.

---

8. Click on the **Save button**. If this is the first time the letter has been saved, the Save File dialog box will open.

9. Type a **filename** for the letter. WordPerfect will assign .frm to the end of the filename to designate it as a form letter.

10. Click on **Save**. The file will be saved.

22

Merging an Address List and Form Letter

It's time to put the first two elements of a Mail Merge together—the data source and the form letter. In this chapter, you'll learn how to:

- Merge names and addresses with a letter
- Merge to specific conditions
- Merge to selected records
- Create envelopes for the merged records

Merging Names and Addresses with a Letter

Merging is the final step to this process. The merge process creates a separate letter for each record in the data file.

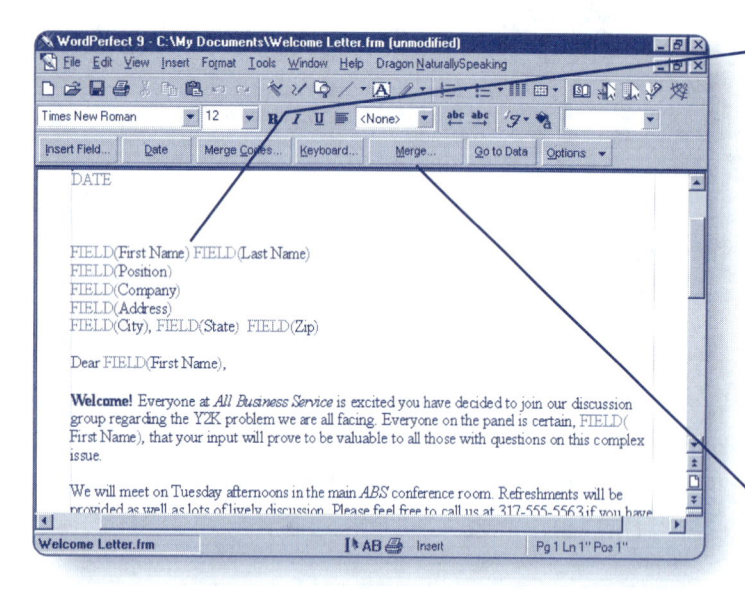

1. Open the **form file**. In our example, we are using the form letter we created in the previous chapter.

NOTE

When merging, it doesn't matter whether the data file is open.

2. Click on **Merge**. The Perform Merge dialog box will open.

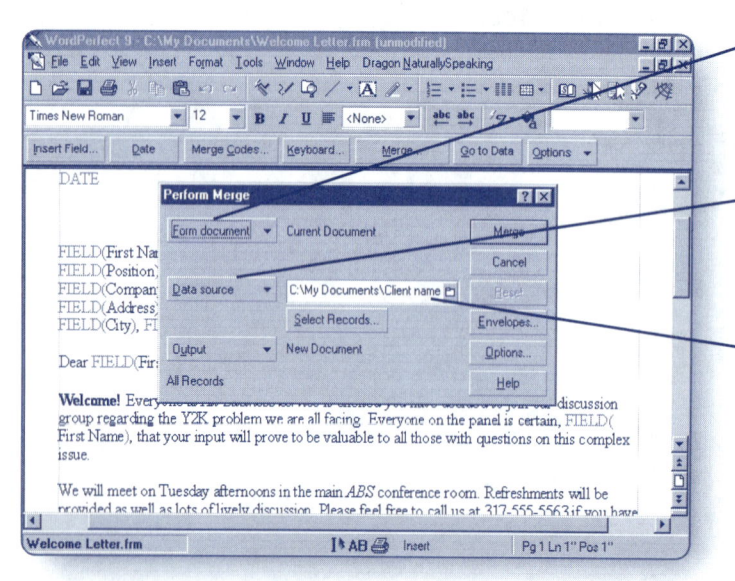

The Form Document button allows you to select which form letter you are using.

The Data Source button allows you to select the location of the data file.

Notice the link to our sample data file—Client name.dat.

MERGING NAMES AND ADDRESSES WITH A LETTER   243

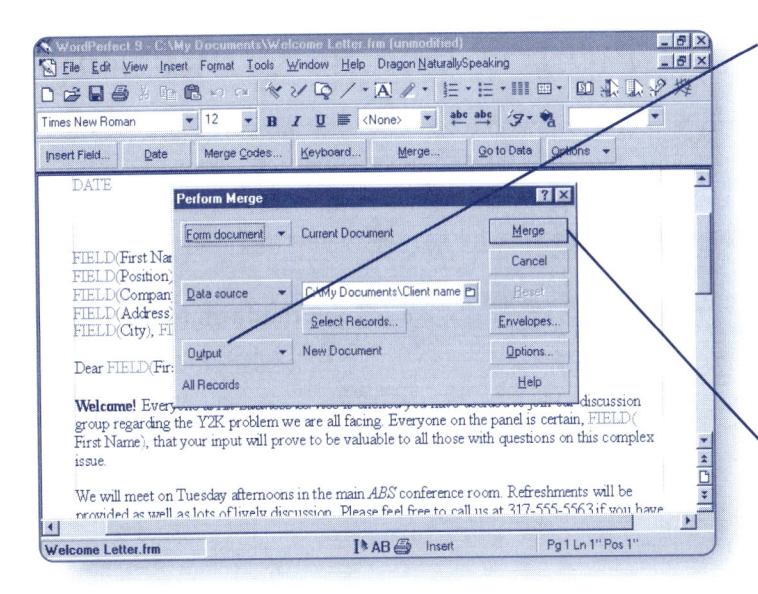

The Output Button allows you to direct the final merge.

> **TIP**
>
> I recommend merging to a new document first to double-check for any errors.

3. Click on **Merge**. The merge process will begin.

4. Press the **Ctrl + Home keys**. The insertion point will move to the beginning of the merged document.

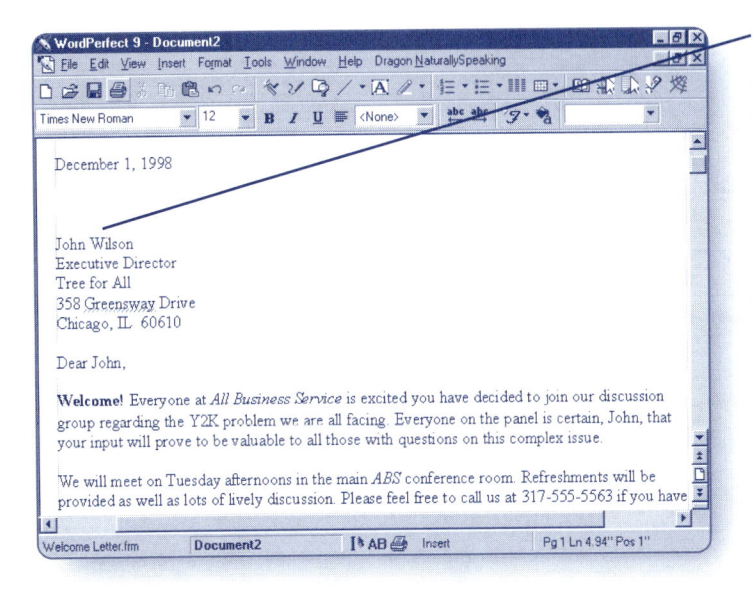

A new document has been created with one letter for each record in the data file.

You will now want to examine the document for any errors or omissions you may have made in the form or data file. If you find any problems, close the merged file, correct the errors, and merge again.

Merging to Specific Conditions

WordPerfect allows you to choose which records you want to merge with the form letter. Perhaps you only want to send this letter to the people who live in a certain city, say Chicago, or only the people who have a last name of Smith.

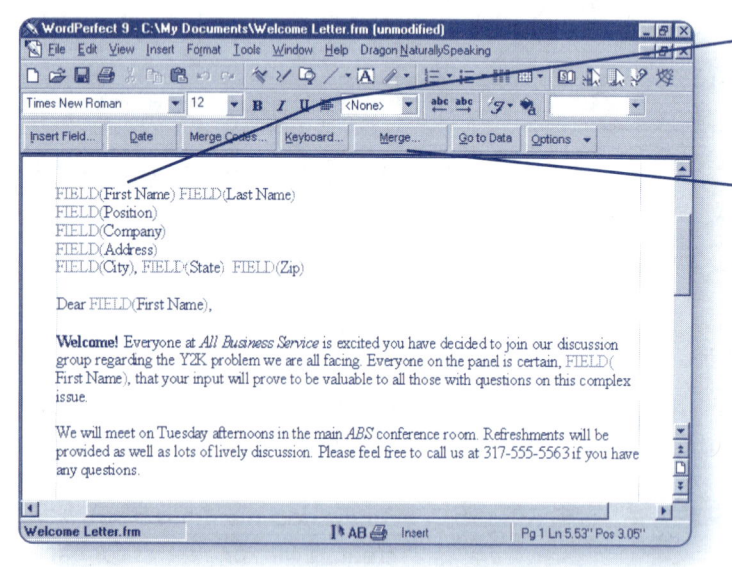

1. Open the **form letter**. The form letter will appear on the screen.

2. Click on **Merge**. The Perform Merge dialog box will open.

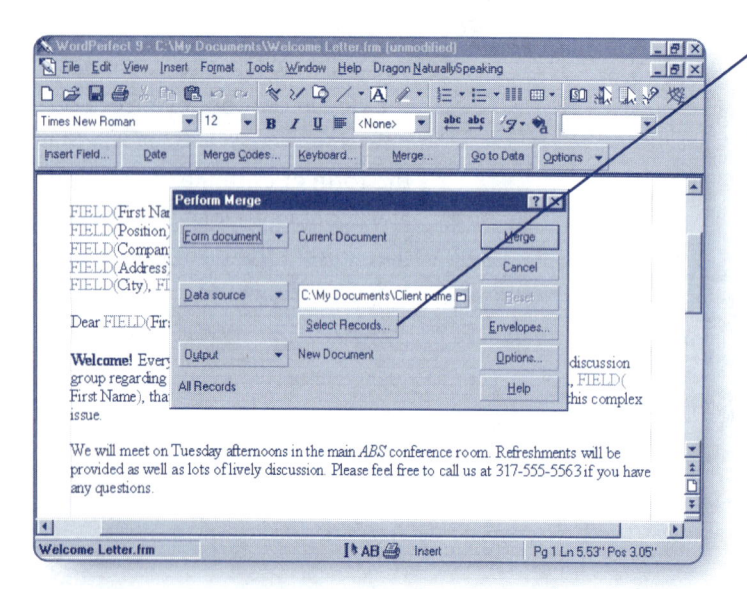

3. Click on **Select Records**. The Select Records dialog box will open.

MERGING TO SPECIFIC CONDITIONS 245

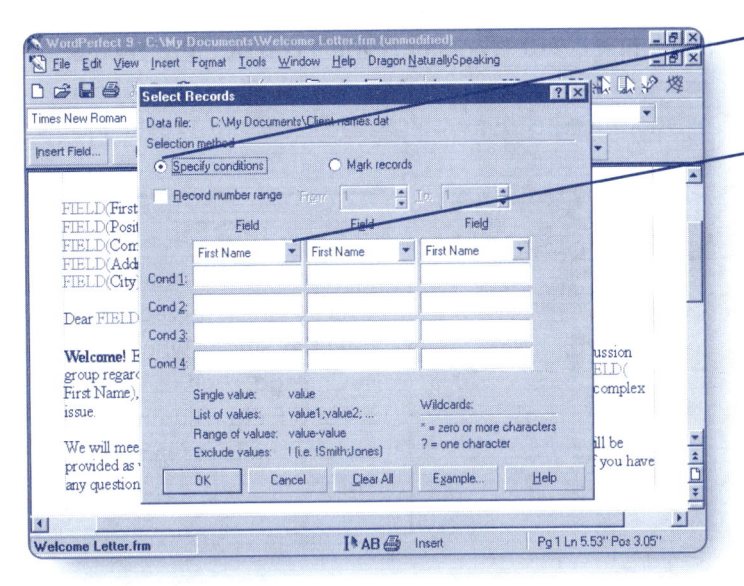

4. Click on **Specify conditions**. The option will be selected.

5. Click on the **down arrow** (▼) in the first field column. A list of fields will appear.

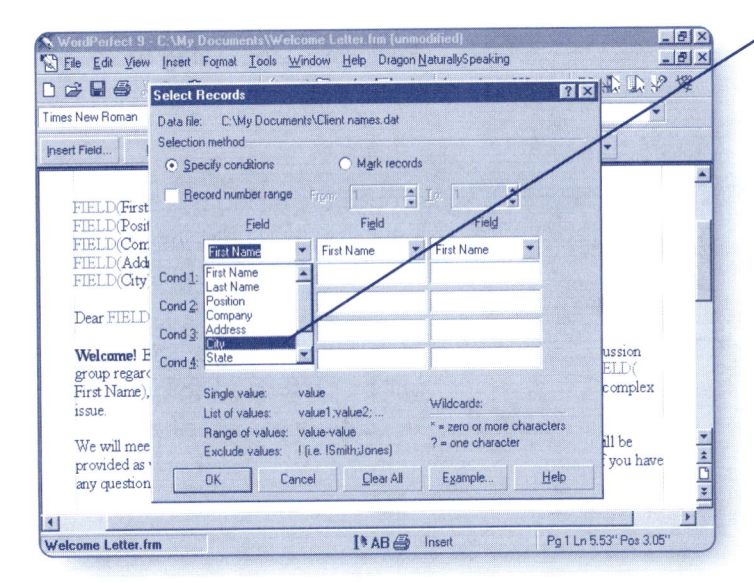

6. Click on the **field** you want to specify the records from. The field name will appear in the first column.

CHAPTER 22: MERGING AN ADDRESS LIST AND FORM LETTER

7. In the first Cond 1: column, **type** a **condition to be met.** For example, if you want only the records of people who live in Chicago, then just type Chicago in the Cond 1: column.

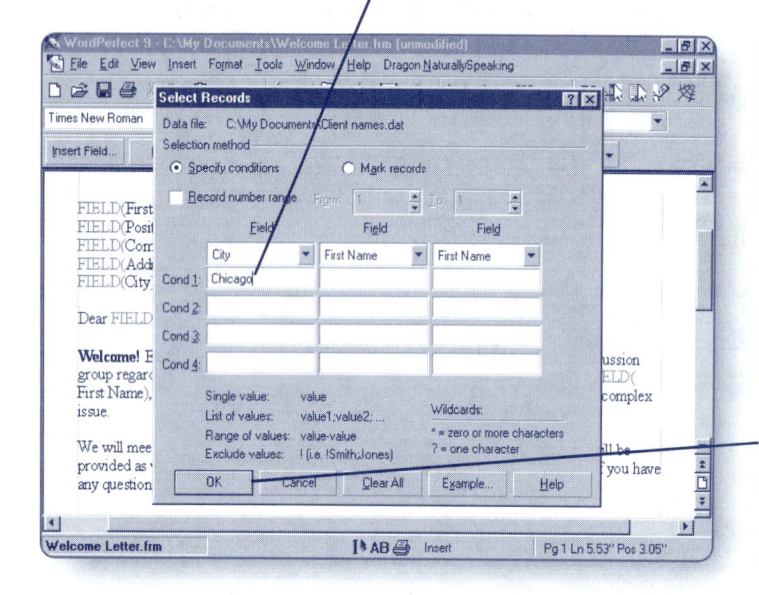

> **NOTE**
> If you want to further specify which records, say only the Smiths who live in Chicago, then use the second Field column to specify the Last Name of Smith.

8. Click on **OK**. The Select Records dialog box will close, and you will be returned to the Perform Merge dialog box.

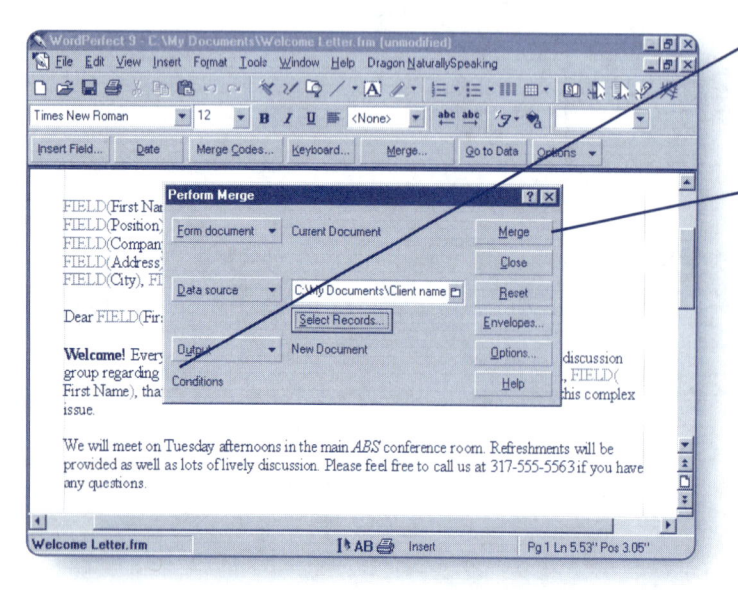

Notice the dialog box specifies that certain conditions are to be met.

9. Click on **Merge**. The merge will be performed according to the criteria you specified.

Merging to Selected Records

Another way to specify which records to merge with is to mark the desired records. This allows you to pick and choose which records without them having any matching criteria.

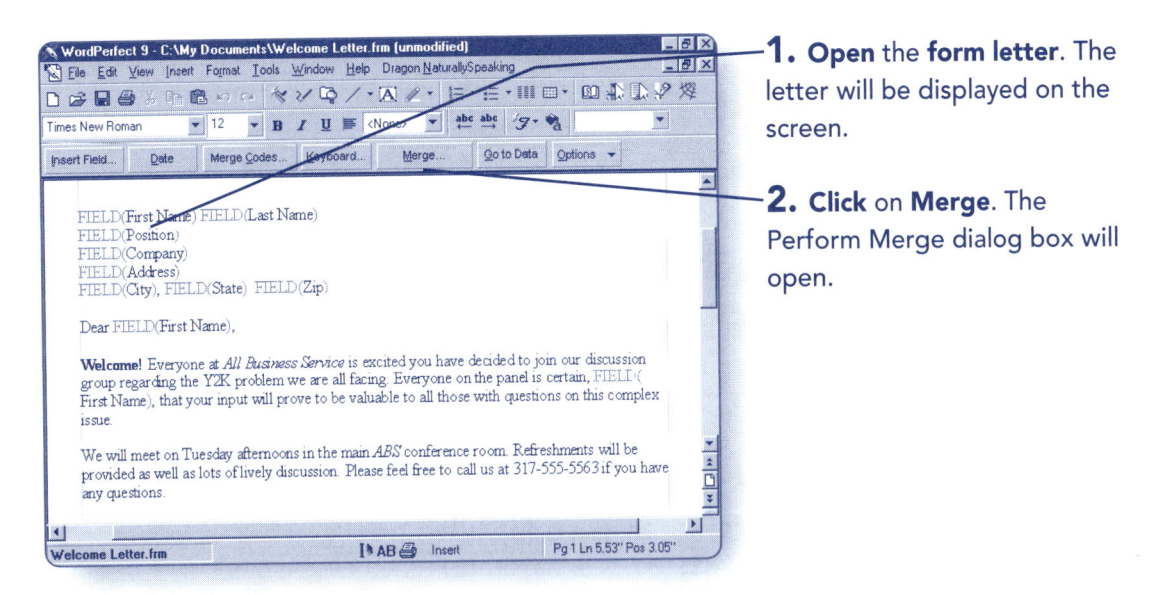

1. Open the **form letter**. The letter will be displayed on the screen.

2. Click on **Merge**. The Perform Merge dialog box will open.

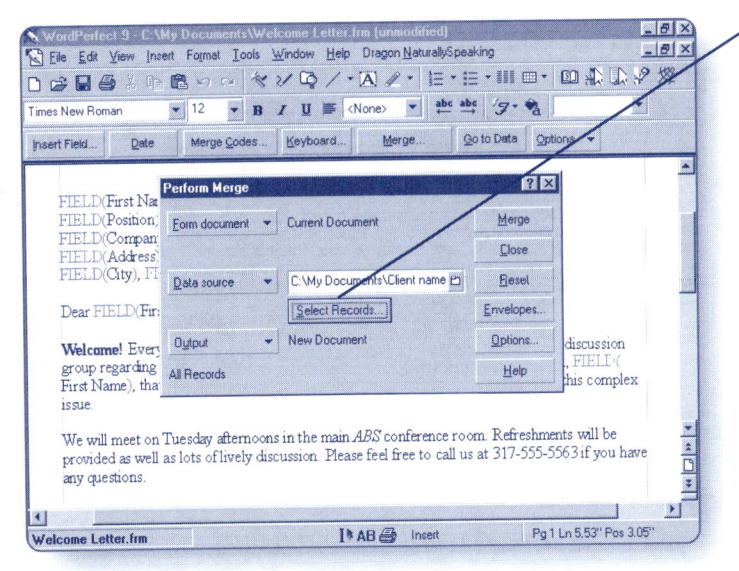

3. Click on **Select Records**. The Select Records dialog box will open.

248 CHAPTER 22: MERGING AN ADDRESS LIST AND FORM LETTER

4. Click on **Mark records**. The dialog box will change to show a representation of each record in the data file.

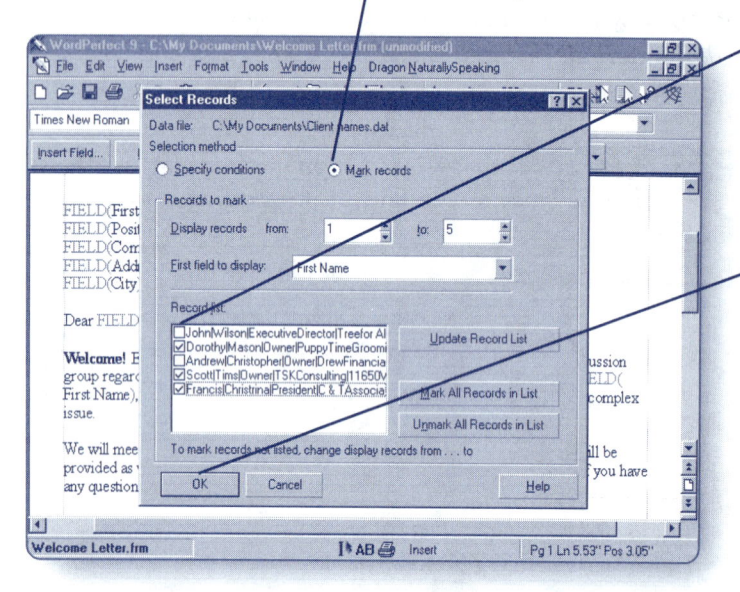

5. Click on the **names** of the records you want to merge from the Record list: box. A ✔ will appear beside each name you choose.

6. Click on **OK**. The Select Records dialog box will close, and you will be returned to the Perform Merge dialog box.

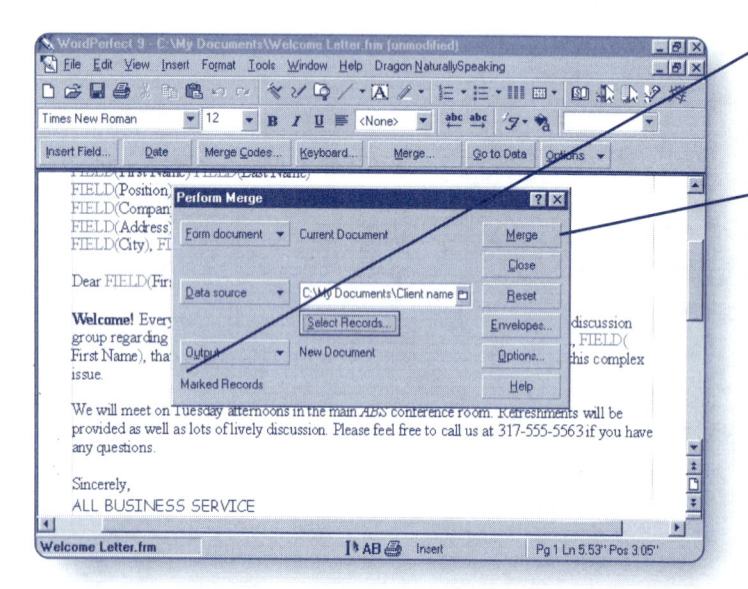

This time the Merge dialog box specifies that certain records are marked for merging.

7. Click on **Merge**. The merge will be performed with the records you selected.

Creating Envelopes for the Merged Records

You can create envelopes along with the letter each time you merge.

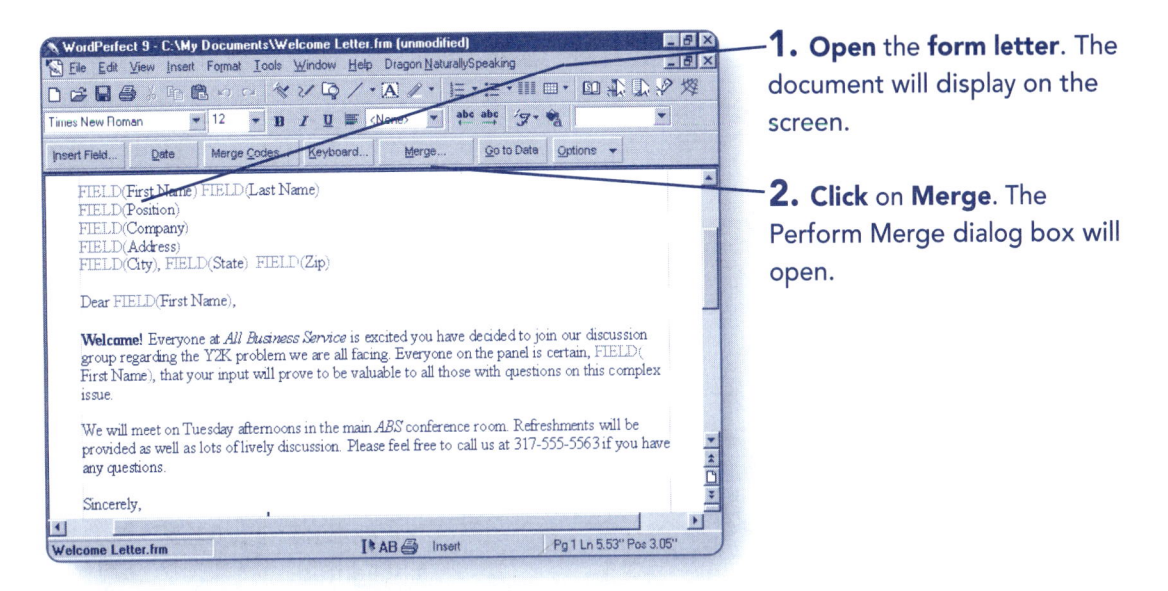

1. Open the **form letter**. The document will display on the screen.

2. Click on **Merge**. The Perform Merge dialog box will open.

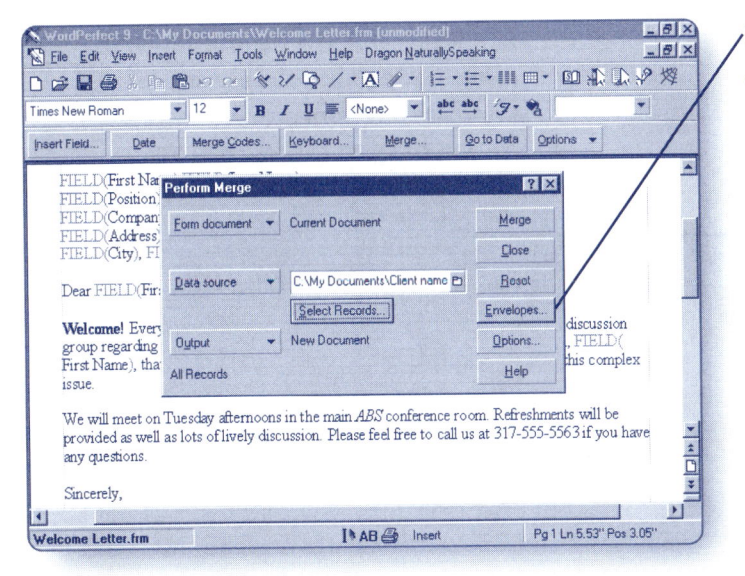

3. Click on **Envelopes**. A blank envelope will display.

CHAPTER 22: MERGING AN ADDRESS LIST AND FORM LETTER

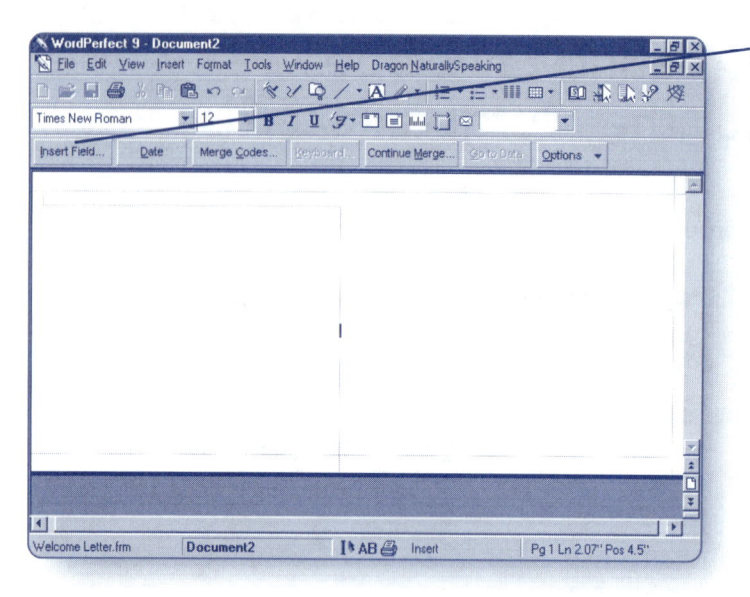

4. Click on **Insert Field**. The Insert Field Name or Number dialog box will open.

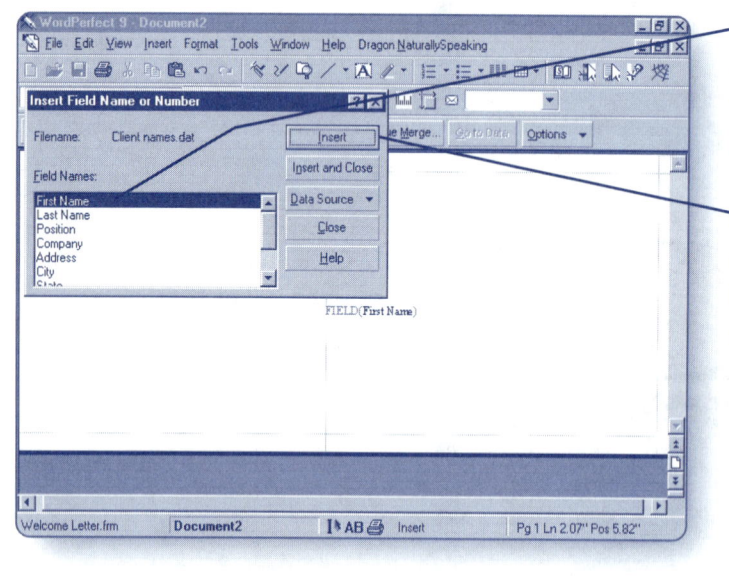

5. Click on the **first field name** to be inserted in the envelope. The field name will be highlighted.

6. Click on **Insert**. The field name will be inserted in the Mailing Address area of the envelope.

CREATING ENVELOPES FOR THE MERGED RECORDS   251

7. Repeat steps 5 and **6** as needed to insert the proper fields in the envelope. The field names will display in the envelope.

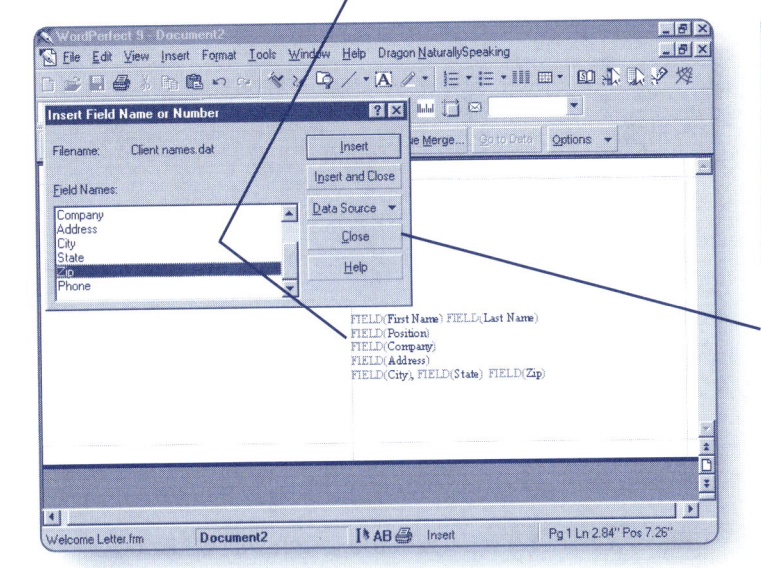

NOTE
This process is similar to the steps you took to insert the fields in the body of the letter.

8. Click on **Close**. The Insert Field Name or Number dialog box will close.

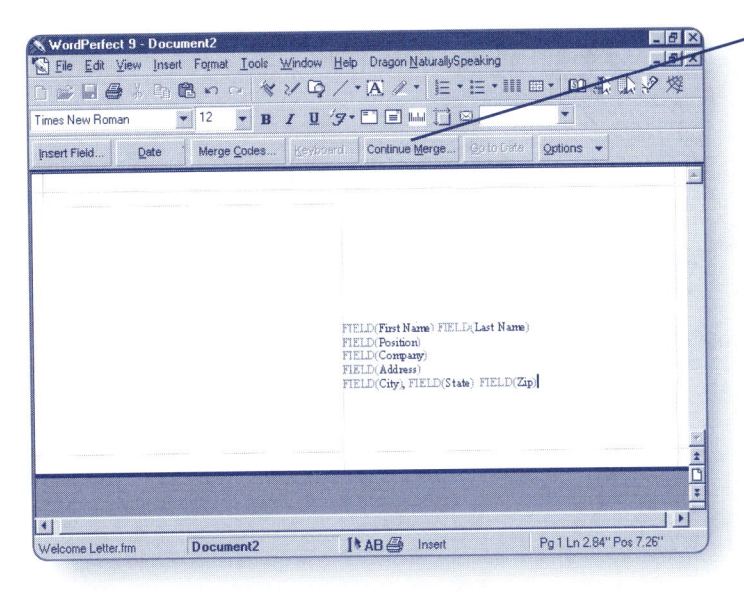

9. Click on **Continue Merge**. The Perform Merge dialog box will reappear.

CHAPTER 22: MERGING AN ADDRESS LIST AND FORM LETTER

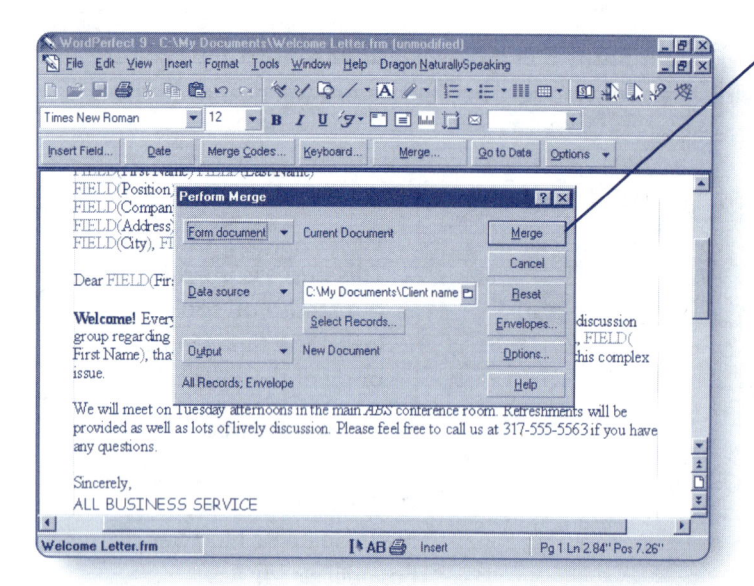

10. Click on **Merge**. WordPerfect will perform the actual merge.

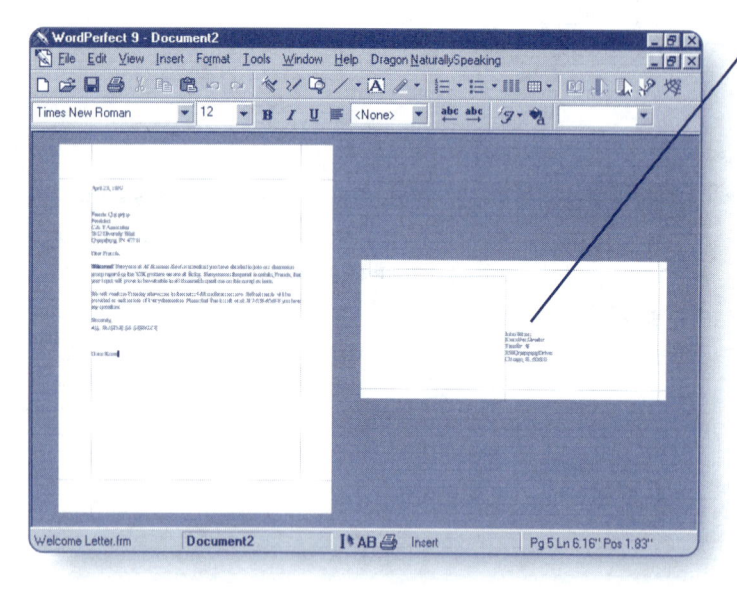

All the letters will be listed together, followed by all the envelopes at the bottom of the new document.

Part IV Review Questions

1. What is stored in a data file? *See "Creating a Data File" in Chapter 20*

2. If you create your data file in a table, what is stored in each column? *See "Naming Data Fields" in Chapter 20*

3. What letters are added to the end of a data file when you save it? *See "Using QuickData Entry" in Chapter 20*

4. What type of information is stored in the form document? *See "Creating a Form Letter" in Chapter 21*

5. What does an "association" do? *See "Creating a Form Letter" in Chapter 21*

6. What does a dynamic merge date do? *See "Using Automatic Dates" in Chapter 21*

7. Does every field in a data file need to be inserted into the form file? *See "Inserting Data Fields" in Chapter 21*

8. Does the data file need to be opened before you can merge? *See "Merging Names and Addresses with a Letter" in Chapter 22*

9. Why should you merge to a new document before you print? *See "Merging Names and Addresses with a Letter" in Chapter 22*

10. Which item prints first during a merge—letters or envelopes? *See "Creating Envelopes for the Merged Records" in Chapter 22*

PART V
Getting Creative with Graphics

Chapter 23
   Working with Graphic Lines **257**

Chapter 24
   Working with Graphic Images. **271**

Chapter 25
   Working with TextArt **283**

23
Working with Graphic Lines

WordPerfect has a drawing layer feature that includes the capability to add horizontal, vertical, or diagonal lines of any size, thickness, or color anywhere in your document. You can also add shaped objects such as arrows, rectangles, polygons, or circles. In this chapter, you'll learn how to:

- Add and move graphic lines
- Edit the thickness, style, and attributes of graphic lines
- Delete a graphic line
- Add a shaped object

Adding a Graphic Line

You can add a horizontal line or vertical line. When you know how to do that, it's easy to work with diagonal lines and other shapes.

1. Click the **mouse pointer** in the document where you want the graphic line to be located. The blinking insertion point will appear.

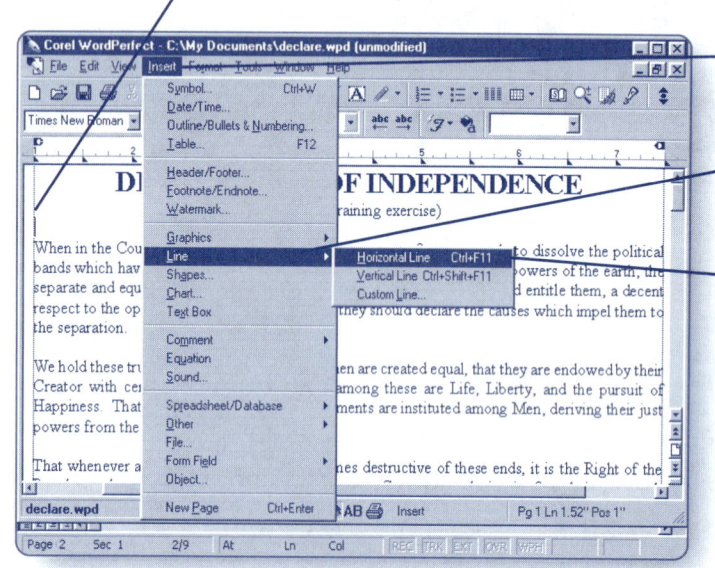

2. Click on **Insert**. The Insert menu will appear.

3. Click on **Line**. The Line cascading menu will appear.

4a. Click on **Horizontal Line**. A horizontal line will be inserted into your document at the position of the insertion point.

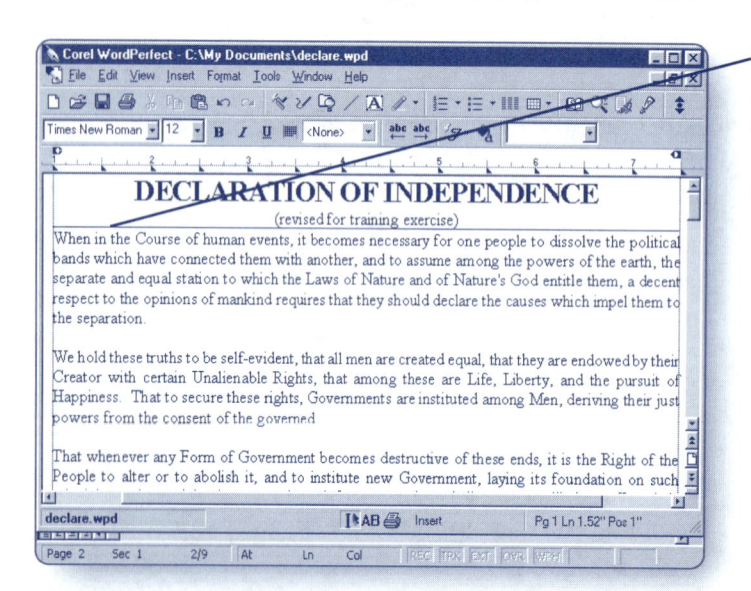

The line will be inserted in your document from the left margin to the right margin.

OR

ADDING A GRAPHIC LINE 259

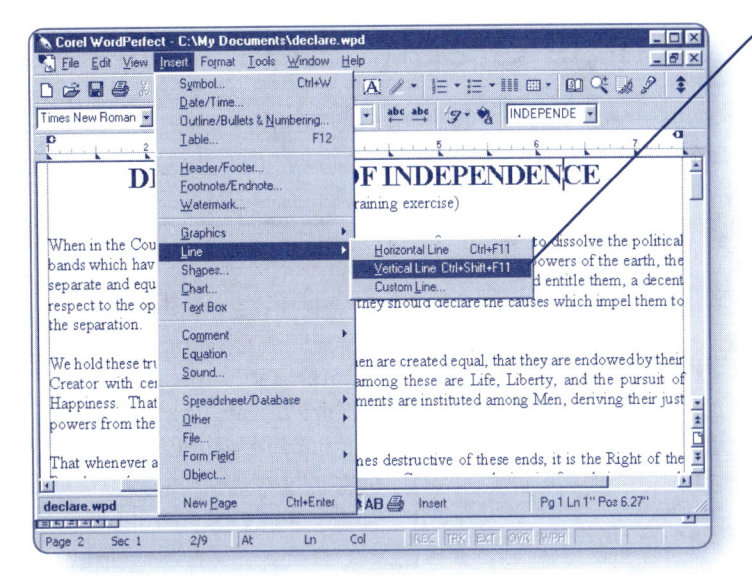

4b. Click on **Vertical Line**. A vertical line will be inserted into your document at the position of the insertion point.

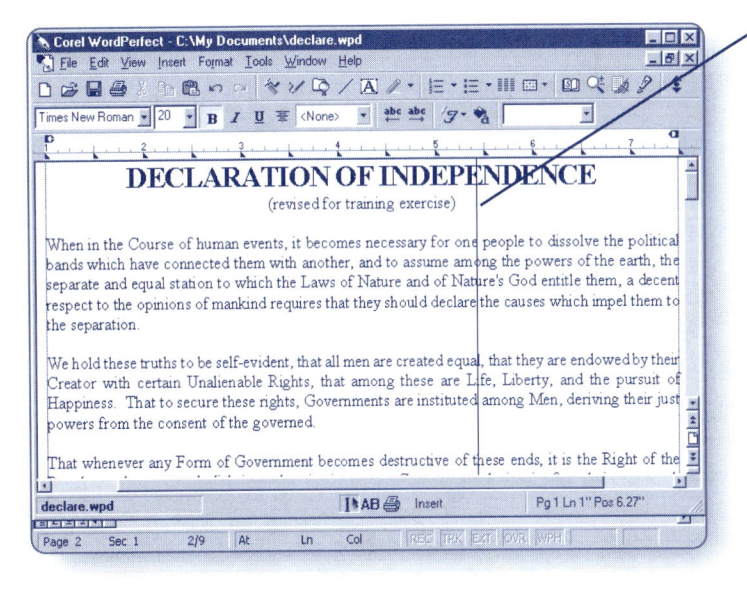

The line will be inserted in your document from the top to the bottom margin.

CHAPTER 23: WORKING WITH GRAPHIC LINES

Moving a Graphic Line

If you inserted the graphic line at the wrong position in your document, you can move it.

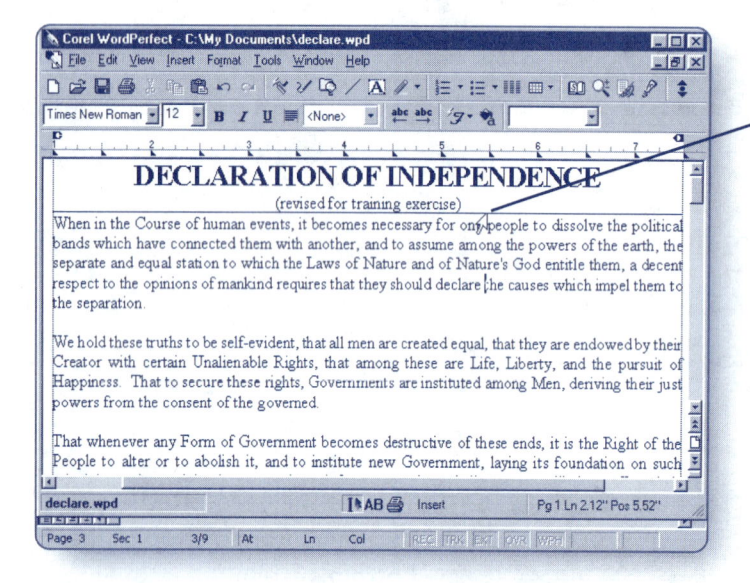

TIP

To select the graphic line, make sure that the mouse pointer is in the shape of a white arrow, not the standard I-beam you normally see when working in a document.

1. Click on the **graphic line**. The graphic line will be selected.

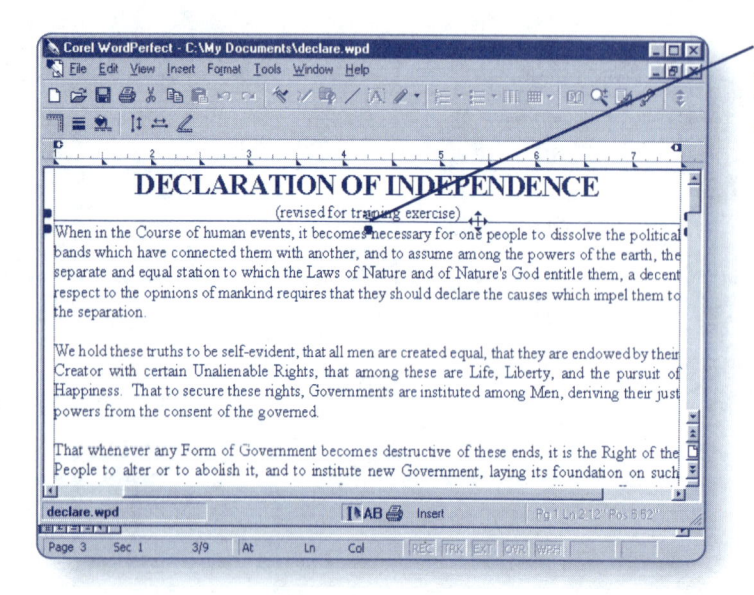

A selected object will have six black boxes called *handles* around it.

MOVING A GRAPHIC LINE   261

Notice the change in the property bar. It now reflects choices applicable to graphic lines.

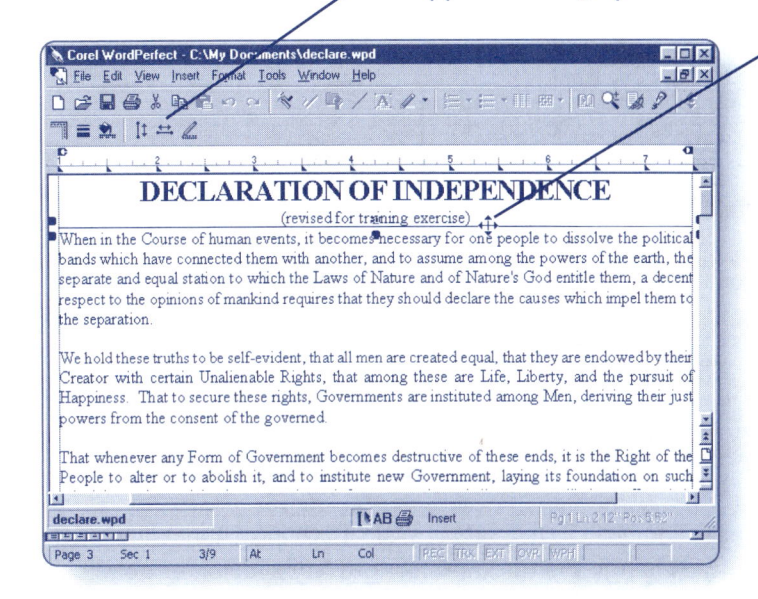

2. Position the **mouse pointer** anywhere on the line but *not* on the little black boxes. The mouse pointer will turn into a cross with four arrowheads on it.

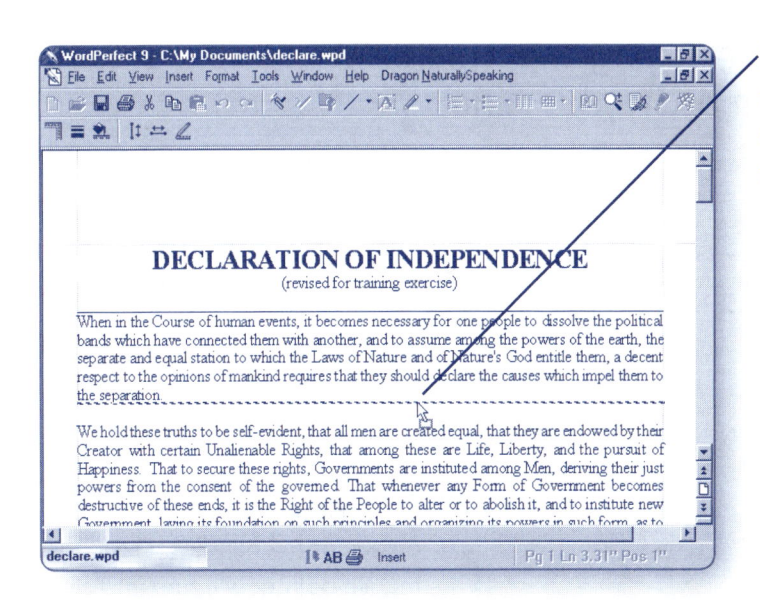

3. Click and drag the line to the new position. A dotted line will show the new position of the line.

CHAPTER 23: WORKING WITH GRAPHIC LINES

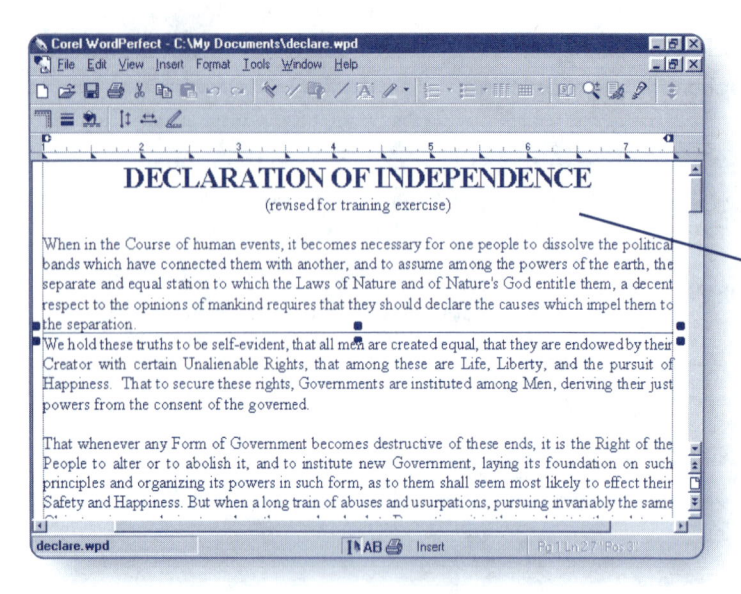

4. Release the **mouse button**. The line will be moved into the new position.

TIP

Click anywhere outside the graphic line to deselect it. The black handles will disappear.

Editing Graphic Lines

After a line has been created, you can change it in many ways. You can change the thickness, length, style, color, or position on the page.

Changing the Thickness of a Graphic Line

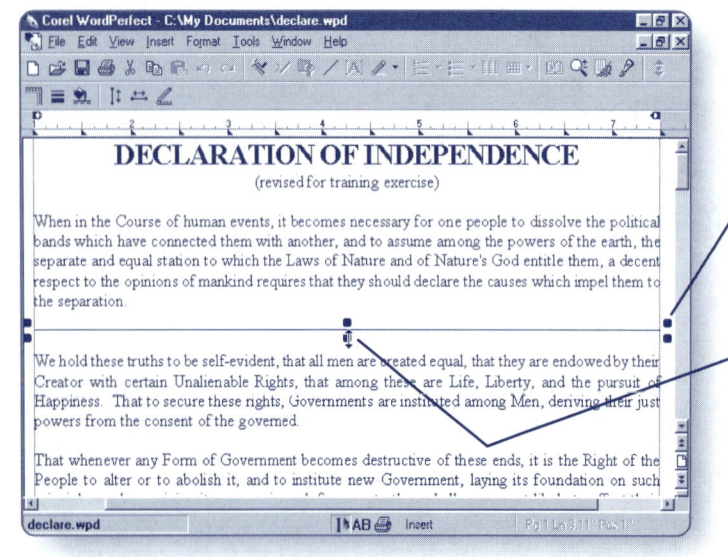

By default, a graphic line is .013-inch thick, or *hairline* thickness. You can change the thickness of the line to whatever you want.

1. Click on the **graphic line**. Six black handles will appear around the line.

2. Position the **mouse pointer** on any of the handles. The mouse pointer will turn into a double-headed arrow.

EDITING GRAPHIC LINES   263

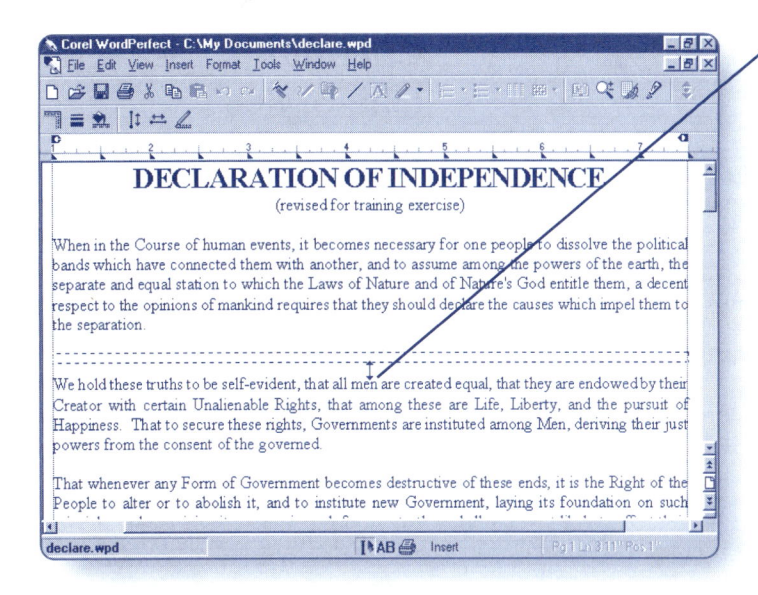

3. Click and drag the **handle** until you get the desired thickness. A dotted box will show the new thickness of the line.

4. Release the **mouse button**. The dotted box will disappear, and the line will be changed to the new thickness.

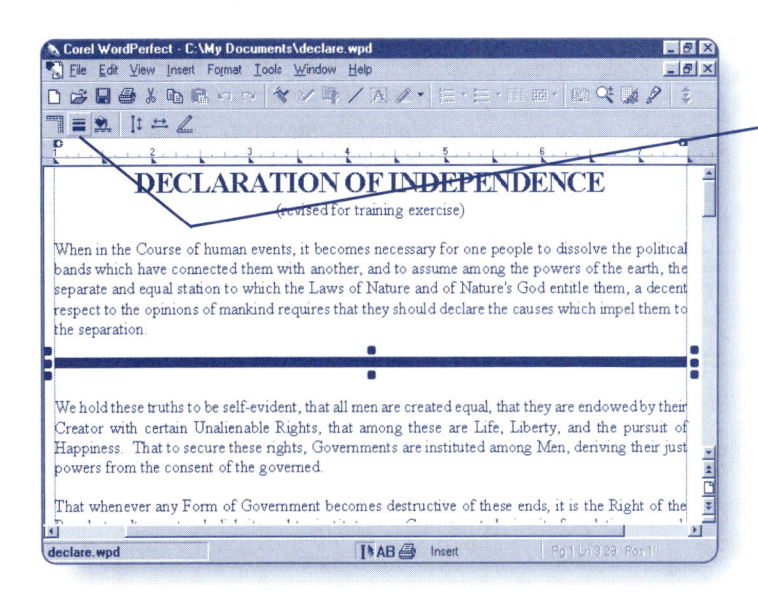

TIP
Another way to change the thickness of a line is to make a selection from the Line Thickness button.

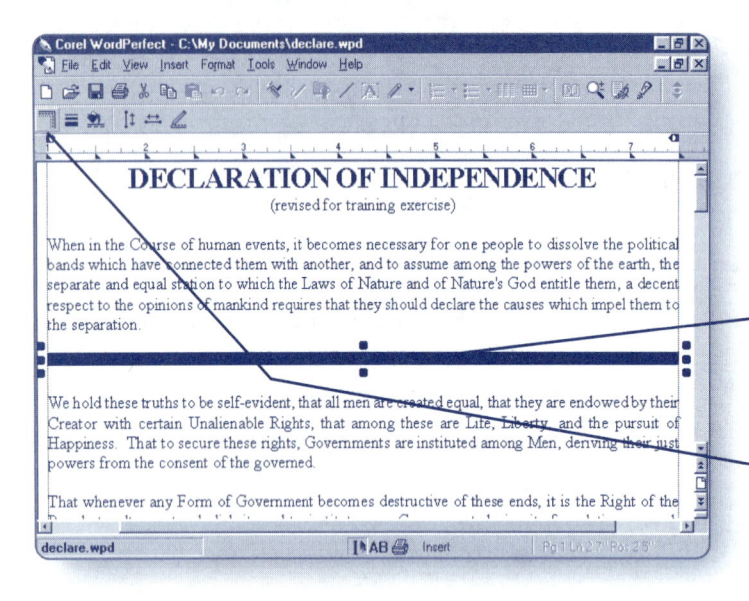

Changing Line Styles

A graphic line is a single line by default, but there are many different styles you can apply.

1. Click on the **graphic line**. Six black handles will appear around the line.

2. Click on the **Line Style button**. A box will appear with many of the line style choices.

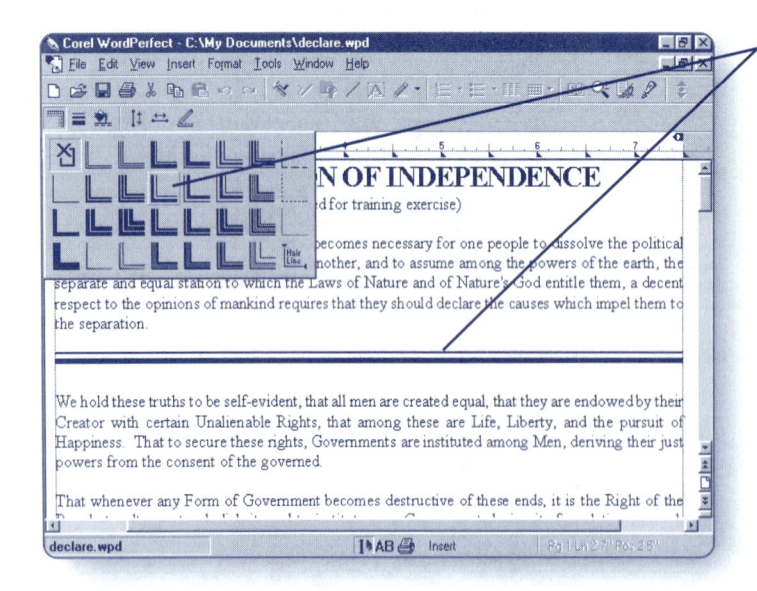

3. Click on the **line style** you want for your graphic line. The line will change to the style you selected.

EDITING GRAPHIC LINES

Editing Line Attributes

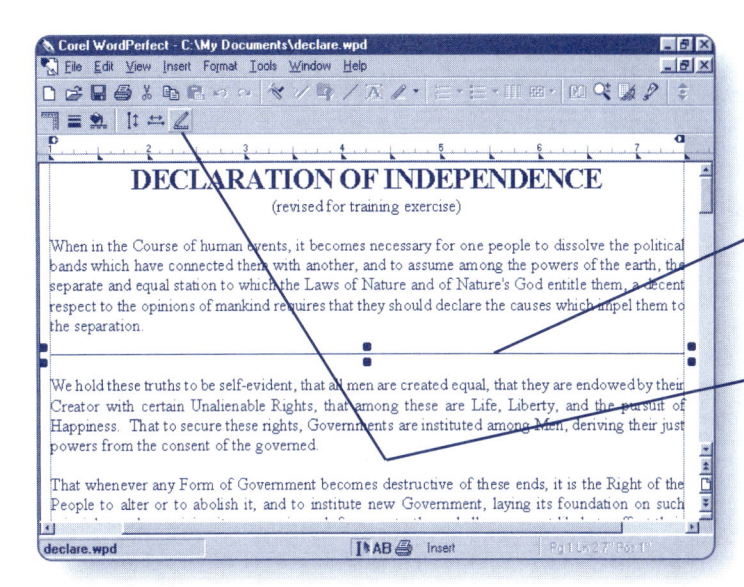

You can change all the attributes of a line from one dialog box, including the color, thickness, and style.

1. Click on the **graphic line**. Six black handles will appear around the line.

2. Click on the **Line Graphic Edit button**. The Edit Graphics Line dialog box will open.

TIP
Optionally, click on the Edit menu and choose Edit Graphic Line.

You can make many changes from this dialog box.

Change a horizontal line to a vertical line or a vertical line to a horizontal line.

Change the style of your graphic line.

Change the color of your graphic line.

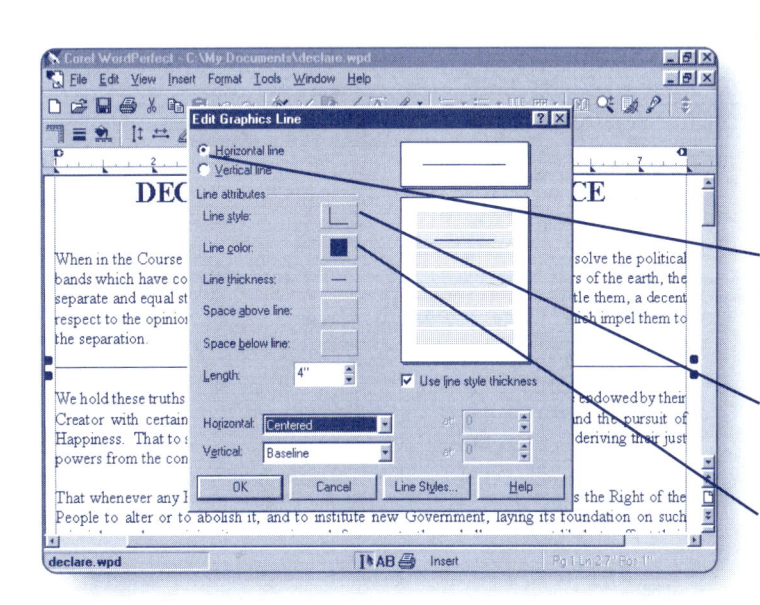

CHAPTER 23: WORKING WITH GRAPHIC LINES

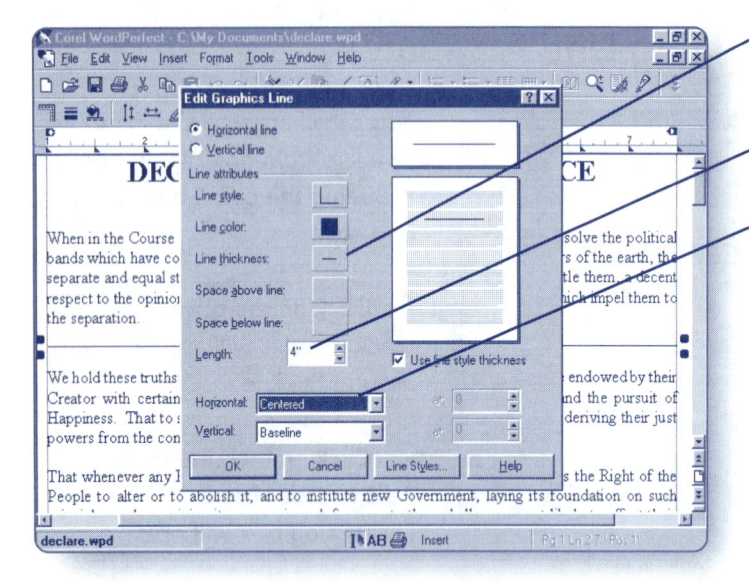

Change the thickness of your graphic line.

Change the length of the line.

Set the position of your line on the page.

3. Make any desired **changes** to the line. The options will be selected.

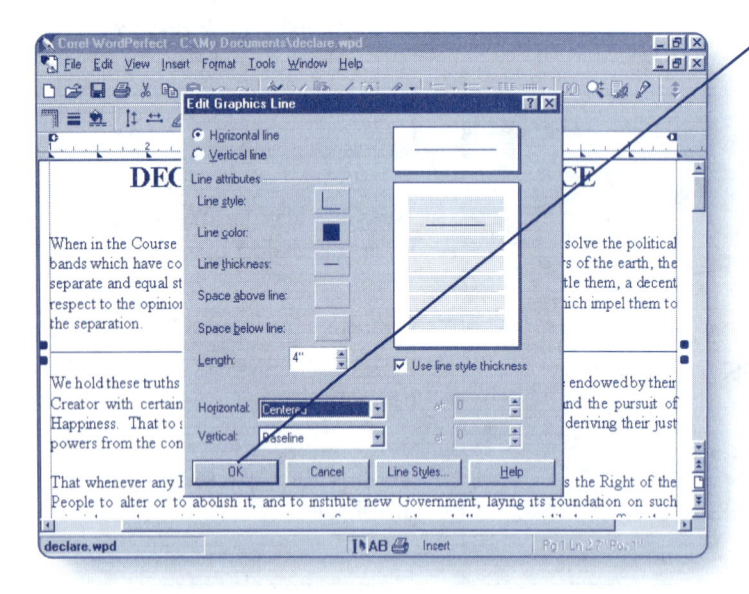

4. Click on **OK**. The Edit Graphics Line dialog box will close.

DELETING GRAPHIC LINES   267

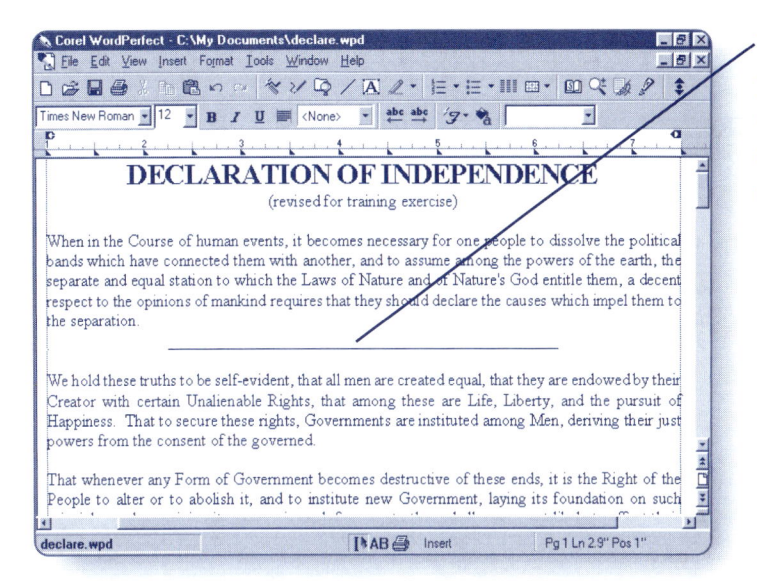

The changes will be in effect for your graphic line. In this example, I changed the length to four inches and centered the line.

Deleting Graphic Lines

If you no longer want the graphic line in your document, you can delete it.

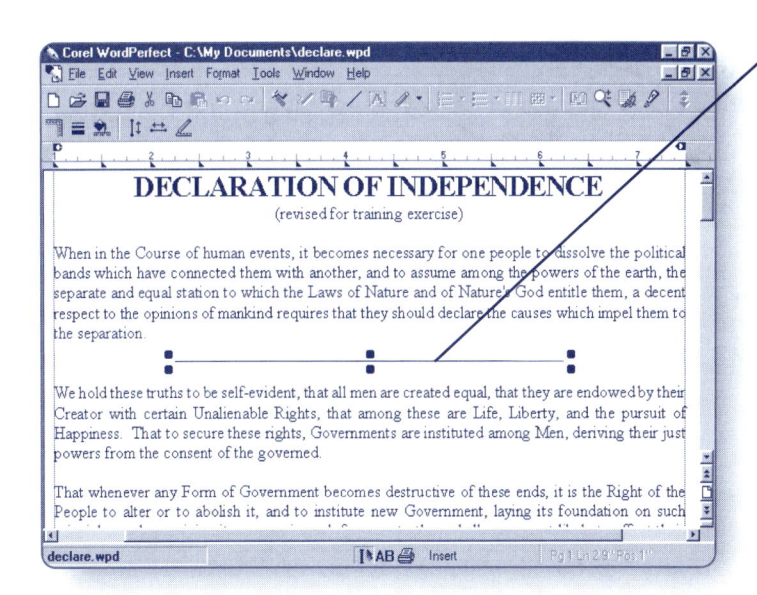

1. Click on the **graphic line**. Six black handles will appear around the line.

2. Press the **Delete key**. The line will be deleted.

Adding a Shaped Object

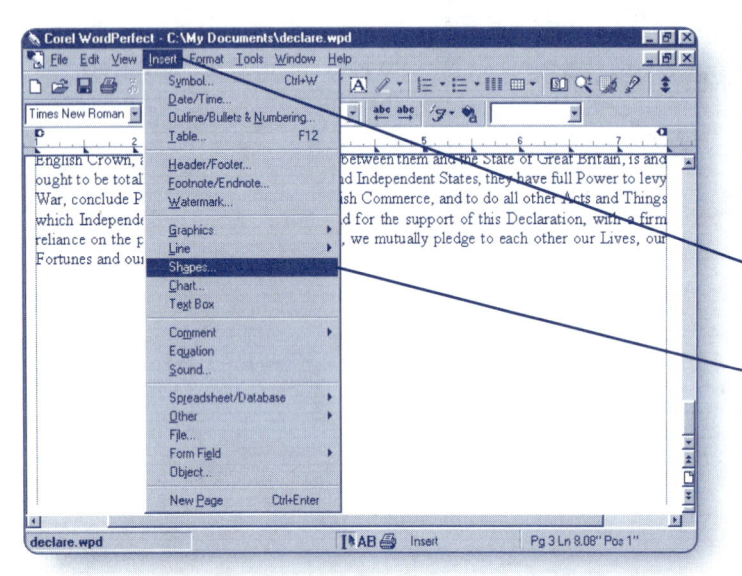

You can draw arrows, stars, hearts, smiley faces, and many other shaped objects to call attention to something in your document.

1. Click on **Insert**. The Insert menu will appear.

2. Click on **Shapes**. The Draw Object Shapes dialog box will open.

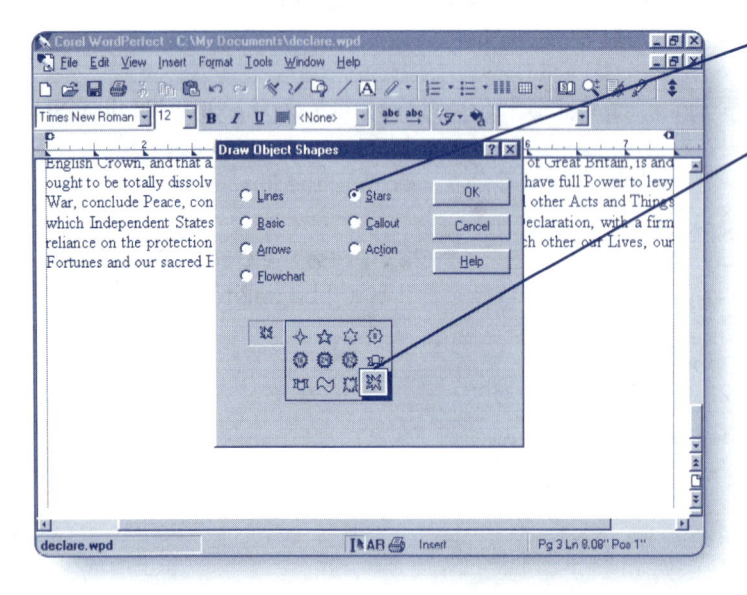

3. Click on a **shape**. A collection of shapes will appear.

4. Click on a **Style**. The option will appear in the box on the left side.

ADDING A SHAPED OBJECT   269

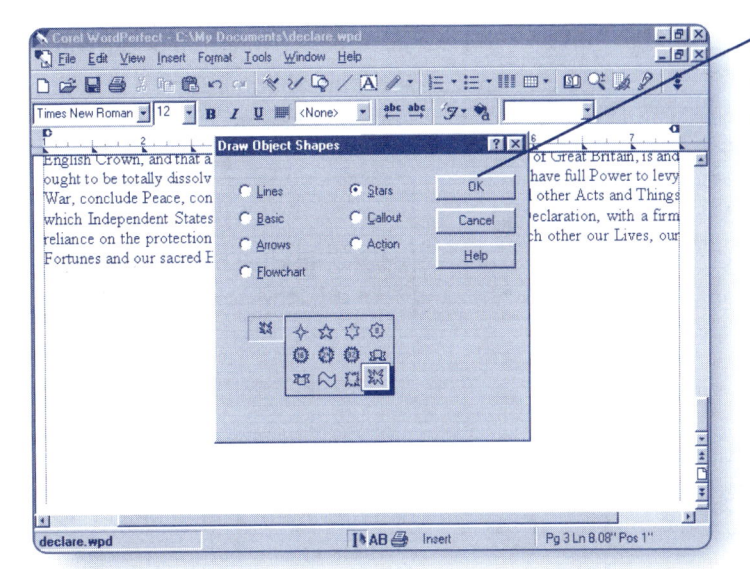

5. Click on **OK**. The menu will close, and the mouse pointer will turn into a black cross.

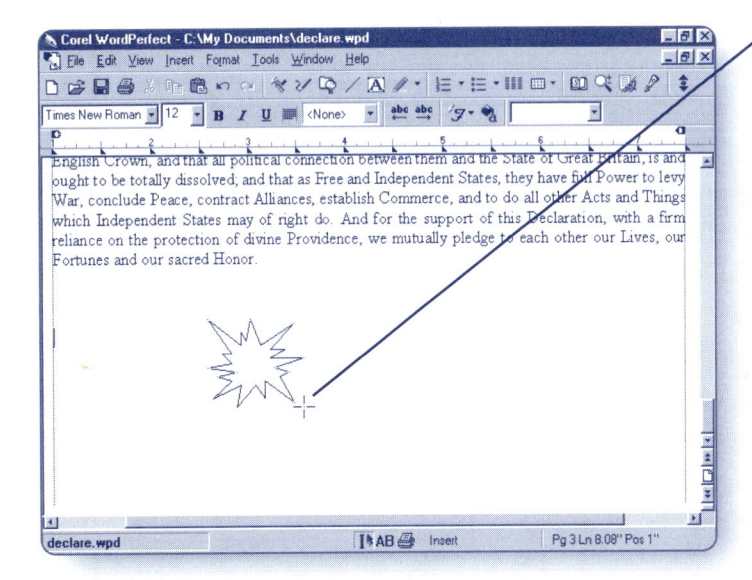

6. Click and **drag** the **mouse pointer** across the area where you want the object to appear. The outline of your shape will appear as you are dragging the mouse.

270 CHAPTER 23: WORKING WITH GRAPHIC LINES

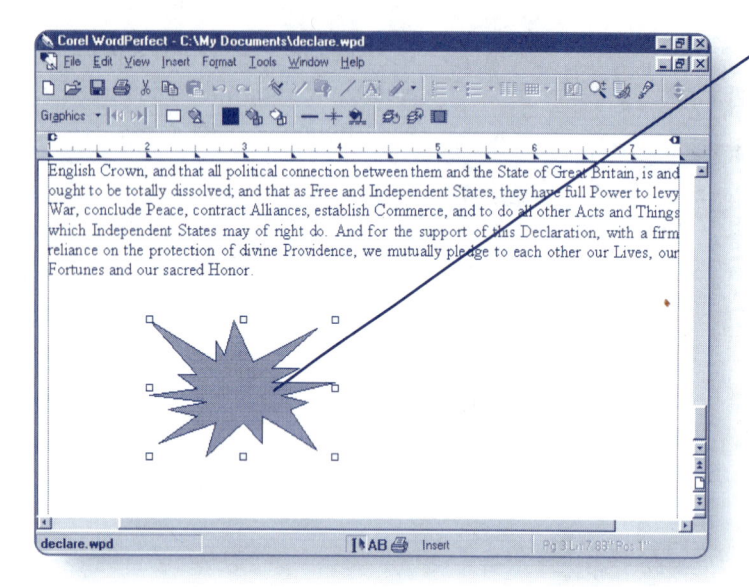

7. Release the **mouse button**. A shape will be inserted into your document.

TIP
Double-click on the object to edit the colors and fill attributes.

The shaped object can be selected, moved, sized, or deleted in the same manner as a graphic line.

24

Working with Graphic Images

Thousands of clip art images and hundreds of photos are provided with WordPerfect. During a standard installation, however, only some of these are copied to your hard drive. Most of these clip art images are stored on the Corel WordPerfect Suite CD. In this chapter, you'll learn how to:

- Add, resize, and move a graphic image
- Change the border, shadow, and fill of an image
- Wrap text around a graphic image

CHAPTER 24: WORKING WITH GRAPHIC IMAGES

Adding a Graphic Image

You can insert many types of graphic images into your document. WordPerfect can automatically convert and read images in many standard formats, including .wpg, .wmf, .jpg, .gif, .tif, .bmp, and .pcx.

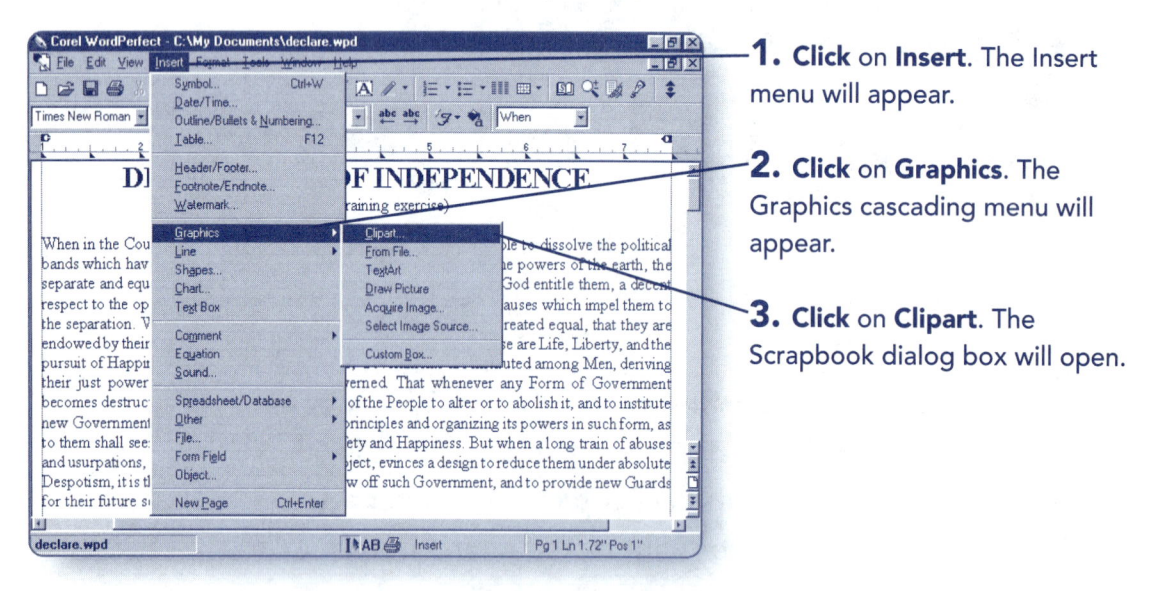

1. Click on **Insert**. The Insert menu will appear.

2. Click on **Graphics**. The Graphics cascading menu will appear.

3. Click on **Clipart**. The Scrapbook dialog box will open.

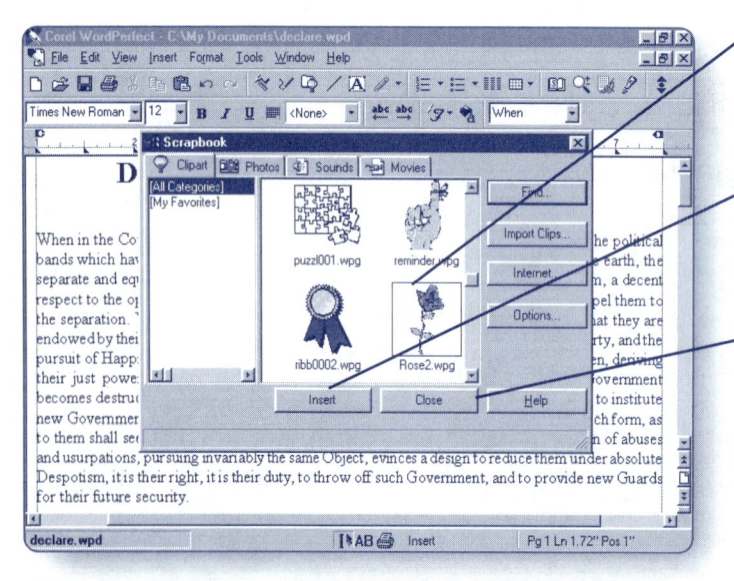

4. Click on the **graphic image** you want to insert. A box will surround the selected image.

5. Click on **Insert**. The graphic image will be inserted into your document.

6. Click on **Close**. The Scrapbook dialog box will close.

RESIZING A GRAPHIC IMAGE 273

A Graphics property bar will display.

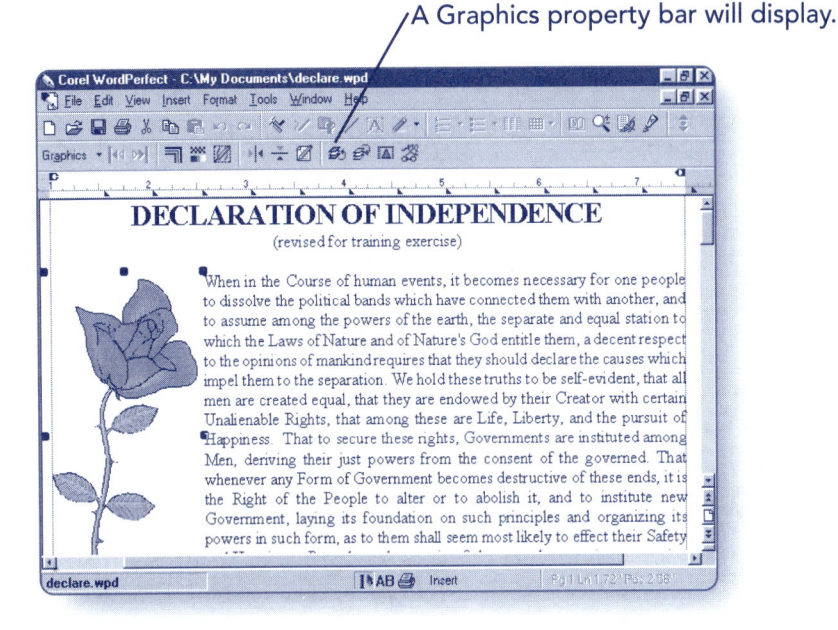

Resizing a Graphic Image

Resize the graphic image to fit appropriately in your document.

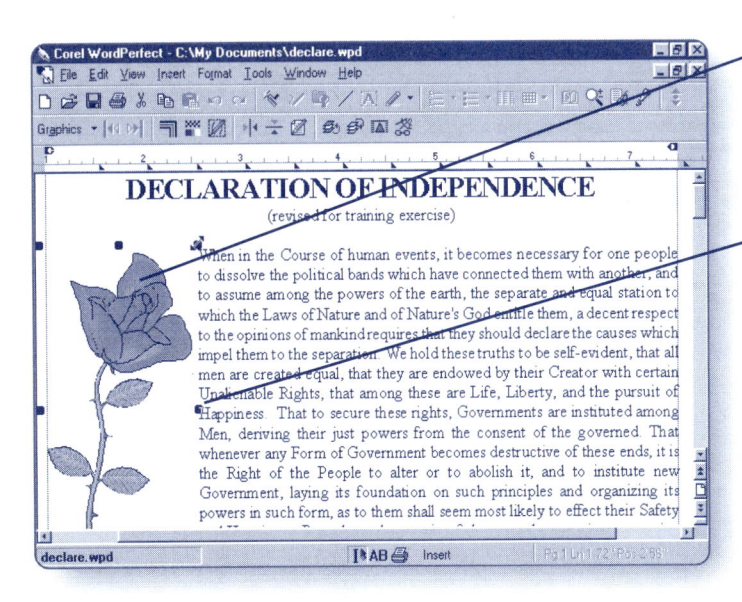

1. If necessary, **click** on the **graphic**. Eight small sizing handles will appear around the image.

2. Position the **mouse pointer** on one of the sizing handles. The mouse pointer will turn into a double-headed arrow.

CHAPTER 24: WORKING WITH GRAPHIC IMAGES

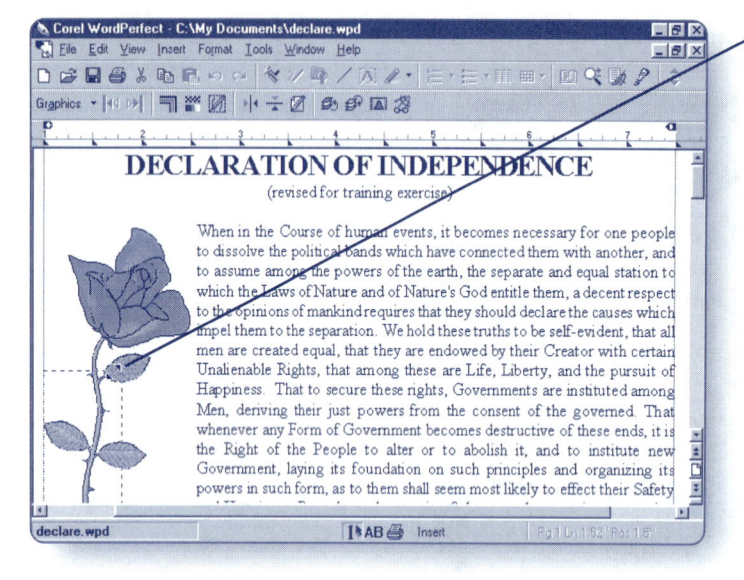

3. Drag the **sizing handle** to change the size of the graphic box. A dotted box will show the new size of the box.

TIP

Be sure to place the pointer directly on a handle when you drag. Use the corner handles to resize a box so as to preserve the current height-width ratio of the box and keep the original proportions of the image.

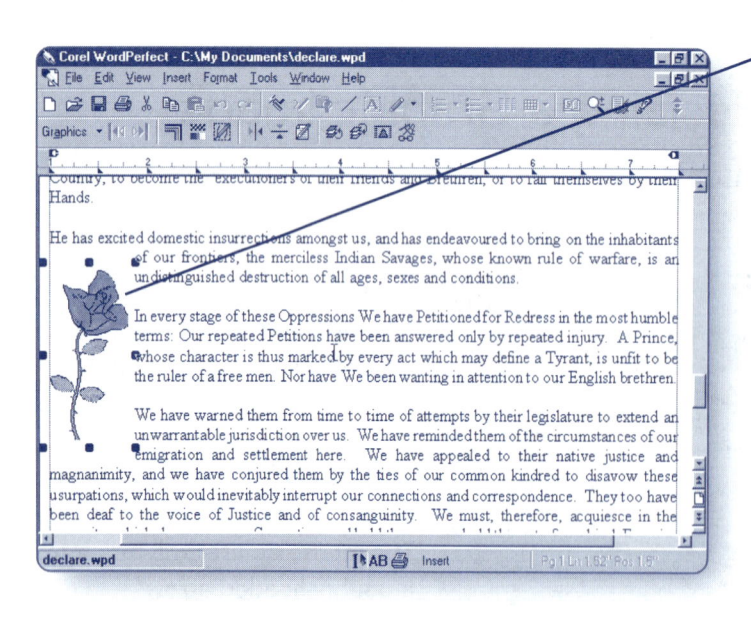

4. Release the **mouse button**. The graphic image will be resized.

Moving a Graphic Image

The graphic image can be moved to any position on your page.

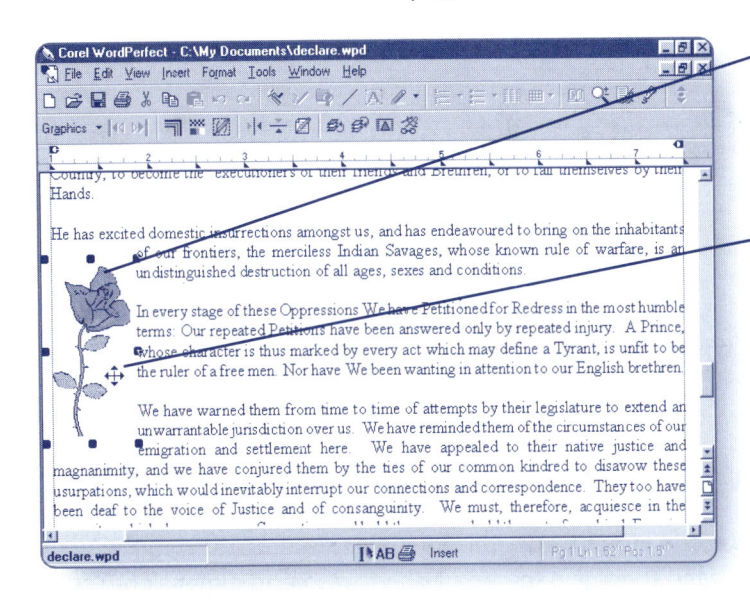

1. If necessary, **click** on the **graphic**. Eight small sizing handles will appear around the image.

2. Position the **mouse pointer** anywhere on the graphic box *except* on any of the sizing handles. The mouse pointer will turn into a black cross with four arrowheads.

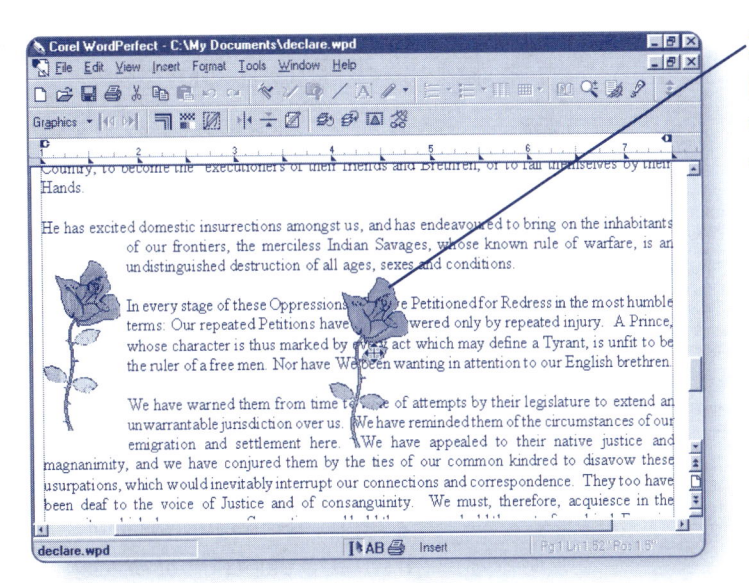

3. Drag the **graphic** to the new location. A replica of the image will indicate where the graphic will be placed.

CHAPTER 24: WORKING WITH GRAPHIC IMAGES

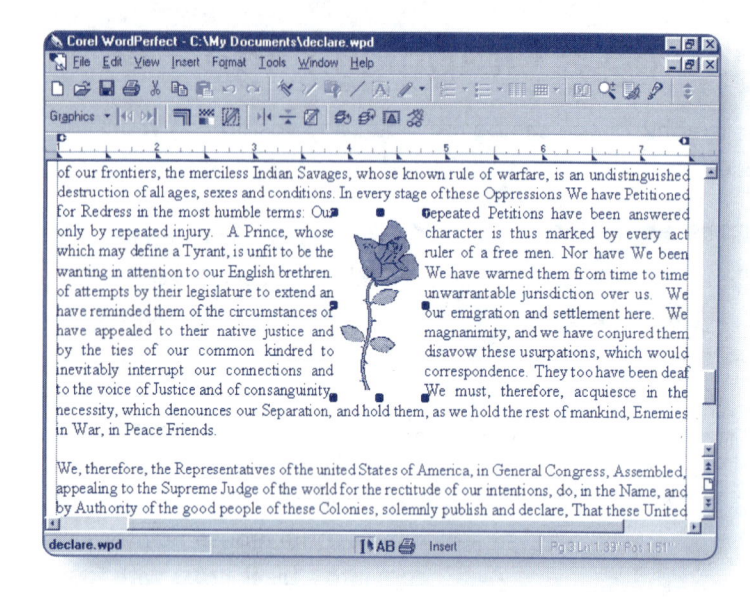

4. Release the **mouse button**. The graphic will be moved to the new location.

Working with Borders and Fills

Set a box around a graphic image to set it apart from the text, and then give the box a shadow to add dimension. You can even add background shading to the box surrounding the graphic image.

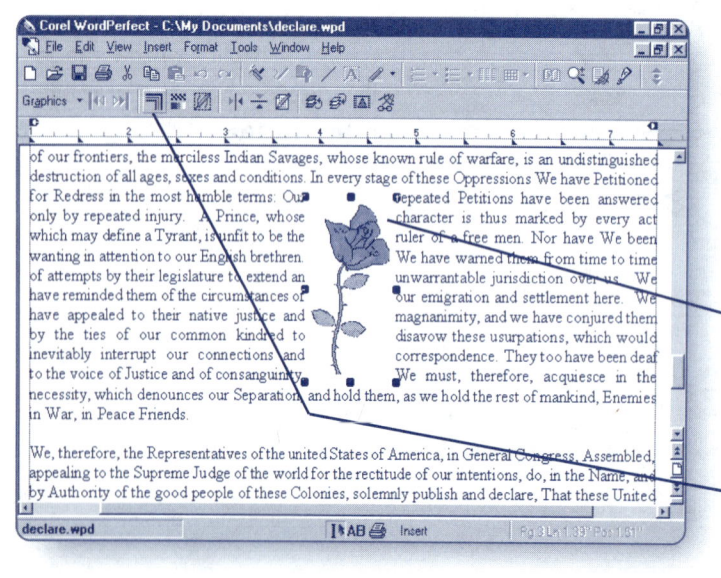

Adding a Border

The graphic box does not have a border around it, but there are many different styles of borders you can apply to your graphic image.

1. If necessary, **click** on the **graphic**. Eight small sizing handles will appear around the image.

2. Click on the **Border Style button**. A selection of border styles will be displayed.

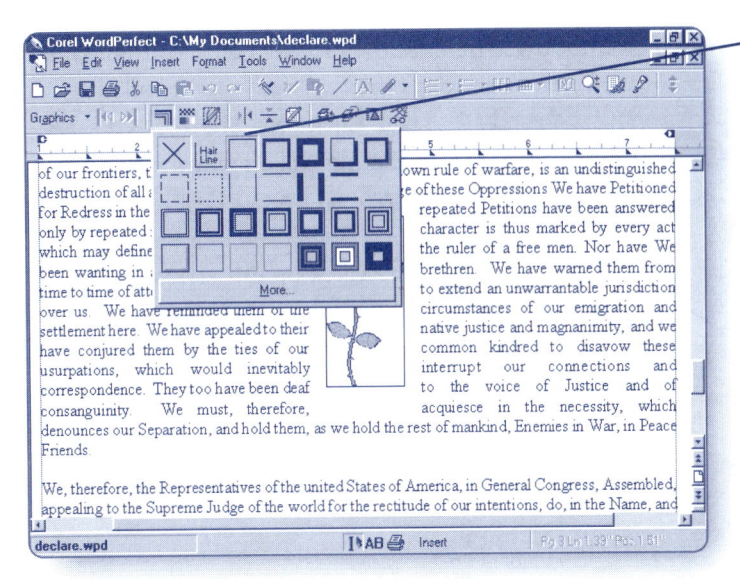

WORKING WITH BORDERS AND FILLS 277

3. Click on the desired **border style**. The selected border will be applied to your graphic image.

Adding a Shadow to a Graphic Box

Adding a shadow gives a three-dimensional effect to your graphic. The image itself will not have a shadow, only the box surrounding it.

> **NOTE**
> Before a shadow can be applied, the image must have a border around it.

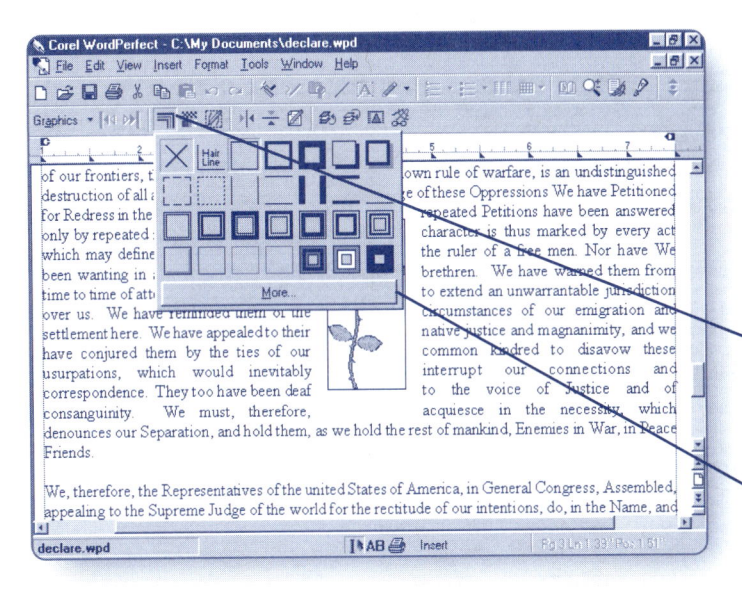

1. If necessary, **click** on the **graphic**. Eight small sizing handles will appear around the image.

2. Click on the **Border Style button**. A selection of border styles will be displayed.

3. Click on **More**. The Box Border/Fill dialog box will open.

CHAPTER 24: WORKING WITH GRAPHIC IMAGES

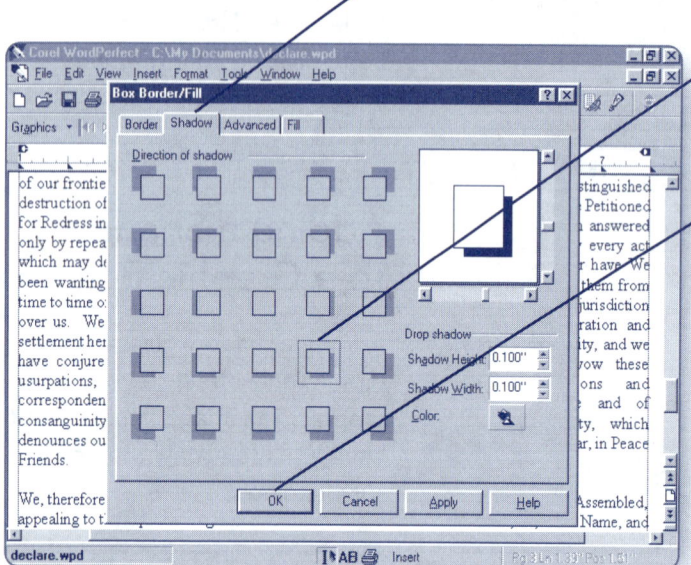

4. Click on **Shadow**. The Shadow tab will come to the front.

5. Click on a **Shadow style**. A sample will display in the preview box.

6. Click on **OK**. The dialog box will close, and the image box will have a shadow.

Applying Fill Patterns

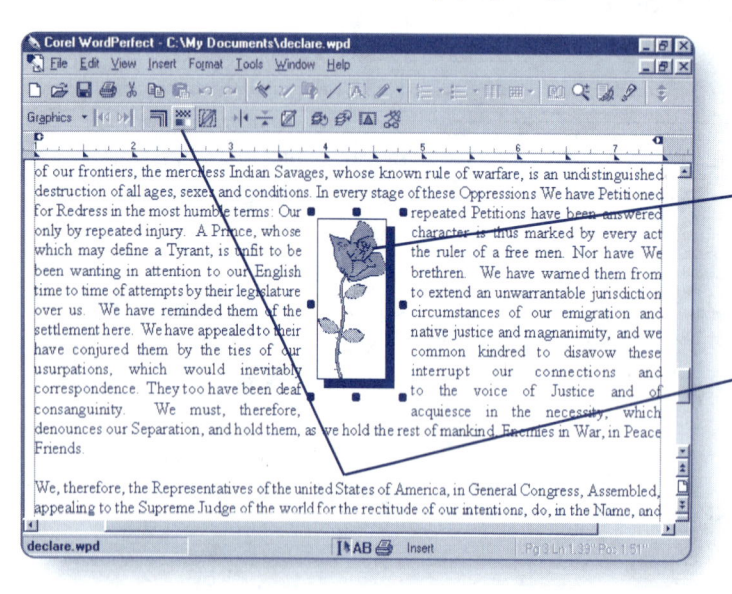

Separate the box from the image by adding a fill pattern to the interior of the box.

1. If necessary, **click** on the **graphic**. Eight small sizing handles will appear around the image.

2. Click on the **Box Fill button**. A selection of choices will appear.

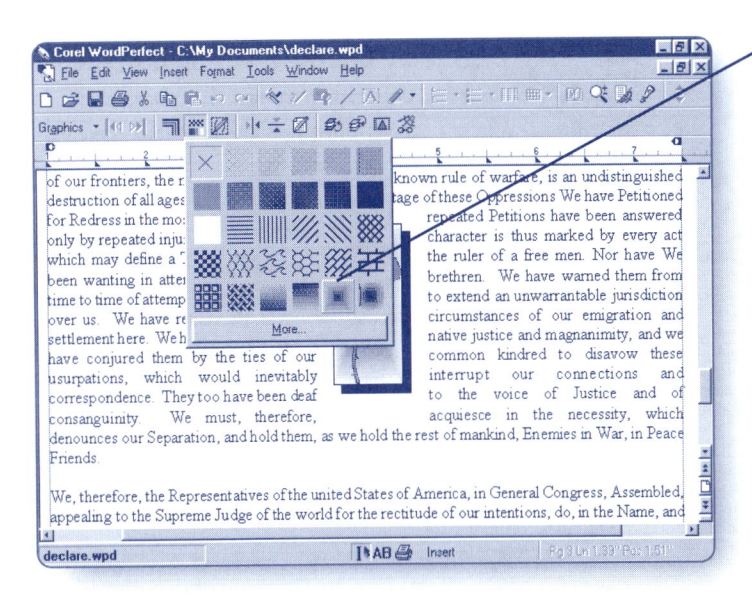

WRAPPING TEXT AROUND THE GRAPHIC IMAGE 279

3. Click on a **Fill Style**. The selection will be applied to the graphic box.

Wrapping Text Around the Graphic Image

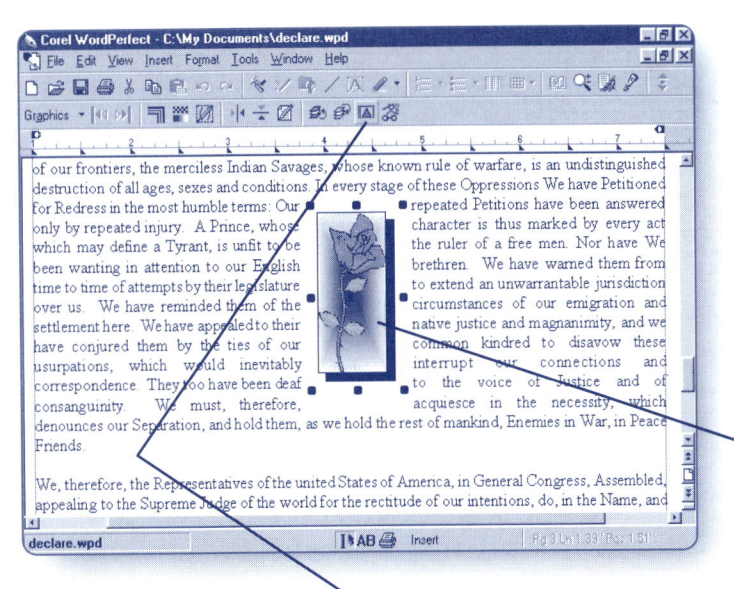

By default, the text will appear on both sides of a graphic image. Several selections are available for the wrapping of text, including contouring. Contouring text eliminates the extra white space around a graphic. Any borders are removed, and the text will wrap around the image.

1. If necessary, **click** on the **graphic**. Eight small sizing handles will appear around the image.

2. Click on the **Wrap button**. A menu of choices will appear.

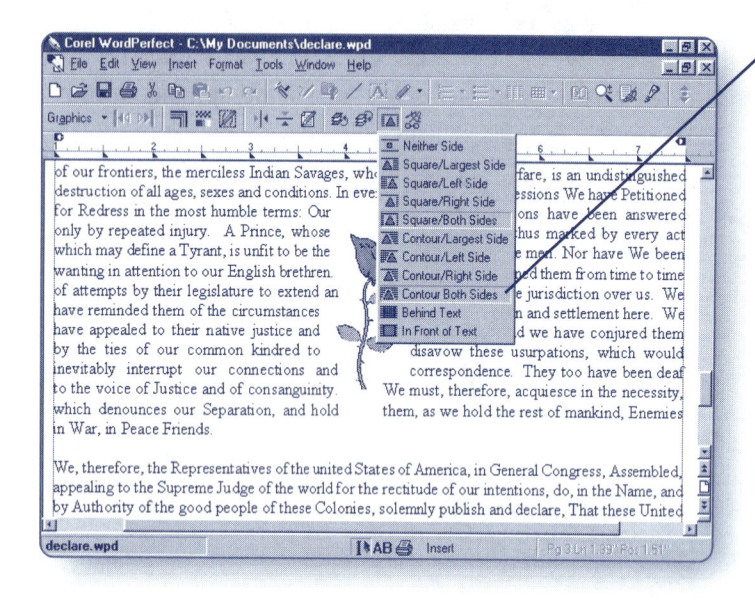

3. Choose a Wrapping Type. This determines the shape the text will take around the graphic image.

> **NOTE**
>
> Contoured text will not work if the box border has rounded corners or separate top and bottom lines.

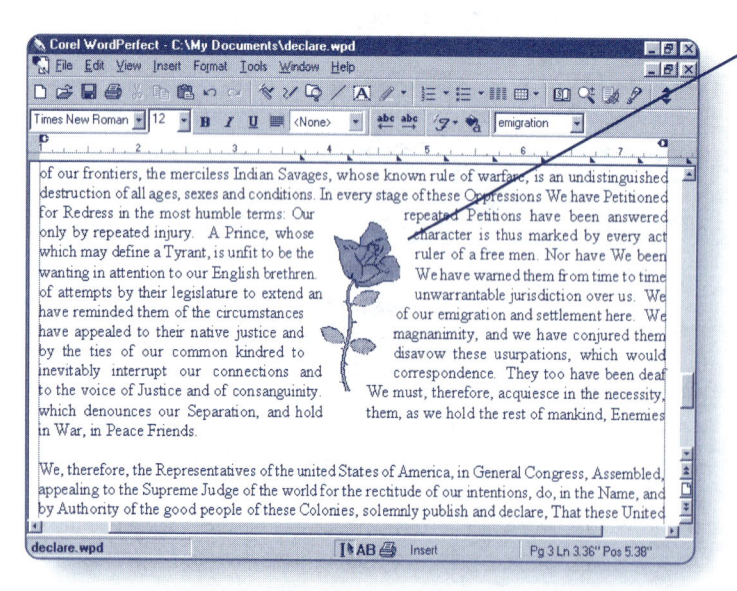

In this example, the text is contoured around the graphic. Any border previously placed around the image is removed.

Tightening Text Contour

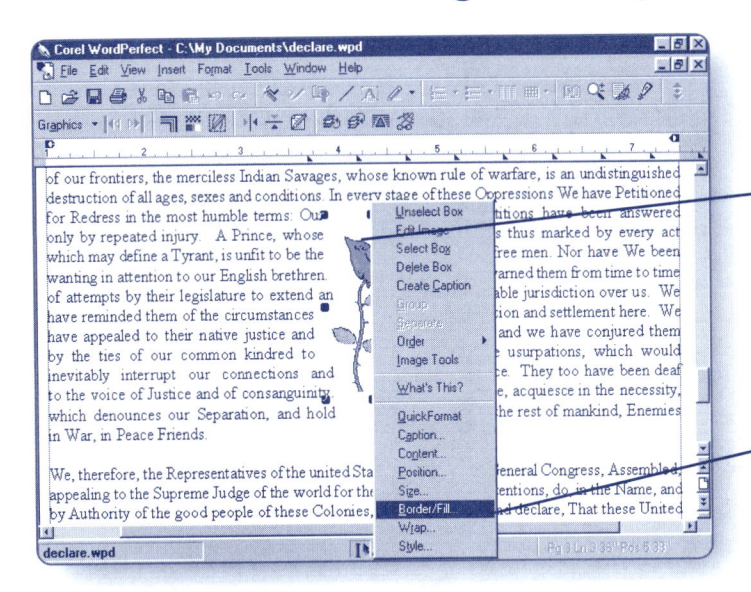

WordPerfect allows you to choose how close the image will appear to the document text.

1. Position the **mouse pointer** on top of the graphic image.

2. Click the **right mouse button**. A shortcut menu will appear.

3. Click on **Border/Fill**. The Box Border/Fill dialog box will open.

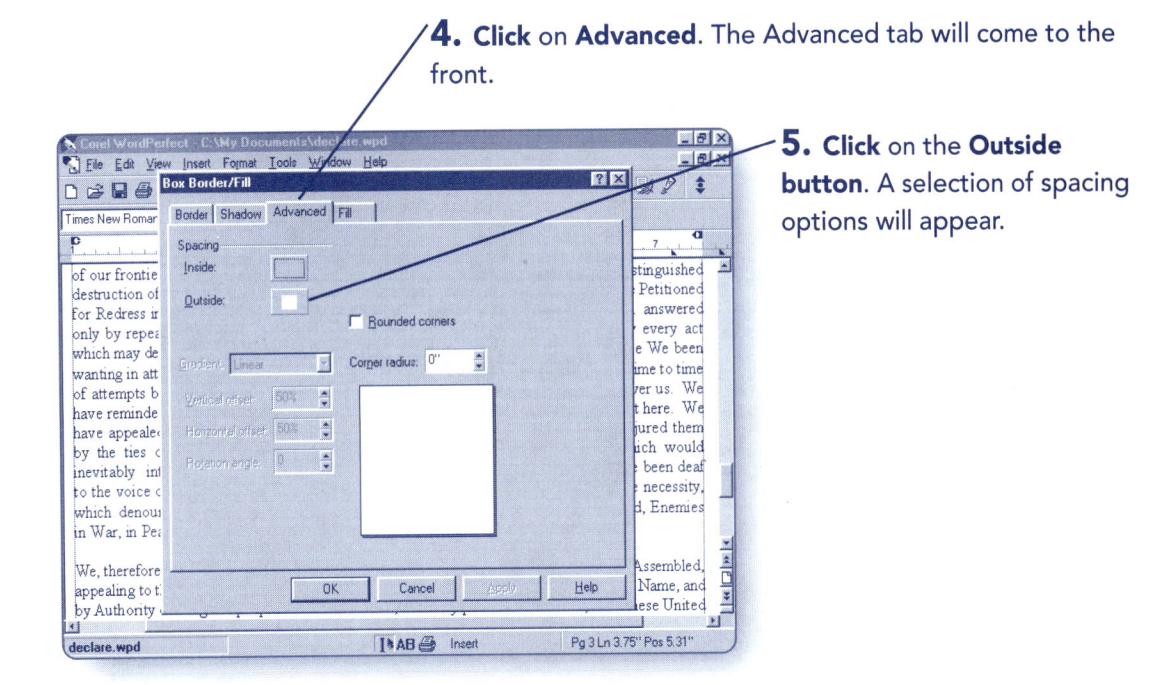

4. Click on **Advanced**. The Advanced tab will come to the front.

5. Click on the **Outside button**. A selection of spacing options will appear.

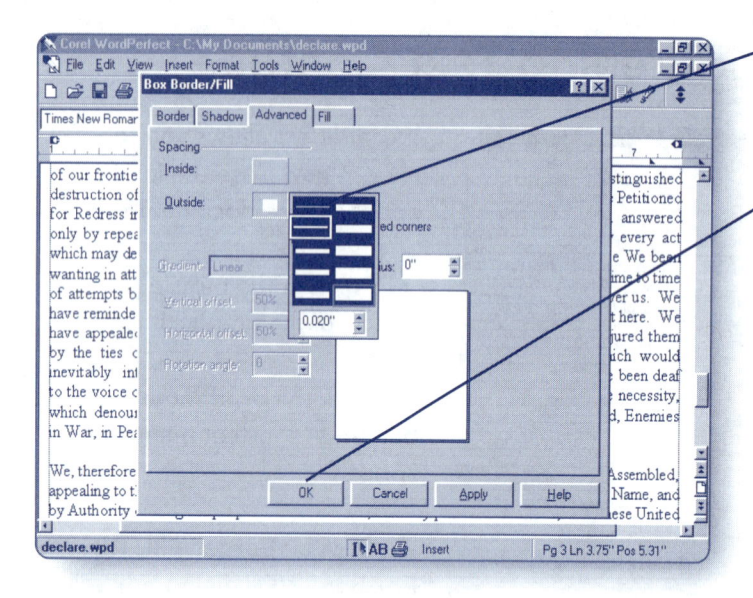

6. Click on **one** of the first three spacing **options**. The option will be selected.

7. Click on **OK**. The Box Border/Fill dialog box will close, and the text will be pulled closer to the image.

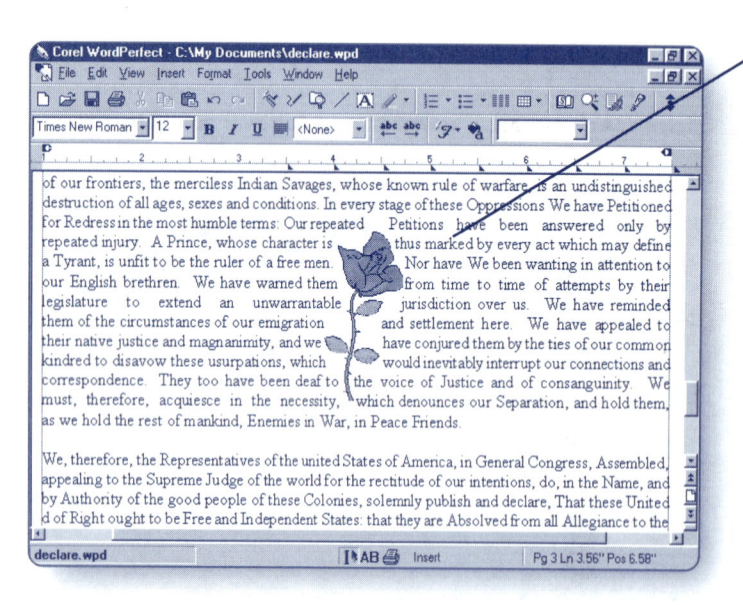

8. Click anywhere **outside** the graphic **image**. The image will be deselected.

25

Working with TextArt

TextArt is used to change words in your documents into graphic designs. You can create both two-dimensional and three-dimensional TextArt shapes. The image can be molded from a wide variety of interesting shapes and modified more using patterns, colors, and other options. In this chapter, you'll learn how to:

- Create TextArt text
- Change TextArt shapes
- Change 2-D options
- Change 3-D options

Creating TextArt Text

TextArt's special effects can be applied to text you have already typed in your document.

1. Click the **mouse pointer** where you want the TextArt object to be located. A blinking insertion point will appear.

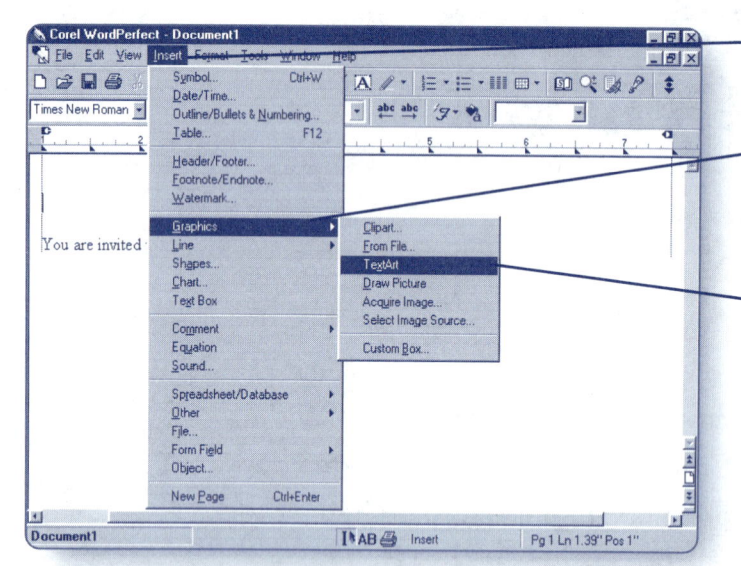

2. Click on **Insert**. The Insert menu will appear.

3. Click on **Graphics**. The Graphics cascading menu will appear.

4. Click on **TextArt**. The Corel TextArt 9.0 dialog box will open.

5. Type your **text** in the Type here: area. Your text will appear in a predefined TextArt shape.

EDITING TEXTART

> **TIP**
> Use short lines of text if possible. Too much text in a TextArt graphic box is hard to read.

Editing TextArt

You can edit TextArt in many ways. Change the shape, color, or font, or even make it three-dimensional.

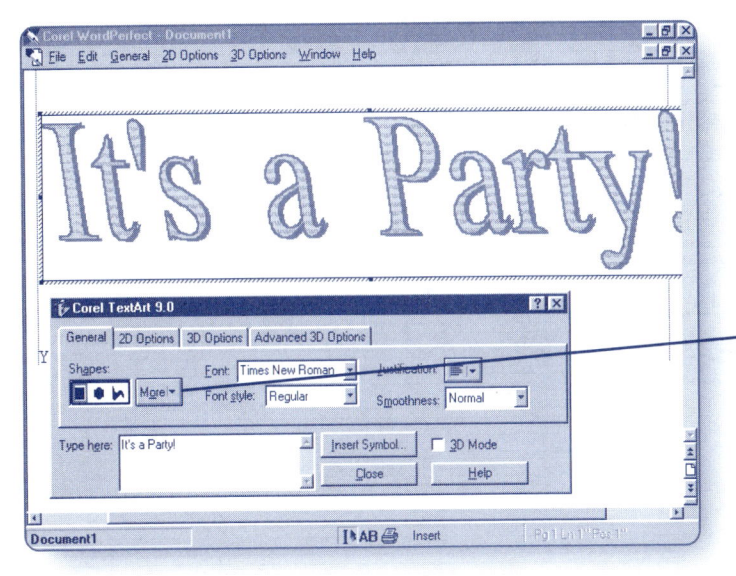

Changing TextArt Shapes

TextArt offers 57 possible shapes for your text. Choose the one that best fits your purpose.

1. Click on **More**. The additional shapes box will appear.

286 CHAPTER 25: WORKING WITH TEXTART

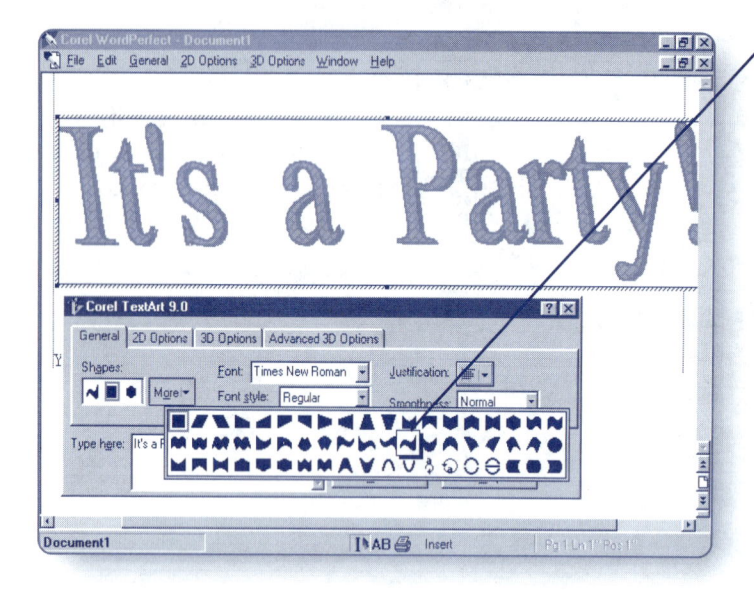

2. Click on a **shape**. Click on the various shapes and watch your text change.

3. Click on **Close**. The TextArt dialog box will close, and the object will be inserted into your document.

Editing TextArt Attributes

Any font you have installed on your machine can be applied to your TextArt object for an additional effect!

1. Double-click on the **TextArt object**. The Corel TextArt 9.0 dialog box will open.

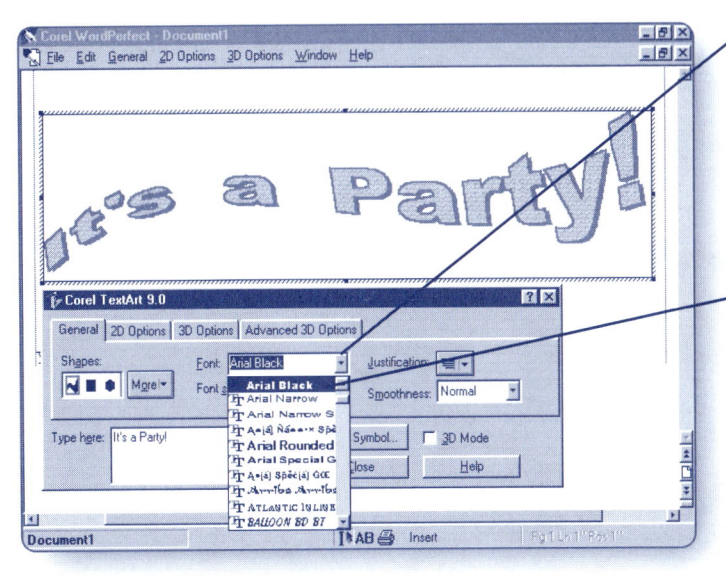

2. Click on the **down arrow** (▼) next to the Font: list box. A list of your available fonts will appear. Your font choices may vary from the ones you see in this figure.

3. Click on a **font** for your text. The TextArt will reflect the newly selected font.

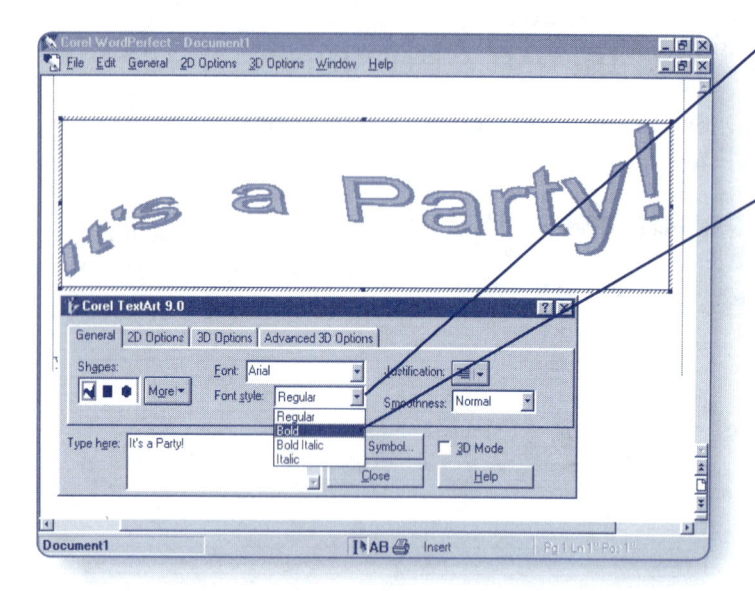

4. Click on the **Font style: box**. A list of available style choices will appear.

5. Choose a **font style** such as bold or italic. The new style will be applied to your TextArt.

Changing 2-D Options

Two-dimensional options include choices such as color or pattern of your text.

1. Click on the **2D Options tab**. The tab will come to the front.

2. Click on the **Preset: button**. Five predefined color and shape options will appear.

EDITING TEXTART 289

3. Click on an **option**. The TextArt object will change.

4. Click on the **Text color: button**. A list of available background color options will appear.

5. Click on a **color**. The background of the object will change.

6. Click on the **Pattern: button**. A series of pattern possibilities will appear.

7. Click on a **Pattern**. The TextArt object will change.

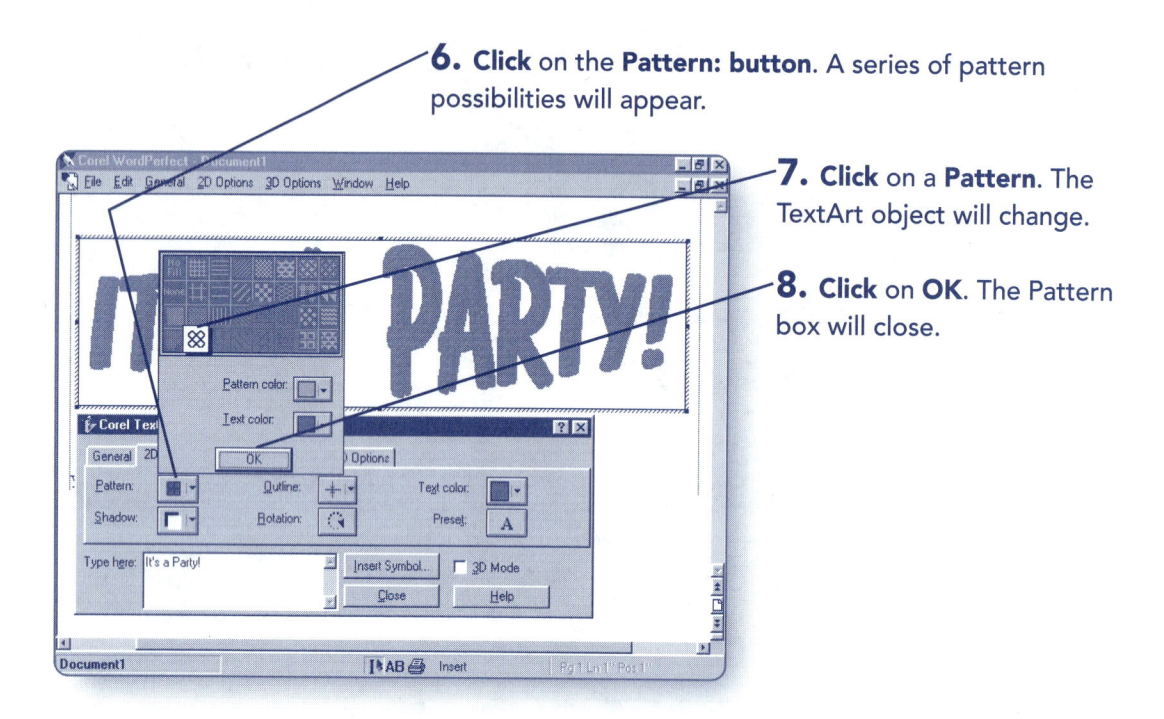

8. Click on **OK**. The Pattern box will close.

Changing 3-D Options

For even more design, add a three-dimensional effect to your text.

1. Click on the **3D Options tab**. The 3D Options tab will come to the front.

2. Click on **3D Mode** to activate three-dimensional options. Your text is automatically converted to a three-dimensional shape.

EDITING TEXTART   291

> **NOTE**
> A message box may display. Adding three-dimensional effects to TextArt substantially increases the size of your file. For example, a file that started as 2K in size was increased to 26K when a two-dimensional TextArt object was added, and then to 277K when a three-dimensional object was added.

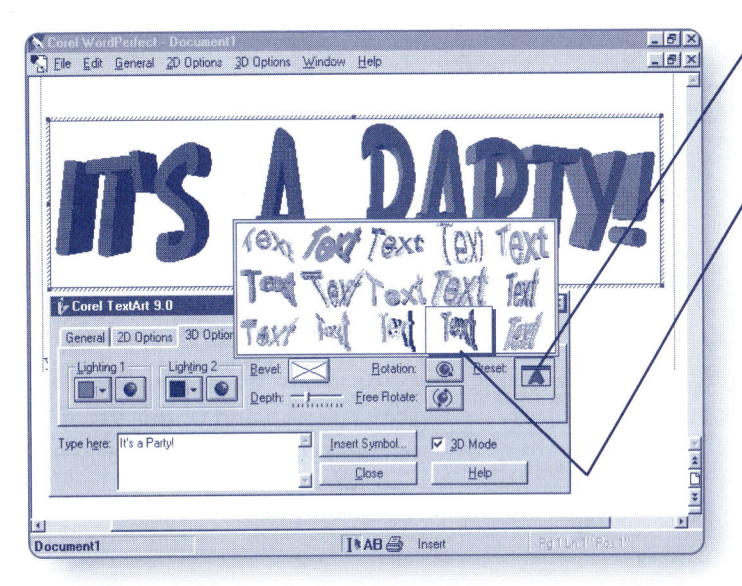

3. Click on the **Preset: button**. A selection of 15 predefined colors and shapes will appear.

4. Click on a **shape**. The 3-D text will change.

To add even more effect, you can increase or decrease the bevel depth of the three-dimensional text.

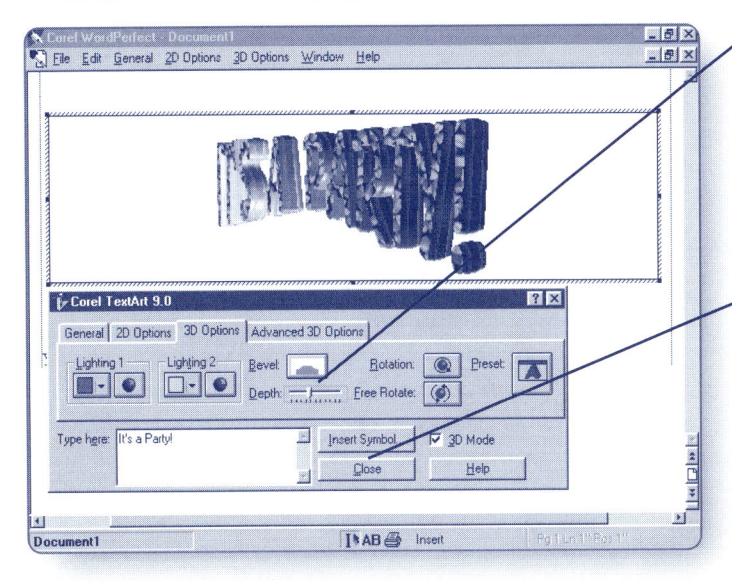

5. Click and drag the **depth slider bar.** Dragging to the left will decrease the depth of the characters, whereas dragging to the right will increase the depth of the characters.

6. Click on **Close**. The dialog box will close, and you will be returned to the WordPerfect document.

7. Click anywhere **outside the TextArt box**. The object will be deselected.

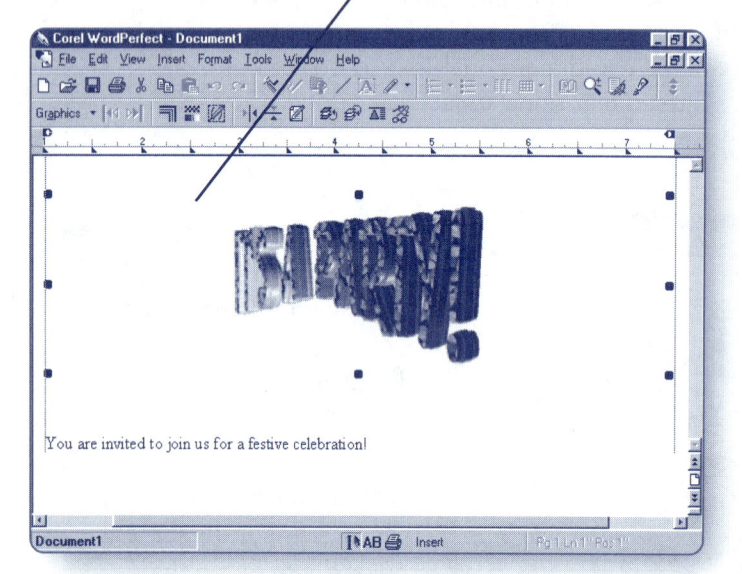

TIP
To further edit the TextArt object, double-click on the TextArt object. The Corel TextArt 9.0 box will reopen.

A TextArt object is like any of the other graphic objects you have worked with. It can be resized, moved, or deleted as you discovered in Chapter 24, "Working with Graphic Images." You can also add borders to it or change the way text wraps around it.

Part V Review Questions

1. What type of line runs from left margin to right margin? *See "Adding a Graphic Line" in Chapter 23*

2. What should the mouse pointer look like before you select a graphic line? *See "Moving a Graphic Line" in Chapter 23*

3. After selecting a graphic line, what key do you press to delete it? *See "Deleting Graphic Lines" in Chapter 23*

4. What happens to the graphic when you resize it? *See "Resizing a Graphic Image" in Chapter 24*

5. When moving a graphic box, where should the mouse pointer *not* be positioned? *See "Moving a Graphic Image" in Chapter 24*

6. What does contouring text do to the graphic? *See "Wrapping Text Around the Graphic Image" in Chapter 24*

7. Why should you use short lines of text when creating a TextArt object? *See "Creating TextArt Text" in Chapter 25*

8. What does clicking on the Preset button do? *See "Changing 2-D Options" in Chapter 25*

9. Which TextArt file will be larger in size: a two-dimensional or a three-dimensional one? *See "Changing 3-D Options" in Chapter 25*

10. If a TextArt object has been deselected in a WordPerfect document, what must you do to further edit the object? *See "Changing 3-D Options" in Chapter 25*

PART VI
Working on the Internet

Chapter 26
    Using SpeedLinks **297**

Chapter 27
    Creating a Simple Web Page **311**

26

Using SpeedLinks

With the SpeedLink feature, you can automatically create hyperlinks when you type certain kinds of text. For example, when you type text that begins with "www," "ftp," "http," or "mailto," SpeedLinks automatically converts it to an Internet link. In this chapter, you'll learn how to:

- Create a SpeedLink
- Edit a SpeedLink
- Add a SpeedLink in a document
- Use a SpeedLink

Creating a SpeedLink

Use SpeedLinks to set up frequently used Internet links or even links to other WordPerfect documents.

Creating an Internet SpeedLink

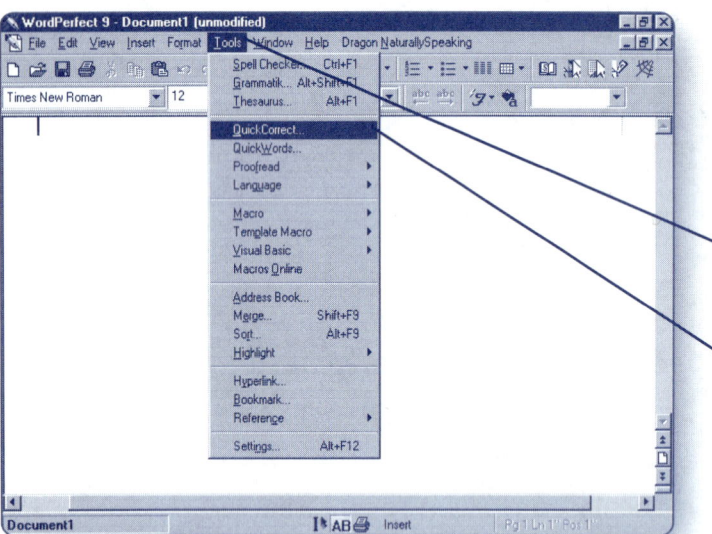

An Internet SpeedLink might be one to the White House at www.whitehouse.gov or Prima Publishing at www.primapublishing.com.

1. Click on **Tools**. The Tools menu will appear.

2. Click on **QuickCorrect**. The QuickCorrect dialog box will open.

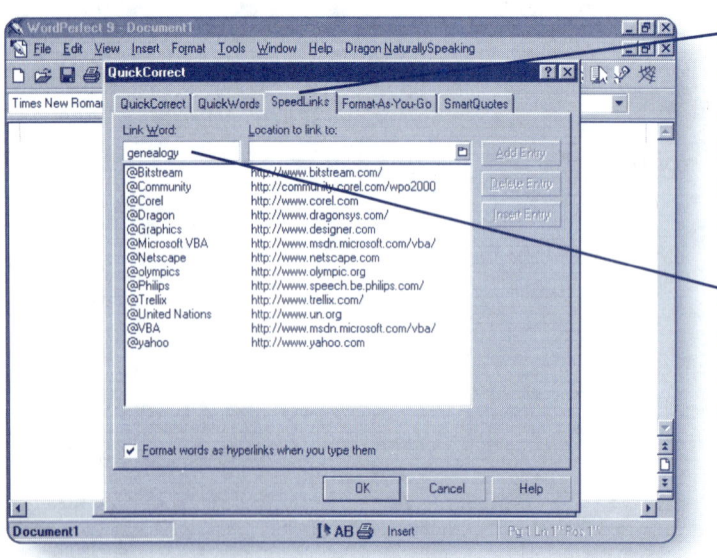

3. Click on the **SpeedLinks tab**. The SpeedLinks tab will come to the front. WordPerfect has already included several Internet SpeedLinks for you to use.

4. Type the **word** you want to type in your document to create a link. The word will appear in the Link Word: text box.

CREATING A SPEEDLINK 299

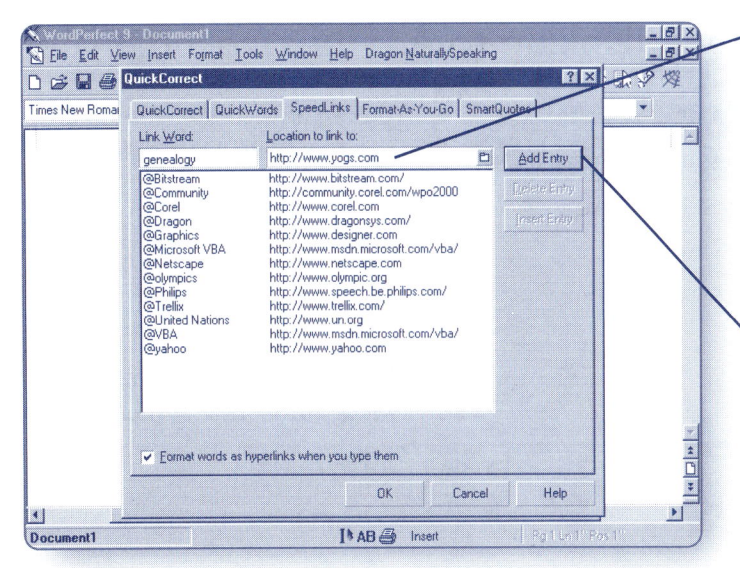

5. Type the **actual address** in the Location to link to: text box. For example, you could specify that typing USPS automatically sets up a link to the United States Postal Service at http://www.usps.gov.

6. Click on **Add Entry**. The entry will be added to the existing list.

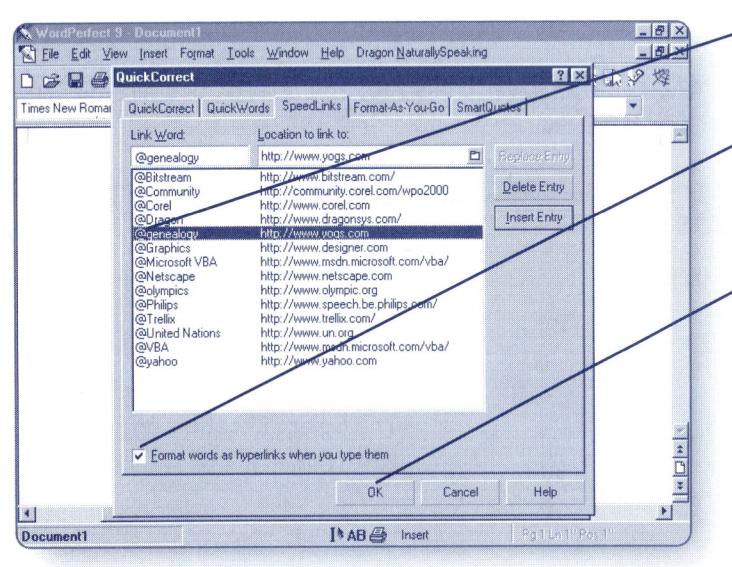

The @ character is inserted at the beginning of the link word.

Make sure that Format words as hyperlinks when you type them is turned on.

7. Click on **OK**. The QuickCorrect dialog box will close.

CHAPTER 26: USING SPEEDLINKS

SpeedLinking to Another Document

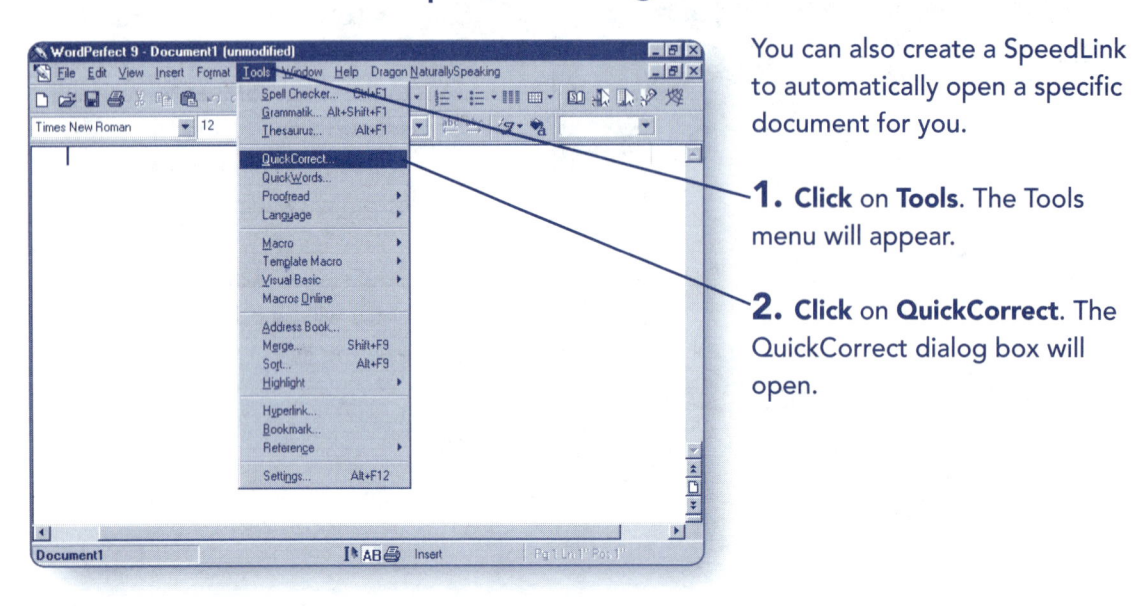

You can also create a SpeedLink to automatically open a specific document for you.

1. Click on **Tools**. The Tools menu will appear.

2. Click on **QuickCorrect**. The QuickCorrect dialog box will open.

3. Click on the **SpeedLinks tab**. The SpeedLinks tab will come to the front.

4. Type the **word** you want to type in your document to create a link. The word will appear in the Link Word: text box.

5. Click on the **Browse folder**. The Select Location or File to Link to dialog box will open.

CREATING A SPEEDLINK 301

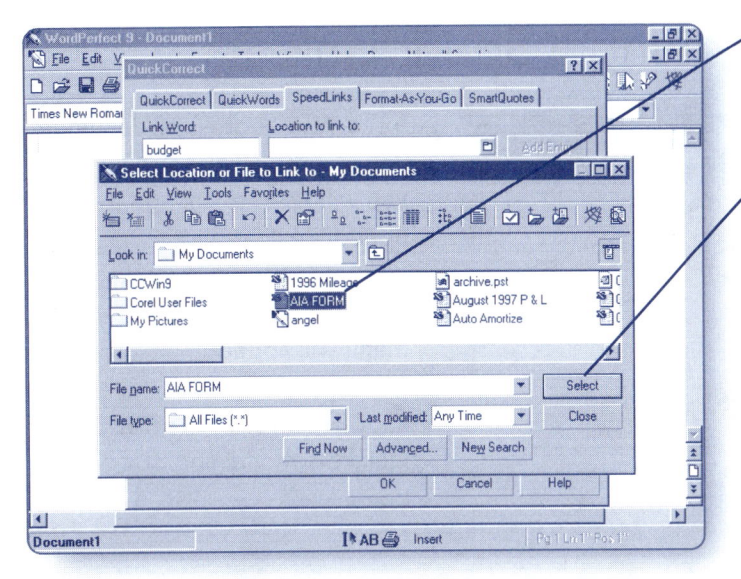

6. Click on the **document** to be opened. The document filename will be highlighted.

7. Click on **Select**. The dialog box will close.

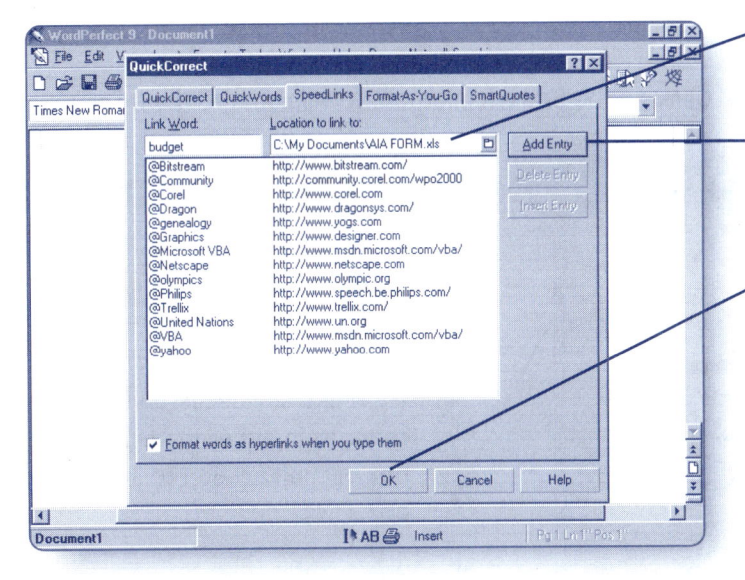

The file path will be displayed in the Location to link to: box.

8. Click on **Add Entry**. The entry will be added to the existing list.

9. Click on **OK**. The QuickCorrect dialog box will close.

Editing a SpeedLink

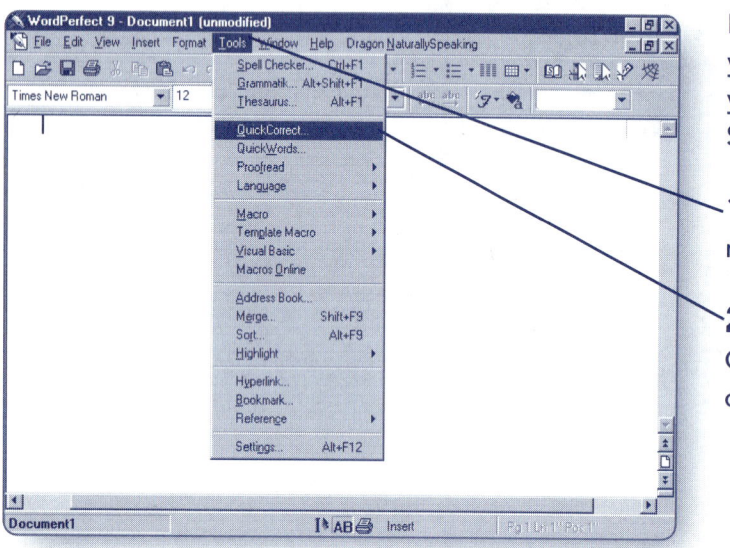

If the Web address or document you created a link to changes, you will need to change the SpeedLink.

1. Click on **Tools**. The Tools menu will appear.

2. Click on **QuickCorrect**. The QuickCorrect dialog box will open.

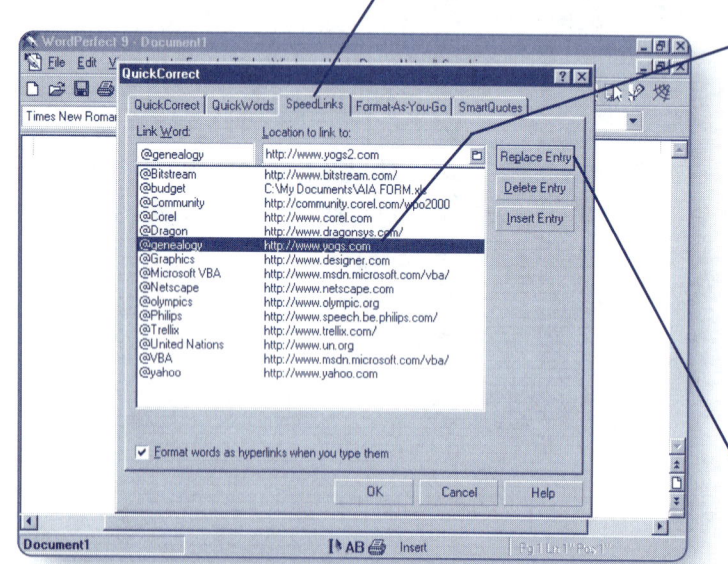

3. Click on the **SpeedLinks tab**. It will come to the front.

4. Click on the **link** to be changed. The current information appears in the Link Word: and Location to link to: boxes.

5. Make any necessary **changes** in either the Link Word: box or the Location to link to: box.

6. Click on **Replace Entry**. The SpeedLink will be modified.

ADDING A SPEEDLINK TO A DOCUMENT   303

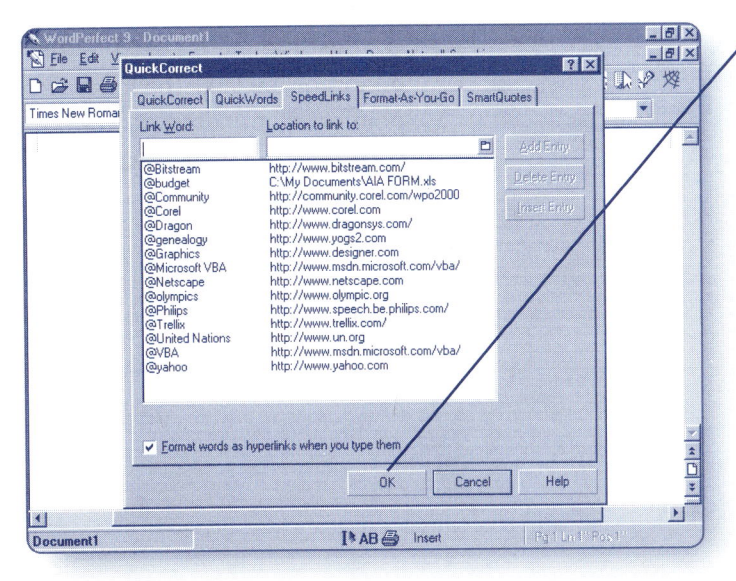

7. Click on **OK**. The QuickCorrect dialog box will close.

Adding a SpeedLink to a Document

SpeedLinks can be inserted quickly into your WordPerfect document. There are two methods available to add the SpeedLink.

Typing a SpeedLink

As you type the shortcut link word, WordPerfect automatically converts the word to a hyperlink.

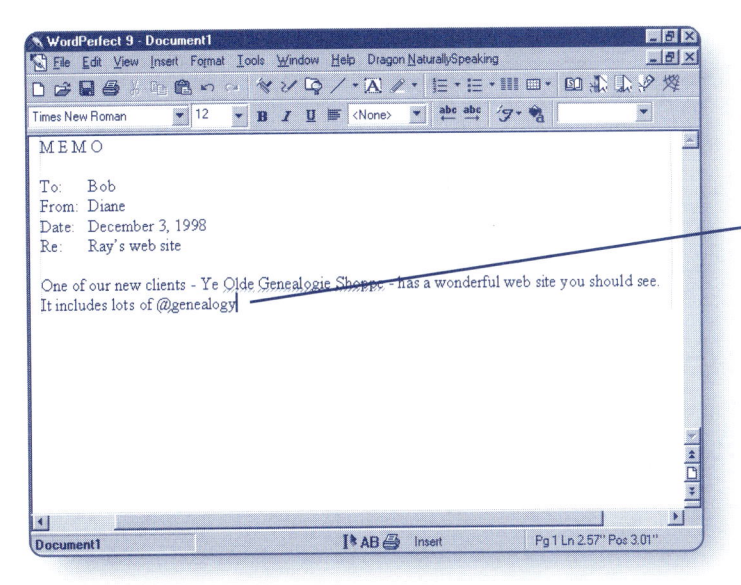

1. Click the **mouse pointer** in the document where the link is to be created. The blinking insertion point will appear.

2. Type the **link word** you created. Be sure to include the @ symbol at the beginning.

3. Press the **spacebar** or the **Enter key**. The link word will turn blue and be underlined, indicating that it is a link to the location you specified. The @ symbol will be removed.

CHAPTER 26: USING SPEEDLINKS

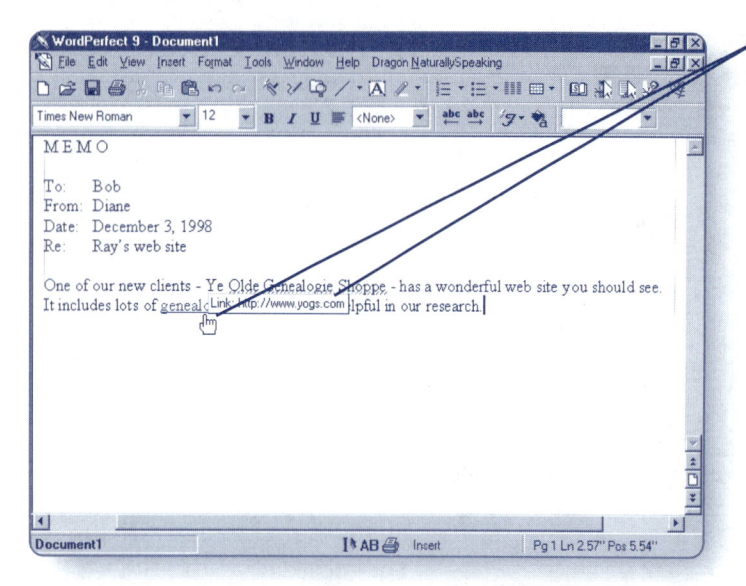

4. Position the **mouse pointer** on top of the link. The mouse pointer will turn into a small hand, and the actual location of the link will be specified in a pop-up box.

Inserting a SpeedLink

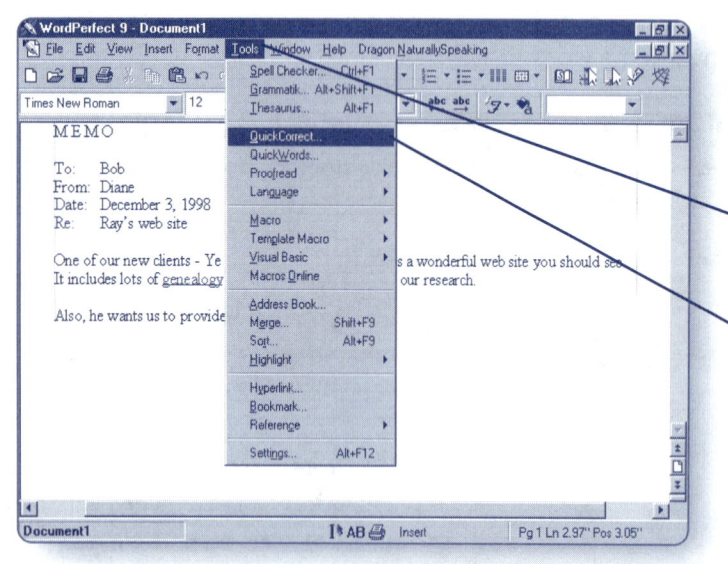

Another way to add a SpeedLink to your document is to insert it through the QuickCorrect dialog box.

1. Click on **Tools**. The Tools menu will appear.

2. Click on **QuickCorrect**. The QuickCorrect dialog box will open.

ADDING A SPEEDLINK TO A DOCUMENT   305

3. Click on the **SpeedLinks tab**. It will come to the front.

4. Click on the **link** to be inserted. The link will be highlighted.

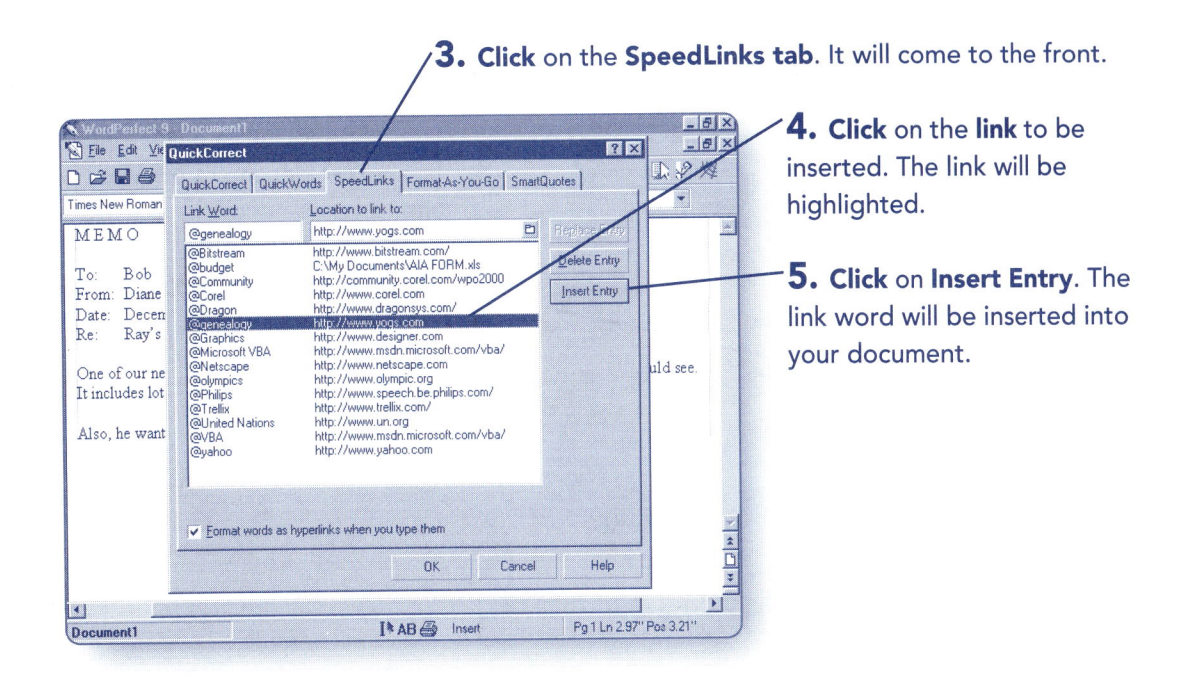

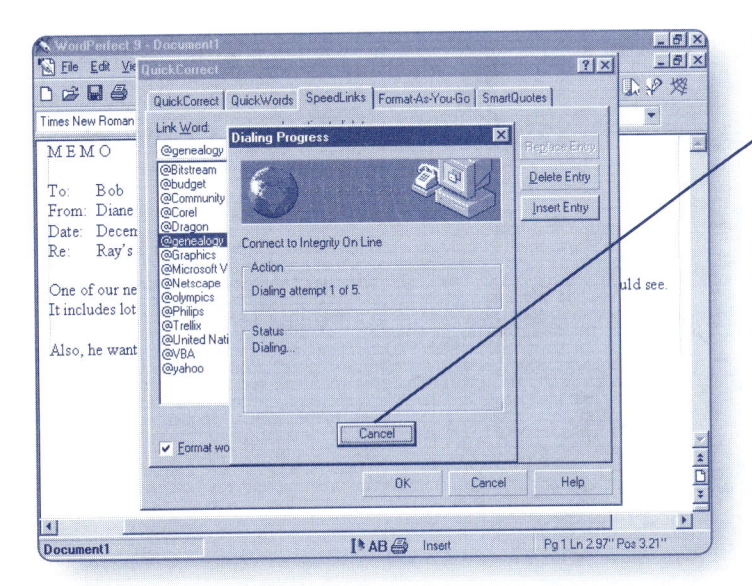

5. Click on **Insert Entry**. The link word will be inserted into your document.

NOTE

The first time an Internet link is inserted using the preceding method, WordPerfect may attempt to verify its accuracy by launching your Web browser and, if necessary, connecting to your Internet service provider. Click on Cancel.

CHAPTER 26: USING SPEEDLINKS

Using a SpeedLink

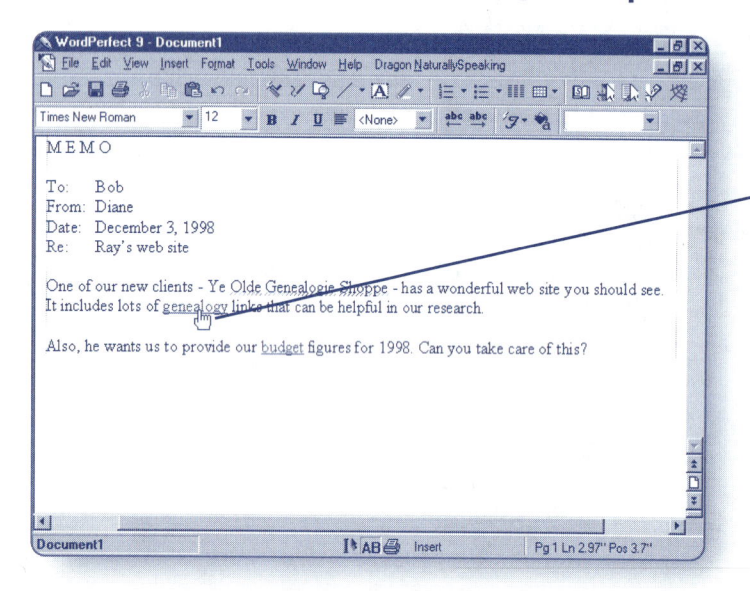

Use a SpeedLink to quickly jump to another document or Web site.

1. Click on the **SpeedLink**. Several things could happen at this point:

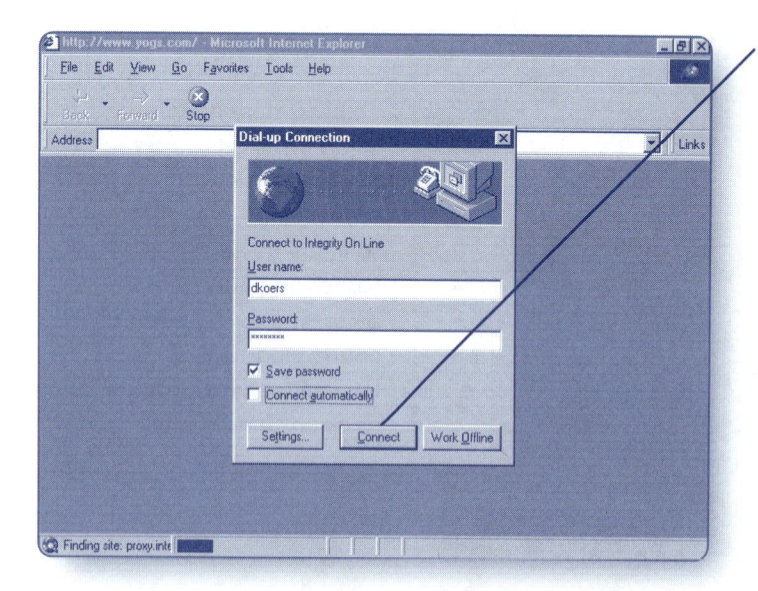

- If the link is an Internet link and you are not yet connected to the Internet, WordPerfect will first launch your Internet browser and then will attempt to launch a connection. It will then jump to the link location.

USING A SPEEDLINK 307

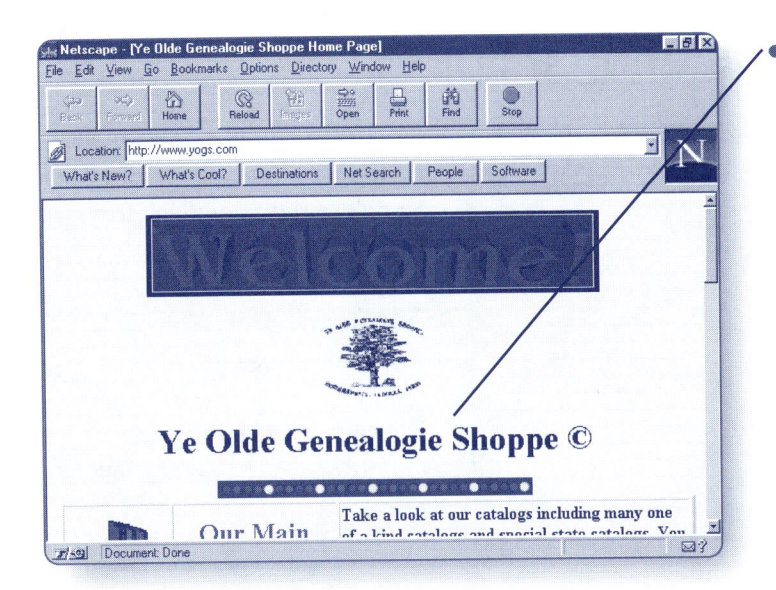

- If the link is an Internet link and you are already connected to the Internet, WordPerfect will launch your Internet browser program and jump to the link location.

- If the link is to another WordPerfect document, the referenced link document will open.

CHAPTER 26: USING SPEEDLINKS

Deleting a SpeedLink

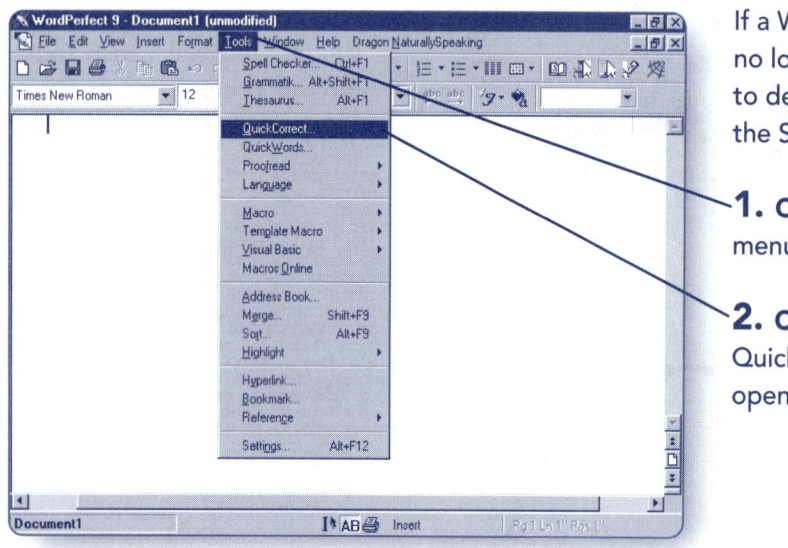

If a Web location or document no longer exists, you might want to delete the SpeedLink from the SpeedLink list.

1. Click on **Tools**. The Tools menu will appear.

2. Click on **QuickCorrect**. The QuickCorrect dialog box will open.

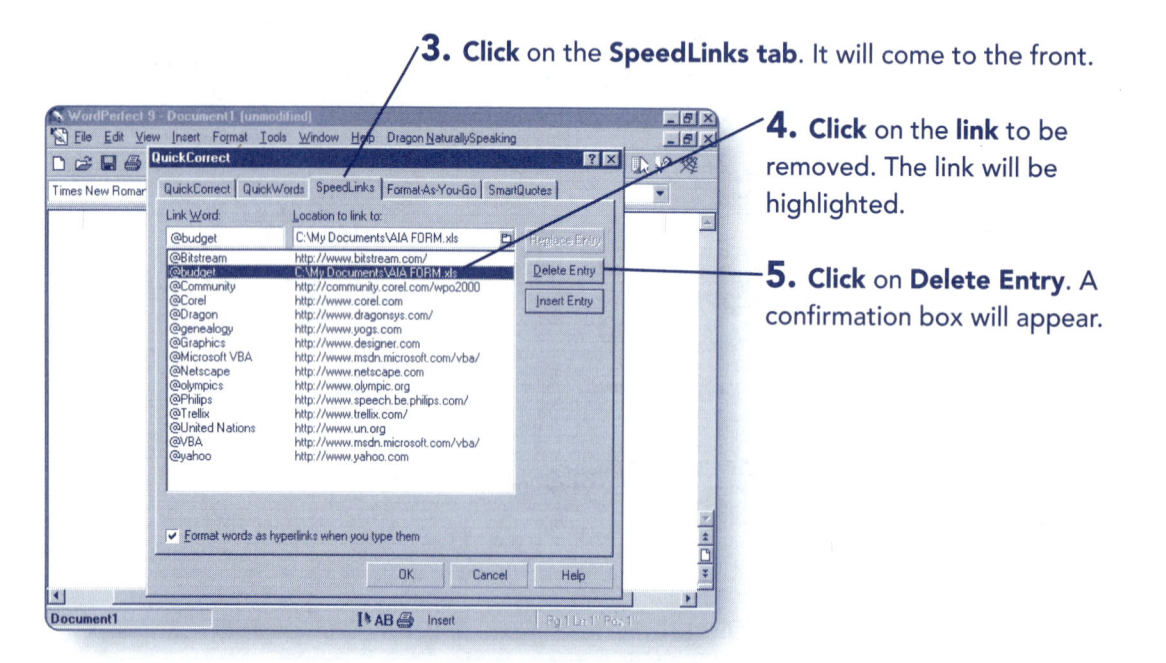

3. Click on the **SpeedLinks tab**. It will come to the front.

4. Click on the **link** to be removed. The link will be highlighted.

5. Click on **Delete Entry**. A confirmation box will appear.

DELETING A SPEEDLINK 309

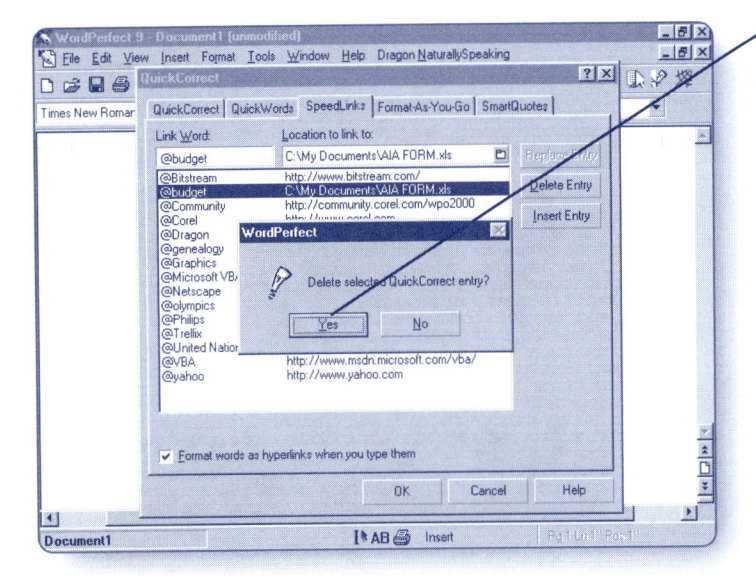

6. Click on **Yes**. The SpeedLink entry will be deleted.

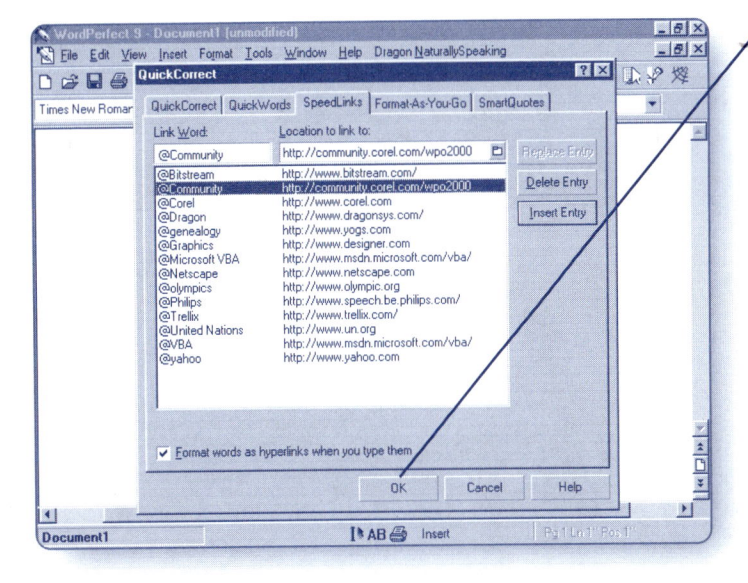

7. Click on **OK**. The SpeedLink dialog box will close.

27

Creating a Simple Web Page

In the not so distant past, to create a Web page you had to learn a type of programming language called HTML (Hypertext Markup Language). WordPerfect has eliminated the need to learn HTML by having the capability to convert regular text on the screen to the HTML code for you. You can now create Web pages by simply creating a WordPerfect document. In this chapter, you'll learn how to:

- Change the background color and the wallpaper of a Web page
- Add text and graphic images to a Web page
- Create hyperlinks
- Publish to HTML
- View the document in a Web browser

CHAPTER 27: CREATING A SIMPLE WEB PAGE

Beginning the PerfectExpert

Some people think that only an expert can understand all the ins and outs of the World Wide Web. However, WordPerfect gives you the ability to become a master Web page builder — by using the Web page PerfectExpert.

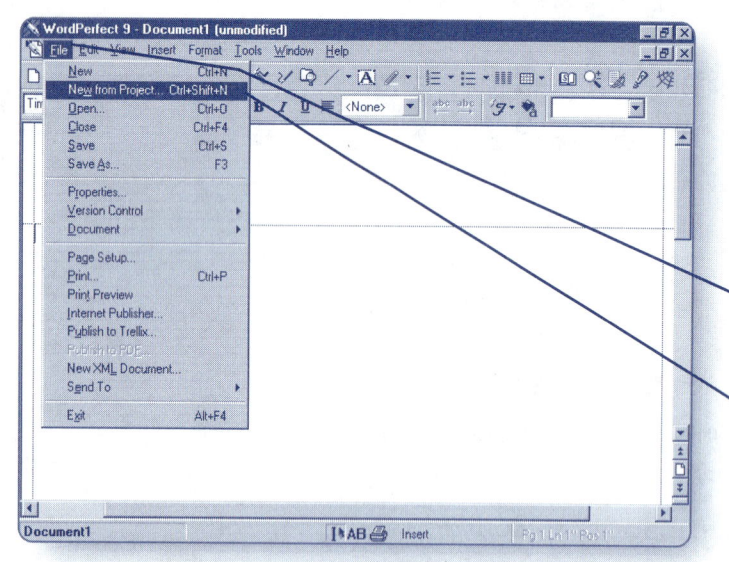

The PerfectExpert assists you in designing your own Web page. You learned about some other PerfectExpert projects in Chapter 15, "Saving Time with Templates."

1. Click on **File**. The File menu will appear.

2. Click on **New from Project**. The Corel PerfectExpert dialog box will open.

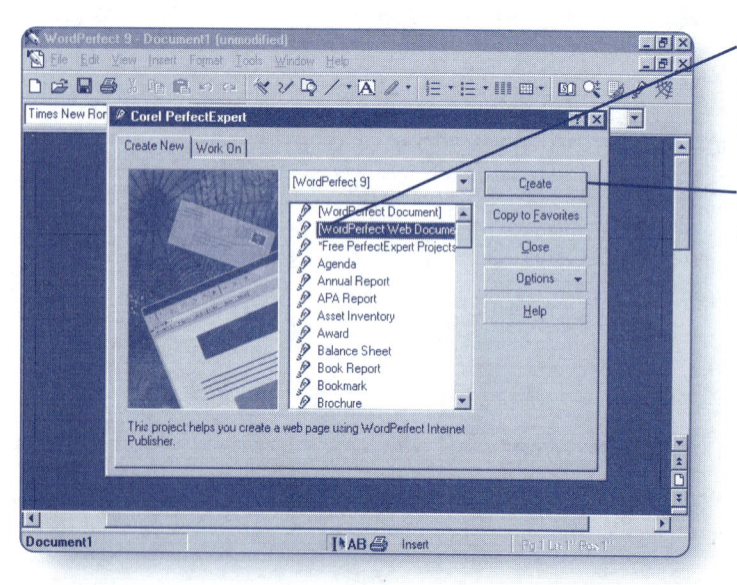

3. Click on **WordPerfect Web Document**. The item will be highlighted.

4. Click on **Create**. A blank Web page will appear.

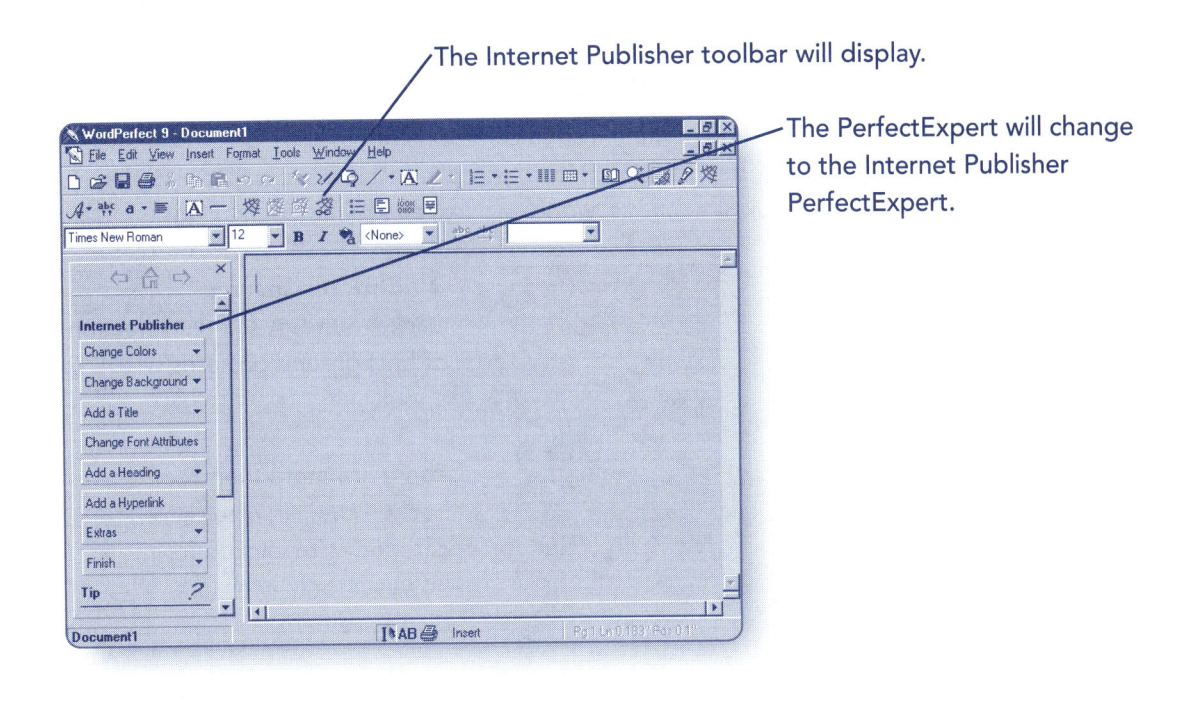

CHANGING THE COLORS 313

The Internet Publisher toolbar will display.

The PerfectExpert will change to the Internet Publisher PerfectExpert.

Changing the Colors

By default, the background of a Web page is gray with black text. You can create your own color combinations or use one of the predesigned color schemes supplied with WordPerfect.

1. Click on **Change Colors**. A menu of color choices will appear.

2. Click on the **Background color** of your choice. The blank document screen will automatically update to your background color selection.

Changing the Wallpaper

Instead of a plain solid color background, try one of the many wallpapers WordPerfect supplies. There are wallpapers that look like fabrics, wood, stones, and many other things.

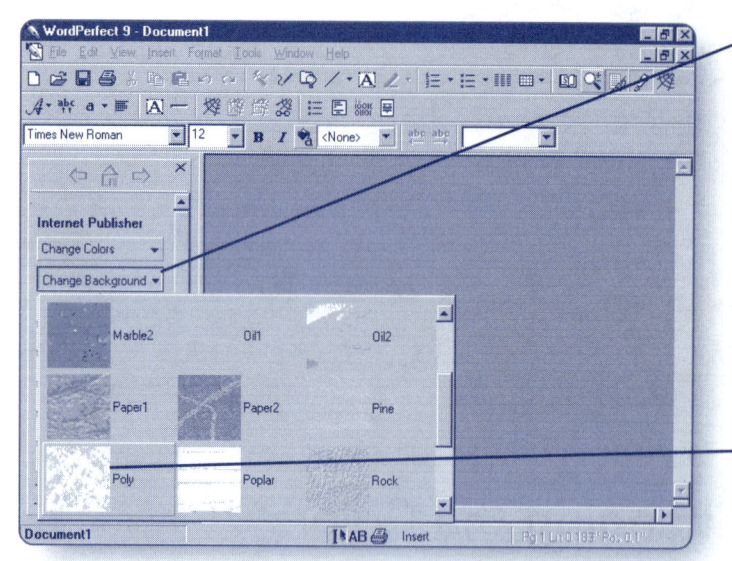

1. Click on **Change Background**. A sample selection of background patterns will appear.

There are more than 350 backgrounds in nine different categories to choose from; however, only a few are displayed here.

2. Click on the background **wallpaper** you want for your Web page.

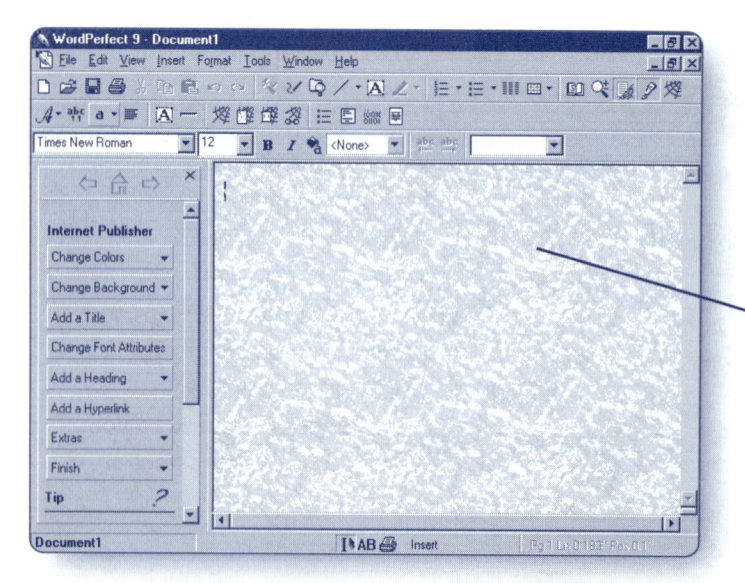

TIP
Click on the Other option to choose from additional wallpaper selections.

The wallpaper will be displayed in your document.

Working with Text

Generally, each Web page contains a single topic or "chunk" of information. Adding text to a Web page is the same as typing in any WordPerfect document; however, not as many formatting choices are available in an HTML document as in a standard WordPerfect document.

Adding and Formatting Text

The Internet Publisher does not apply formatting the same as a standard WordPerfect document. Formatting is applied one paragraph at a time unless more than one is selected.

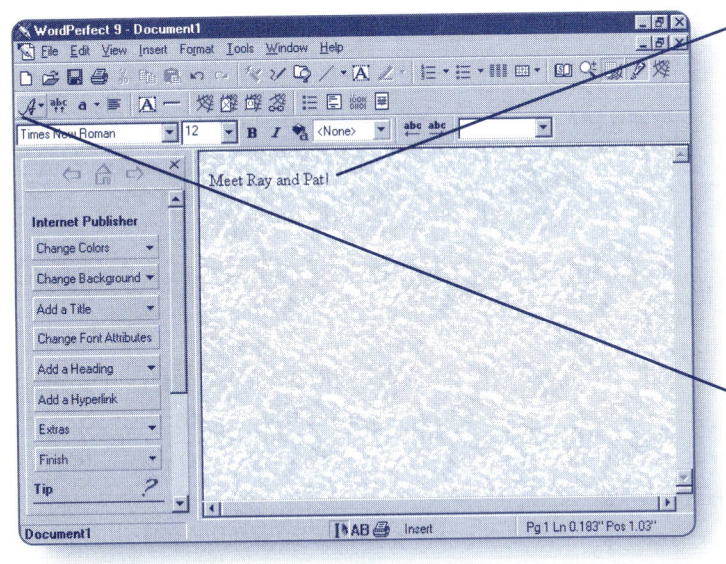

1. Type the desired text in the same manner you would in a regular WordPerfect document. The text will appear in the body of the document.

2. Click in the paragraph to be formatted. The blinking insertion point will appear.

3. Click on the **Font/Size button** on the Internet Publisher toolbar. A list of available styles will appear showing you a sample of each style.

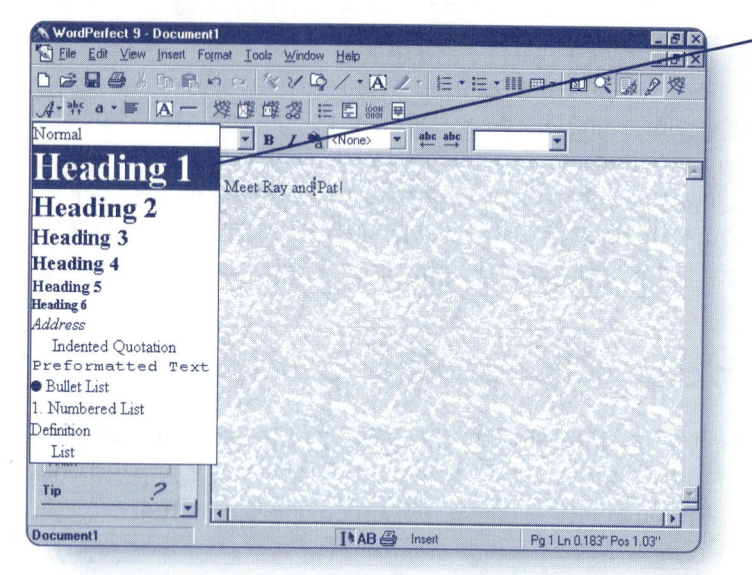

4. Click on a **style** for your text. The current paragraph will change to the selected style.

The current paragraph style is reflected in the status bar.

5. Continue typing any additional text in the Web page document. The text will appear in the document.

6. Format as directed in **steps 2** through **4**. The formatted text will appear as you designated.

A sample Web page is shown with several different styles applied.

Creating Bulleted Lists

In Chapter 12, "Adding Bullets, Numbering, and Borders," you learned how to work with bulleted lists. Bulleted text is frequently used when creating Web pages.

1. Select the **text** to be bulleted. The text will be highlighted.

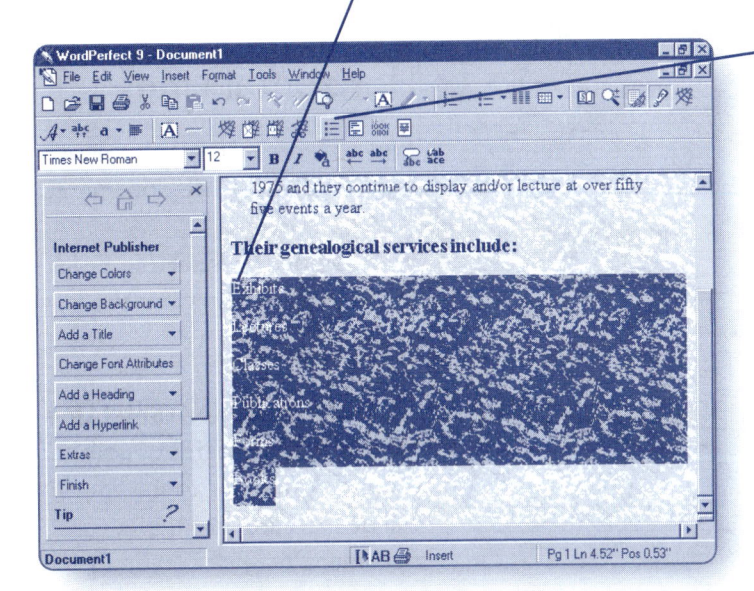

2. Click on the **Bullet button** on the Internet Publisher toolbar. The items will have bullet points.

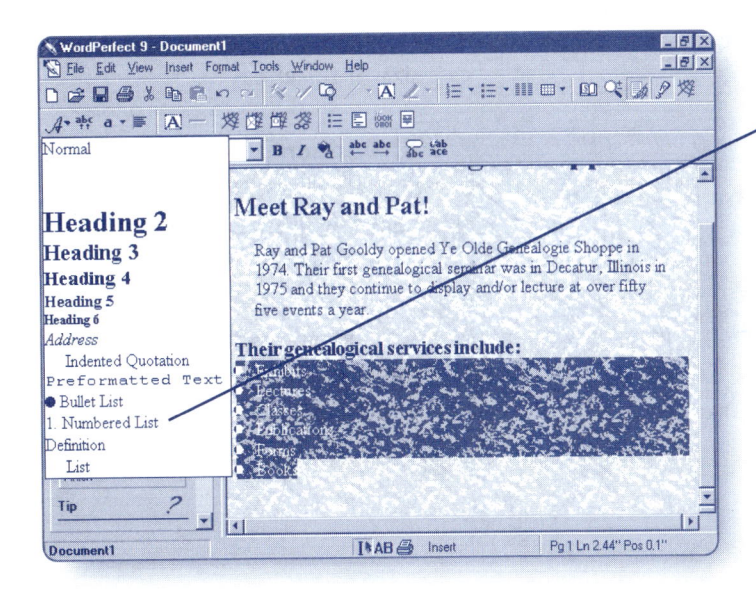

TIP
You can create a numbered list by selecting Numbered List from the Font/Size list.

Adding Graphic Images

Studies have shown that Web surfers lose patience with Web pages that take longer than 20 seconds to load, so try to design Web pages that load quickly. Large graphic images are often the culprits that slow down viewing a Web page.

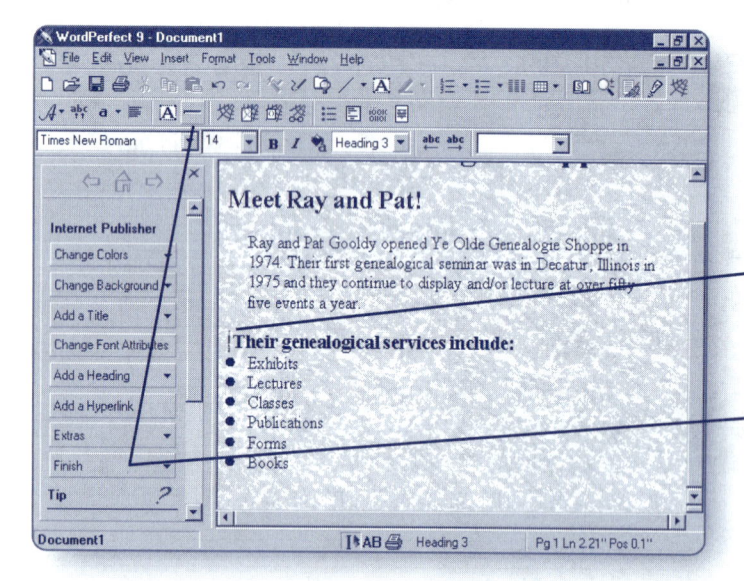

Adding Horizontal Lines

Add horizontal lines to separate sections of an HTML document.

1. Position the **insertion point** at the location you want the line to appear.

2. Click on the **Horizontal Line button** on the Internet Publisher toolbar. A thin horizontal line will be inserted into the document.

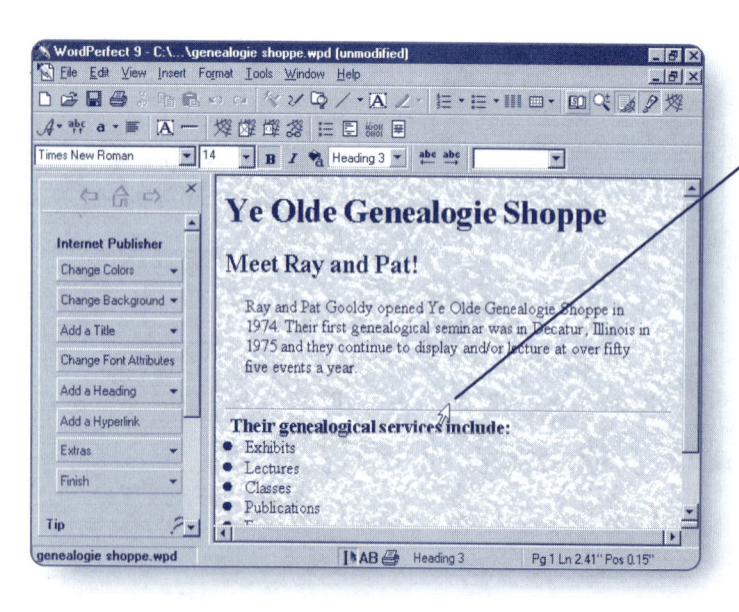

The line can be edited to any size or thickness.

3. Position the **mouse** over the horizontal line. The mouse pointer will change to a white arrow pointing right.

4. Click the **mouse button**. The line will be selected, as indicated by six sizing handles.

ADDING GRAPHIC IMAGES 319

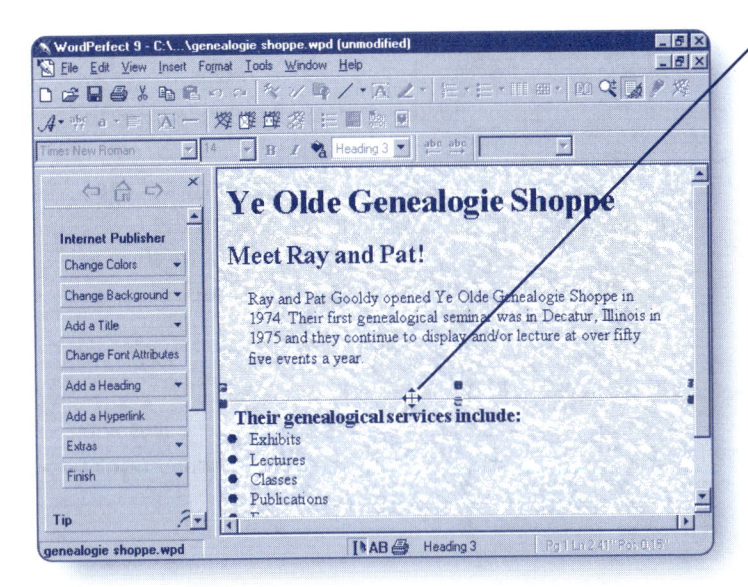

5. Position the **mouse** over the selected line. The mouse pointer will change to a black cross with four arrowheads.

6. Double-click the **mouse**. The Edit Graphics Line dialog box will open.

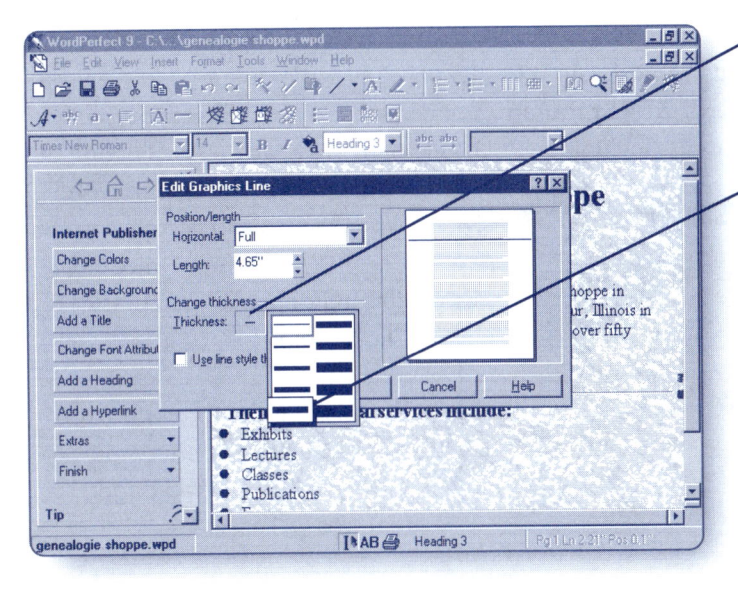

7. Click on the **Thickness button**. A selection of line thickness options will display.

8. Click on a **line thickness**. The option will be selected.

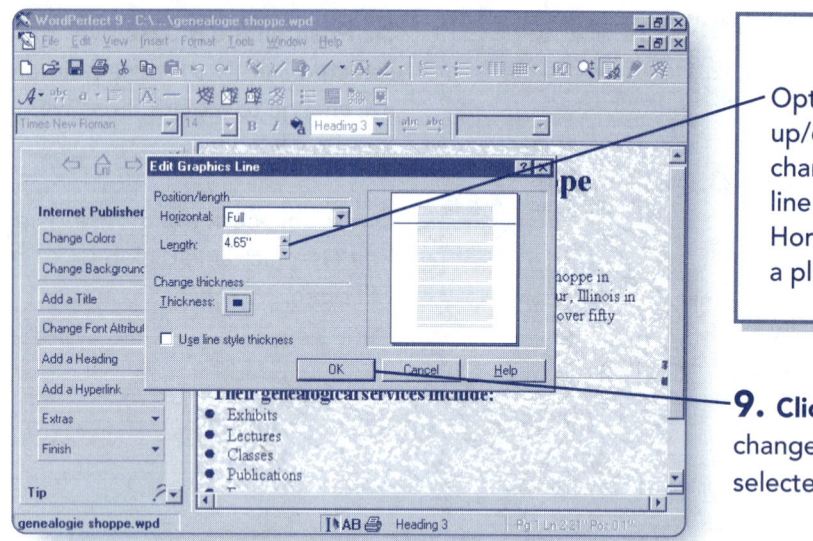

TIP

Optionally, click on the up/down arrows (◆) to change the length of the line and click on the Horizontal: box to choose a placement option.

9. Click on **OK**. The line will change to the specifications you selected.

Adding Clip Art

You can add your own clip art or one that is supplied with the WordPerfect program. You can insert many different types of graphics including JPEG, GIF, or WMF images. A collection of WMF images is included with WordPerfect and is stored in the Corel\WordPerfect Office 2000\Graphics\Clipart\Basic Clipart folder.

1. Click on the **Extras button** on the PerfectExpert window. A list of additional Web page features will appear.

2. Click on **Add a Graphic from File**. The Insert Image – basic clipart dialog box will open.

ADDING GRAPHIC IMAGES 321

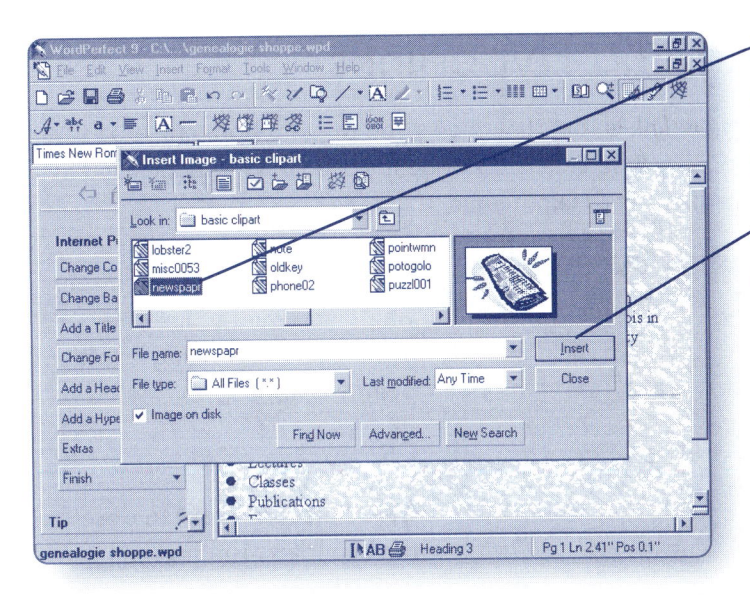

3. Locate and **click** on the **graphic** you want to appear on your Web page document. The image will be selected.

4. Click on **Insert**. The dialog box will close.

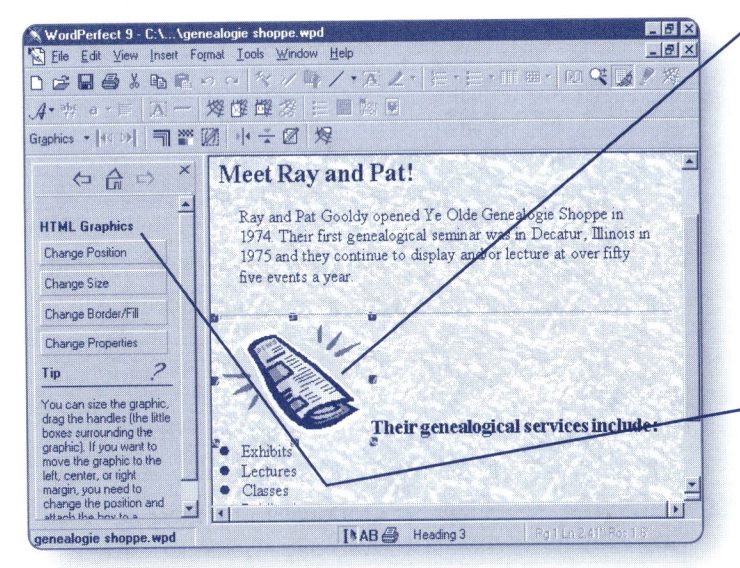

The graphic will be inserted into your document. The graphic image can be resized or deleted like any other graphic. Graphic images are discussed in Chapter 24, "Working with Graphic Images."

NOTE

When a graphic image is selected, the Internet Publisher toolbar changes to display graphic options.

Adding Hyperlinks

A *hyperlink* is text that allows you to jump from one area to another. Hyperlinks are frequently used in Web pages and in WordPerfect's Help menus.

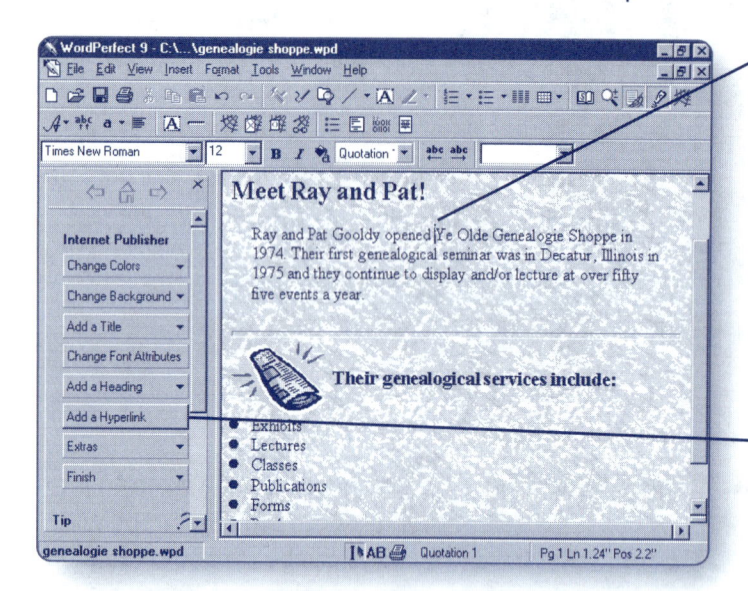

1a. **Click** the **mouse pointer** where you want to insert a hyperlink. The blinking insertion point will appear.

OR

1b. **Select** the **text** to describe the hyperlink. The text will be highlighted.

2. Click on **Add a Hyperlink**. The Hyperlink Properties dialog box will open.

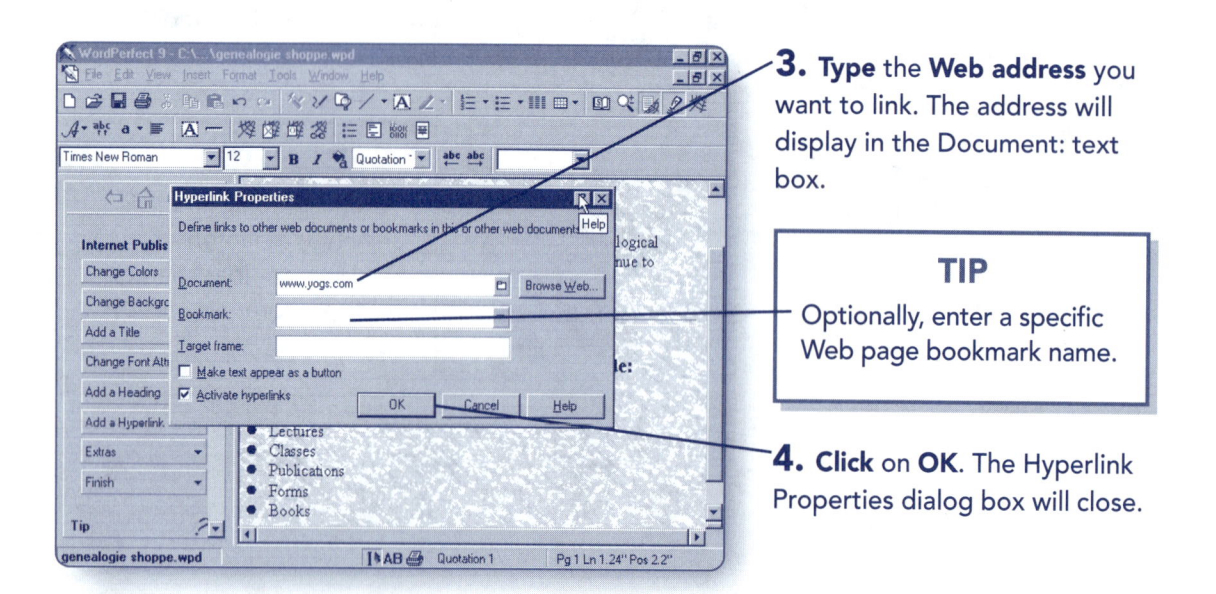

3. Type the **Web address** you want to link. The address will display in the Document: text box.

TIP
Optionally, enter a specific Web page bookmark name.

4. Click on **OK**. The Hyperlink Properties dialog box will close.

ADDING HYPERLINKS 323

If you did not select text before creating the hyperlink, you'll need to type the text to designate the link.

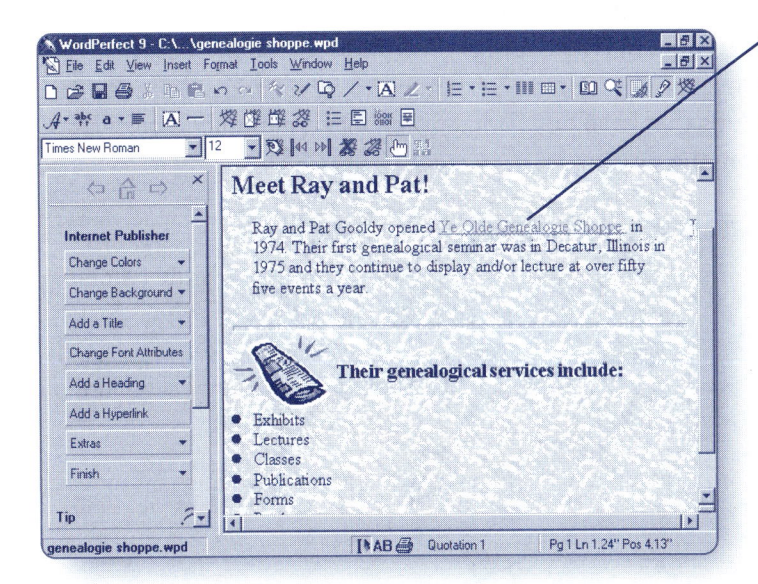

5. Type the **text** you want to associate with the hyperlink. The text will appear in the document as underlined link text.

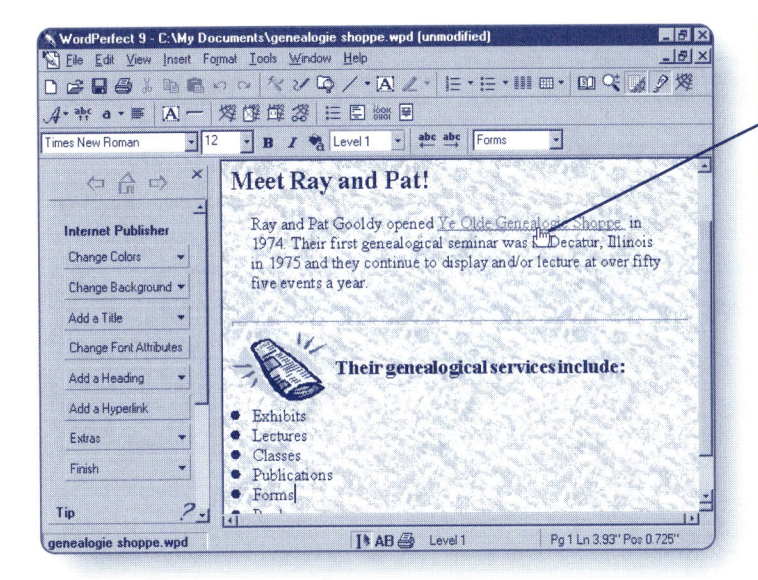

TIP

Positioning the mouse over the link reveals the white hand that is used to display links.

Publishing to HTML

When you publish to HTML, a copy of the current document is re-created in HTML format. WordPerfect automatically converts WordPerfect formatting to HTML tags. WordPerfect codes that have no HTML equivalents are modified or deleted from the document.

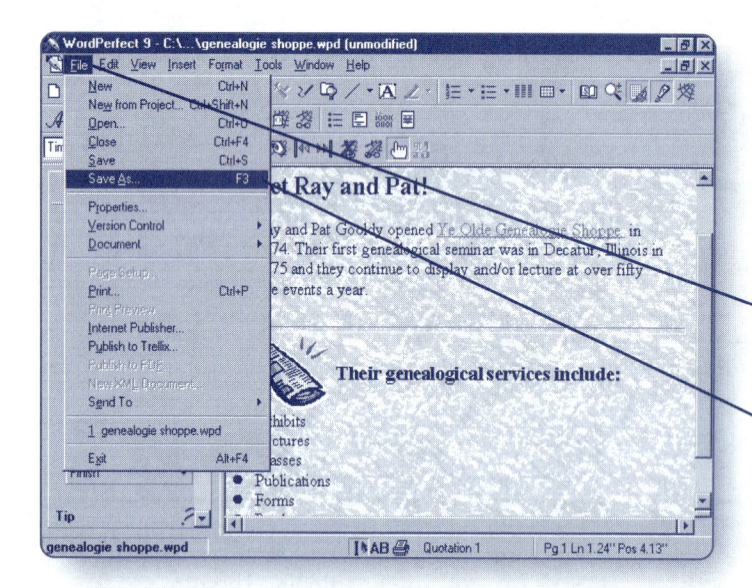

The default name of the new HTML document is the name of the current WordPerfect document with a .htm extension. Any graphic images are saved in the folder you specify.

1. Click on **File**. The File menu will appear.

2. Click on **Save As**. The Save As dialog box will open.

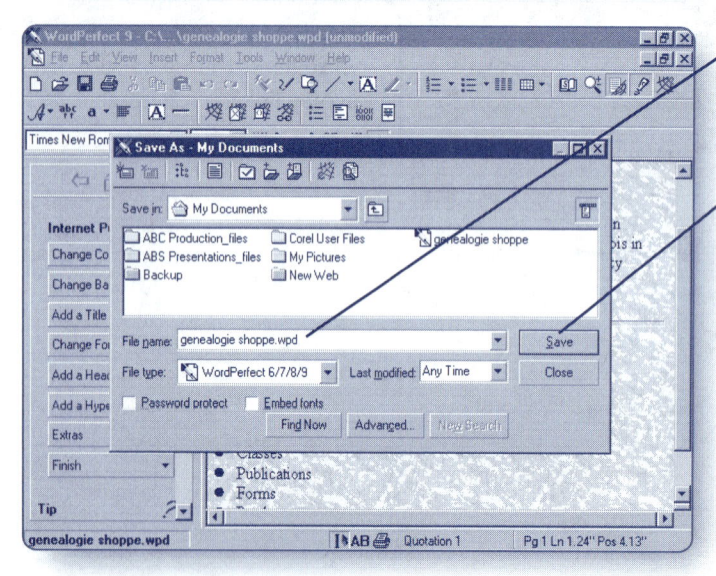

3. Type a name for your document. The text will display in the File name: box.

4. Click on **Save**. The document will be saved in a WordPerfect format.

PUBLISHING TO HTML 325

5. Click on the **Publish to HTML button**. The Publish to HTML dialog box will open.

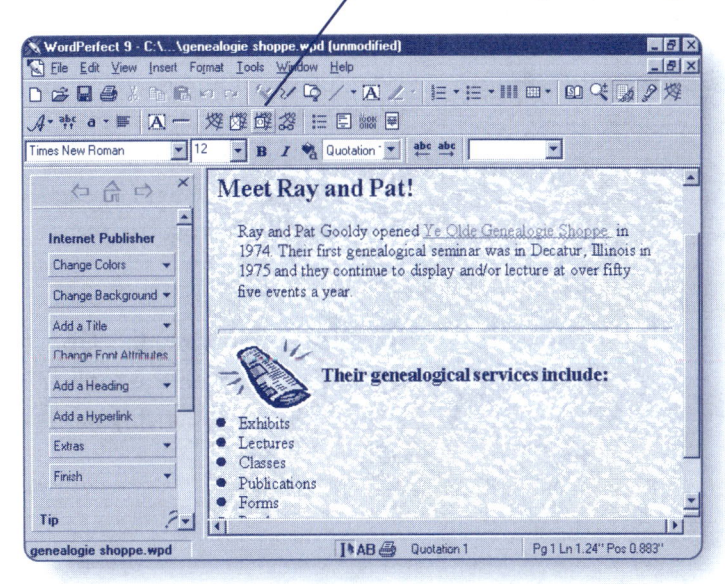

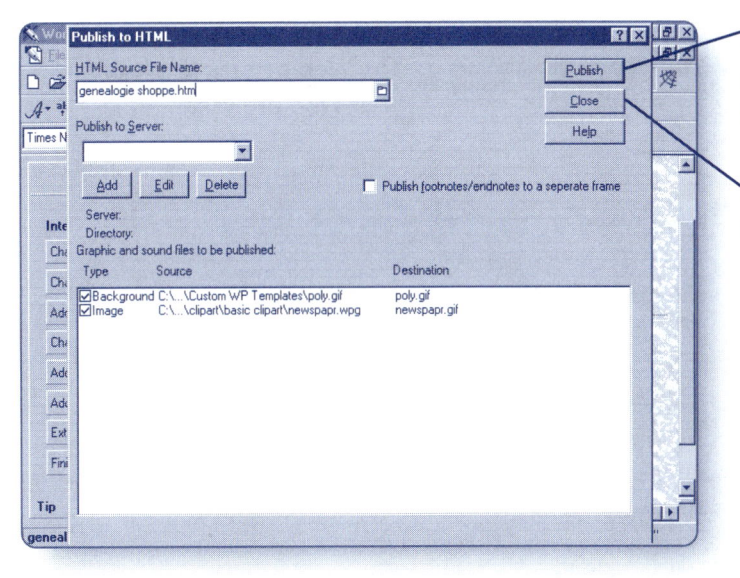

6. Click on **Publish** to save the document with the settings WordPerfect has suggested.

7. Click on **Close**. The Publish to HTML dialog box will close.

Viewing the Document in a Web Browser

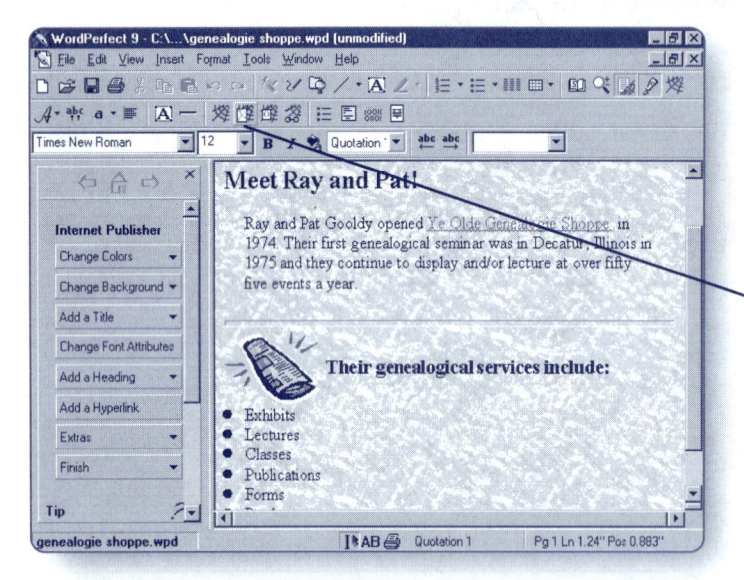

How the document looks in the WordPerfect window is not necessarily how it will look in a Web browser such as Netscape Navigator or Microsoft Internet Explorer.

1. Click on the **View in Web Browser button** on the toolbar. WordPerfect will launch your default browser.

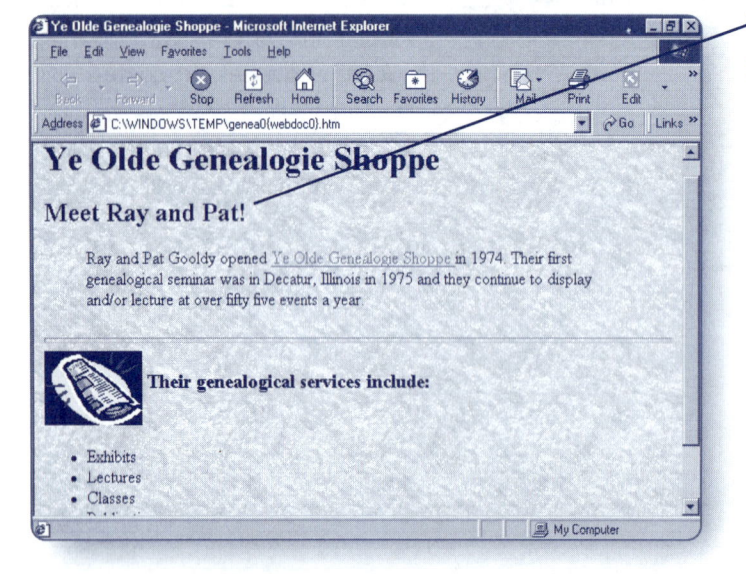

The Web page is displayed in your Web browser.

VIEWING THE DOCUMENT IN A WEB BROWSER

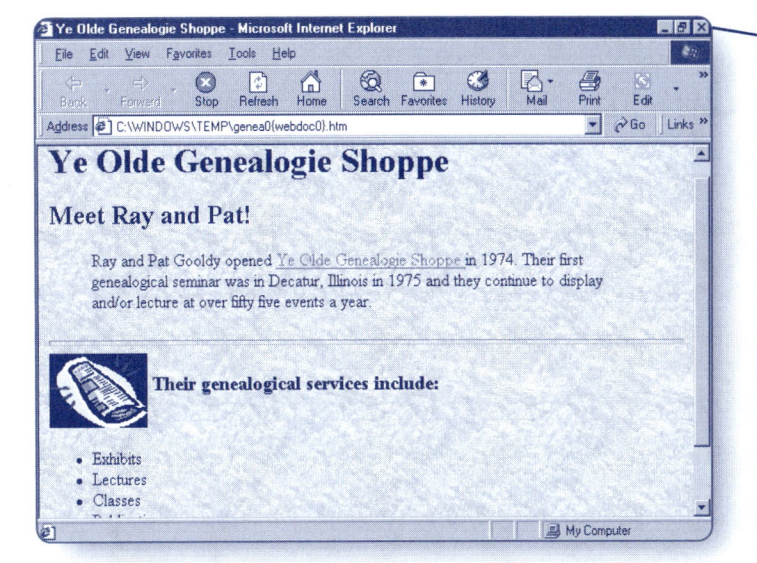

2. Click on the **Close button** (X) of the Web browser. The display will return to the WordPerfect document.

> **TIP**
> Because HTML documents look different in different Web browsers, even between different versions of the same Web browser, try to view your HTML document in as many different browsers as possible.

Contact your Web administrator or Internet service provider (ISP) for instructions on uploading to your server.

> **NOTE**
> You may want to explore a product included with PerfectOffice 2000 called Telix that also helps you create Web pages.

Part VI Review Questions

1. What feature does WordPerfect use to automatically create hyperlinks? *See the introduction in Chapter 26*

2. Can SpeedLinks only be used to access Internet links? *See "Creating a SpeedLink" in Chapter 26*

3. What will happen if you click on an Internet link and you are not yet connected to the Internet? *See "Using a SpeedLink" in Chapter 26*

4. What programming language is used to create Web pages? *See the introduction in Chapter 27*

5. What toolbar appears when you use the PerfectExpert to create a Web page? *See "Beginning the PerfectExpert" in Chapter 27*

6. How many categories of backgrounds does WordPerfect supply? *See "Changing the Wallpaper" in Chapter 27*

7. Why are small graphic images better to use than larger ones? *See "Adding Graphic Images" in Chapter 27*

8. What happens to the mouse pointer when you position it over a hyperlink? *See "Adding Hyperlinks" in Chapter 27*

9. Why should you try to view your HTML document in as many Web browsers as possible? *See "Viewing the Document in a Web Browser" in Chapter 27*

10. What other product is included with PerfectOffice 2000 to help you create Web pages? *See "Viewing the Document in a Web Browser" in Chapter 27*

Appendixes

Appendix A
Installing WordPerfect **331**

Appendix B
Working with Dragon
NaturallySpeaking **349**

Appendix C
Discovering WordPerfect
Tips and Tricks **381**

A
Installing WordPerfect

WordPerfect 9 is a component item of the WordPerfect Office 2000 suite of products. When installing the product, you can elect to install the entire Office suite, or you can install only WordPerfect. In this chapter, you'll learn how to:

- Install WordPerfect Office or WordPerfect
- Uninstall WordPerfect Office

System Requirements

The following is a list of minimum requirements to install and run WordPerfect Office 2000:

- Windows 95 or Windows NT 4.0
- Minimum 486/66
- Minimum 8 MB RAM (16 MB for the Professional version)
- VGA monitor or higher
- Minimum 39 MB of hard disk space for Compact installation, 108 MB for Typical installation, 347 MB for a full Custom installation, and 21 MB for a Run from Network installation. (The Professional version needs 95, 231, 546, and 32 MB, respectively.)
- CD-ROM drive

Beginning the Installation Process

Before installing WordPerfect Office, be sure to temporarily disable any antivirus programs running on your computer.

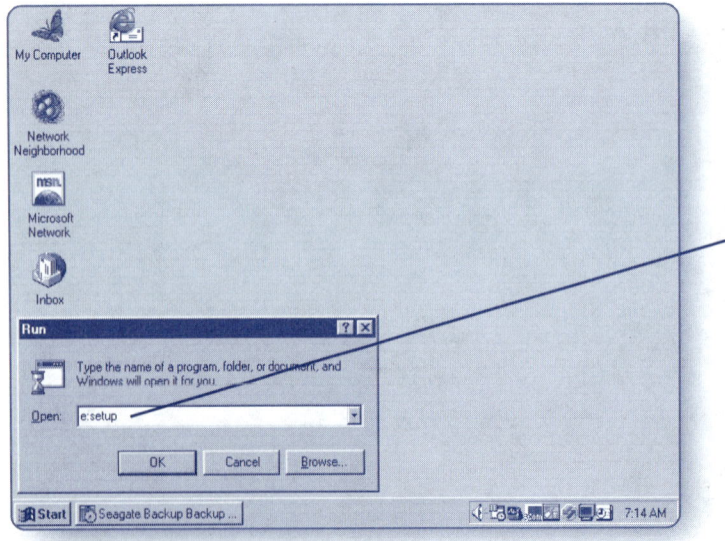

1. Insert the **WordPerfect Office 2000 CD**. The Corel installer will launch.

> **TIP**
> If your installer does not begin after a short period of time (30 seconds), you'll have to launch it manually. Click on Start then click on Run. In the command line type e:\setup (substituting e: for your CD-ROM drive letter).

BEGINNING THE INSTALLATION PROCESS 333

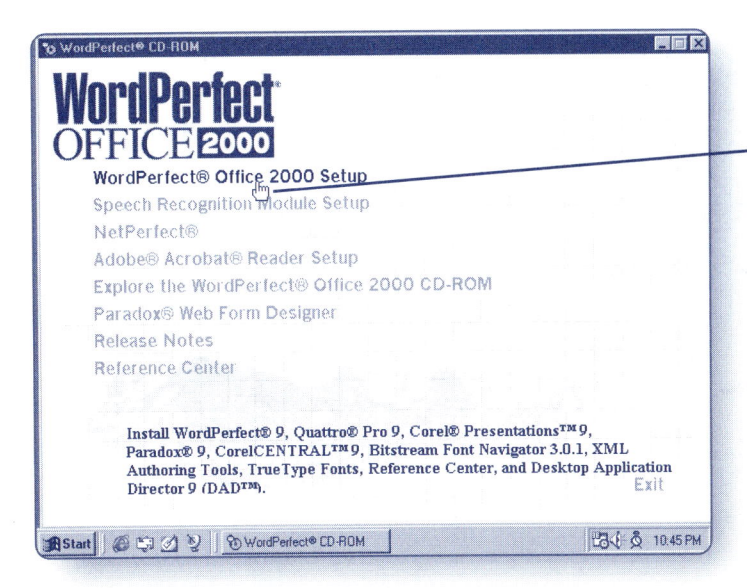

The WordPerfect Office 2000 options window will appear.

2. Click on **WordPerfect Office 2000 Setup**. The Corel Setup Wizard will launch.

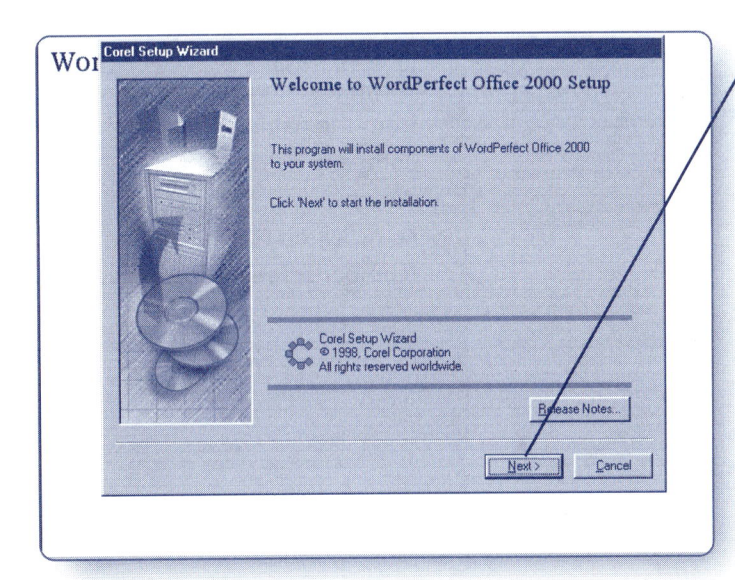

3. Click on **Next**. The license agreement will appear.

334 APPENDIX A: INSTALLING WORDPERFECT

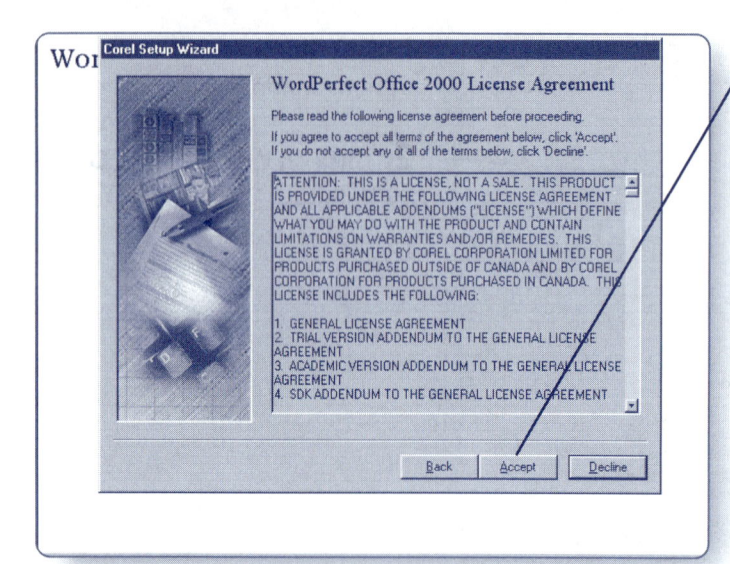

4. Read the license **agreement**, **then click** on **Accept**. The personalization screen will appear.

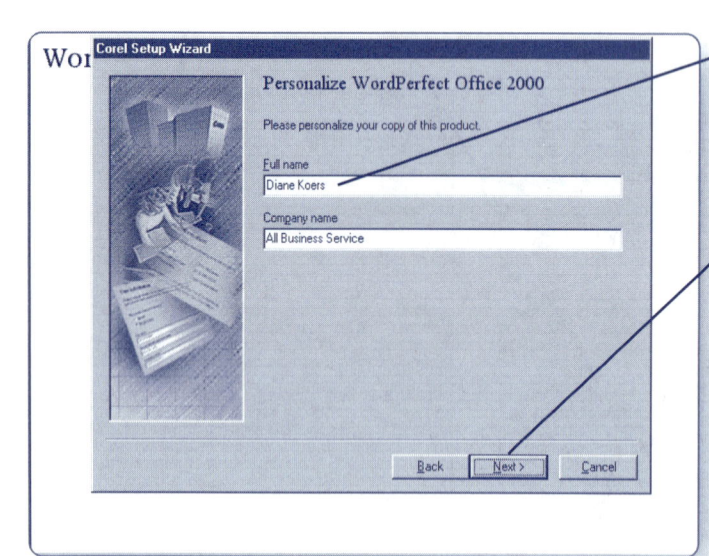

5. Type your **name and company.** Press Tab to move from the name field to the company field.

6. Click on **Next**. The Serial Number screen will appear.

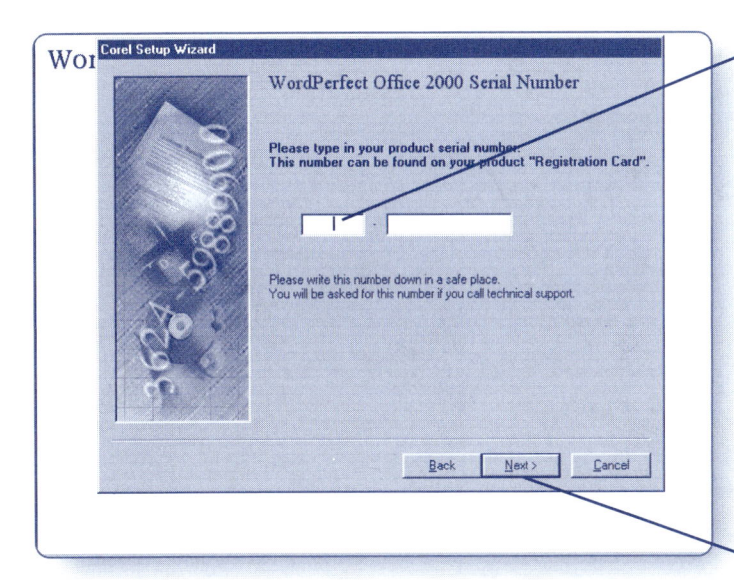

7. Type your product **serial number**. The number is located on your product registration card.

> **NOTE**
> The product serial number can be typed in upper- or lowercase characters. WordPerfect automatically converts it to uppercase letters.

8. Click on **Next**. The Setup Options will appear.

Installing the Complete WordPerfect Office 2000

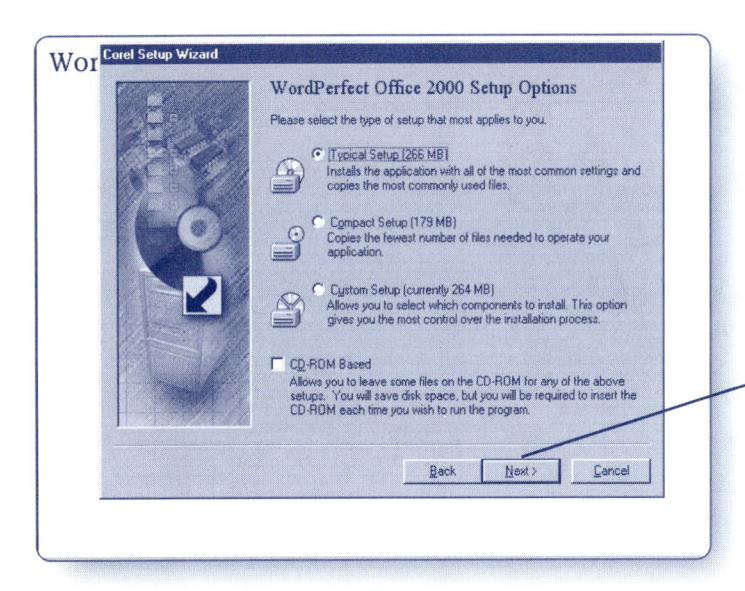

The fastest method to install is using the Typical Setup utility, which installs the most commonly used features of Office including WordPerfect, Quattro Pro, Presentations, and Corel Central. Typical Setup is the default selection.

1. Click on **Next**. The Writing Tools Selection screen will appear.

APPENDIX A: INSTALLING WORDPERFECT

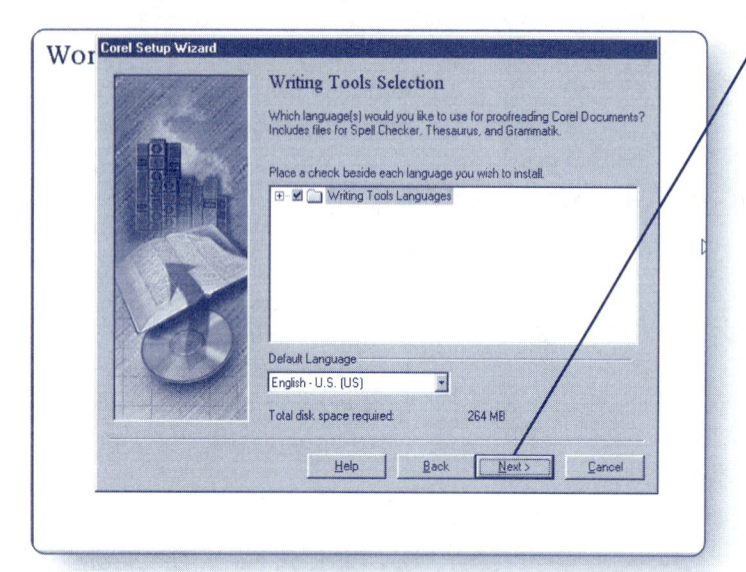

2. Click on **Next**. The Destination Folder screen will appear.

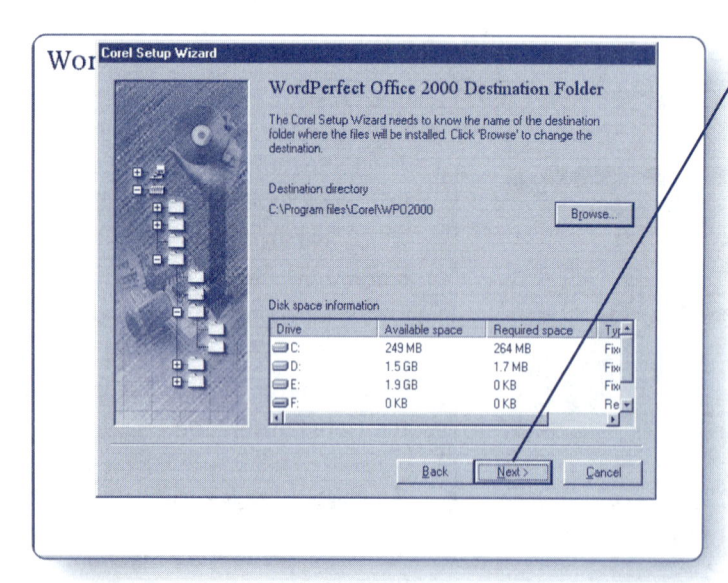

3. Click on **Next**. The Shortcut Folder screen will appear.

BEGINNING THE INSTALLATION PROCESS   337

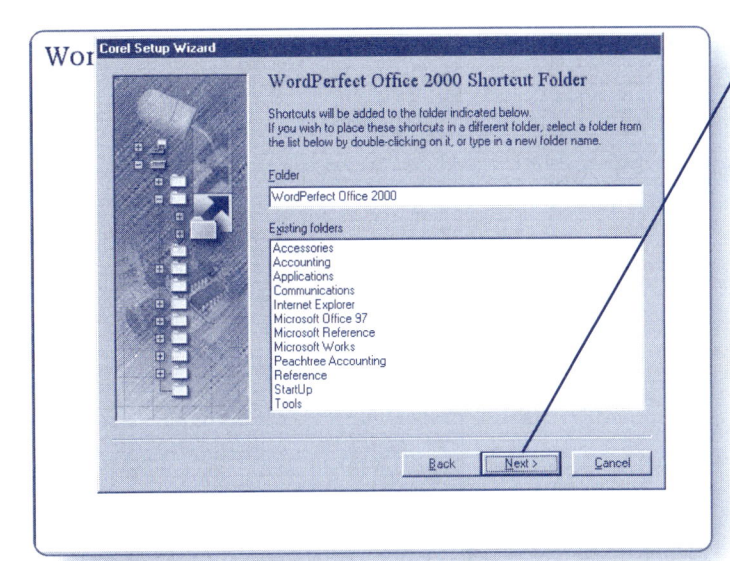

4. Click on **Next**. WordPerfect Office will be ready to install.

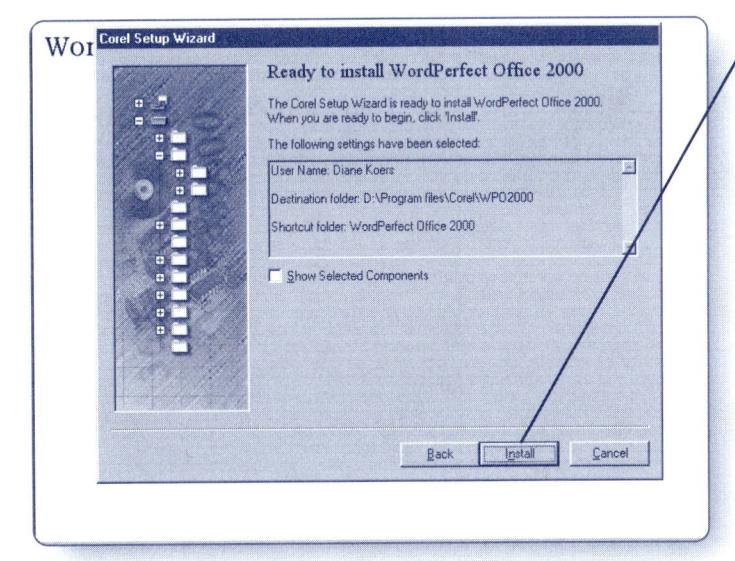

5. Click on **Install**. The Installation process will begin.

> **NOTE**
>
> Be patient. This process could take anywhere from 10 to 50 minutes to complete.

When the installation is complete, a message box will appear.

APPENDIX A: INSTALLING WORDPERFECT

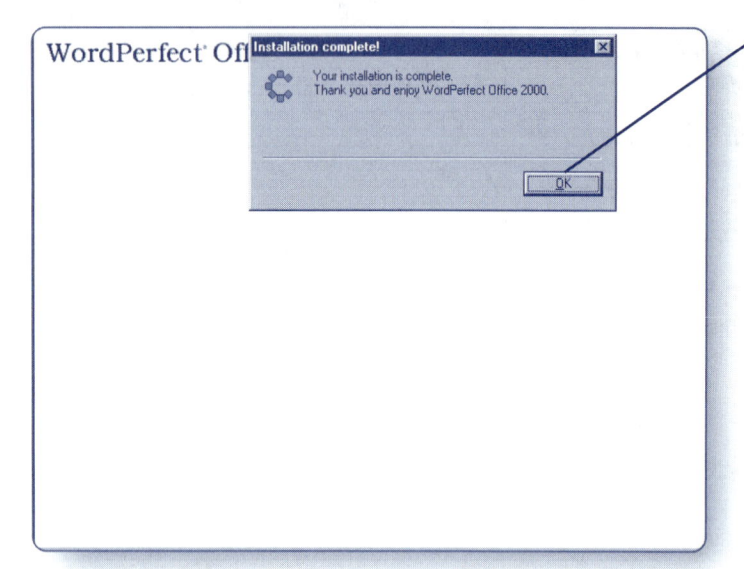

6. Click on **OK**. You will be prompted to restart your system.

7. Click on **Yes**. Your system will restart, and you'll be ready to use WordPerfect Office 2000.

Installing Only the WordPerfect Component

If you are not going to use all the components of WordPerfect Office 2000, you can customize the installation process and elect to only install WordPerfect and any other specific options.

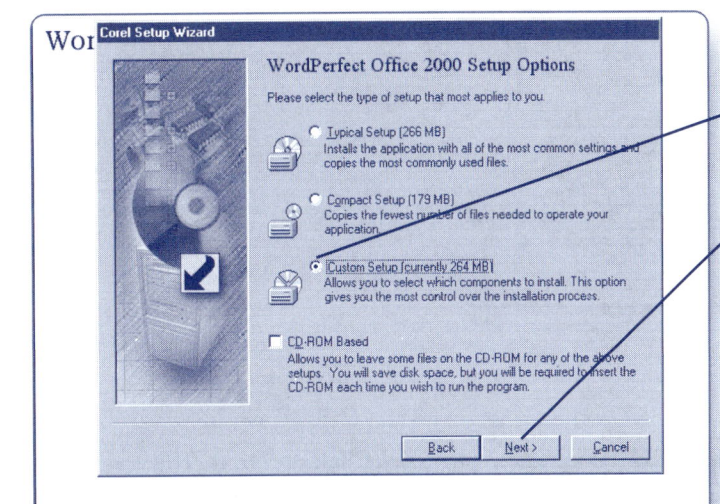

1. Click on **Custom Setup**. The option will be selected.

2. Click on **Next**. The WordPerfect Office 2000 components screen will appear.

WordPerfect Office 2000 is still assuming that you want to install most of its components.

Options that are preselected for you are indicated with a ✔.

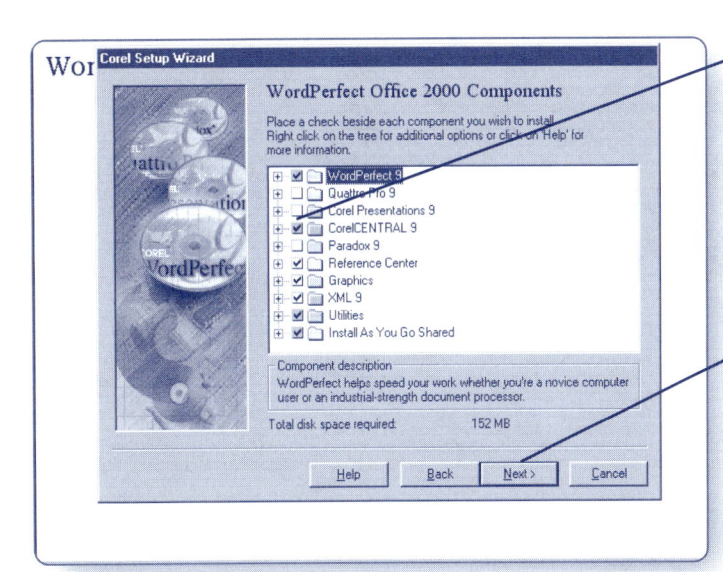

3. Click on any selected **item** that you do not want to install. The ✔ will be removed.

Only the items you want to install should have a ✔ in the box.

4. Click on **Next**. The Conversion Filters screen will appear.

APPENDIX A: INSTALLING WORDPERFECT

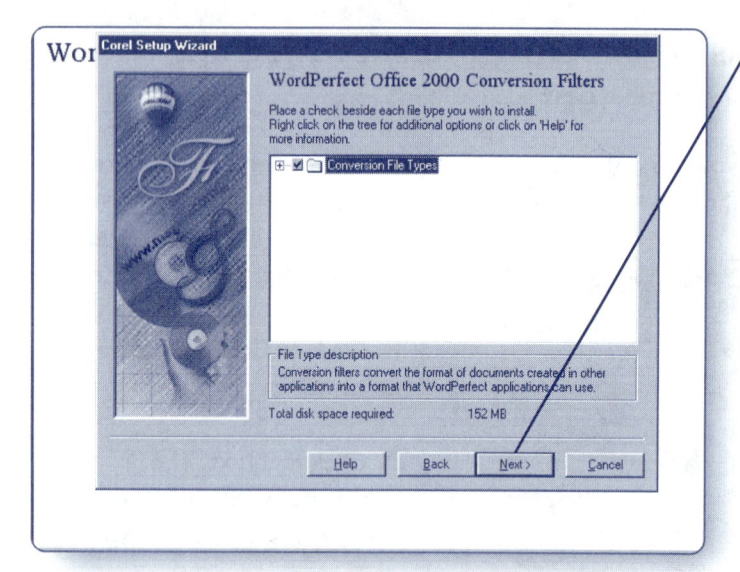

5. Click on **Next**. The Writing Tools Selection screen will appear.

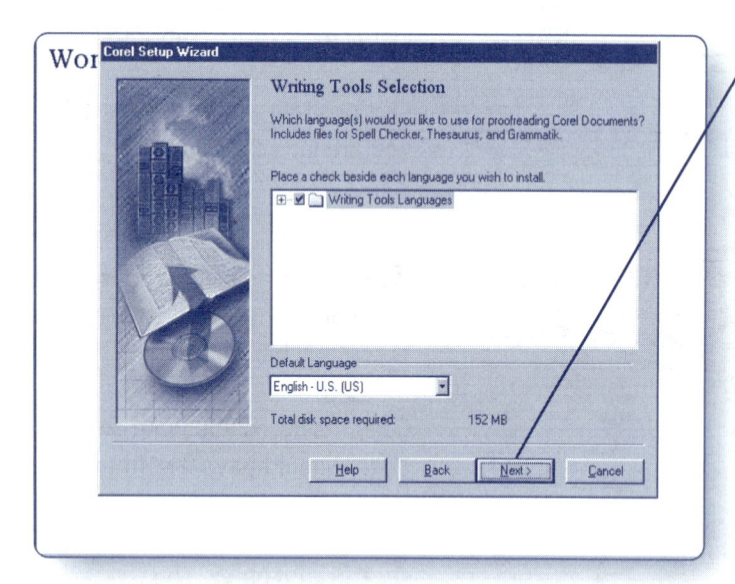

6. Click on **Next**. The WordPerfect Office 2000 Fonts screen will appear.

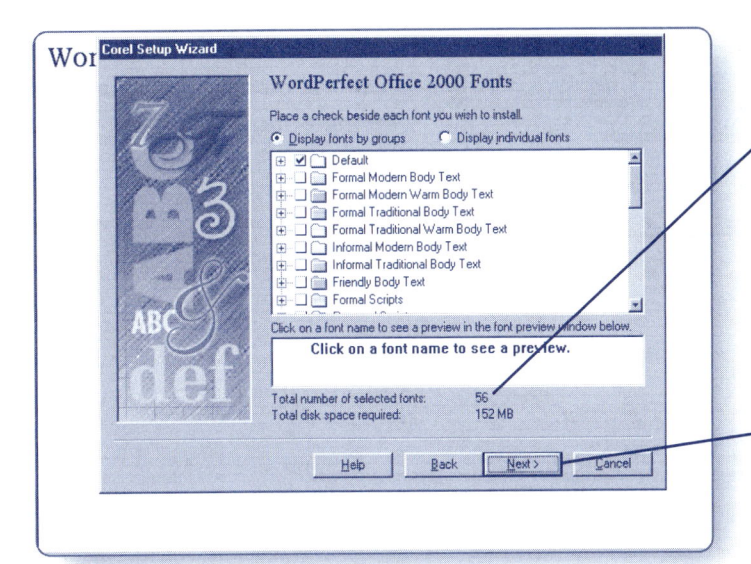

BEGINNING THE INSTALLATION PROCESS 341

TIP

By default, WordPerfect installs 56 new fonts for you to use; however, you can manually select any fonts from the list by clicking on the individual fonts.

7. Click on **Next**. The Destination Folder screen will appear.

Optionally, you can specify a different disk drive or folder to install WordPerfect.

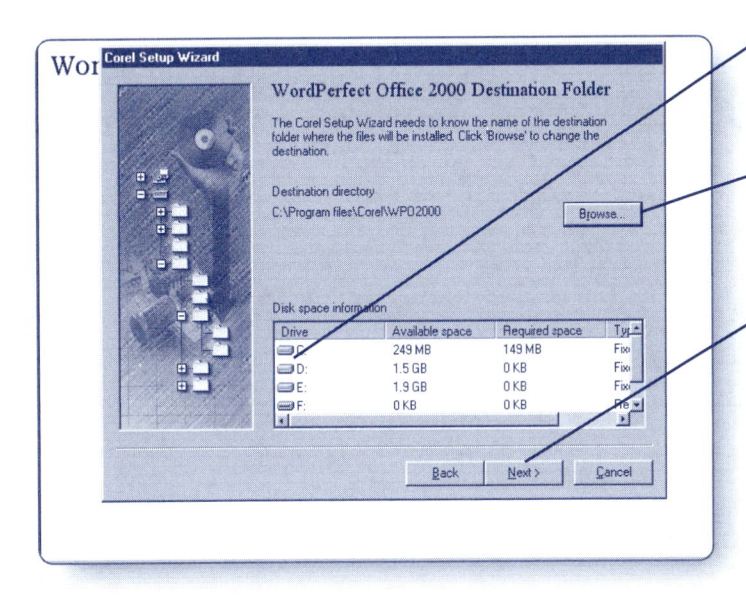

- Double-click on a disk drive letter. WordPerfect will install on a specified disk drive.

- Click on Browse and specify a different folder for the product to be installed on.

8. Click on **Next**. The Shortcut Folder screen will appear.

APPENDIX A: INSTALLING WORDPERFECT

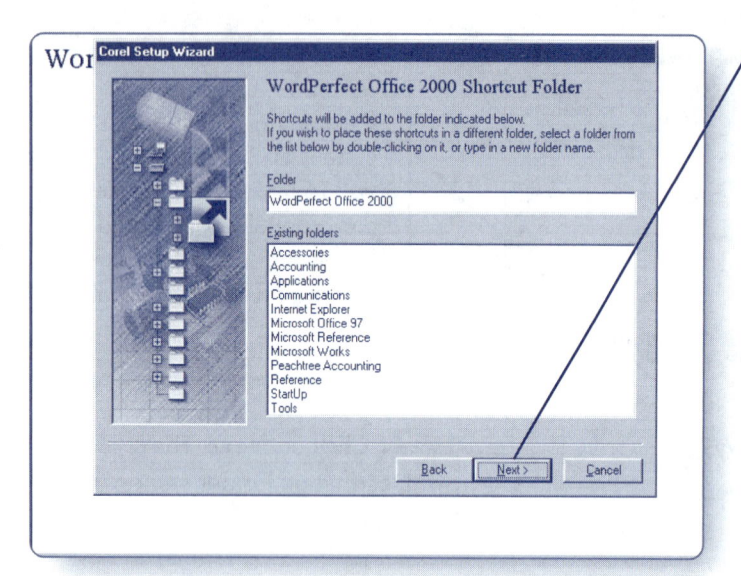

9. Click on **Next**. WordPerfect Office will be ready to install with the options you have selected.

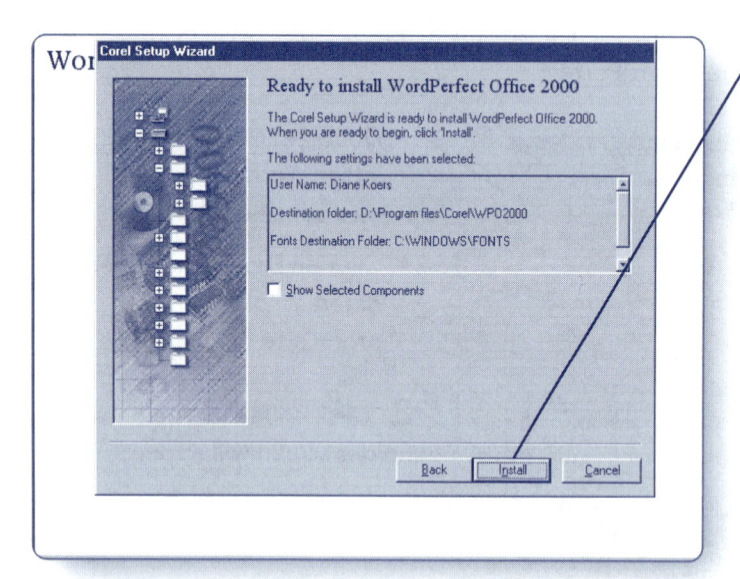

10. Click on **Install**. The Installation process will begin.

When the installation is complete, a message box will appear.

BEGINNING THE INSTALLATION PROCESS 343

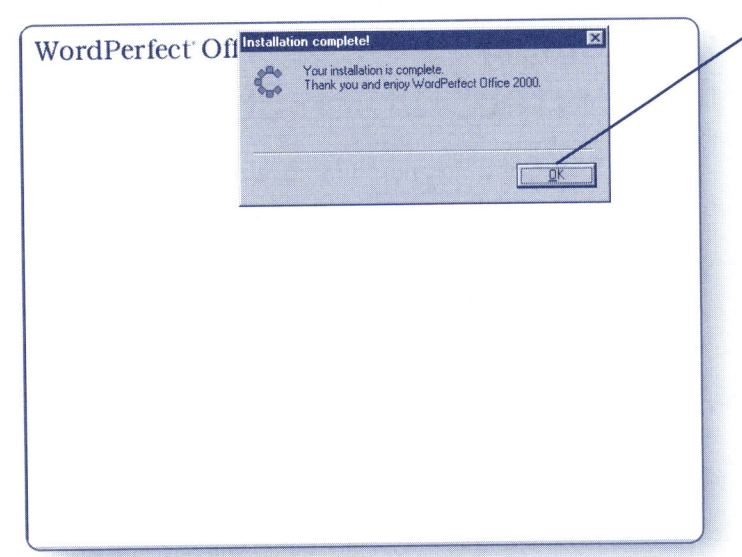

11. Click on **OK**. You'll be prompted to restart your system.

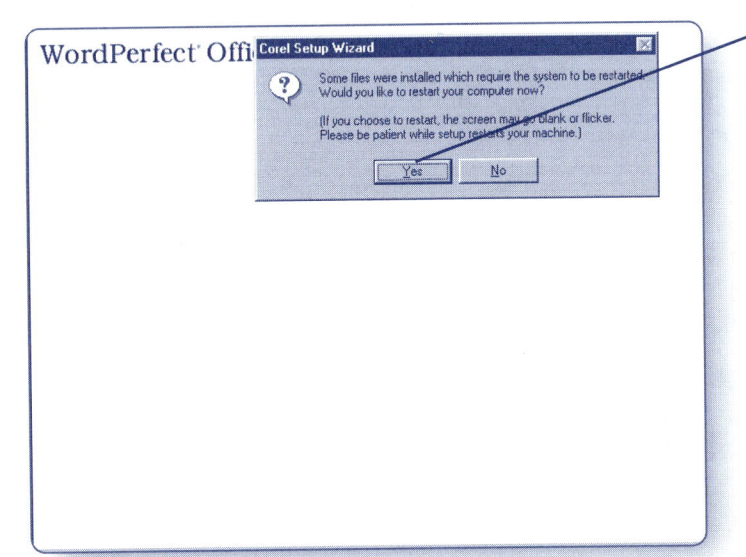

12. Click on **Yes**. Your system will restart, and you'll be ready to use WordPerfect Office 2000.

Uninstalling WordPerfect Office 2000

Use the Windows Control Panel to remove the installation of WordPerfect Office 2000 or any of its components.

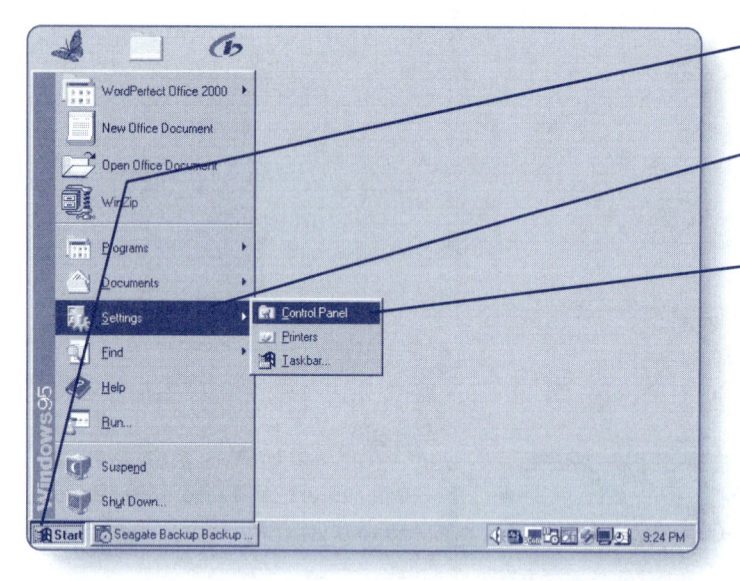

1. Click on **Start**. The Start menu will appear.

2. Click on **Settings**. The Settings submenu will appear.

3. Click on **Control Panel**. The Control Panel window will open.

4. Double-click on **Add/Remove Programs**. The Add/Remove Programs Properties dialog box will open.

UNINSTALLING WORDPERFECT OFFICE 2000

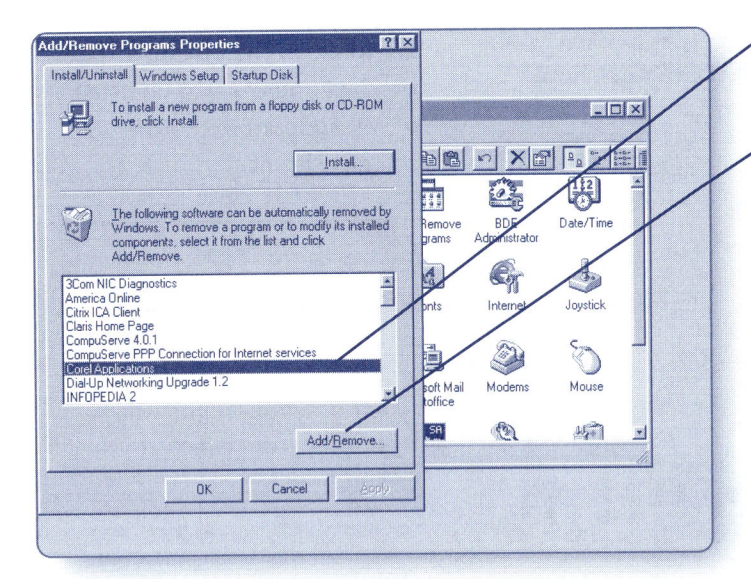

5. Click on **Corel Applications**. The option will be selected.

6. Click on **Add/Remove**. The Corel Uninstaller will launch.

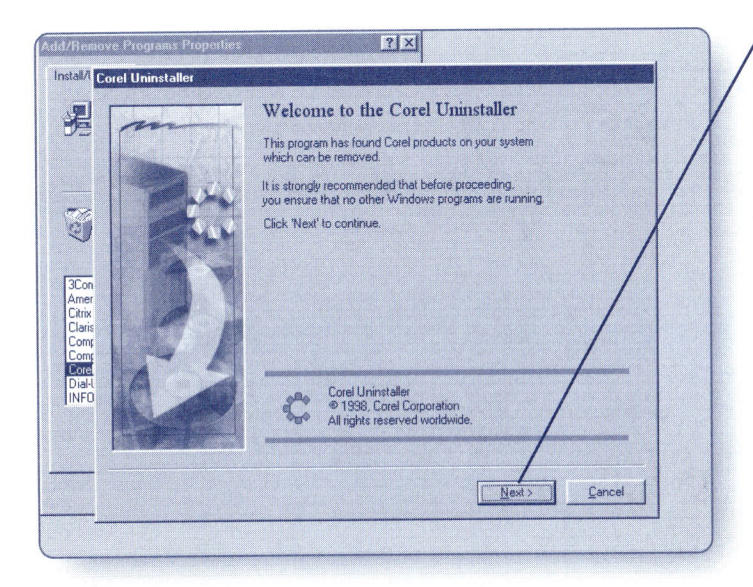

7. Click on **Next**. The Select Products to Remove screen will appear.

APPENDIX A: INSTALLING WORDPERFECT

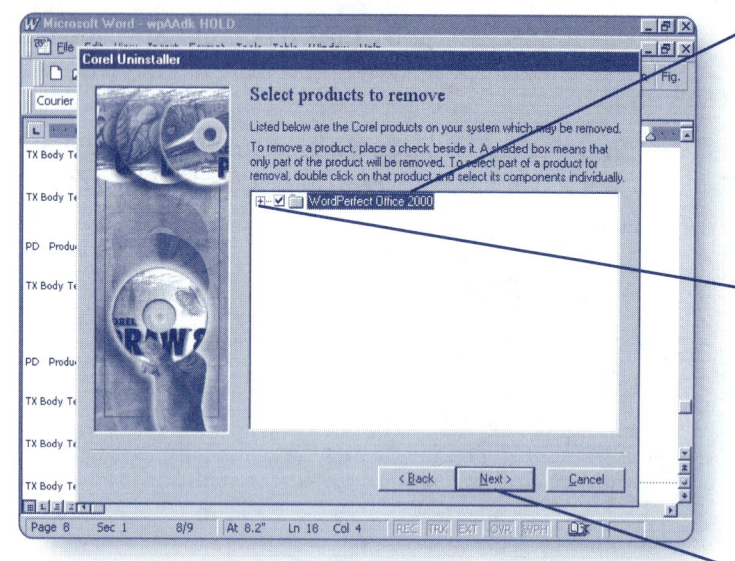

8. Click on the box next to the product you want to uninstall. A ✔ will appear next to the selected items.

TIP

To uninstall components, click on the + sign next to the installed product. A list of components will display from which you can select.

9. Click on **Next**. A confirmation screen will appear.

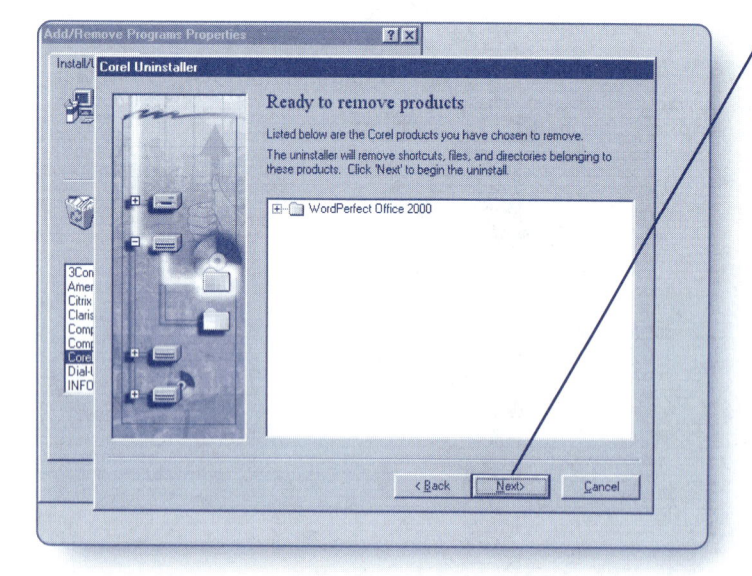

10. Click on **Next**. The Corel Uninstaller will begin removing the selected components.

UNINSTALLING WORDPERFECT OFFICE 2000

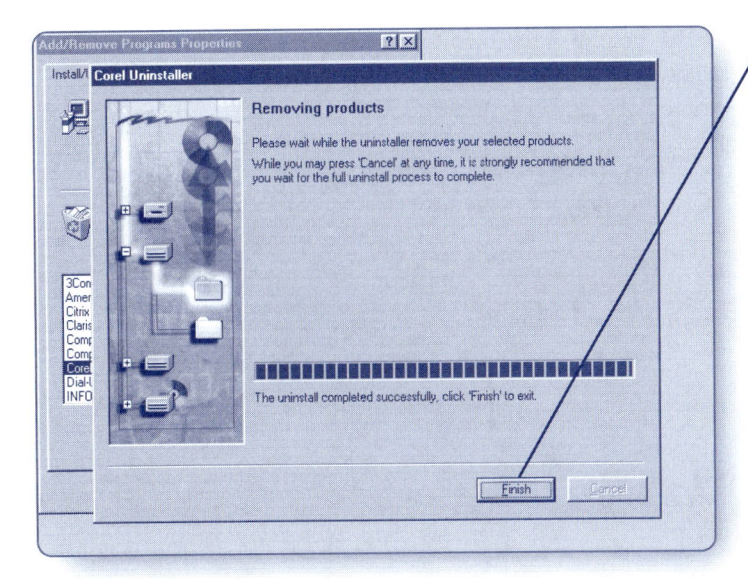

11. Click on **Finish**. You'll be prompted to restart your computer.

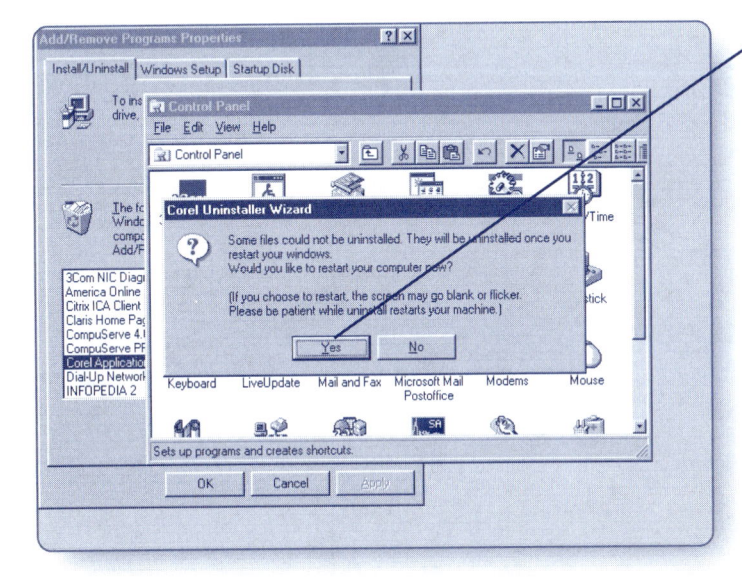

12. Click on **Yes**. Your computer will restart.

NOTE

After your computer restarts, you'll need to close the Control Panel window by clicking on its Close box (X).

B

Working with Dragon NaturallySpeaking

Do you talk to your computer? Most of us do. Dragon NaturallySpeaking is a speech-recognition program that allows you to talk to your computer without feeling like you've gone crazy! You can dictate text right into your document without typing. With Dragon NaturallySpeaking, you can dictate and edit text and more, all without touching the keyboard or mouse! In this chapter, you'll learn how to:

- Install Dragon NaturallySpeaking
- Set up and test your microphone
- Teach Dragon NaturallySpeaking how you speak
- Use Dragon NaturallySpeaking with WordPerfect
- Correct Errors

Installing Dragon NaturallySpeaking

Although the Dragon NaturallySpeaking software is included with WordPerfect 2000, you'll need to install it separately from the Perfect program. Your computer will also need to have a sound card installed, as well as a microphone and speakers.

1. **Insert** the PerfectOffice **CD** marked Voice Recognition. The loading program will appear.

2. **Click** on **Install Dragon NaturallySpeaking**. The Setup Wizard will begin.

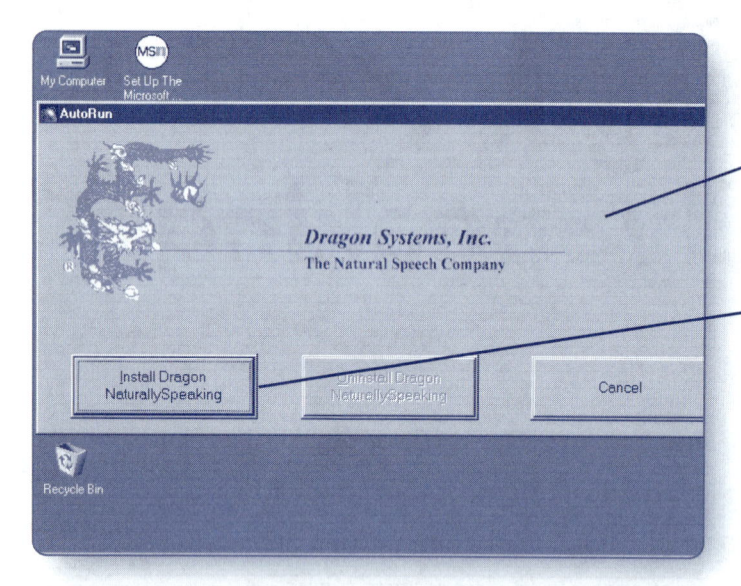

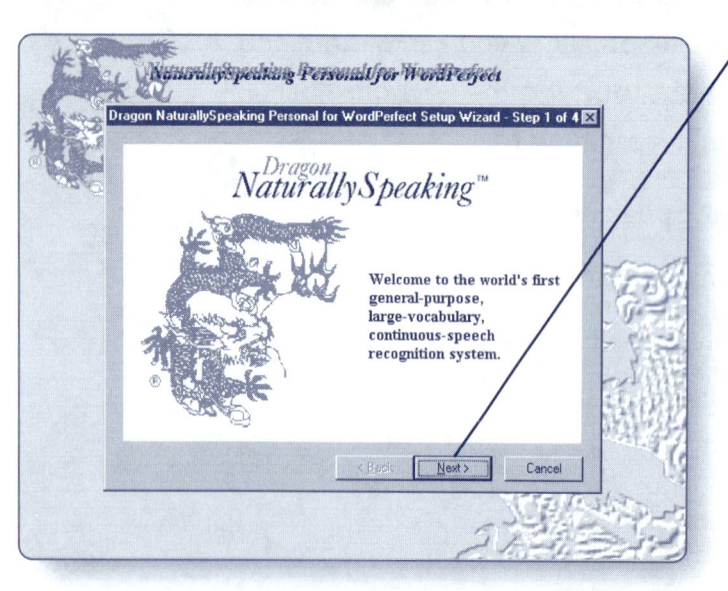

3. **Click** on **Next**. Step 2 of the Setup Wizard will appear.

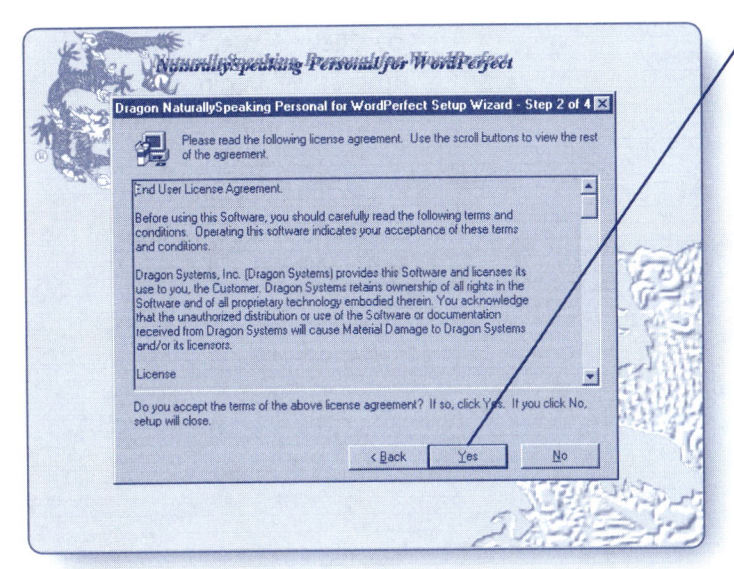

INSTALLING DRAGON NATURALLYSPEAKING 351

4. Read the License Agreement and **then click** on **Yes**. Step 3 of the Setup Wizard will appear.

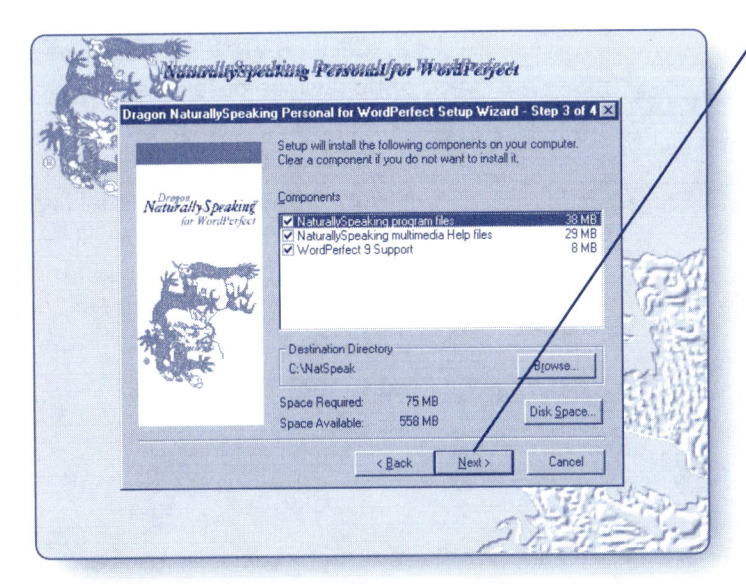

5. Click on **Next**. A message box will appear.

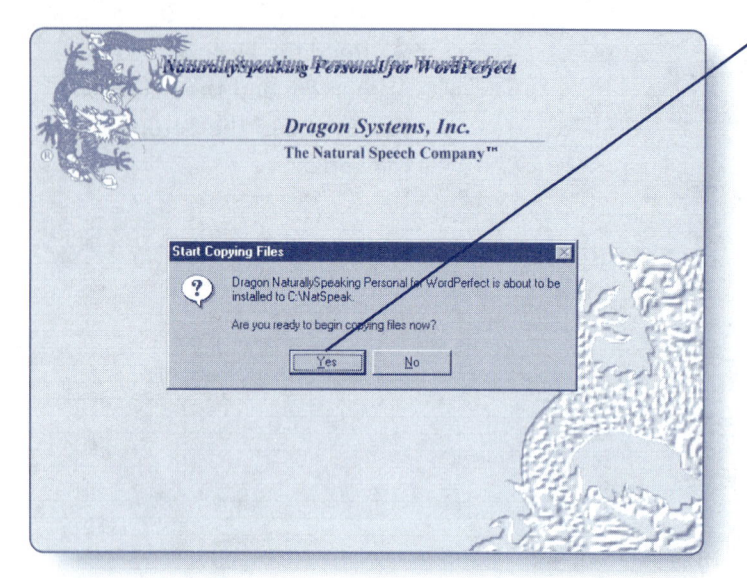

6. **Click** on **Yes**. The installation process will begin, and files will be copied to your system.

When the copy process is completed, the final step of the Setup Wizard will display.

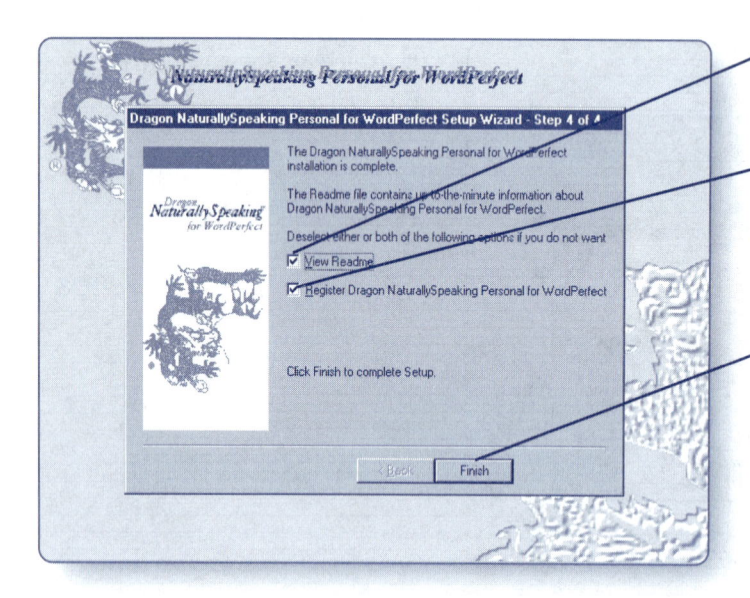

7. **Click** on **View Readme**. The option will be deselected.

8. **Click** on **Register Dragon NaturallySpeaking Personal for WordPerfect**. The option will be selected.

9. **Click** on **Finish**. A registration message will appear.

TRAINING TO YOUR VOICE

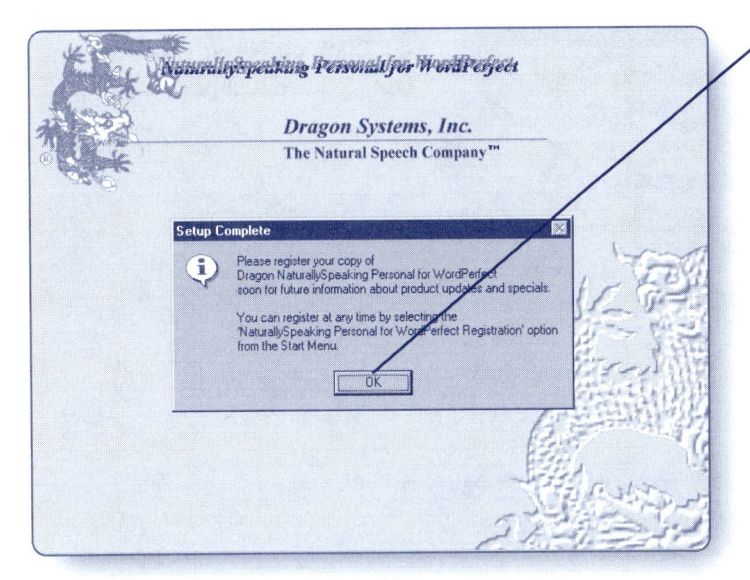

10. Click on **OK**. You can now launch WordPerfect and begin training NaturallySpeaking to your voice.

Training to Your Voice

Each of us has a different tone to our voice and different ways of enunciating words. Before you can use the NaturallySpeaking program, you'll need to teach it how you talk. The Audio Setup Wizard will assist you.

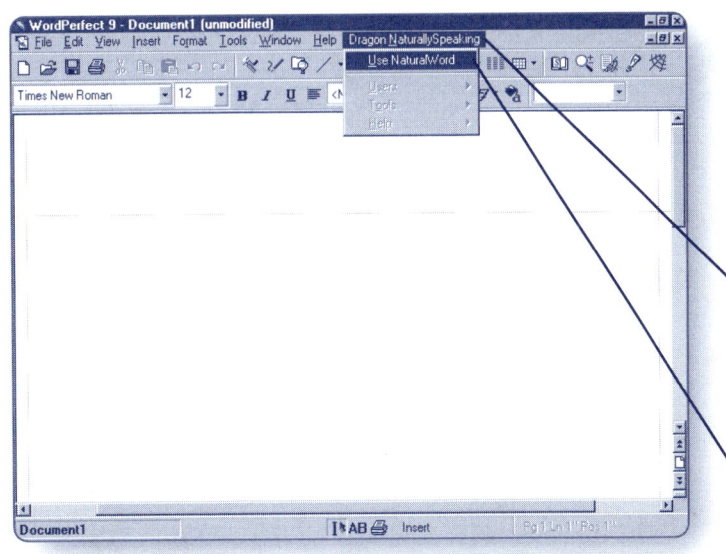

Creating Speech Files

NaturallySpeaking needs to create a speech file to store information about the way you pronounce your words.

1. Click on **Dragon NaturallySpeaking**. The Dragon NaturallySpeaking menu will appear.

2. Click on **Use NaturalWord**. The Open User dialog box will open.

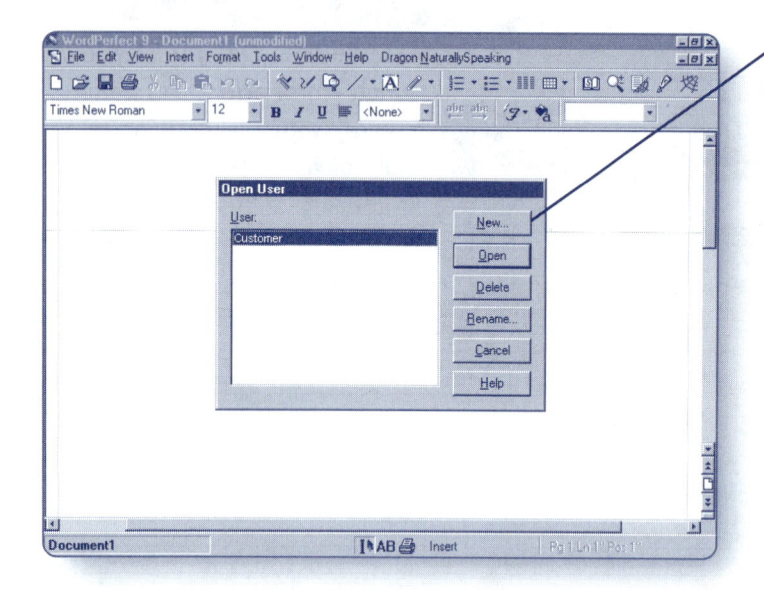

354 APPENDIX B: WORKING WITH DRAGON NATURALLYSPEAKING

3. Click on **New**. The New User Wizard will begin.

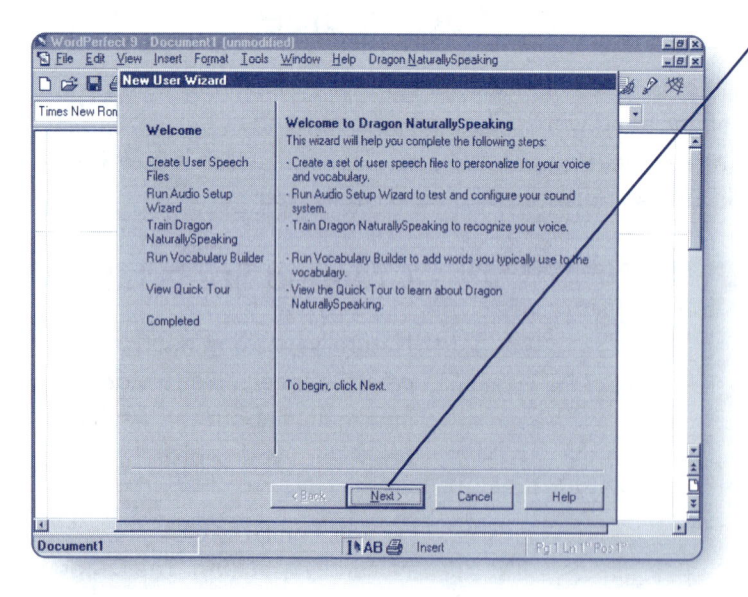

4. Click on **Next**. The next page of the Wizard will appear.

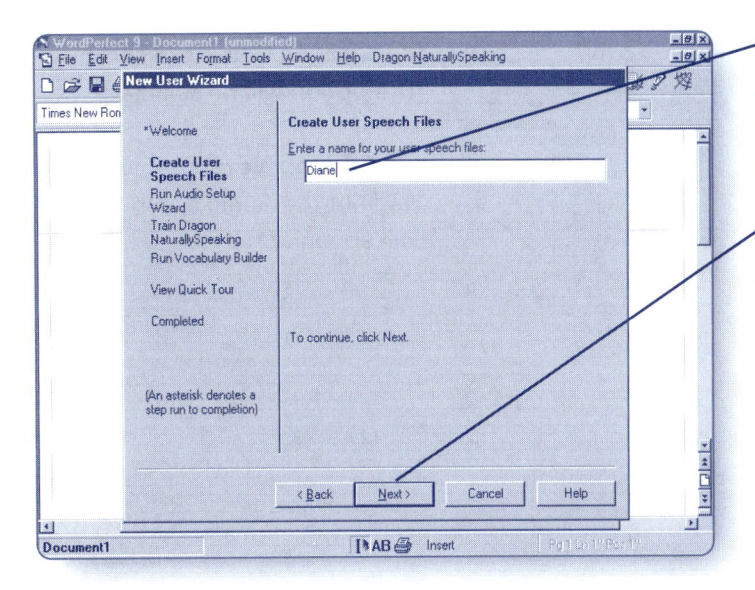

5. Type your **name**. The text will appear in the Enter a name for your user speech files: text box.

6. Click on **Next**. The Audio Setup Wizard page will appear.

Running the Audio Setup Wizard

The Audio Setup Wizard tests and adjusts your system to make sure that the sound is working and your computer can hear your voice.

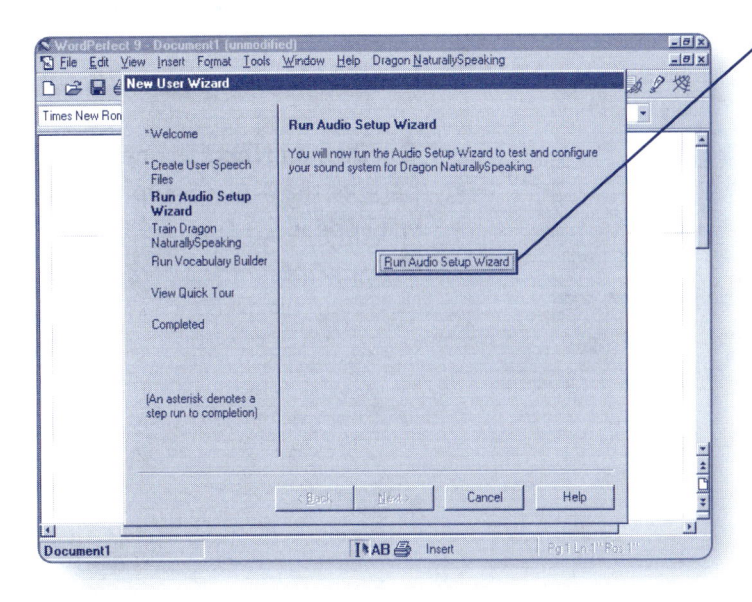

1. Click on **Run Audio Setup Wizard**. The next page of the Audio Setup Wizard will appear.

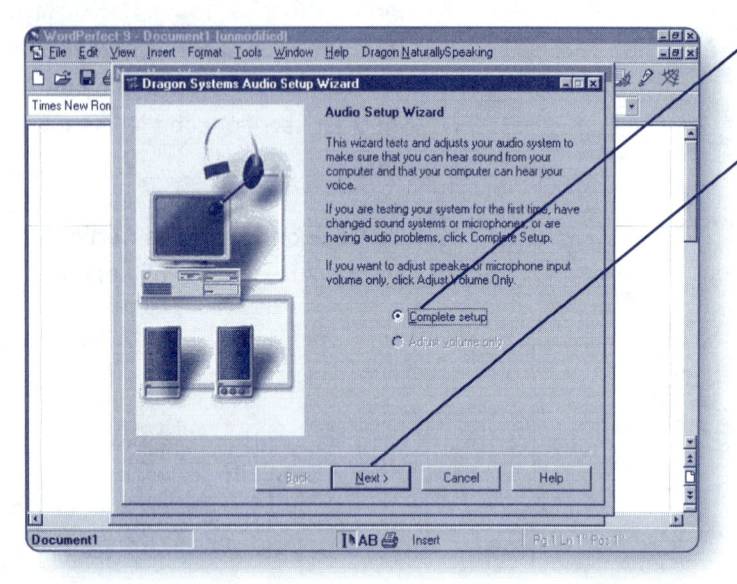

APPENDIX B: WORKING WITH DRAGON NATURALLYSPEAKING

2. Click on **Complete setup**. The option will be selected.

3. Click on **Next**. The next page of the Audio Setup Wizard will appear.

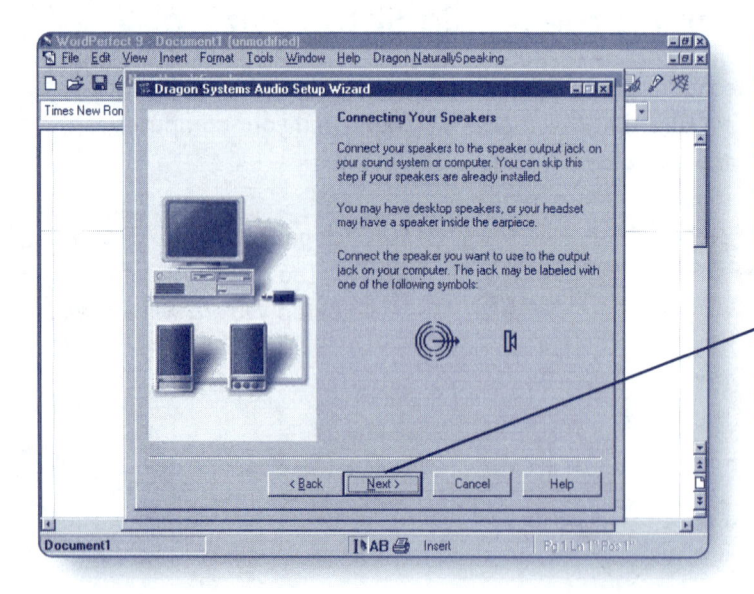

> **TIP**
>
> If your speakers are not connected to your computer, you'll need to plug them in now.

4. Click on **Next**. The next page of the Audio Setup Wizard will appear.

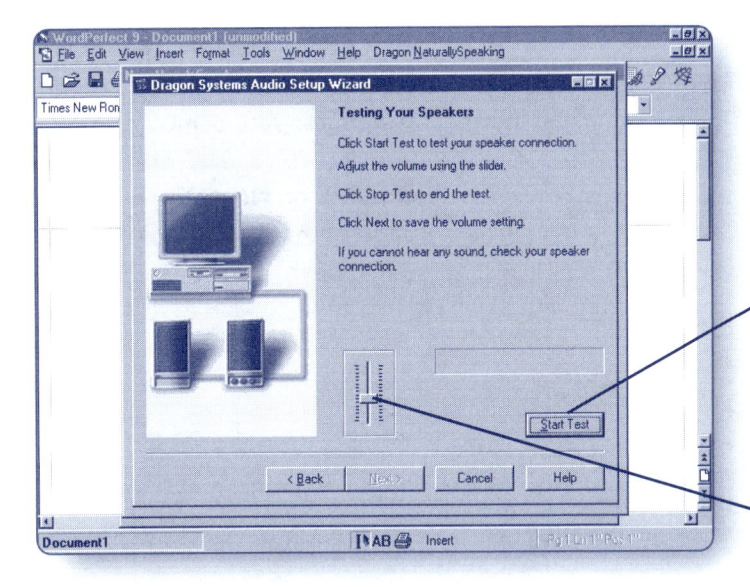

TRAINING TO YOUR VOICE 357

Testing Speaker Connections

Now you need to test the speaker connection and set the volume to your liking.

1. Click on **Start Test**. You should be able to hear sound from your speakers.

TIP

Drag the volume slider up to increase the volume or down to decrease the volume.

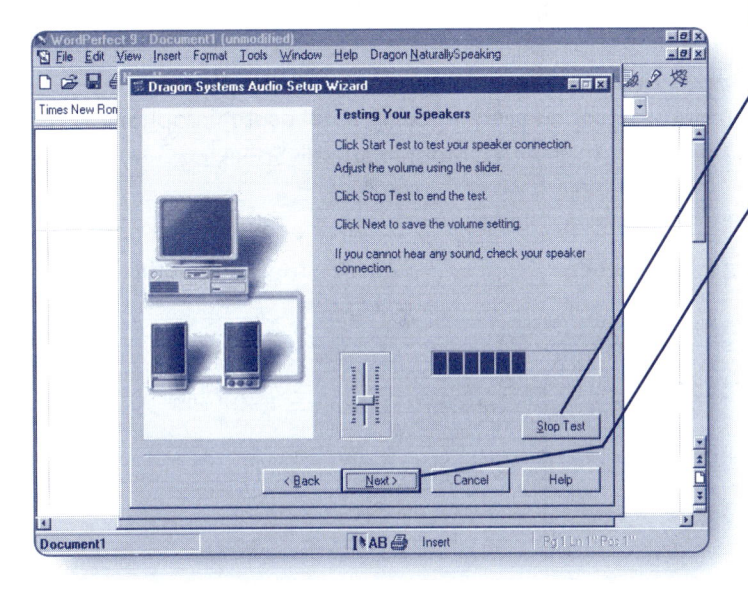

2. Click on **Stop Test**. The speaker test will end.

3. Click on **Next**. The next page of the Audio Setup Wizard will appear.

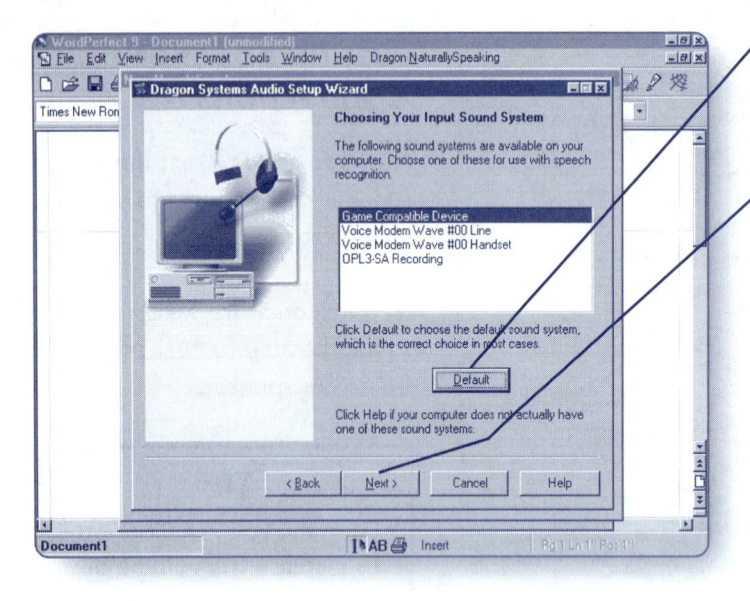

358 APPENDIX B: WORKING WITH DRAGON NATURALLYSPEAKING

4. Click on **Default**. The Audio Setup Wizard will select a sound system for your computer.

5. Click on **Next**. The next page of the Audio Setup Wizard will appear.

Testing the Microphone

Make sure that your microphone is plugged into your computer or sound system. Using a headset microphone is the best way to talk to Dragon NaturallySpeaking.

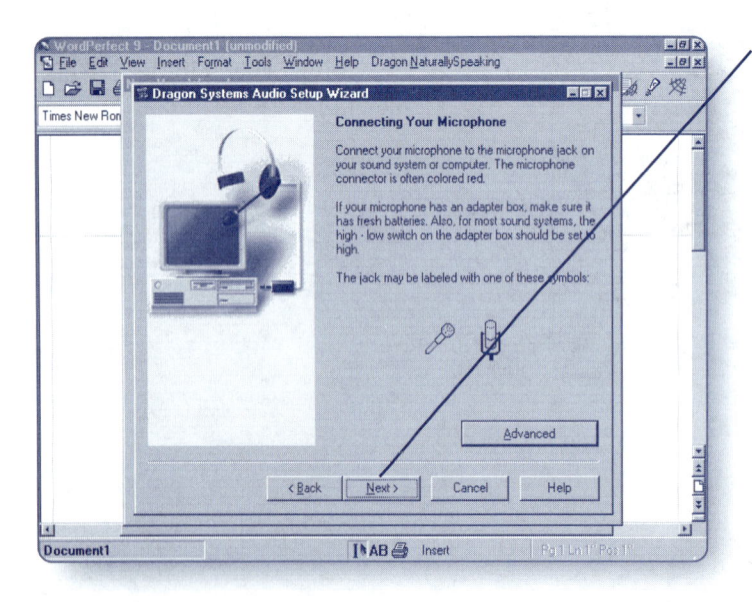

1. Click on **Next**. The next page of the Audio Setup Wizard will appear.

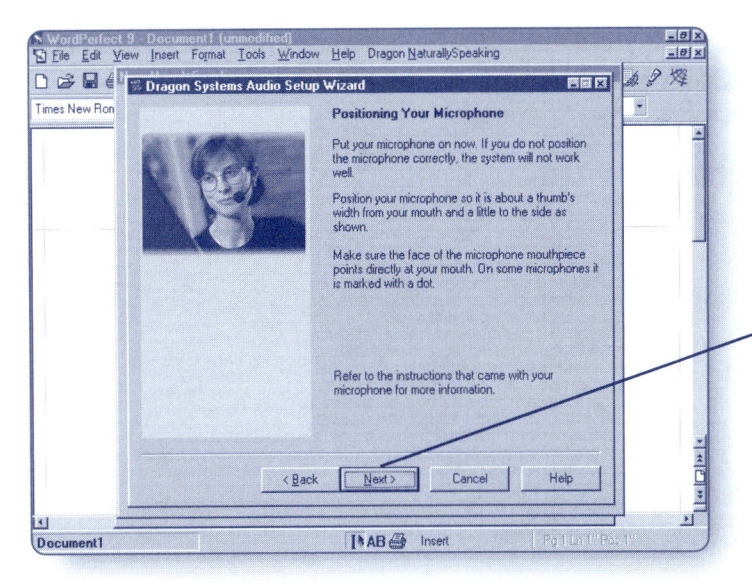

TRAINING TO YOUR VOICE   359

Positioning the microphone correctly each time you use it is one of the most important things you can do to make sure that NaturallySpeaking accurately hears everything you say.

2. Click on **Next**. The next page of the Audio Setup Wizard will display.

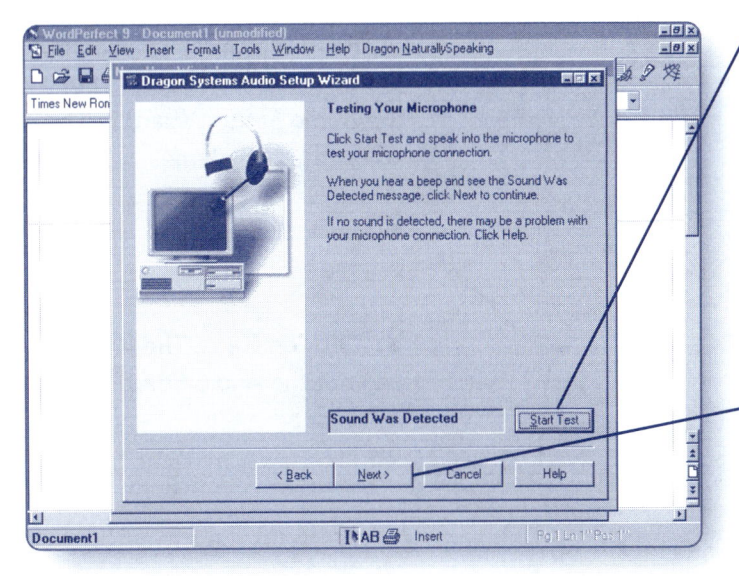

3. Click on **Start Test**. The microphone test will begin.

4. Speak into the microphone. You can say your name, the Pledge of Allegiance or anything you want. When your voice is detected, a Sound Was Detected message will display.

5. Click on **Next**. The next page of the Audio Setup Wizard will appear.

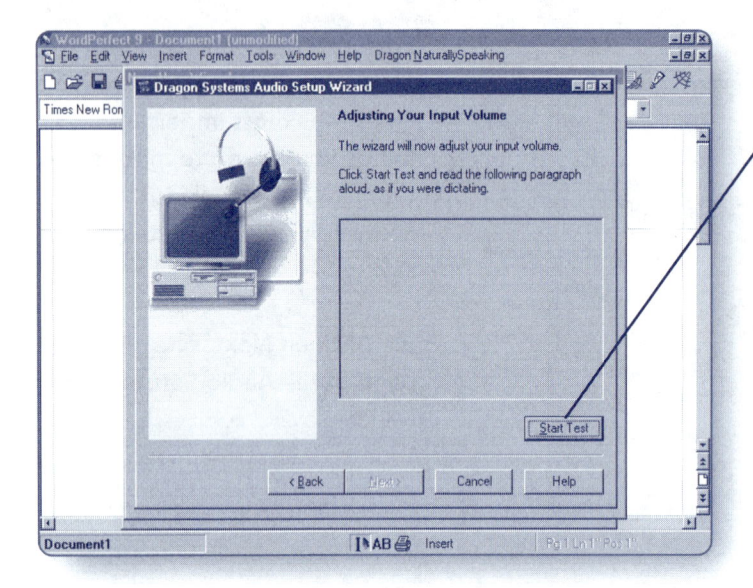

360 APPENDIX B: WORKING WITH DRAGON NATURALLYSPEAKING

The wizard will next adjust the sound level of your voice.

6. Click on **Start Test**. Text will appear in the large box.

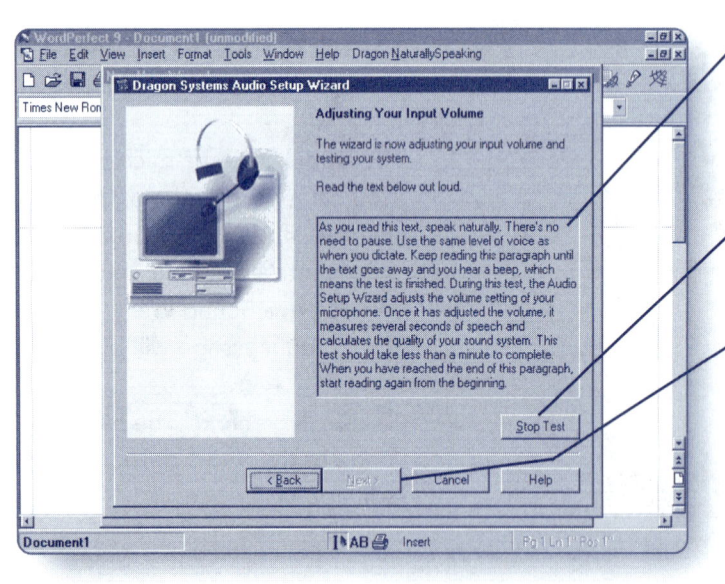

7. Read the **text** displayed in the box. You won't see it, but the Audio Setup Wizard will be adjusting the volume.

8. Click on **Stop Test**. The volume test will stop.

9. Click on **Next**. The final page of the Audio Setup Wizard will appear.

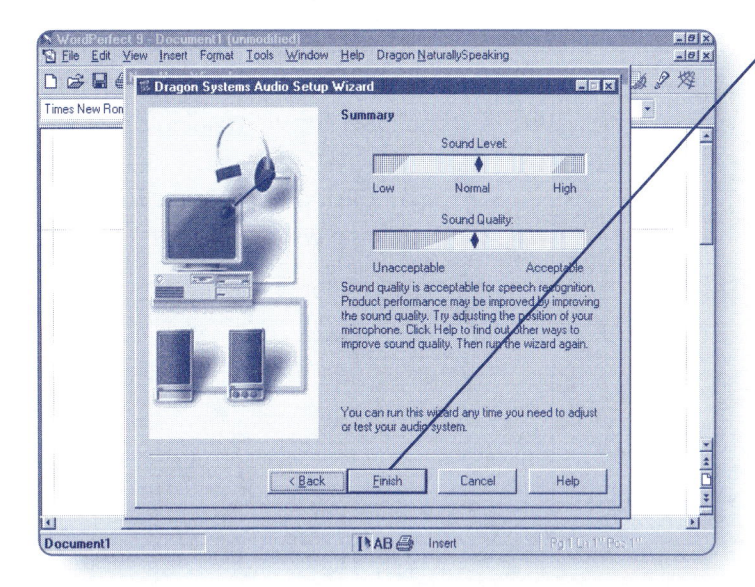

10. Click on **Finish**. The Audio Setup Wizard will close, and the New User Wizard will begin.

Running the New User Wizard

Training NaturallySpeaking to your voice takes several steps. These steps take a little time, approximately 45 minutes, but are necessary to teach the software your voice patterns.

Running General Training

During General Training, you dictate a number of text screens that appear on your screen.

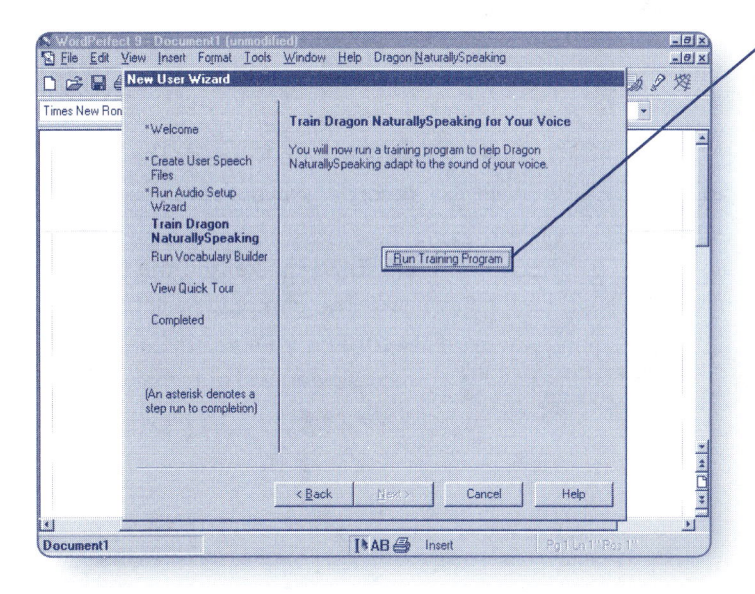

1. Click on **Run Training Program**. An instruction screen will appear.

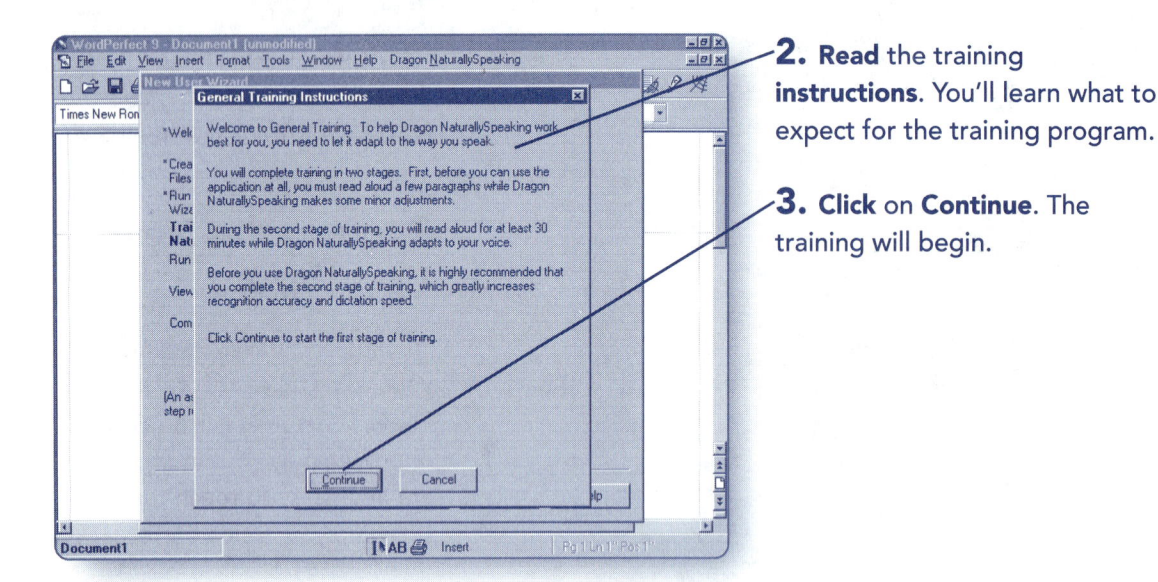

APPENDIX B: WORKING WITH DRAGON NATURALLYSPEAKING

2. Read the training **instructions**. You'll learn what to expect for the training program.

3. Click on **Continue**. The training will begin.

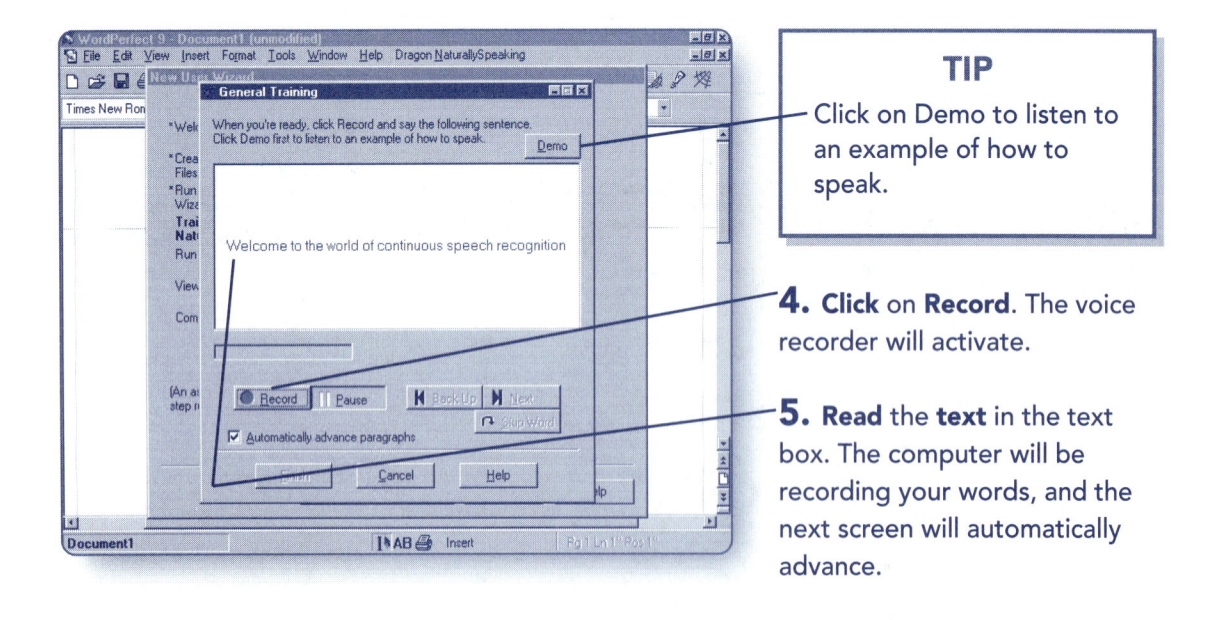

TIP

Click on Demo to listen to an example of how to speak.

4. Click on **Record**. The voice recorder will activate.

5. Read the **text** in the text box. The computer will be recording your words, and the next screen will automatically advance.

TRAINING TO YOUR VOICE

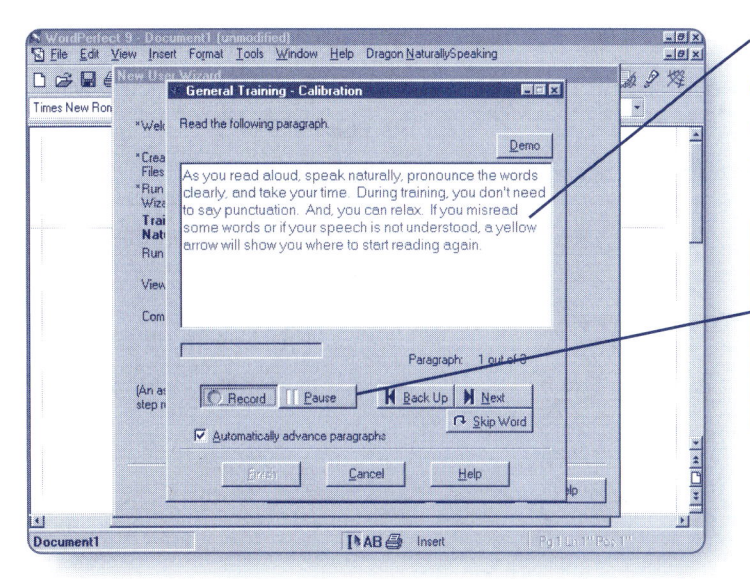

6. Continue reading the text in the text boxes. Each screen will automatically advance to the next one.

> **TIP**
> Click on Pause if you need to temporarily stop the training.

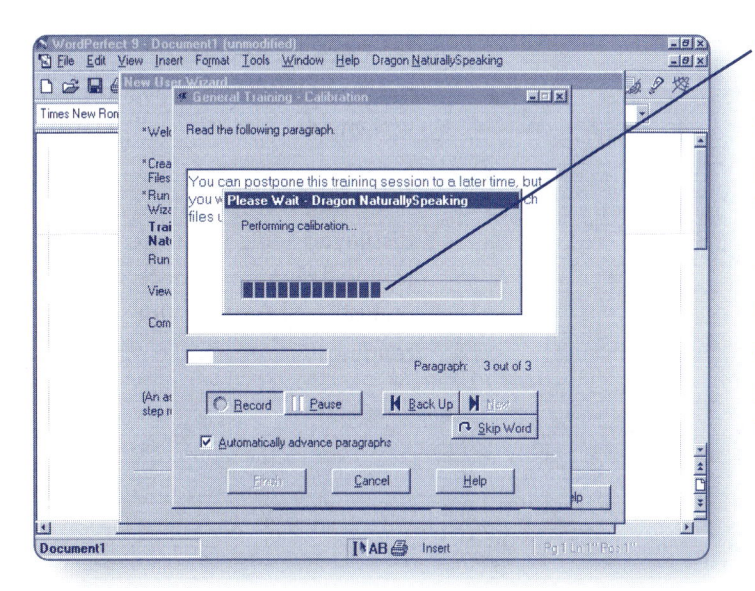

When you have completed reading the three paragraphs, the program automatically performs a calibration to your voice.

The next stage of training begins. This step takes approximately 30 minutes, and you'll be asked to read text from one of three documents.

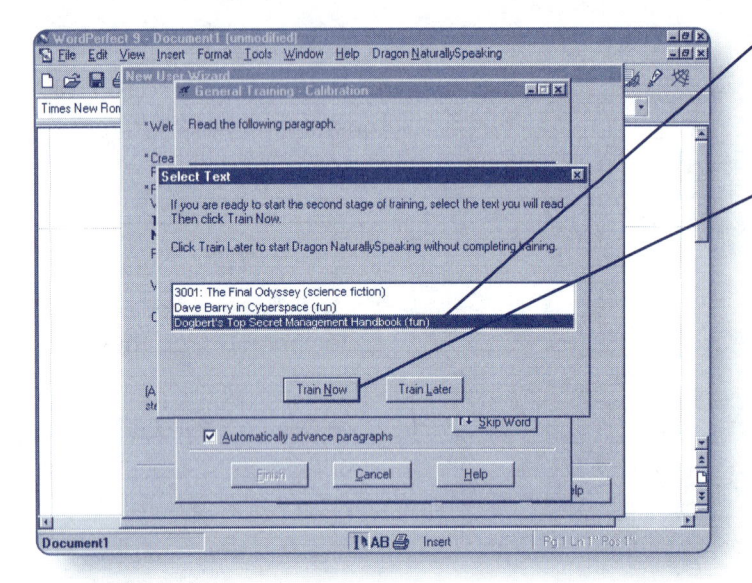

364 APPENDIX B: WORKING WITH DRAGON NATURALLYSPEAKING

7. Click on a **document** to read. The document name will be highlighted.

8. Click on **Train Now**. A page of text will appear on the screen.

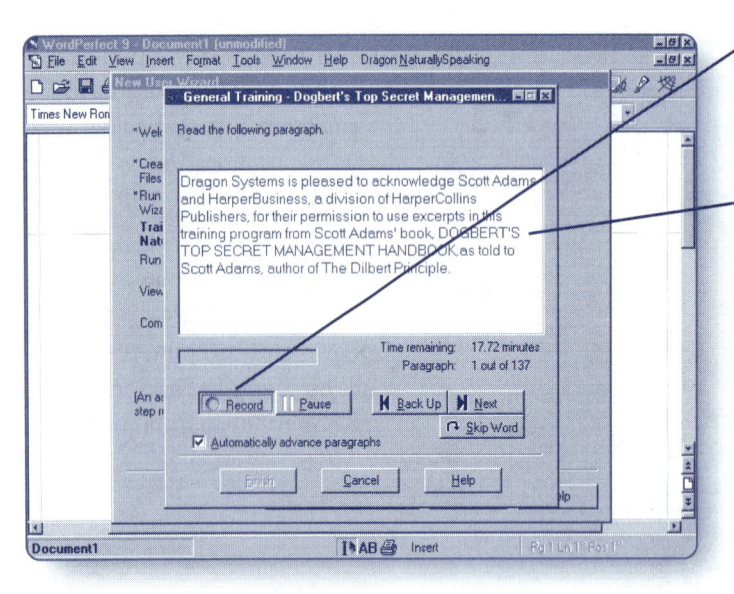

9. Click on **Record**. The microphone recorder will be activated.

10. Begin reading the displayed text. The onscreen text will change color as the computer interprets your reading.

TRAINING TO YOUR VOICE 365

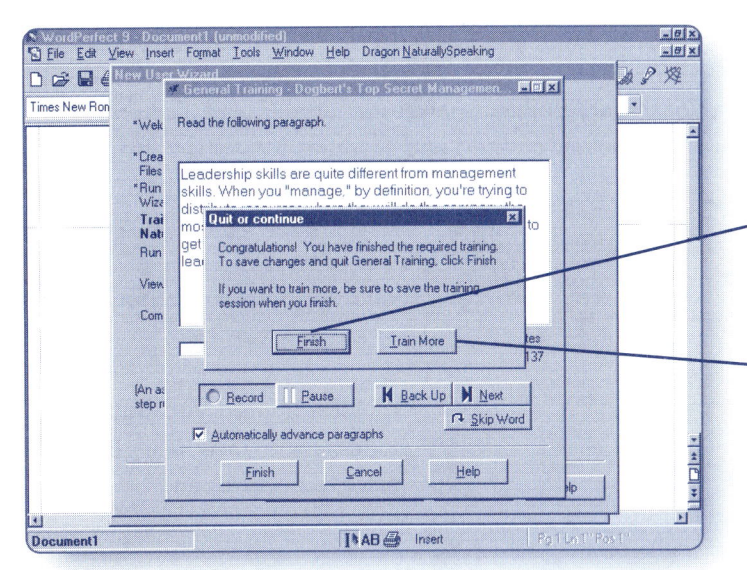

When you have read enough text for NaturallySpeaking to understand your speech pattern, a dialog box will open.

11. **Click** on **Finish**.

NOTE

Optionally, click on Train More to dictate additional text. Remember that the more you dictate, the more the software will understand you.

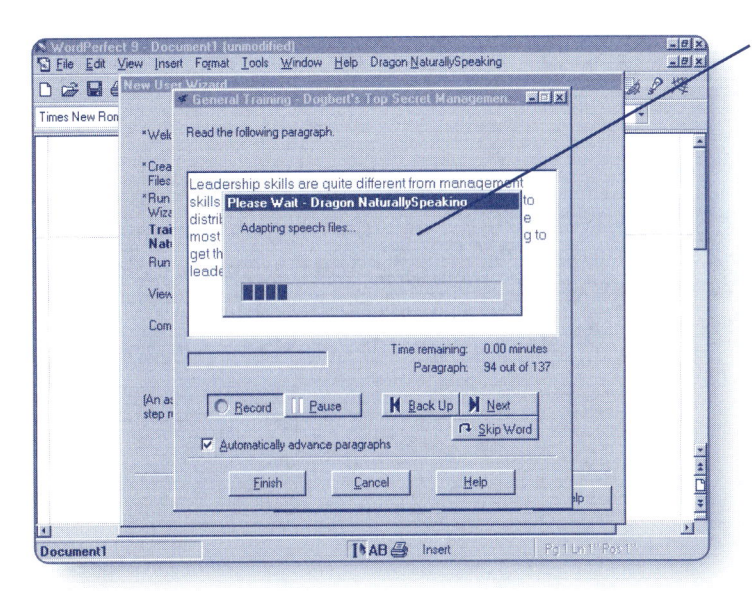

NaturallySpeaking now runs an internal step to adapt the speech files you've dictated. Be patient, this step could take a number of minutes.

Running the Vocabulary Builder

The Vocabulary Builder analyzes a number of documents you've previously created and searches for word patterns, unusual words, and your general writing style. This step is not a requirement to run NaturallySpeaking, but it greatly increases accuracy.

1. Click on **Run Vocabulary Builder**. The Vocabulary Builder dialog box will open.

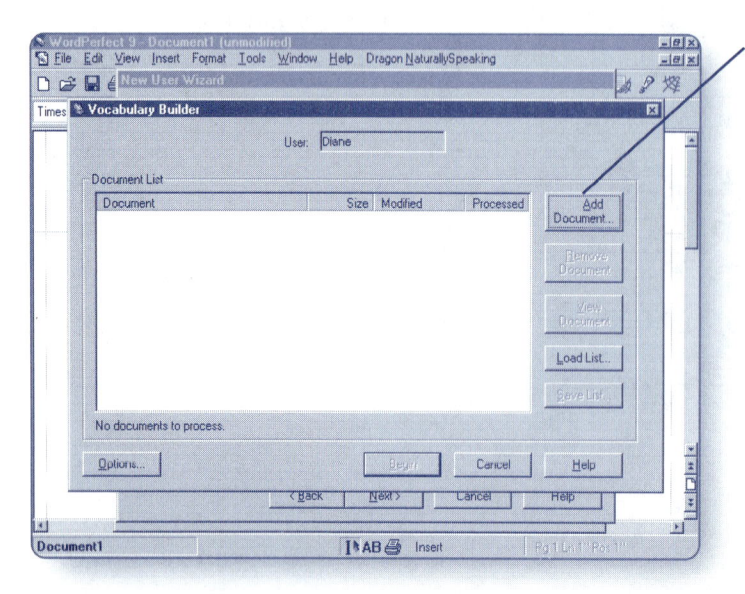

2. Click on **Add Document**. The Add Documents dialog box will open.

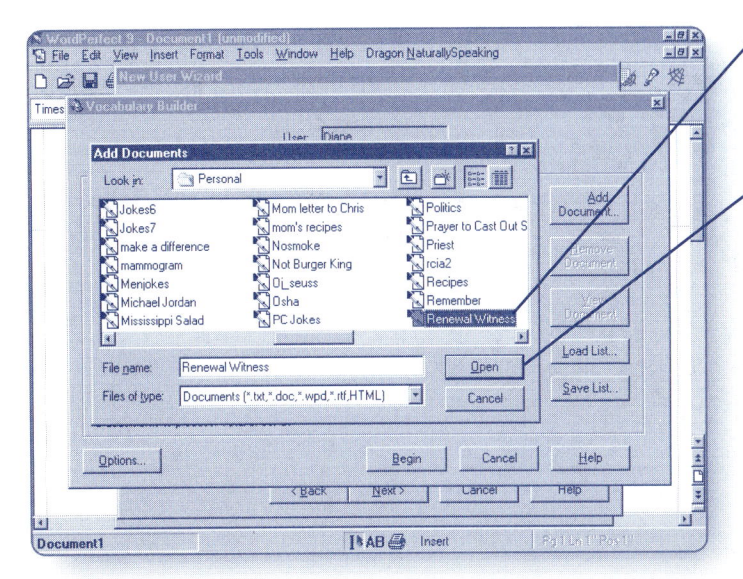

TRAINING TO YOUR VOICE 367

3. Click on a **document** you've written. The document name will be highlighted.

4. Click on **Open**. The document name will be added to the Vocabulary Builder dialog box.

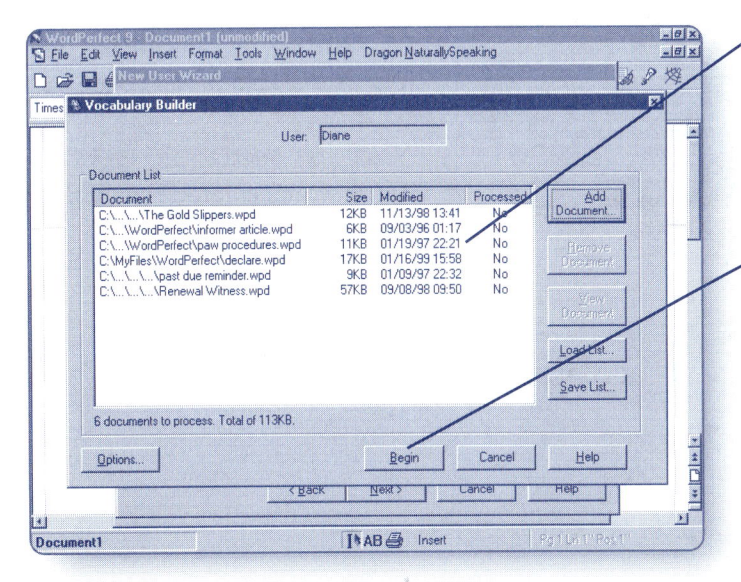

5. Repeat steps 2 through **4** for each document you want to add. Each document name will appear in the Vocabulary Builder dialog box.

6. Click on **Begin**. The New Words from Documents dialog box will open.

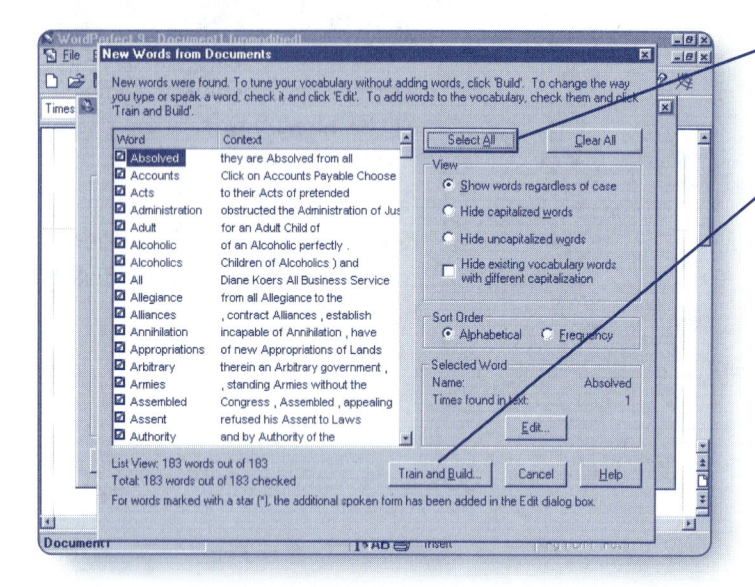

APPENDIX B: WORKING WITH DRAGON NATURALLYSPEAKING

7. Click on **Select All**. Each word in the word list will have a ✔ next to it.

8. Click on **Train and Build**. A message box will appear.

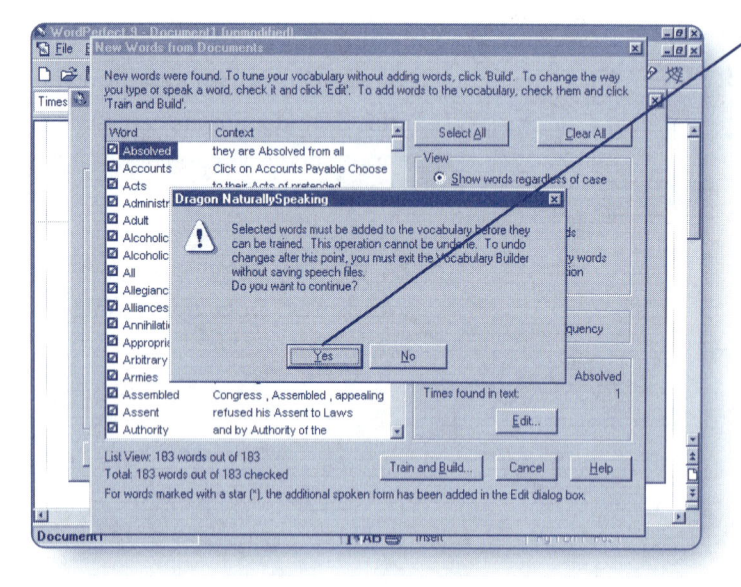

9. Click on **Yes**. The Train Words dialog box will open.

You'll now need to dictate the list of words created from your documents.

TRAINING TO YOUR VOICE 369

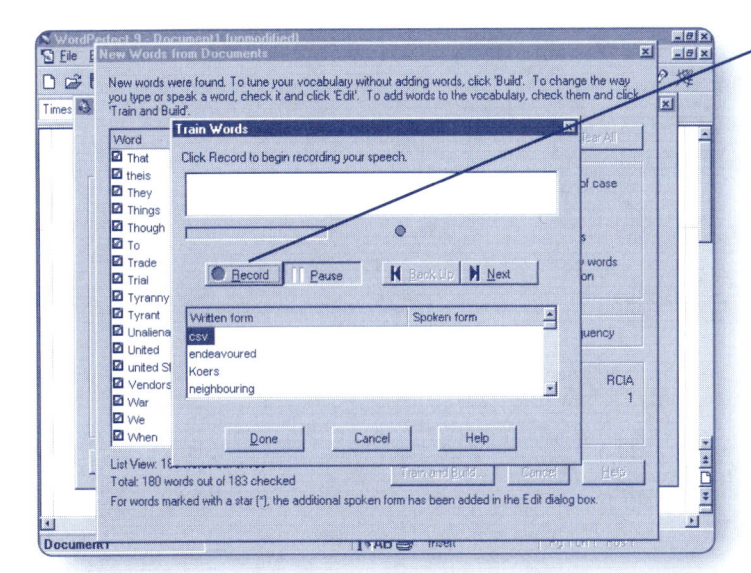

10. Click on **Record**. The speech recorder will begin.

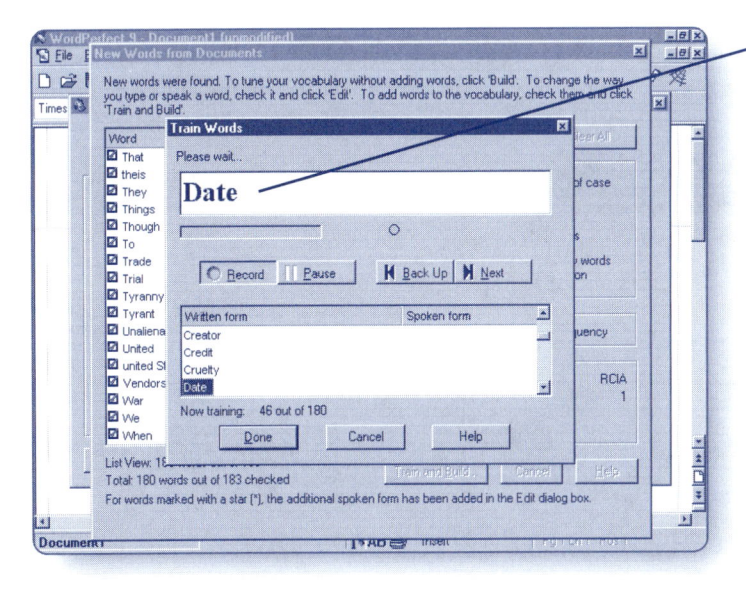

11. Dictate each **word** as it appears in the dictation box. The next word in the list will automatically appear.

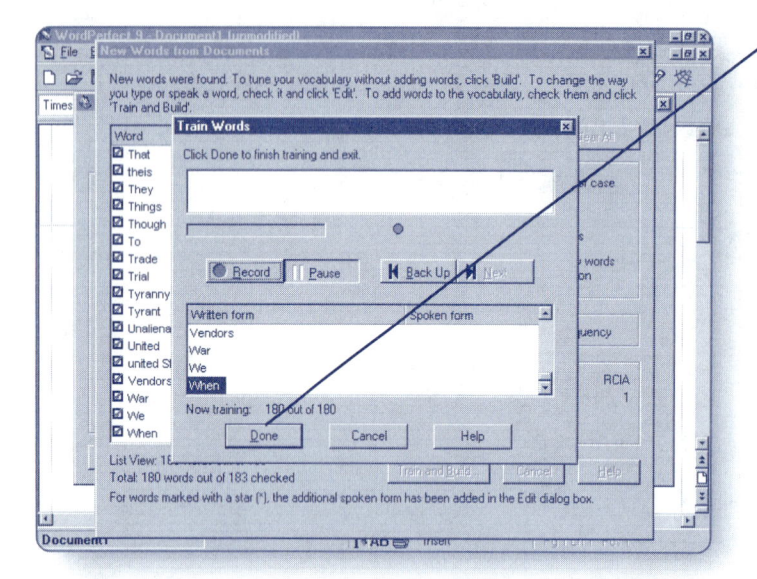

APPENDIX B: WORKING WITH DRAGON NATURALLYSPEAKING

12. Click on **Done**. A message to save your speech files will appear.

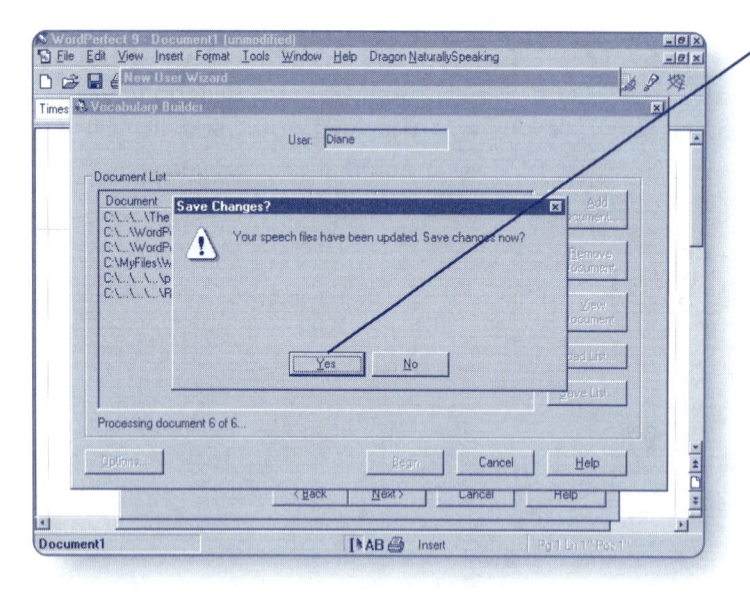

13. Click on **Yes**. The speech files will be saved, and a message box will appear.

TRAINING TO YOUR VOICE 371

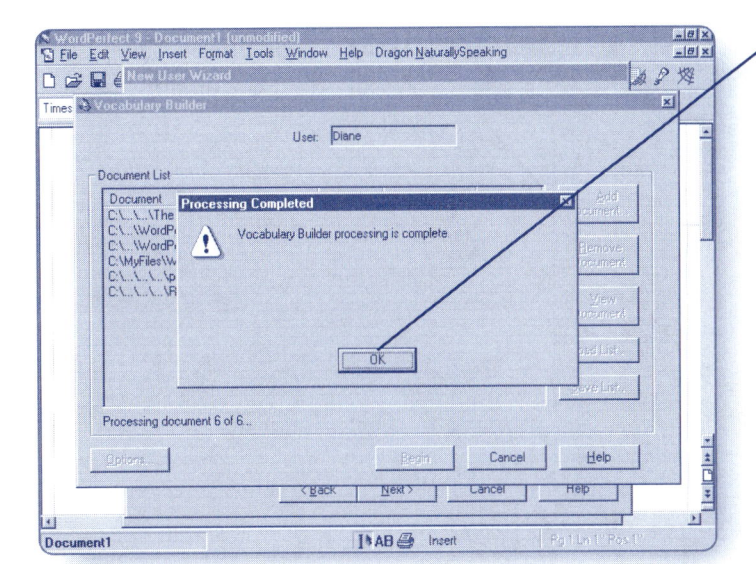

14. Click on **OK**. The New User Wizard will reappear.

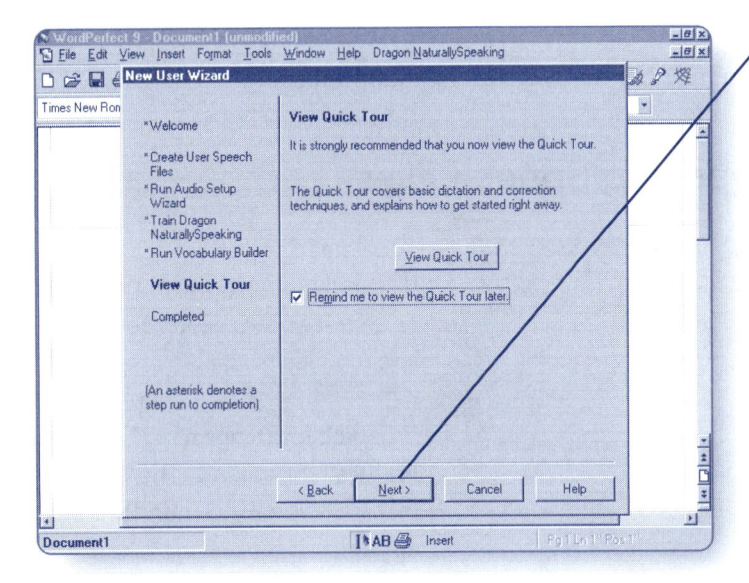

15. Click on **Next**. The final screen of the New User Wizard will appear.

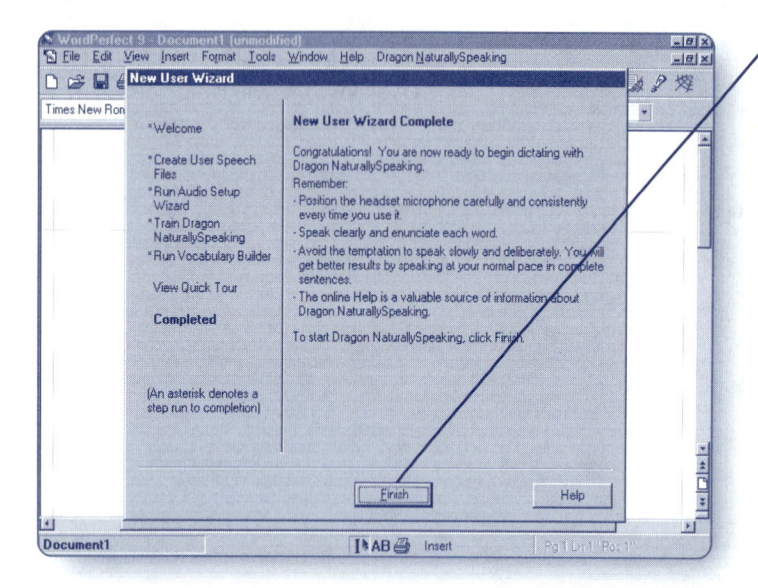

372 APPENDIX B: WORKING WITH DRAGON NATURALLYSPEAKING

16. Click on **Finish**. The WordPerfect document screen will reappear.

Dictating into WordPerfect

You're finally ready to use NaturallySpeaking!

Opening Speech Files

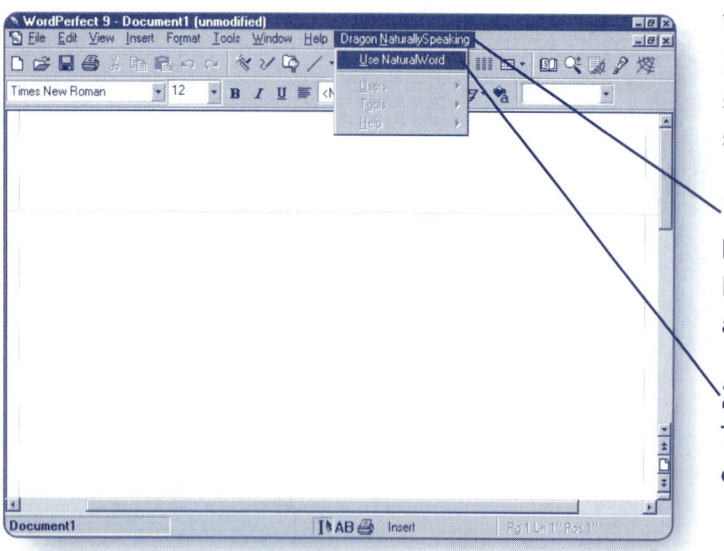

You'll need to tell NaturallySpeaking who you are, so that it knows which set of speech files to use.

1. Click on **Dragon NaturallySpeaking**. The Dragon NaturallySpeaking menu will appear.

2. Click on **Use NaturalWord**. The Open User dialog box will open.

DICTATING INTO WORDPERFECT   373

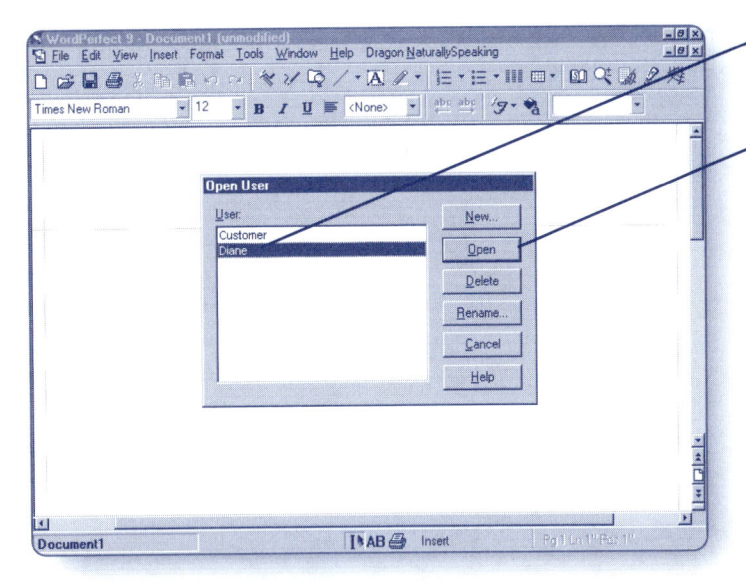

3. Click on your **name**. Your name will be highlighted.

4. Click on **Open**. NaturallySpeaking will activate your speech files and be listening for you to speak.

Turning the Microphone On and Off

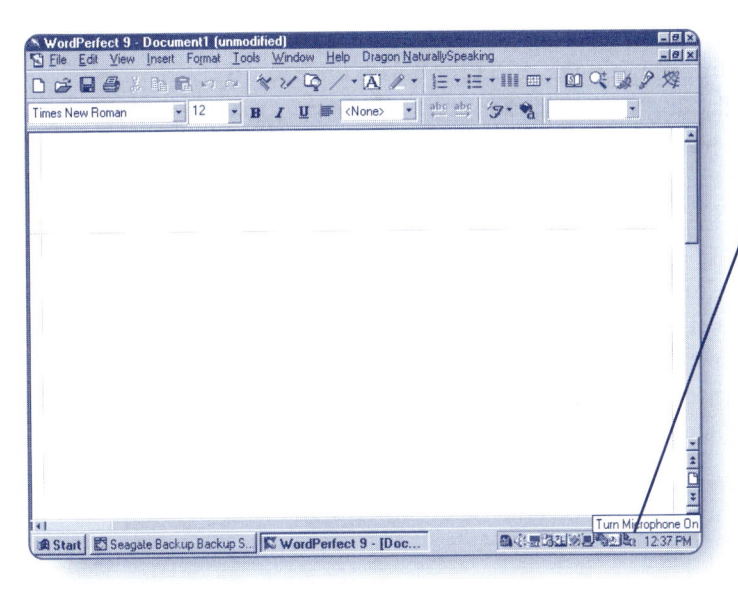

For NaturallySpeaking to hear you, you must first turn on the microphone. You cannot turn on the microphone by voice.

1. Click on the **microphone icon** on the Windows system tray. The microphone icon will stand up.

TIP
Optionally, press the plus key (+) on the numeric keypad.

When the microphone is on, NaturallySpeaking hears everything you say.

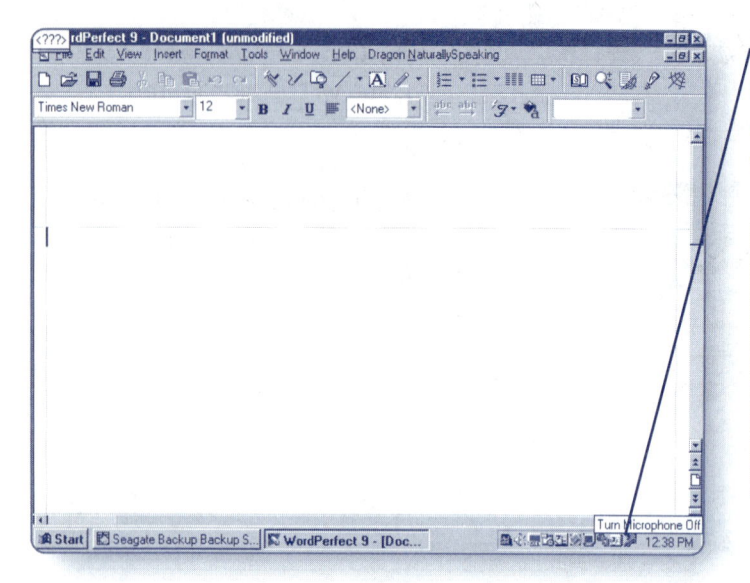

APPENDIX B: WORKING WITH DRAGON NATURALLYSPEAKING

2. Click on the **microphone icon** on the Windows system tray. The microphone icon will fall down.

> **TIP**
> To temporarily deactivate the microphone, say "Go To Sleep." To reactivate the microphone, say the voice command "Wake Up."

Dictating Text

To dictate text, just speak in your normal voice, at a comfortable pace, and pronounce each word clearly. The following table includes some of the punctuation and special commands you can use.

> **TIP**
> For the software to hear you, the WordPerfect window into which you are dictating must be active. If you are dictating and find that nothing is happening, the program window may not be active. Click anywhere in the window to activate it.

DICTATING TEXT

Say this	To display this
Period	.
Comma	,
Semicolon	;
Colon	:
Question mark	?
Exclamation point	!
New line	Inserts a hard return and moves the insertion point down one line
New paragraph	Inserts two hard returns and moves the insertion point down two lines

1. Speak text into the microphone. The text as NaturallySpeaking understands it will appear in the WordPerfect document.

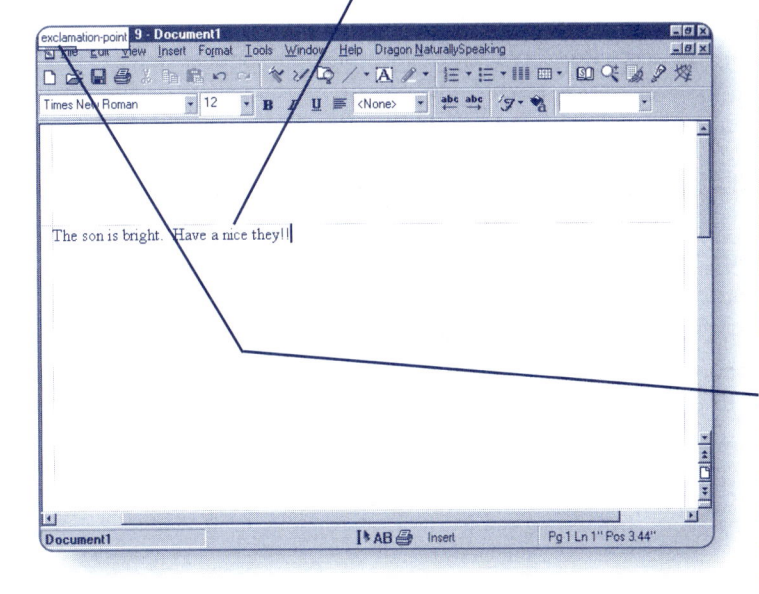

NOTE

NaturallySpeaking automatically capitalizes the first word of a new sentence and inserts the correct number of spaces after each punctuation mark.

As you dictate, NaturallySpeaking previews your words in a small yellow window called the Results box before displaying them in your document. In the Results box, NaturallySpeaking may adjust its interpretation of your words according to their context before entering them into your document.

> **NOTE**
>
> In this example, I said: "the sun is bright **period** have a nice day **exclamation point exclamation point**" but it came out, "The son is bright. Have a nice they!!" You learn how to correct the errors in the next section.

NaturallySpeaking includes formatting of numbers, including fractions, currency, telephone numbers, and times of day. Dictate most numbers in a natural manner—for example, say "three hundred thousand and twenty five" to get 300,025.

It also formats e-mail and Web addresses. Dictate e-mail and Web addresses as you would normally speak them.

Editing Text

Speech recognition technology is still very new. The words you speak may come out on the screen entirely different. You'll need to keep teaching NaturallySpeaking until it recognizes your speech patterns.

Moving Around a Document

You can move the insertion point simply by telling NaturallySpeaking where to move it. Moving the insertion point is useful when you want to scroll through a long document or cut and paste text.

The following table lists some of the Navigation commands:

EDITING TEXT

Say this	To move the insertion point here
Go to top	To the top of the document
Go to bottom	To the bottom of the document
Move left one character	To the left one character
Move right one character	To the right one character
Up one line	Up one line
Down one line	Down one line

Revising Text

When you reconsider what you want to say, revise your text by using "Select-and-Say"™. Simply select the text you want to revise and then say your changes.

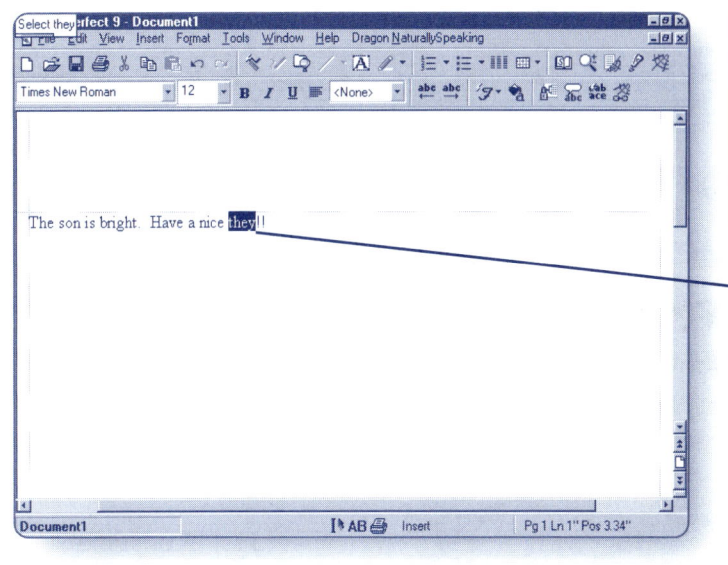

NOTE
The way you revise text differs from the way you correct recognition errors.

1. Say "**Select**" and the **word or phrase** to be modified. The word or phrase will be highlighted.

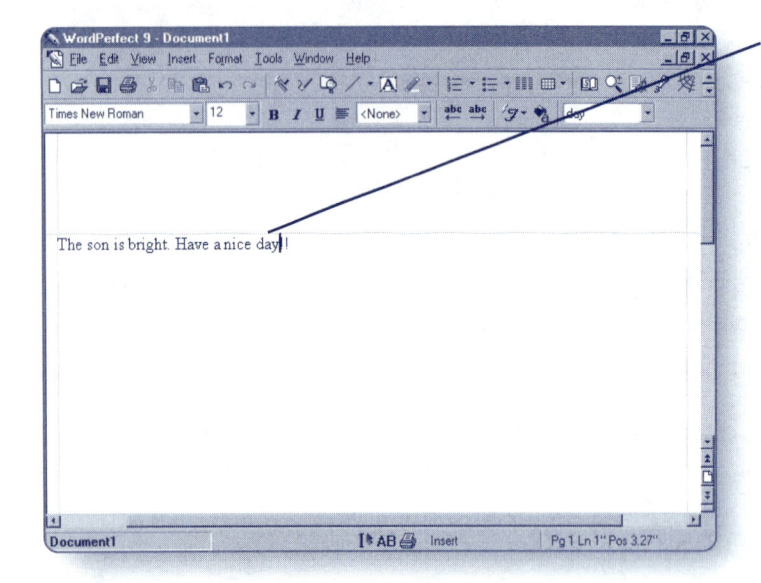

378 APPENDIX B: WORKING WITH DRAGON NATURALLYSPEAKING

2. Say the **new text**. The highlighted text will be replaced with the new text.

Correcting Recognition Errors

If NaturallySpeaking does not recognize one of your words and enters an incorrect word into your document, correct the mistaken word using the Correction dialog box. By using the Correction dialog box, you can train NaturallySpeaking to recognize the word the next time you say it.

> **NOTE**
> The way you correct text differs from the way you revise text.

1. Say "Correct" and the **word or phrase** to be corrected. The text will be highlighted, and the Correction dialog box will open. In this example, I said "correct son."

A numbered list of possible corrections will appear.

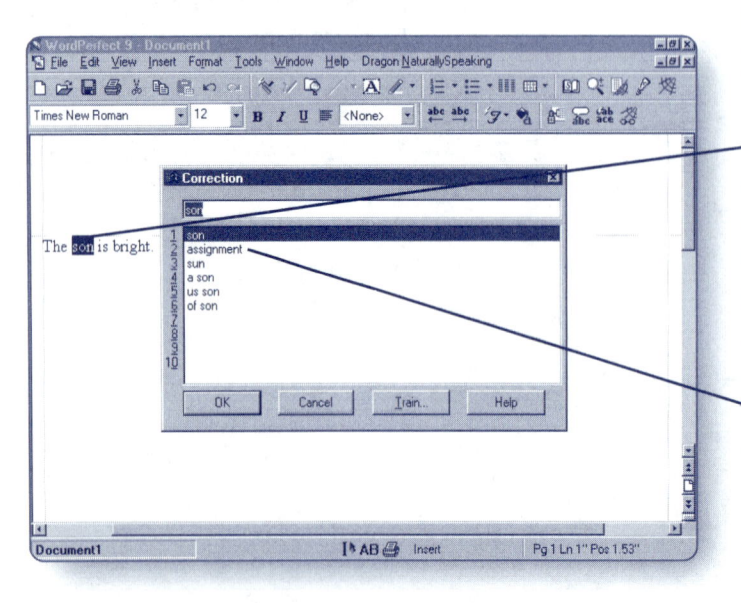

EDITING TEXT 379

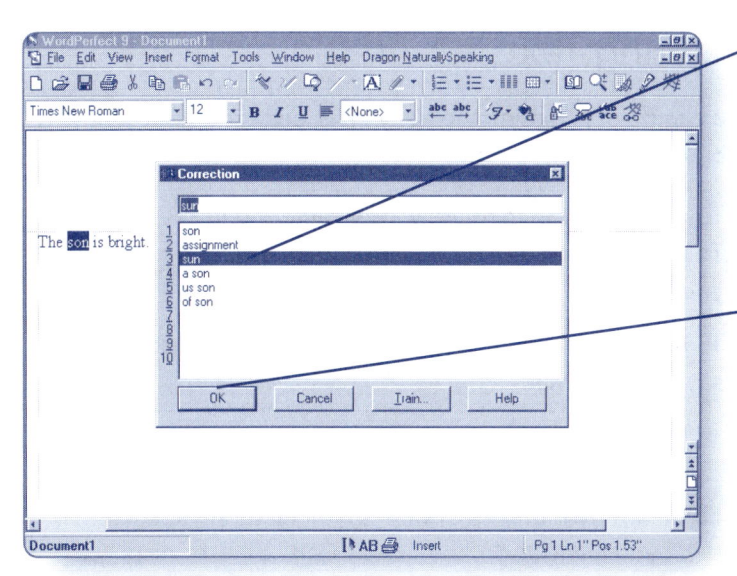

2. Say "Select" and the **number** of the correct replacement. The indicated replacement will be highlighted. In this example, I said "select three."

3. Say "Click on OK." The mouse pointer will automatically move to the OK button, and the dialog box will close.

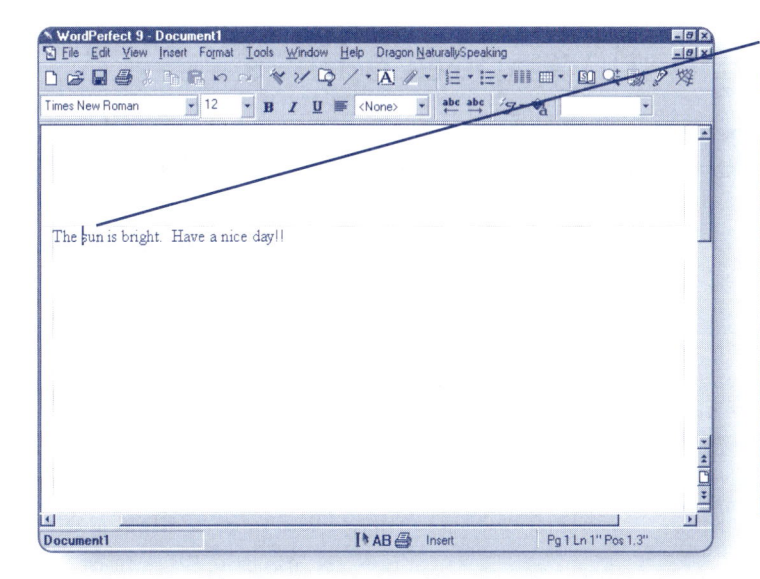

The correct text will appear in your document.

> **NOTE**
> It would have been faster to manually type the correction of this error, but using the preceding method also teaches NaturallySpeaking for future occurrences of the misinterpreted word.

Deleting Text

You can delete text immediately after dictating it, or delete it later, at any time.

- To delete text immediately after dictating it, say "Scratch That." You can say "Scratch That" up to 10 times to delete your 10 most recent phrases.

- To delete text you dictated earlier, select the text and then say "Delete That."

> **TIP**
> If you are ever unsure of how to tell NaturallySpeaking what you want to do, say "What Can I Say" to display a list of available voice commands.

Updating Speech Files

When you close the WordPerfect program, you'll be prompted to save the changes you've made to your speech files.

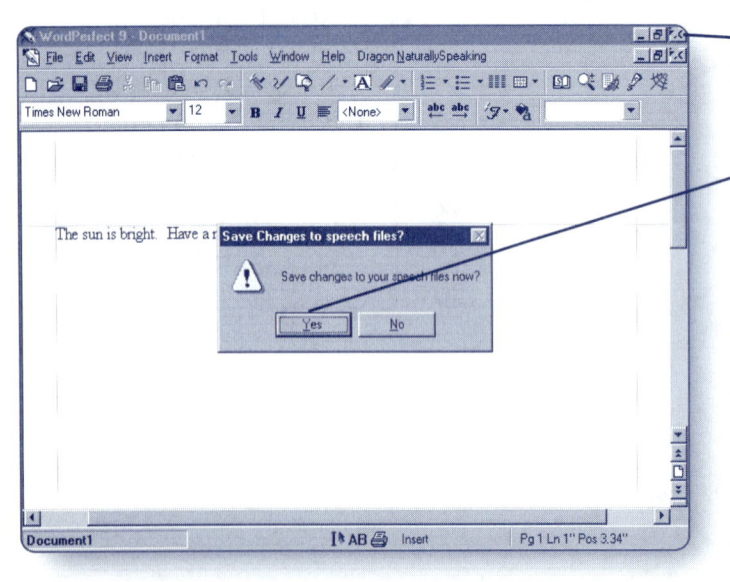

1. Click on the **Program Close box** ([X]). A message box will appear.

2. Click on **Yes**. The speech files will be updated with changes you've made.

Again, speech recognition is still a new technology. Be patient with this product. It does get better with time and usage. Just keep working with it and don't give up! The more you teach it, the better it will respond to you.

C

Discovering WordPerfect Tips and Tricks

I have put together a few of my favorite hints, tips, and tricks for you. I hope you enjoy them! In this appendix, you'll learn how to:

- Keep two words together
- Look at all your fonts
- Add a drop cap to a paragraph
- Stretch a heading

Keeping Two Words Together

To prevent word wrap from splitting a phone number or hyphenated name from one line to the next, hold down the Ctrl key while you are pressing the hyphen (-). This tells WordPerfect not to break up these two words. You can use the same feature for two words with a space between them. Instead of pressing the spacebar by itself, hold down the Ctrl key while you press the spacebar. This is called a *hard hyphen* or *hard space*.

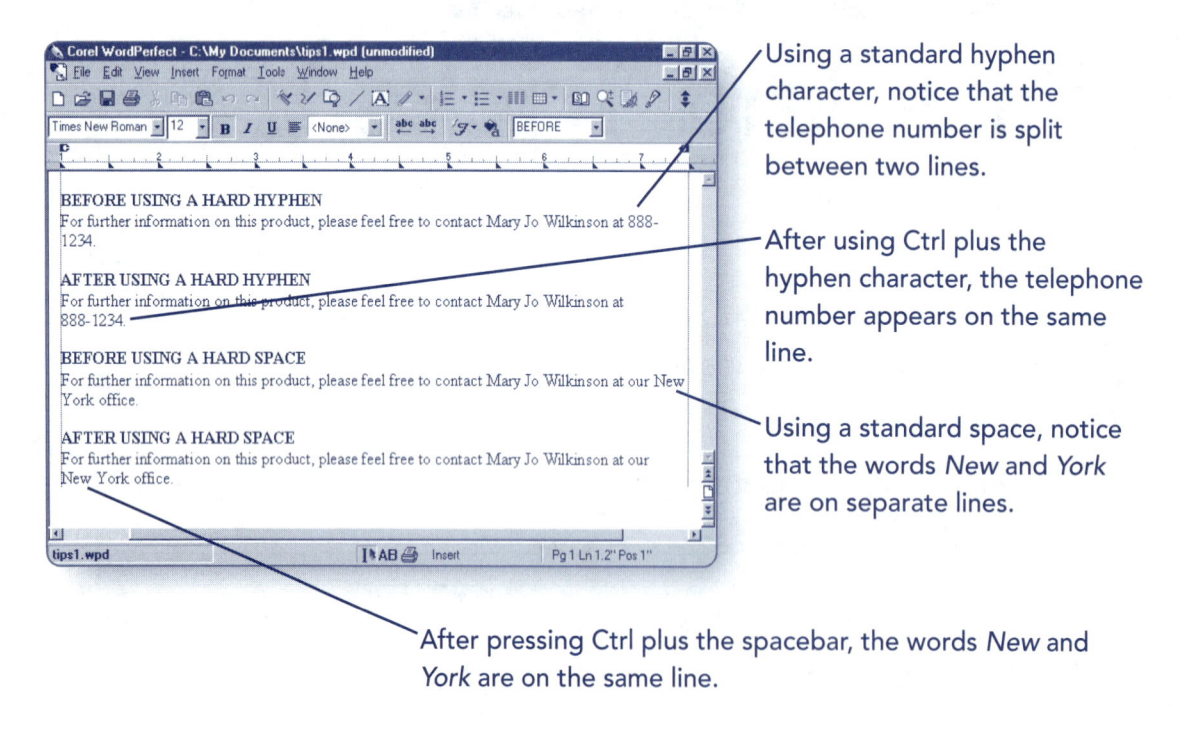

Using a standard hyphen character, notice that the telephone number is split between two lines.

After using Ctrl plus the hyphen character, the telephone number appears on the same line.

Using a standard space, notice that the words *New* and *York* are on separate lines.

After pressing Ctrl plus the spacebar, the words *New* and *York* are on the same line.

Looking at All Your Fonts

If you are a "font junkie" like I am, you have hundreds of fonts on your system. WordPerfect has included a macro that creates a document with a sample of every font you have available.

LOOKING AT ALL YOUR FONTS 383

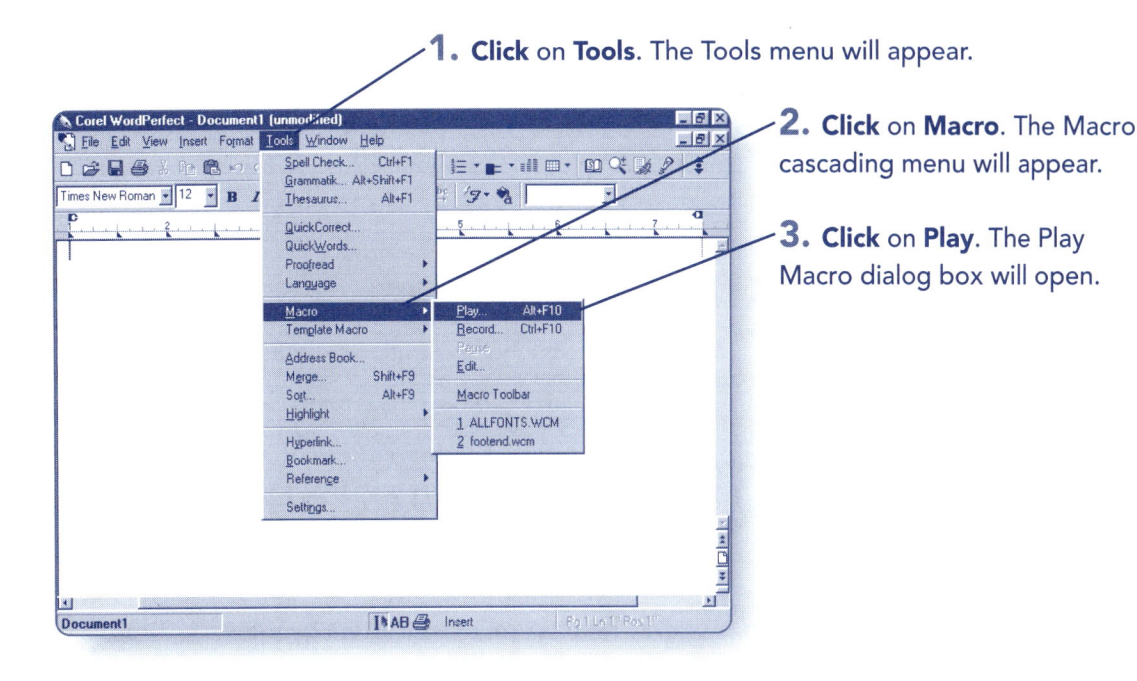

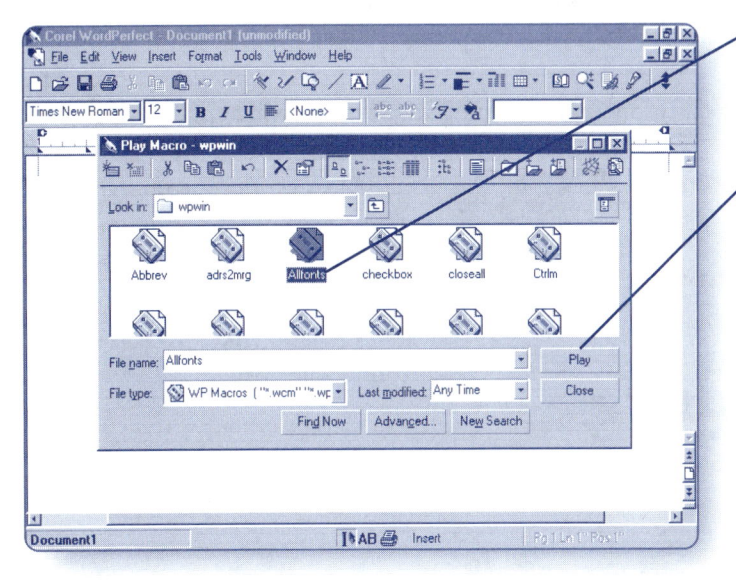

1. Click on **Tools**. The Tools menu will appear.

2. Click on **Macro**. The Macro cascading menu will appear.

3. Click on **Play**. The Play Macro dialog box will open.

4. Click on the macro named **Allfonts**. The macro will be selected.

5. Click on **Play**. The macro will execute, and you will see a document with sample fonts.

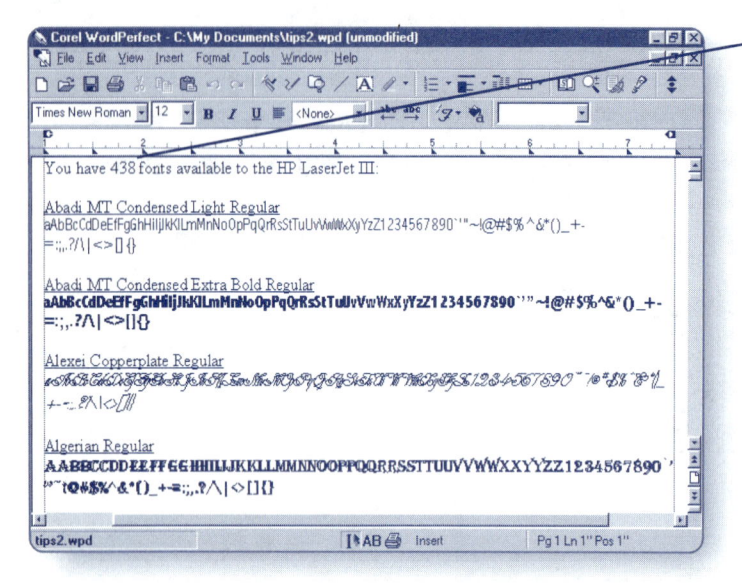

The macro tells you how many fonts you have on your system. (See, I told you I was a font junkie!)

Adding a Drop Cap

You can really liven up your newsletters by using the Drop Cap feature.

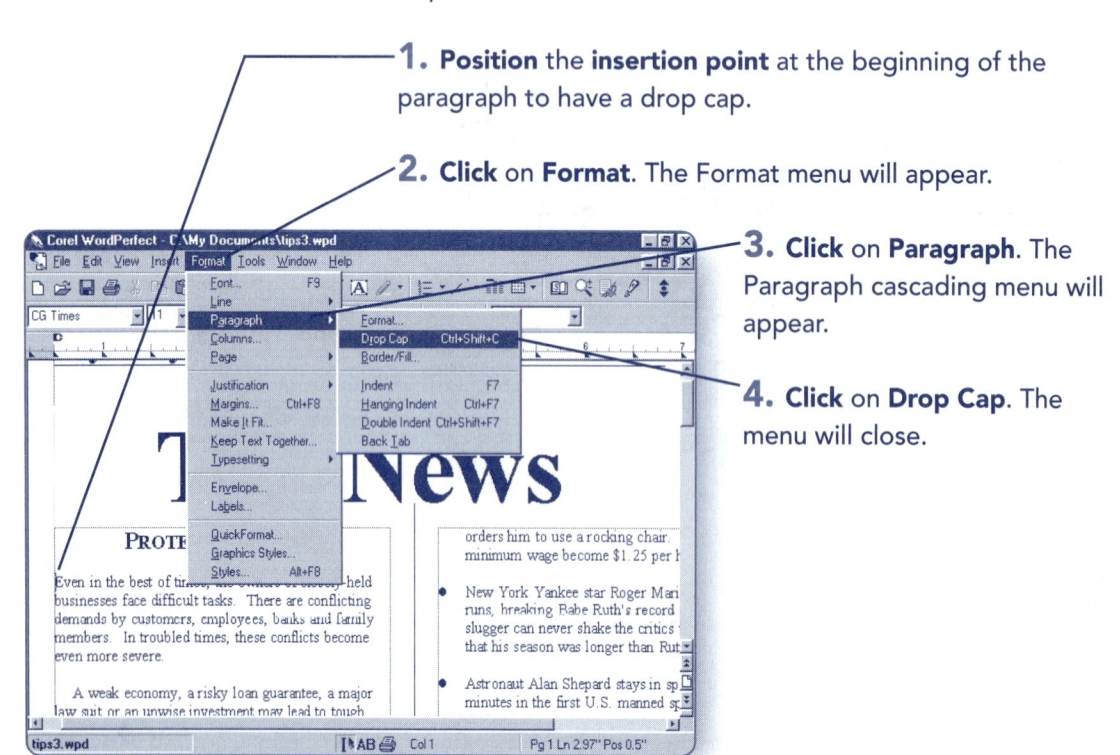

1. Position the **insertion point** at the beginning of the paragraph to have a drop cap.

2. Click on **Format**. The Format menu will appear.

3. Click on **Paragraph**. The Paragraph cascading menu will appear.

4. Click on **Drop Cap**. The menu will close.

ADDING A DROP CAP 385

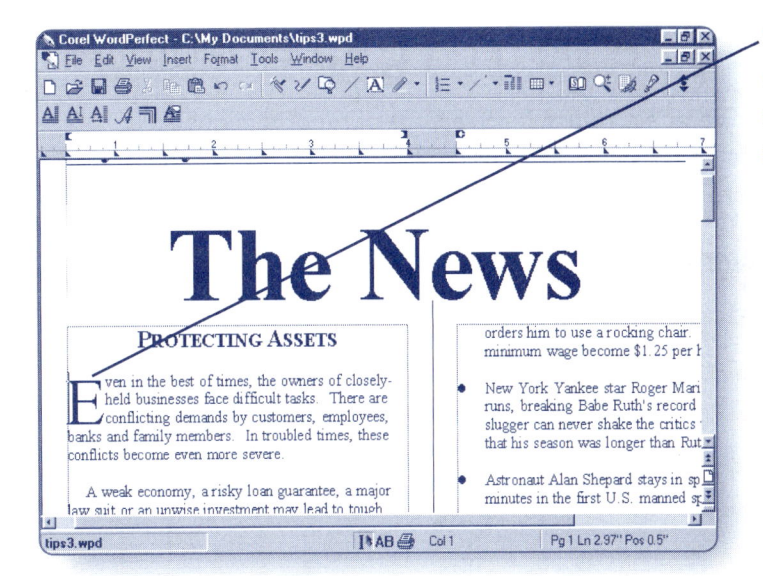

The first letter of the sentence will be converted to a drop cap, and the rest of the text will be shoved over to make room for it.

Several drop cap options appear on the property bar.

"Stretching" a Heading

A nice effect to use for headings of reports might be to stretch the heading across the entire width of a page. WordPerfect has a feature called *justify all* to do this for you.

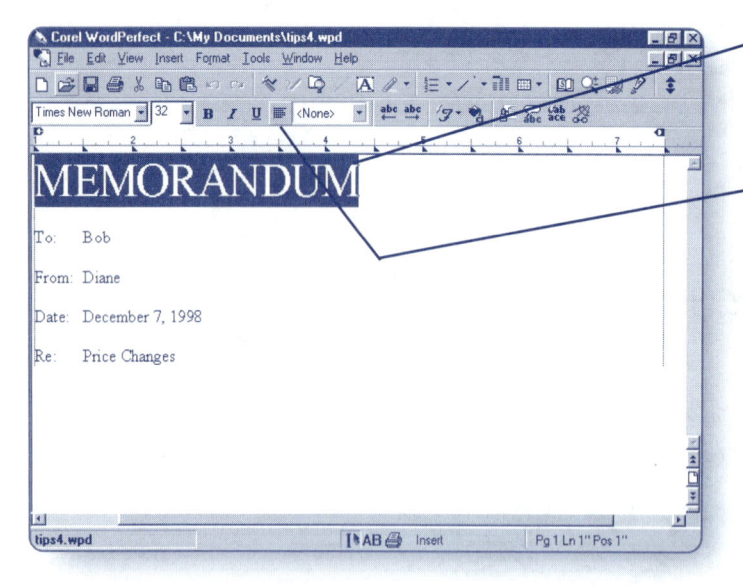

1. Select the **heading** to be stretched. The text will be highlighted.

2. Click on the **Justification button** on the toolbar. The justification options will drop down.

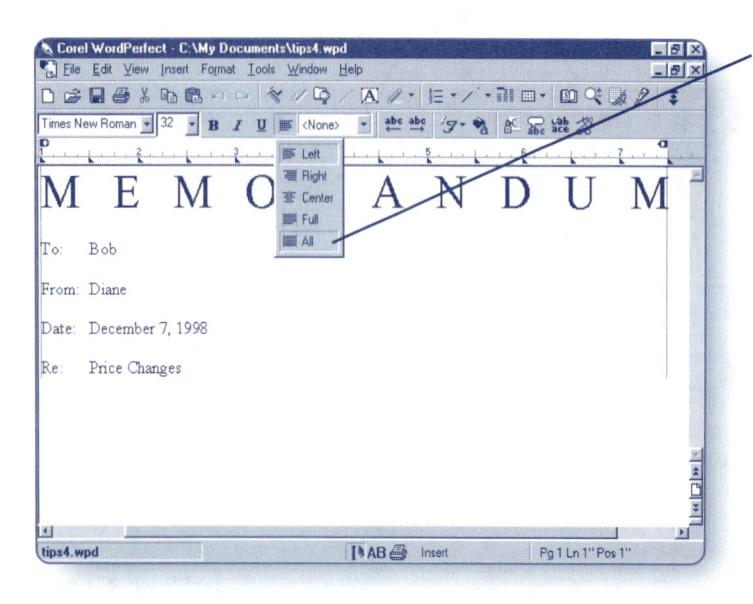

3. Click on **All**. The heading will be stretched from margin to margin.

Adding Dot Leaders to Text on the Right Margin

The Flush Right with Dot Leaders feature is used to line up a portion of a line to the right margin and add dot leaders to it. This is similar to what you might see in a table of contents.

1. Click the **mouse pointer** at the portion of the line to be right aligned. The blinking insertion point will appear.

2. Click on **Format**. The Format menu will appear.

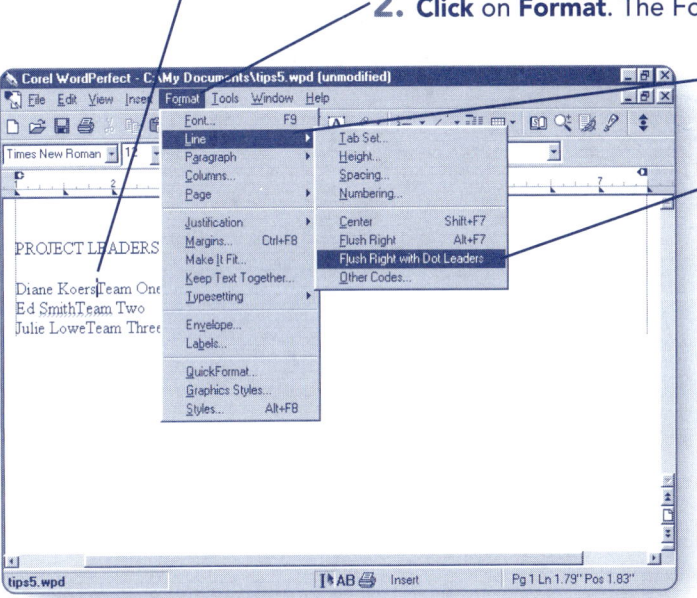

3. Click on **Line**. The Line cascading menu will appear.

4. Click on **Flush Right with Dot Leaders**. The balance of the line from the right of the insertion point will be moved to the right margin with dots leading up to it.

APPENDIX C: DISCOVERING WORDPERFECT TIPS AND TRICKS

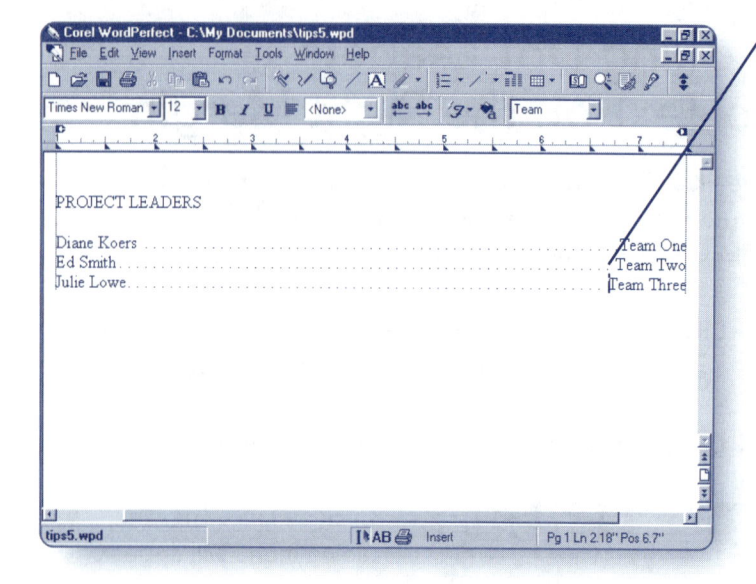

5. **Repeat** the preceding **steps** for each line to be right aligned.

Glossary

A

Address Book. Stores names, addresses, and phone numbers in one handy location.

Alignment. The arrangement of text to the margins of a document or the edges of a table cell. Also called justification.

Append. To add text to the end of the Clipboard contents instead of replacing it.

Attributes. Items that determine the appearance of text such as bolding, underlining, italics, or point size.

B

Bold. A font attribute that makes text thicker and brighter.

Bookmark. Use Bookmark to mark a place in a document so that you can return to that location quickly.

Border. A line surrounding paragraphs, pages, or objects.

Bullet. A small black circle or other character that precedes each item in a list.

C

Cell. The intersection of a row and column in a table or spreadsheet.

Choose. To use the mouse or keyboard to pick a menu item or option in a dialog box.

Clip art. A piece of artwork to be inserted into a WordPerfect document.

Clipboard. An area of computer memory where text or graphics can be temporarily stored.

Close. Used to shut down or exit a dialog box, window, or application.

Columns. Used to divide text vertically on a page.

Comment. Used to add annotations to a document. Comments do not print with the document.

Copy. To take a selection from the document and duplicate it on the Clipboard.

Cut. To take a selection from the document and move it to the Clipboard.

D

Data file. A file that stores a collection of information called records with individual pieces of information called fields. Used in the mail merge process with a form file.

Default. A setting or action predetermined by the program unless changed by the user.

Desktop. The screen background and main area of Windows where you can open and manage files and programs.

Dialog box. A box that appears and lets you select options, or displays warnings and messages.

Document. A letter, memo, proposal, or other file that is created in the WordPerfect program.

Double indent. Used to move an entire paragraph in one tab stop from both the left and right margins.

Draft view. A perspective of your document that does not display certain features such as footers, headers, and watermarks even though they might exist in the document. Because not all features display, working in Draft view is often faster than working in Page view.

Drag and drop. To move text or an object by positioning the mouse pointer on the item you want to move, pressing and holding down the mouse button, moving the mouse, and then releasing the mouse button to drop the item into its new location.

Drop cap. Single letters that decorate text at the beginning of a line or paragraph.

E

Endnote. Reference information that prints at the end of a document.

F

Field. A piece of information used in a data file or a form file for the purpose of mail merge.

File format. The arrangement and organization of information in a file. File format is determined by the application that created the file.

File. Information stored on a disk under a single name.

Fill. The background color or pattern of an object such as a cell of a table or a paragraph.

Font. A group of letters, numbers, and symbols with a common typeface.

Footer. Text entered in an area of the document that will be displayed at the bottom of each page of the document.

Footnote. Reference information that prints at the bottom of the page.

Form file. A file used in the merge process that can be made up of text, formatting, graphics, and merge codes. A form file is created just like a regular document, but instead of placing specific information in certain places, you insert a field or code that is replaced by information from the data source when you perform the merge.

Format. To change the appearance of text or objects with features such as the font, style, color, borders, and size.

G

Go To. A feature that enables you to jump to a specific page or location of your document quickly.

Grammatik. The grammar checking feature of the WordPerfect program.

Gridlines. The lines dividing rows and columns in a table.

H

Handle. Small black squares that appear when you select an object that will enable you to resize the object.

Hanging indent. Used to move all but the first line of a paragraph one tab stop to the right.

Header. Text entered in an area of the document that will be displayed at the top of each page of the document.

Highlight. Puts a bar of transparent color over text.

Hypertext link. Used to provide a connection from the current document to another document or to a document on the World Wide Web.

I

Icon. A small graphic image that represents an application, command, or tool. An action is performed when an icon is clicked or double-clicked.

Indent. Used to move a complete paragraph one tab stop to the right.

Internet Publisher. Used to create and edit documents for the World Wide Web and launch Web browser software to browse the World Wide Web.

J

Justification. See Alignment.

L

Landscape. Orientation of a page in which the long edge of the paper runs horizontally.

Line height. The distance between the top of one line of text and the top of the next line of text. Ordinarily, it is set according to the font being used.

Line numbering. Used to number the lines in a document and print each line number.

Line spacing. The amount of space between lines of text.

M

Macro. A series of commands and keystrokes stored in a file that can be replayed by a few keystrokes or a mouse click.

Mail Merge. A feature that uses data from a data file and combines it with a document called a form file to produce personalized letters.

Margin. The width of blank space from the edge of the page to the edge of the text. All four sides of a paper have a margin.

Mouse pointer. A symbol that indicates a position onscreen as you move the mouse around on your desk.

O

Open. To start an application, to insert a document into a new document window, or to access a dialog box.

Orientation. A setting that designates whether a document will print with text running along the long or short side of a piece of paper.

P

Page break. A command that tells WordPerfect to begin a new page.

Page view. Displays a document the way it will look when printed. Page view displays fonts and appearance features, headers, footers, footnotes, watermarks, rotated text, and label arrangement.

Paste. The process of retrieving the information stored on the Clipboard and inserting a copy of it into a WordPerfect document.

PerfectExpert. A built-in Help program for WordPerfect that lets you type in your own words to ask for the Help information you need. The PerfectExpert searches through all the main Help files and then lists topics that are the best match for your question.

Point size. A unit of measurement used to indicate font size. One point is 1/72-inch in height.

Point. To move the mouse until the tip of the mouse pointer rests on an item.

Portrait. The orientation of the page in which the long edge of the page runs vertically.

Print Preview. Enables you to see a preview of how your printed document will look onscreen before you print it.

Prompt-As-You-Go. A feature on the property bar that displays suggestions while you type. Prompt-As-You-Go can act as a spell checker, a grammar checker, or a thesaurus, depending on where the insertion point is placed.

Property bar. Appears at the top of the application window and is used to access the features available in WordPerfect. Similar to a toolbar. The property bar changes according to the current task.

Q

QuickCorrect. A feature of WordPerfect that automatically corrects common spelling mistakes (such as "teh" for "the").

QuickFormat. Enables you to easily copy formatting applied to text to any other text.

R

Redo. Used to reverse the last Undo action.

Reveal Codes. A feature that allows you to see the hidden markers that control how a document appears on the screen and prints.

Right aligned. Text that is lined up with the right side of a tab setting or document margin, as with a row of numbers in a column.

Ruler. Used to change page format elements such as tabs and margins.

S

Save. The process of taking a document residing in the memory of the computer and creating a file to be stored on a disk.

Scrapbook. A collection of clip art provided by WordPerfect.

Scroll bar. The bars on the right side and bottom of a window that let you move vertically and horizontally through a document.

Shadow cursor. The icon that moves through the document as you move the mouse on your desk. This cursor shows exactly where the insertion point will go when you click the mouse. You can click anywhere to start typing text, or drag to insert clip art, a text box, or a table.

Shape. Items such as circles, rectangles, lines, polygons, and polylines in your document.

Sort. To arrange data in alphabetical order.

SpeedFormat. Enables you to apply predefined sets of formatting to a table.

SpeedLinks. Used to automatically create hyperlinks when you type certain kinds of text.

Spell Check. A feature of WordPerfect that checks the spelling of words in your document against a dictionary and flags possible errors for correction.

Status bar. The line at the bottom of a document window that shows information such as the page, line, and vertical and horizontal position of the insertion point.

Style. A way to format similar types of text, such as headings and lists.

Suppress. The capability to temporarily turn off a header, footer, watermark, or page number.

Symbol. Used to access characters that are not on your keyboard, such as iconic symbols, phonetic characters, and characters in other alphabets.

T

Tab. Settings in your document to determine where the insertion point moves.

Table. Consists of rows and columns of cells that you fill in with text, numbers, or graphics.

Template. A document file with customized format, content, and features. Frequently used to create faxes, memos, and proposals.

Text box. A type of graphics box that can be used for placing and rotating text.

TextArt. Used for adding special effects to text, such as curving the text or making text three-dimensional.

Thesaurus. Used to find synonyms (words that are alike) and antonyms (words that are opposite).

Toolbar. Appears at the top of the application window and is used to access the features available in WordPerfect. Similar to a property bar, except that it does not change according to the current task.

U

Undo. To reverse the last editing action.

Undo/Redo History. Use Undo/Redo History to reverse up to 300 actions in your document. You can save a history of those actions with a document so that you can undo or redo actions after closing the document and then opening it again.

Uppercase. A capital letter.

V

Views. Ways of displaying documents to see different perspectives of the information in that document.

W

Watermark. A background image behind the text on a page. Clip art images, an existing file, or text can be used for the watermark.

Word wrap. The capability of WordPerfect to determine where the right margin is located and drop the current text to the next line when the margin is reached.

Z

Zoom. Used to enlarge or reduce the way the text is displayed on the screen. It does not affect how the document will print.

Index

* (asterisk), in formulas, 210
- (minus sign/hyphen), in formulas, 210
+ (plus sign), in formulas, 210
/ (slash), in formulas, 210
#10 business envelope, 62
@ character, in SpeedLink link word, 299, 303
2D options, TextArt, 288–290
3D options, TextArt, 290–292

A

abbreviations, 73–76
Add Entry button, 301
addition, 205, 206–209, 210, 211
address, envelope, 59, 61
address list, 217. *See also* data file; Mail Merge.
    creating, 217–224
    editing, 224–233
    merging with form letter, 242–248
alignment
    cell, 201–202
    table, 196–197, 201–202
    text, 109, 111–112
antonyms, 83
application bar, 5
associating data file/form letter, 236, 238

asterisk (*), in formulas, 210
attributes
    fill, 270
    font, 53
    line, 265
    TextArt, 287–288
Auto Look Up feature, Thesaurus, 84
Auto Replace, Spell Check, 79
automatic date/time, 6–7, 237
Autoscroll, 32–34
Award Certificate template, 156–161

B

Back button, 35
background color, 313
background fill, 120, 122–123
background image. *See* watermark.
Backspace key, 42
bar code, 60
block, selecting text, 42
.bmp files, 272
Bold button, 95
bold text style, 95–96
bookmark, 322

border
    award certificate, 160
    graphic image, 276–278
    page, 124–125
    paragraph, 120–122
    table, 199
Border Style button, 276, 277
Box Border/Fill dialog box, 277–278, 281–282
Box Fill button, 278
boxes
    around graphic images, 276–278
    using shadow cursor to position, 37
breaks, page, 9
browser. *See* Web browser.
bullets, 118–119, 317
business envelope, #10, 62

C

capitalization
    changing, 43–44
    fixing with QuickCorrect, 72
case, changing
    with Convert Case, 43–44
    with Find and Replace, 52
cells. *See also* table.
    aligning numbers in, 201–202
    determining address of specific, 208
    filling automatically with QuickFill, 181–183
    joining for table heading, 202–203
    selecting/deselecting, 182, 183, 194
Center Page(s) dialog box, 114
centering
    document heading, 110–111
    page, 114–115
certificate, award, 156–161
clip art. *See also* graphic images; TextArt.
    and Award Certificate, 161
    sources of, 271, 320
    using shadow cursor to position, 37

    and watermark, 146, 147–148
    and Web pages, 320–321
Clipboard, 45–47
Close Document button, 17
Close Program button, 20
closing documents, 16–17
color
    fill, 122–123
    graphic line, 265
    highlight, 98–100
    TextArt, 288–289, 291
    Web page background, 313
columns. *See also* table.
    adding with QuickSum, 206–209
    changing width of, 196–198
    inserting/deleting, 185–187
commands. *See* dialog boxes; specific commands.
compression, document, 56–57
computer memory. *See* memory.
conditions, Mail Merge, 244–246
contour, text, 279–282
Convert Case command, 44
Copy button, 47
Copy Formula dialog box, 212–213
copying
    formulas, 212–213
    text
        with Copy/Paste buttons, 47
        with drag and drop, 48
        with shortcut menu, 49–50
copyright symbol, 9
Corel
    Quattro Pro, 188
    Technical Support, 27
    Web site, 27
    WordPerfect suite, 4, 271
Corel TextArt 9.0 dialog box, 284–292
Create Data File dialog box, 218

INDEX

Create Table dialog box, 177–178
cursor, shadow, 36–38
cut and paste, 45–46, 49–50
Cut button, 46

D

daisy wheel, 91
.dat files, 223
data entry, 221–224, 226–232
data file
    adding/deleting fields, 226–232
    associating with form file, 236, 238
    creating, 218
    defined, 217
    editing, 224–226
    entering data, 221–223
    inserting information in form letter, 237–240
    naming/renaming fields, 219–221, 232–233
    saving, 223–224
Data Source button, 242
Date button, 237
Date/Time dialog box, 7–8
definitions, 83, 84
Delete key, 40, 42–43
Delete Structure/Contents dialog box, 187
deleting
    field, 229–232
    footnotes/endnotes, 134
    graphic lines, 267
    record, 225
    shape, 270
    SpeedLink, 308–309
    tab stops, 174
    table columns/rows, 187
    text, 42–43
    TextArt, 292
desktop. *See* Windows desktop.
diagonal lines, 257

dialog boxes
    Border/Fill, 121–123
    Box Border/Fill, 277–278, 281–282
    Center Page(s), 114
    Copy Formula, 212–213
    Corel TextArt 9.0, 284–292
    Create Data File, 218
    Create Table, 177–178
    Date/Time, 7–8
    Delete Structure/Contents, 187
    Draw Object Shapes, 268–269
    Edit Field Names, 227, 229–231
    Edit Graphics Line, 265–266
    Find and Replace, 50–54
    Font, 96–97
    Footnote/Endnote, 128
    Go To, 35–36
    Headers/Footers, 138–139, 145
    Help, 22, 25–27
    Hyperlink Properties, 322
    Import Data, 188–190
    Insert Columns/Rows, 185–186
    Insert Field Name or Number, 238–239, 250–251
    Insert Image-ClipArt, 147–148
    Line Spacing, 115–116
    Make it Fit, 56–57
    Merge, 218
    Open, 18–19
    Page Border/Fill, 124–125
    Page Setup, 102–103, 104–105
    PerfectExpert, 152, 312
    Perform Merge, 242–243, 244, 247, 249
    Play Macro, 134–135
    POSTNET Bar Code, 60–61
    Print, 24, 58
    Properties, 85–86
    Properties for Table Format, 196–197
    Publish to HTML, 325

dialog boxes *(continued)*
    Quick Data Entry, 221–224, 226–232
    QuickCorrect, 72–73, 74–75, 298–303, 308
    Save As, 16
    Save File, 14–15, 223
    Scrapbook, 272
    Select Data Filename, 189
    Select Page Numbering Format, 106–108
    Select Records, 244–246, 247–248
    SpeedFormat, 192–193
    Suppress, 144
    Tab Set, 166–168, 170–171
    Watermark, 146–147
dictionary, Spell Check, 79
division, 205, 209, 210, 211
document
    centering on page, 114–115
    closing, 16–17
    compressing/expanding, 56–57
    double spacing, 116
    editing, 40–50
    entering date/time, 7–8
    finding/correcting mistakes, 71–83
    header/footer, 137–145
    inserting special characters, 9–12
    moving around, 29–38
    naming, 14–15
    numbering pages, 64, 105–108, 139–141
    opening, 4–5, 18–19
    printing, 57–58
    saving, 14–16
    searching for text in, 50–54
    selecting entire, 42
    setting paper size/margins, 101–105
    SpeedLinking to, 300–301
    statistics, 85–86
    typing text into, 6–7, 40
    viewing, 63–70
document screen, 5

dot leader, tab, 169, 172
double indent, 112, 113
double spacing, 116
Draft view, 63–65, 67, 108
drag and drop, 48
Draw Object Shapes dialog box, 268–269
drawing layer, 257
dynamic merge date, 237
dynamic path/filename, 142

E

Edit Field Names dialog box, 227, 229–231
Edit Graphics Line dialog box, 265–266
editing
    address list, 224–233
    data file, 224–226
    envelope, 59
    footnote/endnote, 131
    graphic line, 262–267
    header/footer, 143
    SpeedLink, 302–303
    TextArt, 285–292
e-mailing memo, 155
endfoot macro, 135
endnotes
    converting to footnotes, 134–135
    creating, 128–130
    editing, 131
    moving, 132–134
    purpose of, 127
Enter key, 6, 76
Envelope Size button, 62
envelopes
    adding bar code, 60–61
    creating, 59, 249–252
    for form letters, 249–252
    including return address, 61
    selecting size, 62
Equal button, Page Setup, 105

INDEX

errors, correcting
　with Grammatik, 81–83
　with QuickCorrect, 72–73
　with Spell As You Go, 76–77
　with Spell Check, 78–80
　with Undo, 44–45, 112
exiting program, 19–20
expansion, document, 56–57

F

F1 key, 25
faxing memo, 155
field
　adding/deleting, 226–232
　defined, 219
　naming/renaming, 219–221, 232–233
Field Names button, 229
file. *See also* data file; document.
　naming, 14–15
　opening, 18–19
　saving, 14–16, 17
File menu, 19
filename
　inserting in header/footer, 142
　saving/displaying, 14–15
fill patterns/color, 120, 122–123, 270, 278–279, 313–314
Find and Replace dialog box, 50–54
folder, MyFiles, 15
font
　changing size of, 93–94, 97
　default typeface/size, 92, 93
　finding/replacing, 52–53
　previewing before changing, 96–97
　for TextArt objects, 287–288
Font/Size button, 315
footer. *See* header/footer.
Footnote/Endnote dialog box, 128–129

footnotes
　converting to endnotes, 134–135
　creating, 128–130
　displaying, 64, 131
　editing, 131
　moving, 132–134
　purpose of, 127
　renumbering, 133
foreign language characters, 9–10
Form Document button, 242
form file, 217, 242. *See also* form letter.
form letter. *See also* Mail Merge.
　associating with data file, 236, 238
　formatting, 240
　inserting data fields, 237–240
　merging with address list, 242–248
　saving, 240
　using automatic dates, 237
Format menu, 97, 104, 114, 115
formatting
　form letter, 240
　numbers, 200
　page numbers, 106–108
　table, 191–193
　text, 91–97, 315–317
　Web page, 315–317
　words as hyperlinks, 299
Formula toolbar, 207–208, 210
formulas
　altering calculation sequence, 211
　copying, 212–213
　creating, 209–211
　purpose of, 205
Forward button, 35
Full Page view, 67–68, 115

G

.gif files, 272
GIF images, 320

Go To command, 35–36
Go To Form button, 236
grammatical errors, 81–83
Grammatik, 81–83
graphic images. *See also* clip art; TextArt; watermark.
    adding, 272–273
    applying borders and fills, 276–279
    moving, 275–276
    resizing, 273–274
    standard formats, 272
    and Web pages, 318–321
    wrapping text around, 279–282
graphic lines
    adding, 258–259
    deleting, 267
    editing, 262–267
    moving, 260–262
    selecting/deselecting, 260, 262
    types of, 257
Greek symbols, 10

H

handles, 148, 260, 273–274, 275
hanging indent, 112, 113
header/footer
    and automatic page numbering, 139–141
    creating, 138–141
    discontinuing, 145
    editing, 143
    inserting path/filename, 142
    suppressing on specific page, 143–144
    viewing, 64, 149
Headers/Footers dialog box, 138–139, 145
heading
    document, 110–111
    memo, 153
    table, 202–203

Help dialog box, 22, 25–27
Help menu, 22
Help Topics
    accessing, 25
    printing, 24
    searching, 22–23, 26–27
Highlight button, 98, 99
highlighting text, 95, 98–100
horizontal lines, 257, 258, 265, 318–320
horizontal scroll bar, 30–31
.htm files, 324
HTML, 311, 315, 324–325, 327
hyperlink, 297, 322–323. *See also* SpeedLink.
Hyperlink Properties dialog box, 322
Hypertext Markup Language. *See* HTML.
hyphen character (-), in formulas, 210

I

images. *See* clip art; graphic images.
Import Data dialog box, 188–190
importing spreadsheet, 188–190
indentation, paragraph, 112–113
Index, Help Topics, 26
Insert button/menu, 7
Insert Columns/Rows dialog box, 185–186
Insert Field button, 238
Insert Field Name or Number dialog box, 238–239, 250–251
Insert Image-ClipArt dialog box, 147–148
insert mode, 40
Insert Row button, 184
insertion point
    and font changes, 92
    moving, 30
    purpose of/location, 5
Internet Publisher toolbar, 313, 315, 317, 318, 321
Internet SpeedLink, 297–298, 306–307

INDEX 401

ISP, 327
Italic button, 95
italic text style, 95–96

J

Japanese symbols, 10
JPEG images, 320
.jpg files, 272
Justification button, 110, 111, 201

K

keyboard shortcuts. *See* shortcut keys.

L

Landscape orientation, 103
language tools, 78, 81, 83
letter. *See also* form letter; Mail Merge.
    creating, 6–9
    expanding/compressing to fit specific number of pages, 56–57
line count, 86
line spacing, 115–116
Line Style button, 264
Line Thickness button, 263, 319
lines. *See* graphic lines.
link word, SpeedLink, 299, 303
linking spreadsheet, 188
links. *See* SpeedLink.
lists
    bulleted, 118–119, 317
    numbered, 119–120, 317
Lotus 1-2-3, 188

M

macro, for footnote/endnote conversion, 134–135
Mail Merge
    checking for errors/omissions, 243
    creating data file, 218–224
    creating/associating form letter, 236–240
    formatting letter, 240
    marking records for, 247–248
    merging data file and form letter, 242–248
    overview of process, 217
    specifying conditions for, 244–246
Make It Fit, 56–57
Margin Width zoom setting, 70
margins, 64, 70, 104–105
mass mailing. *See* Mail Merge.
Match options, Find and Replace, 51–52
mathematical formulas. *See* formulas.
mathematical symbols, 10
memo
    choosing style for, 155
    creating with template, 152–154
    printing, 155
    sending, 155
    spell-checking, 155
memory
    freeing up, 19
    temporary storage of documents in, 13
merge date, dynamic, 237
Merge dialog box, 218
Merge Tools, 224
Microsoft Excel, 188
Minimum button, Page Setup, 105
minus sign (-), in formulas, 210
misspelled words, 72–73, 76–80
mistakes, fixing
    with Grammatik, 81–83
    with QuickCorrect, 72–73
    with Spell As You Go, 76–77
    with Spell Check, 78–80
    with Undo, 44–45, 112
months, entering in table, 181–183
mouse pointer, 5
Move shortcut keys, 30

moving
    within a document, 30–32
    endnote/footnote, 132–134
    graphic image, 275–276
    graphic line, 260–262
    insertion point, 30
    tab stop, 173
    text, 45–46
    TextArt, 292
multinational alphabet characters, 9–10
multiplication, 205, 209, 210, 211
MyFiles folder, 15

N

names
    data-file fields, 219–221, 232–233
    document/file, 14–15
Next Page button, 68
numbered list, 119–120, 317
numbering, page, 64, 105–108, 139–141
numbers
    adding, 206–209
    aligning in cells, 201–202
    formatting, 200
Numeric button, 200

O

Open dialog box, 18–19
opening documents, 18–19
orientation, paper, 103
Output button, 243
Outside Lines button, 199

P

Page Border/Fill dialog box, 124–125
page break, 9, 65
Page Number button, 140, 141
Page Setup dialog box, 102–103, 104–105
Page view, 63–65, 67

pages
    centering, 114–115
    numbering, 64, 105–108, 139–141
    putting border around, 124–125
    viewing, 63–68, 115
paper size, 102
paragraphs
    adding border/fill, 120–123
    ending, 6
    getting count of, 86
    indenting, 112–113
    inserting blank line between, 6
    selecting, 41
Paste button, 46, 47. *See also* cut and paste.
path/filename, inserting in header/footer, 142
.pcx files, 272
PerfectExpert
    and Award Certificate template, 156–161
    and Help Topics, 22–25
    and Memo template, 152–156
    and Web pages, 312–313
Perform Merge dialog box, 242–243, 244, 247, 249
Play Macro dialog box, 134–135
plus sign (+), in formulas, 210
point size, font, 93
Portrait orientation, 103
POSTNET Bar Code, 60–61
power failures, 13
Preset: button, 288
Previous Page button, 68
Prima Publishing Web site, 298
Print button, 58
Print dialog box, 24, 58
Print Preview, 67
printing
    document, 57–58, 70
    Help Topics, 24
    memo, 155
proofreading, 77, 83

INDEX

Properties dialog box, 85–86
Properties for Table Format dialog box, 196–197
property bars, 5
Publish to HTML dialog box, 325
punctuation, between fields in form letters, 239

Q

Quattro Pro, 188
questions. *See* review questions.
Quick Data Entry, 221–224, 226–232
Quick Entry button, 224, 229
QuickCorrect, 72–73, 298–303, 308
QuickCreate, Table, 178–179
QuickFill, Table, 181–183
QuickJoin button, 202
QuickSum, 206–209
QuickWords, 73–76

R

records
    adding/deleting, 224–225
    defined, 219
    entering data, 221–223
    merging selected, 244–248
Redo button, 45
reference number, footnote, 129, 130, 132, 133
registered trademark symbol, 9
replacing text, 50–54
return address, envelope, 61
review questions
    Part I, Creating the Perfect Document, 87
    Part II, Formatting a Report, 162
    Part III, Working with Tables, 214
    Part IV, Using Mail Merge, 253
    Part V, Getting Creative with Graphics, 293
    Part VI, Working on the Internet, 328

rows. *See also* table.
    adding with QuickSum, 206
    changing height, 198
    inserting/deleting, 183–185, 187
ruler bar, 166, 168

S

Save As dialog box, 16
Save button, 16
Save File dialog box, 14–15, 223
saving
    data file, 223–224
    form letter, 240
    memo, 155
    Web page, 324
Scrapbook dialog box, 272
scroll bars, 5, 30–32
searching
    document text, 50–54
    Help Topics, 22–23, 26–27
Select Data Filename dialog box, 189
Select Records dialog box, 244–246, 247–248
selecting
    document, 42
    graphic line, 260
    shape, 270
    table cells, 182, 194
    text, 41–42
sentences
    getting count of, 86
    selecting, 41
shadow cursor, 36–38
shadows, 277–278
shapes, 257, 268–270, 283. *See also* TextArt.
shortcut keys
    for accessing special characters, 10
    for bold, italics, and underline, 95
    for displaying Go To dialog box, 35
    for moving around in documents, 30

shortcut menu, 49–50
sizing handles, 273–274, 275
slash (/), in formulas, 210
spacebar, 76
special characters, 9–12
SpeedFormat, 192–193
SpeedLink
    adding to document, 303–305
    creating, 298–299
    deleting, 308–309
    editing, 302–303
    jumping to Web site with, 306–307
    opening document with, 300–301, 306–307
    purpose of, 297–298
Spell Check, 78–80, 155
Spell-As-You-Go feature, 76–77
spreadsheet. *See also* table.
    importing to table, 175, 188–190
    linking to table, 188
Start button/menu, 4
statistics, document, 85–86
style
    border, 125, 199, 276–277
    fill, 279
    font, 288
    graphic line, 264, 265
    memo, 155
    shadow, 278
    table, 193
    table numbers, 200
    text, 95–96, 316
style buttons, 95–96
subtraction, 205, 209, 210, 211
Suppress dialog box, 144
symbols, 9–12
synonyms, 83–85

T

Tab Set dialog box, 166–168, 170–171
tab stops. *See* tabs.

table
    adding/deleting rows and columns, 183–187
    aligning numbers, 201–202
    changing size of columns and rows, 196–198
    creating
        with Create Table dialog box, 177–178
        with Table QuickCreate, 178–179
        with tabs, 173
    filling cells automatically with QuickFill, 181–183
    formatting, 191–193, 200
    importing/linking spreadsheet, 188–190
    joining cells for heading, 202–203
    positioning, 37, 196–197
    selecting border style, 199
    selecting/modifying parts of, 194–195
    typing data into, 180–181
Table button, 192, 206
Table QuickCreate, 178–179
Table QuickFill, 181–183
tabs
    changing default, 166–168
    clearing, 170
    contrasted with indents, 112
    creating custom, 169–173
    deleting, 174
    displaying current settings, 166
    illustration of types, 169
    moving, 173
tags, HTML, 324
Technical Support, Corel, 27
Telix, 327
templates
    Award Certificate, 156–161
    Memo, 152–156
text
    aligning, 109–112
    changing appearance, 92–97
    changing case, 43–44, 52

INDEX 405

copying, 47–50
deleting, 42–43
editing, 40–50
finding/replacing, 50–54
highlighting, 95, 98–100
inserting blank lines, 6
moving, 45–46
restoring with Undo, 44–45
selecting, 41–42
typing, 6–7
for Web pages, 315–317
wrapping around graphic image, 279–282

text boxes, positioning, 37

TextArt
2D/3D options, 288–292
choosing font, 287–288
compared to other graphic objects, 292
creating, 284–285
deleting, 292
editing, 285–292
file-size considerations, 291
moving, 292
purpose of, 283
resizing, 292
wrapping text around, 292

Thesaurus, 83–85

thickness, line, 262–263, 266, 319

Thickness button, 319

three-dimensional options, TextArt, 290–292

.tif files, 272

time, inserting automatically, 7–8

Times New Roman, 92

tips
alignment, indentation, and spacing
applying new line spacing to one section of document, 115
centering text, 110
indenting several paragraphs, 113
using Undo to reverse a change, 112
viewing vertically centered pages, 115

bullets, numbering, and borders
choosing fill color, 123
creating bulleted lists, 119
displaying border-style options, 125

editing
copying text with drag and drop, 48
deleting text with Backspace key, 42
deselecting text, 42
making changes to envelopes, 59
pasting text without formatting, 50
using Replace All command, 53
using Replace menu to select different font/attribute, 53

fonts/formatting
applying bold, italics, and underline text styles, 95, 96
changing typeface, 92
highlighting block of text, 99
using Replace menu to select different font/attribute, 53

footnotes/endnotes, using endfoot macro to convert, 135

general WordPerfect
keeping dates current, 8
saving document with new name/folder, 16
using Open button to access Open dialog box, 18
using shortcut keys to access special characters, 10

graphics
editing a shape's color and fill attributes, 270
editing line attributes, 265
resizing graphic images, 274
selecting/deselecting graphic lines, 260, 262
using Line Thickness button, 263
using short lines of text for TextArt, 285

406 INDEX

tips *(continued)*
    headers, footers, and watermarks
        inserting page number and total pages in header/footer, 141
        previewing watermark image, 148
    help features
        getting additional information, 25, 27
        using F1 key to access, 25
    mail merge
        checking for errors, 243
        formatting form (rather than data) document, 240
    moving around
        using shadow cursor to identify horizontal center, 37
        using shortcut key to display Go To dialog box, 35
    paper size/margins
        accessing Page Setup dialog box, 102
        mixing and matching, 103
        using Equal/Minimum buttons to set margins, 105
    printing
        expanding/compressing documents to fit specific number of pages, 56, 57
        opening Print dialog box, 58
        using Margin Width zoom setting for Landscape printing, 70
    proofreading, 83
    table
        determining cell address, 208
        linking spreadsheet to allow for automatic updating, 188
        modifying row height, 198
        moving from cell to cell, 181
        moving tab stops, 173
        selecting/deselecting cells, 182, 183, 194
    viewing documents, using PageUp/PageDown keys, 66

Web page
    adding hyperlinks, 322
    creating numbered list, 317
    displaying links, 323
    displaying wallpaper options, 314
    placing horizontal lines, 320
    testing with different browsers, 327
Tips and Tricks, Corel, 27
title page, 114
toolbars
    Formula, 207–208, 210
    Internet Publisher, 313, 315, 317, 318, 321
    purpose of/location, 4
trademark symbol, 9
Two Page view, 66, 67, 115
two-dimensional options, TextArt, 288–290
typeface, 92–93
typing
    errors, 72–73
    and use of Enter key, 6–7
typographic symbols, 11–12

U

Underline button, 95
underline text style, 95–96
Undo button, 44–45, 112
United States Postal Service Web site, 299
user interface, 4–5
USPS Web site, 299

V

vertical lines, 257, 259, 265
vertical scroll bar, 30–31
View in Web Browser button, 326
View menu, 64, 65
views
    Draft, 63–65, 67, 108
    Full Page, 67–68, 115

Page, 63–65, 67
Two Page, 66, 67, 115

W

wallpaper, 314
watermark
    creating, 146–149
    for odd/even pages, 147
    purpose of, 137
    viewing, 149
Web browser
    and SpeedLink, 305, 306–307
    viewing Web page document with, 326–327
Web page
    background color/pattern, 313–314
    bulleted/numbered lists, 317
    creating, 312–313
    graphic images, 318–321
    horizontal lines, 318–320
    hyperlinks, 322–323
    publishing, 324–325
    saving, 324
    testing with different browsers, 327
    text, adding/formatting, 315–317
    uploading to server, 327
    viewing in Web browser, 326–327
Web sites
    accessing with SpeedLink, 305, 306–307
    Corel WordPerfect, 27
    Prima Publishing, 298
    United States Postal Service, 299
    White House, 298
White House Web site, 298
Whole Word match, 51
Windows 95/98, 4–5
Windows Clipboard, 45–47
Windows desktop, 3, 4
.wmf files, 272
WMF images, 320
word
    applying text style to, 96
    finding/replacing, 51
    selecting, 41
word count, 85
word wrap, 6, 8, 180
WordPerfect 9
    exiting, 19–20
    starting, 4
    suite *vs.* program, 4
    user interface, 4–5
World Wide Web. *See* Web browser; Web sites.
.wpg files, 272
Wrap button, 279
wrapping text, 279–280. *See also* word wrap.
writing tools, 71. *See also* specific tools.

Z

Zoom button, 68, 69, 70
zooming in/out, 67–70

The Essential Books
Smart Solutions, *Fast!*

An **ESSENTIAL** book from PRIMA TECH isn't merely another reference book. It is organized around everyday work tasks, rather than software features. Every book enables you to quickly create customized, commonly used business documents. Order your **ESSENTIAL** book now and start producing professional-quality materials right away!

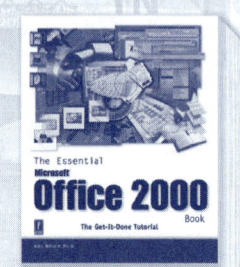

Call now to order
(800)632-8676
ext. 4444

PRIMA TECH
A Division of Prima Publishing
www.prima-tech.com

Prima Publishing is a trademark of Prima Communications, Inc. All other product and company names are trademarks of their respective companies.

Essential Office 2000
0-7615-1886-X
$29.99 (Can. $41.95)

Essential Word 2000
0-7615-1760-X
$24.99 (Can. $34.95)

Essential Excel 2000
0-7615-1889-4
$24.99 (Can. $34.95)

Essential Windows 98
0-7615-0967-4
$24.99 (Can. $34.95)

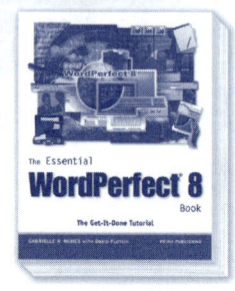

Essential WordPerfect 8
0-7615-0425-7
$24.99 (Can. $34.95)

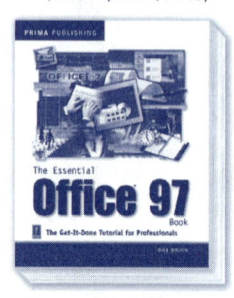

Essential Office 97
0-7615-0969-0
$27.99 (Can. $38.95)

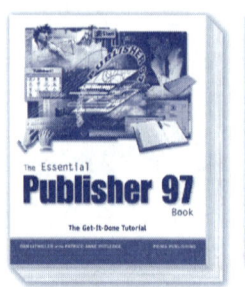

Essential Publisher 97
0-7615-1136-9
$24.99 (Can. $34.95)

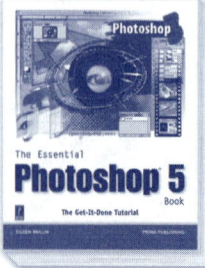

Essential Photoshop 5
0-7615-1396-5
$34.99 (Can. $48.95)

Managing with Microsoft Project 98
0-7615-1420-1
$29.99 (Can. $41.95)

In a Weekend

Learn HTML In a Weekend, Rev. Ed.
0-7615-1800-2
$19.99 (Can. $27.95)

Learn Digital Photography In a Weekend
0-7615-1532-1
$19.99 (Can. $27.95)

Learn the Internet In a Weekend
0-7615-1295-0
$19.99 (Can. $27.95)

Create Your First Web Page In a Weekend, Rev. Ed.
0-7615-1388-2 • CD-ROM
$24.99 (Can. $34.95)

Create FrontPage 2000 Web Pages In a Weekend
0-7615-1929-7 • CD-ROM
$24.99 (Can. $34.95)

Also Available

- Create Web Animations In a Weekend with Microsoft Liquid Motion
- Get Your Family on the Internet In a Weekend
- Learn Windows 98 In a Weekend
- Upgrade Your PC In a Weekend, Revised Edition
- Prepare Your Taxes with TurboTax In a Weekend

GOOD NEWS! You can master the skills you need to achieve your goals in just a weekend! PRIMA TECH's unique IN A WEEKEND series offers practical fast-track guides dedicated to showing you how to complete your projects in a weekend or less!

PRIMA TECH

Call now to order **(800) 632-8676** ext. 4444
A Division of Prima Publishing   www.prima-tech.com

Prima Publishing and In a Weekend are registered trademarks of Prima Communications, Inc. All other product and company names are trademarks of their respective companies.

fast & easy

Relax. Learning new software is now a breeze. You are looking at a series of books dedicated to one idea: To help you learn to use software as quickly and as easily as possible. No need to wade through endless pages of boring text. With PRIMA TECH's FAST & EASY series, you simply look and learn.

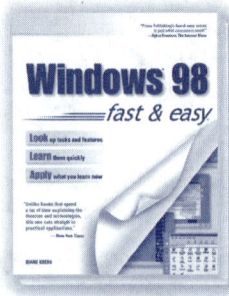

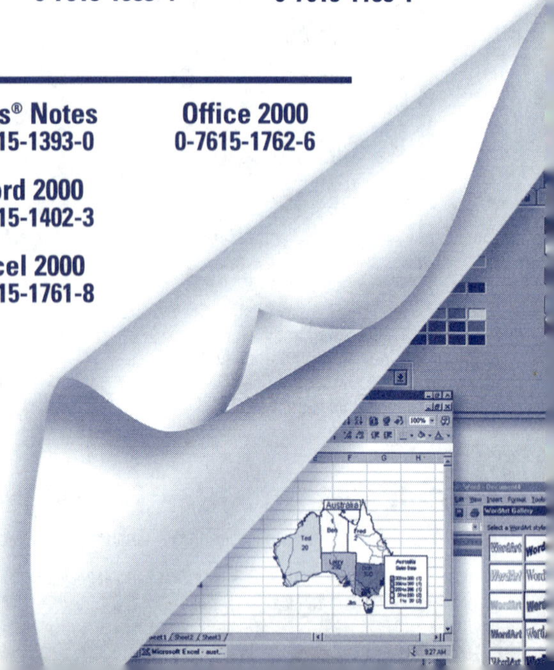

PRIMA TECH
A Division of Prima Publishing
www.prima-tech.com

Call now to order
(800) 632-8676 ext. **4444**

Prima Publishing and Fast & Easy are trademarks of Prima Communications, Inc.
All other product and company names are trademarks of their respective companies.

Windows® 98
0-7615-1006-0
$16.99 (Can. $23.95)

Microsoft® Internet Explorer 5
0-7615-1742-1
$16.99 (Can. $23.95)

Quicken® Deluxe 99
0-7615-1787-1
$16.99 (Can. $23.95)

Microsoft® Money 99
0-7615-1799-5
$16.99 (Can. $23.95)

Also Available

Netscape Navigator® 4.0	WordPerfect® 8	WordPerfect Suite® 8
0-7615-1382-5	0-7615-1083-4	0-7615-1188-1

Coming Soon

FrontPage® 2000
0-7615-1931-9

Lotus® Notes
0-7615-1393-0

Office 2000
0-7615-1762-6

PowerPoint 2000
0-7615-1763-4

Word 2000
0-7615-1402-3

Outlook 2000
0-7615-1927-0

Excel 2000
0-7615-1761-8

Access 2000
0-7615-1404-X

Publisher 2000
0-7615-2033-3